WITH WALT WHITMAN
IN CAMDEN

From a Photograph by Sarony

WALT WHITMAN

WITH
WALT WHITMAN
IN CAMDEN

(July 16, 1888—October 31, 1888)

—

HORACE TRAUBEL

NEW YORK
MITCHELL KENNERLEY
1915

Published February, 1908

THE · PLIMPTON · PRESS
NORWOOD · MASS · U · S · A

ILLUSTRATIONS CONTAINED IN THIS VOLUME

LETTERS CONTAINED IN THIS VOLUME (INCLUDING OTHER MANUSCRIPTS OF WALT WHITMAN)

LETTERS AND MANUSCRIPTS

" It won't be long and I will be dead and gone: then they will hale you into court—put you into the witness box—ply you with questions—try to mix you up with questions: this Walt Whitman—this scamp poet—this arch-pretender—what did you make him out to be? and you will have to answer—and be sure you answer honest, so help you God!"

"You'll be speaking for me many a time after I am dead: do not be afraid to tell the truth—any sort of truth good or bad, for or against: only be afraid not to tell the truth."

W. W. to H. T.

WITH WALT WHITMAN
IN CAMDEN

Sunday, July 15, 1888.

"So far as good meals and a relish of them would prove," said W., as evening wore on, "this has been for me a better day—a best day altogether." Said he was getting "venturesome," enjoying "high hopes of a positive rally." "But," he wound up with saying, "we had better not brag." "I read over the entire Sands at Seventy this afternoon, doing so to get them in total view—to see them together in their proportions, places—to get their general atmosphere. I find myself much better able to appreciate a piece if I put it aside for a time after it is written— for months, even years: returning to it with fresh spirit." Spoke of the Harneds—"parents and children: their constant, untiring attentions." Again: "I ought to die but I have promised you to live to finish this book."

I had been out on the Wissahickon with Anne Montgomerie. "That reminds me," said W., "that years ago I thought some of pitching my own tent out there—squatting—loafing the rest of my days in that vicinity. I cannot be said even now to have wholly given up the idea: though I don't suppose that it matters much where I happen to spend the rest of my days. And you are right, too, Horace, about abandon—the giving in to the hour —steering clear of mental botheration—particularly of the botheration how to be good and all that. Oh! I love that beautiful country—that long road along the creek—even the very fence—(the long lines of the fence up hill and down—the rugged, knotty lines): some of my happiest hours have been spent there —some of my freest hours."

Reference being made to O'Connor's Hamlet's Note-Book W. said: "I have never read it myself: I have very little faculty or liking for books which require charts, comparisons, references —close application—the observance of rules of logic: in the immortal words Swinton addressed to me in a peevish humor: I have a damned ill-regulated mind. The volume was the result of some correspondence between William and Mrs. Pott. Take Donnelly's Cryptogram: I could read the first part but never the cipher business—I could not unravel such a devilish tangle." Getting to the subject by a question I asked him W. said: "Goethe suggests books—carries the aroma of books about with him—seems to be a great man with books, by books, from books. Now, whatever Shake-speare was or was not, he was not that sort of man: he came, with all his scholarship, direct from nature. To me that means oh! so much: to come straight from life—to be rooted in an immediate fact. Bucke sees a great deal more in Goethe than I do—sees Goethe as if come fresh from the soil— regards him in a more liberal light: insists that he articulates the soundest philosophy of the modern world. Bucke says my trouble is in the fact that I cannot read German—that Goethe cannot be translated."

Baker goes to-day. My reference to the fact drew from W. the remark in a grieved tone: "It is inexplicable." Added: "I do not understand it. I thought it might have been caused by something I had said or done—but no, Mary says it is not that. I wished him to stay—he is welcome to stay: I am indeed fond of him. I had hoped he would stay until I got on my feet again— or," here he stopped an instant—"until you buried me." The new nurse, whose name is Musgrove, is an older man than Baker. W. hates to have his routine disturbed. Upon my remonstrance he said: "I will make it a religion to like the new man."

I trod on a Sarony portrait of Bryant face down on the floor, saying to W. of it: "That ought to be put where it will be safe." He took it out of my hand, scanned it, handed it back. "Maybe you have some place at home where you can keep it safe." Then he talked a bit about Bryant: "Some one who was in here and saw that picture said: 'That's you, Walt, when you're finished.' He thought that if a goldbeater got at me, hammered me down some, I might get a polish that would turn me into a real man. There's no use talking: I won't do but Bryant will do. Don't you like the picture? It is every way like the old man—every way: it has a sort of Thanatopsis look. Take this now—this picture"—he reached forward towards me a soiled old photograph of himself: "Do you think this could ever be tinkered into that? —that this loafer, this lubber, could ever be transmuted into that gentleman? All I've got to say is, that I wouldn't like to undertake the contract. Bryant was very masterful in his own way— wrote a few things that time cannot kill—but after all his contribution was not novel—it was nature song, philosophy, of rather a formal cast. I always go back to Emerson—say of Emerson: he was our one man to do a particular job wholly on his own account."

W. laughed about our labors together. "If I die in the midst of things you may fall heir to all my work: think of that: all my work!" I took the old portrait of W. along with the Bryant.

Monday July 16, 1888.

W.'s worst day for a week. Digestion poor and pulse low. Depressed. Change of nurses has something to do with this. Musgrove is a cloudy man. I asked how M. got on. W. evaded the question by some general remark. Baker came in and afterwards had dinner with me. When W. was offered medicine by Musgrove he asked what it was for &c. M. said he did not know. He is only a nurse—not a doctor. W. motioned the medicine away. Baker had always met such questions with answers. Have now reached the end of the reprint for the book. Hicks next in order, though not ready. "I take it up daily but no day so far have been able to stick to it. I want to get it into general view again—then give it final form. Give me a day or two more: I will do my best to be good. Considering the terrible fuss, hubbub, talk, I have made about this piece it would be pretty to have it go out too full of sins. A few sins won't hurt but we must not overload it with our imperfections. Horace, I feel that I am living for but one thing now—for one thing only: to finish this book—to make it what it should be—the little book: not to let it discredit us. Rather than have the Hicks too damned bad I'll close with the printers where I am and burn this up. I find it sadly out of joint—good enough, what there is of it, but crying for this or that right along—everywhere: something to weld the pieces into a total. Talk to the printers to-morrow. You know what to say. Tell them I am sick—oh! very sick—and sore: tell them I feel as if the whole ground had been swept from under my feet—as if I stood on nothing." Later he said of his eyes: "I seem to be approaching a semi-blindness. I experience whole hours every day during which I can scarcely see anything: then I am fully recovered again."

W. has received a copy of To-day (London) containing a paper by Reginald A. Beckett: Walt Whitman as a Socialist Poet. Says: "Yes, I read every word of it—not, however, because of its literary quality (though that is respectable enough) but just to see how I look to one who sees all things from the standpoint of the socialist. Of course I find I'm a good deal more of a socialist than I thought I was: maybe not technically, politically, so, but intrinsically, in my meanings." I asked W.: "Are you the last of your race?" "Neither the last nor the first." "Will there be more poets or less?" "More—more: and greater poets than have ever been." "What kind? Your kind?" "I don't know about that: some *free* kind, sure: they are bound to come—to come soon." After a silent minute or two: "I think I'll get there. The stylists object to me—but they lack just what Matthew Arnold lacks. They talk about form, rule, canons, and all the time forget the real point, which is the substance of poetry. I do not look for a vast audience— for great numbers of endorsers, absorbers—just now—perhaps not even after awhile. But here and there, every now and then, one, several, will raise the standard. Leaves of Grass will

finally make its way. The book is like the flukes of a whale—
if not graceful at least effective: never super-refined or ashamed
of the animal energy that imparts power to expression."

Kennedy returned me Harrison Morris' American piece with
comments. I read them to W., who said: "They are bright—
they have quite a sparkle. Take them over—show them to
Morris." I seemed to hesitate. W. added: "Do so—do so:
Morris will be glad to see them—they will do him good: he'll
know how to take them. Then we must reflect that Kennedy
may be wrong and Morris may be right. We must face all the
objections—they require to be said. Even the other Morris—
Charles—who damns me without reading me, we must not pro-
hibit: let him come in—cheer his oration. What I object to are
the sneakers—the men who hit from the rear. Criticism is a
matter of course—often the best food: the right negative word
spoken at the right time saves many a soul. Criticism is a necessary test—the passage of fire: we have got to meet it—there
is no escape. I do say with regard to myself that I must be
judged elementally—that the Arnolds, the disciples of books as
books, the second and third hand men, the scholars pure and
simple, the lovers of art for art's sake, cannot understand me—
cannot take me in—I elude their circumscriptions. Even
Goethe, in loving beauty, art, literature, for their own inherent
significance, is not as close to nature as I conceive he should be.
I say this with all due respect for Dr. Bucke, who reads Goethe
in the German and declares to me that I have but very little
conception of Goethe's real place in the spiritual history of the
race. Well, maybe I have. I care less and less for books as
books—more and more for people as people. When I go to my
tailor I lay down a law to him: that among prime requisites of a
suit of clothes are pockets, buttons, thread—but the tailor
always wants to make me up his own way anyhow. The objections to me are the objections made to all men who choose to go
their own road—make their own choice of methods. I ought
to be very readily understood by young men and women, but"—
Here he stopped. I put in nothing. He resumed: "A few take

it in—just a few—but to most of them I still seem ridiculous—perhaps even vicious."

W. put Morris's address into his note book. Did he keep a diary? "No—not that—nothing as formidable as that: just a book for memoranda—statistics—memory things, so to speak: naked figures—the briefest entries." He always keeps the book about. Another book near by is very old—crammed with written notes, scraps of print-stuff, and so forth. Harned said to him today about it: "I'll bet that's a gold mine, Walt." W. responded; "You might look at it that way: the roots of Leaves of Grass are in that book."

I read him letters received today from Kennedy and Morse, he, as usual, being much interested. He for his part produced an old letter, of which he said: "This is already a letter of long ago: this was Bucke's first appearance on the scene. You will notice, he comes in quite frankly, quite frankly, without flattering adjectives, yet also without impudence. To Bucke, to me, this document is historic. Read it aloud to me: I would like to hear it again before you take it away." I read:

SARNIA, December 19, 1870.

WALT WHITMAN,

Dear Sir; Will you please send to the enclosed address, two copies of Leaves of Grass, one copy of Passage to India and one copy of Democratic Vistas. Enclosed you will find $7.25—$6.75 for the books and fifty cents for postage. I do not know exactly what this last item will be but I fancy fifty cents will be enough to pay for it. I am an old reader of your works, and a very great admirer of them. About two years ago I borrowed a copy of the 1855 edition of Leaves of Grass and I have a great ambition to own a copy of this edition myself; would it be possible to get one? Before getting that the only thing I had ever seen of yours was Rossetti's selection. Lately I have got a copy of the 1867 edition of Leaves of Grass, and I have compared the Walt Whitman in that with the same poem in the 1855 edition, and I must say that I like the earlier edition best. I have an idea that I shall be in Washington in the course of 1871; if I am it would give me much pleasure to see you, if you would not object. I am afraid, however, that, like other celebrities, you have more people call upon you than you care about seeing; in that case I should not wish to annoy you. At all events believe me

Faithfully Yours,

R. M. BUCKE.

When I was through W. said: "Try to think what that innocent letter has led on to—what it was finally to mean to Maurice, what it has long meant, means today, to me—and to you, too, Horace, God help you: for we are all aboard the same ship—be it frail or strong, aboard the same ship." As I was about to leave W. said: "I also laid out a little Whittier letter for you, but it seems to have got astray among the papers again. I guess it will last, I guess you will last, till to-morrow." He smiled on me. "I am always poking fun at your appetite, Horace, but, after all, I respect it." I asked W.: "Does Whittier commit himself to Leaves of Grass in that letter?" "Good heavens no! He has too much respect for himself, for his puritan conscience, to take such a leap." W. was playful. Then he concluded seriously: "But Whittier has a right to his conscience—God bless 'im!—and the letter—well, the letter was written in good faith—touched me."

Tuesday, July 17, 1888.

W. rallied somewhat from yesterday's depression. "I am not grown strong: I am only easier. I am keeping a watchful eye on myself." Still complains of his eyes. Held a letter gleefully up before my face. "Here is the Whittier," he said: "Take it—be satisfied." Laughing: "Yet there's lots more to come, Horace. In spite of all I have lost and all that has been stolen—" "Stolen?" I broke in. He said gravely: "Yes, stolen. Every now and then after some respectable visitor has come and gone something disappears and never turns up again—some book —some document or other." I expressed some astonishment but W. rallied me by saying: "Don't let's bother about that.

7

Just sit down over there and read the Whittier letter. You will be pleased to see how successfully the old man steers clear of trouble."

OAK KNOLL, DANVERS, MASS., Jan. 13, 1888.

Dear Friend. But for illness I should have thanked thee before this for thy vigorous lines of greeting in Munyon's Illustrated World, combining as they do the cradle and evening song of my life. My brother writers have been very generous to me and I heartily thank them for it.

With all good wishes I am thy friend

JOHN G. WHITTIER.

When I had finished reading I said: "I see no harm, no shortcoming, in that letter. If you'd been writing him on the same subject you wouldn't have said anything about his poetry." This half-nettled W. "Maybe I wouldn't—then maybe I would. What I said of the letter was not so much intended for that letter as for things that went before and come after—Whittier's general attitude towards me, with his friends, with my friends: it has been made a part of his business to keep me at a distance—to discredit my work." W. showed a little feeling here which I disputed. "Generally you are very stoical as toward criticism—sometimes your wall of indifference crumbles." This immediately aroused W. He said: "Horace, you are right I am wrong: for a minute I forgot my own principles—I was wrong, wrong. I am not thin-skinned about opposition: it is being misunderstood—that's what tantalizes me. I know from this or that quoted from Whittier about me—words not so much of censure as of regret—that he got started wrong with the Leaves and never recovered." "But wouldn't you be rather surprised after all if a man of Whittier's spiritual bent understood you? Wouldn't he have to change his bent in order to understand you?" W. was very still. Was slow to answer. "I don't know but that's about the best summing up that could be: we would not travel well harnessed to the same rig."

W. spoke of a letter received from Burroughs. "John used

to be so equable, quiet, buoyant, happy: so like a strong, helpful stream of water: all eyes for joyous reassurances—a grown man with a boy's soul. Now much of that beautiful John is gone: I could not tell why. He was so wise, so gay, though never boisterous, in those times. We were thrown much together—very much—in Washington: were like chips off the same block —members of a common family. Why is John's faith less sea-worthy than it was then? The material must all be there still—all of it. Why does he put it aside—refuse to make use of it? I am sure he still stands for me, even with affection, or something akin to it." No more was said about B. We were both silent for awhile. Then he suddenly exclaimed: "Horace, all the fellows think I am on my last legs—at the jumping off place—about to make a total surrender, soul and baggage. But I, for my part—we—must not play the game with that end in view. I am not at all disposed to make concessions before I must—con-cessions, good or bad—especially bad."

Mitchell not in today. W. was "glad." "For," said he, "Mitchell is inclined to drug me—to fill me with the doctor poisons—which is no help, in fact always an injury, to me, as I too bitterly know. Osler respected my objection." Box of flowers from Charlotte Fiske Bates. Spoke of them affection-ately. "From Cambridge," he said—then with a twinkle in his blue eyes: "From under the shadow of Harvard." "You talk as if you had no right to expect things from Harvard." "Have I? Ask yourself that question." W. said to Mrs. Davis: "Drop in every now and then, Mary, if only for a look. It's hard papers up here nowadays: a big lubber like me, so used to moving about freely, confined to one room, denied every outdoor indulgence, deserves some pity." Made some attempt on the Hicks today. It would not go. Read three galleys of proof, however, and four pages of the revise. "You will have to justify me to the printers again." What did I make out of the To-day piece? "I do not seem to get the thing very clearly in my own mind: it eludes me."

Discussed Sands at Seventy. "O'Connor kicks against them

—is unfavorable—seems to regard the new poems as in some sense a contradiction of the old—alien to the earlier poems—as if I had gone back on myself in my old age. I do not feel that way about them: I have examined the whole matter over again—over, over—without any prejudice in favor of myself—from every side—weighing every possible argument in the negative—and I give the decision to my book. I am sure of myself—that the poems are all right—that the pain, the sickness, the sorrow, the misery, are not too prominently paraded—not in fact predominant. After all I cannot suit everybody nor am conscious that I have wished to or should. So the line is unbroken, so the new chapter of my story fits with the chapter just before it, as I am confident it does, I am satisfied. I love O'-Connor—love them all—like to be told about myself as I seem in other peoples' eyes—but in the end I must go my own road with such light as I have. William resented the Emperor piece. Why? Because he had not quite got hold of my philos phy—missed one of its important minor streams. And yet," he cried with great vehemence, "if I thought anything in my last work disgraced the Leaves as it stood in its prime—ran counter to the original statement of the book, from which I am conscious of no deviation whatever—I would end the whole thing here and now, without a single regret."

I called his attention to some errors on page 37, in Precedent Songs Farewell and An Evening Lull. These poems were written when he was in his very worst recent condition. Several bad breaks. He said of it: "I have no doubt you are right: I will give the poems my attention. Considering how I felt at the time—how I was shaken up (the last timber in me trembling with the force of the earthquake)—it is not surprising that I should have sinned more or less. Be good to me: give me time to straighten out all the warps."

Wednesday, July 18, 1888.

8 p. m. Day reasonably good for W. Ate quite fairly. Up a good part of the time. Complained, however: "While that is

true, my vim and strength do not return: I despair of recovering them." I looked skeptical. "Now what's the matter?" he asked. "You promised not to despair: despair is the worst medicine." This rallied him. He laughed quietly: "You are a good doctor: I am willing to take your medicine." Had made another try at the Hicks. "It don't go very well: my brain is not equal to it: could not cope with it—gets tired, takes my pen out of my hand." Yet he said he had read considerably. "Reading only passively tires me: writing is an active assault." "Some evening," he went on, "you will come here to be told that I have pitched the Hicks into the fire. If it eludes me much longer, fools me, rejects me"—here he stopped because I interrupted him: "Nonsense! you'll do nothing of the kind!" He repeated my exclamation smilingly and replied to it: "Well, maybe I won't do that—won't be as extreme as that—but." There he stopped. "At least, before I do it I will let you look it over. I think if you saw it in its present condition you would advise me to destroy it." Finally: "Hicks is entitled to my best—not my worst. My best would be too little—my worst would be an insult."

Still insists that O'Connor "misses his cue on Sands at Seventy." I happened to say of O'C.'s Good Gray Poet: "It is so eloquent—vocal: when I read it I want to, I do, *hear* it." This elicited his immediate response. "Exactly: that's just it: that's what we all felt—feel. William is in the best sense an orator—is eminently passionate, pictorial, electric. I'd rather hear O'Connor argue for what I consider wrong than hear most other people argue for what I think right: he has charm, color, vigor: he possesses himself of the field: he pierces you to the vitals and you thank him for doing it. I think he learned all that in the anti-slavery school—whether for good or bad I do not know—learned it all there, in the clash of classes—won his spurs in the struggles of the abolition period. But that is not the whole story. William is also a book man—profoundly so—the most bookish of all my friends, I believe (to use the word 'bookish' in an allowable way). The post-Elizabethan era in England

—especially in England though not confined to that one country—developed a great many men, whole classes of men, polite, educated, conventional, keen, haughty—who became exquisite fencers, exquisite literary swordsmen—men not particular what they struck or in what cause, whether for wrong or right—contented if they but displayed agility, skill, and threw their man. O'Connor, one side of him, is quite like those old literary mercenaries—that is, like them on the score of expertness, shrewdness, acumen, polish, scholastic acumen, with a distinct moral nobility added. Dr. Johnson was of the same class—in fact, one of that class before all else." I asked him: "Was Johnson a fencer or a pugilist?" W. laughed and answered: "Perhaps a bit of a pugilist, at the worst, but, at his best, a fencer, I should say: he was not clumsy—was one of the ripest examples of the school—a master graduate."

It seems our talk on this line was all to lead up to an old O'Connor letter which W. had been reading today. This letter he handed to me with the remark: "It is one of the most splendid of all William's splendid letters: it hits you like meeting with something possessing identity in the midst of a crowd—like a sunburst on a dark day." Then: "William could not do even the comparatively innocent things without the air, the authority, of a sovereign will. Stay right where you are—read the letter—see if it is not a proud example in point." I read a large part of the letter aloud, W. listening intently, several times exclaiming "bravo!"

WASHINGTON, D. C., May 20, 1882.

Dear Walt: I have yours of the 17th., and also your picture, for which many thanks. It is a fine presentment.

My article has gone to the Tribune with a note to Whitelaw Reid, and we await the result. I hope, if it appears, you will like it. Of course, you are not in any way responsible for it, and this is the position for you to take. Learning the facts, I use the independent privilege of a friend, and of a citizen, to criticise the offenders. *I alone am responsible.*

I composed the article under great affliction, for as the devil would have it, there were several days of shocking raw weather, followed by five consecutive days of rain, and I got the influenza, and was half dead with headache, a racking cough and all the accompaniments. Nothing therefore was right for composition but the heart. Despite conditions, Charley Eldridge, who got here from California in time to read what I have written, and of whose cool-headedness and judgmatical quality I think highly, considers it the best thing I have done, which I hope will prove true. At all events, if it gets printed, it will be the opening gun in a tremendous cannonade, and we will have war on the enemy in England at any rate, which is what will hurt Oliver Stevens and company here.

My object is to smoke the hidden movers in this business out of their holes, and I kept this in mind through the whole composition. Hence, although I knew that Marston was behind the Boston attorney, I took care not to even mention his name, but focussed all my fire right upon Oliver Stevens, who, you know, is the only one that appears officially in the transaction. He will never endure to be exclusively blistered in this way, but will in defence inculpate the State Attorney General. The minute he brings him forward, I will give them both the devil. In the present article I have been very guarded, and have interwoven fury with moderation, but when we get Marston to the front, there will be augmented fire for his hide, and I hope to make it so intolerable for him, that he will in self-defence peach on the holy citizens who have egged him on. Then, when we get their names, will be the time for punishment, memorable and terrible. They shall never be forgotten. The whole gang shall hang in chains for all time.

This must be our object—to discover the history of this persecution—the names of the subterranean movers. You must help me in this all you can. Perhaps Lathrop can discover.

You are quite right in feeling as you do towards Osgood and Company, besides being magnanimous, but it is not for me, nor for anyone else, to approve their course, which has simply been on the lowest plane of huckster providence. You had grounds against them for an action for damages. They solicited your book, they knew its character, they agreed to non-expurgation, and at the first breath of trouble, they flunked. It is all right for you to take such an attitude as you do toward them—for *you* personally: but my part, and the part of all your friends, is to whale them. You, of course, are not responsible.

I have a strong suspicion that when the truth comes to be known, the Reverend Thomas Wentworth Higginson will be found behind the State Attorney General as an instigator. His tone toward you, in the Woman's Journal article (and the Nation was probably his,) shows extreme venom. I know him, and know just where he is vulnerable, and will in due time plant a javelin where it will do him good.

I have seen and read twice your article in the N. A. Review. It is splendid, and cannot fail to do good. I only wish the style was a little clearer. I like better your earlier manner, so free from sub-clauses, involutions, parentheses— so direct and simple. In this country, in this age, when the necessity is upon us of addressing the whole people, and not the college professors or bookmen merely, I set extreme value upon communication. To be readily apprehended by your auditory, is, the truth being yours, the whole battle.

Your position in the Review article is impregnable. Gibraltar is less strong. It only remains to show the relations of poetic statements to these didactic truths. With many excellent people, especially when devoid of imagination, the trouble is to accept a passional expression, though they are quite willing to accept one simply descriptive, as in a physiological treatise. We live in a cursed abyss of society. Everything is sophisticated, everything polluted. To a sane man or woman it is simply monstrous that the august and tender supra-mortal experience of a nuptial night cannot be put into living poetry.

I hope my Tribune letter will appear and be satisfactory to you. It cost me great pain, as I had to move gingerly and with audacity at the same time. You will see how I have worked Emerson's letter against Stevens like an engine.

You must be careful in what you say of Emerson's position toward your amative passages. You have often told us that in his talk with you on the Common he had nothing to say on intrinsic grounds against these passages, but only on commercial or popular grounds. I remember your telling me that it was the saddest thing you ever heard that Emerson had nothing to urge in all his vehement talk, but that the exclusion of these passages would make the book *sell* better. Nor could he have had. These passages are capable of the most unanswerable vindication on purely intellectual grounds merely, not to go deeper, and this Emerson knew. In his letter to you he approves them. What else does his panegyric on your *"courage of treatment"* mean? I mention this because I have thought from your way of mentioning the matter, that the enemy might say that you had allowed that Emerson was opposed to these passages on moral grounds, which would be untrue.

Good-bye.

Yours Faithfully,

W. D. O'Connor.

I said to W.: "O'Connor gives your style a rap." He smiled over this. "So he does, so he does—but then my style has got nothing but raps from the start, so I am well used by this time to the man who says no. O'Connor himself would fly into a fury over my literary sins—give me hell about some comma I did use or some comma I didn't use. You mustn't suppose that because William is so staunchly my friend he will stand for everything I do. Somehow, it always nettles me some to be lectured about my style—to have much said about style anyhow —said pro, said con. I am willing they should all take a fly at it—only I wish they would meanwhile let me alone—not bother me about it. A plague on the whole worriment—the worriment of blame, the worriment of applause—both: a plague on 'em!" I said to W.: "I suppose William is right about Emerson. You have always explained the incident to me in the same way." "Exactly right—right to the letter. In fact, Emerson distinctly said to me that I was not to construe any of his objections to be against the purport of the book. He repeated that assurance to me over and once again, in different ways—seemed anxious on that point beyond any other to be rightly understood."

Talked of Voltaire. "Now there was a great man, too," said W.: "an emancipator—a shining spiritual light: a miraculous man whose ridicule did more for justice than the battles of armies." "Voltaire never was of a mind to condone Shake-speare: Shake-speare's crudities were offensive to him: there was something crude, powerful, drastic, in the Shakes-speare plays: Voltaire could not reconcile his nerves to their brutal might. But you cannot shift such luminaries from their orbit by a sneer—by an adjective. Do you think Leaves of Grass was ever really hurt by the people who went at it with a club?"

Had he met George Bancroft in Washington? "No—we never met—though I have seen him many times. If the way had been open I would have introduced myself. Even as it is, today, were I eligible, I would take the trouble to write, if do no more by him. Bancroft is a man of sagacity—honest—rather prosy and slow: a plodding hewer of wood and drawer of water—yet an indispensable collector—a man going before to gather materials for philosophy." Had Bancroft any opinion of Leaves of Grass? "None that I ever heard of." What of Holmes? Had Holmes such an opinion? "Holmes seems to prefer to keep his mouth shut—to say nothing." But Lowell? "Ah! there we are on surer ground. Lowell says no to me in ways anybody can understand."

W. threatens each day to take a trip down stairs. Each day I jolly him about it. "Set the day," I said: "I want to be around." He was merry over it. "That's what I dare not do. I am a poor hand to make promises: I never make a promise that I can avoid. I guess that's the reason I never got married; if I had set apart a day I might have begged off when the date arrived." I rose to go. Kissed W. for good-night. He said: "Sometime there will be a last good-night. Then you'll have to keep up the story alone." I said however: "But that don't worry you: a man who isn't afraid of life isn't afraid of death." He fervently answered: "No indeed: I do not worry—I am not afraid: it all belongs to the same scheme: we've got to see it through in the spirit of the cheerfullest faith."

Thursday, July 19, 1888.

8 p.m. Not frisky today though inclined to eat well. Spoke of his head again as "sore." When I entered he was making for the bed, his cane in one hand and a chair in the other. "Navigation grows increasingly difficult. It now takes all my energy merely to get to the chair and back to the bed again. I am not hopeless, however: I am a good wrestler." Read papers today but did not work. Hicks untouched. Brought me Bucke and Burroughs letters, which he thought I should see—"though there's nothing of importance in either"—adding: "I think we all like to have letters whether they amount to much or not." I could not see in the Burroughs' letter the "depression" of which W. spoke—"the sentence of death," as he called it. W. pointed out to me a passage in Bucke's letter of the 9th: "It is a great comfort to me to know that you are at last being looked after. In this regard I feel sure nothing could be better than Baker and Traubel, and I think we are most fortunate in getting the assistance of these two young fellows." "That," said W., "is where you come in in fine feather—and rightly, too. I am not saying much myself about it these days but I think I know even better than Doctor how true his remark is."

Had I read Ossian? Was very circumstantial in talking about the book. "Macpherson was a sort of a rascal—had scamp qualities. There was a great Ossianic debate. I have always had an Ossian about me, though I can't say I ever read it with any great fervor. It was a curious controversy—there were great men on both sides of it—many things were said both pro and con—ideas it did no harm to ventilate. Ossian is of the Biblical order—is best to one who would come freshly upon it—to one who knew nothing of the Hebrew Bible. I don't think Ossian would satisfy the modern young man—the radical—the new man with the new spirit. Ossian's fame lasts—he is still sold— I am told he has been highly thought of by continental critics— very highly. You say you can no longer read Milton—the bigger poems. Well you mustn't feel bad and guilty about that—you're not alone in that fix: there are plenty like you: you may count your uncle here in for the same complaint." He laughed. "Let's be honest with each other," said W., "even if the book is a bigwig. If we think a book's damned tiresome let's say it's damned tiresome and not say 'how do you do?—come again.'"

Referring to the Hicks: "What a poor disjointed fact it is if fact at all. As the old woman said, I don't know yet whether it will be a be. There's one voice which says, don't do it: there's another voice which says, yes, do—and that's where I stand right now, listening both ways." "I knew the habitats of Hicks so well—my grand-parents knew him personally so well—the shore up there, Jericho, the whole tone of the life of the time and place—all is so familiar to me: I have got to look upon myself as sort of chosen to do a job as the Hicksite historian. I have seemed, to myself at least, to be particularly equipped for doing just this thing and doing it as it should be done—have felt that no one else living is exactly so well appointed for it. Now it threatens to go up in smoke! Do you know anything about the method of the Quaker meetings? Well, if you do, you know that they never take a vote: they discuss questions (one this side, one that) —or sometimes most of them on one side and only a few on the other: then the moderator (I think they call him that—at any rate, the man who presides) announces the result, yes or no, as he sees it in the balance of feeling this way or that. It is remarkable, I think, in the history of the sect, that these decisions have never in a single instance been appealed from. If there's not a pretty ardent leaning one way or the other, the moderator reserves judgment: that is the only guard. They seem to select their most judicial men for the place—men who cannot be swayed by momentary passions, interests, prejudices, even sympathies. What all this comes to is, that just that sort of a debate is going on in my mind now, whether to condemn or save the Hicks—whether to send it to the printer or throw it into the stove—a debate not to be put into figures or votes, but real, with a decision pending which I must abide by at last. Tell the printer to give me till Monday—this is Thursday: till then it will be a life and death struggle. For thirty years I have had it in my plans to write a book about Hicks. Now here I am at last, after all the procrastinations, stranded, with nothing but a few runaway thoughts on the subject to show for my good resolutions. Well—if I can't do all I started off to do I may be able to do some little towards it—give at least some hint, glimpse, odor, of the larger scheme." He paused a minute then asked me: "Do you know Quaker women? The women are the cream of the sect. It was not Lucretia Mott alone—I knew her just a little: she was a gracious, superb character: but she was not exceptional: it distinguishes most of the women—seems to appear in them inevitably. Did you know (but I guess you did not) that when I was a young fellow up on the Long Island shore I seriously debated whether I was not by spiritual bent a Quaker?—whether if not one I should not become one? But the question went its way again: I put it aside as impossible: I was never made to live inside a fence." "If you had turned Quaker would Leaves of Grass ever have been written?" "It is more than likely not— quite probably not—almost certainly not. I guess you are right, Horace: you have hit the nail on the head. We must go outside the lines before we can know the best things that are within."

W. gave me before I left a little war-time card photo of his brother George "in his sojer clothes," as W. said. "We have just been talking Quakerism—peace—no war: now look at this picture by way of contrast. You will see, it is a New York picture —made by Bogardus." I said to W.: "I have sometimes tried to imagine you in a uniform but could never make it go." W. first smiled, then grew quite serious: "I should hope not— thank God, thank God, not—not—not!" I was stirred by his vehemence. "Yet they say you condoned the war." "They say that, do they? Well—they say many things, many things. Thank God, Horace, you could never make it go: thank God, thank God!"

Friday, July 20, 1888.

Bad day again: "A great languidness, feebleness, weariness besetting me at the start and lasting all day." He also said: "It has been almost two months since I tangled myself into this snarl and I am still without the first show of substantial strength —though it is true the acute phases of my trouble are passed. I am still in the battle, though—not conquered but badly banged." Yet he advised me to write to Burroughs and say: "Tell him I send my love—tell him I suspect that I am slowly on the mend." W. remarked: "Mrs. Stafford was in today—paid me a long visit, which did me good. Mrs. Stafford is not literary—I account that one of her merits." But did she know the W. W. of Leaves of Grass? "Yes, indeed, essentially knows it well: I think she takes it in—reads nearly all my books. I always say that it is significant when a woman accepts me." Recurring to Burroughs' letter of the other day: "It's the least vital of all the notes I ever got from John. He wanted to write—felt it to be a duty to write—but, having nothing to say, this was the result. Sometimes it's better sense for a fellow to simply yell hello and then stop. I am often in the hello mood myself."

Horace Howard Furness over yesterday but did not see W. No callers today except Mrs. Stafford. Reporters drop in occasionally. Tom Harned of course. Speaking of Harlan W. said: "That act sunk him a thousand fathoms deep and he never came up. The literary fellers in Washington (there were many of them there—there are many of them there still)—hundreds of scribblers of one sort or another who today are not even a memory—writers for papers, hacks, penny-a-liners: they were all generous, frank, quick to resent a wrong: they almost instantly came to my aid, with very few exceptions indeed."

As to criticisms of his style: "I care little for a man's means so the end comes around in its time. You might tell your friend

Morris, the point is, not to prove your possession of a style, but to move the people along the line of their nobler impulses. The style will readily enough accommodate itself. Napoleon didn't study rules first: he first of all studied his task. And there was Lincoln, too: see how he went his own lonely road, disregarding all the usual ways—refusing the guides, accepting no warnings: just keeping his appointment with himself every time. I can hear the advisers saying scornful things to him. They offered him ready-made methods. But Lincoln would only retort: 'I want that battle fought—I want that battle won: I don't care how or when: but fought and won!'"

No work on the Hicks today but had got ready a little manuscript not originally intended to go into the book—notes made in Washington in August and September, 1865, and a brief statement on the Harlan case not before printed: the first headed: Small Memoranda: Thousands Lost—Here One or Two Preserved: the second called A Glint Inside of Abraham Lincoln's Cabinet Before—One Item of Many. Had read some page proofs. No letters. "I tried to write Burroughs but could not nerve myself to it." Spoke of swimming: "I was never what you could call a skillful swimmer but was quite good. I always hugely enjoyed swimming. My forte was—if I can say it that way—in floating. I possessed almost unlimited capacity for floating on my back—for however long: could almost take a nap meanwhile"—laughed: "That is to say I was very much at home in the water. I never could do any of the surprising stunts of the other boys when I was young but I was a first-rate aquatic loafer."

Proud Music of the Storm appeared in The Atlantic Monthly, February, 1868. W. gave me some little correspondence attaching to it. It seems that he asked Emerson to intercede for him and that Emerson took the poem to Fields. W. said of the affair: "It went through without a flurry. After I had written my letter to Emerson I wondered if I had not overdone my call. But Emerson proceeded without delay: he evidently had no qualms: then Fields took the matter up offhand, writing me at once, as you see. The whole business was done in about a week." "How did you happen to appeal to Emerson as a mediator?" He laughed. "For several reasons, I may say. But the best reason I had was in his own suggestion that I should permit him to do such things for me when the moment seemed ripe for it." W. first writes Emerson. Fields then writes W. W. then writes Fields.

WASHINGTON, Nov. 30, '68
sent Dec. 2.

Dear Mr. Emerson: On the eve of sending the enclosed piece abroad I have taken a notion to first offer it to the Atlantic and, if not too great a liberty, to solicit your services for that purpose. I would be obliged if you would take it in to Mr. Fields the first time you go to Boston. If available at all, I propose it for the February number of the magazine. The price is one hundred dollars; and thirty copies of the number in which it may be printed. Of course Mr. F. may read this letter.

I shall require an answer from Mr. Fields within a week from the time of the reception of the piece.

I scrupulously reserve the right to print the piece in the future in my book.

BOSTON, Dec. 5, 1868.

My Dear Sir: Mr. Emerson has handed me the poem which you offer to the Atlantic Monthly; which I shall gladly publish in our February number, and enclose herewith, check for one hundred dollars, the sum named in your letter to Mr. Emerson.

With best wishes, I am

Very sincerely yours
JAMES T. FIELDS.

J. T. FIELDS,   Sent Dec. 8, '68.

Dear Sir: Your letter has come to hand, with the check for one hundred dollars, as payment in full for the piece "Proud Music of the Sea-Storm"—leaving me, however, the right to print it in future book.

Please when ready send me proof, which I will return forthwith. [W. had added and then excised this with two penstrokes: "Please send me, by express, thirty copies of the number, when ready, to my address here. With thanks and best respects."]

Saturday, July 21, 1888.

Day favorable, W. at last tackling the Hicks manuscript. "I have been wondering whether I should write some prefatory note or not. I started something with that end in view, but my condition at the time was rather dubious, so that I am not sure whether it may not have to be rejected. I find that as soon as I can do any work at all I want to do too much. The Hicks needs little re-writing but many after-touches."

Letters to W. today from Bucke, Rhys and Charlotte Fiske Bates. He said of the latter: "She is itching to write books—does write poetry some, I think. It is always a serious disease—sometimes even fatal: a few recover entirely unhurt—but very few." Growls about Bucke's handwriting. "It's all in up and down angles—sharp, like his voice: I never get used to it." I said I had no trouble with it. W. smiled and replied: "That's right—contradict me." He went on to say something about his own hand. "My writing has been clear from the start—almost from boyhood: not beautiful, but legible." He called my attention to a letter from the West and called it "empty". "People often sit down to write letters much as the professional author sits down to work: they have nothing to say but say a great deal about saying nothing." Speaking of his brain inertia he said: "It's as though you tried to make something fluid out of something all slush, squid." Handed me a book—Specimens of Early English Metrical Romances: Bohn, 1848. "You have read it? No? Well take it along—look through it. I think it is better than Percy's Reliques: richer, deeper, larger. But you should have a copy of your own."

Talked some about the tariff. "The politicians do not deal fair with the people, though that is nothing new. They keep the question of the tariff remote, distant, like a priesthood: they

23

won't let the subject reach the people in the right way. Republican newspapers are now all flings, libels, slanders, smart paragraphs, light assertions: not one of them ever stops its humbug to make a respectable statement." Then referred to newspapers generally: "They are all getting into the hands of millionaires. God help our liberties when money has finally got our institutions in its clutch."

A good day having come at last after much waiting he tried to improve its hours. Pushed along a bit on the Hicks. "I see the importance of going while I can. I can never know when the door will be banged shut in my face." W. gave me a Dante portrait which Symonds had once sent him. It bears this on the reverse, in S.'s own hand: "Portrait of Dante copied from a fine Lithograph (published by the Arundel Society) of a fresco Portrait Discovered in Florence 1840 or 1848 said to be painted by Giotto vide Longfellow's notes to his translation of Dante." "The face is wonderfully clean-cut," said W.: "the face of a man who was quits with the impurities of life. To get that in a face much has to be lost as well as won. Dante is unquestionably one of the first-class men, if there are classes in men: he is up on the peak—high up: emancipated, in a way, from the tendencies of the flesh. I do not make too much of that—attach any exclusive importance to it: the flesh, too, has its divine (who knows, maybe the divinest) uses: still, the Dantesque sort of man is vital, must be reckoned with, stands in this thing or that for the supreme ideals. They are not my ideals but they are ideals—very lofty ideals."

Sunday, July 22, 1888.

A good day but no strength gained. Worked enough to get the Hicks piece into shape for the printer—at least as much of it as related to Hicks direct. Originally the study embraced both Hicks and George Fox. W. now decides to halve the paper. I am to take the Hicks to Ferguson. Yesterday afternoon and today wrote a prefatory note. "The text is a little mixed up," W. said of it apologetically: "My mind is not now-a-days a perfect machine." He has had some trouble finding it a satisfactory head-line but at last struck upon one that relieves the paper of assumption without convicting it of weakness. The manuscript is on sheets of various sizes, thicknesses, and colors. The old matter was written with an indelible pencil—purple. That is, the matter written before his illness. The new is in ink. The old phrasing is "vigorous and sure," as he says of it himself. The new is less certain, "unkempt-like," in his own words. "My brain often takes speed and is away—gets rein-free and flies without will or plan—and I am helpless for it all."

W. received today from the Century people proofs of the War Memoranda—Army Hospitals and Cases they have so long held up. It is to appear in October. W. read the four galleys "and did not detect a single error." He had not originally intended putting this matter into November Boughs but thinks he can now do so. Will write Gilder for permission. Gilder had added underneath the headline: "By Walt Whitman, volunteer hospital nurse." This excited W.'s ire. "My whole soul revolts against that line: my very first feeling was one of utter disgust." I laughed. He asked: "What do you mean by that laugh?" "That you take the matter too seriously." He queried: "Do you say that too? That's what Talcott Williams says. He was here today with Mrs. Williams."

W. then talked about the War itself: As the period of the War recedes I am more than ever convinced that it is important for those of us who were on the scene to put our experiences on record." W. said the Harlan piece sent to the printer the other day was his "first public expression in that matter," adding: "And even that I put forth, not because it has any personal significance, but for its bearing on the events of its day—as one evidence of the curious things thrown to the surface in an era of major disturbance. There is infinite treasure—oh! inestimable riches—in that mine. And the secret of it all is, to write in the gush, the throb, the flood, of the moment—to put things down without deliberation—without worrying about their style—without waiting for a fit time or place. I always worked that way. I took the first scrap of paper, the first doorstep, the first desk, and wrote—wrote, wrote. No prepared picture, no elaborated poem, no after-narrative, could be what the thing itself is. You want to catch its first spirit—to tally its birth. By writing at the instant the very heart-beat of life is caught. My place in Washington was a peculiar one—my reasons for being there, my doing there what I did do. I do not think I quite had my match. People went there for all sorts of reasons, none of which were my reasons: went to convert, to proselyte, to observe, to do good, to sentimentalize, from a sense of duty, from philanthropic motives: women, preachers, emotionalists, gushing girls: and I honor them all—all: knew them, hundreds of them, well, and in many cases came to love them. But no one—at least no one that I met—went just from my own reasons—from a profound conviction of necessity, affinity—coming into closest relations—relations oh! so close and dear!—with the whole strange welter of life gathered to that mad focus. I could not expect to do more for my own part at this late day than collect a little of the driftwood of that epoch and pass it down to the future."

So he talked on, in monologue, I putting in scarcely a word. Then Harlan was mentioned again. "Harlan was a despicable man—had a sort of penny-a-line character: was made for little issues, was set for small victories. He was a child of the Methodistic order. The Methodists were entitled to Lincoln's attention—not his alone but everybody's—for their loyalty in the War—their abounding loyalty, which marked them out in a crowd of other sects in the North. What I put into that little piece I got chiefly from Philbrick, a clerk at the White House, who was always favorably disposed towards me—often met and talked with me in those days. Nicolay I did not know in Washington—Nicolay, who probably has as little use for me now as he had then—would hardly perhaps remember my name. I did meet Hay in Washington during the war—talked with him frequently at the White House. Hay and Nicolay were for Harlan at that time, but Hay, at least, warmed towards me later on and has been nobly loyal ever since." W. full of fervent reminiscence. Still kept on: "Life is seen more richly in Washington than at any other one point on this continent, taking it all in all—except, perhaps, if we include the great Southern bar-rooms: for instance, those in New Orleans—the acre-large bar-rooms—in which come all classes, for talk, discussion: and the listeners, too, silent, inarticulate. I have known men in such places to be speaking to a group of a hundred and more people, spontaneously gathered together—several groups like that—no one group interrupted by any other group. Some of this life was mad, wild, hellish, to contemplate—to diagnose." He remarked "the propensity of certain kinds of men—especially the kinds that hang round a capital like Washington, living on their wits—to desert sinking ships—to scamper from declining reputations." Then: "Take a case like Harlan's. Time has now made it possible for us to see why it was inevitable that he should be deserted, fall from his high place, sink into total obscurity: but on the stage, at the moment, while the play was going on, he seemed like a chief figure to which ruin was impossible."

I spoke of an unconventional photographer who had met with hot professional opposition in making experiments looking towards the progress of his art. W. forcibly exclaimed: "There it is over again—the same old bark: the canons: sticking to the old road—the prior claims of rule, custom: the old anti-Napoleonic objurgation: 'He ought to lose the battle—ought to lose it even if he does not—because he don't prepare to win it according to rules!'" Feeling better W. is beginning to see his way towards an enlargement of the book. "Why, I'm feeling so good today I'm almost nasty. A day or two more like this and I'll fight!"

Monday July 23, 1888.

W. passed a good day in all respects except as to strength. Complains of appalling weakness. Wonderfully cheerful in the evening on my arrival, talking most freely for more than an hour. Little work done. Read some papers. Wrote notes, one to Mrs. Stafford. Letters received from Gilchrist and Pearsall

Smith. Answered Smith at once. Wrote Gilder about war piece. "It was a delicate matter: some of the publishers won't consider such requests: but in this case I hope to make my point. It seems so fit and proper to put that piece in November Boughs. I struck out the 'volunteer hospital nurse' line. My last thought confirmed my first: it seemed like supererogation to impose such a statement upon the headlines." Spoke of the memoranda itself: "I like it well. It has lain there in New York nearly two years—perhaps over. Now it comes back fresh to me—almost like a new thought, a new story. It stirs, moves, me—even me—just as though I had had no hand myself in writing it down. I have been sitting here today and saying to myself: 'If that is all so, it must have a value, a pertinency, to others fully as great.'"

Gilchrist reported in his letter that Rhys had said to Baron Sternbach: "I gained a fortune in America and lost it." What did he mean? W. had "no idea." Was it a compliment directed toward W.? "I think not—am sure not. You know, Rhys is not one of my thick and thin admirers—he don't swallow me whole—is not overflowing in his endorsements—not swept away by Leaves of Grass, as are some English people. Rhys is very interesting to me—I easily love him. He is not original—brilliant. He is young—he may still go on to greater things—but he is rather a plodder than a dreamer. How he and Kennedy fell afoul of each other was a caution! Kennedy does not like Rhys—and for that matter Rhys does not like Kennedy —which squares 'em up. Rhys thinks the Kennedys the nervousest couple he ever came across (as perhaps they are) and Kennedy thinks Rhys the stolidest dullhead he ever came across (as maybe he is) but for all that both of them sit with equal prestige in my parliament. Kennedy evidently thinks the center, the core, of Rhys is selfishness—that he is in for the make —that whatever he does is done with certain definite returns in view. I am sure Kennedy got his glasses on his nose upside down when he sat in judgment on Rhys. Rhys should come to America and stay—he belongs here. He is bright, smart, wideawake, with an instinct for new things, delighting in strange doctrines. He was intensely interested in America—saw what was to come—was not disturbed by inharmonies. Rhys is very modern, the best of him—very modern—though I must say of him that he has too deeply dipped into Elizabethan literature —into the literature of stilts, as some of it is: Dekker and those others—does that sort of work right along for the Walter Scott publishers there in London. Those old writers were made for an age of smartness: they write in sounding phrases, make stiff speeches: they are full of the affectations, false humors, wittinesses of the swell boudoirs and reading rooms."

He spoke of the cities he liked best: Brooklyn, Washington, New Orleans, St. Louis, New York. "Camden was originally an accident—but I shall never be sorry I was left over in Camden! It has brought me blessed returns." He looked at me affectionately. "But Washington, New Orleans, Brooklyn— they are my cities of romance. They are the cities of things begun—this is the city of things finished." He paused. Then said: "Of things finished—yes, that's it: soon I will be all finished!"

If the Century people will give him the War Memoranda he will insert it ahead of the Hicks piece. "I want to have the book end with the Fox paper." Sent his "best respects and love" to Myrick, the printer. Could not "muster up the courage" to write Burroughs. "I still have the instinct, the grasp, the pith, of the printer. It is like swimming—the stroke comes back however long and many the years since may have been." Speaking of original writers W. said he thought that "Tennyson in England and Emerson in America constitute the best recent examples—or possible examples, if a fellow has a little doubt left!" Asked me who were yet to be heard from in the American symposium. I knew of Agnes Repplier and Lüders—not of others. W. had never heard of Lüders but said of Miss Repplier: "She is the woman who talks and talks at meetings and then talks again—eh? ain't she? I don't seem to like smart people and I hear that she is damned smart—damned. Yet they belong to the great whole and must have their fling."

He asked me some questions about my health. "When you come in, each day, any time, when I ask you, as I always do: How have you been? your invariable answer is: Well, always well. Are you always so well? It is so great—so superb—to be always well. However, these are your years to expect it—from eighteen to forty-five—halcyon days, sure enough—and if there's anything in a man, physically or mentally, it's sure to come out, to give an account of itself, along through that stretch of life." Just as I was leaving W. gave me three letters in a bunch, saying of them: "They are safer among your papers than among mine. They are three of the letters Rhys wrote me while he was in America. They are memoranda of travel—very interesting, too, though short: in one of them—maybe in two—you will find a little look in on the Colonel, who seems to have taken Rhys by storm as he does everybody else—except, I suppose, the parsons, who have for business reasons"—laughing—"to dissemble their love. After the much talk we have had about Rhys to-night these letters are in point." Here is the first of the Rhys letters:

St. Botolph Club, Boston, 3rd April, '88.

Dear Walt Whitman, Thanks for note forwarded,—reached me this morning. Here in Boston I have had some queer ups and downs. The notorious blizzard ruined one lecture completely, but since then two have passed off with good success, and I am safe from bankruptcy,—glad to be able to get off with a whole skin to England and home. I think of leaving here for New York next Monday or Tuesday, and then taking a trip to Washington, returning via Philadelphia for a last visit of two or three days. Spring is probably more forward with you, than up here; I hope the brighter weather is giving you good cheer,— after the long imprisonment of winter,

Kennedy has not crossed my sight very recently; I hope to spend an evening with him before I leave. He went with me the other day to see the collection of Jean Francois Millet's paintings at Mr. Quincy Shaw's, Brookline. A grand array

they make,—giving one new insight into the human environment of earth and sky and water. How paltry this life of parlors and carpets in comparison!

The note from H. Gilchrist, which you sent on the other day, shows him full of work and good spirits. Of course he ends with "Love to Walt" as usual. Several other young fellows over there, who have written lately, have also sent greetings and love, to which adding my own, I am, as always,

Yours affectionately,

ERNEST RHYS.

W. said: "That reference to the Millet pictures made me home-sick. I, too, have seen those pictures—seen them in that same place. Millet excites all the religion in me—excites me to a greater self-respect. I could not stand before a Millet picture with my hat on."

Tuesday, July 24, 1888.

The second of the three Rhys letters given me by W. yesterday follows. It contains a poem for W.'s birthday.

THE UNION LEAGUE CLUB,
NEW YORK, 30th May, '88.

Dear Poet, I write to wish you all that you wish for yourself—all that is best, on your birthday to-morrow! I meant to have had the lines overleaf complete to send you for the day, but somehow they do not fall into the right order. However, you will take the will for the deed, I know; and perhaps in a day or two I may be able to render them in a better shape, when I write again to tell you of my doings since I saw you last. A splendid time to-night at Metropolitan Opera House, listening to Col. Bob Ingersoll. (Vide morning papers!) More of this anon. I am at Stedman's. He sends birthday greetings. With great love,

ERNEST RHYS.

31

TO WALT WHITMAN-

On his 69th birthday.

Here health I bring you in one draught of song
Caught in my rhymster's cup from earth's delight
Where English fields are green the whole year long,—
The wine of might
That the new-come Spring distills most sweet and strong
In the viewless avis alembic wrought too fine for sight.

Now shall all pain be gone for this one day,
As, drinking deep of this brimm'd wassail cup,
You feel the years uncoil and their travailing pass away,
Till, ere you drink it up,
Again the sun's quick fires you feel pulse brainword through
the blood,
Again, as when in youth they pulsed, making the world seem
good.

For this the Magic wine,
That, tasted by the chosen lips, makes Life as long as
Thought,—
Elixir this long sought,
Filled of the sun and the wind and all green growing things,
The salt of the sea and the sweet of the earth,
And the potencies of death and birth,—
That tasted once makes men as gods and the common world
divine.

W. was inclined to see a merry side to the Rhys poem. "You
see, if I can't write poetry I can inspire it." "So you like this
poem?" "Yes, don't you?" He spoke particularly of the last
verse, and of the descriptive lines: "All green growing things,
the salt of the sea and the sweet of the earth." I had these
letters in my pocket when I saw him today. Letter three he
had me read aloud. "I like to hear such things about the
Colonel. He is always a marvel of a man to me—a sort of child
man who is honest with himself: who acts out according to his
nature—is on the square—has neither false reserve nor false
parade."

THE UNION LEAGUE CLUB,
NEW YORK, 7th June, 1888.

Dear Mr. Whitman, These last days have been so crowded with work and play that there has been no fair chance to do any writing. What with Stedman—who celebrated my last night in America yesterday by toasting me with mint-juleps at the Hoffman House, and Col. Bob Ingersoll, who has been giving me all sorts of wrinkles in oratory at his own house and in public. (It was a great experience to hear him speak to an audience of actors at Madison Square Theater on Tuesday,)—and what with endless other episodes of a friendly and delightful kind, it is a wonder that I have the heart to say Goodbye to America at all. At last the end has come however. I sail by the Crystal this afternoon at three o'clock for Leith, and with this news I must say once more Goodbye, and be silent again for awhile. With much love!

ERNEST RHYS.

W. said, commenting again on this letter: "Do you notice, Horace, nobody ever says of Ingersoll: 'He took me round to the club,' or 'he bowled me off with a big dinner somewhere or other,' or such things? Ingersoll seems to have no taste for that sort of life—he lives too close to nature. No doubt he lives a full life—is comfortable—all that: but he seems to disdain the sham pleasures, the sickly sophistications, of the professional man-about-town, who is seen everywhere at resorts, who is a good fellow to all the literary swells. God bless the Colonel for his simple heart!" W. still resting upon the slender thread of an improvement that imparts no strength. But says his "mind is easier" and "for that a man should be grateful." "I am like Mary Davis' old woman," he added, "who says: Don't talk to me about trouble and trial—I am too busy with my blessings!" Harned rallying him on his possible vote for Harrison W. retorted: "Don't be too damned sure on that score. I was inclined to Harrison at one time but now I hold off. I couldn't swallow him at the best without gagging."

I was visited last evening by a press reporter—a son of Rebecca Harding Davis. He brought a letter of introduction from Talcott Williams. W. said: "Yes, he was here too—but I didn't know that was what he was here for. I asked him his name: he said he was Richard Harding Davis." "He asked me if you had any political opinions. I said, 'No—none of a decided sort that I knew: I knew you were a free trader but that was all.'" "That was about right—you said about all that could be said. You might have said also that if Walt Whitman has any political or religious opinions, he would like to have some one tell him what they are." "I told him I thought you had a great faith but that your stock of opinions had run out." W. was very merry over this: "That was mighty good—better still, was mighty true. I wonder if the young man took it in?" "The boy brought a photographer with him," further explained W. "Yes—he got a view of the house." "Is that so? Then I'd bet he took it from the most detestable point of the compass." "You talk like a victim." This made him laugh. "Probably I do. But I have had some tough experiences with reporters and illustrators." After a pause he added: "So you say that was the son of Rebecca Harding Davis? I thought him an Irish boy: I liked him—he was so candid, so interesting. Such tall, wholesome looking fellows are rare among American youngsters."

Harned broached the subject of the restriction of immigration, and happening to say, "most people believe in it—it's very unpopular now-a-days not to believe in it," W. exclaimed contemptuously: "*All*, did you say, Tom—or *almost* all? Well, here's one who spits it all out, contract labor, pauper labor, or anything else, notwithstanding." Harned said: "I did not say I believe in restriction—I said most people do." W. went on vehemently: "Well for you, Tom, that you do not say it. I have no fears of America—not the slightest. America is for one thing only—and if not for that for what? America must welcome all—Chinese, Irish, German, pauper or not, criminal or not—all, all, without exceptions: become an asylum for all who choose to come. We may have drifted away from this principle temporarily but time will bring us back. The tide may rise and rise again and still again and again after that, but at last there is an ebb—the low water comes at last. Think of it— think of it: how little of the land of the United States is cultivated —how much of it is still utterly untilled. When you go West you sometimes travel whole days at lightning speed across vast spaces where not an acre is plowed, not a tree is touched, not a sign of a house is anywhere detected. America is not for special types, for the castes, but for the great mass of people—the vast, surging, hopeful, army of workers. Dare we deny them a home —close the doors in their face—take possession of all and fence it in and then sit down satisfied with our system—convinced that we have solved our problem? I for my part refuse to connect America with such a failure—such a tragedy, for tragedy it would be." W. spoke with the greatest energy. It is a subject that always warms him up. "You see," he said finally, "that the immigrant, too, like the writer, comes up against the canons, and has to last them out."

W. read some proof today. In reading proofs W. rarely consults his copy. Yet he seems by instinct to catch the printer's aberrations. "I rely a good deal upon my general feeling about a piece when it comes back to me in type." In generally easy mood all through our rather vigorous talk. He said: "The best medicine is time: let us not rob time of its due." Harned had brought in some pears: "They seem right from God Almighty— are the best I have ever eaten—beautiful to look upon and quite as fine to taste." W. wrote to Bucke today. Says he rarely hears from O'Connor. "William has his own troubles." I wrote to Burroughs for W. yesterday. "For years and years John has seemed to avoid me. I never try to guess why. Sometimes I think he is a little afraid of my friends. You, for instance, Horace—Bucke: you are too boisterously radical!" "But you don't think he is afraid of *you?*" To this he instantly said: "It never occurred to me that he could be: I do not think I have any reason for believing John's attitude towards my work or towards me has changed."

Wednesday, July 25, 1888.

W. reasonably well. "My head is behaving itself right decently just now. But it's funny, how unambitious my body is. I am possessed of an incredible inclination to flop. I am like a wet rag—I seem to be eligible to do anything except stand erect. Bucke has evidently got scared about me. You haven't been telling him things to scare him? Don't do it. Just send him hurrahs. I got a letter from him today or yesterday, in which he says to me: 'Stop—stop all labor: your mind won't stand it: put the Hicks aside instantly—the book—let Horace finish it— let anybody finish it—but stop, stop, stop at once!'" W. laughed heartily. "Why, Maurice wouldn't a' made more fuss if the town was afire. I have written him that the work is doing me no harm. Why, I have been here for six weeks or more— imprisoned, practically—with nothing to think of but this. Instead of a hindrance it has been a tonic in all the dreary days. I would have died sure if I had not had this book to do. The siege is a long one—I don't know how long or when or where I shall get through with it: but I am satisfied whatever eventuates so I get my book out before the curtain is rung down."

Spoke regretfully of the Hicks. "My infernal laziness, neglect, inanition, for thirty years or fifty or more has put this off and off till now it is no longer possible. My fatal procrastination has tripped me up at last. I wanted to write of Hicks as a democrat—the only real democrat among all religious teachers: the democrat in religion as Jefferson was the democrat in politics— and not merely to say it as I say it to you now, assertively, nakedly, but to show it, picture it, follow the lines of evidence. No one, no writer, I mean no writer of the requisite quality, has done this for Hicks. The Quakers themselves, with their damnable worldliness and fashions (or no fashions) do not understand Hicks—even those who go by his name rather fear him, do not comprehend the gospel he preached and lived. Hicks was a greater hero than any man Carlyle celebrated in his book. But is does not surprise me that nobody has written him up: he was not sensational—he was too commonplace—too much like the rest of the people in his bravery to be taken for an official hero. I would have had a lot to say about his democracy. There were features in his mysticism with which I had little sympathy but the purport of his message had my entire approval. Hicks was in the last degree a simple character—carried no aureole or shrine about with him—liked to be taken for one of the crowd. He kept a house over his head and a little money in bank. He was not irresponsible—he did not default in his obligations: he lived the plainest life and he paid his bills." Had worked on the Fox today. "My notes are very accurate. I have found by experience that when I undertook to make a historic statement my facts were straight. I have made a headline, George Fox (and Shakspere) just as I once wrote of Father Taylor (and oratory)."

W. had a letter "from the German-Japanese Sadakichi Hartmann" today. Spoke of Hartmann's attempted Whitman club in Boston. "I want no club founded in my name." "Suppose a Whitman club could be founded without a Whitman doctrine— how would that strike you?" "That might strike me—but it is impossible." Again: "There's Sylvester Baxter—he's a theosophist and says I'm one. I had a letter from London the other day —from a young man there. He says he's a socialist—then says I'm a socialist, too. Tucker sees anarchism in the Leaves—sees me for an anarchist. So it goes." "Every man thinks you are his personal fellowman, Walt. You are in the Plato class—the world class. You include all if you can't be included." "Do you say that, knowing all it implies? Thank God! I hope I make room for all—include all—exclude nobody—nobody whatever— shut no door. If I have not achieved all I hoped for in that direction I hope I have hinted of it, started for it, made some motion as if to break the way." W. spoke of Boyle O'Reilly and O'Connor as "like as two peas in some ways"—said they both belong to the "tempest class." "Ardent Irish natures— clean, clear, afire with ideals of justice—willing, eager, anytime to live or die for justice." This was called out by a letter which W. told me to "take along and pigeon-hole."

THE PILOT EDITORIAL ROOMS,
March 5th, 1885.

Dear Mr. Whitman: I am delighted to hear from you—and that you are well. The books came all right. I enclose check for them.

Phil. Bagenal writes me from London that he has lost your picture by an accident to his house—fire, I suppose; and he wants another copy, with your autograph addressed to him. (You remember that I introduced Bagenal to you; he wrote an article about you in The Gentleman's Magazine; and he was an old friend of Standish O'Grady, &c. His name is O. H. Bagenal. He is now, by the way, doing well: assistant editor of the St. James Gazette, and private Sec. of the Earl of Dunraven.)

When sending the photo for him, I wish you would send one to me also with your autograph, and one to Dr. Kelly. It will gratify him exceedingly. I enclose the price of the photographs. Good bye. Love to you.

JOHN BOYLE O'REILLY.

"If you take a pinch of the best Irish salt you get the best salt of the earth," said W., again referring to O'Connor and O'Reilly. Then talked of his paralysis and the blood poisoning that led up to it. "The surgeons there in the hospitals got on to my trouble before I did myself. I seem to be remarkably constituted in one way—for being slow to affect things or be affected. I would never take a disease in a hurry—never make a convert in a hurry —and so on, so on. The trouble at Washington was the culmination of an unusual sympathetic and emotional expenditure of vital energy during those years 63–4–5: partly this and perhaps directly from the singular humor of a New York lad there in the hospitals who demanded to have me—would accept no one but me—to see him through his trouble—a whim quite frequently encountered in sick people. I attended to him—bound his wounds—did everything possible for him. He was an extreme case—an awful case—dangerous at any time as a charge. The effect upon me was slow, though one of the surgeons there finally called my attention to my own peril. He said that what would have made itself manifest in most others at once took a long time to appear in me. Even now, when they give me medicine, which in other men acts in an hour or two, it sometimes takes a day or two for that medicine to take effect. I always was deliberate—except for my vigor much as you see me now. I can see why Clifford said the other day that I made him think of Socrates. I never was nervous or quick. On the other hand I had, I may say, an unusual capacity for standing still, rooted on a spot, at a rest, for a long spell, to ruminate—hours in and out sometimes. The stories of Socrates—of his courage, invincibility, nerve, inertia—are very credible: they seem quite possible: and, as you say, Horace, the non-miraculous garb in which they have come down to us does in some degree attest them."

I heard a preacher speak of a man who was a "centerstance" rather than a "circumstance" in the universe. This struck W. as "very good" though "a bit too premeditated, deliberate." How could Clifford, being so free, talking with such freedom, stay even in a Unitarian pulpit? "It is phenomenal—it is indeed—but I do not look upon it as a condition that can last. The church is against freedom—the best church—against free interpretation—Clifford will some day rub the fur of the wrong fellow or fellows among his church-folk and then he will have to step out. It must happen sooner or later." We discussed the book. W. said: "Nobody can know our anxieties—we know: you know, I know: but, like Lincoln, while the hour is on we stick to the task resolutely and forget the hard ways by which we must effect it." Brought over today proof of pages 105, 6, 7, 8—also four galleys of the Hicks. "I see you do not mean that I shall get out of work." W. will put final touch on the Fox to-morrow. W. said, raising his right arm: "Nowhere but in this hand, wrist, arm, do I notice anything like physical vigor left: all the rest of my body has felt the irremediable nature of my recent losses. My left arm never fully recovered from the shock of 1873, though it has always been a useful remnant. My left leg was never itself again—was not restored—never reawakened."

Again expressed disappointment with the Hicks: "Let Clifford see the proofs. He may find a note or two for a text for a sermon. It is not without fear and trembling that I let it go—watch its course—send it on its voyage. What will be its effect? God knows. I have more fears than hopes. Horace, one of these days, after I am dead, when you find yourself saying things for me, say this for me—say this about Hicks: tell them how I planned for one thing and did another: repeat to them the words I have addressed to you about Hicks' democracy."

Thursday, July 26, 1888.

W. still weak though mainly well. Century proofs arrived. Gilder acquiesces in W.'s wish to use the War Memoranda in the book. "Some kind words from my friend William Carey there—William Carey. So I set to and rearranged the piece: discarded some parts, changed the position of certain paragraphs, besides inserting here and there a new sentence or dropping a bit." The George Fox is finished. Fixed it with minute directions to the printer. This completes the copy for the book. In the Century piece—Army Hospitals and Cases—he has changed the title for the book to Last of the War Cases. He thought the new title called for because of the many changes made in the text.

Had a letter from "a Western professor", he said, giving him "some sound advice concerning the prosody of Leaves of Grass." "Did he offer to come on?" "No—but he intimated that if what he said in this letter was not convincing he had other material to back it up." "What a shame you did not call a council of the school-masters before you wrote your book!" He laughed a good deal. "Yes—yes: and now it's too late! The harm's now about all done!" "You get lots of letters of advice?" "Lots of 'em! and not all of 'em mere letters of advice. Some of 'em are even threatening. You take this advice, Walt Whitman, or, God damn you, we'll know the reason why! That kind of a gentle gentleman emerges from a schoolroom or a study once in a while to take me in hand." "But you are so stubborn. Why don't you do what they demand!" "I would—I would—but they can never agree together as to what they want. Some don't like my long lines, some do: some don't like my commas, some do: some cuss my long catalogues, some think them holy: some call Children of Adam decent, some call Children of Adam obscene: and so on, and so on, and so on. Nothing I have done but a lot of somebodies have objected—nothing I have done but a lot of nobodies have praised. What's the use? What's the use?" He was first serious then merry over it. Wound up with saying: "My old daddy used to say it's some comfort to a man if he must be an ass anyhow to be his own kind of an ass!"

Saw the Photo-Engraving Company today about the reproduction of the Hicks. They sent some samples over to W. who looked at them with great interest. Some of them were landscapes. W. said: "They make me feel home-sick for the open air. My proper habitat is out-of-doors." We found that the photo of the bust made by Frank Harned would not reproduce well. When I repeated this to W. he replied; "Never mind: I've got something that will serve better anyway." Reached for his batch of Hicks notes, opened it, and took out an old steel-plate portrait. "After all this is better adapted to our uses in the book." Along with the engraving was a letter from Sidney Morse, a portrait of Hicks with a hat on, a small oil of Hicks, made by Morse, a replica of some original he found in the West. W. said: "This is a batch of stuff for a curio."

W. spoke of Cortland Palmer, just dead. "He was kind and friendly to me—was very hospitable—expressed every sort of desire to have me visit him, to have me as his guest. They all say great things of Palmer—of his big-minded, big-hearted ways. He and Ingersoll were dear friends, I am told. I have heard many stories about him and they were all the right kind—all on the side of love. Yes, he was the founder, the father, the good genius of the Nineteenth Century Club, the purpose of which, his purpose, was eternally fine. Palmer was what they call a free-thinker—and a free-thinker he indeed was. He left his

41

impression on the public life of New York—of America, in fact. Such a man is a vital influence. He don't write books or paint pictures but he does something a big sight more important. They may bury Palmer—they will bury him—and I do not feel like crying over his grave. There's only one word for some graves—hurrah is that word. Hurrah is the word for brave Palmer!"

Letters today, among others, from Bucke, O'Connor, Kennedy —the latter containing an enclosure of a note from Rhys, dated 4th July, coming from New-Castle-on-Tyne. "I laid them here for you—you need not bring them back. They don't contain anything special, but then we all like to read what is said by the other fellows who are in the swim with us—afloat on the same stream, gyrating in the same circle." We talked about the mechanics of the book. W.'s memory for present things has not been first class for a few weeks. He fights a bit with me over details. Then he caves. Tells me of the Hicks: "Some of these bits were written as many as thirty years ago. Some of them I have written within the past year. They are a miscellaneous lot but they all belong in the same stream." Gave me a portrait of John Forney bearing F.'s autograph and W.'s own note on the reverse: "John W. Forney, Philadelphia 1879–80–81." "Forney was of the high-class journalistic type—a type that is passing off the stage. We no longer associate newspapers with great men but with great pocket books. The Greeley Raymond Forney sort of newspaper is gone for good—gone, rather, for evil. I do not suppose anybody pretends that the present newspaper with all its parts—and it has parts—I concede them: great parts—stands for that something or other above money and the monitions of money which controlled and inspired the journalists of the ideal stamp. Forney was not the last of his line but certainly was one of the last. Personally, to me, he was always noble, gracious, conciliatory: he had in a certain sense the grand manner, as polite writers are pleased to call it, but was a simple man of most lovable traits under all hauteurs." Giving me an old Burroughs letter he said: "That is like a visit to John:

it is just as if I took a trip with him into the woods. I can taste his fruit—I can hear the birds sing. It is an old letter—it has been about this room now many a year. John was fresh at Esopus then: he had a tussle there at first—but he has won out: he is a master vine-dresser these days: and all the time his grip on himself has grown firmer—his intuitions have grown cuter. John is a wood wizard: things come out of their holes—present themselves—ask for orders—when John goes into the woods." W. had written on this letter: "ans. May 21."

Esopus, N. Y. May 17, '74.

Dear Walt: I rec'd a magazine (the Galaxy) from you yesterday, which I have been peeping in a little today, but the day has been so beautiful and the charm of the open air so great that I could not long keep my eyes on the printed page. The season is at last fairly in for it, and the fruit trees are all getting in bloom. My bees are working like beavers and there is a stream of golden thighs passing into the hive all the time. I can do almost anything with them and they won't sting me. Yesterday I turned a hive up and pruned it, that is cut out a lot of old dirty comb; the little fellows were badly frightened and came pouring out in great consternation, but did not offer to sting me. I am going to transfer a swarm in a day or two to a new style of hive. I spend all my time at work about the place and like it much. I run over to M. to look after bank matters for a day or two then back here. The house is being plastered and will be finished during the summer. The wrens and robins and phoebe birds have already taken possession of various nooks of it, and if they are allowed to go on with their building I must stop mine. During that snowstorm the last of April the hermit thrush took refuge in it. We are surrounded with birds here and they are a great comfort and delight to me.

Your room is ready for you and your breakfast plate warmed. When will you come? I know the change would do you good and your presence would certainly do us good. We are counting on your coming; do not disappoint us. I will meet you in New

York if you will tell me when. Let us hear from you soon. Ursula sends love.

As ever,

JOHN BURROUGHS.

W. said further about J. B.: "Did you stop to take a second look at that line in the letter, 'a stream of golden thighs passing into the hive'? John's power is in his simplicity. He writes well because he does not try to write." "Do you mean that a man should not be deliberate? Your writing is deliberate enough." He replied: "I may say it this way—that we should try to secure expression but that we should not try to make an impression." "But don't expression make an impression?" "I see I have not said the thing very well myself. Let me say it another way. We make one sort of impression by sincerity and another sort of impression by trickery. I mean that we should not try to make an impression by trickery." Seeing I was satisfied he went on about Burroughs: "John never bowls you over with any vivid passion of speech—it is not in him to do it —but he calms and soothes you—takes you out into the open where things are in an amiable mood. John might get real mad —his kettle boil over—but his language would remain conciliatory. William O'Connor under the same excitation would blow fiercely and leave his mark on the landscape." "But don't both ways lead to clear weather?" He laughed. "Yes, they do, and I was about to say so, but you took it out of my mouth. Why do you take all the good things out of my mouth?"

Friday, July 27, 1888.

W. much today as on other days this week but not quite so much interested in general matters. No mail, except a note from Frank Gilman, asking W. to autograph a photo, which W. did without hesitation. An autograph letter yesterday started, "I am glad to see that you are about again," and then said, "would you be kind enough," &c. This made W. laugh. "He thinks I'm about again just for that." But running a pen-line ing to transfer a swarm in a day or two a new style of hive, I spend all my time at work about the place & like it much. I run over to M. to look after bank matters for a day or two then back here. The house is being plastered & will be finished during the summer. The wrens & robins & phoebe birds have already taken possession of various nooks of it, & even if they are allowed to go on with their building, I must stop mine. During that snow storm the last of april the Hermit thrush took refuge in it, the are surrounded with birds here & they are a great comfort & delight to me.

Your room is ready for you & your breakfast plate warmed. When will you come? I know the change would do you good & your presence would certainly do us good. We are counting on your coming & do not disappoint us. I will meet you in N.Y. if you will tell me when. Let us hear from you soon Ursula sends love.

As Ever   John Burroughs

A PAGE FROM A BURROUGHS LETTER TO WALT WHITMAN.

across the written page and pointing to the reverse side of the sheet, W. said: "Those fellows have one virtue—they always use good paper: and on that I manage to do a good deal of my writing." He averages two or three letters of this character a day. I saw the process people about the Hicks picture with a result which induced W. to say: "I guess we may take it as decided that the Inman is our picture. If the reproduction comes anywhere near it I shall be satisfied." We are to pay four or five dollars for the work. W. talked of the Hicks: "Hicks I remember as a presence rather than in outline as a concrete body. I do not know that such a picture as this would in itself have been recognizable. I was too young when I saw Hicks. But Inman was a famous man in his day—one of the greatest of the artists —and I do not know but he is still highly regarded. I have always understood that this particular portrait of Hicks is as good as it is rare—and it is rare indeed. What a study it all is—this of portraits: no two of them identical: every interpreter getting another view. What amazing differences develope in the attempt of a dozen observers to tell the same story!" The engravers today said of the Morse and Inman portraits: "They are too unlike to be of the same person." W. replied: "Not so—not so: there are as many views as there are people to take them." W. was "not proud of the photographs of" himself. "I've been taken and taken beyond count—taken from every side—even from my blind side"—laughing—"taken in utter wretchedness of posture for the most part. No man has been photographed more than I have or photographed worse: I've run the whole gamut of photographic fol-de-rol." I kicked. "It seems to me many of your pictures are better than good—better than you deserve, maybe." He regarded me with great merriment. "Better than I deserve, no doubt—that's what consoles me—but still damnable."

Spoke of Last of the War Cases. He had put "last" into the title because the incidents cited "were left over after the close of the war, having to do with the final batch of the injured and needy." In this connection W. remarked: "By the way I have saved you another document of the war period: here it is now—take it along in your pocket." He handed me an envelope on which he had written: "Oct 5, '63 Margaret S Curtis care Charles P Curtis Boston, Mass." He got the impression that I proposed to sit right down and read it. It was a rather long letter. "You can read it when you get home. We had better finish our talk first." He had the Hicks proofs on his lap. Was he satisfied with it? "I am not disappointed—I could not say I am disappointed—but I am not enthused, either. It is so far—so very far—from the thing I dreamed of doing. It was to have been a very complete story—I had the largest hopes, designs, for it—still, as I read it now, it's not so bad (though bad enough) as I feared it would be. I must be satisfied now if I have succeeded in hinting at matters which it was a part of my original scheme to enlarge upon. On the whole, it is not a radical failure—neither is it a radical success."

Having read the full account of Cortland Palmer's funeral yesterday W. confessed that he was "aroused by Ingersoll's speech." "Ingersoll certainly has what I would call a genius for such a function: all his funeral addresses are marvels of beauty: short, musical, rich in cadence, pithy, never too much, never too little: and the best part of Ingersoll is, I don't think anybody ever loses interest in him who hears him speak—ever goes to sleep—ever goes wool-gathering to other scenes in his presence. He is one of the very few—the very select few—who are alive and keep others alive with them." W. did not like Phillips as well. "He was haughty, noble, powerful, but without Ingersoll's jovial reactions. He never spoke but to cut—cut somewhere: with a keen blade, infallibly cut."

Called my attention to a newspaper clipping in which he was again taken to task for not going to the front and fighting during the war. "I had my temptations, but they were not strong enough to tempt. I could never think of myself as firing a gun or drawing a sword on another man. Higginson has more than once, and in print, too, called me to the same account, quoting my record decisively to my discredit, seeming to regard it as an argu-

ment entitled to a great deal of weight—indeed, as being final."
He pointed to a haversack on the wall. "That's a souvenir of
those days: it was given to me by Allen, of the Commissary Department, I think. I often used it at that time in going about
Washington—in the hospitals—among the soldier boys: slung
it over my shoulder in a way to make it comfortable. I have
never once used it since I came to Camden. [Several years afterwards W. presented me with the haversack and it has ever since
hung on my wall. 1906]

Ingram called today but was not admitted to W.'s room. W.
sent his regrets. Ingram was hurt, Musgrove tells me. But
W. explained to me: "I love the old man but cannot stand his
busy talk in my present mess of mind." Hinted that he might
"make a try towards going down stairs to-morrow." W. and I
had a little jollification over a bit of his writing that I picked up
off the floor. "Burst in lecture (or poem)" it was called. This
is the way it reads:

"We talk of our age's materialism—and it is too true—in
gloomy hours—how, amid all the sordidness, the entire devotion
of America, at any price, to mere pecuniary success—merchan-
dise disregarding all but direct business and profit—how for a
bare idea and abstraction or mere heroic dream and reminiscence
—this war burst forth in its great devouring flame and conflagra-
tion, quickly and fiercely spreading and raging, and enveloping
all, [break] into two great ideas—that of the Union cause—and
the other—a strange, deadly Interrogation point, hard to define
what—have we not now safely confest it?—Even that other, with
magnificent rays, streaks, of noblest heroism, fortitude, persever-
ance and even conscientiousness, shedding flashes of light
through its pervadingly malignant darkness. Was there not
something grand—and a perennial proof of American grandeur
—in that war."

"That," said W., "is a piece of an unborn oration: it was to be
a burst, but the bomb never exploded—though I don't know

but the substance of it got into the books somewhere anyhow."
"You often gave yourself advice on paper." "I suppose I did:
I wrote things down: I saw them better in my handwriting than
in my mind's eye—could tell better whether they suited me or
not." "Ingersoll once asked me whether your writing
was pretty well finished before you wrote at all or whether you
wrote mainly, and revised, on paper. I told him I thought you
made lots of use of pens, inks and papers." W. smiled and assented. "So I do—so I do: your answer was the answer I would
have made myself." As I left W. said: "We are not keeping
Ferguson on the anxious bench nowadays. He is a patient man.
He suffered a heap from us, didn't he?"

Saturday, July 28, 1888.

This is the Curtis letter W. gave me yesterday:

WASHINGTON, ARMORY SQ HOSPITAL,
Sunday Evening Oct 4

Dear Madam, Your letter reached me this forenoon with the
$30 for my dear boys, for very dear they have become to me,
wounded and sick here in the government hospitals.—As it happens I find myself rapidly making acknowledgment of your
welcome letter and contribution from the midst of those it was
sent to aid—and best by a sample of actual hospital life on the
spot, and of my own goings around the last two or three hours—
As I write I sit in a large pretty well-filled ward by the cot of a
lad of 18 belonging to Company M 2d N Y cavalry, wounded
three weeks ago today at Culpeper—hit by fragment of a shell
in the leg below the knee—a large part of the calf of the leg is
torn away, (it killed his horse)—still no bones broken, but a
pretty large ugly wound—I have been writing to his mother at
Comac, Suffolk co. N Y—. She must have a letter just as if
from him, about every three days—it pleases the boy very
much—he has four married sisters—them also I have to write
to occasionally—Although so young he has been in many fights
and tells me shrewdly about them, but only when I ask him. He

is a cheerful good-natured child—has to lie in bed constantly his leg in a box—I bring him things—he says little or nothing in the way of thanks—is a country boy—always smiles and brightens much when I appear—looks straight in my face and never at what I may have in my hand for him—I mention him for a specimen as he is within reach of my hand and I can see that his eyes have been steadily fixed on me from his cot ever since I began to write this letter. This youngster is no special favorite —only a needful case—it will not do at all to show partiality here—there are some 25 or 30 wards, barracks, tents, &c in this hospital—This is ward C, has beds for 60 patients—they are mostly full—most of the other principal wards about the same—so you see a U S general hospital here is quite an establishment—this has a regular police, armed sentries at the gates and in the passages &c,—and a great staff of surgeons, cadets, women and men nurses &c &c. I come here pretty regularly because this hospital receives I think the worst cases and is one of the least visited—there is not much hospital visiting here now—it has become an old story—the principal here, Dr. Bliss, is a very fine operating surgeon—sometimes he performs several amputations or other operations of importance in a day —amputations, blood, death are nothing to him—you will see a group absorbed in playing cards up at the other end of the room.

I visit the sick every day or evening—sometimes I stay far in the night, on special occasions. I believe I have not missed more than two days in past six months. It is quite an art to visit the hospitals to advantage. The amount of sickness, and the number of poor, wounded, dying young men is appalling. One often feels lost, despondent, his labors not even a drop in the bucket—the wretched little he can do in proportion.

I believe I mentioned in my letter to Dr. Russell that I try to distribute something, even if but the merest trifle, all round, without missing any, when I visit a ward, going round rather rapidly—and then devoting myself more at leisure to the cases that need special attention. One who is experienced may find in almost any ward at any time one or two patients or more who are at that time trembling in the balance, the crisis of the wound, recovery uncertain, yet death also uncertain. I will confess to you madam that I think I have an instinct and faculty for these cases. Poor young men, how many have I seen and know—how pitiful it is to see them,—one must be calm and cheerful, and not let on how their case really is, must stop much with them, find out their idiosyncrasies—do anything for them—nourish them— judiciously give them the right things to drink,—bringing in the affections, soothe them, brace them up, kiss them, discard all ceremony, and fight for them, as it were, with all weapons. I need not tell your womanly soul that such work blesses him that works as much as the object of it. I have never been happier than in some of these hospital ministering hours.

It is now between 8 and 9 evening—the atmosphere is rather solemn here to-night—there are some very sick men here—the scene is a curious one—the ward is perhaps 120 or 30 feet long— the cots each have their white mosquito curtains—all is quite still—an occasional sigh or groan—up in the middle of the ward the lady nurse sits at a little table with a shaded lamp, reading— the walls, roof, &c are all whitewashed—the light up and down the ward from a few gas-burners about half turned down—It is Sunday evening—to-day I have been in the hospital, one part or another, since three o'clock—to a few of the men, pretty sick, or just convalescing and with delicate stomachs or perhaps badly wounded arms, I have fed their suppers—partly peaches peeled, and cut up with powdered sugar, very cool and refresh- ing,—they like to have me sit by them and peel them, cut them in a glass, and sprinkle on the sugar—(all these little items maybe may interest you).

I have given three of the men this afternoon, small sums of money—I provide myself with a lot of bright new 10 ct and 5 ct bills, and when I give little sums of change I give the bright new bills. Every little thing even must be taken advantage of— to give bright fresh 10 ct bills instead of any other helps break the dullness of hospital life—

I said to W.: "What you said the other day about Burroughs I think also applies to you. This letter is alive all through—every word of it. It carries me back with you into that old experience. I think I can see you there writing in the hospital and see that boy looking at you and smell the medicines" —W. broke in: "Good for me if you can do all that: good enough for me! My main motive would be to say things: not to say them prettily—not to stun the reader with surprises—with fancy turns of speech—with unusual, unaccustomed words—but to say them—to shoot my gun without a flourish and reach the mark if I can. The days in the hospitals were too serious for that."

W. spoke of this as his "best day since the throw-down." "I took a bath as I like to—alone, quietly." Resents the attentions of Musgrove. He got to like Baker but Musgrove rubs him the wrong way. Did not go down stairs yesterday. For the first time fully dressed this evening—gray coat and all—as he sat in his chair. "If I remind myself of it I can see that my mind is not quite all right, but otherwise I can be as chipper as a well man." Feeling weak but very cheerful. I had with me concluding proofs of Last of the War Cases. Letters from Bucke and Logan Smith today. The latter writes from London. W. laughed: "The fellows abroad have an idea, all of them, that we're roasting here. Every letter I receive condoles with me over the heat by which I am tortured." He stopped to pick up his knife that had fallen to the floor. He often plays with his penknife, opening and shutting it as he talks. "This is on the contrary the most remarkable July I have ever known—so far it has been entirely comfortable."

Speaking of churches: "I never made any vows to go or not to go: I went, at intervals, but anywhere—to no one place: was a wanderer: went oftenest in my earlier life—gradually dropped off altogether: today a church is a sort of offense to me. I never had any 'views'—was always free—made no pledges, adopted no creeds, never joined parties or 'bodies.' Many years ago a reporter came to me about some comments *anent* me that appeared in Appleton's Journal: how did I dress when I was young, how now, what were my habits—and more like that. I said to him: I always dressed as I do now and spoke and acted as I do now—that's all I know about it—that's all I can tell you. And that's what I could say now about churches and views: I am as I was: I have not changed. I have met many preachers in my time—some of the sleek kind, but many of them personally good fellows, who treated me well. Always remember, though I hate preaching I do not hate preachers." Pointed out to me an editorial paragraph in the Tribune: "I regret that anybody is willing to accept the doctrine of protection no matter what may be its good fruits—that anybody in America is willing to acknowledge no obligations to other lands, other peoples, demanding protection, welfare, for themselves, no matter how it is secured. America should be an example not an echo— therein lies her chief function—not to follow, oh no, but to lead the way." W. believes in "free Sundays. The boys should have their ball or any frolic they choose: the grown folks should do very much as they please: theaters should be open— there should be plenty of music. Sunday should be a light, not a dark, day. Any law that interferes with innocent enjoyment is a barbarous law no matter who is in favor of it. I would wipe such laws out with a sponge—every one of them—if I could."

Some one asked W. if Emerson's manner lacked in emotion, W. answering: "I do not think so: it had the true ring: Emerson would satisfy all demands of that sort I could make of him. I did think that Thoreau and Emerson, both of them, years ago, in the Brooklyn days, were a little bookish in their expression of love: I say I used to think so, for I don't know how the thing would strike me now." W. has not read Carlyle's Sterling or his Frederick. Said he would "like to read the Sterling—indeed, thought" he "should do it," but imagined "the Frederick is much too big a big thing for" him "to tackle at this late day." "I do not believe the book would interest me a great deal anyhow: I have looked it over—Carlyle makes too much of the battles. My experiences on the field have shown me that the writers catch very little of the real atmosphere of a battle. It is an assault, an immense noise, somebody driven off the field—a victory won: that is all. It is like trying to photograph a tempest."

I said to W. this evening: "Your style is not very new—it is very old." He laughed, shaking a finger towards me: "That is wicked: who told you? Who put you on to my secret?" "It's not even a secret—anybody might know it who looked." To which he replied: "So they might—so they might—if they would only forget their canons, rules, for awhile. It's a great thought, Horace,—you have said it all. I am willing to acquiesce in Heine's notions of criticism. Heine would ask of a book and its writer, not, 'has he written it as I would like him to do it?' but first: ' had he an idea, a point of view, a central thought?' and then, 'has he said what he undertook to say?— done what he undertook to do?' Heine had no doctrine of art with which to flay the rebel: he let the rebel alone: he knew that the rebel was a rebel for reasons."

W. wondered "what the Germans would think of Lewes' Life of Goethe," adding: "I have my own troubles with the German poets: I ought to read them a lot but the translations do not satisfy me. Leland's translation of the Reisebilder is, however, a joy and a delight. My nature, my temperament, my blood, should take me close to the Teuton." "It is singular," said W. suddenly, "how people may get to believe they are saying a new thing when they are simply rehashing a very ancient text. Take Democracy, for instance: the American, the average American, thinks he has a new idea. The truth is that even our proud modern definitions of democracy are antiquated—can be heard reflected in the language of the Elizabethan period in England—in the atmosphere created by Bacon, Ben Jonson, and the rest of that crowd. I would not like to say there might not have been latent in the utterances of that group of men the seed stuff of our American liberty—not to speak of the still older suggestions of it to be found in Greek and Roman sources." Referring to an Italian who had been murdered: "The poor

Italian immigrants! The popular fury now seems to be applied to them—and what have they done, indeed? I wonder if our people really believe the Chinese menace our institutions—the industrious, quiet, inoffensive Chinese? Maybe our institutions ain't no good if they're as thin-skinned as that."

Pointing to a scrapbook on the floor at his feet: "It is a strange miscellany—a hodge-podge, some of it only pulp, some of it very vital: curious, rejected reviews, critiques, odds and ends of newspaper gossip—all of it in the past, the far past—gathered together fifty years ago and on from that time for many years. I have always had it about me as a book for personal reference. It was mislaid for a long time, then reappeared—has been fished out of its barrel again lately: I am again making use of it." "What has that particular book to do with Leaves of Grass?" "Oh! everything! is full of its beginnings—is the a b c of the book—contains the first lisps of the song. How much of it has come and gone like last night's rain!" he exclaimed. "But," I protested, "that was sweet and useful." "Yes—so it was—and so was the book—sweet and useful! Here was my first tally of life—here were my first tries with the lute—in that book I am just like a man tuning up his instrument before the play begins." [The contents of the book were afterwards included by Dr. Bucke in Notes and Fragments. 1906] Finally he said as I was about to withdraw: "Our talk to-night has not been a song without words. I have talked like a man with a new dictionary—have celebrated my re-entrance into clothes by tooting for two hours on my tin horn."

Sunday, July 29, 1888.

W. spent a pretty good day reading proof and writing letters, the almost inevitable note to Bucke among them. Appetite not bad. Still weak. He stepped into the hallway yesterday and threw some soiled clothes down stairs. Mrs. Davis cried: "You must be feeling stronger!" but he demurred: "I'm not, Mary: I feel as weak as a cat." Said he had "a few vague suspicions of returning strength but very few." Gave me a Bucke letter mostly talking about W.'s health. He had read the Press article about himself today. It contained a good picture of the house and lots of cheap talk about W. and his habits since the attack in June. W. asked: "Could we call that *flat?* it certainly is stale and unprofitable: but we should not complain—it could so easily have been worse: we may congratulate ourselves upon being let off with such slight damage." Then he laughed and added: "We could do better than that ourselves." Told me he had been reading Moore, Scott and Burns today. "I go to them again and again in certain humors: they are very consoling." Added a paragraph to the prefatory Note going with the Hicks. Changes not many—several of them, however, characteristic: for instance, where he had "father and mother" he made it now "dear, dear father and mother." Read eight galleys of the Hicks and four of the Last of the War Cases. Nothing left to go into type except the Hicks notes and the Fox paper.

W. asked me whether I had seen The American this week? "Here it is—and it contains a paper by Miss Repplier. It is curious and unfortunate that this should be the best of the lot so far." He read a tariff interview had by some reporter with Ingersoll. "I like Ingersoll, sure enough, but his logic in this matter is queer, to say the least. What will America do? Is she for the great mass of men?—the race, the whole globe? No man is a democrat, a true democrat, who forgets that he is interested in the welfare of the race. Who asks only, what is best for America? instead of, what is best for man—the whole of man? Is a man a citizen of Camden only? No—no indeed. And if not of Camden, not of New Jersey, nor even of America. No—no—no—no: a man is no democrat if he takes the narrow in preference to the broad view. He may talk of democracy, of the people, but it's all a lie—all false—nothing but nuts crackling under a pot. I am not interested in what Carnegie is doing to establish libraries abroad but in what he is doing to keep peace with and render justice to his men here. My item in Specimen Days asking what the working man gets out of the tariff still holds good. I haven't grown conservative on that question with age."

W. answering my inquiry said: "No, I didn't go down stairs today. To-morrow I'm going to make a motion for doing so though I don't know as the motion will be carried: I must go, if only for a few minutes. I want to prove to you fellows—to myself—that I've not entirely gone up the spout." I protested some. He laughed. "Oh! it won't hurt me: my caution, you remember, is six and over! I shall go only when the spirit moves me: if it don't move then not at all. I find the best way to spend my days—at least did long ago—is the free way: not to make plans, but to go this path or that as the mood dictates." Gave me the Hicks picture—the Inman—with many admonitions to me to see that the engraver took good care of it. On a November Boughs proof page given me for size W. wrote: "Size of page Nov: Boughs to picture is illustrate." That's the way his phrases mix up occasionally, especially in writing. When he speaks a confused sentence he corrects it at once. I suggested that he should preserve the manuscript of November Boughs. He acquiesced. "The first manuscript copy of the Leaves—1855—the first edition—is gone—irretrievably lost—went to the ragman: the copy for the Osgood edition I think is still about somewhere. But I make nothing of that— of the money value of the manuscripts—attach no importance to curios. The collectors are inflamed with the curio desire but to me the appetite is unwholesome—at least never excited even my momentary interest. And yet," he reflected, "for Eddy's sake it might be wise for me to husband such stuff—though I don't know: even that seems to me rather wide of the mark. I have for years done so many things with reference to Eddy— have stinted, spared, saved, put by, cherished, watched—so that I might not slip cable some day with him unprovided for. Eddy is helpless: has been at Moorestown—is shortly to go elsewhere: was a poor, stunted boy almost from the first. He had the convulsions—it was all up with him—the infernal, damnable, fits, that left him not half himself from that time on forever." I said to W.: "There is a line in Faces that always makes me think of Eddy." He replied: "There should be several. Eddy had much to do with the inspiration of that poem." I quoted this: "I knew of the agents that emptied and broke my brother." "Yes," said W. "that's one line—you might take the whole verse." I reminded W. of one of my sisters similarly afflicted. "Yes, I remember: Tillie: poor dear little Tillie! but she never was so far gone as Eddy, who practically has never had any mental life at all: who has lived in darkness, eclipsed almost from the start." Paused. "And so I turn every thing I can into provisioning for him. The little property—Lord knows it's little enough: all, all, for Eddy—for such boon as it may bring to him after I am gone." I found on the floor a slip containing a prose paragraph which may be taken as the origin of the first stanza of By Blue Ontario's Shore. I made this guess to W. He said: "Let me see it." Took it—looked it over—handed it back. "No doubt you are right: I remember. Get the book—let's hear how the poem reads." A copy of the book was on the table in front of him. I read to him. He concluded: "You guessed right first time. That's more than I could have done." This is the way the slip read:

"A song America demands that breathes her native air—an utterance to invigorate Democracy. Democracy, the destined conqueror—(yet treacherous lip-smiles everywhere, and death and infidelity at every step.) Of such a song let me, (for I have had that dream,) initiate here the NOVICE'S ATTEMPT,—and bravos to the bards, who coming after me, do better far."

The last phrase had originally read: "to those who, coming after me, do better." As I was leaving W. remarked: "I was destroying some papers today but I saved a few for you." I kicked at once. "I knew you would growl—but no matter—you growl but you do not bite. I am, in fact, Horace, saving you all the essential things—the things that make history: what

I chuck away or burn up is not worth while keeping either for your purposes or mine. Here—take this bunch with my blessing and be happy. He was ahungry and I gave him meat: I feed you with the food you love!" He seemed to enjoy himself a big lot while he was saying this. Then he passed a little package over to me. "You can carry the stuff along with you in your side pocket. If they arouse any questions you can put your questions to me to-morrow." The packet tied with a string contained several Redpath letters and single letters from Rolleston, O'Connor, G. C. Macaulay, W. W., and a receipt to Allen Thorndike Rice from W. W. I looked them over a bit before going home and said to W.: "Yes, this is a full meal." He chuckled gleefully. "I am glad to satisfy you now and then. One of my main concerns in life nowadays is to keep you in good humor."

Monday, July 30, 1888.

This has been one of W.'s worst days. "It may be the weather—it is most likely something else. I haven't cast out all of my devils yet." Brought him new proofs which he at once glanced over. Was astonished to find that the Last of the War Cases made nine pages. "I do little nowadays but sit and thank my stars that I have fallen into such good hands in the time of my need." Today for the first time since taking Baker's place Musgrove found W. willing to invite assistance. Harned and his little girl Anna came in. No letter from Bucke. Spoke of it. Bucke's letters have become a part of W.'s routine. "I sent off a package of papers to Nellie O'Connor—O'Connor's wife." Harned asked: "Is she a bright woman?" "Bright? Quite so—remarkably so—interested in the big things always— a rare beautiful woman: sweet, equable, calm." After a pause: "Did you know O'Connor is writing a long reply to Donnelly's critics in this Shakespeare business? I have no doubt it will be very bright—brighter than Donnelly himself, by far. William is thoroughly grounded in the lore of that period—no man more so: I am convinced that he understands the philosophy of that question much better than Donnelly himself. But while Donnelly's knowledge is not novel, he has put it better than any of his predecessors—than Delia Bacon, for instance, to cite one of them. To me Donnelly's general argument was conclusive: I was in fact ready to be convinced and he passed along and drew me after him. Mine was no sudden conversion, however —it was the outcome of years of study and thought: I drifted, drifted, always in one direction, and arrived at last." W. very animated. Harned sat down. They went on for some time about Bacon.

W. said of yesterday's Press piece: "The more you look at it the worse it seems." Did he expect to make any money out of November Boughs? He laughed: "If I get out of it what I put into it I will be lucky: if I got in addition a little fob of bills for my vest-pocket here I would feel like a millionaire." Harned put in: "I suppose the book will be a dollar and a half." W. shook his head. "No—that's too much: not more than a dollar and a quarter at the most—a dollar if possible." W. added, answering another question of Harned's: "I like to keep my prices down to the level of my real friends. The people with money wouldn't buy me anyhow. I must make it possible for the people without money to buy me."

W. expressed great happiness over what he construed to be O'Connor's "improved condition." "They are a part of me— I am a part of them—William, Nellie. They received me with open arms when I was rejected—they were my dearest, dearest friends, staunchest from the start. They have had their profound sorrows—children lost, two children, one of them a girl, a fine girl who almost grew up." Spoke of the precautions necessary for him to maintain his health. "I must do nothing now to stop the book: I mustn't be the cow to upset the pail of my own milk." Asked Harned to bring him some pears. "They are divine food when the stomach is ready for prayer." Did not go down stairs today, as he threatened last night. "The fact is, I forgot all about it—the spirit did not move me." Harned remarked that the campaign was cool now but would be brot in the fall. W. denied it. "No—cool then, too. What is there for anybody to enthuse over? The real issues are not in politics yet. I notice the Press has its flings, slanders—prods itself into anger: but what does that amount to?" Harned withdrew with his youngster. We then had some talk over the letters he gave me yesterday. I spoke in such enthusiastic terms of the O'Connor letter that W. said: "Read it to me again—I would like to hear it read again: I have read it to myself a dozen times." He smiled quietly: "When William gets going he is more exciting than an alarm of fire. Read it." So I read.

WASHINGTON, D. C., July 20, 1882.

Dear Walt: I just have your postal of the 19th, announcing the first edition out and gone in a day! Hooray! Come on, Vice Society!

I am rejoiced. Rees, Welsh and Co ought to have printed more, but no matter. If they manage right now, they can secure a prodigious sale. The main thing is not to be afraid, but to face persecution. The thunderstorm mounts against the wind.

Comstock is here, probably merely on Post Office business, he being a special agent. If he is moving against your book, I shall hear of it. But the Department is in his way, as he will find. He ought to be pitched out of the public service. . . . I just want a square chance—a clear sight—to embalm him in a letter. Properly shown up he would be bounced.

I have a bad dose in preparation for Tobey. There has been some delay, work presses me so much, together with the load of the dog-day weather, and I have been really quite ill for a week with a severe cold. I wish I could go North for a while to recover.

I got the Press you sent with the Rev. Mr. Morrow's remarks, which I had already seen in the Tribune. He is a pearl among clergymen, and I feel grateful to him. I heard a story once how the brilliant Douglas Jerrold astonished an evening party in London by a constant fire of *jeu de mots* for hours, which continued until every person in the room, man or woman, had been the subject of a jest or epigram, always splendid and nearly always tart. Finally, when the admired wit was leaving, every eye fixed upon him, every ear bent to hear whatever he might utter, Charles Knight, the historian, whose sweetness of nature made him loved by all, standing near the door, said to him with a smile, "You've said something this evening about everyone here except me, Douglas; have you nothing to say about me?" "Yes," replied Jerrold, tenderly pressing his hand as he went away, "Good Knight!" I feel like imitating this wit, and saying, not in parting but in welcome, to our new friend, "Good Morrow."

I have an immensely cordial letter from Dr. Channing, who says he is going to write to you.

Send me one of the new edition when you can.

Faithfully,
W. D. O'CONNOR.

"Yes," said W., "I was selling books then: they went like hot cakes. I never sold them before, I have never sold them since. The next thing to being fashionable is to be unfashionable. Did you notice William's fling at Comstock? What a foolish question—of course you noticed it. The best or the worst of it is, it is all deserved. Of course we should always admit with regard to Comstock that he is what he is for reasons: he is quite honest in all his imbecility." W. thought the "Good Morrow" incident in the letter, "most characteristic of William—most beautiful: just like him in every way," adding: "You know William never stopped to invent, to manufacture, such things—they just came to him, were in and out in a flash." When I asked him about G. C. Macaulay W. said: "He once wrote a paper about me and published it somewhere or other—I don't this minute just recollect where. Didn't you like his letter? It was very warm—very comfortable: like a fire for your backbone when you go in out of the cold. I just nestle up to some letters as if I needed them the worst way. Then you must remember that more things are coming our way now than five or ten or twenty years ago." W. likes to have me read letters to him. He settles himself comfortably in his chair or on the bed listening, sometimes interrupting with comments, though inarticulate. So he had me read Macaulay, though he was quite well aware of the contents of the letter.

RUGBY, ENGLAND, Jan. 9th, 1883.

Sir: I have received the copy of Specimen Days and Collect which you were so kind as to send me, and I hope to have the opportunity soon of saying what I think about it in some English periodical. ["Funny," said W., breaking in, "he did write but I can't for the life of me think of the magazine he got his essay into"]. I have been deeply interested in the book, especially in so far as it supplies the "embryons" of Leaves of Grass, and I am especially gratified to receive it from yourself. My acquaintance with Leaves of Grass dates from my early university days some ten years ago, when having come across Rossetti's edition of selections I was induced soon after to get a complete edition. Since then I have never neglected them, and often enjoyed the effect of awakening others to a perception of its great force and beauty, which being accompanied by so much which (justly or unjustly) excites prejudice, are too often overlooked. As regards the new book, which I have eagerly read, some of it was familiar to me already, e. g. Democratic Vistas— but Specimen Days was entirely new and altogether delightful. I am inclined to think that it will place many readers in a better position to appreciate Leaves of Grass than heretofore. With thanks both for this book and for former benefits received, I remain—

Yours faithfully,
G. C. MACAULAY.

After I was through reading the letter I had to get out to meet an engagement. I wanted to talk with W. some about the Rolleston and Redpath letters but put it off. Before I left he said: "You must never drop the reins—I am depending upon your firm hand in our affairs to bring this journey to a successful finish." He asked me: "Do you go to New York sometimes?" and after my answer said: "You should some day drop in on the Gilders—they would be glad to see you. You mustn't suppose Watson is the only member of the household who is worth while: after you see Mrs. Watson you will find yourself acknowledging a divided allegiance. Women are often the silent partners but they are quite as essential to the business of life as the men-crowd with their incessant catawauling. Look at me—sitting here all my days now, talking, talking, like a dictionary with legs on and a mouth."

Tuesday, July 31, 1888.

Favorable change in W. today. Still no letter from Bucke. W. wrote to Burroughs, "not," as he said, "so much to say any-thing myself (for I said very little) but to enclose the note from Nellie O'Connor, which I knew he would like to see. I believe I told you O'Connor is better than for a long time. It is as though he had reached a high plateau with a clear stretch of country ahead of him, the winds blowing free, the air tonic. William might now go to his journey's end uninterrupted." Before leaving O'Connor W. added: "I don't know whether his criticism of the critics will be a book or a pamphlet: whatever it comes to in the end it will be sharp and fierce, we may rest as-sured—stronger than anything Donnelly has written. I believe William knows a good lot more than Donnelly about the subject —draws deeper water." Mentioned the Lady Mount Temple's vest: "It was never made for me—the owner has not been found yet."

I had been stirred by the last paragraph of the Fox. "It's splendid: perfect strength and eloquence—you never went higher than that." W. exclaimed: "Ah! you find that all there —just as you say it? I am glad—glad: glad there is at least that much to it all. I have never made any full statement on religion in any of my writings but I have always intended to." "But your whole book is religion. We do not want the figures for it.

We are satisfied with the spirit." "You say that, too? Well—maybe, maybe. No doubt I have said enough on the subject—said really all there was in me to say: a few figures more would not have helped. In the days when I was planning to write and deliver lectures I designed one lecture at least on religion—indeed, collected a great mass of material for it. I never felt as though the discussion of religion should be left to the priests: it never seemed to me safe in their hands:"

Took him this evening the Hicks notes and the Fox paper, which together make three galleys. This puts the whole book in type. W. very happy over it. "But we will go right on," he said, "without pauses, stoppages, which at this stage of the game would be dangerous." Discussed press-work, binding and so forth. Gave me his flexible Epictetus for sample of paper but said: "Don't leave it with the printers—show it to them—then bring it back: it's a precious book to me—I don't want to even risk losing it." W. has an idea of putting the Hicks-Fox matter eventually into a special pamphlet. Made many changes of the make-up in order to get the Hicks started on an odd page. This is one of his memorandums to the printer: "begin making up Elias Hicks on page 119 I will supply something for page 118—(*if it suits well and prints well* we will put the now being made portrait of Elias Hicks on page 118)—don't mind on page 118 nor wait for it—but go on making up with E H &c when ready." A blank space occurred on a made-up page between two notes. Instead of having it closed in by shifting the pages he simply added a line. He always knows the easiest way out of printer's puzzles.

Harned brings him fruit almost daily. W. says: "Most people think Tom rough: underneath his rough exterior he is as sweet as the fruit he brings." H. comes generally after dinner in the early evening, with one or both of the children. W. always kisses the youngsters warmly and has dear things to say to them. He is not backward at any time in asking Harned for any choice bit of food he craves. H. says: "That's what I'm here for," and W. replies: "I take you at your word, Tom—

God bless you!" Last week's pears hit him hard. "Yes, bring me pears—pears are good for me—but pears like those you'll never get again."

I quoted something Huxley said about evolution—that he did not hold it as a dogma but as a working hypothesis. W. exclaimed: "It is beautiful—beautiful—such a confession as that: the most glorious and satisfying spiritual statement of the nineteenth century. Can the churches, the priests, the dogmatists, produce anything to match it? How can we ever forget Darwin? Was ever a great man a more simple man than Darwin? Was ever a beautiful character a more simple character than Darwin? He was one of the *acme* men—he was at the top. I could hope for no better fate for my book than that it should grow strong in so beneficent an atmosphere—breathe the breath of its life." Again: "Dr. Mitchell was over today and tells me of a letter from his father—S. Weir—who is in Italy now and encountered there a furious snow-storm which drove him over the mountains. When Mitchell first came he thought he should do something, so ordered several drugs, none of which I would take. I took calomel and calomel until it was of no effect. Drugs are not for me nor I for them—Mitchell himself now admits it. They do me no good. Of course I do not set it down as a doctrine for everyone to observe, under all circumstances, but I do insist upon it for now, to meet existing conditions."

W. never seems to be as easy with Musgrove as with Baker. W. referred to Musgrove this evening as "the gentleman who is here to assist me." This is the first allusion made to M. in two weeks. Talked of Bucke: "Bucke is a marked man —a man you would accept as such from his mere appearance— but not contemplative in any severe sense, though including contemplation, too. Bucke I should describe as an *ensemblist* with supreme steadiness and nerve force—not brutally but always truly heroic. We usually associate courage with battles or brawls but Bucke shows courage in peace—never quails before anything life can crowd on him—the worst, the most tragic. This force he derived not from books but from life, from experience, from cute observation, from broad interests. Bucke includes the whole of life in his province: he is vehement, eager, inquisitive, even militant in the best sense of that violent word. You ask about Mrs. Bucke? She gives me the ideal of maternity. While not a striking woman in what are called intellectual matters she is a great mother—a noble mother. Do you know anything in all this universe superior to a noble mother? I have seen Mrs. Bucke and a group of the children going about together there in London, and the manner of it all was to me most beautiful, convincing. Bucke is a man of sane habits—disbelieves in stimulants for young or old, sick or well—don't dogmatise about it or impose his theory on others—leaves the other doctors up there who work with him perfect freedom to use stimulants if they want to do so with patients in their charge—yet is firm, unyielding, exacting, with himself. And after all that is a thing for which there can be no rule—no rule to use, no rule not to use."

W. handed me W. E. Henley's book of poems inscribed to "Walt Whitman from the author": "It is peculiar—a third or so of it about hospital cases, the work of doctors, and so forth—a curio, I should say, in work of that sort: not wanting in power, yet not all-powerful." So much of the book he had looked over but no more. Eddy was here today and was to remain over night. Is being transferred from Moorestown to Blackwoodtown. The meeting between the brothers mostly and impressively silent—Eddy mentally inarticulate, W. sadly ruminative. They talked in monosyllables. I noticed that while Walt will kiss Jeff he merely takes Eddy's hand and holds it and says nothing. He talked to me of Eddy. "The poor boy—the poor boy." As the evening wore on W. grew more and more uncommunitive as towards Eddy. Finally he said to Mrs. Davis: "I think you had better go now," and to Eddy: "Good-bye, boy—I will send for you soon again: you shall come whenever you choose: good-bye! good-bye!" W. saying of it to me: "Eddy appeals to my heart, to my two arms: I seem to want to reach out and help him."

I said to W.: "That was a noble letter you gave me the other day—Rolleston's letter." "I say so too: we won't quarrel about that." "He takes you to task a bit about your strictures on the American poets." "Yes, I remember it quite clearly. I deserved his whip, maybe." "You say 'maybe'. I don't believe you believe you deserved his whip." W. laughed. "Not literally deserved it, possibly: but, you know, there is another side to everything. Have you got the letter in your pocket?" "Yes— I wanted to talk with you about it." "You did, eh? Well— don't let's talk just yet: read the letter to me—let me hear it again." He settled in his chair. W. had written on the envelope in red ink: "Oct. 80—from Rolleston, Dresden—has some good paragraphs about the poets &c: can be printed." I read:

DRESDEN, October 16, '80.

I was very glad to hear that you had been so well this summer —so comparatively well. Paralysis, even partial, must be a terrible enemy to fight against. I should think it would put a man's faith in the sources of spiritual joy to a very severe test. Yet I have sometimes felt as if I wished that some such calamity would overtake me—it seems so very easy to be free and happy when one has perfect health and strength—and how can one say to a suffering friend: "Be strong," without seeming to speak impertinently? But for myself I do not feel that I could be overwhelmed by any misfortune that left my mind untouched. Insanity however is sometimes a terrible problem to me. To think that

> However we have writ the style of Gods
> And made a push at chance and sufferance,

our impregnable fortress, the mind, can be attacked at its very center: that accident, heredity, a little meddling with the cortex of the brain, can reduce the proudest stoic that ever lived to a helpless, soulless idiot! There is a cynical irony in it, as if man seeking to assert himself in the universe, saying "Here at least, in the spirit, I have freedom and empire inalienable," were to find that there most of all he is enslaved—the sport of the blind forces of materialism. Yet sometimes when I seem to see that there *is* no such thing as "materialism," your passage about the insane in Faces seems sun-clear to me—one must live in the faith of one's hours of brightest insight.

I am sending you herewith a translation of the Encheiridion of Epictetus which I have been working at for sometime. I came across the book this last summer, and it laid hold of my mind so that I could not put it away till I had finished as good a translation as I can make of it. I have had a dozen copies printed here as I want to ask the opinion of one or two friends about publishing it as a little book, a "hand-book" as the Greek name describes it. Read with sympathy and understanding I think it is very valuable—at least it has given me some solid nutriment, and might to others. The copies only came home this day. I had for some time intended to write to you when that would happen.

I saw in the Academy a paragraph saying you were going to write something about the English poets of the XIX Century in one of the London Magazines. I shall look out with great interest for that. I hope you mean English *writing* poets for I should greatly like to hear some of your definite ideas about the Americans. To say the truth, I never could quite accept your utter condemnation of all American authors, expressed both in prose and poetry. I certainly see that tried by a right democratic standard they fail. Longfellow, Whittier, &c., are just as much poets of Europe as poets of America, if not more. But then you do not condemn the non-democratic European poets in that wholesale manner—for so far forth as they are poets, so far forth as they help to put ideas of beauty, nobleness, love, into our minds, they help mankind, democracy even included. And do not Americans do this also to a certain extent? I am not by any means a worshiper of Emerson, but can it really be said of him that he "expresses nothing characteristic, suffices only the lowest level of vacant minds?" And Thoreau, surely he is something, very much. Shall we not thank men for what they are? (though emphatically demanding something more).

Do you ever hear of what passes in Ireland? Things are at a lamentable pass there now, and the House of Lords stands like a block in the way of deliverance. I venture to say their late action has made England take a great stride in the direction of republicanism. Indeed I sometimes think that time is very close now; people are beginning at last to find out that our "constitutional sovereigns" are a little ridiculous, and that £500,000 is rather a large annuity to pay a monarch for having the goodness to do nothing. If the scattered republicans in England could unite their forces and (say) found a paper in which politics, literature &c would all be treated from the highest republican standpoint, it might do much—I have the idea at some time of trying to found some such thing. But at twenty-three years one has not experience enough for carrying out such schemes. Besides, I don't know whether I won't give up any idea of a literary life entirely and take to farming in the backwoods. Anyhow, I shall be here for six months longer, and I will not forbear to say how much I should like now and then to write to you, and sometimes to hear of you.

Yours always,

T. W. ROLLESTON.

"Yes", said W., "you are right: he gives me a good sound rap on the sconce. I seem to have various feelings about Emerson but I am always loyal at last. Emerson gratified me as a young man by what he did—he sometimes tantalized me as an old man by what he failed to do. You see, I both blaspheme and worship." I reminded him: "You once addressed Emerson as Master." He nodded his assent. "So I did—and master he was, for me, then. But I got my roots stronger in the earth—master would not do anymore: no, not then: would no longer do." "And when you say your last word about Emerson—just before you shut up shop for good—what will it be?" He laughed mildly. "It will be loyal," he said: "after all the impatiences, loyal, loyal."

Wednesday, August 1, 1888.

W. lay on the bed, this evening throughout our talk but seemed at ease and was communicative and rather more cheerful than yesterday and day before. The staple of our talk was the book, but he wandered off from time to time into general matters, and I did not try to stop him. My method all along has been to not trespass and not to ply him too closely with questions necessary or unnecessary. When a lull occurs I sometimes get him going again by making a remark that is not a question. Other times we sit together for long seances of silence, neither saying anything. One evening during which we had not done much more than sit together, he on his chair, I on his bed, he said: "We have had a beautiful talk—a beautiful talk." I called it "a Quaker talk." He smiled quietly: "That will describe it! But oh! how precious!" Spoke of his 1881 trip to Boston: "I was there four or five weeks—went about in leisurely fashion—seeing what was to be seen—people, places—doing my work and having my jaunts together. I could get about then, a few blocks, anyway, which is more than I can do now. The Leaves of Grass we made then was very vigilantly proof-read—I gave it more than my usual attention: examined it, word for word, with the copy in my hand, which is an unusual caution for me."

Replying to a question: "I am curious to know the result of the Burroughs-Kennedy camping out venture—what will come if it, especially for Kennedy. There is a good deal in what Rhys told us here about Kennedy's irritability: Kennedy has nerves (damn nerves!): I do not know how his nerves would succeed with Burroughs, who is such a different sort of person—who is so calm, so poised, so much at home with himself, so much a familiar spirit of the forests." "How would you feel about it if I was to go in Kennedy's place?" "Oh, perfectly safe: I would not feel in the least uncertain about you." W. said further: "I see John—Burroughs—breaks out again in the August Century: but he is not at his best there, nor has he been recently. Some subtle change seems to have come over John—he manifests less of his old buoyancy, joyousness." "Do you mean a permanent change —or a mood?" "A mood, rather—a difference of mood, perhaps. John has a reputation to keep up and sometimes a hundred dollars to earn (I don't mean that in any evil sense)—therefore, he cannot always be at his best. He keeps on writing, mostly for the periodicals, his books bringing him in so little of themselves. I can see where John's charm should be for a young fellow of your years and tastes: he is a big man just calculated to do a peculiar work. He is a child of the woods, fields, hills—native to them in a rare sense (in a sense almost of miracle). My own favorite loafing places have always been the rivers, the wharves, the boats—I like sailors, stevedores. I have never lived away from a big river."

Took up Brinton's suggestion that W.'s philosophy "lacks in definiteness." "Well, it is true, I guess—indeed, true without the shadow of a doubt: the more I turn it over the more convinced am I. Of all things, I imagine I am most lacking in what is called definiteness, in so far as that applies to special theories of life and death. As I grow older I am more firmly than ever fixed in my belief that all things tend to good, that no bad is forever bad, that the universe has its own ends to subserve and will subserve them well. Beyond that, when it comes to launching out into mathematics—tying philosophy to the multiplication table—I am lost—lost utterly. Let them all whack away—I am satisfied: if they can explain, let them explain: if they can explain they can do more than I can do. I am not Anarchist, not Methodist, not anything you can name. Yet I see why all the ists and isms and haters and dogmatists exist —can see why they must exist and why I must include all."

Referring to the Encheiridion sent W. by Rolleston: "Epictetus is the one of all my old cronies who has lasted to this day without cutting a diminished figure in my perspective. He belongs with the best—the best of great teachers—is a universe in himself. He sets me free in a flood of light—of life, of vista. Even the preface of that little book is good—Rolleston's little book." Was Epictetus a youthful favorite? "Yes, quite so—

I think even at sixteen. I do not remember when I first read the book. It was far, far back. I first discovered my bookself in the second hand book stores of Brooklyn and New York: I was familiar with them all—searched them through and through. One day or other I found an Epictetus—I know it was at that period: found an Epictetus. It was like being born again." His Epictetus has been all underscored with purple pencillings. He has inscribed it: "Walt Whitman (sent me by my friend the translator T. W. H. Rolleston, from Dresden Saxony,) 1881." There is another memorandum below: "March 1886—T. W. R. is now in Ireland (Delgany, County Wicklow)—and edits the Dublin University Review."

Spoke of Moncure Conway: "He is very brilliant, and, I think, if not favorable, at least not averse, to me. I have met him, know him: at one time I wondered whether he really knew me at all—knew Leaves of Grass—what I stood for, what I stood against, if I may say it in that partial way. But however that was settled, he has been kind to me. Conway's fault is that he lacks the scientific spirit—has had a glimpse of it, now and then makes use of it, but lacks it as a characteristic. He is the advocate, the debater—more anxious to have his case or his man proved true than to *be* true. There is in him a strong vein of the sensational—he likes to take odd views because they are odd." "How do you know his motive in taking odd views?" "That's so—how do I know? I don't know—I only feel—it. You mustn't think I object to odd views when they come natural to a man—are a part of a man. I only object to them when they are put on for effect. As I said, Moncure is brilliant—he shines—he is used to having his eminent lustre admired."

W. jokingly remarked: "I was quite a hero today—I took a bath—I washed myself all over with my own hands: now what have you got to say?" Finally had a little talk with W. about the Redpath letters which he gave me last Sunday. He said of them: "They are a choice bit of our history." Then he had me take them up, the first date first and so on, and read them all to him. "I seem to get a mighty sight better idea of some things when I let you be my better eyes to read for me while I concentrate on what is being said." The correspondence follows.

WILLARD'S HOTEL,
WASHINGTON, June 30, '85.

Dear Walt Whitman: I intended to call over and see you yesterday when I was in Philadelphia, but I was unexpectedly detained by one man and forced to go to Washington so as to reach here last night.

I will call on you on my way back to New York.

But I write now to tell you why, because my visit will be on business.

I believe you have never met Mr. Rice, proprietor of the North American Review, altho' nominally he may have corresponded with you—that is, his office editor may have written to you in his name, as he always does, even when Mr. Rice is in Europe. It is at Mr. Rice's instance that I will call on you.

He has conceived the plan of procuring a collection of papers that, united in one volume, will be a permanent memorial of Lincoln. He has set about to secure the reminiscences of all eminent Americans who came into personal relations with him— each man to tell his story, whether it shall be short or long.

That's what he calls his *Lincoln Series*. Some of these papers he may publish in the North American Review, and others in the North American Review Syndicate: a group of influential papers which he supplies and that publish simultaneously articles from famous men whom ordinarily newspapers cannot reach—nor afford to pay separately even if they did reach them. All the articles that you see marked "Copyright" in the New York Tribune or Philadelphia Times (Sunday editions) are supplied by Mr. Rice.

Next: he intends to secure a series of papers giving the civil history of the Civil War—legislation, &c.

He wants me to see you and ask you to write a paper on your experiences of the Civil War—the hospital life, and other phases that you witnessed and have not yet described.

Could you write an article giving your recollections of Lincoln and also your memories of the War? Short or long it will be gladly accepted and liberally paid for. He will take it, whether it is a page or a hundred pages.

I shall be here a week. I suppose I shall have no difficulty in finding the good grey poet in Camden.

Ever truly yours,

JAMES REDPATH.

The second letter was endorsed in this way by W.: "from James Redpath abt articles on Lincoln and on War incidents—both articles sent accepted and paid for." The letter above was all written in Redpath's own hand. The two letters that follow were dictated to a stenographer and signed by Redpath.

NORTH AMERICAN REVIEW,
NEW YORK, July 16, 1885.

Dear Walt Whitman: I got your letter when I was in Washington and fully expected to stay over and see you on my return, but I was kept so much longer than I thought I would be kept and so much more work was thrown on me that I was compelled to hurry back to New York by night. It is possible that I may be in Philadelphia this week—indeed it is probable—and in that case I shall certainly cross the ferry; but in the meantime why should you be idle? I shall not presume to give you any hints as to how to write; I think you know what I want:

1st, Lincoln: Mr. Rice has got the ambition of editing a work that can never be superseded. He proposes to get every man of note now living who ever met Lincoln to write down in plain words and as accurately as the human memory will record, just what Lincoln did; just how Lincoln looked; just what impression Lincoln made on him. However, he does not want the last clause (that is to say, the impression) recorded by anybody but only by men whose names will go down into history. Like Gradgrind, "what he wants is facts." You, of course, are among the favored few whose impressions will be acceptable;

so you see, if you will write down an account of every interview you ever had with Lincoln, *that* will complete what I ask of you in his name on that subject.

2nd, Memories of the War. He would like from you an account of some phase of the Civil War which you witnessed. But I will see you before you have time, probably, to write the second article, and, possibly, I may be able to suggest the best topic from his point of view to begin with.

Now, my dear Walt Whitman, won't you go to work at once because Rice is chained lightning in a dress suit and damned impatient.

Yours Ever,

JAMES REDPATH.

NORTH AMERICAN REVIEW.

NEW YORK, August 11, 1885.

Dear Walt Whitman: I wrote you several days ago asking you to tell me whether one hundred dollars was your lowest price. I think I said also that if you charged lower than that price I could sell a great many more articles for you than I could at these rates. I enclose a check for sixty dollars, which is payment for the article according to your own estimate of three thousand words, at the rate of twenty dollars a thousand, which is the very highest rate they pay. I had to decide within ten minutes whether I would accept it or not, as Mr. Ferris, who is in charge of the syndicate, was just about to start for Mount McGregor. I told him, however, that if you refused to sell the article for less I should consider myself responsible for the balance and expect payment for it either from him or from Mr. Rice.

So my dear old friend I have protected your interests to the best of my judgment and if you want me to follow orders and break owners in the future let me know and I shall do it. The great problem that the universe is asking you this moment is whether I am to regard this check as payment in full or payment on account. I would also like you to answer my letters. I have no interest whatever in the syndicate to which I sold the manuscript.

Ever yours truly,
JAMES REDPATH.

This was W.'s reply and receipt sent in answer to the last letter:

sent James Redpath
August 12, 1885.

All right my dear J. R.—$60 for the Booth article will do, in full—(I reserve the right of printing it in future collections of my writings—this is indispensable) I have been and am lingering under the miserable inertia following my sunstroke—otherwise should have sent you one or two articles—have them on the stocks—Am very slowly gaining the tally of my previous strength—had none to spare before.

Thank you, dear friend, for your services and affectionate good will.

Aug: '85

Received from Allen Thorndike Rice—by Mr. Ferris attorney and through James Redpath—Sixty Dollars for article *Booth and the Old Bowery*—of which article I reserve the right to include and print in future collections of my writings.

I read all the letters aloud to W., who interrupted me now and then to say, "let me hear that sentence once more," or to say, "yes, yes," or, "I was not sure but I yielded," winding up with this remark: "There you have the psychology of some of my pieces and the psychology of dear Jim Redpath, who was a friend among friends. Redpath said to me once when he was here: 'Walt if you have any money scrapes I want to help you out of 'em.' This he did—did it again and again. Redpath was one of your radical crowd—he was way out and beyond in all his ideas—stalwart, searching—a sort of pioneer, going on and on, always in the advance. Some men stay in the rear with

76

the beef and beans but that was not Redpath's style. Didn't you tell me that Redpath and Ingersoll were great friends? I shouldn't wonder—they have much in common." I said to W.: "You said, 'your crowd.' Why didn't you say 'our crowd.' Don't you belong with us?" He laughed gently: "Yes, yes I do —but not in whole and part. Sometimes I think some of you fellows have outstripped even me—have gone on even beyond me flaunting your red flag of revolt." "Do you mean that for a rebuke or a blessing?" He replied without hesitation: "For a blessing, to be sure: God bless the red flag of revolt!"

Thursday, August 2, 1888.

W. stayed on his bed this evening as we talked. Was free enough, and easy, but weak. "I have had one of the feeblest days of all—one of the very feeblest." Added: "But I do not growl—it might be worse: as long as better is not worse I can enjoy better even if it is not best." Has done little work. "Here are the proofs—but, Horace, do not rely upon my readings. Take the proofs along—scan them for yourself." Still refers every now and then to Eddy. "Poor Eddy! I wonder how he is getting on today?" Returned him Henley's poems. Told him I had read the book through. He exclaimed: "All through? Why, I had no idea anybody was capable of that. I read only the fore part of it—the hospital pieces—was peculiarly, intensely, interested in that—but as for the rest—" After a pause: "It struck me as extremely deliberate verse—verse written of malice prepense—all laid out, designed, on mathematical principles. Did you get that impression of it? Or did it carry you right along as if you could not help it?" Referring to Agnes Repplier: "She is a woman who tries for smartness at all hazards—that is her caliber, the most or the whole of it: and that is what they are all doing, all society, all professionalism, in books, poems, sermons—a strain to make an impression—everything loved that will dazzle the beholder, everything hated that will not." Why had he left his name off the title page of McKay's Leaves? "It was deliberate—not an accident. It would be sacrilege to put a name there—it would seem just like putting a name on the universe. It would be ridiculous to think of Leaves of Grass belonging to any one person: at the most I am only a mouth-piece. My name occurs inside the book—that is enough if not more than enough. I like the feeling of a general partnership—as if the Leaves was anybody's who chooses just as truly as mine." He said this: "I don't care which sea the ship comes on so it finally gets home—I don't care who brings the wheat or by what route it is brought so the wheat is good to the man who brings and the man who receives it."

Speaking of his War pieces he said himself: "Their merit is not chiefly literary—if they have merit—it is chiefly human—it is a presence—statement reduced to its last simplicity—some-times a mere recital of names, dates, incidents—no dress put on anywhere to complicate or beautify it. And by the way, talking of the War—have you seen what Conway has to say about that? It is Conway's opinion that the Rebellion was in great part a war that could have been avoided—a war of the politicians. I want Conway to say it all, of course—preach, write, argue, for his point of view—put in his negative in any form he chooses—but still I am forced to dissent. The War was the boil—that was all: not the root. The War was not the cause of the War: the cause lay deeper—could not have been shifted from its purposes. There are cute historical writers—very cute ones, the best of the whole group—who trace events in modern history back to the Crusades—establish a definite and conclusive connection. So it must be with our Rebellion: to try to consider it without considering what preceded it is only to dally with the truth. There is one thing I shall always regret for myself—always reproach myself for having neglected. I had some brief experience in the South—an intimate experience while it lasted—was convinced that the 'poor white' there, so-called, had never had justice done him in our histories, news-papers, official documents—in our war-talk and after war-talk. Everybody everywhere seems to be interested in crushing him down and keeping him crushed down. If I could I would even undertake the job yet—even yet make some record on its side to show how I hate the tyranny that has oppressed it—pay some tribute to a class so thoroughly, so universally, misunderstood. The horrible *patois* attributed to the 'poor white' there in the South (and not to them only—to Western and Northern classes also) I never found—never encountered. I discovered courtesy, chivalry, generosity, and by no means such external ugliness as is usually charged to them. In fact, all my experiences South— all my experiences in the hospitals, among the soldiers, in the crowds of the cities, with the masses, in the great centers of population—allowing for all idiosyncrasies, idiocrasies, passions, what-not, the very worst—have only served to confirm my faith in man—in the average of men. Take the hospital drill I went through—take the mixtures of men there, men often supposed to be of contrary types—how impressive was the fact of their likeness, their uniformity of essential nature—the same basic traits in them all—in the Northern man, in the Southern man, in the Western man—all of one instinct, one color—addicted to the same vices, ennobled by the same virtues: the dignity, courtesy, open-handedness, radical in all, beautiful in all. When I first went to Washington I had a great dislike for the typical Yankee—had always had it, years back, from the start—but in my very first contact with the human Yankee all my prejudices were put to flight."

W. said: "In talking with you the other day about great editors I forgot to speak of one man who is maybe the greatest of all —and who is besides my dear friend. I mean Dana—Charles Dana. Dana's Sun has always stuck to it that Walt Whitman is some punkins no matter what the scorners said. Bryant once said to me that he supposed that Dana on the whole was the imperial master of the craft. I don't like to take sides with any greatest man of all—I don't say Dana is greatest of all—but I put in my vote for him as a tremendous force. Dana has a hissing, hating, side, that I don't like at all—it goes against my grain —but it is not the chief thing in the man, and when his total is made up cuts only a small figure." W. reached his hand under the pillow and drew out a letter which he handed to me. "Take it over to the light—turn the light up—read it to me." I looked at the signature—Dowden's. Then read.

MONTENOTTE, CORK,
Sept. 3, 1872.

My dear Mr. Whitman, I can hardly understand how I have left your most welcome letter so long unanswered. In Paris two months ago I saw one morning in a newspaper that "the American Poet Walt Whitman would shortly visit England," and there and then I sat down and wrote part of a letter to you, but the weariness of illness (I was ailing a good deal) caused it to remain unended and unsent. Now I have just heard from Mr. Burroughs that there is, or may be, a fair chance of your coming to us, and of your giving readings from your poems. As far as my own opinion goes, I would say that there is a certainty of success, a sufficient success at the least, and perhaps a complete one, in Dublin. Do come. You do not know how welcome you would be to many of us. ["God bless 'em!" exclaimed W. as I read]. I need not say that if you would come to our house in Dublin, my wife and I would be made abundantly happy, and would remember 1872 as a year good to think of.

There are several things for which I owe you thanks—two copies of Democratic Vistas and newspapers from time to time. Each I assure you has been valued, (though my thanks are tardy); and your letter has been read or heard of by those who would care for its contents.

Mr. Burroughs tells me that you have been not as well as heretofore since the great summer heat. I trust that it is only a slight and temporary yielding of your health. You will be best able to feel yourself whether a run across the Atlantic, and the absorbing of new life and scenery in England and Ireland, would not be just the tonic you require. We at all events are interested in believing this, and think that *you* are just the communicator of vitality and joy that *we* require. I mean by this, besides its more direct personal meaning, that such influences as yours are precisely what our poetry in its latest development needs to make it sane and masculine. And I have not a doubt that your personal presence in England would do much towards bringing the time when the recognition of your power and soundness in art and literature must become general.

I have written to Mr. Burroughs anything about myself that I thought would interest him, and I will not write the same again to you. Also I have sent him two or three things I have written, and if he thinks you would care to see them he will give them to you.

I will write to you again before long. I hope you will continue to let me see or hear of such things of yours as otherwise I might miss. The Mystic Trumpeter I was very glad to have seen. But chiefly I hope to hear that you are coming, and coming to us.

My address is as before, 50, Wellington Road, Dublin.

This has been a year of comparative loss to me as regards physical health, but I am well again now; and in other respects it has been a year of gain and progress. But I don't in the least find that, with progress, I slip aside or away from your poems.

I am dear Mr. Whitman

Very sincerely yours,

EDWARD DOWDEN.

"One of the interesting things about Dowden," said W., "is his simple acceptance of my work. He don't say maybe I ought to maybe I ought not—he is not forever weighing pros against cons—he takes me for granted and then stops. Even some of the men on this side who call themselves my friends seem to be looking about all the time to see whether their endorsement may not be a mistake. Dowden never made any fuss, never got excited about it, was just affirmative, just nodded yes and let it go at that. I don't mind the simple, straight-out negative—indeed, I like it: I don't mind the fellows who say without a tremor: 'Here, damn you, Walt Whitman, what do you mean by all this nonsense. To hell with you, Walt Whitman: to hell with you! to hell with you!' That don't sound bad—on the contrary it sounds very good—it is tonic. But when a fellow comes along, convinced and not convinced, hungry for your society and afraid of your society, blowing hot and cold, with praise on his lips that had better be blame, you are at your wit's end to know how to meet him. As I say, Dowden didn't come along with a brass band—a flourish of flags. No, not that way: he just came along simply by himself, said how d'ye do, and stayed without a question. That's better than having an army on your side."

As I was going W. said: "I'm nursing up a surprise for you." "Good or bad?" "We shall see—we shall see! In the meantime, brace up—it may break on you any day now." He reached under his pillow again and handed me a paper. "What's that?" he asked—"look at it—tell me." It was too dark where he was. Taking it to the light I answered: "It's your rough draft of a letter to Schmidt." "That's right—that's what I meant it to be: take it along with you. I was tearing up some useless odds and ends today—saved this out of the mess for you. I like you to know just how our crowd got along with each other —what we were saying to each other in those old days of battle. You had not then flashed on the scene—you were a youngster then—but you ought to be informed of all the whys and wherefores so that by and by when the right word needs to be said about us you will be in a position to say it." Put the Schmidt note in my pocket. W. said: "Come, kiss me for good night." He was still lying down. I reached over him and we kissed. He took my hand—pressed it fervently. "I am in luck. Are you? I guess God just sent us for each other."

Friday, August 3, 1888.

W. brighter physically than yesterday, yet "still strangely languid." "It is getting to be difficult for me even to walk across the room." Very cheerful. Almost merry here and there in the talk. "My today's mail has been chiefly an autograph mail. I did get a letter from Bucke and that was a consolation (the first letter from Bucke for three or four days). Not a day but the autograph hunter is on my trail—chases me, dogs me! sometimes two or three appear in the very same mail. Their subterfuges, deceptions, hypocrisies, are curious, nasty, yes damnable. I will get a letter from a young child—a young reader—this is her first book—she has got fond of me—she should be encouraged in her fine ambitions—would I not &c &c —and I would *not*, of course—why should I? I can see the grin of an old deceiver in such letters." Today a woman came in whose husband had been one of W.'s fellow clerks in Washington. She asked for an autograph, which W. gave her on a slip of paper. "And a sentiment," she added, offering to pass the slip back. W. took no notice of the slip but quietly said: "That is all." She withdrew. Autographed Harrison Morris' copy of the Leaves. Is generally quite willing to give his autograph but hates to be worked. "Sometimes two or three letters will come together in one mail and I say to myself: Here's a fillip for a few thoughts. I settle myself in my chair, get the glasses on my nose, and lo! every note is for an autograph. One man the other day wrote: 'I am very sick—liable to die soon—it would be a great comfort to me to have your signature on this card.'" "Did you send the signature?" "Yes, I did. I felt quite sure the man was lying but I didn't want to run no chances in so serious a case." Laughed. I told W. I did not agree with what he said of Burroughs' Century paper. "Maybe I was too quick—did not, perhaps, look it over carefully enough. After hearing what you say about it I am inclined to think I should take it up again and see if my second impression is better than the first." W. spoke of B's "berry farm" as he calls it— "up on the Hudson, embowered in beauty."

Harned brought some pears. Then talked with W. about politics. W. spoke with great force. "There is no enthusiasm —they cannot work it up—though they blow all their breaths together they cannot work it up—neither side—though the tariff men seem to be straining with might and main to create an issue. The Clevelandites are wise to lay low—to remain quiet. The big shindig they have been arranging for Blaine in New York sounds interesting. If I was not beyond managing myself I would go over to New York—down the harbor and back—around—to get the feel of such a vast popular outpouring. Yet there's a lot of humbug thrown in to spice it all. As things are the working classes, as such, belong to neither party—are not billed to either. I am glad to see that it is getting through their wool that the tariff, for instance, is more for capital than for labor—has always been so. The great country, the greatest country, the richest country, is not that which has the most capitalists, monopolists, immense grabbings, vast fortunes, with its sad, sad foil of extreme, degrading, damning poverty, but the land in which there are the most homesteads, freeholds—where wealth does not show such contrasts high and low, where all men have enough—a modest living—and no man is made possessor beyond the sane and beautiful necessities of the simple body and the simple soul. The great country, in fact, is the country of free labor—of free laborers: negro, white, Chinese, or other. To use the word 'great' to describe any other sort of country is to my mind a confession of ignorance or hypocrisy. I do not mean this to be counted as an expression of despair: men are in the main decent, pure, or want to be. Things are about as good as they can be under present conditions (of course man can always change the conditions). Systems, institutions, even the vile ones, have a work to do—do the work." Harned asked: "What place do you find for corruption in politics?" W. answered: "I do not need to find a place for it: it has found a place for itself. But there's more to the story than that, Tom—oh! much more. The spiritual influences back of everything else—subtle, unseen, invisible, mainly discredited—they finally arbitrate the social order. Science tells us about excretions—the throwings off of the body—that the chief results are secured in the form of invisible exhalations—the whole flesh casting it forth. That strange, inarticulate, force is not less operative in the institutions of society—in politics, literature, music, science, art—than in the physical realm. We must not forget such forces—not one of them. Society throws off some of its ephemera, its corruption, through politics—the process is

From a Photograph

RUDOLF SCHMIDT
(1872)

offensive—we shudder over it—but it may be true, it is still true, that the interior system throwing off its excreta this way is sound, wholly sound, prepared for the proper work of its own purification." I asked W. something about the letter to Schmidt which he gave to me yesterday.

To RUDOLF SCHMIDT.

Feb. 2, 1872

Dear Mr. Rudolf Schmidt, Your note of Jan. 5, acknowledging receipt of "papers", and enclosing to me your photograph, is just received. I like your photograph and thank you for it—I like indeed the good frank way of sending such pictures when interested and curious. I wish to know whether you have safely received the particular copy of the last edition of my poems, in one volume with loose sheet photos enclosed, which I sent you by Mr. Clausen. Mr. Clausen tells me that he put up the various matter I furnished in three parcels—if you have got the three it is all right. I mailed you a letter of some length, Jan. 16. I shall send you, probably by next mail, my latest piece, in a Western Magazine for February. Also a second copy of my pamphlet "Democratic Vistas"—If the first copy reached you, send the second to Mr. Bjornson—if not, not. Yes, I am sure I should like your friend Bjornson much.

I am going next week to New York to stay there until April 10 —my address there will be 107 *North* Portland av. Brooklyn, New York, U. S. Amer—about April 10, I shall return here again and my address will be——

I am writing this at my desk—as above, Treasury Building, middle of afternoon. From my great south window I can see a far-stretching and noble view, many, many miles of open ground, the Potomac river, the hilly banks, the mountains of Virginia, &c. We are having a severe cold spell. Everything is white with snow but the sun has been clear and dazzling all day. The hour of office-closing is nigh and I too must close. I have much pleasure in writing to you and expecting yours. Adieu.

I said to W.: "I came today prepared for my surprise—but you have not yet surprised me. Am I still to be kept in suspense?" He laughed quietly. "I am afraid so—it looks that way: but I've put a couple of letters in this string to assuage your feelings —one is from Dowden, the other from John Burroughs. You will like what John says about 'style': it is very deep—oh! very deep: I guess nothing goes below it: it is the last foundation on the last foundation." "Shall I read them now?" "No—not now— take them with you—put them where they belong. My mind advises me that I must suspend operations for to-night. Take my love to your mother: and how about Anne Montgomerie? She has not been here for ten days. When she was here last she brought me a bunch of roses, which were very beautiful, very beautiful—though she was more beautiful than her roses. She has cheeks like the prettiest peach in the orchard." I will put the Burroughs letter right in here. I was so curious from what W. had said that I stopped under the street lamp at the corner and read it.

WEST PARK, N. Y.
Dec. 31st, 1885.

Dear Walt: A happy new year to you, and many returns of the same. I was right glad to get your letter and to know your eyes were so much better. I feel certain that if you eat little or no meat, you will be greatly the gainer. It will not do to take in sail in one's activities &c unless he takes in sail in his food also.

We are all pretty well here this winter so far. I have just sent off the copy for my new vol: I think I shall stick to Signs and Seasons for the title, as this covers all the articles.

Kennedy sent me his article on The Poet as Craftsman. I liked it pretty well: what he has to say about you is excellent. He wanted my opinion about the argument of the essay, so I told him that I never felt like quarreling with a real poet about his form; let him take the form he can use best; any form is good if it holds good poetry and any form is bad if it holds bad poetry. I would not have Tennyson or Longfellow or Burns use other forms than they do. If a man excels in prose he is pretty sure to use prose. Coleridge is greater in prose than in poetry. Poe is greater in poetry than in prose. Carlyle tried the poetic form and gave it up.

I hope you will keep well and that I will see you before long. How much I wish you was here to eat a New Year's dinner with us. I wrote to Herbert Gilchrist the other day. These must be dark days for him and Grace. To me a black shadow seems to have settled on all England since I read of the death of Mrs. Gilchrist.

I wish you would send me by mail or express those books of Emerson, the Essays and the Miscellanies. I want to use them. I am going to re-read Emerson, and see how he strikes me now.

With much love

JOHN BURROUGHS.

Saturday, August, 4, 1888.

In the progress of W.'s disease this has been one of his worst days. Till three o'clock—all through the morning and the hours of the early afternoon—he "felt utterly exhausted—sick in head and body—with everything promising another spell except the spell itself." To-night complains of being "melted and weak though better." The day very hot. Has done practically nothing except write to Bucke. Read no proofs. "On the whole I feel like Abe Lincoln who would not growl over the scars and the losses but thought that the government was lucky to come out of its troubles alive." Went on: "I have been incessantly thinking of that fearful, frightful tragedy in New York—that terrible fire in the tenements last night. I often wonder how the people in those foul rookeries manage to exist anyhow in such weather. I have often been accused of turning a deaf ear to that side of life—of being too unconcerned—of treating it as if it was not. Lately, as I have sat here thinking, it has come upon me that there must be some truth in the charge—that I should have studied that strata of life more directly—seen what it signifies, what it starts from, what it means as a part of the social fabric. I have seen a lot of the rich-poor—of the people who have plenty yet have little—of the miseries of the well-to-do, who are supposed to be exempt from creature troubles. One of the painful facts in connection with this human misery—a fact insisted upon by the men who know most and who know what to do with their knowledge—is that the evil cannot be remedied by any one change, one reform, or even half a dozen changes and reforms, but must be accomplished by countless forces working towards the one effect. Hygiene will help—oh! help much. But how will we get our hygiene? I am quite well aware that there are economic considerations, also, to be taken into account. It strikes me again, as it always has struck me, that the whole business finally comes back to the good body—not back to wealth, to poverty, but to the strong body— the sane, sufficient body." I said: "You don't expect the sane body in the tenements, do you?" "No—I do not. The tenements are hot-beds of disease—scrofula, syphilis, of everything, almost: disease just fattens in the tenements. You have touched the nerve of the trouble." "Then isn't it possible to produce social conditions which will make the sane body possible?" "Surely—surely: that is the problem. I think all the scientists would agree with me, as I agree with the scientists, that a beautiful, competent, sufficing, body is the prime force making towards the virtues in civilization, life, history, I think I now see better what you mean when you speak of the economic problems as coming before all the rest and though I have not stated it in that extreme way myself I do not doubt your position: I have great faith in science—real science: the science that is the science of the soul as well as the science of the body (you know many men of half sciences seem to forget the soul)."

O'Connor writes W. of Charles Eldridge's 1889 calendar quoted from Leaves of Grass. W. says: "It is a dubious experiment—I don't shine in bits (there are no 'gems' in Leaves of Grass) though O'Connor says this collection is a strong one. I was at first inclined to demur powerfully but suppose such an experiment may best be left to find its own level." He talked of the propositions to take him away: "I look now for a hot siege of it—for sultry weather: but after going this far we must not admit that such a little thing can keep us from going to the end. As to leaving this place just now—it is impossible—out of the question: my legs would not take me if I wished to go, as I do not. Besides, the compensation would not fit the case: while gaining something in the mountains or at the sea shore, I would lose more than I gain—lose the sense of being on a spot of my own earth, of doing what I choose—and what a comfort that is! If I went off somewhere into more complaisant surroundings— had servants at my beck, the best of food, a down bed to sleep on —what would it all come to? I might be tempted some—I could not be tempted enough to go—my decision would be finally reverse."

W. said regarding a certain passage in Leaves of Grass which I thought particularly effective: "I am glad to hear you say that. It has often happened, often happens—not with me alone—that an author thinks himself very simple, clear, true, at a point considered by others of all points silly, befogged, inane." Referring to another paper in the American series on W. W. "Well, let them go on. It is interesting to be in court and find that none of the witnesses called know anything about the case." I remarked: "You had a lot of good and right things to say about the Burroughs letter yesterday but you said nothing about Dowden's. Had you no amen for Dowden's letter?" He replied: "I am guilty—put me down for guilty. The fact is, Dowden's letter is of the best sort. I happened to say extra much of Burroughs because of what he wrote about style, which seemed to me the best first and the best last thing to be said on the subject. Dowden has a wonderful passage in his letter—a passage about death. Read it to me again, won't you? just that one bit. The whole letter is human—it is not the letter of one literary man to another but of one simple man to a man as simple as himself. Won't you read the letter?" I answered "yes". "I like to get all my relations with people personal, human. I hate to think I can possibly excite any professional feeling in another." I read the whole letter again to myself and the particular part he asked for aloud to W.

WINSTEAD, TEMPLE ROAD,
RATHMINES, DUBLIN,
Oct. 4, 1876.

My dear Mr. Whitman. Some days ago came my parcel—many thanks—Mr. Grosairt's books included. That for Mr. Graves had come previously. I have waited a few days expecting to hear from my brother (from Edinburgh) of the arrival of his copies, but it is sometimes his way to put off writing to me too long, and I have little doubt he has got the books safely.

Rossetti let me know from time to time any news of you that reached him, and I have to thank you for some newspapers now and again.

It was a real sorrow to us, dear friend, to hear of the death of your little nephew and namesake. A friend of mine, Harold Littledale, watched this summer by the side of a little sister (about twenty years younger than himself) who died and he told me that in the presence of death and with its consciousness enveloping him it was words of yours which expressed the deepest truths of the hour and the event. Littledale is President this year of our principal society of students in Trinity College, the Philosophical Society, and I believe his opening address, which is the event of the session, is to be partly concerned with your poetry. It was a great satisfaction to me this year, also, to get a kind of confession or self-revelation from one of the most promising men in my class of the really saving and delivering power of your writings when he was lapsing in that lethargy and cynicism which is one of the diseases of youth in our *Old* World, if not in your *New* one—(but in both I should suppose).

I have done too little this last summer. I copied out about 200 pp. of verse, and am about to have them published. I will send you a copy, but I doubt whether you will care for them—I don't claim to be an "Answerer," but I do assert a right to be one of the tribe of the singers—"Eye-singer, ear-singer, head-

will care for them — I don't claim
to be an "Answerer"; but I do assert
a right to be one of the tribe of the
singers — "eye-singer, ear-singer, head-singer,
sweet-singer, echo-singer, parlor-singer,
love-singer, or something else". And
these have their place & raison d'être.
Probably my next bit of work will
be the arranging for publication a
volume of Essays on 19th century
~~poet~~ writers, including Tennyson &
Browning, Victor Hugo, & the Westminster
article (somewhat altered) on your
poetry.
You asked for O'Grady's address.
I don't know it at this moment;
but he would like to get your
photograph (of which you spoke) & if you
address it to my care he will get
it.
I hope the cooler weather (after so hot a
summer) may do your ~~~~ health good.
We are all well. Always affectionately yours
Edward Dowden

A PAGE FROM A DOWDEN LETTER TO WALT WHITMAN.

singer, sweet-singer, echo-singer, parlor-singer, love-singer," or something else. And these have their place and *raison d'etre*. Probably my next bit of work will be the arranging for publication a volume of essays on 19th century writers, including Tennyson and Browning, Victor Hugo, and the Westminister article (somewhat altered) on your poetry.

You asked for O'Grady's address. I don't know it at this moment; but he would like to get your photograph (of which you spoke)—if you address it to my care he will get it.

I hope the cooler weather (after so hot a summer) may do your health good. We are all well.

Always affectionately yours,
EDWARD DOWDEN.

I repeated to W. that phrase—"the really saving and delivering power of your writings," and he repeated it back again, and still again, finally saying of it: "It has gospel beauty and beat: I hope I deserve it—oh! deserve it, deserve it."

Sunday, August 5, 1888.

Very hot sultry day. W. a little stronger and less languid. He stayed on his bed—talked fully an hour, cheerfully, of matters general and particular. He asked me: "What do you mean by the word 'enervation'?" adding after my reply: "I see I am all right: I often use the word and yet lose the sense of it. I feel enervated—the weather melts me—melts me completely. This is the kind of weather from which people want to escape somewhere, anywhere, only to get off—to get beyond the ordinary tones and semi-tones of life. It is a study—a profound study—the play in life as much as the work in life—and it is all right, too, that the people should go—should have the gala-days. They talk of the extravagance of the people. Nonsense. The people spend their money—help each other—save something—are generous, sacrificial—in so far as they can be are most lavish. Sometimes you don't pay too much for play if you pay your last cent for it."

Letter from Elmina Slenker today. "She is in Virginia—has read some of the—highly-colored reports in the papers—is afraid that I'm pegging out—so writes me, wishing me well in the most friendly fashion. I am inclined to be agreeably impressed—she seems interested and interesting. She approaches me freely—is an aged woman—she has given much time to the study of sexual matters (sees a hint in that direction in Leaves of Grass): she has done her work, her good work, and is now hale, placid, companionable, in every way rounded, on all sides. The old woman is always the best woman, certain other things being equal." Again W. said: "It is curious, what are people's likes and dislikes—how their hates appear and remain, as well as their loves. You will find one man who hates another worse than the devil, exhibiting almost a snake-like poisonous antipathy, and yet can give no reason for it, has no reason for it —simply knows he feels it, that is all. I have myself been the victim of such humors in the human critter—repeatedly the victim—so that nowadays I attach very little significance to the phenomenon. A man came to me in Washington once and said: 'Walt Whitman, I hate myself for hating you, but I hate you!' I assumed at first that he was joking but he would not let it go that way. 'It's no joke, no mistake,' he said, 'somehow there's something in you, in your work, to excite me to a fierce animosity: I don't like it, but it exists.' Wasn't that a touch of psychology for the initiated? I never quite made it out myself."

Spoke of Philadelphia Ledger. "The Ledger fights shy of me. It is queer, too, Childs being so unmistakably my friend. But the Ledger, as a paper, is McKean's work, I suppose, and he don't like me, has no time for me—is, in fact, devoutly opposed to me. I imagine that it is an act of religion in McKean not to patronize a man of my make. I like the Ledger—some of it—but not its tariff. It is probably a tariff paper under pressure. Some of my enemies are malignants—for instance, Littlebill Winter, as O'Connor calls him, and Stoddard, and others of that stripe—violently on the other side—Winter especially—Winter, who is a little man in all ways: little in body, little in soul, little in spirit—a dried-up cadaverous school-master who flourishes his nasty doctrines threateningly over the heads of the anointed."

Read a poem by Florence Earle Coates in The Century. "I am told she bears me in mind and is of a disposition to look with something of favor on my work—which I might say, quoting one of William's playful quips, 'shows her good sense.' They tell me Mrs. Coates is quite a woman among women—is beautiful, shines with great brightness, and, by those who know her well, is admired and cherished. I used to meet Mrs. Winter, now and then—found her quite attractive, though I never could reconcile myself to the literary fiddle-faddle for which her husband in common with so many New Yorkers and others stood and which he swore by. I always found Gilder and Stedman in a group by themselves in that New York art delirium—two always sane men in the general madness."

I asked W. whether he had read Browning's Paracelsus. He talked then of Browning: "You should read The Ring and The Book. That, at least, it would repay anybody who had the leisure to read. Browning is in some respects utterly free—free not to explain: free to put down his statement where it may be seen and then let the world find its own way to a meaning—free of the desire to be at once or ever understood. Browning was also free of humor as an architect of verse, though I feel that his freedom here drifts him rather towards an angular than a facile result. Browning has what O'Connor calls 'elements'—powers of the first class—virility, fiber. I think it would mean a hard tussle for anyone to take Browning up in the bulk—attempt to take him in in the large—the whole of him for better or for worse. I don't believe I could do it. I don't find Browning's technique easy—it beats me sore, bruises me—though I don't make much of that: the fault is mainly my own. I have friends who dose themselves with Browning to the bitter end and regard him as the most invigorating influence in the modern world of books. Browning is full of Italy—knows it—writes of it—has something of its air, its sky, in his work, his soul. And there is even to me a great charm in Italy, in things Italian, in the simple Italian immigrant, in so far as I can get the feel of the country at this distance. When I got sick that time and went down to the Staffords' on Timber Creek, there was a gang of Italian laborers came along to work on the narrow gauge railroad then just being laid: a number of Italians came, all sorts—they lived in huts there, accessible, of course, to me, and I, as you may well believe, was only too ready to seize the opportunity and prospect among them a little. Oh! the good talks we had together! We became almost intimate. I found in them the same courtesy, the same charm, the same poetic flavor, that have always been associated with Italy and things Italian. I often read of accidents on the road—accidents in which the little Italians are the main victims. They are accorded but scant sympathy—nobody seems to care: it makes me sad and mad—riles me. Yes, they are the 'damned dagoes'—always so harmless, quiet, inoffensive. Italy seems in some things to represent qualities the exact opposite of qualities we cultivate here in America: the Italians are more fervent, tenderer, gentler, more considerate—less mercenary: it runs through the whole race, cultivated and ignorant—this manifest superiority."

W. always gets exasperated when he reads a protection argument. He said: "I believe in the higher patriotism—not, my country whether or no, God bless it and damn the rest!—no, not that—but my country, to be kept big, to grow bigger, to lead the procession, not in conquest, however, but in inspiration. If Patrick Ford rightly reports himself in his North American Review article when he attributes the miseries of Ireland to English free trade, then Pat Ford is the biggest fool of the whole lot of fools—then Pat Ford is the prize fool of our time. As for Ireland, who can point out the queen bee in the clusters of reasons for her condition? The reasons come by many ways, mysterious reasons, plain reasons—each reason important with other reasons—no one reason telling the whole rank tale." "Then you think the Irish have a grievance? that the tale is really rank?" "Rank? Rank as hell!"

W. is terribly persecuted for autographs. "If the thing gets any worse I shall be driven to an old trick. I used to put portraits containing my autograph with the folks out at the Children's Home, turning all applications over to the Home, which asked a dollar apiece for the pictures, and, often, got it." Talked of Burns: "He was all heart—Scotch from top to toe, which means human from top to toe: with limitations, to be sure, but limitations that seemed to rather perfect than mar him. James Hunter was here today—you know Hunter?—Scotch, too, as he is, to the bone: hearty, merry, laughing, canny (using 'canny' in the right sense): pouring over your troubled waters the oil of a pacifying humor." I asked W.: "Would you say the best man would be imperfect with humor left out of his composition?" "I don't know: would I?" "Or could a man without humor be a best man?" "I don't know: could he? You are driving me hard with major questions." "Emerson thought it a defect in Jesus that he lacked humor—if the records are correct." "I am not so sure: the idea startles me." "Emerson don't mean laughter or guffawing but that something or other which oils life—gets rid of its angles and incongruities—a sort of lubricator." "Does he make humor to mean that?" "I make it to mean that after reading Emerson." "Good! Good! that is a noble distinction to make: I don't know but having the distinction made that way I am prepared to accept it."

W. asked me if the Boston Investigator is still in existence. "It is of the free-thinking bigoted order—much needed, of course, but very narrow and very small in some of its definitions. We seem to require all kinds of bigots to complete the chapter of our sorrows—Methodist bigots, Presbyterian bigots, the bigots for the Bible, the bigots against the Bible, Quaker bigots stiffer than their hats: all sorts, all sorts: we need them all to finish off the ornament of our hari-kari world." I laughed. "Is that all?" I asked. "It stands for all, I guess. We ought not to neglect to include the political party newspapers—they are as bad as the worst."

W. gave me a war-time letter from B. P. Shillaber. Asked

8 95

me if I knew Shillaber. I was familiar with his Mrs. Partington fictions. Had also visited him once at Chelsea with Sidney Morse. W. said: "That interests me. Some day you will have to tell me about it. They say he was a good deal of a man. You will remember about the soldier Babbitt he mentions in the letter—I asked someone up there (was it the Curtis or the Wigglesworth women?) to look him up. Shillaber found him—found that he remembered me (God bless 'im). Do you know, Horace, such things as that—just little things, insignificant things—are the big things of life after all? Babbitt didn't say I wrote beautiful poems or did anything that people looked at but just 'brightened up' on hearing my name mentioned. Ain't that a thousand times better than writing poems—just that—to brighten up those who suffer?" "Except it happens that the poems also brighten them up." "Well, that is a reasonable amendment. But the man always comes before and always remains after the poem."

This is Shillaber's letter:

BOSTON, December 10, 1863.

WALT WHITMAN—

My dear sir—I went to the hospital in Pemberton Square yesterday and saw your friend Babbitt. I found him in a bad way. For two months, he tells me, he has been unable to do any thing for himself on account of giddiness if he attempts to rise. He therefor is confined to one position—poor fellow!—flat on his back, but is cheerful nevertheless, and on hearing your name he brightened up and gave me a warm welcome. He was in Barre some time after his return from under your care, and among his friends he grew better—was able to go about; but the ride—some sixty miles, I think—so unsettled his nervous organization that for three weeks it seemed to him that he was still on the cars. He has not sat up since. He was very grateful for your interest, and his last words to me were—"tell him to write to me." He cannot speak a loud word owing to his diseased throat. He looks pretty well, however, and his hand was strong and honest when I shook it at parting. His case I think a very painful one—how much harder than though he had gone into the battle and lost his life or a limb! There seems a sort of hopelessness about this, and being unused to hospitals my feelings were far from cheerful, though I tried to say brave and encouraging things to him and uttered the customary platitudes—the "Be thou clothed" and "Be thou fed" formulas,—without giving a rag or a crumb else. I asked if I could do anything for him. He told me no, thanking me. His thought seemed most on getting a letter from you.

If you are in the Armory Hospital and inquire for Frank McDonald, Ward E., I believe you may say a kind word to a friend of mine.

Hoping what I have written may interest you, I remain with much regard

Yours

B. P. SHILLABER.

Monday, August 6, 1888.

Heat still excessive. W. says: "There is some peculiar atmospherical influence which reacts strangely upon the chemistry of my body. The days go on from bad to bad, from early morning until about four in the afternoon, when I experience a sudden rally: from then on to bedtime I am another man." Took some proofs from me. Stuck them in his pocket. "The Herald man was over this late afternoon—Browning, their Philadelphia representative. He wanted something from me on Sheridan. At first I said it was impossible—really felt that it was out of the question—but after he had gone I turned the matter over in my mind and after all wrote a dozen lines or so, which I have just sent up to the post office by the nurse here—glad, to be sure, as I am, to squeeze a word or two for Sheridan out of the damning lethargy of these trying days. Sheridan was in many respects our soldier of soldiers—was the most dashing of the lot—though as I sit here nowadays I am wondering if the whole soldier business is not cursed beyond palliation."

Had been reading Carlyle's Sterling, which I took to him last evening—was reading it when I arrived. "Yes, it is interesting —sort of: I have been going through it—skimming what invites me, getting glimpses of it." Asked me: "Do you know much about Aaron Burr? There's a man, now, who is only damned and damned again in history and yet who had his parts. I have always designed writing something about him to show I did not stand in the jam of his vilifiers. I had a piece on him which should have gone into this book. You don't know (I guess I never told you) that when I was a lad, working in a lawyer's office, it fell to me to go over the river now and then with messages for Burr. Burr was very gentle—persuasive. He had a way of giving me a bit of fruit on these visits—an apple or a pear. I can see him clearly, still—his stateliness, gray hair, courtesy, consideration. Two or three years ago I wrote up some reminiscences but the manuscript got buried with other manuscripts down stairs. Sometime I must hunt it up."

A copy of Hollyer's etching of W. came today. W. said of it: "My mind is a slow one—it never hustles: I don't seem to know yet what I think of the portrait." Delighted over our success with the Hicks. "I had for several days been fighting off a damnable suspicion that it was to be a failure—a slouch, a botch, job." Then: "I want you to say that to the man for me. I should like to send something over to him: what shall it be? Something above his bill"—after a pause adding: "Get the candle, Horace. I have in the other room a whole pile of books —copies of As a Strong Bird on Pinions Free: how would one of them do? And one for you, too, if you say so." He got up from his chair in rather painful fashion, took my arm, and went with me into the back room. The books were found. We returned in the same way to his chair. He dropped into it heavily with a sigh of relief: "God! what a strain that was—and only a few feet of walk, too. How sweet is this chair—how I hunger for it!" Inscribed the books: "Walt Whitman, Aug: '88" "I made that singular excursion to Dartmouth—delivered the little poem you see here. I wonder how it happened that I was chosen for the poem there? It was never quite clear to me. But I went—was royally received. When I returned to New York I produced this little volume. Nobody wanted it—nobody cared for it— even my friends mostly left it unread—and so five hundred copies or so fell into my hands—five hundred, which I have given away right and left until now only a hundred or less remain." The "something else in view" of which W. spoke to me yesterday was a portrait of himself for frontispiece—a sitting portrait taken he could no longer tell by whom, in Philadelphia, last year—which he designs to print with this inscription: "Walt Whitman in his 70th year." He gave me a sheet of suggestions to submit to the engraver, saying: "That picture is in the nature of a surprise: my niece was here the other day—found it lying around—asked for it. It seems to me a satisfying picture, all in all. Do you and the man over in the city put your heads together and make what you can of it, using your own best taste. I rely upon you particularly, Horace, because I know you have lived among pictures and are not easily satisfied." Examined the Hicks: "A number of the fellows in England are off after Blake—after the work of Blake's time: but, if I do not err, some of that art is not sufficiently admirable to be imitated. Blake is great—very, very—and is not to be imitated: Blake began and ended in Blake. As for this"—holding up the Hicks proof— "I would think myself replying to a reproach if I said: This is what it is because of four dollars and a half and for no other reason."

Had he ever seen Theodore Parker? "Yes indeed. When I visited Boston those days I would alternate between Father Taylor's and Theodore Parker's meetings. I clearly remember seeing Emerson at one of the Parker meetings. I find my memory sometimes playing me tricks—working a little rusty: I may be saying to myself, 'it was thus or so,' yet for the life of me I can produce no supporting evidence. Then again, if I don't try to bring it back all comes back." He is "afraid" Bucke's expectations as to the quality of the Hicks will be disappointed: "There's an expression among the boys—I heard it often enough when I was a boy myself—'taking chances,' 'taking his chances' (how good it is, too, don't you think so?)—and so, though I tremble and am afraid this is all going amiss, that none of you will realize from it what you expect, yet I 'take chances,' 'take chances,' and must wait and see what all my gamble comes to." He had "another anxiety:" "If the Century should not use the Memoranda in October what a stew it would put us in! It is true the piece has been so cut and changed it has become another piece: still I feel pledged to them—there is a principle involved. Yes, they said October—but even that don't clear it for me. I always give the publishers all that is due them if not more." "You always prefer if you err at all to err on the side of bankruptcy." He laughed with great glee: "Good! Good! That's what keeps me poor: it is also what keeps me happy."

Bucke said in his letter to W.: "I do not understand your plans about publishing. You say you may not publish for awhile 'for reasons.' I think myself a good idea would be print a hundred or two hundred copies on good (and large) paper, bind them nicely, and sell them yourself for five or even ten dollars with autograph, by and by publishing through McKay or another." W. remarked: "In these days of cheap printing, when such beautiful books are so easily and reasonably produced and sold, we can't hold ourselves too high. I for my part don't want to be either haughty or humble. I had thought of an edition for a dollar—and Lord only knows, that dollar may be more than any number of people would care to pay. Bucke does not seem to realize that I am still a rejected quantity in the market."

Dr. Baker came in. B. thinks W. "preceptibly improved." B. asked W. if he had been down stairs yet. "I have not but should have been—I shall in fact make a try for it to-morrow, not to stay, not to brag, but just to convince myself and you fellows that I am not as Horace says 'all paid up' yet." Baker protested: "Don't be reckless." W. smiled. "There's no danger: the phrenologists mark my caution at six to seven—nearer to seven than six—which amounts to cowardice." Showing me a copy of the English Hobby Horse Guild he said: "I never have thought of it with respect to what it contains but in connection with its mechanical beauty—and yet the motive of the thing after all is its only reality: if it lacks in high motive it will always deserve to be kept flat on the ground whatever its convincing mechanism." Letter from John Baker, Penfield, New York, saying he had suffered from an affliction similar to W's and wondered what it was had, as he heard, "improved" W. Gave me O'Connor's letter of the 3rd. "It is about the calendar— will give you the latest news about the calendar. William is always wideawake—always plants both of his two eyes on life. Bucke's letters often go off into words—off into the air—but William is always true to the scent of himself." This is O'Connor's letter:

WASHINGTON, D. C.,
LIFE SAVING SERVICE,
Aug. 3, 1888.

Dear Walt: I enclose for your information a letter I got yesterday from Dr. Channing about the calendar, which reads well.

Today I have a letter from Stedman, in which he cordially undertakes the task of getting a publisher. I think this very good of him, as he is quite driven with all sorts of commissions.

I feel sorry that the delay of last year prevented our getting Mr. Stetson to draw the picture I wrote you of for the card, because he is a man of singular genius, and appreciates deeply Leaves of Grass, the central sun of which, and permeating all its parts without exception, is, he thinks, Spirituality. I think he would have given us something really good—something artistically bold, any way, though maybe not. But he cannot do it this year, and I understand is getting ready to go for study to Italy.

I did not know the Ms. of the calendar was to be placed in Stedman's hands, but it could not be in better nor friendlier.

Send me back the letter when you have done with it, that I may write to Dr. Channing, who has been very laborious and earnest in the matter. Grace [Grace Ellery Channing] the cherub deviser of the scheme, is now up at Bristol, Rhode Island.

101

I have been much comforted by the newspaper reports about you, as by your card of the 27th ultimo, though I realize how badly ill you still must be. But I have strong hopes. If you can but weather the summer!

I am myself pretty bad—very back-achey and weak leggy. But, like Webster, we still live, and who can get us under!

I am glad you can sit up and work a little on your book, which must be a comfort.

I have another letter from Dr. Bucke, whom I treat disgracefully, not answering promptly. But it is pretty hard to write and keep the office stone rolled up the hill daily.

All consolation! all cheer!

Affectionately yours,

W. D. O'Connor.

Tuesday, August 7, 1888.

Harned come in to see me after dinner and we went down to W.'s together at 8. W. a trifle easier than yesterday but still, as he says, "silly weak." Then he said: "Mary Davis and I agree in one thing—that, all the drawbacks considered, I am getting along well—as well as could be expected—yes, even improving, I may say. Yet, such are the drains of the heat on my small treasure of strength, that the vim I had (Lord knows it was little enough!) threatens to go—to go completely— so that if this weather continues I guess I won't." "I have been reading for a couple of hours this afternoon Gabriel Harrison's Life of John Howard Paine. I have had the book a couple of years (Gabriel sent it to me himself: he is my personal friend) but have never until now taken it up in a right mood of appreciation. It appeals to me greatly—even the sadness of it, the pathos of it, which element is very considerably interwoven with its texture."

W.'s Sheridan not in The Herald today. His first question was about it. "Well, well, it's all right if it appears to-morrow, all right if it does not appear at all." Harned asked: "What have you been doing to The Herald?" W. replied: "Now I can tell you nothing about that: I doubt if I would recognize it my-self if I saw it again. It was eked out the last thing, in the last ten minutes, before darkness set in: without weighing, testing, changing it, I mailed it off, to let what would come come." This led him to speak about Sheridan: "He was in essentials a genius: he had almost phenomenal directness, and genius is almost a hundred per cent directness—nothing more. He was characterized by a rough candor which always meant what it appeared to mean. Of all the major men developed by the War he was closest to the top. The War brought out a lot of ability of its own kind. There was Hancock: Hancock was not as distinctly individual as Sheridan but was nevertheless a splendid soldier—a soldier born, rarely bettered upon. Grant, I suppose, take him for all and all, was our most comprehensive man—took in most, was composed and potent. Grant was just spared being too considerate: McClellan was not—was therefore a failure."

Reference being made to Ireland W. remarked: "A search for the cause of the misery of Ireland would be like a search for the cause of the weather: a history of the one would be a history of the other." "Well, but you must see that there are economic and political ingredients to the problem." "No doubt—but what are they? Do you know?" I looked at him without answering: "I have no doubt you radicals have a theory about it that would settle the whole trouble by daybreak." "You talk like an Irish landlord, Walt." "Well, I don't feel like one—I feel more like an Irish pauper. And as for all that I may say, that though I haven't any theory in the matter you can't hit a landlord too often, Irish or American, and if you hit and don't hear my amen that's because I didn't see what you were about." Harned raised his hand in mock horror: "Walt, you are a bloody Fenian!" W. seriously: "There were the Fenians, yes: God knows they didn't come too soon or without a reason."

W. does not acquiesce in the recent revival of Bewick and William Blake. "It is as if a fellow started out of a morning and said to himself: 'I've lots of money but I don't like the railroad and so I will betake myself to a coach or go afoot'—though the distance be a thousand miles. Our friend Blake in Chicago —the Unitarian preacher there—objects to the present current style of writing, that it has ceased to be archaic or classic and has become journalistic. I do not think we will ever go back to Chaucer or Shakespeare—nor back to Dryden or that ilk—nor back at all." Harned suggested sending up a stenographer to help W. through with some of his work. W. replied: "It's decent of you, Tom, to propose that, but it would not do—I could not make it work: your dog here is too old to learn any new tricks: to stop at the door of the tomb and study a new a b c." W. replied to Harned anent November Boughs: "I must see to it, rather that I am suited than that the public is suited. I don't know if a fellow ought to say it, but if it might be allowed I would say: so I please myself I don't care a damn what the public thinks of me." Spielman writes:

LONDON, July 24, 1888.

WALT WHITMAN, ESQ.,

Dear Sir, After some months' delay I publish in this month's Magazine of Art (which will be next month's in America) your poem of "twenty years;" and I should be glad to hear from you if you think the drawing in any way adequately expresses your feelings.

In the hope that your health has improved, I remain,

Faithfully yours,

M. H. SPIELMAN.

W. said: "I hope he will have the good grace to send me a copy or two when it appears." I told him I took the Magazine. "Ah well—that will do: keep a sharp look-out for the poem." Gave him messages from Kennedy and Burroughs. No letter from Bucke. Put the photo for the frontispiece in my hands: "I leave it all to you fellows to do right with: if you do wrong, God help you! Though slow I am fierce in anger." Brown sent thanks back for the book. W. said: "Isn't it in Shakespeare, in one of the comedies, where some one speaks of 'poor things, poor things! but mine own, mine own'?" Harned left. I picked a bit of W's manuscript off the floor and reading it laughed. "Now what's up?" asked W. "Nothing much. This is a place where you have put yourself under a magnifier." "Let me see—let me see. No—it's dark over here—read it to me." He had got back on the bed. I read.

"It is not when matched with other verse and tested by the ordinary intellectual or esthetic lineaments they compare favorably with that verse; probably by those tests indeed they do not equal the best poems. But the impalpable atmosphere which every page of Leaves of Grass has sprung from, and which it exhales forever, makes a spell, a fascination, to one capable of appreciating it, that certainly belongs to no other poet, no other poem, ever yet known."

W. laughed heartily about this: "That's where I lift myself by my suspenders and put myself on a pedestal of my own make." I waited to see if he would say more, which he did, this time in an entirely serious vein: "It is a kind of self analysis which may amount to much or little according to whose perspective it gets into. You know I have said from the first that Leaves of Grass was not to achieve a negative recognition—was bound to be either a howling success or a stupendous failure. When I wrote that paragraph I must have felt prosperous." Gravely humorous. I left soon after. Found a little picture of Emerson on the floor. Recognized it as a waif from Morse's collection worked with when he was here. Smeared with clay. W. said I "might as well have it as consign it again to the floor, where it seems destined to remain," explaining: "I picked it up a dozen times and put it on the table here but it always seems to get back to the floor. It is a noble little bit of portraiture—shows Emerson at his best: radiant, clean, with that far-in-the-future look which seemed to possess him in the best hours. Emerson's face always seemed to me so clean—as if God had just washed it off. When you looked at Emerson it never occurred to you that there could be any villainies in the world."

Wednesday, August 8, 1888.

Stormy when I went to W. this evening. W. sat by the window, a fan in his hand, and talked cheerfully of the fallen temperature and his immediate physical response to it. The lightning flashed. W.'s head stood out against the northern sky. The rain fell in torrents. For the first time in a week the air was fresh and inspiring. "How sweet it is, boy!" exclaimed W. "My body is a splendid barometer." Gave him today's Herald containing the Sheridan piece. "I don't know too much about Sheridan, personally: we met, met several times, but that is all. You know I don't enthuse over him or over any military man— simply military man—any more than over a sword, a cannon, a bombshell. Sheridan had Napoleonic dash, nerve—as a soldier was a good one. He was psychically an uncommon character —had military philosophy as well as military ardor—was always cool in action, never lost his head, always knew what to do when the unexpected turned up."

Still reading Carlyle. "Today I struck upon the chapter on Coleridge—was intensely interested. It mainly hits the nail on the head—is just as true as it is enjoyable. I do not find anything in Carlyle's style to criticise. I never found any difficulties in it—or in the thought either, for that matter. It seems to me Carlyle's style is the expression of the man—natural, strong, right, for him. I know what is everywhere being said about his style, but I do not see what the objectors want. Do they mean that Carlyle should have turned about face just on their say-so? It is too much to ask of a man. Carlyle was not an accident—he was law, design."

"For years and years," said W., gravely, "I have argued with myself whether to write a prefatory note for Leaves of Grass. I never wrote one, never even got it laid out, but never forgot my intention. Should I make some such statement of my original purpose as would in the end account for all the mysteries of my book? I always decided against it—always came round to one conclusion—always planted my heel on the temptation at last: no, no, nothing *there:* if there's a thing to be said say it in your prose—don't trespass on the integrity of the Leaves—don't! don't! I was once driven down a steep hill by a friend of mine: he hurried the horses along at a breakneck pace, I protesting. 'Ain't you afraid to go so fast?' I asked. 'No—not a bit of it' he answered: 'I'm afraid to go slow. That's the only way I can overcome the difficulties of the road.' So it is with the Leaves—it must drive on, drive on, without protest, without explanations, without hesitations, on and on—no apologies, no dickers, no compromises—just drive on and on, no matter how rough, how dangerous, the road may be." W. said he had never dedicated a book. "I do not know why—probably there was no why. Dedications have gone out of vogue—are no longer regarded as necessary."

Referring to Notes and Queries: "Hunter has gone to work on it: God save him! I see no place for a paper of the sort. A literary class in America always strikes me with a laugh or with nausea: it is a forced product—does not belong here. We should not have professional art in a republic: it seems anti to the people—a threat offered our dearest ideals." W. wrote postals to Bucke and Mrs. Heyde. "She is afraid I am going to die— is always anxious and trembling." No letters today. "No mail at all, in fact, but Tucker's Liberty. I read his defense of Cortland Palmer—that though he was a man of great wealth he was profoundly concerned over the economic problems. The best of that statement is its truth—it is every word true. Palmer was a man of vista: he saw far ahead of all the commonplaces of the day." If Brown does well with the W. W. portrait W. will have him try the Eakins. Looked over a photo-engraving cata- logue. "It is beautiful stuff. Art will be democratized. The people will yet some day get a look in on the best art of the world: the castes will have to get out of the way of the crowd." Novem- ber Boughs complete ran to page 139—end of the Fox paper. W. thought it should go over to page 140, so prepared an additional "note" to go in with the Hicks—part of it written many years ago, part of it today. Likewise re-arranged page 118. From the first W. has been displeased with page 118—that A Backward Glance ending there fills the page. "I shall alter the plates—get a little blank at the foot of the page." To get that blank he today sacrificed this bit of text:

"I hope to go on record for something different—something better, if I may dare to say so. If I rested 'Leaves of Grass' on the usual claims—if I did not feel that the deepest moral, social, political purposes of America are the underlying endeavors at least of my pages: that the geography and hydrography of this continent, the Prairies, the St. Lawrence, Ohio, the Carolinas, Texas, Missouri are their real veins and current concrete—I should not dare to have them put in type, and printed, and offer'd for sale."

W. added explanatorily: "We want to do our best with the book. I want it mechanically so well done, so carefully thought out, that we may show the English printers that we, too, can do creditable work—that we, too, can make conclusive books." I said to W.: "It is interesting about Shillaber that though he was so broken up by his sympathies when he visited the hospital to see Babbitt for you he was real game when he was sick himself. When Morse and I visited him in Chelsea he was all gone to pieces, roomfast, waiting to die, but he was full of reminiscence, fun, even of a certain kind of hope." This interested W. "I see what it all means—it is in accord with my own experience with men: a man of heart often suffers more pain seeing sickness than being sick." At the time I went with Morse to see Shillaber Morse was making a bust of the old man. W. suddenly said: "It's rather odd you should have referred to Shillaber and Babbitt again as it reminds me of a letter I have laid out on the table for you. Look for it over there yourself—on the other side: yes, that's it: the yellow envelope. It's from Trowbridge—also about Babbitt." I opened the letter and started to read it to myself. W. said: "Let me hear it again, too—read it aloud."

Boston, Dec. 21, 1863.

Dear Walt, I am here at the bedside of your friend Babbitt in the Mason Hospital. I read him your letter; and he wishes me to say to you that he would be glad to answer your letters to him if he was able. He is in about the same condition he has been in for three months. He wishes to go home to his friends in Barre, and could get his discharge, but Dr. Bliss, of the Armory Square Hospital, neglects to send on his descriptive list, although the surgeon here has written to him for it. No doubt you can see to having it sent. Mr. Babbitt's father, who has been out with the 53rd, is going out again, and he is anxious to get his son home before he leaves. The descriptive list is the only thing necessary now to procure his discharge. Your friend wishes you to see Dr. Bliss, and write to him what he says about it. I shall come and see him whenever I come to town. What he needs is sympathizing friends around him. He is very lonesome lying here with no Walt Whitman to cheer him up.

I have been to see about getting together a package of books for you, but the booksellers are so busy it will be several days before I can get them packed and sent.

Let me hear from you. I write in haste with numb fingers— it is bitter cold here today.

Yours,
J. T. Trowbridge.

The letter was addressed to W. at Washington care of Major Hapgood. I said to W.: "I know one sentence in the letter that pleased you." "I do too." "'He is very lonesome ——'" "That's it," said W., delighted: "You are a firstrate guesser: you keep a little ahead of me every time." Said again to W.: "I am still waiting for that surprise." "Why, so you are—I had almost forgotten. A day or two more and you may come to your own." W. called my attention to a little

109

slip of paper which he had endorsed in red ink: "from O'Connor from Washington Nov: '82." This is what O'Connor had written:

"That was a mighty good thing the President said about Tobey after his visit recently: 'Is that the damned old fool that threw Whitman's book out of the mails?' So like Arthur too—the urban Arthur—the gentleman and man-of-the-world Arthur."

Thursday, August 9, 1888.

The cooler day has had a brightening effect upon W. He regains no strength, but feels less depressed physically. He deplored his weakness, though quite satisfied to have things as well as they are. He makes no motion, however, towards going down stairs. Read and wrote more considerably than usual today. Is quite interested in the Blaine reception at New York. "Is the ship yet in? Is the grand to-do yet done?" Seemed to take it as the prime event of the week. He sat much of the day across the room from the bed working in a mild way. His raw product is about him, on the table, the floor, in boxes and baskets, on chairs, and pretty nearly all things he may need are within reaching distance. At his foot is the pitcher of ordinary (never iced) water, which he takes up from time to time and draws from copiously. Books are piled promiscuously about, his will remains on the box-corner where he placed it when it was drawn up—letters, envelopes, are scattered over the floor,—autographed volumes hang on the edges of the table-leaves, chairs, the sofa—everything seeming in disorder. My impression of W's appearance at this date is a favorable one: though it is clear enough that his recent severe trials have added burdens to his life. His face is not so full as it was: he has nervous irritations: there are lines, down-lines, never until now in his cheeks. His complexion, though often as ruddy and strong as it was a year ago, is less to be depended upon, is unstable. W's room is a large one, considering the house—it has three north windows—

one door opening from it into the hallway, another into a connecting apartment. In this latter (he never works here) are most of his stored papers, books, and with them the Morse heads—three or four of them—and boxes more or less laden with letters, &c. Often he points me about the rooms: "Poor as these are, they are a comfort to me—my own—giving me freedom: such freedom as I am competent yet to enjoy. Why, then, should I leave them now for strange scenes—scenes in which I might gain much but would surely lose much more?"

W. wrote a Sheridam poem to-day and intimated to the Herald that he wished it printed Saturday, the day of the funeral. "Keep a sharp look-out for the paper," he said to me: "And another thing, Horace—take a wink or two at the Cosmopolitan, which, Tom says, has been taking a fly at me: then tell me what you think of it. If it's mere frippery, smartness, let it go—don't speak to me about it, forget it: but if it's worth attention, whether because it's strongly for or against, bring the magazine to me. You know what I like, what I can read—endure: you know me better than all the rest: so, anytime, anywhere, if you pick up odds and ends of stuff which you think belongs by rights to me, cart it into this room—give me my little see-saw with it."

He spoke of George Ripley as a man superlatively equipped for the office of critic. "I met him here and there but we were never on close terms. His great learning always impressed me —but that was where Ripley stopped: with the learning: he never talked of life direct: he talked of the talk of life. He was a sort of news-carrier—and I do not deny that he carried the news well and that the news was worth carrying." "Did you ever notice," W. went on, "—or perhaps you haven't (you're younger than I am)—that the bitterest, most severe, most malignant, conservatives—old conservatives—are made out of men who in their youth were the extremest radicals—radicals of radicals? I don't know what will become of you—no doubt you will come out all right—but that has been the history of some of the best friends of my own youth—men who started with me—the best of them." I quoted Emerson: "The old conservative is the young radical gone to seed." W. exclaimed: "How good! how good! And dear Emerson, too. Well, there was a man who never lost his youth."

I had a letter from Edward Coates, husband of Florence Earle. Quoted it to W., who said: "I don't know Mr. Coates but I know the wife—a beautiful, true woman, I have always believed her. We have had several talks together—or maybe only one talk: I am not clear about that now—but I shall always remember what she said—the effect of her talk, which was mainly about Matthew Arnold, who was her guest in Germantown. Arnold is a man for whom I never seem to be able to get up any stir—with whom I never have had and never could have a thorough-going affinity. But Mrs. Coates gave me the other side of him—the social side, the personal side, the intellectual side—the side of deportment, behavior—the side which I ought perhaps most to hear about and did willingly and gladly hear of from her. For every man has that better thing to be said of him—is entitled to all it may mean, signify, explain."

W. remarked: "I think The Critic is rather doubtful of me if not actually adverse—seems to delight to quote this squid and that making light of my work. You can detect the bent of the editorial mind with perfect ease by what it quotes. Littell's used to quote consistently the meanest things that were being said about me. Anyhow—I have no idea that Joe Gilder cares a fig for me. Jennie is more favorable, though not red-hot at all, nor anywhere near it. My only uncompromising friend in the family is probably Watson—he swears to me—not everything in me, but to me—without shame. There are critics and critics. You don't know the tribe as I do—the damned mean stuff they are often made of—the very poison (not the salt) of the earth. Some of my opponents are fairly on the other side—belong there, are honest, I respect them: others are malignants—are of the snake order. Look at Stoddard and Winter—at Winter, particularly, who is the smallest of the crowd, however you try him, whether for brain or emotion. If you have not experienced a direct encounter with the monitors, critics, censors, you can have no idea of the venoms, jealousies, meannesses, spites, which chiefly characterize their opposition. It has been a rallying cry with a little group of men in this country: down Walt Whitman—down him in any way, by any method, with any weapon you can—but down him—drive him into obscurity, hurry him into oblivion! But suppose Walt Whitman stays, stays, is stubborn, stays again, stays again, will not be downed?"

He seemed to greatly enjoy the idea that he was not to be downed. But happening to pick up an illustrated paper containing some Tyrolean pictures which attracted him he got right off on another subject: "These great hills are wonderful but not exceptional—you don't need to go to Europe to find them. Take the Rockies, for instance—they sweep along the horizon like cloud: to the novice they would be no more than grand cloud effects: sometimes they even puzzle the initiated. You know what worlds live in the cloudlands—worlds as real as ours while they last. We do not need to travel to find these worlds—they are always just where we are. Cross the Delaware almost any night and you will become a discoverer: there are no wonders anywhere greater than the wonders you see right over your head as you cross the river in the boat. When I was in Denver I spent my longest hours in contemplation of the mountain ranges."

Then he talked of his mother. Where were the letters he wrote his mother in Brooklyn from the War? "They are here—I have them—I got them after she died—a hundred or more: all scrupulously kept together—still about somewhere with my manuscripts. The reality, the simplicity, the transparency, of my dear, dear mother's life, was responsible for the main things in the letters as in Leaves of Grass itself. How much I owe her! It could not be put in a scale—weighed: it could not be measured—be even put in the best words: it can only be apprehended through the intuitions. Leaves of Grass is the flower of her temperament active in me. My mother was illiterate in the formal sense but strangely knowing: she excelled in narrative—

had great mimetic power: she could tell stories, impersonate: she was very eloquent in the utterance of noble moral axioms— was very original in her manner, her style. It was through my mother that I learned of Hicks: when she found I liked to hear about him she seemed to like to speak. I wonder what Leaves of Grass would have been if I had been born of some other mother and had never met William O'Connor?"

Letter from Bucke to W. in which B. says: "I am glad you are getting cheerful letters from O'Connor. I am sorry he is worrying himself about the Cryptogram, which I fear is more or less of a fraud, though not perhaps intentionally so on Donnelly's part." W. asked: "What does Bucke mean by fraud—fraud? I would like to hear him say fraud to O'Connor: there would be an explosion." "You do not say anything about the cipher yourself—pro or con." "No I don't—it's beyond me: but I don't cry fraud. I like, agree with, the plain English of Donnelly's book —the mathematics are too much for me."

W. gave me some directions concerning our work at Ferguson's, saying laughingly afterwards: "The things I don't tell you to do you do anyway and do right, so I do not have any anxieties. You seem some ways to know better what I want than I do myself: I have to try and try: you go straight to the mark." I took off my hat to the compliment. He reaffirmed: "It's not flattery, Horace—not even praise: it's the everyday truth." I kissed him for good night and left the room. When I got out in the hallway I heard his call: "Horace! Horace!" and hurried back. "Here," he said, still sitting near the table, handing me a little bunch of letters or something tied in a red string: "Here is a prize package for you: put it in your pocket: don't let the police catch you with it. If you draw a jewel I'll go halves!" Seemed very jovial. "And one thing more—before you go for good help me over to the bed."

Friday, August 10, 1888.

I have been writing Bucke frankly about W.'s condition. Bucke today referred to my letters in writing to W. This was a mistake. W. consequently a little reticent. When I quizzed him he said frankly: "I don't want Bucke to know the worst until the worst is hopeless: he worries over bad news: write him in a cheerful vein—lie to him, buoy him up." "Lie to him?" "Well—lies won't help, I suppose—but don't tell him the evil until there's no more any good to tell about." W. is reading and writing again, almost steadily, for several hours of each day. Said he worked too hard yesterday. "It told on me so that I got up this morning feeling stale." Sometimes W. suffers a sort of aphasia—can't get his words without a search: but his mind is always clear. Lay on the bed most of or all the time of our talk. Was at times even hilarious. He has been interested in the Blaine reception in New York, but says: "I doubt if there are even a few of the noisy hurrahers who could stop their noise for a minute or two and tell us why their great man is great." Then: "The working class is slow to learn—they are cheated, swindled, robbed, pay all the pipers' bills and hear none of the music—yet go on year after year putting their robbers back in Congress, in the legislatures—making them mayors and what not."

Spoke of Kennedy's W. W. "It seems to come to nothing. And Kennedy himself—what's the matter with him? He writes a trite message—then ends." Said he was not in favor of the W. W. calendar: "I not only don't enthuse—I do not even approve. Leaves of Grass does not lend itself to piecemeal quotation: can only find its reflection in ensemble, ensemble: cannot be rendered by any selection of pretty lines, strange allusions, passages from here and there: it belongs to bulk, mass, unity: must be seen with reference to its eligibility to express world-meanings rather than literary prettinesses. It is true O'Connor thinks a good deal of the calendar: it comes from his nieces: and then Grace Channing is a bright, good girl, too, and might to trusted to do what could be done in that sort of work and with Leaves of Grass. But my first impression was a bad one and I have not moved from it. I shall not interfere (I did not interfere with the Walt Whitman Club in Boston) but I shall have my friends know that I don't endorse calendars or any other such miniaturing from Leaves of Grass." He thinks: "The New York fellers regard me as an oddity—most of them—even those who more than half like me. No one can know Leaves of Grass who judges it piecemeal: it makes no revelations to the merely literary eye."

Asked me questions about Wagner operas. "So many of my friends say Wagner is Leaves of Grass done into music that I begin to suspect there must be something in it. Doctor Bucke, who don't go much on operas, banks a lot on Wagner. I was never wholly convinced—there was always a remaining question. I have got rather off the field—the Wagner opera has had its vogue only in these later years since I got out of the way of going to the theater. Do you figure out Wagner to be a force making for democracy or the opposite? O'Connor swears to the democracy—swears to it with a big oath. Others have said to me that Wagner's art was distinctly the art of a caste—for the few. What am I to believe? I confess that I have heard bits here and there at concerts, from orchestras, bands, which have astonished, ravished me, like the discovery of a new world. The masters keep on coming and coming again: nature can always do better than her best: is prodigal, exhaustless."

I have started a Whitman fund—am trying to get a small monthly guarantee each from a group of people to pay for the nurse and the extras required by W.'s persistent illness. W. does not know about the fund. He knows the nurse is put here by his friends. I have not explained anything to him in detail. Hard to find the friends, however. Many excuse themselves when approached on the subject. I said to W.: "I sometimes find that certain people who profess a big conviction about you do not back it up." He laughed. "Are you just learning that? A lot of the Whitman talk is simply glamor (I call it that: is it a right use of the word?)—pretense, good nature, and so on—not being willing to justify itself in a crisis. I do not complain—only I like to know a fact for a fact. A man wrote in a paper the other day: 'All this English talk about Walt Whitman is a fraud:

the English accept Whitman as an eccentric, a rough, something different. He is not sincerely considered: he pleases a whim and when that whim has fed itself full good-bye Whitman in England.' That's about what was said. Whether true or not, the truth of it, the falsity of it, will find a proper level in time—like water whatever its troubles finds its level at last." Again: "They used to load all their indecent stories on Lincoln: now some people are loading all their indecent interpretations on me."

I said to W.: "Ferguson lets us have our own way in his place." "That is true—and we appreciate—yes, respect the concession. Such treatment involves reciprocal obligations: it removes our relations to a plane above trade." "The 'prize package' yesterday contained four jewels instead of one jewel," I said to W. He appeared pleased. "Which half do you want?" I asked him. He remembered that he had said he would go me halves if I found a jewel. "My half is in seeing you tickled," he replied. Then he asked me seriously: "You found something there worth preserving? It all contributes towards the history. It won't be long and I will be dead and gone: then they will hale you into court—put you into the witness box—ply you with questions—try to mix you up with questions: this Walt Whitman —this scamp poet—this arch-pretender—what did you make him out to be? And you will have to answer—and be sure you answer honest, so help you God!"

One of the jewels was a portrait which W. had endorsed in this way: "Rudolph Schmidt Copenhagen Denmark April 5 '74." He said of it: "It is simple, imperative, pleasing: is the face of a man not too much in doubt about himself—a telling autobiographical item. I always remember that Schmidt has broken several lances in my interest off in that strange country." The other jewels were letters from William Michael Rossetti and Mrs. Watson Gilder to W. and a never-delivered letter from William Swinton to Charles Sumner "to introduce Walt Whitman." When I got talking of these letters to-night he had me start reading them to him. I first took the Gilder letter. He had written in red ink on a blank page: "From Mr. and Mrs. Gilder New York (Gilder you know is a sort of chief literary man now on Scribner's)."

"KAYWOOD," STATEN ISLAND,
Nov. 20th, '80.

Dear Mr. Whitman, We were delighted at receiving your books—and *from you*. We have always intended owning them and were only waiting to return to our little house in town, as we have now a volume belonging to Mr. Burroughs. Your poems have a great hold on us, and grow more and more to us in value.

In London last winter we saw the Gilchrists several times and of course talked of you. Mrs. Gilchrist spoke most enthusiastically and affectionately of you, and Mme. Modjeska who was acting there wanted us to remind you of her having had the pleasure of meeting you. She is making a great success.

We read some of your poems to a group of people—artists etc. —in London, who were all intensely interested and impressed. One, Alfred Hunt, the landscape painter, was much moved over some of the descriptions of nature, the mocking bird and the pine trees especially. Richard talked about you with William M. Rossetti, your good friend, and others, who all were anxious to hear from you. Richard is very desirous to know whether you got some of your poems done into Provencal, by W. C. Bonaparte Wyse. Would you write a line of acknowledgment to the latter, to be forwarded through Richard? Mr. Wyse would value it very greatly.

Mr. Burroughs and Richard were camping out in September and there was a great deal of talk of W. W. under the pine trees beside the little Ulster Co. lake.

I know you love children and I wish I could show you my little boy, of whom I am very proud.

In February we will be again in our house—hope to see you there once more.

With renewed thanks I am dear Mr. Whitman one of your sincerest admirers

HELENA deKAY GILDER.

We are both greatly obliged to you and I endorse the foregoing.   R. W. G.

"Horace," said W., "you must never forget this of the Gilders—that at a time when most everybody else in their set was throwing me down they were nobly and unhesitatingly hospitable. This letter gives you a clue—a fine clue. It was about that same period some other woman in New York invited me to a dinner but just as I was about to start off for the trip sent me a second letter withdrawing the invitation on the ground that some guests who were indispensable to the success of the dinner refused to sit at the table with me." The story seemed incredible. While I was wondering what to say W. added: "It was God's truth, Horace—God's amazing truth! Nor was the affair a solitary one—I had dozens of such or similar rubs if I had two. Now, the Gilders were without pride and without shame—they just asked me along in the natural way. It was beautiful, beautiful. You know how at one time the church was an asylum for fugitives—the church, God's right arm, fending the innocent. I was such an innocent and the Gilders took me in." While I was reading the Swinton letter W. said: "William just let himself go—kept nothing vital back. I never delivered the letter. I felt that I would rather own the letter than have the job it asked for. Would you have supposed the school-bookman—Swinton—William—could ever so forget himself—wax so eloquent, make such a darling hullaballoo—about a man like your uncle? Some of my friends when they fairly got going about me made the stars look faint. My friends were fewer than my enemies but they blew a trumpet loud enough for everybody to hear." Swinton's letter was enclosed in a New York Times envelope.

119

WASHINGTON, Jany 6th, 1863.

HON. CHARLES SUMNER:

My Dear Sir: The bearer of this is Walt Whitman—of New York—a poet and absolute devotee to literature in the sense of giving America something genuinely her own—something that is robust while full of feeling and idiomatic while universal. He is the author of Leaves of Grass. He is ardent for future poetic works—I think noble and enduring ones. In New York the young men count with faith upon his future.

Mr. Whitman has for years remained poor. He is in Washington seeking to push his fortune,—to get some clerk-ship, appointment or whatnot. His claim rests upon literary grounds, not political ones—though he is and has long been a Republican in politics.

I have known him for years and know that he is an honorable and trustworthy man in all relations and in the highest sense.

Finding him here without access to the great quarters, I have taken the liberty to give him this note to one so well fitted to advise him; and although I see and know what demands are made upon your time and influence, I am sure you will not confound Mr. Whitman with the ordinary herd of Washington axe-grinders.

With best respects and regards,

WILLIAM SWINTON.

It was getting after ten. W. looked tired, I said: "Let's lay over the Rossetti letter until to-morrow." He acquiesced: "All right—to-morrow. Did you particularly notice in William's letter—'robust while full of feeling and individual while universal'? That fits my intentions to a t—describes my ideal absolutely. Leaves of Grass must answer to that call or be forgotten. Don't you think it was a bold thing for a man to say at that time: 'The young men count with faith upon his future'? That letter is a capital example of what I call let-go. A man who will talk that way in the face of a general opposition must care very very much or very very little for his reputation." W. finally said: "Take care of the book—the book's the thing!"

Saturday, August 11, 1888.

W. still holding his own, though weak. Busy reading and writing. Took him a bundle of page proofs, up to 140. Page 118 contains the Hicks portrait. W. said: "I would not be surprised either way with the portrait—surprised for good, surprised for bad." Still debating whether he would write a preface for November Boughs. "Why should I?—the book itself explains all I wish explained: is personal, confessional: a variegated product, in fact—streaks of white and black, light and darkness, threads of evil and good running in and out and across and through achieving in the end some sort of unity. I have often, especially in recent years, asked myself whether in rounding up Leaves of Grass I should not add a prologue and an epilogue—some fore-cast and resumé reasserting the designed and achieved tempo—some closing transcript of the aspirations, intuitions, that went and go to the making of the book—the appreciation of its message. But why should I? The same question—the same answer: no, no: I feel the no without defining it—and no is best, is best."

The Sheridan poem was not in today's Herald. "Not today? To-morrow then, or next day—or maybe not at all (why at all?) —which would be all right, too." Harned came in. Talk got on politics. W. said: "What about Blaine, Tom? Tell me the news about Blaine." He didn't wait for the news but went on: "Blaine has a wonderful intuition concerning current affairs and people—concerning the average thought, the everyday passions and prejudices of the street—yet the longer I live the more contemptible, the more utterly contemptible, seem his style and make-up, the instrument upon which he plays, the flagrant insincerity of his ambitions." Harned asked: "But hasn't he brains?" "Yes, brains—but of the superficial, sharp, evanescent kind. Take that matter of protection. After awhile it will strike the masses that protection does bring money to somebody but not to them—that the benefit is all one way and not their way—and then the throne will fall. I give protection ten or twenty more robbing years—not more than twenty, nor less than ten. There is always the wave and the counterwave—the tide goes up the tide goes down—the storm arrives, the storm departs. Protection had to come and has to go. Protection talk comes with bad grace from a man like Blaine having his clean or dirty twenty thousand a year—from the easy, comfortable elite of our money world who clap their hands over their hearts and say: 'Don't disturb any of these things: we're having a good time of it—plenty to eat, drink, wear: palaces to live in, servants to flatter and fawn upon us—luxury, yachts, money in the bank: don't disturb things as they are—don't ask questions—don't riot within the sacred precincts of our success.'" "They don't see the end," I said. "What is the end?" "Revolution." "Or evolution—which means the same thing in its results."

Harned withdrew. He had the two children with him. W. called them "the darlings" and kissed them good night. Henry George said in a speech in New York the other night: "The republic should lead the world to freedom." W. reaffirmed: "It will lead the world to freedom or to hell—I prefer freedom." Asked me questions about Lew Wallace: "I had Ben Hur here once and started to read it but before I had got along far it disappeared—whether through being stolen or lost or given away I do not know. I thought it really interesting and well done. I don't know but in reading the best method is to simply let the mind caper about and do as it chooses—or as it don't choose, as it must. I never try to create interest for myself in a book: if the interest don't come of its own account I drop my experiment: I would no more force my reading than my writing. I read the papers in the forenoon, about ten: I sort of toy with them—amuse myself with them—dawdle with them."

W. spoke doubtfully of Wagner's choice of Niebelungen themes for his operas: "I question the wisdom of selecting the Jack and the Beanstalk stories and putting them into this modern medium. Without a doubt there are points here which I have not considered—which are not quite familiar table-talk to me—but my first impression, my original instinct, (I can only give that) is adverse, critical, though not, of course, absolutely negative." This led him to ask me a question: "You speak of young Neumayer as a true bass. Is he that? pure, strong, without being coarse? Oh! the true bass is the most precious of all voices because the rarest of all. I have known so many yet so few—so few with the full equipment—one or two (not more than two) in all my experience." Allusion to the Leaves: "I am much less concerned to have them believed true than to have them true—much less concerned to have people recognize the good things than to have them there: and yet I like to have applause, too—like to hear the hurrahs that I don't have to go back and meet." I said to W.: "I've still got the Rossetti letter in my pocket." He said: "Yes—read it: I want to hear it once more before you take it away for good."

56 Euston Sq.
London, N. W., April 12, 1868.

Dear Walt Whitman, I received with thanks, and read with much interest, the article by Mr. Hinton which you sent me. Besides Mr. Hinton's own share in the article, I was particularly glad to see in full Emerson's letter written on the first appearance of Leaves of Grass. Of this I had hitherto only seen an expression or two extracted.

Will you allow me to respond by sending two English notices of the selection. The one in the Academia I find is written by a Mr. Robertson whom I have met occasionally—a Scotchman of acute intellectual sympathies. The alterations noted in ink in his article are reproduced by me from the copy which he himself sent me: I infer that they are in conformity with the original Ms., but cut out by a less ardent editor. The Sunday Times is edited by a Mr. Knight, of whom also I have some slight personal knowledge. I think the review in that paper is very likely done by Mr. Knight himself. The Academia is a recently started paper, chiefly scholastic, and I suppose of restricted circulation. The Sunday Times has no doubt a very large circulation, and a good standing among weekly newspapers—not being however a specially *literary* organ.

You will, I think, have seen through Mr. Conway the notice, also eulogistic, in the London Review. I am told of a hostile one in the Express (evening edition of the Daily News) but have not seen it: the Morning Star (the paper most closely connected with John Bright) had a very handsome notice about a week ago —but, like all literary reviews in that paper, a brief one. These are all the notices I know of at present. Perhaps I ought to apologize for saying so much to you about a matter which I know plays but the smallest part in your thought and interest as a poet.

As to the sale of the book I really know nothing as yet—not having once seen the publisher since the volume was issued.

A glance at the Sunday Times notice recalls to my attention a sentence therein which I should perhaps refer to—about your having given express sanction &c. Where the writer gets this from I know not—certainly not from me: indeed the P. S. to the selection asserts the exact contrary, and I have not so much as seen Mr. Knight for (I dare say) a couple of years.

With warmest regard and friendship,
yours

W. M. ROSSETTI.

"That was twenty years ago," said W., "and Rossetti is still serving under the flag—a pirate flag, somebody said: but it is hardly that: it is more like the red flag—the flag of revolution. The best of Rossetti is in the natural way he takes this whole Leaves of Grass business, without apologizing for, without glorifying, me."

Sunday, August 12, 1888.

10.30 A. M. Went in to W. early to take him his N. Y. Herald containing Taps for Sheridan. He sat in his armchair reading the Press, but at once took the Herald out of my hands. "The poem amounts to nothing in itself: was the work of ten minutes or so the other day: but I was quite anxious to have it appear in the Herald, which has been so kind to me." Then he saw how conspicuously it had been placed, at the head of the long story describing the Sheridan obsequies: "They've gone and done it after all—the very worst thing—the thing I especially *didn't* want them to do. It was my desire to have it come into the personal column—to appear there casually as something swept along in the current and picked up and set into a place."

Paul R. Cleveland refers to W. in the August Cosmopolitan as "a vagabond." I quoted this to W. "The sad fact about the story that I never made a living through literature is, that it is for the most part true. That has been made the staple complaint of numerous old and new accusers of Leaves of Grass. If I should care to make a guess, I should say that Paul R. Cleveland it not an actual person—that the name is an assumed one. If the article was not poorly written, as you say, I should ascribe it to Stoddard: but Stoddard writes well. And yet I am sure that if Stoddard did not write he at least dictated it—is at least responsible for it—Stoddard or some one or several of that group. It is a sore thing to some of them that I got along at all—much worse, that I got along so well."

Examined a rough proof of the Hicks and said: "It makes him look like a cross between an Injun and a Nigger, without a drop of white blood in his veins. There's one reason in particular why I want this picture to appear. With the damnable unreason of a sect the Quakers—too many of them—are fiercely opposed to pictures, music, in their houses. I want this head, therefore, to flaunt itself right in the faces of the Quakers who see this book—who read November Boughs."

"Horace," said W., suddenly, "I think the time has come for the American magazine—for a magazine designed to reflect America—its mechanics, its great labor masses—to give the smack of the heath—the native heath: to get its color from a life particularly American and offer the result to the world. Americana in the best sense—that we need. It's about time we had outgrown the Lord Adolphus Fitznoodle business—the Dobson, Lang, ballade, villanelle, business: the looking abroad for suggestions, for models, for ideals. Oh! I can see that such a venture would even pay for itself in money in time, not to speak of the other pay—not today, not to-morrow, but finally, after a tussle, in the long run. We are so commercialized in this country that we will do nothing without the pay is in sight—nothing, nothing: the profits must be near enough to grab: we seem to lack that great faculty of wait, wait, wait, which distinguishes and accounts for the world-power of the English merchant. Yet there are signs of an awakening. We may soon have to revise our notions on this score. Some day we may rise to the standards of moral, spiritual, profit, letting all the baser standards fall into disuse. By and bye the American magazine will come as the gift of some far-sighted far-hearted individual, who is willing to throw away all the vulgar prizes of the market for the sake of a cause, a future."

Advised me to meet Browning, the Herald's Philadelphia representative. "He is a fine, dark-browed, vital, affectionate sort of a man—a newspaper man made of the real stuff. The Herald people have always treated me as if I was what the boys call the real thing." W. laughed heartily when I told him Bucke said Walt Whitman never took advice: "In a way he is right: but again he is not. I do not object to advice but to having it made imperative. I claim the final privilege—claim the right to pass upon the advice that is passed up to me. I can honestly say that I like to hear all that is to be said in criticism of my work, my life: but you know well enough that it is impossible for a man to get down on his hands and knees before the advisers." W. thinks he has but two copies of Drum Taps left. "If there should be more I want you to have one—the first beyond the two that turns up shall be yours." The two he has are flung about different places in the room from day to day— on the round table, on the chairs, on the bed, on the floor. "As a Strong Bird I still possess in some quantity: you can take three or four or more of them any time you choose."

Letter from Bucke to W. today. Bucke says: "I should like to hear that you are gaining strength. I do not hear that. How is it?" W. repeated: "How is it? I don't know. Do you? Tell Maurice we've given up guessing here: let him make a guess in Canada." We had a little talk over one of his War letters, the rough draft of which I turned up in trying to find a Camelot book for him. It was in sheets pinned together, without an envelope or any sign of an address attached. W. turned it over and over mystified: "I don't know for sure who it was written to—probably one of those Boston women—the Curtis people, it may be. Is it of any use to you?" He passed it over. I was eager for it at once. This excited his remark: "Did I ever know you to decline anything like that? I don't believe you know how to decline." I replied: "I don't—I don't." My vehemence amused him. "Well, you must pay the penalty: sit right down there under the light and read me the letter. That will be my good-bye to the letter. After all, for your purposes, I don't suppose it matters at all who it was meant for at the time—its history is just as good for whoever. I guessed a Massachusetts name because I notice I make a point of mentioning the Yankee boys." I read the letter, W. closing his eyes and listening, breaking in every now and then with monosyllabic ejaculations:

Dear Friend. I am going to write to you to ask any friends you may be in communication with for aid for my soldiers. I remain here in Washington still occupied among the hospitals —I have now been engaged in this over seven months. As time passes on it seems as if sad cases of old and lingering wounded accumulate, regularly recruited with new ones every week—I have been most of this day in Armory Square Hospital Seventh st. I seldom miss a day or evening. Out of the six or seven hundred in this Hospital I try to give a word or a trifle to every one without exception, making regular rounds among them all. I give all kinds of sustenance, blackberries, peaches, lemons and sugar, wines, all kinds of preserves, pickles, brandy, milk, shirts and all articles of underclothing, tobacco, tea, handkerchiefs, &c &c &c. I always give paper, envelopes, stamps, &c. I want a supply for this purpose. To many I give (when I have it) small sums of money—half of the soldiers in hospital have not a cent. There are many returned prisoners sick, lost all—and every day squads of men from the front, cavalry or infantry—brought in wounded or sick, generally without a cent of money. I select the most needy cases and devote my time and services much to them. I find it tells best—some are mere lads, 17, 18, 19, or 20—some are silent, sick, heavy-hearted, (things, attentions, &c. are very rude in the army and hospitals, nothing but the mere hard routine, no time for tenderness or extras)—so I go round, —some of my boys die, some get well.

O what a sweet unwonted love (those good American boys of good stock, decent, clean, well-raised boys, so near to me)— what an attachment grows up between us, started from hospital cots, where pale young faces lie and wounded or sick bodies. My brave young American soldiers—now for so many months I have gone around among them, where they lie. I have long discarded all stiff conventions (they and I are too near to each other, there is no time to lose, and death and anguish dissipate ceremony here between my lads and me)—I pet them, some of them it does so much good, they are so faint and lonesome— at parting at night sometimes I kiss them right and left— The doctors tell me I supply the patients with a medicine which all their drugs and bottles and powders are helpless to yield.

I wish you would ask anybody you know who is likely to contribute—It is a good holy cause, surely nothing nobler—I desire you if possible could raise for me, forthwith, for application to these wounded and sick here, (they are from Massachusetts and all the New England states, there is not a day but I am with some Yankee boys, and doing some trifle for them)—

a sum—if possible fifty dollars—if not then less—thirty dollars
—or indeed any amount—

I am at present curiously almost alone here, as visitor and
consolator to Hospitals—the work of the different Reliefs and
Commissions is nearly all off in the field—and as to private
visitors, there are few or none—I wish you or some of your
friends could just make a round with me, for an hour or so,
at some of my hospitals or camps—I go among all our own dear
soldiers, hospital camps and any, our teamsters' hospitals,
among sick and dying, the rebels, the contrabands, &c &c.
What I reach is necessarily but a drop in the bucket but it is
done in good faith, and with now some experience and I hope
with good heart.

When I started to go W. asked: "Going, Horace? *Where*
are you going?" And when I answered, "To Harned's for
dinner," he seemed reminded of something and commenced to
rummage among his papers. "Is there something to go?"
I asked. "Nothing I have particularly looked for: I was only
trying to get my hands on something to send Tom"—then,
as his eyes fell upon the table: "Ah! yes! this!" picking up
Symonds' Wine, Women and Song and handing it to me:
"This: Symonds sent it to me: I have read a great deal of it:
take it to Tom." "For him to read?" "Yes—to read and
to keep: and for you to read, too. It is a little loose, but not
much so: not bad: not out of place with those French books
at Tom's—the beautiful books from that Parisian publisher."
I reminded W. that I was losing sleep and meals in my anxiety
over the "surprise" that he still held back. "Still harping on
my daughter" he exclaimed and said no more.

Evening, 7.30. Harned with W., who was in vigorous talking humor. Went on for an hour. The death of Dick Spofford everywhere spoken of in today's papers aroused W. to some
affectionate reminiscence: "Dick was bright—had a mind like a
star, so clear was its radiance. His body was very frail—you
could break it almost like a pipe-stem: yet his brain was so

active, effective, you never remarked his bodily defects. Dick was a Walt-Whitmaniac in the common ways of life—consciously or unconsciously that: hospitable to all sorts of men, all forms of thought, all contrasts of life: a brilliant apparition: always kind to me, thoughtful, friend of my friends as well as directly (while not intimately) friendly to me." W. sceptical about Blaine's declaration that "if the tariff goes down it can only be by the failure of the working man to sustain it." "A wonderful remark!—and the Press seizes on it and prints it in Italics as a watchword—God help us! Alas! what have we come to! The day of emancipation is yet way off. The tariff must still hang over us, prescribing its petty principles—just as Methodism, Presbyterianism, hold on like the devil though without a leg to stand on."

W. spoke of Emerson: "I shall never forget the first visit he paid me—the call, the first call: it was in Brooklyn: no, I can never forget it. I can hear his gentle knock still—the soft knock—so"—indicating it on the chair-arm—"and the slow sweet voice, as my mother stood there by the door: and the words, 'I came to see Mr. Whitman': and the response, 'He is here'—the simple unaffected greeting on both sides—'How are you, Mr. Whitman,' 'How are you, Waldo'—the hour's talk or so —the taste of lovableness he left behind when he was gone. I can easily see how Carlyle should have likened Emerson's appearance in their household to the apparition of an angel." W. thought Cabot's presentation of the anti-controversial Emerson "capital": "That was like him: he would take a stand, he would not hit out." W. said: "I always hated formal controversy anyhow." "I like to see the scuffle—I feel the necessity of hearing the last word of challenge—but am not to be lured into the fight. The world must move on without my fighting for it."

He said he had "resolved" today "to keep that unprecedented thing, a scrap-book." "I started it with the two Herald pieces on Sheridan." Harned spoke of English Traits as "the best study of English character extant." W. objected: "I do not think so: it never struck me so forcibly as that." But he added: "Emerson was a great vessel: he held a lot. When a man is dead we begin to see what a buffer he is." Then: "You should sometime get John Burroughs, when he is in his best humor, to tell you of his visit with Conway to Carlyle: it is so full of interest—so rich in touches of Carlyle's character. John speaks of Carlyle's laugh—the hearty, roaring, indescribable laugh, about which Horace has just given us Emerson's description. I remember one incident John told me of the visit. Conway spoke of him to Carlyle as an ornithologist, whereupon Carlyle had a story to tell. He had gone a long journey—the purpose of the journey was defeated—he had been forced to walk home—was despondent, depressed, dispirited. Suddenly the song of a bird in the distance came upon him—the fresh clear notes of a song—and swept his heart clean of its debris, so that a journey's end which was threatened with sorrow was accomplished with gladness. It was wonderful to me —the undertone, the overtone, of that story. Mrs. Gilchrist will not hear to it—that Carlyle was what the average world makes him out to be: will not yield an inch to the clamor. She gives a clean bill to both of them—to Thomas, to Jean: she says the stories of their dissensions are vagaries, malicious and impossible: that she knew—that she was their neighbor, a frequent visitor in their home."

W. finally has something to say about the Hollyer etching. "I do not think it good enough to be good—this is especially true of the eyes—they are too glaring: I have a dull not a glaring eye." Harned asked: "After all, Walt, don't you think you're very much photographed and very little caught?" "Exactly, Tom—very rarely. Tom—Horace has the best picture of all: the Gardner picture—the Washington picture. I remember well the afternoon that was taken. When a reporter saw it in the case by and bye he wrote that Walt Whitman had been photographed in his night-dress. The Gardner people were fiery mad over it—to me it seemed funny." Back to the Hollyer: "It is not first class as an etching—far from first class as a portrait. It is taken from the Lear original. Do you know, it was Mary Costelloe who gave that picture its name?—a good name, too, as most of my friends have allowed."

Discussed November Boughs. Thought we might try a flexible cover for it. Then looked over plans for the full-edition Whitman—a one volume W. W. to contain all the prose and verse up to the date of issue. We are to go to work on it at once. "It's a new baby to be born," said W., "and we must get to work at once to prepare its clothes." Attempted to walk round the house today but got no farther than the bathroom. The first daring venture. Said of it: "I am a lame though not yet quite a dead duck." Gave me a Bucke letter: "Tell me what you make of Bucke's warnings and objurgations."

Monday, August 13, 1888.

Day wonderfully cool. W. like a child in his joy. "For the first time I feel sassy with returning vigor. I take the benefits as they come: when they do not come I do not worry reaching out for them." Harned came in. Applauded the Herald poem. "So you think the old dog is at his tricks—and that that is a sign of improvement? Well—let it go at that: you can't teach me new but I won't forget the old tricks." When I arrived he lay on his bed and we had an earnest talk, no one else being present, about the big book. W. is fully resolved. "Tell Ferguson we'll back him up for the best he can do: tell him the story of the old woman who said to the hen: 'This time I'm going to give you a chance to fling yourself!'—so let Ferguson fling. A few dollars more or less—what do they amount to?" He laughed. I said: "A few dollars more mean a good deal if you ain't got 'em." "I should say! and don't I know? hasn't my prosperity walked on its uppers almost from the start?" Still: "I think I've got enough to see the book through so let's see it through right. I am familiar with the small economies, meannesses, of publishers: but we are not publishers: let us travel over the best road." I secured a rough estimate today on a book of nine hundred pages. W. satisfied. "That seems reasonable: hitch up—let's start." The idea is to issue a limited edition including Leaves of Grass, Specimen Days, and November Boughs: press work first class, paper good, margins liberal, with "powerful but modest portraits" ("if any: are portraits indispensable?" he asks): the books to sell for five or ten dollars and be autographed. This is an old idea revived. We discussed and abandoned it while W. was sick and seemed to be getting hopelessly worse. Gave me multiplied cautions to see that the Hicks portrait comes up right in the printing. "I have set my heart on that head—on its satisfactory presentation: I would rather leave it out altogether than have it go in bad."

"Though always objecting to prefaces," he said, "I think I shall have to write some note amounting to a preface for this de luxe edition." He waited for me to notice his "de luxe." I said nothing. "What's the matter with de luxe? I thought you would say amen to it." Said further of prefaces: "They are much like bowing and scraping a man in through your open door. The door being open, that should be enough. I tie myself to no rule in such a matter but I believe that they are mainly superfluous. This seems to be a case where a preface —some explanation—is in order." When he came to light up his gas he said quickly: "Hullo! I haven't turned the facet against the wall"—he has a table jet attached—"What a thing is habit!—how habit makes monkeys of us all! We forget once or twice to turn the facet—after that we always forget it: it has become a habit. From that time on we are slaves. Curiously, it is harder to break away from your vices than from your virtues: sometimes it seems easier to go to the Devil than to go to God!"

Harned came in and after a bit called the children up. Then there was a great munching of molasses candy—yellow jack— W. partaking most heartily. "How extra good it is, too, kiddies: ain't it better than the usual run?" Anna laughed and replied: "Oh yes! this kind you can only buy three cents worth of: you can't buy a cent's worth of this!" W. clapped his hand down on the big arm of his chair. "That explains it—I thought we were enjoying an extra extra treat!"

W. gave me his notions of a cover for November Boughs. Again produced the little Epictetus volume. "The book is precious to me—I think is one out of an edition of a hundred printed especially for Rolleston. Take it along however—show it to the binders—but don't take any risks with it." He called my attention to Twenty Years, which appears in the Magazine of Art, a copy of which he received today. "I like the drawing as drawing, though it is far enough away from anything I thought of when I wrote the piece. The general make-up of the page is very flattering. The boy there in the shrouds—he is best of all: splendid, easy, natural. It is true, too, as you say, that this figure down here on the shore—this strong, straight somebody with his hands in his pockets—is a try at me —of me as you know me in that Leaves of Grass portrait. Do you remember, the Magazine man said he would like to be informed whether the page pleased me? Well, I am pleased—much pleased—and you can say so to him or anyone. I don't mind it that he chose his own way of illustrating the poem—that was his own little privilege: he tried his hand at explication. The picture is like Hamlet—it has various ways of being interpreted. I used to make a fellow I knew mad by saying there were as many Hamlets as there were actors to act Hamlet, but he would not have it so: there was but one Hamlet, only one, and God help the man who didn't act that one! Winter is one of the worst of that crowd of jackasses. I have felt Salvini and Rossi to be all the greater for preferring their own Lears, Hamlets, Othellos to the heroes of the critics."

W. of Stedman: "Stedman would I think be freer and easier with me if it was not for the rabid crowd of literary wolves by which he is surrounded in New York—that crowd of yellers and screamers who declare that Walt Whitman is no good—is to be in no way endorsed, tolerated, commended. Even Stedman could not resist all that pressure. Yet he is noble, generous, lavish of his love. I shall never forget his kindness to me—his many kindnesses: why, he once paid thirty dollars I am told for a single special copy of Leaves of Grass. That was surely an act of great faith. The worst I hear about Stedman is not that he has failed in business but that he is sick." W. gave me an 1887 letter from James Grant Wilson: "I knew Wilson very well—he was a cordial and convincing character. This letter was sweetened by a touch of frank cameraderie— no more but that truely. Wilson belongs to the conventional literary old guard in New York." "You never broke into that crowd?" "No—they broke into me. I find them here and there hospitable, conciliatory: as a rule they are haughtily set against my claims—which is all right too, for their denial may in the end be confirmed." Wilson's letter was written on the stationery of Appleton's Cyclopedia.

NEW YORK, April 8, [1887]

My dear Mr. Whitman: Am glad to see by a morning journal that you are well enough to undertake a visit to New York, and the delivery of your address on Lincoln. If you have no better place to go, I shall be happy to give you shelter under my roof No. 15, East Seventy-fourth st, where I think you spent an hour some years ago. In any event, I hope to hear your address and to see you at my office. I am anxious to have one or more contributions from you for my Cyclopedia for which we pay ten dollars per printed page. Will you suggest some that you would like to write? Prospectus enclosed.

Very faithfully yours,

JAS. GRANT WILSON.

P. S. I can offer you a large chamber on the second floor, with a bathroom connected with it, for your exclusive use!

"I might have written up Paine, Hicks, Burr, Frances Wright —the unpopulars—but do you think the book would have stood for it? I'm afraid my pen let loose would have seemed out of character in such a place: my pen tied up I haven't to sell." "But," added W., "while the conventionals, on their side, are generally too timid, we, the radicals of us, on our side, are often too cocky." He shook his finger at me: "Be cocky, you young quarrelers—be cocky, be cocky, don't be too damned cocky!"

W. gave me a bit of his writing which proved to be a draft of his Garfield poem, The Sobbing of the Bells. I found it was written on the reverse of a letter written to W. by Boyle O'Reilly. Spoke of it to W. "Yes, so I see. That must have been in the eighties, while I was in Boston. Yes, we want art: I saw the Millet pictures at Shaw's: it was a great day." As W. had cut the Boyle letter and pieced it together again irregularly it is now difficult to make out. Up in the corner of the letter O'R. wrote: "Shall see you at Bartlett's Thursday." This is the letter as I have got it together with perhaps a word or two not literally in place:

THE PILOT EDITORIAL ROOMS,
BOSTON, Sept. 21.

Dear Mr. Whitman: Can you come, with Bartlett, Kate, and a charming lady and myself, to see Mr. Quincey Shaw's pictures on Friday at 2 p.m.? I shall call for you with carriage. Don't say no: you'll enjoy it. If you don't answer I shall take it for yes.

BOYLE O'REILLY.

Regarding the manuscript W. said: "Some of my enemies who think I write in the dark without premeditation ought to see that sheet of paper: there ain't a word there that seems to have had an easy time of it—that wasn't subjected to catawauling. I tell you, Horace, it's no fun for words when they get in my hands, though the howlers may not know it."

Tuesday, August 14, 1888.

To W.'s at one o'clock. Sat in chair. Bright and chatty— "garrulous," he said of himself. He had been rooting in an old basket of odds and ends, "destroying a lot of stuff, saving some" —looking at me with reassuring eyes: "I haven't destroyed anything it was better to keep." Gave me galley prints of Bur-

ORIGINAL MANUSCRIPT OF WHITMAN'S POEM, "THE SOBBING OF THE BELLS"

roughs' Science and Theology. "I have never read it," said W., "I can't get up an interest in such subjects: Ingersoll and Huxley seem to be my only exceptions for anti-theological reading. Do you take John along with you—read him: if you can make anything particular out of him there tell me of it. I would rather go with John among the birds and beasts than among the parsons."

He showed me several of his little improvised note-books of the war-time. One was marked "September & October, 1863." He read some memoranda from it to me. "I carried sometimes half a dozen such books in my pocket at one time—never was without one of them: I took notes as I went along—often as I sat—talking, maybe, as with you here now—I writing while the other fellow told his story. I would take the best paper (you can see, the best I could find) and make it up into these books, tying them with string or tape or getting someone (often it was Nellie O'Connor) to stitch them for me. My little books were beginnings—they were the ground into which I dropped the seed. See, here is a little poem itself"—he handed me the book: "Probably it is included in the Leaves somewhere. I would work in this way when I was out in the crowds, then put the stuff together at home. Drum Taps was all written in that manner— all of it—all put together by fits and starts, on the field, in the hospitals, as I worked with the soldier boys. Some days I was more emotional than others, then I would suffer all the extra horrors of my experience—I would try to write, blind, blind, with my own tears. O Horace! Horace! Horace! Should I ever get to Washington again I must look up my old cherry tree there —the great old tree under which I used to sit and write, write long, write. I want to give you one, several, of these books, if you would like to have them from me. They are more than precious—precious because they recall the old years—bring back the pictures of agony and death—reassociate me with the scenes and human actors of that tragic period."

He spelled out a name from the book—Lige Fox: "Yes, I remember Lige—he was from the Northwest—very free-going, very honest-like. Some day I'll gather all the stories of these books together and give them out: what a jail delivery there will be! There's the story of Lige: it plays the dickens with the character of Stonewall Jackson—taking him down (whipping him off) the pedestal he has decorated by general consent. Everybody in Washington wanted to think well of Jackson—I with the rest—and we were inclined to the very last to distrust the many stories which seemed to reflect upon his glory. But Lige's tale was so modestly told I could not doubt it—was told so entirely without brag, bad temper—without any desire for revenge—in fact, without any consciousness that Jackson had done anything but what was usual and right. Lige had been captured. Jackson subjected him to an inquisition—wanted information—would have it—would, would, would, whether or no. Lige only said and kept on saying: 'I'm a Union soldier and can't do it.' Finding he could get nothing from Lige Jackson punished him by making him walk the ten miles to Richmond while the others were conveyed. I could never think the same of Jackson after hearing that—after seeing how he resented in Lige what was a credit to him—what Lige could not have given and what Jackson could not have taken and either remain honest. And think of it, too! Jackson such a praying man—going off into the woods, flopping on his knees everywhere and anywhere to pray! There are a number of reputations I could prick in that same fashion. It always struck me in the War, how honest and direct the private soldiers were—how superior they were, in the main, to their officers. They would freely unbosom to me—tell me of their experiences—perhaps go into minutest details—always, however, as if everything was a matter of fact, was of no value—as if nothing was of enough significance to be bragged of. Their stories justified themselves—did not need to be argued about. My intuitions rarely made a mistake: I believed or did not believe in certain men because—and that was all the reason I had for it. I could always distinguish between a veteran and a tyro: the don't-cry, the calmness, the entire absence of priggishness in the veteran was obvious, conclusive, at once."

W. contrasted the punctiliousness of Lee and the freedom of Grant. "Grant was the typical Western man: the plainest, the most efficient: was the least imposed upon by appearances, was most impressive in the severe simplicity of his flannel shirt and his utter disregard for formal military etiquette. Lee had great qualities his own but these were the greatest. I could appreciate such contrasts: I lived in the time, on the spot: I lived in the midst of the life and death vigils of those fearful years—in the camps, in the hospitals, in the fiercest ferment of events."

We talked some about a Miller letter—an old letter. W. said of it: "It takes me back and sets me forward. Joaquin himself lit a pretty good torch at the divine fire. The singers come sometimes in streams—spiritual streams: are swept into the world, out of the world again, fortified by anonymous inspirations, not great or little in themselves, seeming to be in the round-up only a voice to utter the dreams, hopes, faiths, of the people. If you look at it that way the best man is not enough best to be vain of his performances." Asked me: "Can you read Miller's letter? I always have trouble with his handwriting."

N. Y. Apr. 16, '76.

My dear Walt Whitman: I met a mutual friend last evening who informed me he had just procured your books from you by mail, and I directed him, since he had been so fortunate and knew how to do it, to write at once for me and have the books sent to the Windsor Hotel.

Well, I am *not* living at the Windsor, and in fact have no fixed abode. Besides, I want your name written in the books if not asking too much for so little. And so on reflection I have decided to write you that when you receive my order through Mr. Johnston, you will please write in the books, saying they are from you to me, and then lay them to one side and I will call and get them next month. For when the Centennial opens I want to bring you some friends who are so anxious to meet the good and the *great* gray Poet. Thine.

Of course it is idle for me to congratulate you on your accession to immortality and your well deserved renown. I will only say that my soul and my sympathy all go out towards you and I often think of you as the one lone tree that tops us all, battered by storm and blown but still holding your place, serene and satisfied.

Hoping to see you early in May—Good bye and the gods be with you.

JOAQUIN MILLER.

W. laughed as he said: "Some newspaper man in New York who wrote as though he saw Miller with me somewhere said: 'Their poetry may be no good but there's no discount on their curls.' And he said something more. He said: 'If hair is poetry then Walt Whitman ought to be a great success.' So you see everybody is not deceived by our disguise. I can't make out all the arguments on the other side: some of them are not clear: but this man was a good shot. Don't you think he was good shot enough to bring down his game? Or maybe he was a barber in masquerade." So W. talked amusedly. I had a letter from Stedman today. Read some of it to W. who said: "I disapprove of the calendar anyway—will therefore not grieve if it fails to go through. Stedman is generous to take an interest in it. I am proud, you know, Horace, when I think of Stedman as my friend—but you know the wife, mother, of that household is no less my friend: that sets me up extra high. I have been more than lucky in the women I have met: a woman is always heaven or hell to a man—mostly heaven: she don't spend much of her time on the border-lines." W. asked me to write to Burroughs. "Tell him that for the past week I have really been getting a certain sort of grip on things again. Tell him it looked like total ruin but that our stock threatens to retrieve itself." Signed for me two portraits I received from Mrs Talcott Williams. Also give me a five pound note to have cashed for him. "I got rooting into old things today by accident. I asked Mary for something that was down stairs and she brought up an entire basket, which I am now sorting out. You are liable to get a number of rag-babies before I get through with my scavengering." This is the Stedman letter:

44 East 26th st.,
NEW YORK, Aug. 12, '88.

Dear Mr. Traubel, My thanks for your very good note. But surely I still possess the means and the privilege of joining, for the present, in a matter which you make so light for each member of the Circle. I only meant to intimate that I am unable to apply any noteworthy sum, in view of my obligations. . . . . Nor can I pledge any contributions for an indefinite period. But I can easily spare three dollars a month, and must beg you to receive now the enclosed six dollars for August and September, and also to let me know if any special sum is needed at any time.

Don't speak to Walt of the following. The calendar reached me August 1st, long after all Christmas books &c. had been arranged for by the book-trade. The Scribners say that they think it admirable, and more likely to "take" than any other calendar that could be devised; but that the calendar idea has been worked to death, overdone, and they have resolved not to issue one henceforth. The Cassell's are now considering the matter, but I fear it is quite too late for this year.

You may tell Walt that I have selected thirteen pages of his poetry, with great care, for our Library of American Literature, and am going to have him well represented. I hope Linton will let us use his engraving. If not we will make a new engraving of W. W. for vol. VIII.

Sincerely yours,
E. C. STEDMAN.

I did not read W. the first part of Stedman's letter. He does not know how I am paying for the nurse. The "circle" is my own creation. I read him the calendar matter, in spite of Stedman's interdiction, because I knew he was not stuck on the idea of piecemeal selections made from his book—would rather

have the scheme fail than succeed. W. said of the letter:
"The cut belongs to me still—it is not Linton's: say yes to
Stedman—yes, yes. Have you read all the note, Horace. All
I should hear? Eh? Just so—just so. Give him my love.
I haven't things ready-made to say to him. Just give him my
love. Let him know too—or I will let him know—that his
hospitality to me, to the Leaves, in his big book is taken by me
for what it is intended to signify." W. every now and then will
reel out this couplet:

"Not heaven itself upon the past has power,
But what has been has been—and I have had my hour."

Today I found it written in his hand on an old slip of paper
with this superscription: "Horace, translated (improved) by
Dryden."

Wednesday, August 15, 1888.

W. physically bad today. Called at 10.30. Sat reading
papers. Nurse said he stayed up unusually late last evening.
Generally turns in about ten. Last night it was eleven. When
I asked W. how he felt he replied: "How do I feel? only so-so,
only so-so." He had read Lüders' paper in last Saturday's
American. "Somebody sent it to me—it came in Sunday's
mail: I read it—not critically—scanned it, ran over it. It's
not bad—only it lacks guts." "I like the way some people say
no better than the way some other people say yes," I put in.
"Exactly—exactly: so do I: this man says neither in a way to
excite my admiration. I admire a good many of my enemies
more than I admire some of my friends. If these fellows would
only read Leaves of Grass—read it through their eyes rather
than through their prejudices: but when they condemn it without reading it—that's what nettles me. Lüders (how do you
pronounce his name?) gags at my 'catalogues.' Oh God! how
tired I get of hearing that said about the 'catalogues!' I resolved
at the start to diagnose, recognize, state, the case of the mechan-

ics, laborers, artisans, of America—to get into the stream with them—give them a voice in literature: not an echoed voice—no: their own voice—that which they had never had before. I meant to do this naturally, however—not with apologies—not to lug them in by the neck and heels, in season and out of season, where they did belong and where they didn't belong—but to welcome them to their legitimate superior place—to give them entrance and lodgment by all fair means. Maybe I have failed, maybe I have succeeded—but whatever, my intention has always remained clear, unshakable. I have often heard the dismal growl—here, Walt Whitman, what do you mean?—the shadow of the same axe has always been on my head: has been made the staple of quite a number of the brilliant assaults of which I have been the victim. I have never budged—never. I have had five or six chances to revise—to concede a point here and there to conciliate the howlers: Leaves of Grass has gone through a number of editions since those objections were first promulged: but the more I consider my purpose, my early and now confirmed end, aim, hope, the more the propriety, the justice, the inevitability, of all I have done is driven in upon me."

He paused. I was wholly silent. He then went on with the same line of thought: "I have a deeper reason than all that, however: a reason deeper than reasons—a reason that always seems conclusive, to say the last word—the conviction that the thing is because it is, being what it is because it must be just that—as a tree is a tree, a river a river, the sky the sky. A curious affinity exists right there between me and the Quakers, who always say, this is so or so because of some inner justifying fact—because it could not be otherwise. I remember a beautiful old Quakeress saying to me once: 'Walt—I feel thee is right—I could not tell why but I feel thee is right!'—and that seemed to me to be more significant than much that passes for reason in the world."

I wrote to Stedman and Burroughs today repeating his messages. W. said: "John particularly will be glad to hear I am on the mend. Tell him all the favorable things you can but don't brag." W. copied Taps for Donaldson today. "I don't know what got into his noddle, but he seemed to be particularly urgent in the matter. He did not come over—he wrote." Handed him cash for the English note. Alluding to one of his poems I said: "Things you write sometimes may lack the formal body but they certainly contain the soul of a poem." "Do you say that deliberately? The trouble with most poems is that they are nothing but poems—all poetry, all literary, not in any way human." Not entirely satisfied with the Linton portrait: "It is good—I have always thought it good—rather rough as a wood-cut, but if rough then like me. It fails in one thing surely, if in no other thing—in the eyes—and fails there as much and much in the same fashion as Hollyer does. My eyes are by no means bright, liquid, startling—no, not a bit that sort of eyes: they are rather dull—rather sluggish—to be pictured, as I often say, by what they are not rather than by what they are."

The Herald poem now being copied everywhere as Taps was sent in as Interpolations. "What are taps?" he asked me. "I have a dim notion of the truth in my brain but I am not confident I know. I want you to ask the first soldier you meet for a lucid explanation—then I want you to repeat his explanation to me. As I guess at it now it is a military good-night—a last sort of ceremony before turning in—the final message of the drums before sleep. It has a certain kind of solemn significance: I notice that the soldiers attach great sentiment to it—regard it with great respect."

An actor, Nestor Lennon, sent up his name. W. handed the card to me. "Who is it—do you know?" Musgrove intervened: "He says he's in the profession." "*The* profession," smiling —"yes, I see—that's the way they speak of it: the Jews speak of *the* people. Anyhow," finally said W., "tell him to come up— it won't hurt—but tell him, too, it must be only for a minute— or two minutes." Lennon came up—stayed ten minutes. He made a lot of formal remarks to W., who took them with rather a bored air. He then asked for some autographs. W. gave him three. Lennon said: "One of these is for Steele Mackaye."

W. thereupon monologued a bit: "I have a weakness for actors —they seem to have a weakness for me: that makes our meetings rather like family affairs." Then asked Lennon: "Do you like your business real well?" When Lennon got up to go he cleared his throat, hitched his trousers, scratched his head, and blurted out to W. as if it was a hard job to get his message delivered right: "Mr. Whitman, do you need money? I've been delegated to ask you whether you need money. I know a hundred actors in places about and in New York who would like to get together and give you a benefit." W. was visibly touched. He frankly offered Lennon his hand and said with a voice that was shaken with emotion: "God bless you—God bless you all— for that! I have enough money, more than enough, for all my earthly wants, so I need not acquiesce in your beautiful plans: but you make me happy, nevertheless. I shall feed on your good will for many a day to come. Tell all the boys what I have said to you about that—give them my love." As Lennon was withdrawing W. added: "The English theatrical people have always seemed to like me—Irving has been here—Wilson Barrett, too: I have had letters from Ellen Terry: then there is Bram Stoker—he has treated me like a best son." Lennon was not to be outdone: "Yes, I know, Mr. Whitman: they like you, no doubt—*like* you: but we—we *love* you." After Lennon was gone W. said: "Did you notice how he set his American *love* up against the English *like?* It was very pretty, Horace. And his offer—what did you think of that? It was very handsome—it took me unawares—almost bowled me over."

W. pointed to a pile of letters and papers on the table. "That came out of the grab-basket Mary brought up stairs. Most of it will eventually go to you, no doubt: you'd starve to death if I didn't feed you! I will look it all through as I can—report to you on it from time to time. You must possess your soul in patience. And by the way, our 'surprise,' that we have talked so much about, has threatened to be a boomerang." I pricked up my ears. Was the revelation about to come? He saw my interested face. "Are you ready for it?" I laughingly replied:

"I'm leanin' up against myself strong!" He took this in a jolly way. "How good that is—leanin' up against yourself! That's about the best any man can do when he needs support. But to go back to the surprise, I don't mind telling you about it— also, why it has hung fire. You remember I have several times promised you a couple of Bayard Taylor letters I knew I had? The letters turned up one day awhile ago in a mess of things when I wasn't looking for 'em. That night when I first mentioned the surprise to you was the night of the day of the find. I wanted to read the letters again before I passed 'em over to you. The next day when I looked for the letters they were gone. They had evidently got pushed back into chaos again. And so every day until today. Today I found *one* of the letters. Where the devil the other is I don't know. I won't wait for the other before giving you this because we had better secure our prizes when we have them. You will take this along with you and chew on it and tell me how it strikes you. When the other finally shows up again we will put that with this. This rare game seems hard to bag. I have very particular reasons for wishing to get these letters into your hands where they may be kept and used on occasion in the future. Things said of me in the Tribune and by way of gossip attributed to Taylor in recent years will find a foil in the cordial warmth, the enthusiasm almost, of these two volunteered letters." I started to open the letter right where I was. "No, not now," said W., "open it in broad daylight when you can get it in a sunny perspective."

Thursday, August 16, 1888.

Day awful hot. W. about knocked out. Calm, however. Read some, wrote some. W. had a note from the Philadelphia office of the Herald: this:

Aug. 15, 1888.

Dear Mr. Whitman: Won't you read over carefully Amelie Rives' poem in today's Herald and give me an expert's opinion of it for publication in the Herald? I will call for this tomorrow, for I am sure you will have something instructive to say about the poem.

Very truly yours,
C. H. Browning.

W. mad as fire. "Sure? is he? Sure? Damn his 'sure!' I know nothing about Mrs. Chanler—I have never read a thing she has written. Besides, I did not see The Herald—it is not sent here any more. And there was more than that to it, too. The letter seemed to me impertinent, impudent, if not worse: that 'expert' fling, now—what do you make out of that? Browning don't know me or he would have chosen his words and his manners a little better. He sent his message and then would send his boy for the stuff the next day! I was under orders, you see—an 'expert' under orders—to write something about a writer whose writings I had never seen. Well, the boy appeared today, and when Mr. Musgrove came up and said he was there I sent word back that Walt Whitman was a very sick man and had no goods to deliver. I think this is Browning's own little spec: I don't believe it was suggested from headquarters. I sent the Sheridan piece to The Herald because I knew Sheridan, for one reason, and because they asked for that—did not demand it. I don't see why I am to be bothered to put myself on record on any and every subject in order merely to satisfy a newspaper's desire for a sensation." W. said after he was calmed down: "There's a letter from Bucke. Read it."

London, Ont., Aug. 15, 1888.

I received last evening the last pages of the book. I admire the Elias Hicks greatly and think I *understand the drift of it.* Do not think you have ever written better prose. It is altogether an admirable and most valuable piece. I shall write more at length another day. Am rather crowded this morning. I think I shall remodel my piece (that I sent Walsh of Lippincott's) and make it into a review of the new volume. Perhaps in that shape I shall get some "able editor" to print it. I have

147

seen your little piece on Sheridan (one of them). You must be coming round finely to be able to write so vigorously. All well here. A little warmer today.

R. M. BUCKE.

W. said: "Bucke is eligible to approve, to be pleased, to accept: his yeas are not surprises." Concluded to make the first edition of November Boughs a thousand copies. Showed him a Tacoma paper which contained his portrait and a lament over his "approaching death." W. laughed. "Thank you Mr. Critic —you're cheerful! Death is always approaching, but Horace and I have a job of work to do before we bow it into the house and ask it to sit down—eh, Horace?" After a bit he suddenly said: "And, now, Horace, what about the Taylor letter? Did you read it? There was no ahem and ahaw in that letter, do you think? Have you got the letter in your pocket? Yes? Read it to me."

KENNETT SQUARE, PENNA.
Nov. 12, 1866.

My dear Sir: I send to you by the same mail which takes this note, a copy of my last poem The Picture of St. John. I do not know whether the subject of the poem (the growth and development of the artist-nature, and its relations to life) will much interest you, but I hope you will here and there find something drawn immediately from nature. I am, at least, not aware that anything in the book is simulated or forced: whether successful or not, it is an honest conscientious effort.

I value, above all things, *sincerity* in literature; hence I am not one of those who overlook your remarkable powers of expression, your broad, vital reverence for humanity, because some things you have said repel them. The age is over-squeamish, and, for my part, I prefer the honest nude to the suggestive half-draped. I think the proper question to be asked is: does a certain thing *need* to be said? If so, let it be said! The worst form of immorality, I have found, veils itself in decent words.

There is one quality I recognize in you, which warmly and

constantly attracts me. That is, your deep and tender reverence for Man—your unwearied, affectionate, practical fraternity. There is too little of this quality in the world, and the race will be better and happier in proportion as it is manifested.

I shall be in Washington on the 27th of December, to lecture, and hope that I shall then be able to meet you personally. If you can spare me an hour or two after the lecture, you will greatly oblige

Your friend,
BAYARD TAYLOR.

The letter was addressed to W. at Washington. W. endorsed the envelope: "from Bayard Taylor Nov. 16, 1866." As I finished reading W. asked: "Well—what do you say to that? That don't sound like the note of a man who was in great doubt, does it? I don't make too much of such things. They come and go—or they don't come: and if they don't come, that is right too. But I find the Taylor of that time interesting because people say (the gossips say) the Taylor of today won't have me on any terms—hates to hear my name mentioned. I don't know about it all: men do change their minds: the Taylor who did like me may be wrong, the Taylor who does not like me (if there is such a Taylor) may be right. Who knows? Who knows? I wish I had the other letter now for you to read—it puts a finish on the little story. Damn it, I wonder where that letter got to? Sometimes I'm all in a heap here—goods, chattels, anything, myself with everything, all in a heap." After a laugh he added: "No matter what the fellers said, didn't say—no matter for the curses, the blessings—no matter for anything, I had to stick to my business. If I had stopped to dispute with my enemies, even to dally or luxuriate with my friends, the book would have gone begging. The book—the book: that was always the thing!"

Picked up a copy of the Press and threw it down again with a gesture of disgust: "I hate the bigotry of the high-tariffites. Even Blaine, I notice, thinks that a revenue reformer is in

English pay—or says he thinks so: is a foe to the republic—a wilful marplot—bent upon the enslavement of labor. Read this paper: did you ever see anything more absolutely asinine than its attitude on this question? Charles Emory Smith might be a king among asses, but among philosophers—well, I wouldn't like to say what he would be among philosophers. Even Williams, Talcott, seems to have given in to the pressure—the hue and cry of the provincials—yet, if I recollect rightly, Talcott's view of five years ago was quite different. I do not say this from what I know but from what I infer. Talcott always impressed me as being on the liberal side of such questions."

I had a long Wissahickon walk with Harrison Morris today. W. asked me about it. We had talked a great lot about W. I repeated some cardinal things. W. said: "It is likely you got more warmed up on that subject than I do or should. If they call me no poet then no-poet it may be. I don't care what they call me—by one name or another name—it is all one—so that I produce the result—so that I get my word spoken and heard— maybe move men and women. Morris should read Bucke's book—read it without prejudice. Bucke does not argue— does not fuss: makes a calm, almost cold, statement, like a man of exact science—then drops the point. It is hard for a man born, bred, luxuriating in the conventions, to shake that all off. Sloane Kennedy was five or six years ago just where Morris is now—still floundering among the canons—and in the end came around all right. Why, Kennedy was almost violently opposed for a time. Kennedy is a thinker, thoroughly original—a strong man on many sides—and such a student is rather more eligible for the freer processes, more sensitive to the newer intimations, than the ordinary literary dabbler. Yet I feel a little as though Morris left to himself—the reins thrown down, the ways every- where wide open for ingress and egress—may yet escape the professional tangle and take his place with the elect outcasts. The tendency of art is all towards the delicate, the refined, the polished: that I am forced to eschew—it is outside, it would vitiate my purpose. Well, what's the use fighting over the matter? Time will settle it one way or the other—time, and what goes with time: settle it better than any immediate hammering—any high-handed disputation. What people won't see as it stands in the fact they won't see much better if at all in our dogmatism about the fact. As to Leaves of Grass—the literary man pure and simple will never acknowledge it: its premises are so different from those upon which he stakes his theories of art." I said: "It's queer about Morris—when we are walking out in the country he's always complaining of the mathematics of goodness—of the trees planted in a row: but don't Morris plant all his art-trees in a row?" W. laughed several times over and asked: "Did you fellers go walking today just to have it out with each other?—to fight that fight to a finish—to settle that question?"

Tomorrow we get our plate-proofs. Burroughs is to come here for a visit in September. "I expect you and John to take a shine to each other. I need not tell you about your own virtues—but John's virtues? Well, they are many and they are the kind of virtues you like. John is never a gamble—he is always a sure risk." W. asked me: "Horace, what is this Henry George thing—this single tax fandangle: tell me about it: tell me all you know: I hear so much said for it, against it, that I feel as if I should know what all the fireworks are about." I talked for the next half hour about Progress and Poverty. He asked a lot of questions—led me to explain the theory in a way to make it clear to him. Finally he said: "That'll do: now I begin to know what the hullaballoo means. It's a plausible scheme, too, it seems to me, at first blush. I have no doubt the statisticians could come along and disprove it—but what can't they disprove? Somehow men live and think and love and have their being in spite of statistics."

W. spoke dismally of American maternity this evening. "Our women don't seem to be any longer built for child-bearing. We have gone on for so long hurting the body that the job of rehabilitating it seems prodigious if not impossible. The time will come when the whole affair of sex—copulation, reproduction—

will be treated with the respect to which it is entitled. Instead of meaning shame and being apologized for it will mean purity and will be glorified."

Friday, August 17, 1888.

W. sat in his room reading Scott's The Antiquary. 7.45 evening. He laid his book down. "Ah, Horace, is that you? And what have you done, learned, today?" For his own part he had read, written letters and received two reporters—one from the Camden Courier and one from the Philadelphia Press. Gave me a copy of As a Strong Bird, inscribed: "John Clifford, Aug: 21st '88 from Walt Whitman and Horace Traubel." "There is your little book," he said—"is that what you wanted?" "Aunt Mary," an old woman who often comes in to help Mrs. Davis, had a stroke of paralysis in W.'s kitchen this evening. W. concerned but not worried. A carriage drove up to the door. "That's for the old lady," he said: "Go down and see if you can help: I wish I could do so myself." Later on he exclaimed again: "Oh! how I should like to go down to Aunt Mary's home to see how she fares!"

He seemed suddenly to have thought of something in danger of being forgotten. Reached forward to the table—picked up a letter. "Hurrah!" he cried, shaking it in the air. I repeated: "Hurrah!" and then asked: "But what is it?" He laughed gaily. "It's the Taylor letter, damn it—didn't you guess?" and before I could have replied he added: "It was here on the table all the time, of course, under a lot of other things. Now we have it let's keep it." He passed it across to me. "It's a warm letter," he added—"about as warm as the weather. Read it for yourself, read it for yourself! Seeing is believing: just look at it." I quoted my dentist who got off an old saw while he was working on one of my sensitive teeth: "Seeing is believing but feeling is the naked truth." W. laughed again: "That would not be regarded as quite proper but it's true, nevertheless. Read the letter to me: you will feel its naked truth before you get through." I asked W.: "Why is it you have lately had me read so many things to you that you were already perfectly familiar with?" "I don't know—read, read, and ask no questions." So I read.

KENNETT SQUARE, PENNA., Dec. 2, 1866.

My dear Whitman: I find your book and cordial letter, on returning home from a lecturing tour in New York, and heartily thank you for both. I have had the first edition of your Leaves of Grass among my books, since its first appearance, and have read it many times. I may say, frankly, that there are two things in it which I find nowhere else in literature, though I find them in my own nature. I mean the awe and wonder and reverence and beauty of Life, as expressed in the human body, with the physical attraction and delight of mere contact which it inspires, and that tender and noble love of man for man which once certainly existed, but now almost seems to have gone out of the experience of the race. I think there is nothing in your volume which I do not fully comprehend in the sense in which you wrote; I always try to judge an author from his own stand-point rather than mine, but in this case the two nearly coincide. We should differ rather in regard to form than substance, I suspect. There is not one word of your large and beautiful sympathy for men, which I cannot take into my own heart, nor one of those subtle and wonderful physical affinities you describe which I cannot comprehend. I say these things, not in the way of praise, but because I know from my own experience that correct appreciation of an author is less frequent than it should be. It is welcome to me, and may be so to you.

I did not mean to write so much when I commenced, and will only say that I shall be in Washington on the 27th—only for that night—and would be very glad if we can come together for awhile after my lecture is over. I am afraid I shall not arrive in time to call at the Dep't before the lecture, but if I can I will. If not, will you either come to Willard's or tell me where to find you, and oblige   Your friend,

BAYARD TAYLOR.

W. said: "Taylor has been of recent years quoted against me —especially against the sex poems. Now, it is precisely on that point that the declarations of his letter are the most unqualified and decisive. What are we to believe? It would be easy to quote one Taylor against the other—but which against and which for?" He smiled good-naturedly: "I prefer to believe in the Taylor of my letters even if it does smack of egotism for me to do so." "Are you afraid of being accused of egotism?" "Hardly afraid—I am accused. I say just this: I hear all sorts of vague stories about Taylor nowadays—vague stories which may be false or true. Now, here are two letters: they are in his hand, he signed them, they are not vague. Why shouldn't I believe the letters?"

He said reflectively after awhile: "I wouldn't know what to do, how to comport myself, if I lived long enough to become accepted, to get in demand, to ride on the crest of the wave. I would have to go scratching, questioning, hitching about, to see if this was the real critter, the old Walt Whitman—to see if Walt Whitman had not suffered a destructive transformation—become apostate, formal, reconciled to the conventions, subdued from the old independence. I have adjusted myself to the negative condition—have adjusted myself for opposition, denunciation, suspicion: the revolution, therefore, would have to be very violent indeed to whip me round to the other situation." He stopped to laugh. "But I guess there is no immediate danger: I am not very near such a crisis. I remember when Swinburne at last turned against me, John Burroughs said he felt that things were coming right again—that things had got back to their equilibrium—that the inexplicable community of admiration between him and Swinburne had come to its legitimate end—had had to perish of its own dead weight. John seemed to think that for the two of them to say the same things about me would prove either that Burroughs was not Burroughs or Walt Whitman wasn't Walt Whitman. Then came the Swinburne outburst: presto! the air was cleared: John breathed free again! It is a good story to know and tell.

I know from my own experience that correct appreciation of an author is less frequent than it should be. It is welcome to me, and may be so to you.

I did not mean to write so much when I commenced, and will only say that I shall be in Washington on the 27th — only for that night, — and would be very glad if we can come together for awhile after my lecture is over. I am afraid I shall not arrive in time to call at the Dep't before the lecture, but if I can I will. If not, will you either come to Willard's or tell me where to find you, and oblige

Your friend,

Bayard Taylor.

A PAGE FROM A BAYARD TAYLOR LETTER TO WALT WHITMAN

I don't feel myself like damning Swinburne for saving himself!"
W.'s little sallies of humor like this are always quiet. His laugh
is a silent one—yet infectious. "Swinburne has his own big-
ness: he is not to be drummed out of all camps because he does
not find himself comfortable in our camp." I said: "The
people who instance Tennyson and Swinburne as masters of
poetic form should not forget that both of them have in later
years taken all sorts of liberties with the code." W. nodded
an assent: "It is indeed so: so with Swinburne, so with Tennyson: almost phenomenally so."

Commenting on Bucke's approval of the Hicks piece: "I
have not yet adjusted myself to it: I cannot tell today or tomorrow what will be my own matured impression. Judgment
never comes to me in a hurry. My first notion is one of disappointment. That comes because I am at the moment too
sensitive concerning the thing I did not do. Some day I will
get the matter in another perspective—maybe see that it after
all possesses qualities that excuse its creation." Talked of
Browning's letter: "I am glad he did not come over in person:
if he had done so I might have been tempted to see him—then
there would have been a storm—and a storm would earn no
sort of profitable interest on my present capital." Some one
had been in to take W.'s picture. W. said: "So you think every
man will by and by be his own photographer, painter, shoemaker, again? Well—who knows? The world is turning around
again towards the simple—the condition in which each man
may supply his own needs. A day may yet arrive to find
us grown aboriginal again—civilized aboriginal if I may
say so."

W. says he misses Kennedy's "old-time letters." "He used
to write martial letters—warlike letters: was up in arms about
things. He got about a good deal, saw people, had a story to
tell. Now he seems too busy. When Kennedy was passing
through the early stages of his faith in the Leaves—the first
fervors of conversion—he made Whitman the password: opposed to Walt Whitman opposed to me—that sort of chip-on-

the-shoulder business: so that in ways Sloane got unpopular—people avoided him—they didn't want to hear his wild Indian ideas, and so forth." I brought W. over today plate proofs, three sets, to page 125. Has finally decided to make the price of the book one dollar. Has finally decided "no" as to de luxe copies. "I want no autocrat editions." Heat intense all day and evening. "I manage to stay—to hold on—that's about all."

I met Edward Coates today—husband of Florence Earle. He asked me about W.'s autograph editions and the Cox portraits. "The curio collector is from everlasting to everlasting," said W., "but he has his parts, too. Some of my old editions, which I could not give away at the time, now bring fabulous prices, ridiculous prices: it beats the devil, the ups and downs of authorship—especially the downs: I've had my fill and fill again of the downs. Yes, tell the Coates people—Mrs., Mr. Coates—to come over: I will see them." Then said as to the Cox portraits: "Advise Coates to go to see William Carey—no doubt Coates is often in New York (those men are): send him, then, to my friend Carey: Carey puts up with the Century Company—works there. Carey has the photographs, all duly autographed. If Coates goes let him know that I like one of the pictures in particular—the laughing philosopher, I call it—and one other, perhaps as well—my head resting in my hands, forward, this way"—indicating—"and always, of course, the unsilvered copies—always those. And should you want one of the heads, Horace, I want to give it to you." I objected: "It would be robbery." "No—no: I want to and you must let me do it." Again: "Pictures are partial—they give a dash of a man, a phase: many are called but few are chosen: there is a success here and there to a hundred failures. I guess they all hint at the man—even Herbert's, maybe, strange as that may seem. The very worst place in the world to put Herbert's picture would be right next to Eakins'. It would be sure death." W. gave me a Washington relic which he had endorsed as "Pass Burnside's Army Jan. '63." It read this way:

HEADQUARTERS RG D.
NEAR FALMOUTH Dec 27 1862.

Pass the bearer Walter Whitman, a citizen, to Washington
Rail R. and government steamer.

By command of

MAJ GEN SUMNER

I N TAYLOR

CHIEF OF STAFF ACTG—

W. said nothing much about it: "Would you like that for
a curio? It won't pass for money—". I laughed and said
"pass?" and he said "pass?" after me, adding: "Did you
ever know me to pun? It's not in my line at all. I am guilty
of most the real bad sins but that bad sin I never acquired."

Saturday, August 18, 1888.

7 P. M. W. on bed. Greeted me heartily, though quietly,
as usual. Is never boisterous. Said concerning his health:
"I hold on, as you see, but only hold on: I am not slipping down
nor am I climbing up." Both Musgrove and Mrs. Davis
spoke of his pallor all day. The heat is hurting him. Our
talk was mostly in the dark, W. staying on the bed, I sitting over
under the lowered light. Referred sympathetically to the old
Aunt Mary. Then said: "Bucke's book about me is not to be
skipped. I like it better now than I did when it first appeared.
It is strong, suggestive: I have not always realized its full
importance. It is not conclusive, of course: Doctor is a bit
too much on our side, in a sense. I do not lay much stress upon
his explications—upon his inferences—upon his far-away speculations: I esteem the book for its atmosphere, ruggedness,
simplicity—for something that is almost like a wholesome brutality. The best thing about the book would seem to be the fact
that you must go back to it if you would possess yourself of its
whole truth—it has a new suggestiveness each time."

I asked W. what he knew of Kennedy's Whitman. "What
do I know of it?" asked W.: "Well, I know something but not

much. It is full of dash, spirit, side-flash, sparkle: whether it has any spinal thread—of that I am none too certain. Kennedy is like a brilliant soldier—a leader of cavalry—full of ability to go, to push on to an objective point—to invent means, to revise prejudices, to meet unexpected crises." "A Sheridan, perhaps," I suggested. "Yes," nodded W., "a Sheridan—and that is a remarkably good parallel: a Sheridan, full of the fire of action, the romance of achievement: and yet far-seeing, too, and not to have his philosophical importance belittled." I quoted my observation made in a discussion about W. "You fellows admit to me that versification rules do not constitute poetry, and yet you say Whitman is not a poet because he ignores versification rules." W. exclaimed: "What an upset that must have been for their apple carts, to be sure. But I doubt if our hot and heavy arguments in themselves make an impression on the reactionaries.'

W. received copies of Notes and Queries. "I suppose they came from Mr. Hunter. The paper is a mystery to me. I doubt if it can last—there's not enough curiosity of the sort to back it up in this country. It might get on in England because there we are ushered into an entirely different situation—lords with so many thousands a year, leisure, backgrounds of lineage, old colleges—seats of learning—a great literary class: a dawdling, temporizing aristocracy trying and failing to fill out an empty life. The paper takes up the most trivial questions—questions of origins—questions of literary finesse—of words, axioms, proverbs, colloquialisms, slang, and God knows what and God knows what not. After a long debate over the question of the first authorship of this or that famous phrase, for instance— one fellow with two columns, another with four, another (going from worse to worse still) with six—then number one with two columns more: after all this I find myself just where I was before with the confusion become aggravated. There's the word 'flunkey': who first used it, why was it first used: has its meaning remained what it was: and so on and so on and so on: all about flunkey. So they set to, all fours, tooth and nail, and discuss it ad nauseum—in the end with no approach to the truth on either side and little good feeling. This may be compensated for in one way, I suppose, by very interesting and valuable sidelights that may be developed in the course of the controversy: though I must say that, like all argument, or much of it, the results have not at all come up to the value of what was sacrificed in the struggle."

W. let me read and was willing I should take his draft of an old letter to Schmidt. A mem. on the letter said: "Books sent to Mr. Clausen to send." The letter was short:

Dec. 7, 1871.

Rudolf Schmidt,
　　Kopenhagen, Denmark.

Dear Sir: I have received (through Mr. Clausen) your letter of 19th October from Kopenhagen, and I cheerfully forward you my poems Leaves of Grass and a small prose work Democratic Vistas. I also enclose several articles and criticisms, written about my book in England and America, within the last ten years. May I say there is something about your letter and application that has deeply pleased me. How I should like to know your country and people—and especially you yourself, and your poet Björnson and Hans Andersen. How proud I should be to become known to you all. Pray let me hear from you, and if the books and papers reach you.

My address is Washington, D. C. United States of America.

"That" said W., "must have been one of the first letters I wrote Schmidt. The north countries were always miracle countries to me, somehow. I was particularly interested in the Norwegian Björnson. He sent me his picture once. It is that of a Viking: powerful, inflexible, clean: a face of humanity, purpose: a face of the ideal. Norway has made her best men much bigger than her own size—has made them men of world-dimensions: Ibsen, Björnson, the others." One of the things W. had laid out for me from the big budget was a Garland letter:

"The first to me from him, I think: the original avowal. If you don't mind I will have you read it aloud as you sit there under the light. Turn the light up a bit: yes, that is right. I will stay where I am and listen: I'm so confounded comfortable I don't want to move." He had laid the letter on the top of the pile where I had found it at his direction.

JAMAICA PLAIN, BOSTON, MASS.,
Nov. 24, 1886.

Mr. Walt Whitman. It is with profound sorrow that I read in the papers the news that you are again suffering from your old trouble. I trust it is not so serious as reported. My regard for you is so great that I am very sorry not to be able to buy more copies of your book and thus give a more substantial token of sympathy.

I am an enthusiastic reader of your books, both volumes of which I have within reach of hand. I am, everywhere in my talking and writing, making your claims felt and shall continue to do so. I have demonstrated (what of course you know) that there is no veil, no impediment, between your mind and your audience, when your writings are *voiced*. ["That's a point to chew on!" W. exclaimed, breaking in: "Read it again: I want to get it clear in my noddle for keeps!"] The formlessness is only seeming, not real. I have never read a page of your poetry, or quoted a line, that has not commanded admiration. The music is there and the grandeur of thought is there, if the reader reads guided by the sense and not by the external lining or paragraphing. Even very young pupils feel the thrill of the deep rolling music though the thought may be too profound for them to grasp. In a course of lectures before the Boston School of Oratory last summer I made a test of the matter. I do not think a single pupil held out against my arguments supplemented by readings from your work. The trouble is they get at your work through the daily press or through the defenders of Longfellow or Tennyson (whom it is supposed you utterly antagonize). When it is brought to them by one who appreciates and measurably understands your methods and ideals, I do not think there is any doubt of the favorable result. I have found much opposition but it was mostly ignorant or misled.

I am a young man of very ordinary attainments and do not presume to do more than give you a glimpse of the temper of that public which would not do you wrong, deliberately, but who by reason of the causes hinted at above, fail to get at the transcendent power of Leaves of Grass. If I have given you the impression that I believe in you and strive to interpret you, you will not feel that I have over-stepped the privilege of a pupil in the presence of a great teacher.

The enclosed slip is a meagre outline of a volume which I am writing and which I hope to get out this coming spring. As the motto page of this volume I have used a paragraph from your Collect which is entitled Foundation Stages—then Others. While it is not strictly essential to the book, yet I should esteem it a favor if you would consent to its use. One sentence, "In nothing is there more evolution than in the American mind," I have also used in company with Spencer's great law of progress upon my title page. It helped to decide the title, which is: The Evolution of American Thought: an outline study of the leading phases of American literature, etc. In the latter part of the volume I have treated of the Age of Democracy and its thought, taking as foundation the splendid utterances of M. Taine upon the modern age. It is in this chapter that I place your work. I quote from you quite largely both in treating of your writings and in treating the general theme of present and future democratic ideals. I hope to be able to please you with my treatment of your great work. Beside this I am preparing special lectures upon the same subject. Have you any objection to the quotations which I find it necessary to use?

In conclusion let me say that without any bias in your favor (rather the opposite from newspapers) your poems thrilled me, reversed many of my ideas, confirmed me in others, helped to make me what I am. I am a border-man,—born in Wisconsin and raised on the prairie frontier. I am a disciple of Mr. Spencer and therefore strive at comparative methods of criticism. That your poems should thus convert me, is to me a revelation of their power, especially when I can convince others in the same manner.

And now revered friend (for I feel you are a friend) think of me as one who radiates the principles of the modern age, and who will in his best manner (poor at best) strive to make his hearers and readers better aware of the "Good Gray Poet" and his elemental lines.

Your readers are increasing, and may you live to see the circle infinitely extended is my fervent hope. I do not expect a reply to this other than the signification whether I may quote you or not. I wish I might see and talk with you but that is not possible—except through your volumes.

I am most sincerely yours,

HAMLIN GARLAND.

I said to W.: "Garland's practice of reading you aloud is one that Ingersoll, too, has told me he followed." "How so? What did the Colonel say?" "That all great literature lent itself to the lips—that you were never so impressive as when rightly read aloud." "Did he say that? How interesting that is. Is that all he said?" "No—not all. He said that he often argued with people about you—that argument most times did not have much effect. He said that when he found his arguments were making no impression he resorted to your book and read from it: that the argument of the book, given in that way, was many times conclusive." W. exclaimed: "How fine! And that is probably what Garland meant, too. I shouldn't wonder but it's all true. That is a striking theory of the Colonel's: All great utterance in literature lends itself to the lips! I shall never forget that—it is very startling, incisive: it's not difficult to remember anything expressed with such piercing directness." He paused for a spell. Then went on: "Now—wasn't that a dandy letter from Garland? This was his first salutation—this was what he said when he first came along: a first confession:

162

not an obsequious obeisance made to the ground but just a manly equal shake of the hand—like that, no more. Did you notice, too, that he speaks of himself as a borderman?—a child of the western prairies? That appeals to me—hits me hardest where I enjoy being hit. That country out there is my own country though I have mainly had to view it from afar. I always seem to expect the men and women of the West to take me in in—what shall I say?—oh! take me in in one gulp! Where the East might gag over me the West should swallow me with a free throat. That letter of Garland's was two years ago— already two years ago. He ought to do something with the West—get it into great books." "The East is like hope and the West is like more hope!" I said. W. shook his finger off the bed at me. "That's very clever—very true—Horace. Be careful—be careful: they will get you into the papers—quote you—pass you around: then your troubles will begin."

I got up to go. W. said: "If you find a Gilder letter right there on the top of the pile, take it—read it when you get home: I will tell you more about it to-morrow." I found the letter. It had no envelope. W. said again: "Just turn the light down a wee mite: that's it—that's it." I crossed the room to the bed, leaned over, kissed him, and left.

Sunday, August 19, 1888.

Much cooler today. W. more comfortable though still weak. Sat up and read and wrote some, but "irregularly, in snatches." Towards evening started reading the plate proofs. Debated with himself the merits of wet and dry proofs—"I am inclined to the wet." Said: "It is a moot subject among printers: ask the best fellers when you see 'em—ask the Century people some day." Says sometimes his physical body threatens to break him down. But: "If we keep pegging away slowly but persist- ently, the book must in the end come out—if I should last, and I guess I will. But we mustn't crow until we've left the last limit of the woods behind us—till we're clean out into the open. The vicissitudes are many—the certainties few. I have got beyond the point where I make the least calculation for the morrow—for any morrow. Yet it is our chief business to plod ahead, not disturbed, frittered away, with thoughts of things that might be."

"Aunt Mary" died this morning. W. said: "Poverty, old age, trouble, the severe heat—and then the finish! The extreme poor suffer extra burdens of life—carry an unfair load. Some day we will get all that fixed right in the world—some day after many days." W. talked like a tired man—very clear, however. "I always tell you, Horace—don't you notice?—that my mind is bound to last me out whatever becomes of my body." Spoke of the Harneds. "I suppose Tom and Frank are at Atlantic City today? And the children? Ah! the dear dear children! Horace, the Harneds are true as truth itself—they are the best thing in the midst of worst things." W. asked: "Where have you been today?—who seen?—what doing?" I said: "I have met no literary people." "Thank God!" I knew he would take it that way. He always does. But when I added: "I had a long talk with Ed Lindell at the ferry," he was at once animated and said: "Tell me about it—what had Ed to say about things in general?" "He didn't speak about things in general—he spoke mostly about you." Laughed. "That was good in Ed: but things in general would be more interesting." W. said: "When you come in I asked you, howdydo? Ain't that a good word?—howdydo. It has a phonetic significance—has pith, is straight-to. I am told that in some places west the salutation is still further abbreviated. You meet a man: you ask, How?"

No letters today from anyone—"not a wisp." Read the Press. "The Press editorially is an empty barrel: I reach clean to the bottom and find nothing." Spoke of O'Connor: "He is a withering fire to his enemies and a sustaining fire to his friends. William has more right words for right places in him than any man I know of in America." Was delighted that I had established such friendly personal relations with the printers. "You seem to be very free there—free with the workmen themselves. That is good—good. The workman always comes before the boss—though you tell me that Ferguson himself is a fine feller and I believe you. If I could get about I would like to go there myself, to shake hands all around." W. asked me: "You seem to read a lot. Where do you do your reading?" "Most of it as I go about in the boats and cars—often even in walking." "That is right—in the open air—in the midst of things: that is where life meets you in the flush. If there is anything peculiar in my work it lies just in that—in jottings of the moment, made for truth, not made for effect." My father spoke of the Twenty Years' drawings in the Magazine of Art as being "so Scotch." W. assented: "They struck me the same way: God bless the Scotch!" He mentioned the New York Herald as "exceptional among newspapers in that it now and then prints an editorial which a man can read with a clear conscience." I laughed. "I mean it: they are sometimes so good I am impelled to write to the Herald in recognition of its singular virtue." W. asked me: "You took the Gilder letter with you last night: you have said nothing about it: have you nothing to say?" "I was waiting for you to say—" This is the letter.

EDITORIAL DEPARTMENT THE CENTURY MAGAZINE,
UNION SQUARE, NEW YORK,
June 7, '83.

My dear Mr. Whitman: I do not know whether you saw a little paragraph in a recent number of the Critic—in the Lounger's Department. I have not seen Dr. Bucke's book, but I was told that he had done me the honor of quoting some verses of mine. I was asked whether those verses were written for the book, or about yourself, and I said "no—they were published in the magazine some time ago and were suggested by another writer." I am very sorry that paragraph appeared as it did, or at all, as it might look as if I were not a friend and admirer of the subject of the book.

Are you coming north this summer? I wish you would come and see me at Marion, on Buzzard's Bay in Mass. If you will give me the slightest encouragement I will try to get Burroughs there to meet you. Splendid pine woods, good fishing and boating—a quiet little whaling village. Think well of it and let me know by return mail.

Very sincerely yours
R. W. GILDER.

W. said this: "Doctor was quite set in the notion that Gilder originally meant that for me but I said no—no—it didn't seem quite likely. When Gilder himself said no Maurice was furious: he wrote me: 'Your friend has not the courage of his convictions.' I said to Maurice: 'Not so fast, not so fast: you have no right to charge up your accusing inference against Gilder.' It seems the same to me today. Gilder has always been my friend— very good friend—indeed, I may say my 'dear' friend, speaking for myself, for my own affections: but I never felt that he put me quite up where he placed 'the true poet.' He may have meant his poem for somebody in particular—I don't know who, but somebody: or he may have written it at large, to apply to a situation—or maybe it was only prophetic: anyway, I do not see that it fits itself to me, necessarily. I think Maurice finally conceded that I was more right than he was—that his angry reaction of the moment was not quite the mood in which to meet the incident." I asked W.: "Did you go to Marion?" "No— it was out of the question at the time, though tempting in the extreme. With Burroughs along, and the Mrs. Gilder as well as Watson himself, I'd had one of the times of my life. The Gilders have always received me without ifs and buts—I am not dead sure I have always shown them that my appreciation, my love for them, has no ifs and buts either."

[1905. I referred the 1883 letter to Gilder—asked him if he remembered it. Here is his answer:

EDITORIAL DEPARTMENT THE CENTURY MAGAZINE
UNION SQUARE NEW YORK, November 29, 1905.

My dear Traubel: This letter from me I only vaguely remember, but I think it explains itself quite clearly. They (the verses) refer evidently to my poem entitled When the True Poet Comes, which was supposed by some to have been suggested by Walt Whitman, and, when asked, I had to say it was not so suggested, as, indeed, should be evident to anyone who reads the poem carefully, because in it it says: "Manners like other men, an unstrange gear." This means that the particular poet I spoke of was conventional in his dress and bearing, which Whitman was not. I may tell you that I referred to the lack of popular appreciation of Charles DeKay's poetry—a lack which Whitman himself, strangely, as it seems, exemplifies. DeKay is surely one of our most virile and imaginative poets, as well as a great admirer of Whitman, and yet, as you know, Whitman spoke contemptuously of him. Of course I did not know that until I read your manuscript.

I do not remember the paragraph in the Critic. If you can strike the date it would not be impossible, perhaps, to find it. But you see that I say as follows: "I am very sorry that paragraph appeared as it did, or at all, as it might look as if I were not a friend and admirer of the subject of the book." The letter shows that I was such a friend and admirer way back in '83. I wish I could have got Whitman to Marion, as I tried to do. It would have been a delightful memory.

Sincerely yours,
R. W. GILDER.]

W. said to me tonight: "Beware of the literary cliques—keep well in the general crowd: beware of book sympathies, caste sympathies. Some one said here the other day—who was it?—'Mr. Whitman you seem to have sympathy for manhood but not for authorship?' It seems to me that all real authorship is manhood—that my sympathy for manhood includes authorship even if it don't make authorship a preferred object of worship. What is authorship in itself if you cart it away from the main stream of life? It is starved, starved: it is a dead limb off the tree—it is the unquickened seed in the ground."

Monday, August 20, 1888.

W. spent today depressed—physically "played-out like," as he said. Still reading Scott—and sometimes the poets lying about: Moore, Byron. The sudden taking off of Aunt Mary seems to have stumped him some. "There are no signs of a second wind—quite the contrary." Puts on a brave front. While he said to the Courier man that he expected to get out by cold weather he says to me: "Getting out seems more and more unlikely." We talked of the big one-volume Whitman. I said to him: "I guess you should let me do that work, Walt." He replied: "It is not a question of what I will or should, but a compulsion—what I must: I will simply have to put myself in your hands—God knows whether not in other things, and more and more things, as well as in that. I anticipate a time, not very far distant, when I will lose my physical volition altogether —suffer an entire extinguishment of efficient physical energy— find the fire utterly going out or gone out. When there is no fuel left the fire cannot last. You know Bucke's theory about the soul—the theories of men of science—the physical theories. Well, science is too damned fast for truth sometimes. I often feel like saying to the fellers who are so sure they are sure on all that: hold your horses, hold your horses—don't be too confident that you know the whole story—the kernel, the beginning, the end. Then I have a reaction. After the long period in which the other view was upheld—the contempt of the body, the horrible, narrow, filthy, degenerate, poisonous, distaste expressed in ascetic religions for the physical man—I confess that even materialism is a relief, like a new day, like sunlight, like beauty—yes, like truth itself." "And whatever your conviction about the soul, haven't you also just as firm a conviction about the body?" "Yes, just as firm—sometimes for earth reasons firmer. That is what should be and must be: a powerful loyalty to the body—to the body's desires, passions, appetites, all of them, well in rein, but alive, serving the soul, like a faithful steed." Then: "But after all, there's more to it than that—

more to it than these bodies—than the most superb bodies: more than that: and while I cannot argue the matter out, neither can I surrender my profound conviction."

Donnelly has returned to America. W.: "I feel that I for one owe him a great debt. I spent several half days or whole days assiduously reading his big book—the Cryptogram—and the immense mass and value of its information staggered me. I could no longer accept the Shaksperian—the actor—authorship: that is gone—gone forever." I suggested: "But you had come to that conclusion before." "To a certain extent, yes—but not entirely, not entirely. Here everything was systematized— everything was brought together—suspicions so placed as to get the force of certainty. I was already half-convinced—that is true—but convinced in the way a feller is convinced who hears debate, hears controversy-statements, counterstatements—things massed for partisan effect, hotly assailed, even logically proved —logically made unassailable—and yet comes away with his own doubts as active as before. But now, in my case, the instinct is confirmed—it no longer argues with itself—is satisfied—and Donnelly has done that for me." "Bucke wrote me that he thought the cipher a great fraud." "I knew he disapproved of the cipher—I didn't know he went it quite so strong as fraud. But that's a little like Maurice—over emphasis is his failing— going off half-cocked, as we say. You know yourself I do not find the cipher business significant. Not that I know anything about it—anything at all: I somehow have an instinctive aversion to the idea of a cipher and that leads up to my suspicions (which I admit may be all wrong): just as I have an aversion to the church notion of an atonement, because of its essential vulgarity, its wanton treachery to what I take to be high and imperative standards of human action. We say of a certain man: the atonement is not for him by the very fact of his being what he is: he is so made that he is made free. So I would say: the cipher is not for Bacon: by the very fact of his being what he is he is entitled to an exoneration." "Wouldn't O'Connor swear this idea down to the ground." "Down to the ground and under the ground! William would call me by a few strong names and then go to work again with his heresy. But whatever becomes of the cipher, I know what will become of Master Shaksper the actor—what has already become of him. He has gone for good." Adding: "I am just as slow to say yes as no—just as cautious. It took me a long time to say no to Shaksper: the rest of the problem is still unsolved—I have no answer to its questions. I am extremely cautious—weighing every grain before giving in my adhesion."

Bucke writes W. giving him a heap of advice anent the complete book. W. says to me: "We have talked most of those points over here. Doctor suggests that we should repaginate the book—give it consecutive pages. There is no necessity. The books have their own reasons for being—their independent reasons—Leaves of Grass, Specimen Days. They are not parts of a play—acts one, two, three—or chapters of a romance—that they need to be put together palpably by pagination. Then besides that would involve extra expense and trouble which I do not feel prepared to accept just now. All that is required under the present idea, my idea, might be a little preface, stating my reasons for this particular issue of my works."

Talked about reading. "Reading, most of it, by candlelight, indoors, up against a hot register or steam pipes, is a disease: I doubt if it does anyone much good. The best reading seems to need the best open air. When I was down on the Creek—Timber Creek—and roamed out and along the water, I always took a book, a little book, however rarely I made use of it. It might have been once, twice: three, four, five, even nine, times: I passed along the same trail and never opened the book: but then there was a tenth time, always, when nothing *but* a book would do—not tree, or water, or anything else—only a book: and it was for that tenth trip that I carried the book."

Harrison Morris over this evening but W. couldn't see him. "Again—some other time: I feel all knocked up to-night—all used up." W. said I should take an old Burroughs letter that laid on the table before me. "It gives a little look into the

Carlyle country—yes, and a big look into John's soul. John and William are very different men. John is a placid landscape—William is a landscape in a storm. Does that seem to express a difference? The only critical doubt I ever have about John is that sometimes I feel as if I would like to poke him up with a stick or something to get him mad: his writing sometimes seems to go to sleep. It is always attractive to me but always leaves me in a slow mood. William is quite different: he whips me with cords—he makes all my flesh tingle—he is like a soldier who stirs me for war." Then after a pause: "But it is always hopeless—the attempt to put a man into a sentence. William and John stand for such unlike temperaments they can hardly be talked of together: I can be at home with either—equally at home—but on the whole William mixes best with my blood." W. had me read the Burroughs letter aloud.

LONDON, June 16, 1882.

Dear Walt: I have delayed writing to you longer than I intended to. We had a pleasant passage over, and have been as happy as sight-seers can expect to be. We keep pretty well and take things easy. My first taste of the country was at Alloway, Burns' birthplace. We spent a week here in a cosy little inn on the banks of the Doon, surrounded by one of the sweetest and finest farming countries I ever beheld. From there we went up into the Highlands, where I did some mountain climbing: thence around to Edinburgh. From there we went down to Carlyle's country and spent a week at Ecclefechan, arriving there the first day of June just as the first red clover was beginning to bloom. I walked a good deal about Ecclefechan and shall write something about it and weave in certain things I want to say of Carlyle. I enclose a daisy or a spray of speedwell that I gathered from Carlyle's grave. There is no stone yet marking his grave. I saw the graves of eight "Thomas Carlyles." The "Carlyls" as the Scotch call them were a numerous race in this section. They were a stern savage set, not to be trifled with. One old Scotchman said they were "bullies." Then we went down into the Lake region for a few days; and thence to London.

Mr. Carpenter has been up and spent a day and a night with me. He has recently lost his father. He is well. We have been out to Mrs. Gilchrist's twice to tea. She and Grace are alone, Herbert being off in Wales, painting. They chided me for not bringing you, and entertain hopes of seeing you yet. They are well and have a pleasant cheery house. You would have a good time if you were to come. I have seen no one else in London and do not expect to. Rossetti I hear is not well. We shall leave here tomorrow, or I shall, for Haslemere and thence through some of the southern countries for a week; wife and Julian will stay with an old acquaintance of ours at Brentford, near London. I presume we shall be home in August. June has been cold and wet here: no heat, no warmth.

Conway has an article on Emerson in the June Fortnightly Review, but it is hasty and of not much account. I hope to hear yet that Osgood has not thrown up Leaves of Grass. I expect a letter from O'Connor every day. Drop me a line care of Henderson Brothers, 5 Union street, Glasgow, Scotland.

Ever your friend,
JOHN BURROUGHS.

Tuesday, August 21, 1888.

11 A. M. W. got up not feeling extra well. Yet read his daily papers (with them The Critic, which he is fond of) with a relish. Wished he might hear from Morse. "Morse went to Chicago then disappeared! We should send out the bell-man for him." I told W. I had preserved several hundred of Morse's letters. He was enthusiastic. "What a wealth of stuff that collection must be! Morse always writes memorable letters. Is there anything better in literature than the best letters?" After a pause: "Talking of letters, I have had one that will interest you. This is Tuesday the 21st—tomorrow is the 22d: tomorrow Herbert sails—Herbert Gilchrist—intending to come straight to Philadelphia. It seems to have been a sudden

whim—a jump: whether because he has had some success with his work and some dollars I don't know. Ocean travelling nowadays costs practically nothing—if a man has to pay board anyhow he can as cheaply pay it moving about as standing still. Or it may be that Herbert comes for the shaking up —the sea voyage. Herbert's power so far has been chiefly latent—an unuttered force."

Asked for his big blue coat. "This was made for me by my sister. Rhys brought me one over, too—but that I have never worn so far. It is down stairs." While I sat there Musgrove brought in a basket of peaches—luscious, big—that had been left at the door. W. took them, put on the glasses, read the tag. "There's no name but I think they're from Tom—from Mr. Harned. Harned came in with the children last night, and they spoke of peaches, little Annie saying: 'Papa, it's time Mr. Whitman had more fruit,' and she added, 'It should be peaches this time'—making a big circle with her two hands—'that's the kind, papa!'—then laughing over it. Oh the dear, dear children! And there's little Tom, too, full of life—joyous, exulting life! Yes, I know the peaches came from little Annie and the rest of the Harneds: the Harneds, may God bless em!" I spoke of Anna's excellent piano playing, W. taking it up: "Have you noticed that, too, Horace? I thought it was a secret all my own." Laughed gently. "She is full of musical feeling, though very undemonstrative, too. And by the way, Horace— wasn't your father a considerable something of a singer once upon a time?" And to my yes: "Ah! so I thought: and it must have been a great treat to you all. A baritone, was he? It is a noble voice. Ask him for me if he ever heard Badiali: Badiali was the superbest of all superb baritones in my time—in my singing years. Oh! those great days! great, great days! Alboni, Badiali, in particular: no one can tell, know, even suspect, how much they had to do with the making of Leaves of Grass. Badiali was a big, coarse, broad-chested, feller, invested, however, with absolute ease of demeanor—a master of his art—confident, powerful, self-sufficient." I spoke of our contemporary baritone, Galassi. W. nodded: "Yes, I have heard of though I have not heard him: he, too, must have a spark of the same fire in his composition. Badiali I remember chiefly in The Puritans—in what is abominably called 'the trombone duo' by the newspaper scriveners. My younger life was so saturated with the emotions, raptures, up-lifts, of such musical experiences that it would be surprising indeed if all my future work had not been colored by them. A real musician running through Leaves of Grass—a philosopher musician—could put his finger on this and that anywhere in the text no doubt as indicating the activity of the influences I have spoken of."

W. confided to me some of his plans concerning the big book and answered some of my questions. "When you go in to see Ferguson today tell him we want to go right on with it—make the proper, make your own, arrangements with him: you know exactly what we want—you particularly know that we want no delays. Tell him how as Walt Whitman is on the ragged edge and needs to be pampered and shoved along—that while he may relapse into strong life again, the chances are all the other way: that he will drop into the dead sea. Tell Ferguson Walt Whitman is down on his knees saying Ferguson prayers which Ferguson like the gentleman you say he is must answer."

Evening. W. reading The Antiquary. Has fingered the plate proofs some. "I have been thinking of our book today— trying to get it into right relations with myself. I have not yet made up my mind about November Boughs. If I end the voyage with this done I shall be happy: get into port not altogether bereft, with my colors still flying. Is that to be my good fate? I don't force things—don't force even the price of a book, the arrangement of a page of type, anything. Everything must come freely: I take up the incidents of life by the way, as they come along—and what is unwilling, loth, coquettish, I forego—I know is not for me, for my uses."

McKay was over this afternoon. W. says: "I think Dave has treated me all right, and I shall therefore reciprocate—am inclined to treat him right—yes, not only right but generously.

I have about decided to let him have the book—the little book. That is, I think I shall propose that he take the whole edition at forty-three cents—forty-three cents a volume. He may shy at that—regard it suspiciously as too big a demand: but as I have been sitting here, such is the condition that I feel bound to attach to any large or exclusive sale of the book. I shall be glad if I come out even on the job—get the plates even if nothing beyond. I am not worrying, shall not worry, dare not worry. When I have thought this all out for myself I am going to ask you to act it all out for me. For the present we will go on with the book—get it finished. I must have my own way, too: I must be humored. I think there's only one person living who ever browbeats me with success." "Who is that?" "You— you!" Laughed. "My good daddy used to say: 'Oh! what a comfort it is to lie down on your own floor, a floor laid with your own hands, in a house which represents your own handiwork— cellar and walls and roof!' In Long Island they had a phrase, 'to lie on one's own dunghill,' or something like it. I have long teased my brain with visions of a handsome little book at last— like the Epictetus—a dear, strong, aromatic volume, like the Encheiridion, as it is called, for the pocket. That would tend to induce people to take me along with them and read me in the open air: I am nearly always successful with the reader in the open air. I have my own peculiar affection for November Boughs. It is the depository of many dreams and thoughts precious to me—of many sacred aspirational experiences, too holy to be argued about—of sayings, almost of *mots:* of so many unspeakable records, reminiscences, worked into the soil of my matured life and now at last projected in this compact shape. To have such a book—such a book produced in every way according to a feller's simple and unimpeded humors— that has been my idea, is still my idea."

He went on about McKay: "He is young-blooded, careful, wide-awake, vital—has a shrewd eye, a steady hand. I should predict for Dave (you know he is greatly extending, greatly, all the time) that a few years of success will show him up as a big gun among publishers. Dave never shuffles his papers—he keeps his contracts. He has just returned from a trip West—a successful trip. He tells me he is to produce an Emerson—an early Emerson on which the copyright has expired. What a cute—devilishly cute—lot the publishing wolves are. There they are, the whole hungry herd—a dozen sets of eyes straining for a chance to pounce on these things the first minute of freedom."

This, too, was W.'s: "Often when the visitors come—visitors particularly honored and desired—my dear, dear mother, wishing to increase the richness of her cakes, would put in shortening, and keep putting it in, until from excess of attention the whole cake would fall apart. Now—warn the professionals —the artists—the men of finesse—not to put too much shortening in their cakes!" W. gave me an O'Connor letter with the remark: "It is as much your letter as mine. Make it all yours —take it home. William mentions you. This is one of William's least consequential letters, yet has the same inevitable stir of his blood. William will die with a hurrah on his lips." I said: "He'll never know he's dead he'll be so busy with resurrection day." This made W. laugh. "Horace, you ought to write that down: it's a trumpet-note." O'Connor's letter:

WASHINGTON, D. C., LIFE SAVING SERVICE,
July 26, 1888

Dear Walt: I got your card of the 19th (last Thursday's) and was greatly cheered and comforted thereby—the handwriting was so bold and vigorous. I had been feeling depressed and sorrowful—perhaps my own bad state had something to do with it; but anyhow, the brave hand-writing was like Chevy Chase to Sidney, "stirring my heart as with the sound of a trumpet." Since, I saw an item in a paper reporting you better, and am much encouraged. Strong hope is like strong prayer, and I shall hope for you strongly.

I have sent the To-Day to Dr. Bucke. The article was pleasing.

One of the Transcripts you sent had a characteristic speech by Littlebill Winter. He is certainly the Winter of my discontent mentioned by Lord Bacon in his play of Richard III. Small beast! It makes me sad to think how the Devil will suffer when he gets him. For spite of his faults, the prince of darkness is a gentleman, and how can he endure such company!

I hear from Bucke pretty often. He is a saint.

We have had heavenly weather until yesterday, which was a swelterer. But today is good again.

I have been overrun this week, but held back the flying hour by the hair today, just to send you this note.

I had a nice letter this morning from Mr. Traubel, to whom I will write soon.

I hope this will find you comfortable. Au revoir.

Always affectionately,
W. D. O'CONNOR.

"William always has the effect of the open air upon me," said W. "Next to getting out of my room here is to stay in my room and get a letter from William. I don't know which contains the most open air—William or out-doors. I like salient men—the men of elements—oxygenated men: the fellers who come and go like storms come and go: who grow up out of honest roots: not the titillated gentleman of boudoir amours and parlor fripperies: no, not that man: but if need be the rough of the streets who may underneath his coarse skin possess the saving graces of sympathy, service—the first of all, the last of all, the heart of all, personal excellence."

Wednesday, August 22, 1888.

W. perseveres in his reading of Scott. He seemed unusually quiet and feeble. "No—I have not felt well: not for some days past—am unable to write or do anything consecutive. I did write to Bucke today, however—but what had I to tell him? Nothing—no news. How could a feller sitting here in this room, cut off from the world, have news? With me it is but one thing

—one stale thing: if I write I must harp on that alone. I sit here all day, or lie over there"—motioning towards the bed—"and that is what my life amounts to." Has not examined proofs today. "I am on the disabled list for sure. I have taken a little look in on Scott—only a little look: even that would not go."

I read him a Bucke letter. Bucke expects to make money out of Gurd's water meter. W. says of that: "I can imagine no worse fortune for a man who amounts to anything, who hopes to grow and flower, who has in him the stuff of achievement, than to come into an income, ease, goods—be put into pawn to the world's patronage. May God help Bucke to remain a poor man!" "And me—Walt: do you pray for me, too?" "I don't need to: you'll never be rich: you'd run away if you saw riches coming." "Morse used to write me that when our million shiners came in we could pack up and go to Paris together—or something like that." "To Paris? And why to Paris? I don't see what use either one of you could make of Paris. Paris is a good thing to see in order to be through with it—to have it over with: like a fever or a great many evils that afflict us: or like the boy with his first watch, for instance—he can't be cured of it till he has it!"

Someone called his attention to an error in Leaves of Grass. "I see—I see: it must be wrong—but that is one of my idiocrities —to put it there and let it be, wrong or right. Maybe what is wrong for him is right for me: such things, too, do happen." Submitted him samples of paper for the two books. He looked them over. "After all, however, I leave that to you—what you all agree to I will approve. I want you to rub up against the pressman, too—get his advice. Pressmen know the kind of paper they can handle with the best results."

William Winter has been making a speech in England defending America against the negations of Arnold. W. said: "I have seen and read it—part of it, anyway. It came along from Kennedy, in a copy of The Transcript, and I afterwards passed it on to O'Connor. There was nothing in it to stick a pin through.

He made some reference to me, not by name, if I remember rightly, but by innuendo: some statement generously conceding my personal decency, even my goodness, and then dismissing my literary insanity and worse with a shrug of his literary shoulders, and an intimation in words that I was altogether off so far as concerned any serious poetic purpose and reputation."

We had a little talk about Bucke's Man's Moral Nature, W. saying: "Oh yes, I have read it—more than once—more than twice. It is a book you have to chew on—chew on with good teeth, faithfully, loyally: it pays principal and interest in the end if you stick to it. No one can hop skip and jump through it—it needs to be let altogether alone or very seriously read. It is worked out on daring lines—clearly, reverently, impartially. I understand that the scientific men are coming round very generally to the same view. Of course that is not conclusive: they all come, come again, come, come: then a new rebel appears, goes still beyond, and the men of science get up again for another walk. Speculation has its place but is not infallible—goes oftener wrong than right. We feel like saying to the metaphysicians and moralists: hold your horses, keep them well in hand —you never know when you've got to take a sharp turn-about! It's like in medicine—this year's dogma is tomorrow thrown away."

W. much amused by a newspaper editorial someone had sent him from the West. It had a question for a headline: "Who is this Walt Whitman, anyway?" He thought the "furious phosphorescent" inquiry of his assailant "refreshing." "Who is this Walt Whitman, anyway? Well, who is he? Do you know, Horace? Yes, you know—I haven't fooled you. But just see how I have juggled with the rest of the world!" I said: "I know who you are—you are the dirty novel man!" This broke him down utterly. He laughed more heartily than I have known him to do for months. I had reminded him of a story. Years ago—I was a small boy—we were on a ferry-boat together, sitting in front of the cabin. A well-dressed man leaning against the rail had been watching us intently. Finally he motioned to me—called me by crooking his forefinger. I got up and went over to where he stood. "Say," he said—"say, bubby—is that Walt Whitman, the man who writes the dirty novels?" I was convulsed but said "Yes." When I got back Walt remarked: "He was speaking about me—what did he say?" I told him. He took the dose calmly for he saw the man still looking at him. Later on, however, he let himself go in quiet little chuckles of amusement. Again and again afterward he would hand me out manuscripts to look at—poems, often, and say: "There's my latest dirty novel." This was the incident recalled when I said tonight: "You are the dirty novel man."

W. asked me: "What do you know of Lionel Johnson? Is he doing anything in the world that you know anything about?" "Why do you ask?" "Look at this." Handed an open letter to me. It was written on a small note sheet in a very delicate, sensitive hand. "It came two and more years ago, as you see: it was a very remarkable letter—and he was so young, a mere boy. It hits me hard when young people take such a shine to me —makes me feel as if I had to behave myself specially well. But this Johnson—this boy: I felt that he would do, if he had not already done, some signal writing of a sort—he seemed to have writing stuff in him. We must watch for his apparition: it will surely appear. Read the letter and see if I am likely to prove a false prophet."

ROSE COTTAGE, WINCHESTER, HAMPSHIRE, ENGLAND,
OCT. 20th, 1885.

Dear Walt Whitman: I write to you, though personally unknown, as writing to a dear friend: because, though happy to call many about me by the name of friends, I have no truer friend than yourself: if friendship means the receiving of light and delight and strength from the spirit of a brother man. I have lived as yet but eighteen years; yet in all the constant thoughts and acts of my last few years, your words have been my guides and true oracles. I cannot hope to see you face to face and tell you this: but you will at least believe it and feel that I am not writing from an unworthy spirit of self-assertion: but that I should feel shame for myself, were I not to show the reality of my gratitude to you, even through the weakness of words—you, whom I thankfully acknowledge for my veritable master and dear brother.

You, in your age and glorious approach to the sure future of death—you will know that I am speaking neither empty adulation nor shallow shams.

I am proud of belonging to the oldest school of any in England—to the great foundation of the strong priest and ruler, William of Wykeham: and it was under the shadows of the ancient walls of his college, still flourishing through the influence of his powerful personality, that I first received Leaves of Grass from the hands of a most dear friend. And the help and exaltation I have won from it have been won by many another boy and young man, of those in whose hearts rests the immediate history of the coming years—to make it splendid with strong actions and strong asserted truths. It is in your works, as in the great powers of earth and sea, that the inspiring force of no school is to be found; certain to dare all things by the strength of body and soul inseparable.

Whether I am right or not in writing to you, I neither know nor care: I do know that I cannot keep silence.

I am, in love and reverence,

LIONEL JOHNSON.

"That sounds very ripe for a boy of eighteen," said W.— "ripe enough already to shed fruit. It is singular how soon some natures come to a head and how long it takes others to ripen, though I believe, as a rule, the slow fruit is the best. It's not the least flattering feature of my experience that I have been most successful with young people, the just-comers, and least successful with the full done and over done literary masters of ceremony." Finally he said: "Keep a weather eye open for that boy: he will appear again." Asked me if I had ever seen

181

"this" portrait of Rudolf Schmidt. No, I had not. He said: "You might put it away in your Whitman rag-bag: it will be of use to you by and bye when you come of literary age and act as the historian of our many battles." I was present once when a preacher dropped in to see W. The visitor got talking special salvation to W. W. was impatient but held in. Finally the talker stopped as if to invite W.'s comment. W. looked up at the man, who was standing, and simply said: "Oh, hell!" The preacher looked at W. more hurt than horrified. "Is that all you have to say, Mr. Whitman?" W. was by this time thoroughly annoyed, though he only asked: "What more would you have me say, Mr. Ross?" Then the visitor left. W. turned to me and asked wickedly: "Horace, don't you think oh, hell covered the whole case?"

Thursday, August 23, 1888.

Forenoon. W. reading Lippincott's. I asked: "Are you studying the tragedy?"—referring to Amelie Rives' play there printed in full. "Oh no—I am not prepared to tackle that. But who is this Mitchell—Langdon Elwyn Mitchell? The name has a new sound to me." "Is the poem better than the general run of them?" "I think it is—it has some snap and go: it is worth looking over a second time." W. said he had concluded to make the edition of the complete book six instead of five hundred. "Keep your best eye on these details, Horace. I often find I fall down—most people fall down—on details." Looks feeble, tired, this morning. Weather cool. No further work yet done by him on the proofs. W. said: "I had a note from Clifford—it came just awhile ago. He got the book." Then, handing me the letter: "It is written in the style of the Queen Anne fellows period: very complimentary—rich in compliment: but I know it is wholly sincere in him—wholly so. He likes the booklet (and what a word that is, too—booklet!— just exactly says what we want it to!)—and knows just what it comes to, too, I have no doubt." Here is the letter:

FARMINGTON, MAINE,
Aug. 21, 1888.

My dear Mr. Whitman: I am content to have waited forty years for the birthday book which I have from you and Horace. If forty more could hold promise and deserving of such another, I should face them with best hope and patience.

If this coveted but not-to-have-been-asked for autograph means, as it seems to do, that the hand which wrote it is much stronger than when last I felt its generous touch, that token is alone enough to gladden this my little day. Long life and all love!

J. H. CLIFFORD

Clifford addressed the envelope simply "Walt Whitman." W. said: "I like it so. I remember that Tennyson was at first a little shy but ended by coming round and saying, I must speak of you and to you simply as Walt Whitman. Some of my friends still hold on to the belated 'Walter:' some do even worse—say 'Mr.' Whitman. Could anything be more out of place than 'Mr.' Whitman?" After a laugh: "They seem to feel that anything less than 'Mr.' breeds familiarity. My own family is for calling me 'Walt'—all of my family. Dr. Bucke always speaks of me in his book as 'Walt Whitman,' which sounds just right." I reminded W. that Clifford hates the "Rev." W. nodded: "Yes, I remember what he said about it. I do not wonder that a man made up as he is mostly of the simplest material should hate a cant title. Clifford belongs out on the road—does not belong in a church. The church is no place for a man after he has got his growth. I would like to predict of Clifford that if he don't step out of his own accord he will some day be kicked out. He is too ready to say the things which rub pews the wrong way: it is like a perpetual challenge, which will in good time be taken up. Some nabob parishioner will get it into his head that Clifford is dangerous to have about—is not a fit man to act as their spokesman—then Clifford will retire—with honor, maybe, but retire. I never knew a minister extraordinary in a church to make a fight of that kind successfully—and Clifford is a minister extraordinary, don't you think?" W. stopped a minute. I said nothing. Then he went on: "I once said something like this to a woman, a church woman—it may have been Hannah Smith. She asked me: 'Why are you so bitter against religion, Mr. Whitman?' And when I answered, 'I am not talking about religion—I am talking about the church' —she only said: 'I don't see the difference—they are one thing to me.' Nine people out of ten would make the same protest."

Evening. Reading Lippincott's again. "Ah Horace!" he cried in his usual fashion, stretching out his hand: "And what do you bring tonight?" I laid my hat and package on the lounge and produced for him the big envelope containing three missing pages of plate proofs (128-9-30) and proof of frontispiece. Enjoyed them. Some of the proofs on glazed paper, which he hates. He studied the portrait with great care. "That will do," he finally remarked, looking over at me: "We have come out of a great trouble with our skins perfect. Sometimes when things don't go right I find myself saying: 'It's lucky not to have been worse.' I do not need to say that for the picture. The picture is a success. I won't thank anyone for it—it's all a part of our gamble—but I'll thank our stars." He suddenly commenced to poke about among the papers on the floor with his cane. "I had a Post here, Horace: something in it I wanted you to see to. The American Book Maker, it seems, has been printing something about me—a portrait—which Bonsall seems to regard with great favor. We must get a copy of the magazine." After much searching the paper was found under the rocker of his chair. "Ah! here it is: read it." I stood reading. He turned up the light. "Don't that bear out my idea?" Bonsall had written: "The American Book Maker prints a life-like picture of Walt Whitman, which may be among the last, as it certainly is the best, given." Now W. resumed: "Go to Bonsall —borrow his copy: then we may see what we want." W. while he looked for the paper talked of the confusion in the room:

"I think there is a devil—that he some days gets loose in this room."

Expressed a desire to see the Emerson-Carlyle correspondence. Ignatius Donnelly passed through Camden yesterday and this morning an interview appeared in the Press. W. had read it. "Yes, all of it: and it was interesting: but I don't think Donnelly strengthens his case by such interviews—interviews which carry with them the cheaper atmosphere of a second or third class lawyer. Besides, all that English exploiting, noising about, weakens his position. His Cryptogram is a great book in spite of Donnelly himself—the first part of it, I mean, which staggered me and must make any unbiased man pause and consider. After that, William Shaksper is no more for me—for me, at least. But long debates at Oxford, and putting it to a vote, and arguing it up and down, as the case may be, in no wise adds invincibility to the cause. I rely more on the quiet pondering of data, contemporary probabilities, and so forth, than on argument, logic, scholarly pros and cons, even if they are of the very best: on the silent conviction that is possessing many minds—the drift of the more considerable students: the not-to-be-stated but real and unassailable instinct now ripening in men here and there—in Tom, in Dr. Bucke, in you yourself—yes, in me: count me in with the 'considerable.' That seems far more potent and significant to me than the slam-dash controversy of the lawyers. The whole point is, to provide the material—to set it forth so it may be handled—and then turn on the light, which, gathering strength more and more, in its own free way, will drive inevitably to a certain result—is eligible for one result and one only."

Thurman made a big speech on the tariff yesterday at Port Huron. W. read it. "But I fear Thurman is not the man— have always believed he was not the man. There is a great dearth in America of men who will exploit, elucidate, this subject on the highest grounds—of men not intellectual alone, but emotional, sympathetic, bound in by no narrow horizon of a special party, sect, school. We have had cute men—men too damned cute—Sumner was one of them—free traders—but no one clear of alliances, conventional hesitations, limitations of one kind or another: no one without some sort of a bond to qualify the purity of his faith. All the fellers consider the tariff as an affair in itself complete, as if nothing else was involved, as it would be in a library with one shelf only, and all that for books on one subject: and yet there is no policy, no truth, no principle that draws more to itself than the tariff, considered in its real rootgerms and its infinite effects. You mention Henry George. I do not think I should say anything about him: I know so little, practically nothing, of his economic theories. It is my impression of him, however, that he too is the victim of a special twist, bias—not the absolutely direct individuality, personality, I am looking for—America requires. In this campaign it strikes me that the whole batch of the spellbinders and statesmen so-called (God help us, statesmen!) are all wrong, all sides—discussing the problem from a vulgar point of view—poor, petty, unworthy, insincere, insulting in fact. These men never get up high enough to see what the problem in reality is—never recognize it in its international complications—do not see that it is not political but human—that it means something to Bohemia as well as to America."

He stopped here to ejaculate: "Why, damn me, I'm making a speech!" I clapped my hands. He threw his arms out as if in acknowledgment of applause. Then he proceeded: "Anyhow, I am convinced that the best samples of the critter off there in England, Ireland, Scotland, beat us by a good margin—are of more solid substance—are built for a longer stay. The actors for example (there have been lots of them coming here from time to time to see me): tall, broad, plainly dressed, not grammatical in speech (a suit of tweed, perhaps, or even something plainer)—not formal, like our men—generous, lithe, averse to show in all ways—no gammon (oh! no gammon at all—it's unknown to them)—yet men to be depended upon for severe trials, stretches of tremendous labor, splendid unostentatious achievements. And these are features of the general life over there—

inertia, stability. The trouble here with us is our devil of a craze for money—money in everything for every occasion—by hook or by crook, money: and, on top of that, show, show: crowning all that, brilliancy, smartness unsurpassed, repartee, social wish-wash, very misleading, very superficial: the whole situation one to discourage the more efficient factors of character. Of course this is an exaggerated statement—such statements generally are—but it contains the material of a just complaint. We will get out of it—must get out of it: we will escape our defects: I do not croak. There is one thing more to be said —an important thing. Before I was sick, particularly in the year or two previous, I was visited a lot by the better class mechanics—I mean the more serious of the mechanics (the more informed, ambitious, instructed). Frequently they would come in and talk and talk, sometimes like a house afire, of their enthusiasms—socialistic, many of them, perhaps most of them, were—very bright, quick, dead in earnest, able to take care of themselves and more too in an argument. They, their like, the crowd of the grave workingmen of our world—they are the hope, the sole hope, the sufficient hope, of our democracy. Before we despair we have to count them in—after we count them in we won't despair. All will adjust itself. But that image of the typical extra fine Britisher—his brown face, his broad deep chest, his ample limbs, his clear eye, his strong independent mien, his resonant voice—still clings to me. One thing we must remember: we were born in the political sense free—they were not: that creates an altogether different atmosphere—is a fact never to be forgotten. We seem in many ways to have grown careless of our freedom. Some day we will have to stir our croppers and fight to be free again!" I said: "We shook off England. We shook off the slave. What will we shake off next?" "Money!—the dominion of money." I protested: "You kick when I say that: you say I am too radical: you tell me to hold in my horses." He laughed at my dig. "Maybe I do that just after some theorist has been here with an axe to convert me. That always makes me hot—hot: I resent it.

But do you suppose you see any better than I do the menace hanging over our democracy? Yet, Horace, we are safe, safe. The mass, the crowd, the vast multitude that works, is competent to, will, preserve our liberties: they are our prop, mainstay, sure, sure."

Friday, August 24, 1888.

Morning, 10.15. W. sat reading the papers but was ready to talk. I asked him for money for the frontispiece plate. He began to search through his pockets. Adjusted his glasses. He carries his wallet in his inside vest pocket. He found a dollar bill in one pocket and a two dollar bill in one of the other pockets. He found two silver dollars in his trousers pocket. He looked at me, laughing: "I didn't know I was so well off. Money, money, everywhere." Suddenly he held up a single new dollar bill and said: "Ah! this—this was for poor Aunt Mary: I handed it to Mary for her and Mary came back and said the old lady was dead." He finally got the money together and gave me what was required. "I have no letters today— none at all—but there is a Transcript from Kennedy: I don't know what is in it."

I found a poem by Swinburne—A Double Ballad of August. W. said: "Oh yes, I did see that. And if Swinburne had a few grains of thought with all his music wouldn't he be the greatest charmer of all? I never liked him from the first—Swinburne— from the very first: could not take him in, adapt myself to him. I know of nothing I think of so little account as pretty words, pretty thoughts, pretty china, pretty arrangements. I have a friend, a woman—a cute one, too: one of the very cutest—who takes most to Bothwell: thinks Bothwell the one thing most to Swinburne's credit and likely to last, if any: and it is true of Atalanta, as you say, that it is rich in particulars and esteemed by scholars. My taste is alien—on other currents: I do not seem to belong in the Swinburne drift. I find it difficult to account for my dear woman's taste. Did you not hear it said somewhere that Schiller was very fond of rotten apples—had them always about him—the rottener the better? Maybe that is a story which explains her taste."

I had brought him the Carlyle-Emerson correspondence. He handled the volume affectionately: "What a beautiful letter this book is set up in! It's a good sight for my old sore eyes: leaded, double-leaded. After all that is the one reasonable—yes, merciful—method: to spread the lines far apart." I put in: "The merciful reader is merciful to his eyes." W. assented: "Yes, sure enough. I have myself always gone on the other supposition with regard to a type-set page—that it should be solid, in the interest both of condensation and money, but lately it has impressed me that I was wrong." He looked at the portrait: "Sidney's bust of Emerson—Morse's—is a much better portrait than the one they use in this book." Bonsall will find us the Book Maker. I saw him the first thing this morning. W. said: "Don't argue about health, Horace—be healthy. When you argue about health your health is already gone."

Evening. W. reading when I arrived. He put his book down. "What news? What news?" "News? None. What news have you?" "None—none at all: I get nothing—not even letters: not even a letter from Bucke." I paid Brown for the portrait today. I said to B.: "Brown, you know that's a bum portrait: but the old man likes it." Brown said: "It is bum—I wouldn't have been surprised if you had turned it down." I repeated this to W. who only replied: "I have nothing to complain of. The figure's the thing: that will not be criticised. So far as the technicalities go, well—damn the technicalities if the rest is all right!" Brown will try again if this plate is too difficult to print from. W. had settled upon a costly paper for the two books. I brought him an estimate—one hundred and ten dollars for N. B. and two hundred and fifty for the complete W. W. The figures startled him: "I confess that it staggers me—knocks me clean off my feet." I asked: "Well, shall I look for some cheaper stock?" "Who said cheaper stock?" asked W. Then added: "I will see the books through if it takes every cent I possess!"

W. asked me to explain to him the purport of the President's message of retaliation (out today) on the fisheries dispute with Canada. "I can't get it into my noddle what the stir is all about. Do you know and can you tell?" And then after I had gone over the ground briefly: "Well—let them go on: let them push it as hard as they choose: let them run up their walls, obstructions, laws, as high as they choose: in the end all will inure for the best results—we will in fact pluck the flower free trade from the nettle protection. As an individual I feel myself imposed upon, robbed, trampled over, but I can still urge patience, patience. Let them push their theory to the breaking point—for break it must. I myself once fell afoul of an experience with customs officers up there on the Canadian border. Happily Bucke was along and extricated me. He took the officials aside and seemed to settle it that my baggage was not to be disturbed—gave them a few dollars to even up the trouble. The whole thing was quite a source of wonder to me—instructive, baffling: and what struck me most of all was Bucke's ease, suavity, composure, negligé—a sort of taking it for grantedness coolly expressed in his assumption of the manner of a born, tired, traveller. It seemed to me then as it had before and always has since, that here lay one of the worst evils of the system—in its encouragement of lying, bribery, misrepresentation, hypocrisy—just as in the prohibition and other special cases: yet this is a side of the situation no one considers. No one goes to hard pan with the problem—no one is more than cute in handling it—is deep enough to see it all around, in all that it includes, reflects, implies. It is not a fiscal, it is a moral, problem—a problem of the largest humanities."

This led him to dilate on copyright. "What an infernal, outrageous, conspiracy of red-tapeism it is, not only in its initial requisites but in its after demands! It is all a matter of apery: our laws are copied after, modeled upon, the English laws— laws which proceed on the supposition that the people have nothing to do but study the comforts and purses of governments, monarchs, legislatures: the pleasure of lords, ladies, nabobs. What is legality anyway?—puzzle—pretense, snare. Cute thinkers have said (William Leggett—one of the best of 'em: Leggett, of the Post, who always said it so well, irrefutably) that there is no legal writing under heaven—not the carefullest, clearest—but may be overturned, disproved, vitiated, by sharp pleading, unexpected construction. This is so much true that some one has declared that we should never put a word—not a word, not the suspicion of a word—on paper without realizing on the legal side that when the destroyers get to work upon it it may all fall to the ground in confusion and seem to falsify the whole moral code."

W. had been asked a question like this in a letter: Is a man's work ever greater than the man who does the work? He answered the question to me in this way: "It is obvious that the man is always superior. Any fact is superior to a statement of the fact: any statement at its best is only a half-statement." I reminded him of a remark he made to me years ago one noonday on the boat: "If Grant is not himself poet, singer, artist, he at least contains within himself the eligibility, the subject-force, of song, art." He listened intently. "Repeat that," he said. I did so. Then he said: "Yes, I should stand by that. Dowden's Shakspere somewhere exploits a thought like that —a thought that seems to me the most significant and valuable thing in the book. Have you read Dowden? You should: he is a whole literature in himself. I have the Shakspere volume here somewhere. Dowden sent it to me himself: I have always kept it near my chair—I wanted it handy. If you find it take it along and read it. Besides it is a sample of the English printing which I am so fond of."

Not yet done with the N. B. proofs. "I am having a hard time again trying to straighten out their kinks. After all you'll have to round them up with your own eagle eye." Told me my father was here yesterday: "I was glad to see him—he looked so well—was very cheerful. He talked to me about German poetry and music—even sang a bit, a few strains, to illustrate something he was saying. Do you know, Horace, he has a beautiful voice—a baritone? But of course you know—you only haven't happened to say so."

I asked W. if he had ever had any correspondence with Oscar Wilde? "No correspondence, though he has written me letters. Did I never show you a fine letter I had from him while he was making his American trip? No? Well—it is about here in the mess—somewhere about, God knows where: if it ever shows its head I'll grab it—you may have it. I never completely make Wilde out—out for good or bad. He writes exquisitely—is as lucid as a star on a clear night—but there seems to be a little substance lacking at the root—something—what is it? I have no sympathy with the crowd of the scorners who want to crowd him off the earth."

W. gave me a letter from Sylvester Baxter that he has several times spoken about since it came last month. He mentioned it to me originally because of its reference to Bellamy's book. On another occasion he said of it: "Sylvester is on several sides my friend—my friend, I think, for general reasons not one reason alone. You see, some people like this or that in me— like nothing else: as a man might like your leg or arm and forget the body of which they form a part: Baxter is of the other, the large, sort—he sees me whole. Sylvester is a quiet, sane, agreeable make of man—don't get into flusters, don't indulge in bad tempers about humanity—yet is radical, too, if not revolutionary, and looks for some shake-up in the social order before long."

MALDEN, MASS.,
JULY 13, '88.

My dear friend: I have just heard from Kennedy that your illness continues. We had been hoping that the recovery would be more lasting and that the summer days would see you driving out and enjoying the precious sunshine. We had also been looking forward to the pleasure of feeling that you were comfortably domiciled in the desired cottage of your own, away from the stifling and noisy city, but your friends who worked to that end will all feel—as one of them has expressed it—that the thought that the project has given you even the briefest joy, and that it has given you the gratification of building and dwelling therein in the world of your mind—more real than the world of sense—fully compensates them.

I am so glad that you have to help you so devoted a friend as young Traubel, and through you I give him my hand and my thanks.

I have lately been reading a beautiful and noble story by Edward Bellamy, Looking Backward. It goes far in the direction pointed out by your prophetic Democratic Vistas and I hope Traubel will read it and tell you about it.

In these days the glorious words you have spoken about death come up in my mind, and I feel much as must have been felt by the disciples in those calm last hours of Socrates. Whether his coming be near at hand, or later, he can only take your physical presence from us and that which you have given will ever abide with us. To many whose souls you know will be realized your words: "I spring from the pages into your arms—decease calls me forth."

Faithfully yours.
SYLVESTER BAXTER.

W. said: "You must read the Bellamy book and tell me about it." "I have read it already." "So? Well—you must explain it to me—but not now, not today." I asked W. whether he noticed that Death, which to him was a "strong deliveress" was to Baxter a "deliverer—he"? W. laughed. "Horace, I didn't think you'd do it—you are as fussy as a peeking critic. So he does—so he does: but it has no furtive significance: neither he nor she would say it all."

Saturday, August 25, 1888.

Running about all day for W.—first to Bonsall's house for the Book Maker—then across the river for conferences at different places with Ferguson, McKay, Magarge & Green (paper merchants), Brown, Bilstein (plate printers). Struck a paper for seven cents, by which we can save one hundred and forty dollars on the lot required. W. said at once: "If you agree, we will have that—that quality for both books." He endorsed my set of plate-proofs as follows: "First proof-sheets of *November Boughs*—to my friend Horace Traubel who gets out the booklet with me. Walt Whitman Aug: 25, '88." He wrote under a frontispiece proof of his own portrait: "The Seventieth Year—taken from life" He laughed as he did this. "You threaten to be as odd and particular as I am myself. I recollect Count Gurowski, in Washington, once directing me what to write in a book—some damnable Germanicism—and then explaining: 'I know you think it trifling, but then other people attach a great value to just such things'."

Brought over today a number of proofs of the frontispiece plate. W. still quite satisfied with it. Proposes to put it in the big book also. I produced the Book Maker containing Frank Fowler's portrait of W., who just glanced at it and exclaimed vehemently: "That's not me—not like me: I must confess it disappoints me as a portrait. Yet, what a wonderful piece of work it is!—and after all, if not *the* Hamlet it is *a* Hamlet, and that is not without its satisfactions. But what mystifies me about it is, where the devil he got my sitting, my superscription, and when the devil I looked like that. I can't for the life of me remember Fowler—what he is like, that he met me, how he could have encountered me in this or any other fashion. I do have a dim remembrance of having been corraled at Huntington (I think that was in 1881 or thereabouts) by an artist, but I am sure that involves another person, not Fowler: oh yes!—Dora Wheeler: I feel it—*her:* do you know of her?—painter?—artist? How little this all sounds like me: 'Yes', says Walt Whitman, and so forth, and so forth: yet it looks genuine—though how Fowler could have come into possession of it I couldn't guess: the writing is a bit off for me but the sentiment is genuine. The picture itself is not Walt Whitman—is too combed, curled, pretty, for him—lacks his traits, the this or that which you know him by."

Without waiting for me to break in he added: "I have been reading the Emerson-Carlyle letters: they are interesting to me from the word go: historic letters, letters of genius, in some respects the most remarkable letters in all English literature. I find you must get fully into the atmosphere before you can thoroughly enjoy them. But, do you know, I should say here was a chance for the critics, too. If I was myself a critic, was admitted as a critic to the reviews, I would cry out against the whole business as too deliberate, too much prepared, too top-loftical—too infernally top-loftical. God never made men this way: this is the way men are made when they are made over by men—creations of strain, creations for effect. But after that is said all the bad is said: as for the rest, the correspondence is fascinating, elevated, conclusive. I deduct only a little from the total, you see: there is plenty left."

I read him Burroughs' letter of the 23rd closing with a request for W's opinion of B's Arnold in the June Century and admonishing me not to "let him know I put you up to it." I excused myself to W. for reading the whole letter by saying: "I know you're that kind of a man to whom all is never too much." "You are right—right to read it: and how good in John: that part of the letter and all the letter so like him. I once visited Girard College—I think I went with Houghton, Lord Houghton—and the good old President said to me: 'I perceive you come to learn, to investigate. If you meet anywhere with the legend, 'no admittance,' be it just there that you do most quickly betake yourself.' That's the way with John's caution to you—best observed by being violated." B. will send on some pears.

Happening to refer to a paper he had sent to Mary Costelloe W. said: "She has met Tennyson: the two girls went to see him once—I told you of that. Tennyson (the sly old rascal), is a lady's man—is fond of the girls—rather prefers them. They say he particularly affects children—children of ten or eleven or such years—is often seen with one on his knee." W. paused while I asked questions about Tennyson's title. Then: "He has all that in him, the eligibility for all that—for title, place, deference, hauteur—but in the great deeps behind, below, the great spirit pervading all, something more, something truly human, lasting, unerringly true. When I write him, as I have several times, I never address him except as simply Alfred Tennyson. Mrs Gilchrist's talks with me about him were always charmed, touched, as with the contact of an unusual personality."

I asked W. if he had kept any Emerson letters. "Yes, several—I had a number of letters from him, as you know, some of them coming to Washington—two or three of them there. If you like, and I can put my hands on them, the letters may be transferred to your collection. I am pretty certain I still have the original, the first, the great Emerson letter, too—the bravest of them all: but where it just is it would beat my poor brains to say." This revived the old question—had Emerson ever recanted his Whitmanism? W. answered; "It is my final belief that he did not—a belief confirmed by many things, many facts, many side-lights. I shall never forget Lord Houghton's visit of 1876, after a several week's course of meetings with Emerson. He sat opposite me (it was down on Stevens Street) as you do there now—raised his finger this way—and said, in a resolute manner, which was at once clear and emphatic: 'Mark my words, Whitman [or Walt Whitman or Walt]—mark my words, put them down: I want to say them now because I am never likely to see you again: mark my words—Emerson never took the back track—never, never: never swerved, never retreated—is still your friend, as he was and must continue to be, recanting nothing, sticking to his faith. I know what I am talking about—I am not guessing: I have been there, talked with him, understood him and been understood: Whitman, in all the essentials of adhesion Emerson is still on your side, sternly affirming your particular message.' It was just that way, in such warm words, that Lord Houghton spoke to me—almost those very words or words purporting them." Then W. proceeded reflectively: "In substance, in bulk, that is right—is confirmed by my own knowledge. That the literary fellows drove Emerson hard I know—everybody knows: that he was almost driven to cover by the pressure is also a fact not disputed. Yet I am compelled to believe that he remained to the end unmoved in all the essentials of his first loyalty. I do not mean that he always thought the same of me but that he never shifted his point of view to satisfy the protesters. Besides, there's a side to that story which is known to but one person—a side mine, never divulged—a side I have no desire to exploit, made clear by me to O'Connor but to no other person living—and on that alone I could rest much, all. None of the reasons of my friends why Emerson could not have changed can come so close home, can go so near the marrow, the spine, of what is the abiding truth of it all, as some few things, some never exploited minor assurances, whatnot, made by Emerson to me, for me alone—sacredly, wholly for me—not to be blazoned out in any confession or defense."

I read him a Bucke letter dilating on the water meter. W. was not interested. Drifted off at once into other matters. He was in a high mood the whole evening—the best for weeks. "The prospect of an early production of both the books gives me a sense of relief beyond words. I want you to say to all the fellows—the printer men—all of them (be sure you don't forget the proof-reader) that Walt Whitman is grateful for everything they have done—that his pay is not the pay of money but the pay of love. Tell them that—tell even the flinty ones that. I want them to know that I am not in merely trade relations with them." W. was lying down on my arrival but got up at once and hobbled to the chair, asking me what I had to show him. Of his health he said: "It's nothing to brag of—at the best only so-so—has no real up-tides. I feel as if I weighed four hundred pounds."

Bucke has sent W. a pamphlet on the uses of alcohol, negativing it even for sickness. W. says: "Bucke knows I drink—at least that I used to whenever I got the chance—was in the mood. And yet I am not sure but he is right—right even in his extremest extreme statement—that the reaction from drink is always to be feared: always, without question or exception. I know that I dare not touch it myself any more. The champagne that was brought me a couple of weeks ago was tempting and I took a little glass of it, a very little glass of it, a mere fillip—feeling, as I thought, in consequence, uncomfortable, hardly myself, the rest of the day." W. got as far as the bath-room today, going there without any assistance. But he said to me this evening: "If these things—tables, chairs, etc.—were not scattered about the room, if I didn't know every object and spot, I don't believe I could navigate at all. There's no use bawling because the batter's upset, Horace, but it begins to look as if I wasn't much feathers any more physically speaking: my plumage is about all shaken out."

Sunday, August 26, 1888.

When I reached W's. in the evening I met Harned coming off the step. "Walt is in very bad shape to-night," he said. Musgrove indoors said the same thing. I went upstairs, however, and saw W., who sat in his chair reading Scott, and looking, sure enough, very worn, very tired, very much distressed. His greeting was nevertheless prompt and cordial. "Ah! Horace! another day—another day has gone: a damned bad day, too, and I'm not sorry to say good bye to it"—laying his book down and offering me his hand. "Won't you sit down? there's a chair: take it"—pointing. I protested: "No—no—I won't stay to-night—you are not well." He replied: "Oh, nonsense! Not well? Of course not well—but always well to you!" I said: "That's a sweet compliment—I shan't forget it." Then he went on: "Stay a bit of a bit of a time, anyhow—long enough for me to get a look at you. You look very fresh to-night—glowing: it helps my sore eyes to see your face." I still stood up. "Well, if you don't want to sit down I won't force you to. I have had a bad day—a very miserable bad day: but I notice my bad days often come just before my best days—so you see I have reasons for hope as well as reasons for despair."

He handed me a proof of the frontispiece page on which he had written "The 70th year—taken from life." He had penned on it some instructions for the printer: "Under the picture as it seems to me would be best in two lines—the upper one caps, O. S. Roman—say l.p. the lower one lower case Roman (but use your own taste) 'The 70th year Taken from life.'" W. said as to this: "I suggest several things but you need not adopt them if you like your own ideas better." Hunter in today. Did not like the picture. "But that makes no difference to me —not the slightest: the point with me is that I be suited, and when I am suited (and I am suited now), that settles the question. Besides, this picture belongs to this particular book— it has the same air, tone, ring, color: the same ruggedness, unstudiedness, unconventionality. I am more likely any time to be governed by my intuitive than by my critical self, anyhow. On top of all my self-analysis is the fact that Aggie was in today, saw the picture, liked it, said I should use it, and, as a wise, good woman is very apt to do in my case, put a clincher on my own intentions in the matter."

He is anxious to push the books along. Whenever he has a particularly bad day he wants to rush the work. "It admonishes me against delay." Asked me to see McKay. "I should prefer that you deal with him for me—I must be spared the worry of it." He looked at me affectionately and said this: "Whenever I think of your perfect health I think of you as a duplicate of myself as I was at the end of the war"—than after a stop—"or I might say it in another way—I think of myself as your embodied prophet." He related an experience. "It illustrates official lassitude and stupidity—one or both. I have tried again and again to find by inquiry at our post office how long it takes to carry a letter from Camden to London—to Bucke. Nobody can tell me—nobody knows—nobody seems to care to know. They put Mr. Musgrove off without even an attempt to find out or a regret expressed that they do not know." "Someone needs to go into that office with a kicker on the toe of his boot." "That's so: and what's more he needs to exercise it roundly on the whole gang." W. laughed quietly, tiredly: "I get mad at people, then people get mad at me: that's the way we even up."

W. had tied together in a string for me a little bunch of stuff of which he said: "These are acceptances and declinations of editors—invitations to write, invitations not to write, such things: I put them together for you out of this helter-skelter mass thinking you might like to see how some things came and some things didn't come my way. We have often talked of editors—of their curses, their blessings (both deserved, no doubt): the open hand, the clenched fist: the hems and haws of editors who would and who wouldn't and always wound up with wouldn't: such like stuff. That's what you'll find in the bundle. They have no interest except possibly as superficial biographical tattle." I took the stuff out of his hand. "You may get along with this to-night instead of a talk," he said, weariedly: "If you have any questions to ask anent the letters you can ask them another time. I want to give you all the pro and con in these matters that I can—all, all, not withholding anything intentionally. Horace, you are the only person in the world whose questions I tolerate: questions are my bete noir: even you at times, damn you, try me: but I answer your questions because you seem to me to have a superior right to ask them, if anyone has, which may be doubted. Cross-examinations are not in the terms of our contract but you do certainly sometimes put me through the fire in great shape." He laughed. "Now, Horace, you see how much I love you: you have extorted my last secret. You have made me tell why you are an exceptional person—you have forced from me an avowal of affection." He was quite lively for an instant while making this sally. Then he relapsed—looked miserable, as if to go to pieces. I went to him. "Help me to the bed," he said. This I did. He sank on the pillow. Closed his eyes. I reached down and kissed him. He said "Good night" without opening his eyes. I said "Good night" and left. As I stood in the doorway an instant he cried: "And you will come tomorrow again? that everlasting, that sweet, tomorrow! Yes, yes: I'll be cautious"—replying to my injunction—"I'll not do anything reckless: I'll come round by morning, I know."

My sister Agnes had gone today to take W. fruit. He was

very loving with her. Kissed her affectionately—talked freely for fifteen minutes. Alluded to me: "Horace has wonderful intuition: he divines me, perceives me, almost before I divine, perceive, myself." He said to me regarding myself: "Horace, how it happens you fall to my lot—you, being just what you are—now, in my need: who can tell? There certainly was a divinity that shaped this end." To my sister and my father who in these last few days have seen W. for the first time since his present sickness began his bodily decline has seemed shocking. Those of us who have been with him every day have not so well perceived the subtle change. My father says: "His mind to me seemed if anything clearer, firmer, more sure of itself, if possible, than ever before." My father is a materialist in philosophy. So he says: "That was of course not what I expected and it is therefore what I cannot explain." W. handed me what he called "a family memorandum" a day or two ago. "It's nothing—something," he said: "It's only a bit about George—a war bit. Can you make room for it in your bulging pigeon-holes?" He laughed. I will put it in right here:

New York, 16th April, 1862.

Lt. Geo. W. Whitman,
Newbern, N. C.

Lieutenant: Enclosed I have the pleasure of handing you your commission, and congratulate you upon your promotion.

In the 51st, more especially than in almost any other regiment, promotion has been made to depend upon gallant action—and this is now doubly in your favor.

I shall always be glad to hear from you.

I am, Lt. Very Truly Yours

Elliott F. Shepard.

Another letter W. gave me the same day was this from Linton:

New Haven, Conn., Aug: 21, 1875.

My dear Whitman: First—how are you getting on? Second (like a woman's postscript) have I told you at any time that I

201

have been and am preparing a vol: of Amer: poetry up to your Centennial, for English publication? I would like, if I may, to use as frontispiece your head, which will not hurt your fame on the other side; and three thousand miles off will not, I think, interfere with the appearance of the same head here with those new things which I want to see. May I use it? Say honestly yes or no, as you feel. I do not want to do what you might not like, whether in matters of interest or feeling. But I can have nothing I should like so well.

I wish you were here now that the storms seem over. We have had such a spell of bad weather as I have never before been treated to by U. S.

Yours always,

W. J. LINTON.

W's. reply to this was written on the foot of the sheet:

"You are entirely welcome to use the eng: as you desire. I am about as usual—not any worse. Feel or fancy I feel relief already as summer wanes. One of my doctors thinks much of my head trouble the past three months is from the sun. I am almost always easier as day departs."

Monday, August 27, 1888.

Gave Ferguson order for paper today—seven cent paper: heavy weight for November Boughs, light weight for the "complete" Whitman. Also saw Bilstein about the frontispiece. W. spent another very bad day. When I entered was reading Scott again. He put his book down at once. Looked ill, tired, worn, almost haggard. Threatened to go down stairs today but did not go. "I must make a move—the time has come to make a break." Said to me: "If I don't force myself about some I will eventuate by making this room a prison, and that will be my finish." His niece was in to see him this evening early. Harned dropped in as we talked, leaving us after awhile still busy in our arguments. When H. was about to go W. remarked to him:

"It's been a rum go today, Tom, a rum go: I've had a devil of a time of it—a devil of a useless time of it. I've felt brighter since you fellows came in than in all the rest of the day put together: you have cheered me up. I'm like a candle, whose flame is up and down, varying continually, never the same: that candle— that's me."

He spoke of a Bucke letter. "Doctor is absorbed in Willie Gurd's meter—it possesses him body and soul. Even the Leaves must be set aside for this machine. I guess he has a good heap of money put away in it—far away, I'd bet: so far away it'll never be got back, I'm afraid: but Doctor is very optimistic: he sees it all come home to roost with millions added to enrich the nest: God help us! Well, I don't wish Maurice any harm—and I don't wish him any money, either." Talked some about Harned: "Tom is direct—powerfully, unerringly direct— in his work in the law, I should guess. It is a Sir Matthew Hale quality: I have cited it in writing of Hicks—Elias Hicks. It is of supreme importance—perhaps the greatest faculty of all— productive of signal results: a corkscrew certainty of brain, of spirit, going this fashion"—indicating—"through all distractions to the core, to foundations, to roots. What a pity all lawyers, judges, priests (especially priests) did not have it in past ages: how much sorrow would have been saved the world!"

I said to W.: "I didn't write to Burroughs today: I didn't know what to tell him about Arnold." W. laughed. "About me, you mean? My notion of Arnold—of John's paper? Well, what can I say? It has been some time (didn't you say June?) since it appeared. I read it then but have no definite idea of the impression it made upon me." "I remember: I remember that you seemed more occupied with the fact that you differed with Burroughs than with the other merits of the piece." "That is quite possible—no doubt true: I can never bring myself to applaud Arnold. Arnold has his pet word, adopted from the German: Philistine: a word I should apply to him above all others: and a Philistine of that sort I cannot accept, affiliate with. John himself, in spite of himself, has been touched a bit

15

with the frost of the literary clique in New York: Stoddard, Winter, Fawcett, God knows who—the whole crew." I broke in: "But he's not one of 'em!" "No—no indeed: not one of 'em: one *not* of 'em—but touched, touched, bitten: touched as Dowden is in England: the noble, good Dowden, superb as he is in instinct and equipment. John's preeminent features are good nature, good humor, eligibility for friendship: he proposes to include everybody, to accept the meanest creature in the tribe, to draw no lines: he in fact is for the *ensemble:* John's world would have no outcasts." "Yes," I said, "nor would your world—that kind of a Burroughs is Walt Whitman, too." "True: true!—that's me, too: but I am not good natured: no: no: not at all as good and kind as John: I get riled—a fellow like Arnold stirs me up. I accept the world—most of the world—but somehow draw the line somewhere on some of those fellows. John detects in me primarily the lessons of comradeship, the comrade spirit: is drawn to that, sees that as the vitalizing spinal force."

I showed W. an autograph note written by Wendell Phillips to C. C. Burleigh, given to me by the latter's son. "I have heard Burleigh speak," said W., taking off his glasses: "The whole Burleigh family was noble: C. C. was a powerful speaker: he was a grand looking as well as a grand spoken man: most impressive in build and demeanor. In those days I frequented the anti-slavery halls, in New York—heard many of their speakers—people of all qualities, styles—always interesting, always suggestive. It was there I heard Fanny Wright: the noblest Roman of them all, though not of them, except for a time: a woman of the noblest make-up whose orbit was a great deal larger than theirs—too large to be tolerated for long by them: a most maligned, lied-about character—one of the best in history though also one of the least understood. She had a varied career here and in France—married a damned scoundrel, lost her fortune, faced the world with her usual courage. Her crowning sorrow was when the infernal whelp who had been her husband tried in France, through the aid of a priest, to take from her her daughter, charging that the child needed to be protected from the danger of her mother's infidelistic teachings. Think of it! And this time it was a priest not a woman who was at the bottom of the villainy. They say, somebody says, almost everybody says, there's a woman at the bottom of everything. That's the half truth: the whole truth is that there's a man always back of the woman. The scoundrel, through the aid of the French law, which is of all law probably the least favorable to women, got nearly her whole fortune, perhaps the whole of it, so that at the last, when she needed five thousand dollars or so, she had to beg it of him, he even then making the concession reluctantly. But my remembrance of her all centers about New York. She spoke in the old Tammany Hall there, every Sunday, about all sorts of reforms. Her views were very broad—she touched the widest range of themes—spoke informally, colloquially. She published while there the Free Inquirer, which my daddy took and I often read. She has always been to me one of the sweetest of sweet memories: we all loved her: fell down before her: her very appearance seemed to enthrall us. I had a picture of her about here—it is probably somewhere in the house still: a sitting figure—graceful, deer-like: and her countenance! oh! it was very serene. Her hair was put up in the old style, high at the back, so"—gesturing. "You don't know Mary Smith—Mrs. Costelloe?—well, if you could know her, meet her, you might in a general way see Fanny Wright as she always comes back to me." "Did she write anything, Walt?" asked Harned. "Oh, yes! one little book I remember well—a little pamphlet, a mere whiffet for size but sparkling with life: Ten Days in Athens it was called." I said: "Morse gave it to me and said he had given away hundreds of copies." "Did Morse say that to you? Good for Morse! I have myself given some copies around in places where I thought they would do the most good. The book is not great but it is interesting, even fascinating—written, I think, in her eighteenth year—immature, perhaps, crude, but strong."

Harned got up, said good bye to W. and left. W. then went right on with the same line of reminiscence, which seemed of intense interest to him, as it was to me. "I swore when I was a young man that I would sometime—I could not say when but as the opportunity appeared—do public justice to three people—three of the superber characters of my day or America's early days who were either much maligned or much misunderstood. One of them was Thomas Paine: Paine, the chiefest of these: the other two were Elias Hicks and Fanny Wright. I determined that I would bear witness to them—true witness where the great majority have borne false witness—in thick and thin, come what might to me. Some years ago I put in a word for Paine—appeared on the Liberal League platform up town, in Philadelphia—you will find what I said in the Collect of Specimen Days—holding forth, so to speak: talking right out in I think unmistakable words the conviction that had for so long beset me. Now, in our new book, I try in my Hicks to confirm another item of my triple oath. Fanny Wright yet remains: God knows whether I'll ever get to her! If I ever get back to anything like or that seems like strength I shall do for Fanny Wright what I have done for the others—that and more, too, if need be. If a Fanny Wright afternoon or evening should be arranged for anywhere by any group of people who know enough to celebrate her I must try to be about to say my say, even if I must drag myself on my half dead legs to the spot—to put in such full measure of tribute as I know ever, forever, is due to her from me. The Paine piece was very small—written diminuendo, I am aware—yet is choked, brimfull, of such feeling as the moment, the man, the old cherished associations, invoked. The boys over in New York in the Bowery used to have a handsome idiom—'Little, but O hell!' Ain't that richer than the mint? I hope if my Paine piece is little it's also O hell."

W. asked me: "What do you think, Horace—is a preface necessary?—I mean, for the big book?" "Perhaps not necessary but you would make it seem so." "You are a flatterer. I have thought no, I have thought yes: today I have been thinking yes extra strong. But whatever it is, it must be very short: perhaps a bare statement of the purpose, design, of the book (has it a purpose or design?)—then a full stop—would be the best thing to meet the case. My hesitations make me think of a story. The captain of a baseball nine was to be presented with a silver pitcher. The spokesman for the Club had a fine speech written and rehearsed—the captain ditto. The day arrived, the crowd was there, but the program didn't go through. Both the stars of the occasion forgot their speeches: they flustered about, wondering what to do—then finally retreated to first causes, to their simple human nature—the spokesman exclaiming: 'Captain, here's the pitcher!' and the captain exclaiming in reply: 'Is *that* the pitcher?' So the affair was a success after all, though not according to the rule set. I guess I'll have to model my preface on that incident—and if the preface is half as successful as the incident I'll be satisfied. 'Captain, here's the preface!' 'Is *that* the preface?' We want to get the pitcher into the right hands—that's the whole object."

W. is as he says "still mystified by the Fowler portrait and its superscription. I must have been hypnotically handled by somebody." In objecting to a line of type at the foot of the frontispiece portrait W. says: "I don't know why but I know I don't like it. I don't know what I want but I do know what I don't want. I know my game always when I see it but I do not always know how to drive it up a tree. Use your own taste—that's the best way—and when your taste is my taste (for it often enough is, don't you think, Horace?) I'll yell for you to anchor. I resign all this detail to you, to do with it what you can. You will hear from me loud and hard if you fail me but I don't think you will fail me. I have a *sense* of things that seems to precede all judgments—a something or other that does not immediately explain itself but likes, dislikes, not being able to say why. It's the Quaker in me—in me strong here and there."

Though looking bad enough W's. whole talk this evening was vigorous and inspiring. His voice was at times weak. Mary Davis said to me: "You seem to have waked Mr. Whitman up. He was dull enough all day. Miss Jessie came in in the very early evening. She is a bright girl—she, too, cheered him. I have never known him to be more silent than today." Talked some about a Roden Noel portrait which he produced from a pile of papers on the table. "It is Byronic in the extreme: do we not understand that he is somehow of the Byron stock? It is feminine, too—not weakly so, but feminine. Noel hates to have us reckon up our assets without counting him in: you remember how he kicked? He is a virile sort of fellow, too, if I may get a shy in on him through his letters. I gave you a volume of his poems once but you have never told me how they hit you—or if they hit you at all." W. also said, handing me a sheet of paper: "You might put this with the Linton letter I gave you yesterday or day before. I don't know as it's of the least use, but you're so hungry and fussy I feel guilty if I throw the least scrap of paper away without your permission." What he gave me was the draft of one of his own letters.

CAMDEN, Feb. 24 '75.

My dear Linton: I want you to have printed very nicely for me 1000 impressions of the cut, my head, to go into the book. Herewith I send the size of sheet. If convenient I should like to see a proof, fac simile, first.

I am still holding out here—don't get well yet—and don't go under yet.

Love to you—Write immediately on receiving this.

Under the note W. had written: "this sized sheet—print *dark* in color as you think they will stand (I don't like them too weak in color)." W. said: "1875! that was one of my darkest years: I was down, down, down that year: it seemed like a year of surrender. I came out of it—God knows how." Remarked: "You have said nothing of the editorial wish-wash I handed over to you yesterday." I replied: "I haven't come to it yet— I'm getting behind in some things." W. laughed: "I'm in no hurry: anytime or never, it's all one to me."

Tuesday, August 28, 1888.

Two men came in at night-fall—one a Philadelphian, the other a Rev. Andrews, of Belfast, Ireland. W. consented to see them though when they arrived up stairs not inviting them to be seated or talking with them as if he wished them to stay. He was eating his supper at the time. Andrews complimented him—spoke of objections "among the cloth" in England to L. of G.—assured W. that for his part W's. work was unexceptionable: W. saying concerning it all: "They do not seem to comprehend that we are all God's creatures"—but saying little more, he himself finally terminating the conference by pushing out his fist and bidding them good night. A little later W. had another visitor, a Camden printer, who had named his son "Walt Whitman so and so," as W. said. They talked a little but W. could not stand it. "Too much goes a good ways towards satisfying me," he said to me amusingly, describing the incident. "I feel such a strange lethargy—am utterly fagged out—am on the dizzy edge of things today."

Had for him a proof of revised frontispiece page. His face lighted up. "That is right now—right at last"—nodding to me: "Horace, you know just what I want and do in such things: do it: do it just as if it was your own to do." Was in too bad shape today to touch the preface. Read some. "But even reading is difficult." He picks his book up, opens it, puts on his glasses, reads a bit, then suddenly lays his book down again on its open face, removes his glasses, drops his head against the back of the chair, and looks out into space. He does this again and again. Yet when I said: "You seem to have a hard time reading," he replied a bit testily: "Who told you that, I'd like to know?" I asked: "But do you?" He nodded: "I will admit something of that kind but not much."

Bucke is still giving W. advice about the big book. W. remarked: "Maurice lives in a small town and sends me a large advice. If I could sell all the advice I get I might retire from the Leaves of Grass business with a competence." We expect Gilchrist in a few days. W. frequently works his way to the bath room: "But it's a damned painful process: my left leg ain't worth shucks any more—I simply have to drag it along." W. handed me Dowden's Shakspere—his Mind and Art with the suggestion that I should read it. It is full of W.'s pencillings and of newspaper clippings pinned in—but few comments. "That is the sort of book that seems to have funded all the particular, essential, information in its own specialty: a world book in the sense of being rounded, completed, self-sufficient. Dowden could challenge all comers in his own line—no one would dare take him up." Then he stopped, adding, however, after my "I like to hear you say that," "I like to say it, too—it is only the truth. It's the finest thing in the world to be able to do justice to some study—do it whole justice—not exactly exhaust it (that is impossible) but to treat it with a sort of final comprehensiveness, dignity. Dowden has done that much in his book: I do not hesitate to say, in his memorable book. You can see from the thumb marks and other marks in the book how I have practically demonstrated my faith."

We talked a little about the editorial letters he gave me a few days ago. "You have said things now and then about the editors which are not borne out by their letters." He asked: "What things?" "You have talked as if they uniformly turned you down. There are quite as many acceptances as refusals in this budget." He answered: "Are there? Then that is an unusual budget. I suppose I have destroyed the most of the letters that came back with my poems. I was more likely to keep the pleasant than the unpleasant letters. I shouldn't wonder if it proved true that you have in that batch of letters and in a few others I have already given you about all the blessings that have ever come to me by way of editorial correspondence. There is some Galaxy stuff still coming to you: I can't just now just put my hand on it." He complained of his head. I got up to go. He protested: "Before you do so, read me a letter or two for example——." I laughed. "You know them all. Why should I worry you with them over again." But he still said: "Read a few: I want to have my memory refreshed." I read five letters before he stopped me. Several times he asked me to reread a sentence.

FIELDS, OSGOOD & COMPANY,
BOSTON, December 14, 1868.

WALT WHITMAN.

Dear Sir:—In order that your poem shall go into the February number of the Atlantic, it is impossible to risk the time it would take to get the proof to Washington and back, So I promise you the proof shall be read, word for word, and point for point, with your copy, which being in print, there is no chance for an error.

Yours always,
JAMES T. FIELDS.

OFFICE OF THE NEW YORK CITIZEN.
NEW YORK, Nov. 18, 1867.

WALT WHITMAN.

Dear Sir: Do you remember that I wrote to you asking you if you could not give us a poem, and if so, on what terms?

May I call your attention once more to the matter. We should be very glad to have a poem from you, but I don't know how much the proprietors would authorize me to pay.

When you are in town, if you will call on me, I can show you two ladies—one of them my wife—who appreciate your poetry, as I do.

It is only of late years that I have understood it; and I am now enthusiastic over it.

Very respectfully yours,
W. L. ALDEN.
(Associate Editor).

HARPER & BROTHERS' EDITORIAL ROOMS
NEW YORK, Jan. 3, 1885.

Dear Mr. Whitman, I am unable to use After the Supper and Talk to advantage—though it is very happy in the prelusive connection you would give it in your volume.

With thanks, sincerely yours.
H. M. ALDEN.
Editor Harpers' Magazine.

EDITORIAL DEPARTMENT, THE CENTURY MAGAZINE,
MARION, MASS., Aug 9, 1884.

My dear Mr. Whitman, I am glad you can do the *nursing* article. Thanks for the Father Taylor. Should you not include Emerson in the list of his praisers which you give? We will try to find a photograph from life.

Sincerely,

R. W. GILDER.

NEW YORK TRIBUNE.
NEW YORK, July 10, 1876.

Dear Whitman: I was out of town—returning from the West, from the funeral of a near relative—when your note of the 7th came. We shall try to publish the poem on Monday, and if we get it in shall hope to enclose check herewith for the amount. If it doesn't come with this it will be because of my being compelled to go down to Washington as a witness in the Impeachment trial. If by reason of my absence it should be overlooked, pray remind me of it.

Very truly yours,

WHITELAW REID.

When I had got this far W. said: "Thank you, Horace: thanks, thanks. That's enough for the present. They do sort o' bear you out in what you say." He laughed lightly. "I am a little surprised myself at the favorable nature of the letters," he continued, "for they do certainly say yes, yes, in rather a friendly fashion—all except the one, and that one is not a slap. I do not feel sore when I am refused, but I hate to be pitched out head first without a chance to open the door for myself and go out. Most of the editors, in spite of this exhibit, were dead agin me— some even violently so: I ought to know what I am talking about for I was the one who felt the toes of their boots. There were exceptions—maybe I should have turned this over to you as a batch of exceptions." As W. stopped I read him another of the letters:

WITH WALT WHITMAN IN CAMDEN

OFFICE OF THE ATLANTIC MONTHLY.

BOSTON, Oct. 10, 1861.

Mr. WALT WHITMAN—

BROOKLYN, N. Y.

Dear Sir:—We beg to inclose to your address, in two envelopes, the three poems with which you have favored us, but which we could not possibly use before their interest,—which is of the present,—would have passed. Thanking you for your attention, We are, Very truly yours,

EDITORS OF ATLANTIC MONTHLY.

This envelope was addressed in W's. own hand to "Walt Whitman, Portland Avenue, Brooklyn, N. Y.," and was endorsed: "from Atlantic Monthly declining poems." I asked W.: "What were the poems?" and he answered: "I don't just remember: I do remember that the idea that their interest was of the present struck me as being a bit odd: I always have written with something more than a simply contemporary perspective. But there's no use crying over spilled poems. The ways of editors are like the ways of Providence"—"and the poets," I put in—"past finding out." W. laughed at my interjection and cried: "Now what the hell have you got against the poets?" "Just what you've got against the editors," I answered. "Is that all? I've got nothing against the editors." "I've got nothing against the poets." He had brightened up over our sally: "Then what the devil are we quarreling about, Horace?" He was serious and silent after this for a moment: "Horace, if nations stopped long enough when they are mad to ask themselves that question we would have no wars: do you hear? we would have no wars!" He spoke with great earnestness. "Horace, most of our quarrels start with little things and grow in volume by what they feed upon." I said: "Watch the little things and the big things will take care of themselves." He exclaimed: "That's what I was about to say. Why didn't you wait till I said it? You're getting in the habit of taking the best things right out of my mouth and saying them as if they were your own.

How am I going to shine if your light gets too big?" I reminded him: "I haven't finished with the editors." He nodded: "I know—don't finish tonight: I've gone beyond myself in this talk already: I felt miserable when you arrived—you have stirred me up considerably—brightened me lots—but if I don't stop now I'll have to pay for it to-morrow. Besides, Mr. Musgrove will step in presently and put me to bed with or without my consent, and then——". I said: "I don't believe Musgrove or anybody ever does much with you without your consent." He chuckled a bit: "I don't know—I don't know: though your guess, Horace, ain't half bad either."

Wednesday, August 29, 1888.

Little if any change in W. today. Woke up feeling very bad. By and by remarked: "I seem to see my way out: I guess I'll get through." All day in such a negative condition. "I am like a tree fixed in the ground." When I arrived in the evening he remarked after the "Ah Horace, is that you?" "I continue just where I was, but am irritable, irritable." I objected: "I don't believe it's in you to be irritable: I couldn't connect you with irritability." He returned: "Don't be so sure about that—don't let that notion run away with you: you don't know to what depths of devilishness I may not descend if I get going once." "Yes, but you don't get going." "Maybe I don't—maybe I'm slow to get going, but it's not impossible."

He settled himself comfortably in his chair, put on his glasses (which he had taken off as he laid down the Cosmopolitan he was reading on my entrance) and asked: "Now, what have you got for me? I see you have got something." I handed him proofs. Myrick said today: "I'll try the old man with some new-fangled type-faces." Referring to title page design. W. said: "I have no objections to being tried, especially if I am tried this way and so successfully." We talked over details concerning the contents pages. W. said: "I never know what I want until I see it before my eyes. My mind's eye don't serve me in the printing business."

W. still dissenting from Bucke's views concerning the big book. "Doctor is a little too much inclined to special de luxe editions, which I don't care for at all: exclusive editions, editions for the elite, curios, what not. I have thought to get a hundred printed and bound for my own sales to help me out on the expense account. If I could sell a hundred at ten dollars a copy I'd feel like a pampered darling of fortune—it would be a pretty penny for me. Well, well—let us keep the work moving right on—many of the excited things will calm themselves. I always have great faith in *ends:* we miss a lot as we go along— mix up bad and good and indifferent—but the end is sure—the right end."

Musgrove entered with a letter. W. took it, glanced at it, turned to me: "It's from the Doctor—from Bucke." Then after disposing of other things and reading the note deliberately: "There's nothing in it, nothing striking, and yet it is atmospherically so wholesome. A bunch of them take a trip together —have a good time, eating, talking, cutting up: then they go home again, all the better for a break out of routine." After a pause he said: "Did I tell you that Mrs. Coates and Mr. Coates were in today? Well, they were. I saw them—was glad to see them: both of them are so good, cordial, sincere—she particularly. It does my old eyes good to look at such a woman. They said they had come upon your intimation that they might see me. They talked about the books—she did—but Mr. Coates said: 'I have arranged for all that with Mr. Traubel— we will not trouble Mr. Whitman now.' I have reserved for them the books they want—the Centennial edition."

I told W. I was enjoying Dowden's Shakespere. "So? It is fine—fine indeed: Dowden is flesh and blood. His book gives the common sense view of Shakespeare—gives it powerfully, lucidly, musically. I am myself not altogether satisfied with it—I do not follow or endorse his picture, his conclusions: but I esteem the book for what it possesses—for its own inimitable virtues. Dowden is my friend: he quotes me several times —is always cordial: not wholesale, but loyal. How does Dowden compare with Stedman? He is fuller, ampler, holds more—undoubtedly holds more. Burroughs thinks there is no one like Dowden—thinks he's the greatest of the pack—no one approaching him, no one comparable, no one in sight, not even Rossetti. I am not so sure about Rossetti: I shall never give over Rossetti: he is always capacious, liberal—an inevitably broad-acred sort of a man. Rossetti, too, has always declared for me, stood by me, staunchly asserted my right to my own. And did you notice the printing of the book, Horace? The mere printing is a delight—would be a sufficient charm if there was nothing else. It is so honest—so good for bad eyes, or good ones either. American printing is all gloss, glare: the paper is bad, the ink is anemic—pale in the gills: makes me think of the prettiness of drug stores—the polished bottles, the painful glitter."

I asked: "How about the Book Maker portrait: have you come upon an explanation of it yet?" "No, not a sign of one, not a whisper or a hint. But probably I did that"—pointing to the fac-simile autograph—"in one of my 'moods,' though, however done, it was exceptional—not in my usual manner." He added as to the same matter: "I am not surprised that that thing should have got away from me: my memory cuts up strange capers. I wrote to Lockwood thanking him for the copies I received today but said nothing about our mystery—asked no questions. My memory is not what it was—is quite surely shocked or breaking. Indeed, it performs the most astounding antics. To-day I sent copies of the Book Maker to my sisters, to O'Connor, to Bucke and to Kennedy. When I came to Kennedy I couldn't for all I might do remember his name. I could remember Belmont and Massachusetts but it took me five minutes to get the rest. And yet my memory is perfect for old things—clear about things that happened years ago: is a good deal more at home with my old than with my new history—than with affairs I am mixed with (if I mix with anything) nowadays."

W. had been looking for a book he could not find. "I have

From a Photograph

EDWARD DOWDEN
(1889)

had numbers of books stolen." "Stolen?" "Yes, stolen: my own books, books sent me: stolen from down stairs, from the back room here—almost under my eyes." He stopped to laugh, and he laughed with extra heartiness. "I spoke of the defects of my memory, but bad as they are they are not fatal—some ways my memory's as good as ever. These book thieves are not all unknown: in many and many a case I could name the thief if there was need for it: but though I don't do so and wouldn't, I keep up a devil of a thinking."

Some one has sent him Edward J. McPhelim's *America* critique, in which it is said: "Early in life Whitman met Mr. Beecher, and at the outset of their acquaintanceship asked him: 'How does it make you feel when men swear?' Mr. Beecher replied that it shocked him. That was enough for Whitman. He went back to his rough companions and evidently found nothing uncongenial in their conversation." I laughed and asked W.: "Where did he get that from?" W. tapped his forehead: "Here." Then added: "Some men, authors, think they are born to write articles at all hazards so they write articles—write them for ten, twenty, dollars a page. If they have facts, well and good—if they haven't facts, then so much the worse for the facts. Conway is a brilliant example of that class of men—the most brilliant example. He is always writing, always getting into print: thinks it a duty to write whether there's anything to write about or not. Conway seemed intended for a better fate but some screw got loose in the machinery and the result, though not a dead failure, was not what I call the right sort of success."

W., in speaking of the Emerson-Carlyle correspondence, says: "It seems open to one charge from the critic. All through the book we find Emerson saying to Carlyle: 'You're a good fellow, quite a great fellow,' and so forth, and so forth: and then Carlyle returns the compliment in kind, 'You're another—another,' and so forth, and so forth. It's a little like two masters of fashion trying to outbow each other. That's not all there is to the book but that is there." W. says he is considering whether not to interdict all strangers. "They wear me down—I find I can't stand it: we'll have to put a warning up over the front door." Asked me if I still had the remaining editorial letters in my pocket? "If you have you might go on reading them to me. They remind me of my triumphs and my defeats. I still insist that I have had more editorial battles on my list lost than won. But read."

EDITORIAL DEPARTMENT THE CENTURY MAGAZINE,
NEW YORK, July 12, 1884.

WALT WHITMAN, ESQ.,

My dear Sir: We are making preparations for a notable series of papers on the Battles of the War to be written by participants—general officers—including Grant, McClellan, Rosecrans, Beauregard, Longstreet, Joe Johnson and others. These we desire to supplement by short pithy papers on different phases of the War. At Mr. Gilder's request I write to ask if you would not write us a short, comprehensive paper on Hospital Nursing in Washington and on the field—something human and vivid. We should like about four thousand words.

The object of the supplementary papers is to give the life, the spirit, the color, of the War, which may be left out by the generals.

Of course we should like the paper to cover different ground from what you have before written if possible—at least to cover it in a different way.

Yours sincerely,
R. U. JOHNSON.

After reading this I waited for W. to say something, but he was silent, except to exclaim: "Go on—go on: let's hear them all!" So I proceeded.

HARPER & BROTHERS' EDITORIAL ROOMS.
NEW YORK, Oct. 22, 1884.

Dear Mr. Whitman: Please find enclosed Messrs Harper & Brothers' cheque for thirty dollars in payment for your poem

Of That Blithe Throat of Thine. And you have the Messrs
Harpers' permission to use the poem in a collection of your
poems six months (or later) after our publication.

With thanks, sincerely yours,

H. M. ALDEN.

EDITOR OF HARPERS' MAGAZINE.

"That thirty dollars," said W., "I remember quite well,
because Harry Bonsall was here when it arrived and as I flour-
ished it in the air said to me: 'I'd write bad poems myself Walt
if I could get anybody to pay me thirty dollars apiece for 'em.'"
The next letter was headed by a red ink question in W's hand:
"send something?" It was written on the stationery of the
Dublin University Magazine.

LONDON, April 23, 1877.

WALT WHITMAN, ESQ.

Dear Sir:—I have been reading aloud your Whispers of Heavenly Death this evening from the copy which you so kindly sent
me in March, 1876: and it has led me on to ask if you have any
poems still unpublished in the same vein of mystic realism. And
if so, could you spare me one or two for the Magazine which I
represent? I am sorry that but a trifle could be offered for them,
as the Magazine has been neglected of late, and has only recently
come into my hands, to be worked up again by labor and patience.

I trust you are as well as you expect to be and nearly as happy
as you hope.

Yours faithfully,

KENNINGALE COOK.

"Mystic realism" struck W. He said: "Now and then we
get a whole something or other packed tight and sure in a word
or two." I said: "That, again, don't look much like being
kicked out." And as I read the next: "Nor this, either."

219

ONCE A WEEK.

NEW YORK, 30 July, 1887.

Dear Sir. Will you be so good as to let me know if you would be willing to honor us with a contribution for Once A Week and what your terms would be?

Yours faithfully,

NUGENT ROBINSON,

EDITOR.

"Why, he even says 'honor us!' It seems to me these fellows instead of kicking you out went out on the sidewalk and helped you in." W. retorted: "You do well to say 'these fellows:' but what about all the other fellows who did the kicking? Maybe you'd like to hear about them?" "I have heard: you have told me: but this bunch of autocrats seem to me to have handled you in a very mild spirit." Now he laughed. "Damn you, you are determined to have it your way! Go on with the letters and don't say so much!" Next I read another Alden letter, remarking as I did so: "Better and more of it." "Better what?" he asked. "Better courtesy, patronage, good will."

HARPER & BROTHERS' EDITORIAL ROOMS.

NEW YORK, Nov. 30, 1883.

Dear Mr. Whitman, Please find enclosed Messers Harper & Brothers' cheque for fifty dollars in payment for your poem, With Husky-Haughty Lips O Sea!

With thanks and best wishes for your health and holiday cheer.

Sincerely yours,

HENRY M. ALDEN,

EDITOR HARPERS' MAGAZINE.

I still jollied W. "When you gave me this collection of letters the other day I thought from what you said that it was a bunch of sticks. Instead of that it is a bunch of roses." He had at first been just a bit nettled by my comments on these letters but this broke down his dignity. He nodded to me: "It certainly does look bad for my growl, to have all this evidence against it. But it just happens that I have saved the approving letters and thrown the disapproving letters away. If I had saved all my correspondence with editors you would at once see what I meant by my original remark—how that remark was justified by the facts." I desisted from further reading. There were three or four letters left but there didn't seem to be much of him left. I helped him over to the bed. "Have I stayed too long?" "No— it's not that—I am just as apt to get this way without you here as with you here. Besides, there are things we must do together even if we must fight for our lives in getting 'em done." I kissed him good night and started off. I was already in the hallway when I heard him cry: "Horace! Horace!" I hurried back. "I almost forgot," he exclaimed: "you'll find on the table over there a couple of open letters in purple ink. They are Trowbridge letters. You remember, you asked about his letters. There are more here but the two I have laid out there will give you a pretty good idea of the length and breadth and heat of his adhesion to me in my unfashionable days."

Thursday, August 30, 1888.

Received today at office basket of pears from John Burroughs, taking some over to Camden with me in the evening. When I entered W's. room with the burden on my shoulder he laid down his book and looked at me in astonishment. "What in the world have you got there?" he cried: and when I had explained he added: "Ah! so you brought it over—all the way over and by yourself, too?" I set the basket on the floor in front of him. "How good of John! And will you write to him? Yes, do so— and give him my love: tell him I sit here simmering, tallying things as they go, but lame, useless, perhaps not to get about again at all." He spoke calmly but freely about his condition. "I am only so-so—I gain no strength, and, I may say, no heart —lose heart, in fact. I doubt if I shall ever get out of this mess —I am more and more doubtful: it seems to me I am here for a life sentence—here in my prison, as I call it." To Mary Davis he said: "I guess my ship wont sail no more," and to me in conclusion: "It looks as if I'd go on in about this way to the end."

Every time he gets in such a mood about his condition he urges that we hurry our work. Did so this evening. Instead of saying, "let's take our time—time is plenty," he says, "our time may be very short—who knows how short?" and so: "Push everything along with vigor." I showed him samples of paper. He chose one. "I like it—like its feel, like its look: order that. I will give you a check for it any day you say so. One thing more: see that the frontispiece plate is printed. I do not want anything my fault to interfere with your progress. When I'm in the road throw me out—I empower you to throw me out." Bucke wrote him a cheery letter day before yesterday advising him to move down stairs, live in sight of events, go riding occasionally, and so forth. But W. said: "I know better than any others can what I should do, what I care to do. At present I have no desire for change of any sort." Approved of Myrick's title page. "I generally find that if I start by liking a thing I am eventually satisfied with it and let it go." Had read Contents pages today. Reduced the size of "Walt Whitman" on the title. "It's unusual for me to put it on at all but the publishers insist on it—Dave McKay in particular—saying that it secures readers, arrests attention. It never quite approves itself to my eye but I yield. You know, Horace, that I am of a pliable disposition. You do know, don't you?" He stopped to laugh at the idea. As to the big book, he is asking himself if it may not need a special title. "If one pops up I'll nail it—use it —but I won't go looking for it." "I had from Australia today," he said, "a little book (there it is—you have your hand on it now)—a peculiar book: a book of poems, labor poems, written by an anarchist or some such fellow." "Have you read it?" "No—not at all: I rarely read literature of the sort. This man is affectionate: look at his inscription." This was the inscription:

"To Walt Whitman,—to the poet of the first generation of Democracy, to the noble pioneer of a true Civilization, to the splendid singer of the health and freedom of man,—with admiration, affection, reverence."

"The author's name is Adams—Francis Adams," added W. "and the book is called Songs of the Army of the Night. You ought to take the book along with you, Horace: it's more in your line than mine. They all think I am theirs—theirs alone. My own instinct is to avoid books of that nature: they never attracted me: nowadays, when I am almost like a closed bank account, I find them absolutely impossible. You will like to see this particular book: I looked at it enough to see that it is superior in its class: you may even read it: you are so anxious to keep up with everything that's going on—to see what the fellows, all the odds and ends of the fellows, in the world are about."

I gave him a little portrait of myself. "I shall like to have it right here where I can put my hands on it—and my eyes." Then he got back into business again. "I shall send to Washington for the copyright. We need two title pages for that. Then we need title pages for your set and Bucke's and my own, and contents for all. I trust all to you—I am always expecting that you will keep tabs on everything going on in our business together whether I speak of it or not. When the plate printer gets his work done take the sheets to Oldach, as you suggest: I have about fully decided to adopt him: I know about him—like his work." Had he gone over the plate proofs thoroughly? "Not thoroughly, nor do I feel that I shall or ought. It looks bad for you, Horace—as if you'd have to do that part of the job without my assistance." Asked him for an order upon Sherman for the plates of L. of G. to be delivered to Ferguson. "Yes— I'll write you the order: and another thing, Horace"—here he removed his glasses and closed his eyes: "There are still a few slips in Leaves of Grass in spite of all my vigilance and these I shall give you a list of so that they may be looked to in this edition." Wishes me to get him "twenty or more—though not many more" impressions from the frontispiece plate on "extra good paper:" "I have a number of friends I want to send copies to." Told him I enjoyed the Trowbridge letters very much. "So they struck you forcibly, did they? That's the way they struck me at the time." I asked in mock seriousness: "Why don't you say that Trowbridge, too, kicked you out?" He was amused. "You have a long memory Horace—an uncomfortable memory. Don't it hurt you sometimes?" It was my turn to laugh. "I don't know what about that. It's hurting you just now." Still good natured W. said: "Anyhow, the Trowbridge letters are all right, don't you think? Trowbridge is not a master-force in literature but he has mined a lot in honest ground and brought out some real metal." I read the letters aloud at W.'s request.

ARLINGTON, MASS.
Apr. 3rd, 1875.

My dear friend, I think I have all of your books (2 or 3 editions of some) except the last,—specified in my former note,—which alone I had intended to ask for. That might be sent by mail. I write this because on your card you speak of sending me books, and because I really desire only one.

I still go back occasionally to the old Leaves of Grass and find in them the same unfailing freshness and power which repeated readings in no wise dull to the sense—a test which only master strokes in literature can stand. They seem very great to me. I am thankful for them.

Faithfully yours,
J. T. TROWBRIDGE.

ARLINGTON, MASS.
Dec. 2, 1877.

Dear Friend Whitman, By the time you get this I suppose you will have received The Book of Eden which I have ordered for you from the publishing house. I think you will find some things in it that will interest you.

I have heard nothing from the projected bust of you for a long while. The last time I saw it, nearly a year ago, it had quite lost headway. I hope, however, that Morse will take a new departure and finally succeed.

I see that somebody has stepped forward to "defend" you (in a mild way) in the Contributors' Club of the last Atlantic. I am astonished that these latter-day critics should have so little to say of the first Leaves of Grass, or venture to speak of them only apologetically. They still stand to me as the most powerful prophetic utterances in modern literature.

I have now two dear little girls, and we are all pretty well. I trust you are comfortable.

J. T. TROWBRIDGE.

W. said: "Trowbridge was one of the early comers and long stayers, always loved and welcomed. I have had some friends of a secondary character—friends with ifs and buts to be satisfied before they would swear to an allegiance. Trowbridge came with a few others by a straight road. You notice what he says of the first edition. Do you know, I think almost all the fellows who came first like the first edition above all others. Yet the last edition is as necessary to my scheme as the first edition: no one could be superior to another because all are of equal importance in the fulfilment of the design. Yet I think I know what Trowbridge means, too: I do not consider his position unreasonable: there was an immediateness in the 1855 edition, an incisive directness, that was perhaps not repeated in any section of poems afterwards added to the book: a hot, unqualifying temper, an insulting arrogance (to use a few strong words) that would not have been as natural to the periods that followed. We miss that ecstasy of statement in some of the after-work— miss that and get something different, something in some ways undoubtedly better. But what's the use arguing an unarguable question? It either is or isn't and that's the end on't." I called W's. attention to the fact that I had not read all the editorial letters last night. Should I go on with them? "Still harping on my daughter! Yes, go on. But, say, Horace, ain't you nearly done with 'em? I had no idea the story had so many chapters when I handed it over to you." I read.

HARPER & BROTHERS' EDITORIAL ROOMS.
NEW YORK, Sept. 20, 1886.

Dear Mr. Whitman, I am unable to avail myself of your War Memoranda, which I herewith return. The Century Magazine has so strongly occupied this field that we do not wish to enter upon it.

With thanks, sincerely yours,
H. M. ALDEN,
EDITOR HARPERS' MAGAZINE.

"See," said W., "there's a kick: don't you call that a kick?" "If it's a kick it's a sort of kick that don't hurt." He said again: "I suppose I'm thin-skinned too, sometimes: I never get it quite clear in my old head that I am not popular and if editors have any use for me at all it can only be among the minor figures of interest. I do not rank high in market valuations—at the best I am only received on sufferance: I have not yet really got beyond the trial stage."

THE NORTH AMERICAN REVIEW.
NEW YORK, Oct. 5, 1886.

My dear Friend: The syndicate is dissolved. Mr. Rice furnishes articles for the Star only. The price of your article puts it outside of any possible use for it in that paper, as the highest price is ten dollars per thousand. Just wait a few days, however, and I will read it and see if it will not do for the North American. Your Burns article will be, I expect, in the November number.

Very truly yours,
JAMES REDPATH.

"Redpath? yes, Redpath was always partial to me—even went out of his way to curl my hair. He jumped in several times and saved me from bankruptcy—steered things my way that might have gone anywhere: interceded for me, with Rice for instance, often, I suspect, at some cost to himself. O'Connor used to say to me: 'I can count your real friends in America, Walt, on my fingers and toes: Burroughs, Redpath—and so he would go on: I noticed he always included Redpath." I read W. another letter.

THE SATURDAY UNION.
LYNN, MASS., May 26, 1884

MR. WALT WHITMAN:

Dear Sir. I send you with this letter two copies of our paper, both containing notices of your poems. Permit me to thank you warmly for the great inspiration I have received from the reading of Leaves of Grass. In my opinion it makes a new era in American Literature, and is to stand out more and more prominently, as time advances, as the distinctively American book.

Most respectfully,
S. W. Foss.

I asked W.: "Who is Foss?" He answered: "I don't know— a writer, they tell me: writes prose, poetry: I don't seem to have come to close quarters with his work." Then after a pause: "Now let me see, maybe I wrote him—maybe I do know more than that about him: I have, I think, read a few little poems with his name attached—quaint, semi-humorous poems: or do I still get him mixed with somebody else?" I said: "He makes a big claim for you." "Yes, so he does—but will anybody believe him? When I say such things about myself the world looks on and calls me crazy!" He seemed to be a good bit amused with his own fancy, adding: "Time was when I had to say big things about myself in order to be honest with the world—in order to keep in a good frame of mind until the world caught up. A man has sometimes to whistle very loud to keep a stiff upper lip." "When the cries and the silences are all against him?" "Yes— then: the cries and silences: that's just it." I said: "There are a couple of letters left." He looked at his watch—threw up his hand in protest. "No more editors to-night: another time, any time, to-morrow: no more to-night."

Friday, August 31, 1888.

In at Ferguson's today and Bilstein's. Received second proof of title and contents pages, W. expressing himself at once as completely satisfied with both. W. said: "Did you notice what Bucke said about you in that letter yesterday?" "What did he say?" "He said: 'H. is first-class.' I say so too. So now, ain't you some proud of yourself?" Gave me another letter from Bucke, dated London 29th. "He has heard from O'Connor. Read what he says of William." Bucke had written: "I had a letter today from O'Connor. He seems wonderfully bright and lively considering. His letter was all about you and Donnelly. He sticks to you like a grand fellow as he is." W. repeated the phrase: "Like a grand fellow as he is." "Yes! yes! that and more: like a grandest fellow as he is: words are so weak and William is so strong!" Bucke had also written: "I have been thinking over the Riddle Song and have made up my mind that the answer is 'good cause' or 'old cause' or some other words meaning about the same thing.—?——." W. took the letter from me and put his finger down on Bucke's question mark. "Doctor has guessed—thinks he has guessed right. I wonder? I wonder?" I waited for him to say more. "Do you want me to answer him?" I asked. "Yes answer him: but answer him for yourself—don't answer him for me." "Will *you* answer the question?" "Do I ever answer questions?" He laughed quietly. "Horace, I made the puzzle: it's not my business to solve it. Doctor says he has the right answer—well, that ought to satisfy him—the right answer ought to satisfy him." I saw W. was determined to maintain his silence in the matter and said no more. People have often asked him the meaning of the poem There was a Child went Forth and he has always made the same answer: "What is the meaning? I wonder what? I wonder what?" Once he said to Bonsall: "Harry, maybe it has no meaning."

W. went down stairs today for the first time—was there half an hour. "The trip down was harder than the trip up," he explained: "Things are much the same though I miss the litter in the parlor." Mrs Davis had told me of this before I saw W. In W's room I said at once: "I hear you have made a trip to Europe today." He did not at first comprehend—simply looked doubtfully at me: then suddenly his whole face lighted up. "To Europe? yes: down stairs: I did go, I made a venture. Don't you think I was a brave man to undertake such a journey?" "You must be feeling considerable better." "No—I am not: not at all better. But I wanted something down there and thought I would start off on my own hook and get it. Besides, I ought to move about some, ought to walk, must not get fixed in the chair and bed habit, which will soon turn me into a useless invalid. Mary looked scared—I don't believe she is over it yet." What he was looking for down stairs was Symonds' Greek Literature and a copy of Marcus Aurelius. "I wrote Burroughs a postcard," he remarked: "a few words only." I asked him if he contemplated making his quarters down stairs, as Bucke suggested. "I contemplate nothing: I would be a poor one to contemplate: I drift, drift: there's nothing else left me to do."

I told W. I had sent McPhelim's America piece off to Bucke. "Ah! good! But what a mess it is! There are a thousand and one gnats, mosquitoes, camp-followers, hanging about the literary army, and each of 'em thinks he must have a fling at Walt Whitman. They know nothing about him—maylike never read or even looked at his book—but that's no matter: that, in fact, seems to be taken as a special qualification for their carpings and crowings. Walt Whitman is a rowdy, rough—likes common people: is apt to write about indecent, indelicate, things—is odd, dresses informally: they all tell you that, get hold of that—then are done for." McPhelim seems to have an idea that Charles O'Connor and our William O'Connor are the same person. "I was glad to see a little notice of November Boughs," said W., "in the American Stationer: a little, not a big, notice. Take the paper along—see what you can make of it. I always find something to interest me in trade papers. A man goes out of town for six months and when he returns half a dozen new inventions have come and revolutionized his profession."

Still talks of free trade. "Well, I don't promise myself much for this year but I know the baby is born who will strangle this monster. The mass of the people will finally get it rammed into their heads what an infernal humbug the 'American System' is. The man who thinks the free traders do not know what they are about had better keep on thinking—may make a better guess second time: had better take it all out in thinking now: for soon his time will come and there will be no ground left for him to stand on. I have heard it said that reason comes with the forties. I should say as to most men, that reason does not come even then—does not come at all—for I am impressed with the general lack of it."

What is the place of sickness in character? W. asked himself that question. "They speak of Emerson as being sickly, weak, ailing: all biographies repeat the statement: I guess there is something to it. But, do you know, I never think of Emerson as a sick man. I met him twenty and more times: he was always lithe, active, of good complexion, with a clear eye: gave out no notion of dubious health—was physically jubilant, in a quiet way, as was like him. Indeed, Emerson was almost impatient of sickness—was bright, wonderfully bright, to the very last. Why, I can recall the occasion of our last meeting: it was there at Concord: it was the final visit: he was still possessed of the same imperturbable courage. I was reading the correspondence today—and fine it is, too. All the letters were prepared letters—designed, mulled over, worked out and out. Letters were events in those days. There's something peculiar in my notion about this book. I can read with perfect composure Emerson's soft-soaping of Carlyle, but when Carlyle enters into a sort of responding mood of laudation I am mad—find it artificial. Can you explain that? I can't." I said: "Morse prefers the Carlyle letters." "I do not: I always have liked Emerson's letters—they are not formal, they seem just right to be his."

After a pause W. added: "I think Burroughs has written some of the best things about Carlyle. And now, while I'm upon that, let me say: the next time you write Burroughs add this to your letter: 'Walt Whitman advises that you gather together all you have ever written about Carlyle—essays, scraps, notes—and print them in a little volume, booklet, so they may be preserved.' Burroughs' espousal of Carlyle is a queer thing, too, taken one way, though I have always upheld his hands in that—always unequivocally endorsed it. It was not strange that I, for instance, should have found friends in England—should have attracted Mrs. Gilchrist, for one: not strange that I should have attracted any one person: but it is significant that that one person should be a woman, in the first place, and then a woman marked for culture, refinement, scholarship. I have a similar feeling of wonder when I remember that Carlyle's most significant living adherent in America should be a man like John: a scholar, concrete—all of him concrete: materialistic (using that word with its broadest amplifications) to a degree. It is curious about Carlyle, too, that his friends here have been our staunchest Americans—in spite of his mean flings, our best democrats—among whom I hope I deserve to be counted."

W. reminded me of my remark last night that I had a couple of editorial letters still left unread. "Why not read them now," he said, "and be done with 'em?" I replied: "Maybe you would rather not hear them read: they might hurt your feelings." He answered, with a laugh: "I suppose you mean by that that they're both favorable letters?" "Exactly." He was grave for a moment. Then he said: "You seem to have been right about that particular collection of letters—they happened to be in the main or wholly of a pleasant nature: but you may believe me when I say I can more than match 'em with others not only politely haughty but often offensively and vituperatively inimical. An editor wrote me: 'How dare you, Walt Whitman,' and so forth: and another said in an effort to be funny: 'Your poem was submitted to the editor of our joke department but he said he could not see the humor of it so with regrets we return it to

you.'" After W. had somewhat gravely quoted his second incident he added: "Though you won't call that insulting, of
course." I said: "I confess I am not inclined to take it seriously." W. further said before I read the letters: "There was
a New York editor who wrote and assured me that though he
could not get interested in my poems he was sure that if I would
submit some of my short stories to him we could do some business together." "Had you sent the poems?" "No—but he was
afraid I would." Now I read the letters.

THE NORTH AMERICAN REVIEW,
NEW YORK CITY, Oct. 20, 1885.

Dear Mr. Whitman: Enclosed please find a check for fifty
dollars for the article in the November number of the North
American Review on Slang in America. This is the very
highest rate that is paid for contributions, and exactly double
what is paid for nine-tenths of the articles that appear in it. I
trust it is satisfactory. When will you have your article on
Lincoln ready? Mr. Rice is quite impatient for it. If any
question of pay stands in the way won't you please state what
you will ask for it, and then I shall have the matter off my mind.
I wish you would answer this letter today, as I am about to
start on a two weeks' trip to the West.

Yours very truly,
JAMES REDPATH.

MAGAZINE OF ART,
LONDON, E. C., Nov. 30, 1887.

WALT WHITMAN, ESQ.,

Sir, Having added the editorship of this magazine to my duties
on the Pall Mall Gazette my thoughts at once turned to you, in
the hope that you would let me have a poem for publication in
this very widely circulated serial.

Will you have the kindness to inform me if you have such a
poem by you—not too long—and unpublished, of course—and,

preferably, one which would lend itself to illustration? And also on what terms you would let me have such a poem? And, if you haven't this, if you would write one?

I send a copy of the magazine herewith for you to judge of.

Awaiting the favor of your reply, and in the hope that your health is in a satisfactory condition,

I am, Sir, Faithfully yours,

M. H. SPIELMANN,

EDITOR.

As I concluded reading I exclaimed: "Well, Walt, this was not a frost—it was an ovation." How heartily he laughed! "So it was—so it was: I must have put my hand on the wrong bundle when I turned those letters over to you for opposition votes. Horace, I hereby apologize to the bundle! Look at Redpath's letter, anyhow: he paid me 'the very highest rate.' Why, that looks almost like popularity, prosperity! You see, however, that I survived all the letters without a fortune. I answered the Spielmann letter by sending the Twenty Years poem which has just appeared. What stuff of bodies and souls history is made of, Horace! What troubles, labors, doubts, as well as what joys, satisfactions, triumphs! No story is complete without the slaps as well as the kisses."

W. had been reading in a paper about a big free trade meeting in New York addressed by Henry George and William Lloyd Garrison. "I wish you would hunt me up a good report. That man Garrison seems like 'a worth while son to a worth while father,' as you so well said the other day talking of our own Charley Garrison. Sons of the big men are rarely big: it would be curious if William Lloyd Garrison two should get as famous as Garrison one, but I don't expect it. Look at the younger Henry James—I don't see anything above common in him: he has a vogue—but surely his vogue won't last: he don't stand permanently for anything. The elder James must have been quite a man: I know several of his companions: they held him in high esteem. And he had an opinion about me, too."

"Was it a good one?" "No—sharp, discouraging. I had a friend up there—a woman friend—who knew him well and often talked with him about authors—sometimes about me. Her great claim for Walt Whitman was that he asserted virility, health, but James used to say to her as to that: 'That's just the trouble: no man can be a great poet who has not known sickness, disease,' and so on. I was always impressed with the idea—it hit me powerful like—impatient as I have always been towards invalidism. James seemed to think a potentially great poet, before he achieves greatness, must encounter opposition, ostracism, illness: must shed the literal blood from his veins in the cause he upholds: and why isn't he right? Do you know any reason, Horace, for saying he is not right?" I said: "Whatever may have been the case when James applied his theory to you you've had all the prescribed experience since." W. smiled and assented. "Time: time: but that alone does not make the great poet: something must go before!" I added: "Well, Walt, I won't discuss that point with you, except to say that I can accept James' theory and accept Walt Whitman without hurt to the truth." "Do you say that, Horace? But then you are always saying things!"

We put the matter aside here by silence, both. W. was the first to speak. "There's Bucke: Bucke thinks there was a weakening of my pulse already in Drum Taps: that Drum Taps showed a distinct drop in power. No matter for that: I feel myself satisfied to let all go as you find it today—the additions, just as they are, down to the very latest utterance of the Leaves. Of my personal ailments, of sickness as an element, I never spoke a word until the first of the poems I call Sands at Seventy were written, and then some expression of invalidism seemed to be called for. It cannot be skipped—it should not be made too much of. I feel that there is a solid basis for what I have done— a root-idea justifying all—from the first leaf of all the Leaves to the last leaf—the very last: as there must also be for anything that is yet to come. There is another point it's just as well to bear in mind—that a man may be sick for sins a dead generation committed: that admonishes us to be a bit gentle in applying the rod."

Referring to the American-Canadian fisheries dispute W. said: "I expect it to be a mere matter of wind, hollow as hollow can be on both sides." This led him to speak of Canada. "It is a country of characteristics—the landscape has characteristics, the people have characteristics. Canada has been injured by its colonial adhesion to England. I used to walk about when I was up there with Bucke and talk with the people. Canada should be on its own feet, asserting the life which properly belongs to it. I should say that we on this side of the border are too much inclined to minimize its importance. It is good to get about among other peoples: to not take any one nation too much for granted in its superiorities: to take a little off our prejudices here, and put a little on our admirations there— just so's we may finally establish ourselves on the right family basis among the nations."

Recurring to Bucke's opinion of Drum Taps: "I can understand Bucke: he has his reasons, good reasons: but still the conviction abides with me that I am in the end right—must be sustained, convinced, as I feel myself to be, by a logic I cannot state but must stand by, insist upon"—he laughed—"world without end." Then he referred to James again. "He may have been right—certainly was in part right. James was himself sickly, I was always well: we were physically antithetical. It is hard for a perfectly well man to thoroughly understand a perfectly sick man, or vice versa."

He mentioned the visit of the Coateses. "They are so cheery —she particularly: so hopeful, both of them—and fine—I have had them in my mind ever since. The mere atmosphere of such an invasion scatters blessings in my path: a sort of rain of blessings. I know I have felt better for their courtesy." He remarked as I got up to leave: "I shall very likely go down stairs again to-morrow but of course not by laying plans to do so (how can I make plans? plans mean work!) but if and when the mood strikes me." I said to him: "Mrs Harned is nearing her confinement. Her doctor says she is one of the most perfectly organized women physically speaking that she has ever attended —that she is in almost unprecedented condition." W. cried: "Good! good! good! Horace, I can't say good often enough! Who could better realize what that means—who better understand, who more thoroughly rejoice in, what you tell me: who more fully appreciate its significance—than I do—I, whose gospel, if I have a gospel (God help me!) it exemplifies and celebrates? Tell her this for me—congratulate her for me. There are many kinds of mothers, Horace, but there is only one final kind of mother. Give the new mother my love: tell her I glorify her in my thanksgivings—that Walt Whitman glorifies her: tell her that."

Saturday, September 1, 1888.

W. sat reading when I entered (7.45 evening), sitting by a dim light, awake, reflecting. "Ah!"—his accustomed ejaculation— "and what is the good word to-night?" "Your good word?" I returned: "What is that?" He grew serious. "My good word is a bad word: I am not changed for the better: I am still down flat on the ground." I looked doubtfully at him. "Walt— you are getting pessimistic: shake it off! shake it off!" He replied gravely: "You are right: I should make the most of the light as long as there is any left." Next he said: "I had a letter from Kennedy to-day—yes, and letters from others: one from Bucke, one from O'Connor: I have laid them all aside for you to take, along with an old O'Connor letter, which I know you will find some use for. I wrote back to Kennedy, who complains that you do not keep him well enough informed in details regarding my condition. He does not know that you are writing hundreds of letters for me right and left these days— he doesn't know: if he knew he would see how impossible it is for you to write any one letter of great length." He had tied the four letters together with a red string. I asked him: "Why do you feel so blue about yourself to-night?" "I don't know— except that I am facing the truth." "What truth?" "Horace,

I have about reached the end of my rope—the last strand has almost given out. I realize that I am at last on the verge of dissolution: my vim has departed, my strength is gone, life is getting to be impossible on any desirable terms."

Williamson writes asking anxiously about W. W. says: "Horace, tell them the truth when they ask you—hold nothing back: don't make better worse but don't put on an air of assurance when you feel none. You might express it this way: Walt Whitman says that the first alarming symptoms of his trouble no longer possess him, but says further that though succeeding in his fight to shake off that one phase of his disorder it has been but as though to deposit him on a desert island, with far-stretching seas about and no succor possible." Old Age's Lambent Peaks is in The Century out today. W. said as to the idéa of putting it into November Boughs: "I shall think it over to-morrow: give me a day for it: I'm a slow duffer but that's the way I'm built." Gave him ten dollars from Coates for Centennial edition. Also handed him a sheet of paper sent by Mrs. Coates for him to write a copy of Twilight on. He resisted a little. "I have it here in large plain type—The Century printed it: perhaps she would like that"—but after a few words from me: "Well, I'll do it: she's such a cheery body and you ask it," laying the paper and clipping on the table. Handed over the books to me.

W. had gone over a lot of our work. Had Contents proof ready and L. of G. and S. D. volumes containing an order on Sherman for the Leaves plates and corrections to be made by Ferguson in both volumes—about twenty in Specimen Days and about twenty-five or more in Leaves of Grass: spelling, bad type, punctuation—none in any way vital. He likes things well done. "I am sensitive to technical slips, errors—am as ready as anyone to have everything shipshape, or as nearly so as I can make them. I abhor slouchy workmen—always admonish them in offices doing my work: Don't put on a slouchy printer." W. is always saying to me such things as these: "Look out that the binders don't get slouchy," "avoid the slouchy mechanic, whatever you do." Yet he is not squeamish: writes, for instance, to the Ferguson shop: "*To corrector and printer*—I know you have not the exact font of type &c: but you must do the best you can with what you have."

W. paid his respects to Gail Hamilton for her maltreatment of the domestic problem of the Carlyles. "Her presumed *exposé* is all gammon: I have no patience with it. And besides, I feel that I know all about that story, and on good authority, too: from no less a person than Mrs. Gilchrist, who associated with both the Carlyles intimately and was in no sense a woman to be fooled. I attach oh! so great an importance to all she said to me on that subject: facts, pertinent facts, weighty: things she saw, again and again—goings on—enough to turn topsy-turvy the alleged truths of newspaper gossip, the indecent generalizations of scribblers. That Carlyle was high-strung is true, but Mrs. Carlyle, too, had a temper—one, you may be bound, that was not always reined in. Jane Carlyle was the wife of a great man—of one of the greatest men of his time, of any time: a man of ways peculiar to himself, odd fancies, strange whims and humors. That these things were not always fixed in their right relations by a couple both of whom were extremely mettlesome does not surprise me. It is not with the Carlyles alone that there may be said to have been hours, acts, speculations, frictions, upon which the blinds should be dropped. I am confident that after all else—after all the trials, heart-burns, domestic mysteries of the Carlyle history—is dropped, this much will remain to be said for both Jane and Thomas—this much if not more: this much, surely this much, and then silence, silence, upon the whole matter." W. was very much moved by O'Connor's letter. Before I quote what he said I will insert the letter:

WASHINGTON, D. C.
August 31, 1888.

My dear Walt: I got your letter of the 6th, a postal card of the 4th, divers newspapers, and day before yesterday the handsome magazine with the pen-and-ink portrait—a beautiful piece of work, but a bad likeness—in fact, a caricature, which I hope, as Voltaire said of the Letter to Posterity, is a letter that will never reach its address. He has given you a wad for a mouth and made you squint like one of George Borrows' gipsies. Drat his imperence!

I have had it on my mind for a month to write but have had a bad time. I thought of you anxiously during the abominable swelter of August, and felt rejoiced when the cool spell came, hoping it would do you good, though I got a cold out of it, by ill luck, which pulled me back considerably.

Your letter was very comforting. I shall hope to hear good news of you. I sent your messages to Dr. Channing, Grace and Stedman. No news has reached me about the calendar, but I hope it is all right. Grace is expected here in a few days.

Who is it writes of you so friendlily in the editorial notes of Lippincott?

I shall hope for all good things for November Boughs. I wish it were farther along.

I have been using the spare hours when I have felt less weak and woe-begone, than I usually do, and less weighted down with office work, to scratch off in pencil a defense of Donnelly's book for the N. A. Review, if I can only get it in. It has been a bad task, but a duty, for the reviewers have been outrageous.

My hope and heart are high for you. If the weather will only let up!

Good bye. I find that I can't write much, as I hoped to when I began. As the Indian said to Roger Williams when they landed at Seekonk, "What cheer, brother, what cheer!"— meaning all cheer!

Affectionately,
WILLIAM D. O'CONNOR.

Here is what W. said of O'Connor: "William is the last of his race—no one is left but William. I know no other scholar here in America so well based, rock-based, in lines important to the history of literature, to humanity. They are all the rest of them dabblers, talkers, triflers—he drives home to the heart of things. His knowledge of the literature of the Elizabethan period was marvellous, and is: sure, serious, vital: always penetrating the spinal mysteries, powers—never losing hold on the substance of a thing once understood and grasped. There were a couple of years in O'Connor's life when he had nothing to do—was looking for work (that was before he got into his Washington job): it was then he devoted himself exclusively to this one study—and it was an experience profitable to him beyond words. William often says of himself—did say it when we were together: 'I can read him through to the back coat button!' and he could: no one could confuse his vision. How he touches off the Elizabethan fellows (he always calls that 'the age of Bacon') few can realize who have not known him personally—met him, listened to his talk, heard his voice, looked the man in the face. Burroughs thinks William too strenuous—keyed up monotonously too high—but I do not. To me William is self-justified in the truest sense of the word. He is intense, overwhelming—when he wrote the Good Gray Poet, when he wrote the letter for Bucke's book, he was excited and indignant to a degree: but we must remember what it was that called forth his wrath—the consciousness of a great wrong: an inexcusable offense which demanded a corresponding emphasis of resentment. William's onslaught is terrifying—it always means business." "He never charges the enemy with an apology on his lance." "That is the idea—he is fiercely in earnest: nothing can stand against him: when he comes along God help you if you don't get out of his road. He used to handle my skepticism about Poe without gloves: Edgar Poe: he would not have my qualifications: Poe was great this or that, great so and so, or he was nothing, and Walt Whitman be damned. O'Connor's constitutional melancholy, his Irish bardic nature, put extreme color into his thought and speech. See how he accepts Bacon: bribe or no bribe—with all his sins on his head: the master intellect of the modern human world towering above all the measuring-sticks of the historians and the schools. And there was Rabelais, too: Rabelais was William's man: in whatever literary reactions or moralistic humors, he includes, stands for, glorifies, Rabelais. He admits all the superficial charges made against such men and then celebrates them—almost celebrates their sins, as though they constituted an *exposé* of the black pruderies of a humbug social order." W. added: "I imagine that Ben Tucker has some qualities more or less akin to the militant and shining chivalric qualities in William. I often feel as though I would like to see Tucker and have a long, long, long, confab with him, just for the sake of squaring up some old scores (gratitude on my part, gratitude to him): he is remarkable for outright pluck—grit of the real sort: for loyalty, steadfastness. Some day you will meet Tucker and when you do I want you to say these things to him for me."

W. has pinned on page 178 in a copy of Specimen Days in which from time to time he marks changes for future editions—under Carlyle from American Points of View—and marked it in red ink, "Phila. Press June 23, '86," the following printed "study item," as he called it when it was mentioned by me:

"Mr. Larkin, who was for ten years a sort of secretary and intimate associate of Carlyle, says that the open secret of the Scotchman's life was his desire to be a man of affairs rather than a writer. 'Little as some of his critics imagine it,' says Mr. Larkin, 'his heart was sick of perpetually exhorting and admonishing. He longed to be doing something, instead of, as he says, eloquently writing and talking about it; to be a kind of king or leader in the practical activities of life, not a mere prophet, forever and forever prophesying.'"

W. said: "That's not only interesting as applied to Carlyle but interesting to me because it may be applied to my life and may be used as in some byways an explanation of my addiction to the trades and my apprenticeship to the life of the hospitals during the War. It also exemplifies one of my chief doctrines, which is, that we should never become so absorbed in the ornamental occupations as to lose connection with life. Some men lead professional lives—some men just live: I prefer to just live. I never want to be thought to be contending that any amount of isolated esthetic achievement can compensate for the loss of the comrade life of the world: the comrade life, the right life of the one in the crowd, which is of all human ideals the most to be desired, the only one to be finally desired, and perpetuated." Mentioning Bucke's letter again W. said: "It's full of advice— good advice, I admit, but advice—about the big book."

LONDON, ONTARIO, 30 Aug. 1888.

I feel quite anxious about the "complete" works and would like much to hear from you how you will deal with that book. I think:

1 The book should be first-class in all respects.
2 Price should be ten dollars.
3 It should (every copy of it) be autograph.
4 Should contain a number of pictures.
5 Should be sold entirely by yourself.
6 A full advertisement of it should go in "N. B."

If you would tell Horace to write me your decision on each of these points you would relieve my mind very much.

There is nothing new or special here. All jogging on in the old way.

Your friend,
R. M. BUCKE.

"You see," said W. "Maurice simply repeats the advice we have been giving ourselves." "You seem to hate advice, no matter who it comes from or when it is given." "I think I do: I have been trained to resentment through thirty years of experience with advisers. Horace, I have had my life through to keep up a constant warfare with advice." Finally W. said: "You might write Maurice and say to him that we have come to conclusions on most of the points he presents and that he will be surprised to find when the book comes out in how much we agree." "That sounds darn formal," I said. "I know it

242

would please Doctor to have me reply in a way that would sound more like concession but I don't feel to do it, Horace—I don't feel to do it." W. said about Kennedy's letter: "The little querulous complaint of you—you mustn't notice that—let it go. What he says of Scott has my entire approval: Scott is my man, too: I go to him sometimes with a real relish. Scott does not stale for me."

BELMONT, MASS.
August 30, 1888.

Dear Walt Whitman: I long, and have lang syne and every day longed—to know some details of your days now. For some reason Mr. Traubel has never seen fit to tell me anything about your daily doings—whether you sit up or whether you are prone on your back. It is cruel to keep a fellow ignorant. Can't you tell me in a line or two yourself? Thank you for the magazine—Book Maker—with its picture of you. Herbert Gilchrist has sent me a proof of what seems to me the best of the two photogravures of Mrs. Gilchrist. I prize it highly. Any news from *the three?*—Bucke, O'C. or J. B.?

I am reading with tremendous interest and absorption (by bits as I get time) Scott's best novels again, and looking up all the hard Scotch words in Jamieson's Dictionary. They have made my summer glorious. My love of that man is something strong as fate. Indeed I believe the ties of blood draw me to him and to Scotland—my "forbears" being Scotch-Irish (on one side). I am now revelling in the Antiquary which I opine to be the healthiest and most humorous of all, perhaps.

Yours affectionately as ever,
W. S. KENNEDY.

W. said: "That querulous note—it is always present in Kennedy: it breaks in upon his best harmonies. Don't you feel it? You would be surprised to find it in Bucke, John, William: you get to expect it as a matter of course in Kennedy. I once felt that he would weed it out of his composition, or that it

243

would weed itself out, but it seems to be keeping fast hold—will probably never let go its grip. It's a damned shame—it may prevent his real talents from ever fully asserting themselves." When I got up to go W. objected: "Why do you hurry?" and to my answer: "I've bothered you long enough," he protested: "You bother me? you couldn't: you never victimize me—you wake me up. I am far more alert this minute, am feeling better, than I have been at any time during the day." We said nothing about "the old O'Conner letter," which I put in my pocket and took away with me. It was long. The sheets were pinned together. It was 9.45 when I left.

Sunday, September 2, 1888.

2 P. M. Last night W. told me he had not felt up to going over the plate proofs. I went home and worked until two o'clock on them. We have promised them to Ferguson Monday. Worked again until eleven this morning. Now submit them to W. He sat reading the Century as I entered. "So it's Horace again?" Looked rather well. How was he? "Not a bit nifty—not a bit nifty," he replied. Nifty? what was nifty? "Did you never hear that colloquialism—nifty?—n-i-f-t-y—sassy, on edge?" Continued: "I have sat about here, have read some, have dozed more—that is the history of the day." No down-stairs today? "No nothing," he said: "not an adventure —not a single sensational event!" We examined the proofs together. Very particular in certain details. "That's what we're here for, you with me. We won't fuss but we'll be exact." "Does this all worry you?" "Oh no! it rather brightens me up." I did not find him anxious about spellings. "I regret my ignorance of German: German is the one foreign language I am sorry I did not go into when I was young." He objected to some changes I suggested. "They are not wrong—they are only my whims, oddities: as such I must let them pass." When we reached page thirty-seven I tried again to have him see the errors in An Evening Lull. The last line he conceded to be

wrong. "Did I write it that way? It seems impossible."
Fixed it. Did not touch the other line. He is more conscientious in his reading of the verse than of the prose. "That puts us in good shape," he said after we had finished our job together. "I see you look sharply at such matters and it is good to do so." Here he laughed gently: "I wrote to Doctor today: took your advice—addressed him in a rather concessional spirit. I have not finally decided the question of price—whether to make the little book a dollar or more or the big one five or six or ten dollars. I never start out bent upon doing anything by a particular method but let events grow their own way. Bucke takes the book more seriously than we do—is almost agonizing about it: writes me it *must* be so and so—*must* be—or we will all be ruined, or such like rot. That *must* is damned disagreeable no matter who says it! But I don't doubt Bucke's items—they are about correct. Bucke sometimes gives out the show of being precipitate but that does not fairly represent him: he is on the contrary rather Socratic, rather inclined to calm, to accept things as they are while they are, stoically, in fact optimistically."

He suddenly took another turn. "Here is Mrs Coates' piece —I did it for you"—handing it to me from the table—very handsomely copied. While we talked my eye lighted on a pamphlet lying loose among other papers at his feet—Richard II: home-bound in brown wrapping paper. "What is that?" I asked —he looking first at me and then down towards the floor —"This?" picking up the pamphlet. "What a flood of memories it lets loose. It is my old play-book, used many and many times in my itinerant theatre days: Richard: Shakespeare's Richard: one of the best of the plays, I always say—one of the best—in it's vehemence, power, even in it's grace. I took the sheets from a book—a big book—from a book too big to carry— and bound them so for practical use. The book itself should be here somewhere"—commencing to root in a couple of piles of books at his feet—"Ah! here it is"—handing it over to me. The gap was found and the abstracted sheets were put back in their place. "Home again!" he exclaimed, as he closed the book, "home again, after all these years of wandering." The volume was printed in Germany in English text and was called English Classics—Shakespeare, Milton, and others, making up the collection. W. said: "A whole hogshead of precious fluid —the juices of all savors, climes, poured into the one cask— distilled at last into a bottle an inch long—the size of the joint of your thumb! That is Richard—this same Richard. How often I spouted this—these first pages—on the Broadway stage-coaches, in the awful din of the street. In that seething mass— that noise, chaos, bedlam—what is one voice more or less: one single voice added, thrown in, joyously mingled in the amazing chorus?" He continued to finger the book, talking of its German-icisms: "I found several in the preface: see—I have marked them:" alluding also to "its wonderfully legible print—a joy to my bad eyes."

I picked up an old piece of manuscript written on the reverse of a blue billhead of the City of Williamsburgh. Had it ever been used? "Maybe—maybe not." "Have you much unused manuscript about here?" "Not a great deal though I have made a good bit of manuscript that never got directly into print. Think how many things go to produce the weather—east, west, north, south: things unaccounted for, at least to the eye. Out of such a process of selection Leaves of Grass assumed the shape you know." This is what was on the sheet:

"The idea that in the nature of things, through all affairs and deeds, national or individual, good and bad, each has its own inherent law of punishment or reward, which is part of the deed or affair itself, identical with it, and, with its results, goes with that deed, that affair, then and afterwards.

"The idea that the Woman of America is to become the per-fect equal of the man.

"The idea of the good old cause, Liberty—that it is to be honored here, whatever day, whatever question, it presents it-self in—that the relation of master and slave [W. had written on here at a later date: "this was written in 1855"] is to go the same road out of These States that the relation of kings, lords and commons, has gone."

W. mentioned Gilchrist. "I expect him, I may say hourly. What mystifies me is, what calls him over? He comes in the British Prince to Philadelphia. One point occurs to me—he must have made some money—have had some success with his work. Herbert is pretty poor, like most of the fellows, but not extremely so. He came before on the fifty guineas or so paid him by the publishers over there for the Life of his Mother."

Evening at 8. W. sat reading the Emerson-Carlyle correspondence. "Where have you been this afternoon?" "To the Zoo." "You don't say!" "I do say." He smiled. "Well, it's good news—I thought everything in Philadelphia worth while was shut up and barred for Sunday. Sunday—Sunday: we make it the dullest day in the week when it might be made the cheeriest. Will the people ever come to base ball, plays, concerts, yacht races, on Sunday? That would seem like clear weather after a rain. Why do you suppose people are so narrow-minded in their interpretation of the Sunday? If we read about Luther we find that he was not gloomy, not sad-devout, not sickly-religious: but a man full of blood who didn't hesitate to outrage ascetic customs or play games if he felt like it on Sunday. The Catholic regards Sunday with a more nearly sane eye. It does seem as though the Puritan was responsible for our Sunday: the Puritan had his virtues but I for one owe him a grudge or two which I don't hesitate to talk about loud enough to be heard."

W. advised me: "Read Burns—don't skip Burns: Burns will do things for you no one else can do. Hunter always dilates on Burns. Hunter is a sly old dog, after all, and cute, too. I will ask him a question. He will say: 'I don't know anything about that.' Then he will go to work and prove to you that he knows all about it." I laughed. W. asked: "Now, what is there amusing in what I say?" "Nothing—except that Kennedy in a letter to me applied the same expression to you—sly old dog."

W. replied at once: "But it don't fit me: that's not me: I am more outright—especially outright with my ignorance: I don't seem to have enough finesse to throw the least observant person off the track. Hunter has a little flirtiness in his composition—likes to play out his learning diplomatically. Horace, he is a very engaging character to me." "His coquetteries have won you?" "Perhaps it's that—I don't know: it may be said that way! When I first met Hunter I thought he was of little consequence as a scholar, but he led me on and on, by little and little, until I found myself of my present admiring mind about him."

He further said: "You find me cautious—that I do not throw myself at people, events?" "You are willing to take time enough to get the right time." "That's a mighty good way to say it: yes, time enough: I never fire my gun before I cock it—I never cock it until I know just exactly the game I am after." "That is, you have discovered that you're no good in a quick charge but a sure thing in a long siege." W. looked at me fixedly: "That's damned clever, Horace: but look out—you mustn't get yourself in the habit of saying clever things—it's a dangerous practice—lands many a man many a time in a lie. Still, it happens that this clever thing is also true, so I forgive you. Yes, I have made the best of my sluggish pulse by trying to keep it sure, strong. Every man has to learn his own best method: my method is to go slow, extra slow. All great work is cautious work—is done with an eye on all the horizons of the spirit: in the absence of such gravity we become dabblers—the big things don't get said, don't get done." I did not stay longer, though he asked me to. "It does me good to have you here," he said. I don't always think it does. As I left he reached forward and again took up the book he was reading as I entered.

Monday, September 3, 1888.

8 P. M. W. reading when I entered but was at once solicitous for "news." He gave me money for frontispiece presswork. Cheerier than for a week. Had discovered other errors in N. B. I opened up the subject of An Evening Lull again, almost insist-

ing that he change "restless" on second line to "unrest." He said: "I never knew you to be so infernally stubborn before. Let me look at the proof again." I handed it to him. He put on his glasses and looked at the sheet intently. Then his whole face lighted up. "Why yes, Horace—you're right— Myrick's right. How do you suppose I came to pass it again and again? You remember I wrote it on one of my off days." "Now this is an on day and you correct it." "Yes, an on day." He laughed. Took up a pencil. "See—here goes then"— marking the correction. I said: "Bucke wrote me advising against the change. He said the psychologists would find it interesting when they came to write of you in the future." "The psychologists? The devil! They'd never think of it except as a typographical error or an oversight. You mean that it would be significant as showing my condition the day I wrote it? The idea shows that—I do not need to carry the evidence out into the spelling. Bucke," he added, laughing, "is a stickler for verbal inspiration: he raises a hell of a row if I change a comma if it once got in though it may first of all have got in in error."

I saw Browning's card on the chair—the N. Y. Herald's Browning. "Has he been here?" "Yes; he was over today. He said he understood I had written a long piece about Elias Hicks (I wonder how he found it out?) and the Herald wanted a column or two advanced to them." "Will you agree to do it?" "Yes: why not? I shall do it—send it on direct to Chambers rather than through Browning. It worked in my noddle that Browning wanted it as a part of his Philadelphia correspondence, which don't quite recommend itself to me. I will make a selection of matter with great care and put my price on it: they may then print it or not as they choose. It's strange how these newspaper men get on the scent of everything—nothing escapes them: they go everywhere, they never fail. I thought we were keeping it all so mum and yet the cat is out of the bag." I said: "The Press mentioned the piece: that explains Browning's source of knowledge." "Ah! yes: I had forgotten that. It's just as well: we had no particular motive to keep the book in hiding." "I hope the Herald will print intact what I send. Unless a fellow's a damned big gun—like Tennyson, for instance —they treat him pretty shabbily." "Have editors ever revised you?" "I should say so—as much as any man alive. They all think they know better."

I told him of an experience I had with an editor recently. He wanted to entirely recast a paper I had sent him. "But you didn't allow it?" "No—not at all: I had him send it back." "I thought so—that's right. Never knuckle down—always insist upon your way, even if it is the wrong way, as the right way. There's one point, a glorious point, I get from the Emerson-Carlyle correspondence: 'Are we going to give in in our old age?' Not in such words, exactly, but signifying that. 'Are we going to give in in our old age?' It is the fore-dream of my own question: I put that question to myself every day. Emerson's old age was very wonderful, Horace—I told Frank Sanborn I thought it highly beautiful: that in all essentials the forgetful Emerson was still what the remembering Emerson had been: the bearing, the expression, the eye, the hand, the smile, still the same. Something was gone—some quality—but the atmosphere of his noble personality never failed him." I said: "It was just today that I wrote Bucke something of the same tenor about you: that the stern poise that dignified and irradiated your character is still the first thing in all you say, think or do." I shall never forget W.'s look. He said: "Ah! Horace! That is a noble thought: it is worthy of you and more than worthy of me. And if it be true? It would make all the suffering of these days more than easy. It was a month or so ago that you said something of the same purport to me and I have never lost sight of it for an instant since in the temptations incident to such invalidism as mine. I conclude that these last poems which some of the fellows howl so about are justified by the same fact— are found in this way to be integral to the scheme of the book— could not remain unwritten or be dismissed without violating its integrity."

Referring to the poetry in the magazines, W. said: "I read

it nowadays, most of it, mostly for amusement: I expect no other benefit from it. Now and then I am surprised with a bit of verse by a man or woman who seems to have something to say. Scott is my chief pleasure nowadays—the novels: I read them every day, some: read them because they are not so frivolous as to be useless and vulgar, and not so weighty as to set my brains into a snarl." "How about the Emerson-Carlyle correspondence? Under what head do you put that?" "I don't think that heavy—and heavy or not it is wonderfully interesting—it has attracted and absorbed me." After a pause: "And now, by the way, do you see that Whittier is out again about Burns, in a rather long letter, characteristic but weak? He sees nothing beyond the commonplaces of the orthodox scholars. He plasters it on very thick. You know about the McPherson woman who gave the twenty-five thousand dollar statue to Albany? I think Whittier is a wonderful, noble old man, but it always mystified me how he could select Burns, of all men, for his special laudations. Burns was a great 'chiel' but utterly forlorn on the very points which Whittier seems to select for praise. Lust, whiskey, such things, played heavy cards in his game of life. I have no exceptions to take: if anyone tells me he holds Burns in high love and regard I say I do, too—as high as any: for he was a whole-hearted, not a half-hearted, man, after all the rest is said. Whittier has made so conspicuously much of certain virtues for which Burns did not shine that we are entitled to remark the incongruity. Burns was Whittier's first poet—that may account for some of the mystery when nothing else will. None of them understand Burns, however—none of them: his enemies slander him beyond recognition—his friends praise him beyond recognition."

I said to W.: "No one likes the Book Maker head." "Why should they? It might just as well be Jim Blaine as me." Asked me: "Have you the second of Froude's big books on Carlyle? I never read it. The first I got hold of when it first appeared: the second was brought out six months later, never came my way. My impression of it was favorable—not the common one at all. I did not feel as though it had style, brilliancy, and there stopped. It seemed to me to be a real success in stating the facts of Carlyle's personality—in presenting an individual of flesh and blood. Burroughs was here while I was full of the matter and we agreed—unanimously agreed, the two of us—that Froude had not failed: had in fact achieved a notable success. I think I must try to read the second volume: it may undeceive me!"

W. had found someone saying again in print somewhere that he had no humor. "O'Connor has his own way of taking that charge up—says Walt Whitman don't start out to be humorous: humor is no implied part of his scheme: though if it was he would show up for humor as supremely as he had for other qualities: and besides, there's a humor deeper than a laugh which Walt Whitman has—this cannot be questioned: and even the laugh humor is there, as all his personal friends know—no man being more eligible to enter into its spirit. That is the way O'Connor puts it. It is a strong defense: William says of it himself: 'Walt, it puts them all to flight!' The humor in the Shakespearean comedies is very broad, obvious, often brutal, coarse: but in some of the tragedies—take Lear for instance—you will find another kind of humor, a humor more remote (subtle, illusive, not present)—the sort of humor William declares he finds in the Leaves and in me."

W. showed me an English serial publication called Parodies (part 58: Vol. 5) put out by Reeves & Taylor, London—this number devoted to American writers and devoting six double-columned pages to W. "It is a novel affair of its kind: it is conceived in no inimical spirit: gives biographical data and even literal selections from the works of writers parodied. Some of the parodies are well done, too—very well done. I haven't looked them over critically but they seem to me almost uniformly above the average. I am aware that Leaves of Grass lends itself readily to parody—invites parody—given the right man to do the deed."

W. said: "Your father was in today again, Horace. He told me some things about himself—that he comes of Jewish stock, that he quarreled with his parents about religion when he was a mere boy: left home, weathered out life for himself: came to America with nothing but his brains and faith (he had plenty of both): and so on, Horace: so on. It all sounded right: I never thought he was any other kind of a man than just that kind: in our crowd he is initiate—he requires no extra introductions. I would like you and your father to meet Karl Knortz. We should all meet: perhaps it can be arranged yet. It is one of the things I design still to do. My own curiosity to see him is great. Don't you see how impossible it is for me to die just yet, with all these new plans for things little and big pushing out their heads every day?"

W. gave me an old Tucker letter. "I want you to know how staunch his adhesion to me has been. We talked about him the other day: I said nothing quite warm enough then—I shall say nothing now to increase the quantity of my adjectives applied to him—but I want you to know the facts, and such facts are strong enough without words added to embellish them. This letter is a fact—at the time it was a fighting fact—better in peace to me than a file of soldiers in war to an army. Do you mind reading the letter aloud to me? No? Well, go on."

BOSTON, May 25, 1882.

MR. WALT WHITMAN:

Dear Sir, I am a stranger to you but have long been an admirer of your writings. Perhaps you have heard of me as at one time editor of the Radical Review, which published J. B. Marvin's admirable essay entitled Walt Whitman. The action of the Massachusetts authorities and the cowardice of the Osgoods prompt me to write to you. I am ashamed of the whole business. What do you propose to do? Some steps should be at once taken for the republication of your book, from the same plates, in the same locality where it has been struck down. Is there no one that will undertake it? With able counsel to conduct the case I do not believe a jury could be found in Massachusetts to send the publisher of Leaves of Grass to prison. At any rate the question ought to be tested. If I had the means, I would gladly, with your permission, put your book on the market advertised as the suppressed edition, and invite the authorities to dispute my right to do so. What I will do is this, if nothing better can be done. If you will find parties to furnish the means for republication from your plates, advertising the book, and defending it in court, I will become the responsible publisher, and go to prison if necessary. In case the verdict should be against me and I should be fined, I should decline to pay the fine. It seems to me highly important that the people of America should know exactly how far they can safely indulge in the expression of their opinions. What do you say? If you desire to know anything about me before replying to so important a question, you may inquire of S. H. Morse Quincy, Mass., the sculptor, whom you know, and who has long been one of my intimate friends. He does not know of my design in this matter, but he will tell you that I am thoroughly reliable, and no notoriety-hunter or anything of that kind.

Yours indignantly,
BENJ. R. TUCKER.

When I had read it through W. exclaimed: "Good! Good! Bully for Tucker!" just as if he was hearing it for the first time. Then he said: "Ain't that like the challenge of an old knight going out against all comers in behalf of his faith? Like it and better! You didn't know the letter existed, did you? It's none the less a feather in Tucker's cap that it was not necessary for me to acquiesce in his proposition. This is not the letter of a literary man but of a man: a man simply possessed of the first impulse to help make fair play possible in the world. I do not mean by this to belittle Tucker's acquirements, which I am told are most uncommon. Morse says his knowledge is encyclopedic: says he is one of the best, the very best, of translators from the French: and more, much more. Morse spent one of his half days here with me last year, just speaking about Tucker—he giving me an idea in the rough of how Tucker had come in conflict with the authorities by reason of his advanced anarchistic ideas. When I recall the cowardly advice I have in the main received from the literary class concerning the expurgation of Leaves of Grass Tucker's immediate rally to its support, his persistent advocacy in thick and thin, excites me to supreme admiration." As I left to go W. gave me two letters tied in red string of which he said: "I think they were the start of my correspondence with Forman, which has been kept up, though not in any great volume, ever since."

Tuesday, September 4th, 1888.

8 p. m. W. writing a note to his sister when I entered. "The folks went to see Eddy today so I'm writing about that." But was ready enough to drop the letter for the present. "What have *you* got? tell me that." I handed him an envelope containing copies of frontispiece. He opened it—regarded the picture long and carefully. "It is very good: it grows better and better: a little more ink now gives it a little more life: life, life—we want life. I am glad you brought a few: I can enclose them with my letters." I said: "The presswork is first-rate— it has brought out all there is in the cut: if there's anything missing now blame the cut." He smiled: "I'll blame nothing: we'll draw out of the cut what there's in us. I used to know an old German—oh it was a long time ago—and Jeff could tell you of it, too—who had about the wheeziest, damnablest, out-of-tune piano that ever was. Yet the instant the old man sat down and commenced to play everybody would listen—I, too, and Jeff—all the talkers would listen—and we could never get enough of it, never get satiated—would listen for hours. He would draw out of it, out of himself, all there was in it, all there was in him."

W. said of his health: "It was greatly improved Sunday and yesterday but I am not so well today. Some days I get all fagged out, feeling bad enough to give in once for all." Gave me this message for Morse: "Yes, write to Sidney: I send him my love; say to him that I still flourish (if that word can be used in connection with me): that the books are in a fair way to be out soon: that we are both working like beavers (one of us a sick beaver): and that we are waiting to hear from him. Tell Sidney we are fussy—that it is his turn to write!" Gilchrist has not yet arrived though there is mail here for him.

Musgrove entered with a letter for W., who looked at the postmark and said: "It's from Atlantic City: who do we know there? Oh! Mrs. Williams. You know Frank: it's his wife." He started in at once and had read most of the letter aloud to me when he came upon the request that it should be shown to no one. "But it's done! the mischief's done! Yet I wonder why she made the suggestion." After putting the letter back in the envelope he said: "The worst of sickness is its bad humor, its peevishness, its crossness, its irritability." I looked skeptical. "But it's all there, I can assure you, Horace. I'm not all sweetness, by any means: far otherwise: you'll find in me, if you look far enough, a whole hodge-podge of bad impulses—things maybe not seen, but there, active enough, devilish enough, God knows, all the same." Paused. I said nothing. Then he went on: "I once read a story of Socrates—I can't tell where any more: I was young at the time—it was in New York: a story, if I'm not mistaken, from Bacon, or credited to him. Hardly that: it sounds too fishy: but the point is the same. At that time there were travelling phrenologists—they came into the villages, or big business centers, plying their trade. As the story goes it was such a man in old Greece who happened into the Socratian circle—into one of the groups of young fellows who hung about Socrates—who proceeded to annoy and jeer at him—taunt him: what could he do? what were his powers? pshaw! and so forth. But he was not to be downed. They were challenged to produce a subject—accepted the challenge—blindfolded him —brought Socrates in. The phrenologist went to work: here was indeed a pretty subject—a pretty subject indeed. Over the bumps went the wary hand: here was a very glutton, a rascal fond of wine—could drink swinishly: and a lecherous scamp too: you who had nice daughters, have a care!—and so on. The young men were hilarious—took off the bandage—released the phrenologist. 'Do you know who it is you have been saying all these beautiful things about? This is the great, the wise, Socrates, loftiest of mortals.' And they badgered the poor devil so bad he was like to give up. All the time Socrates stood there, with a smile on his face, finally protesting from his place aside. He raised his hand, this way"—indicating—"'Not so fast now, not so fast now: don't be so sure: don't be so sure you know and he don't. Listen to me. I know better than all of you know the real facts. No one knows what is hidden away in me as I do: I tell you all this man says is true, every word of it—and more, too, if he had chosen to go farther. You must not suppose that because I suppress the evidences of it that it does not exist—that there are not in me, too, as much as in anyone, wild growths of poison flowers, mad passions of villainy, to be fought and thrown in the defence of virtue'".

W. told this story with great gusto. "I wish I could remember where it came from: I would like to see, read, it again. It may have been in an old magazine, though that is not likely, for magazine editors would have construed it to be licentious and not consent to give it currency. I say to my friends: Don't be so sure of my innocence: all the bad is there with all the good, only needing to be exposed—all in hiding. There's always a heap in such stories, but this, likely enough, this Socratian story, is fiction, as most of them are."

I picked up a paper-bound book lying on the table—a copy of the 1867 edition of Leaves of Grass. "There was a history and a grief attached to that edition," said W.: "It was got up by a friend of mine, a young fellow, printed from type, in New York. One day I received the intelligence (I was then in Washington) that the place had been seized for debt. I received a portion of the books remaining—the most of them were lost, scattered God knows where, God knows how. But this," he said, picking up another book, "this is the best of the editions, the '72 edition—printed by Green." I read aloud from the title page imprint, "Washington." "No," objected W., "dated

Washington but Green was in New York. I have a few of those copies left—one for you if you want it, if you have none."

We talked of anthologies. "I am usually left out. Bryant, I think, ignored me in early editions, but some later editor seems to have included me. Dana quoted me copiously in his book— was my genial friend." "Why did Emerson ignore you in Parnassus?" "I do not know. I have ceased not only inquiring but caring. I am satisfied to wait—satisfied to have things take their own time. I have never had, nor have, any wish to make a big flare-up: a big flare-up is soon out. I am aware that my work, if it has any stuff in it—any substance that can endure— needs time to make its way, and if it has not is as well dropped now as later." We talked some about the O'Connor letter which he gave me on Sunday. "It is brilliant," said W.— "like a bright star in a clear sky. William is a man who never needs a prod—is always afire: in fence he is a ways ready— his weapons are always on edge. I doubt if America has so far produced another man his equal in the things for which his temperament may be said to stand."

PROVIDENCE, R. I.
April 1, 1883.

Dear Walt: I got your note of the 29th and in the afternoon of the same day (March 30) the package of books came. It was very kind in you to send them. As Dr. Channing's family are ardent friends of you and your book, and have no recent issues, I turned over to them one copy of the poems and the copy of Specimen Days—you know I have both myself (Specimen Days, I regret to say, I have never found time to read, but shall, from the copy you sent me, when I return to Washington, as I shall have more leisure this spring and summer than I had in the dreadful months of labor when the book came.) The other copy of the poems, I shall reserve for some one who shall prove to be worthy: and I hope this disposition of your kind gift will please you.

The Channing family are staunch adherents, and the girls

(Mary and Grace—Mary was recently married and is living in Cambridge—) both gave their cousin, Col. Higginson, (whom I have gone for so savagely in the Introductory) a round talking-to on your account, apropos of his article in The Woman's Journal. But Higginson is incorrigible. I imagine, however, that the rhinosceros spear I have planted in and turned by steam in his hide (in the Introductory) will startle his supercilious composure, especially what I say about his Port Royal experience, and I guess he will be mad as a wet hen. All right: people that live in porcelain towers or crystal palaces, shouldn't throw stones at the "lower horders," such as we are,—we whose armorial legend is: "'eave 'arf a brick at 'im!'"

It was very kind to send Karl Elze's book, which I have read (you know I am a very rapid reader) and will return to you by express. I knew him already by his life of Byron, which I own, and the best thing in which is his perfectly exterminating analysis of Mrs. Stowe's (or rather Lady Byron's) ridiculous slander. Otherwise in this Byron book, as in the book on Shakespeare, he is a perfect Bismarck philistine, with a head of wood just larded with brains. The lack of political freedom, inducing proclivity to aristocratic ideas, and utter lack of sympathy with democratic or republican thought, makes all the Germans, even the great ones (and Elze is not great), perfectly worthless whenever they approach topics connected with the questions of liberty and humanity; and Shakespeare cannot be successfully approached in criticism except in connection with the mighty human movement which made the life of his age—"the world-bettering age," as one of the great Elizabethan. men calls it. Hence this supper of sawdust, such as Carl Elze, and others like him, sets for us. A dull fellow, moreover, which only partly accounts for his slurring notice of Hugo's magnificent book on Shakespeare—Bismarckism being accountable for the rest of it. However, what paralyzes all Shakespearean criticism, Elze's as well as the rest, is the obstinate consideration of the work with that Stratford chucklehead and his chucklehead biography. If we had no notion whatever of the author, we should fare better in understanding the work than we do with William Shakespeare on our brains as an incubus. To know a man is to know his book. To be dead sure in advance that Barnum wrote Hamlet and the Tempest, is to be dead sure of knowing little or nothing of those works forever.

I have heard nothing yet about the Heywood trial. You and McKay *did perfectly right* in keeping aloof and not contributing to the defense. Your connection could not help him and might hurt you. "Against stupidity the gods themselves are powerless," says Euripides, and Heywood is certainly a champion jackass. I am sorry for him, but his bed is his own making, and he should have known what Comstock could do to him if he advertised war on the ovaries. I only hope we shall escape the consequences of his folly.

I suppose the correction has been made, but I noticed in Bucke's Latin motto the error of the diphthong œ (in the fourth line) in the word præclarius. It should be æ not œ. Munro spells it praeclarius without using the diphthong character at all, which is sensible. It is a glorious epigraph.

I have just been down to the Post Office, and got your letter of yesterday, but not the revise, which will not come until to-morrow morning. I am rejoiced at what you say of my contribution, but feel *dreadfully* at the prospect your letter opens of my paragraphing being changed. I could bear with equanimity anything but that—especially the breaking up of my running account of the great books into paragraphs. *That* I never can like. The effect will be horrible. Besides, you told me I was to have my way.

I will write you again after I get the revise. I expect to leave here tomorrow evening and arrive in Washington on Tuesday afternoon: so unless you hear to the contrary, address me at the Office of the Life Saving Service, as usual.

I leave heavy-hearted, for Jeannie is very feeble, and I fear the worst. Yet I must go on to Washington even if I have to return again. I can only hope that she will revive as the days go on (illness has its ebbs and flows,) and be able to journey home. At present she is too ill and weak to leave her bed.

I shall probably return you the revise from Washington, though I may be able to look over it before I leave, if I get it to-morrow morning. Thanks to Protestantism, Sunday knocks post-office usages endways. The post-office can only be open for an hour on God's day, so that I get your letter but not the proof, there not being time for the officials to over-haul postal matter of the second or third or fourth class until Monday!

Goodbye.

Faithfully

W. D. O'CONNOR.

It was the simplest human touch in this letter that hit W. hardest—the reference to Jeannie. "Jeannie's death was the tragedy of their history—and a tragedy in my history, too. Too much must not be said of that or the like of that—it gets down in you where words do not go. Of all the dear, dear friends of those days, Nellie, William, were dearest, dearest." He looked at me: his eyes were full of tears. He turned away. Then he added: "But let's not let go, Horace: we know how to take death, to see death, right, don't we? Let's not let go." W. rarely gives way externally to his extreme emotions.

W. took his broken-backed check book and wrote me out a check for the paper bill—$240.10. When I got up to go I said: "This is the first temptation you have offered me to skip." He laughed and I started off. I got out into the hallway when he called me back. "I was about to say, if you skipped with the check it wouldn't be the check I'd regret but you—the loss of you. I am daily praying that nothing may happen to you until these books are out—yes, until I am all out, too, Horace. I am damned selfish—I want you to live, live, if only for me." "I want to live—if only for you!" Then I asked him a question: "Do you think a right strong young fellow can *think* death even? —even if aware that it may come any time?" He reflected: "No—I don't believe he can: more than that, I don't believe he

261

ought: thinking life is the condition of being alive. It is always my point—don't submit to provocations, irritabilities, black fancies of the superficial day: go your way unmoved—on and on to what you are required to do: the rest will take care of itself."

The Parodies, which we talked about yesterday or day before, starts off with W. W. by a brief biographical statement, which is highly favorable—speaking of his "vigor"—of the "mock modesty" that refuses to include "many of his finest thoughts on the mysteries of nature" in English editions. "Whitman is emphatically a poet for *men* not for 'Select Academies for the Daughters of Gentlemen only' and whilst much that he has written is glorious poetry to those who will, and can, imbibe its spirit freely, to those who cannot so absorb it the Parodies will appear nearly as poetical as the originals." Speaks furthermore of Leaves of Grass as "a marvellous book:" then proceeds to quote in whole or in part Song of Myself, Miracles, A Thanksgiving Day, interspersing remarks—"this is not poetry of the tinkling rhyme"—referring to Tennyson's friendship for W. and Swinburne's before he "took to renouncing all the opinions of his youth"—and quoting the Emerson letter: following all with a dozen parodies from English and American sources. Covers six pages and more.

Wednesday, September 5th, 1888.

8 p. m. W. talking to Mrs. Davis when I entered. She sat on the sofa, her arms folded. W., with his hands resting on the arms of his chair and his eyes raised over his glasses, was telling her a story. The light was only half turned up. His voice was very clear and melodious. Without stopping his talk he extended his right hand and took my own, which he pressed warmly and beckoned me to a seat. After W. finished with Mrs. Davis she took the evening papers and left. As usual, having to answer my question, he spoke first of his health. "Sunday and Monday things looked pretty bright—yesterday much less that way— today only so-so." "How about your weather inside?" "Oh!

that's placid enough—I don't let anything disturb that." Told him I had written to both Kennedy and O'Connor saying that last week's depression was mainly gone. "That was just the thing to say. And that reminds me—I have two letters saved here for you from Dr. Bucke and another from Kennedy: Kennedy's curiously brief. I had still another letter today—it was from Mary Costelloe—from somewhere off in Wales—that I sent to Doctor—Doctor Bucke." "I took Kennedy into our secret." "What secret was that?" "Your trip down stairs on Friday." W. laughed very happily. "It *was* a great feat, wasn't it?—an exploit: almost heroic!" Then he added: "You're sure you haven't given it away to any reporter? They would come over to interview me—insist on knowing my sensations! The reporters are mad for sensations. If you have a belly-ache they want to know your sensations. Of course, you have sensations—decided sensations—with a belly-ache, but what's the use making them cheap by advertising the symptoms in a newspaper?" He was a bit amused by this note:

CAMBRIDGE, Aug. 29th, 1888.

My dear Friend, I send you this comprehensive brevity to tell you how glad I am that you are regaining your old self, and are again able to be at work.

Cordially yours,
CHARLOTTE FISKE BATES.

"The feeling of the note is quite loving and correct, but that 'comprehensive brevity' would surely trouble Polonius as a vile phrase." "We never say things so well when we try to say things as when we let them say themselves." "That's what I would have said if you had given me time, Horace." He spoke of the "good health" of Bucke's notes. "They invariably get in under me and give me a boost." This is Kennedy's "curiously brief" note:

Dear Walt W. I enclose letter from St. Louis—I have begun to copy over (clean) some of the 70 pp of the Whitman MS. (my book). Glad to hear of your new books. Am still reading proof. I don't see much prospect of my book on you seeing the light soon. But——. Regards to Traubel.

W. S. KENNEDY.

W. said: "Bucke makes an allusion to Kennedy's book in one of those letters." I looked it up. This: "I wonder how it is we (at least, I) hear nothing these times of Kennedy and his Walt Whitman? I fear publishers are not smiling upon him. Fifty years from now they would be glad enough to get it." Another passage in one of the Bucke letters hit W. hard: "I am thinking of you a great deal in this lovely September weather, wondering how it is with you, dreaming of that September eight years ago when you were here." W. said: "I am dreaming of it, too, Maurice—God bless you!" Said he had not "yet felt disposed to take up the Hicks matter for The Herald." No work today on the book. Reads from time to time in the old English poets. "To-day, however, I have been reading Virgil and Marcus Aurelius." I had a few dollars change (discount) on the paper bill. Offered it to him. He said: "No—you keep it—give it to the boys—the printers, any of the others. It has always been my practice to give a few dollars here and there on occasion among the men—among the people I fall in with as I do with Ferguson's. Aside from the emotional phases—enough of themselves—there is the policy of it: though that is sordid and is not needed to make up the case. People are always extra helpful—are always doing things no money can pay for: I like to have them see I see it."

Gilchrist turned up today. "He didn't stay long—only a few minutes." Bucke wrote: "Be sure you make it clear Walt is in a bad way and must not be visited too much." W. said: "It is done already—I took care to have them make that clear to him down stairs. Herbert is rather inclined to be long-winded, so I realize the importance of having him understand—cautioned. He has come over, I think, to stay a year or so—will settle—get a room or two rooms in the city and put up a cot there and mainly live in that place—meanwhile painting, studying. After he gets his studio set up you must go to see him. You ought to be very good friends."

W, said: "I have about finally decided that the little book must be one dollar and a quarter. In regard to the big book I am still at sea." I spent some time at Ferguson's today looking over page proofs. November Boughs goes to press to-morrow. W. said: "My eye affects a soft wine color—dark, pure—for the little book." Several visitors. Would not see them. I asked W.: "Do you keep your receipts all together?" He laughed. "I keep nothing together: did you ever know me to keep things together? I keep body and soul together—that's about all." Said that though he had promised me a copy of the 1872 edition he "doubted now whether there was more than one copy about the house—the one there—" pointing to the table. "And yet one may turn up: I am always finding things I thought lost, or things I imagined given away long ago, or things I thought I never possessed." Talked a little about the Forman letters he gave me Monday. "There was a gap of four years between the letters," said W., "and a lot happened in those four years. They were in some ways the four worst years of my life: I was down in the dumps from seventy-three about on to seventy-seven—then I got a bit more spruce again. But read the letters: I'd rather refresh my memory a bit with 'em."

38, MARLBOROUGH HILL,
ST. JOHN'S WOOD,
LONDON N. W., 21 Feb. 72.

WALT WHITMAN, ESQ.

Dear Sir, I send herewith, by book post, a short poem called The Great Peace-Maker, which I have just edited for private distribution.

As a constant reader and great admirer of your poetry, I have had the idea that the practical element in this poem, and also its fervent aspiration after the good of mankind, may commend themselves to you,—while a poem more like the rest of our contemporary verse might not.

I have been a long time trying to persuade one or another of our publishers to print a complete English edition of your works —verbatim, without any retrenchments; and I have gone so far as to offer my poor services in justifying as far as criticism can justify poetry, those portions which they take exception to, *or fear to print*. Supposing I ultimately succeeded, would a verbatim reprint of the latest edition, with an introductory essay, have your approval?

Believe me to be dear sir faithfully yours,

H. Buxton Forman.

"Don't that sound refreshing—verbatim, without any retrenchments? That's no by-your-leave spirit. In a day and month and year of weakness I yielded to the idea that the English reader could not stand a full dose of Walt Whitman. It was an evil decision growing out of the best intentions. 'Verbatim, without any retrenchments.' The book belongs so or does not belong at all. Any edition American or English which for any reason whatever is abridged is abhorrent and inexcusable: none the less inexcusable because I may be the guilty man: none the less abhorrent because I am the one to acquiesce in the mutilation of my own book. Worst of all, any cut made in a book which has been subjected to the peculiar criticism visited upon the Leaves is a confession and I do not see why I should be making confessions." On the envelope of Forman's second letter W. had written: "H. Buxton Forman, Jan. '76. sent paper and circ. Apr 4. (Sent W. J. Press art. May 24, '76)."

LONDON, N. W.
26 January, 1876.

WALT WHITMAN ESQ.

My dear Sir, Some years ago when I had occasion to address you, you were so good as to say you should be happy to hear from me again; and as my admiration of your works and interest in whatever concerns you have rather strengthened than weakened, I feel sure you will not mind my asking you one or two questions.

As a faithful student of your books, I have made it my business to obtain every edition I could, and all portraits and notable accounts and criticisms. But there is one edition in particular which I have never been able to see even,—that mentioned by Rossetti as having been issued in 1856 in 16 mo. The American agent to whom my last application for this was forwarded says: "I don't think there is an 1856 edition. There is one earlier or later in great demand, and at a high price, something like twenty-five or thirty dollars; but I can't find that. There was a copy auctioned the other night at something like the above."

Can you tell me whether there is or is not an edition between that one set up by yourself in 1855 and that of Thayer and Eldridge dated 1860–61? If there is, can you give me any particulars that will help me towards buying it? Also, what is the edition that fetches twenty-five dollars to thirty dollars? Not that of 1855; for I hear that can be had for three or four.

When at my friend Mr. W. B. Scott's a few weeks ago, I saw a proof of a fine portrait of you enlarged by Linton: may I ask what it is from, and where it is published?

I live in hopes of publishing some day a good English edition of your works; and my enquiries about editions are not mere bibliomania. I find they vary considerably; and my experience is that the careful collation of various versions of a poet's work is often a key as well as an incitement to the right understanding of his spirit and intent.

I am at present engaged on an edition of Shelley which will be the handsomest in form, and the most extensive in matter (I hope), yet published; and that takes up most of my time.

With best wishes believe me to be, dear sir, faithfully yours,

H. Buxton Forman.

Thursday, September 6th, 1888.

7.45 p. m. W. had been reading Old Mortality. "Scott again?" "O yes, only to kill time." Laid aside his book and talked. Was he well? "Yes—pretty well—but not quite so cocky as Sunday and Monday." Gilchrist was over. Spoke of Gilchrist's life of his mother: "You should read it—read my copy: Karl Knortz has it now, but we can get it back. You will not find the book to equal your great expectations, if you have any—will perhaps be disappointed. It is true much of the book is made up of things written by Mrs. Gilchrist—but writing was not the best of her. The best of her was her talk—to hear her perfectly say these things which she has only imperfectly written. I shall never forget—never forget: she is over there now, where you are—eyeing me, overflowing with utterance. She was marvellous above other women in traits in which women are marvellous as a rule—immediate perception, emotion, deep inevitable insight. She had such superb judgment—it welled up and out and I only sat off and wondered: welled up from a reservoir of riches, spontaneously, unpremeditatedly. Women are ahead of us in that anyhow—way ahead of us. It was because she was that kind of a woman that I always trusted Mrs. Gilchrist's picture of Carlyle—of the Carlyles. She was not a blind dreamer—a chaser of fancies: she was concrete—spiritually concrete, I might say: not in the sordid sense of it but the big, the high. She was practical enough to know just how to ask that dangerous question, will it pay? and to answer it with high meanings. I know nothing more miserable, sickening, than Will it pay? as it is usually asked. This is not a tonight's opinion: it is premeditated—what I have come to by careful thought: I want you to regard it as much. For me it is conclusive."

I brought W. Froude's Carlyle in London and a copy of this week's Unity containing a poem by Sidney Morse. Along with other things I had pages 16 to 32 November Boughs—first printed sheet. W. was as eager as a child as he examined it. "Good!" "Fine!" "Done at last!" "Hurrah!" "Hunkie-dory!" Many exclamations. I asked: "Where are your doubts now?" "Gone, gone, gone utterly." He was silent. Then: "I count on nothing physical till I see it—not even a promise of marriage till the marriage." And yet he confessed:

"This defied augury, it came out so fine: it's the best press-work I have ever had on any one of my books. Think of the agonies that have led up to it, Horace!" Afterwards he added: "Tell them that when they are all done with the work I'll come over, or send someone over to represent me, and we'll all take a drink together." Felicitated himself upon the arrangement of one of his pages. "My printer's eyes are never deceived." Turning over a few pages. "Yonnondio: you notice that name? They printed it in The Critic first, and the Critic fellows objected to it that my use of the word was not correct, not justified. You remember, see"—pointing—"I make it mean *lament* and so forth: they say, no, that is not it: Yonnondio signifies governor —was an Indian name given to the French governors sent over to this continent in colonial times. No doubt there's considerable to warrant their argument, but"—putting his forefinger down on the poem and looking at me waggishly—"I had already committed myself to my own meaning—written the poem: so here it stands, for right or wrong." I asked him where he got hold of his own construction of the word. He replied: "From an old man—a wise, reticent old man—much learned in Injun tongues, lore—in Injun habits and the history of them so far as known. You never have asked Brinton? I wish you would—for me: he would know—something, at least. The debate is like many others—inconclusive. I never knew a controversy of this character—each side ready to swear to its accuracy, full of the arrogance of learning, equipped with book knowledge—to end in anything like a settlement: the problem was always as wide open at the end as at the start."

Afterwards pointing to the Grant poem he closed the sheet and said: "It was in Harper's Weekly: a young fellow there, who was friendly to me, sent for it. Grant was dying at the time—or thought to be. After I had sent off the poem Grant revived, so, while it was held, I wrote and despatched the after-piece, which was finally printed along with the original lines. Now"—indicating the poem—"it is back to its first shape again: Grant is dead. It was the last thing the Harpers took from me.

This [With Husky Haughty Lips O Sea!] was the last piece proper in the Magazine: the Grant piece went in solely through the friendship of that young man. I have the feeling that the Harpers wish no more of me." W. adds Old Age's Lambent Peaks to go in on the last page preceding After the Supper and Talk. Was he going to include the Sheridan piece? "No—I am not particular about that. The old age poem belongs in the book—is in a sense almost necessary: might be last of all, indeed, following After the Supper and Talk—but somewhere, close to the end: it must go in." I told W. Harrison Morris in telephoning today asked: "What does the poem mean?" "You didn't tell him, did you? I never tell. It's my secret until the next fellow catches on by himself—then it's his secret, too. What does it mean? How should I know? Tell him to tell me."

W. picked up the Pall Mall pamphlet containing a reproduction of Gilchrist's Whitman. "You have seen it? It's pretty doubtful to me—pretty doubtful: Herbert has gone way off to make me rather than staying close by: I am only to be done right close by. Mrs. Coates spoke when she was here of some superb picture. She certainly did not mean this—she could not have called this superb." "Why not? After Bonsall's verdict on Frank Fowler's portrait we might expect anything." W. laughed. "But that was a good piece of work, Horace—well done—splendidly done." "Yes, but it was not *you*." He nodded. "That's right, too: it *was* a bad go as a portrait, wasn't it?" W. said he was "still wondering" what had "brought Herbert over to America." "Herbert must have had a windfall somehow—sold a picture, maybe: maybe borrowed a thousand pounds or so from his brother. Did I ever tell you about Percy Gilchrist? He's another son—invented some steel process—has made a million dollars or more by it, God help 'im! A million dollars is a lot of baggage to get in a man's way, ain't it? A million dollars would spoil me for life. Herbert and Talcott Williams seem to entertain quite a shine for each other. I remember Herbert once said to me: 'I can easily see how a man in England might want to come here but I don't see how a man once on this side would want to go back.' Herbert is a fellow you should know, Horace, though I am not sure you would quite gee together. Herbert is English to the jumping off place: he is aggressively national. Talcott is not an American by birth—Syrian, I think: born, however, of English or American parents."

Intended to write Morse today but had not done so. A letter came from Bucke while I was there. I gave the printers at Ferguson's today a box of cigars as from Walt, who was greatly pleased. "It was right, it was good, and, as the old lady would say, I am glad you had the wit to do it." W. gave me a Swinton letter with the suggestion that I should "notice the jubilant tone of John's mood," adding: "Swinton sometimes seems to get in the dumps awful—is down in the mouth about the tardiness of the people to respond to the appeal of the economic radicals. The people will come along in their own time—yes, and take their time, too." This is what Swinton wrote:

JOHN SWINTON'S PAPER,
NEW YORK, Feb. 13, 1885.

My dear Walt—The last honor that decorates the brow of genius is now yours, and it is that I herewith introduce you to a live New Zealander—a professor from New Zealand—Prof. Brown of Canterbury College, New Zealand. He's an old admirer of the bard of Paumanok (fish-shaped) and is anxious to meet you; and so I give him this note to you. I know you will be glad to meet him. I shake your hand.

JOHN SWINTON.

"That's the way John makes fun and is dead in earnest at the same time," said W.: "New Zealand is pretty far around: some day we will girdle the globe." W. mentioned Weir Mitchell: "He is my friend—has proved it in divers ways: is not quite as easy-going as our crowd—has a social position to maintain: yet I don't know but he's about as near right in most things as most people. I can't say that he's a world-author—he don't hit me for that size—but he's a world-doctor for sure—leastwise everybody says so and I join in." W. sent Musgrove out for some envelopes. When they were brought W. said: "No—they won't do—they don't satisfy me for shape: I like a shapely envelope. What are you laughing about, Horace? Oh, you think I'm fussy? No—I'm only esthetic!" He laughed. "Someways I do, someways I don't care, for things: they hit my eye or they don't: I can't always say why I like or don't like but I am quite firm in my preferences." He has not yet completely arranged the Hicks for the Herald.

I had a long note from Morse today. The minute W. heard me say so he was impatient to have it read. He stopped me again and again with comments. When Morse spoke of being "immersed" in his novel, Jefferson Brown, W. said: "Stop right where you are and tell me about it. Morse never read it or any part of it to me: is it like Mrs. Ward's book?" Morse mentioned "the more Bohemian" of his friends and said: "I feel certain of them." W. asked: "Does he mean us?" He was much interested in Morse's purpose to make a big Emerson bust for Edward Emerson. "His Emerson can't be beat—it's a final triumph." "I rather prefer the big head of Emerson left here by Morse," says W.: "it has great merit." No copies were ever taken. It is here still. Vila Blake said to Morse: "The small head is human, the large divine." "That is striking," said W.: "Tell me about Blake—who he is." W. then talked in a general way about Morse: "I had the idea of getting a piece of ground and having him put up a rig here—a den in which he could have his own way: plenty of floor room—tall ceilings, sky-lights, air: getting everything in character with Sidney's big, generous ideas of work. I was ready to put two or three hundred dollars into it for him. Every literary fellow, artist—every man who has a big job of work to do—should have his own den—a coop entirely his own—with a cot in it, if need be, and a stove: a studio with a human side to it." Morse once had such a studio at Quincy. I spoke of it. W. said: "That all sounds good: that's the same idea. Morse has grown wonderfully the last two years—thrown off a coat or two—developed, evoluted (that's the word: evoluted!)

From a Photograph by Henry Ulke and Bro.

WALT WHITMAN
(1871)

—will go on to the end getting a little higher up all the time. I don't know but Chicago is just the place for him: if he can get a top-floor room somewhere and a landlord who won't worry him too much about the rent. Will you write Morse? Yes? Well—give him my love—tell him I have all sorts of faith in his success. Tell him that we miss him here—that his presence was a benediction: that we have never had any doubt about our love for him."

W. gave me a copy of a Washington (1871) portrait made by Ulke. I said of it: "It has a William Morris lay-out." He replied: "Do you say so? It would please O'Connor to hear you say that. Some of them say my face there has a rogue in it. O'Connor called it my sea-captain face. Some newspaper got hold of a copy of the photograph and said it bore out the notion that Walt Whitman was a sensualist. I offered one to a woman in Washington. She said she'd rather have a picture that had more love in it. It's a little rough and tumble, possibly, but it's not a face I could hate. Could you? Honest Injun, Horace: could you hate it?"

Friday, September 7, 1888.

Saw Oldach today about binding November Boughs. Will give me an estimate to-morrow. Gave Myrick copy for duplicate plates—contents and pagings. Plates of Specimen Days and Leaves of Grass not yet secured from Sherman. November Boughs will be finished by Monday night. Called on W. about eight, evening. Corning and Harned had just gone. Corning has bought W.'s horse and carriage. W. had previously tendered them to Bucke for what Bucke calls "an imaginary debt", Bucke declining. W. said to Corning: "I first offered it to somebody to whom I owed two hundred dollars." Said to me concerning it: "It marks a new epoch in my life: another stage on the down-hill road." "I shouldn't think with your idea of death that you would speak of it as a *down* road." "Sure enough —the word was false: *up* road: up—up: another stage on the up-hill road: that certainly seems more like me and I want to be like myself."

W. sat this evening with his big blue bath-robe on—head thrown rather back: gray hat on: dark red tie, carelessly half-undone: leaning side-wise towards the light: Life in London (Carlyle) in his hand. Said he had just taken the book up this evening and grown instantly interested. "I think the book is going to be one of the events." Harned had not been in for nearly a week. W. had welcomed him as "the prodigal." Speaking of Thurman's sudden sickness in N. Y. last evening when about to speak: "He should go home: he would lose nothing by it and the world would gain. We have passed beyond Thurman: he was left behind by a past dispensation." I told W. Bucke was afraid I was pushing him too strenuously with the book. "Maurice, don't you believe it! Not at all—not at all. It's the best thing for me—it's the only thing that has kept me alive. The work has not weakened, it has strengthened, me: it has steadied my nerves—been a star ahead: sustained me when everything else would have failed." Then he added: "As the sailors say when they are pretty sure of the harbor—we're going to fetch it! We've got past all, or nearly all, the dangers, headlands: our time is coming now: the voyage is near done." Asked me: "Isn't Corning inclined to taffy—soft-soap—something like that? He has been here a number of times: talks volubly, cheerfully (I like his optimism): seems inclined to pile it on pretty thick. That tendency to overpraise—is it usual with him? Yes? I was afraid so: I had that impression myself. What do you attribute it to? I like nearly everything in Corning but this: it is so laboriously sugary: it spoils to the taste in its excess." "It's the minister in him—the hireling minister who has to oblige everybody in his parish." "You talk like a Quaker but I guess you are right: what is first a studied habit may afterwards become second nature. The case is saved if we say Corning is as he is because he must be."

I read W. an Independent editorial. When I came to the close of the third sentence he laughed heartily at the thrust. Before I had gone far he interrupted me to say: "That's Stoddard—Stoddard, I guess: and it's well written, too—he writes well: it bears the marks of his hand. You see, I still pass for a cipher in certain circles." When he found his poem quoted in full he added: "That's fair: give the devil—the Independent —his due: let's thank God for this one touch of grace. The enemy seem to be still about—there are plenty of enemies left— we must still stand to our arms. Horace, read the rest of the piece—let me hear it all: tell me the worst."

"POETICAL FADS.

"One of our magazines announces that it will publish at an early date an article entitled, Has America Produced a Poet? the author being a well-known English critic. While we hope for an affirmative answer to the question, we trust that this Englishman will not, like so many of his countrymen, name Walt Whitman as the poet. It is curious the veneration in which this man's works are held in England, and the reflected glory they obtain in this country on that account. There may be something interesting and venerable in Whitman's personality as there is, undoubtedly, something pathetic in his poverty; but we have always failed to comprehend the interest in his poetry—we call it such by courtesy—that Lord Tennyson and others have frequently manifested. During the winter we commented on one or two of Whitman's effusions that appeared in the Herald. Now another appears in The Century for September—Old Age's Lambent Peaks—that is, indeed, less shocking, but no less involved and unrhythmical. Here it is:

> "'The touch of flame—the illuminating fire—the loftiest look
> at last,
> O'er city, passion, sea—o'er prairie, mountain, wood—the
> earth itself;
> The airy, different, changing hues of all, in falling twilight,
> Objects and groups, bearings, faces, reminiscences;
> The calmer sight—the golden setting, clear and broad;
> So much i' the atmosphere, the points of view, the situations
> whence we scan,
> Bro't out by them alone—so much (perhaps the best) unreck'd
> before;
> The lights indeed from them—old age's lambent peaks.'

"Nothing can be said for these lines except that they are original in their construction and obscurity. They will be read and extolled by a dozen or two Whitmaniacs; but that is all.

"The effort to make a man's poetry great by creating a clique and a claque to sound his praises is bound to be unsuccessful, whether the deity be Browning or Shelley in England and in Boston or Whitman in New York. Writing of this very subject, Mr. J. T. Palgrave, the editor of that incomparable collection of English lyrics known as The Golden Treasury, and at present Professor of Poetry in Oxford University, said, in a recent letter to the editor of The Independent: 'We are deluged in this country just now with criticisms on the poets, and I often regard it as a proof of their essential vitality that they survive the praises of cliques and societies.' As a corollary of this statement, we may say that if a poet's works are worthy they will be recognized and live without any co-operative enthusiasm.

"Editors have a certain duty to the public in their selection of poems for publication. There is no doubt that one of the chief causes of the disrepute into which poetry has fallen is the woful inferiority of the stuff and twaddle published in our periodicals under the name of poetry. Better do as The Atlantic did a few months ago and as it does again for September—omit poetry altogether, if *poetry* can not be found. Editors must be heartless, must be cruel to contributors, in order to be kind to readers."

"That's me," said W.: "Is there any reason for anyone being further deceived in me? That's a good sample indictment: it takes me up in several items and convicts me without qualification. It sounds wonderful like Dick Stoddard—good enough to be his, bad enough to be his." W. said: "A Symonds letter is a red day for my calendar. This is one of them—an old letter." He reached it forward to me. "Symonds is as tall as a mountain peak—and gentle: always gentle. He hasn't got William's guts: he lacks that first brutality of utterance which goes with the initiators and inspirers: but for pure grace and suavity of phrase, for a certain element of literary as distinguished from oratorical eloquence, he is unexcelled. Symonds is a craftsman of the first water—pure as crystal—fine, fine, fine—dangerously near the superfine in his weaker moments. I am always strangely moved by a letter from Symonds: it makes the day, it makes many days, sacred."

CLIFTON HILL HOUSE,
BRISTOL, Oct 7, 1871.

My dear Sir. When a man has ventured to dedicate his work to another without authority or permission, I think he is bound to make confession of the liberty he has taken. This must be my excuse for sending you the crude poem in which you may perchance detect some echo, faint and feeble, of your Calamus. As I have put pen to paper I cannot refrain from saying that since the time when I first took up Leaves of Grass in a friend's room at Trinity College Cambridge six years ago till now, your poems have been my constant companions. I have read them in Italy by the shores of the Mediterranean, under pine trees or in caverns washed by the sea—and in Switzerland among the Alpine pastures and beside the glaciers. At home I have found in them pure air and health—the free breath of the world—when often cramped by illness and the cares of life. What one man can do by communicating to those he loves the treasure he has found, I have done among my friends.

I say this in order that I may, as simply as may be, tell you how much I owe to you. He who makes the words of a man his spiritual food for years is greatly that man's debtor.

As for the poem I send you—it is of course implicit already in your Calamus, especially in Scented Herbage of my Breast. I have but set to an old tune the new divine song: for you know that on this side of the Atlantic at least people most readily listen to the old tunes. I fear greatly I have marred the purity and beauty of your thought by my bad singing.

I am an Englishman, married, with three children, and am aged thirty.

Answer to this I scarcely expect, as I certainly do not deserve it. The poem I send is due for reasons already set forth. It is a printer's proof at present and no more. I am your grateful and attached

JOHN ADDINGTON SYMONDS.

W. said: "That was one of the first, if not the very first, of the Symonds letters. It starts off with the good will which he has never abated of to these very last days. It makes a fellow walk pretty straight when a man like that takes him so dead in earnest. Symonds has always seemed to me a forthright man—unhesitating, without cant: not slushing over, not freezing up. He has written me many letters: they are all of the same character—warm (not too warm), a bit inquisitive, ingratiating." Another letter W. called my attention to was in an envelope endorsed in his own hand: "friendly note from Ward, the sculptor (will send an order and money after May 1)."

140 East 38th Street,
NEW YORK, April 23, 1876.

My dear Mr. Whitman: Your note was received and I am only waiting until the 1st of May when I shall be more "flush" to send you an order for five copies of your complete works.

I am glad that you are publishing your works in this complete form and feel sure that you will be well repaid in every way for the effort.

I hope to do more than this in the way of getting subscribers.
Very Sincerely Yours
J. Q. A. WARD.

I said to W.: "After all a large proportion of the vital people got on your side. The enemies did not understand you, but the people with blood by and bye got a notion that you were some shucks." He was "satisfied to have it said that way," adding: "I have quite well realized that I gradually secured a considerable body of approbation: things never got easy with me, but they did get less cruel." W. gave me an army pass

April 23/76

140 East 38th St

New York

My dear Mr Whitman:

Your note was received and I am only waiting until the 1st of May when I shall be more "flush" to send you an order for five copies of your complete works —

I am glad that you are publishing your works in this complete form — and feel sure that you will be well repaid in every way for the effort — I hope to do more than this in the way of getting subscribers — of

Very truly
y'rs
J. Q. A. Ward

LETTER TO WALT WHITMAN FROM J. Q. A. WARD
20

made out to W. to put among my papers. He had endorsed it: "Pass Burnside's Army Jan '63." It read this way:

PROVOST MARSHALL GENERAL'S OFFICE,
No 330   ARMY OF THE POTOMAC,
               FALMOUTH STATION, Dec 27th, 1862.

The Bearer Walter Whitman has permission to pass from Falmouth Station to Aquia Creek Landing by rail for the purpose of business. This pass will expire this the 29th day of December (twenty-ninth).

By command of M. R. Patrick, Provost Marshall General.
                                   F. C. MILLER.
                         MAJOR AND PROVOST MARSHALL.

W. in mighty good feather this evening. Said he had found an Oscar Wilde letter but "would not give it to" me "just yet." Wanted "to read it again." "Wilde," he said, "may have been some of him fraud at that time but was not all fraud. My letter from him seems wholly sincere. He has extraordinary brilliancy of genius with perhaps rather too little root in eternal soils. Wilde gives up too much to the extrinsic decorative values in art." Also said: "I am laying aside one thing and another for you from day to day. You will do what you will with them—you will throw them away if that seems best to do—you will use them some way—this way or that (perhaps publish them): I do not wish to tie you up at all—to say what you must or may not do: I prefer to leave you free to dispose of anything I may pass over into your hands as you see fit: put it into the fire, put it anywhere: I feel safe in your hands." Before I left he handed me four letters done up in a string. They proved to be one each from Conway, Hotten, William Michael Rossetti and Trowbridge. "You will find that Conway commits himself to Leaves of Grass powerful like in his letter. Hotten writes as a publisher— almost apologizes for himself." Rossetti's envelope was endorsed by W.: "first instalment from W M Rossetti free will offering." I did not stop further to talk about the letters.

Saturday, September 8th, 1888.

8 p. m.   W. reading Life in London, going through it with
for him wonderful avidity, but was very willing to put it down
and hear what I had to say.   "My health has only been so-so,
neither much good nor much bad."   I had been in to see both
the binder and the printer today—brought over specimen book
of colors for cover of November Boughs—samples of cloth: also
saw Brown and got from him the sheet containing the Hicks
head.   W. in high humor.   "Things are progressing: progress
is what I am after—I want to get along—get the work done:
then I will be ready to take in sail for the last harbor."   I got
from Myrick proofs of Annex page, with changed pagings for
duplicate plates.   The instant W. looked at the former he exclaimed: "That will do: I can say so because I trust first impressions and this first impression is a good one."   Chose a dark
wine linen for the cover of the book.   Regarded the Hicks picture intently.   "I can see defects: this forehead, for instance, is
not quite as it should be: but my general notion of the portrait
is a good one: as I often say, I congratulate myself that it's not
so damned bad as it might be."   As so often before he commented upon "the superiority of English presswork."   Has
decided for good on a dollar and a quarter for November Boughs.
"Do you think the world will stand it?"   Oldach asked me today
if W. was of German stock.   W. said of that: "Not German:
no: Dutch: a good lot of the Dutch is in me: I owe some of my
characteristics indubitably to the Dutch.   My mother was a
Van Velsor: I favor her: 'favor' they call it up on Long Island—
a curious word so used, yet a word of great suggestiveness.
Often people would say—men, women, children, would say—
'You are a Whitman: I know you.'   When I asked how they
knew they would up with a finger at me: 'By your features, your
gait, your voice: they are your mother's.'   I think all that was,
is, true: I could see it in myself."

I quoted three references to W. made in The Critic this week.
The Critic speaks of Old Age's Lambent Peaks as in W.'s "best

manner": it quotes James Ward Davidson's book, The Poetry of the Future, and says that "poetry will, while discarding measured verse and terminal rhyme, retain the rhythmical foot": it says of C. Sadakichi Hartmann that he some years ago attempted "to launch a Walt Whitman Society on an unprepared world." W. had nothing much to say on the first two points, but was quick to take up the last: "A world unprepared! Yes, indeed! But I was the fellow who put his foot down on that little plan—who forbade the launching of the enterprise. So Baxter and the fellows there squelched Hartmann. It had always been my contention that I should avoid proselytism—avoid all gospel work that looked like force—do nothing to compel attention: trust all to freedom, growth: then what came would belong to us. For ten years and more there was a suspicion lurking within me—dim, undefined, for a long time, but finally grown clear, convincing—that our whole Whitman business was ticklish, uncertain—hung in the balance, with perhaps only a hair needed to shift the fine measure either way. In all I have written, said, I have exercised the greatest care, lest I go too far, or say too much, or write things damaging to our cause: indeed, I might almost put it, nervous, almost nervous, lest I forget the metes and bounds of our worth: trembling, nervous, nearly, if I could be that (as thank God I never could be!). But since November Boughs has been under way I have had a revulsion of feeling—have gained a sense of security—become convinced that things are all right, the current strong our way, the end beyond a doubt. Though this experience has gone largely, if not wholly, unconfessed, it was being lived through by me in all those years. You can easily imagine, then, how a Walt Whitman Club, a concerted movement, an attempt to beat down the opposition, should be everyhow repugnant to me. But Hartmann is more than the organizer of a Whitman club. I wish you could meet him: his views on things Occidental, as they say, are rare, novel—should be heard. They come from one who has his roots in the other side of the planet—was raised under surprising differences of perspective. Take his ideas of Holland, France, Germany,

England (he has been in all those countries) and you will find them very often just the things we need to have told us. Hartmann has written astonishingly good studies. His observations on America are bright—surprisingly searching—some of them."

I talked to W. of my Japanese friend Tatui Baba. Baba says his first strong impression received in America is of the fearful gap between its rich and poor. "Ah!" exclaimed W.: "Did he say that? Then I am convinced that he put his finger on the sore spot at once. I always come back to the same idea myself: there is the itch—the trouble: there is no mistake: the fact of the matter is the situation is growing worse and worse. And yet," he continued, "we must not forget that the disease is one which may be cured: the cure of it is in our own hands. It is seen at its damnedest in the big cities—New York, Philadelphia, Chicago: but it is bad no matter where. America has got to clean house some day!" I asked him: "Will she do it with a broom or a gun?" He reflected for a minute. "That depends: I am not prepared to say the gun is impossible. I don't like to think about the gun—it is not a pleasant prospect to dream about—but history sometimes has a way of jumping difficulties in a somewhat violent style. I say, if, if, if, it is not the one thing, then it must be, must be, the other. I like the broom best myself."

Oldach says of the cover on the Epictetus: "It is buckram." W. said: "I don't believe it but I am outvoted. But then it's Honest John Davis over again." I looked puzzled. "Don't you know the story? It was one of Wendell Phillips'—one of his best." I still looked blank. "Well—I don't remember its details. Honest John Davis was a senator (many years ago) and Phillips hated him like the devil. 'Honest John Davis' was a nickname—deserved, I believe: he was so cold, austere, stern, strict, clean, hard. Davis was somewhere—it was night: heard an old darky woman call out 'Hot cakes!'—bought one. But the cake was not hot. John turned back. 'See here, my woman, this ain't hot!' 'Law sakes, honey—dey all says dey is!' So he was outvoted—Honest John Davis: Honest Walt Whitman. Phillips told the story beautifully: indeed, I think the best part of Phillips was in the asides, the digressions: they were always fresh, free, powerful."

By some turn in the talk W. got on the subject of the quadroons and octoroons in the South. Did he believe in amalgamation? "I know many who already have it done—critics, reviewers, historians—done, proved: proved as they prove most things, which is not to prove them at all. I don't believe in it—it is not possible. The nigger, like the Injun, will be eliminated: it is the law of races, history, what-not: always so far inexorable—always to be. Someone proves that a superior grade of rats comes and then all the minor rats are cleared out." I said: "That sounds like Darwin." "Does it? It sounds like me, too." W. then proceeded: "I have been in New Orleans—known, seen, all its peculiar phases of life. Of course my report would be forty years old or so. The Octoroon was not a whore, a prostitute, as we call a certain class of women here—and yet *was*, too: a hard class to comprehend: women with splendid bodies—no bustles, no corsets, no enormities of any sort: large, luminous, rich eyes: face a rich olive: habits indolent, yet not lazy as we define laziness North: fascinating, magnetic, sexual, ignorant, illiterate: always more than pretty—'pretty' is too weak a word to apply to them. Do you tell me that amalgamation is likely? I do not see it. The American white and the Southern black will *mix* but not *ally*. I have considered the problem from all sides. It is wonderful the readiness with which French and Negro, or Spanish and Negro, will marry—interlock—and the results are always good. It is the same with the Injun and Nigger—they too will ask no questions: they, too, achieve equally fine reproductivities. New Orleans, in my day, was divided into three municipalities, arrondissements. In one of these were the French and here were those great women—a full acceptance of them. Now, the Southern white does not encourage such intermixtures: there are psychological, physiological, reasons for it—back of all psychologies, physiologies, some deeper fact. They are a study, too—the poor whites South: lank, sallow, coughing, spitting, with no bellies (and bellies seem a sine qua non): hang on and on into the sixties and seventies: seem to defy all auguries, theories, which attempt to set them aside or limit their future. For all that is said to discountenance them they maintain their independence, stand aloof, are not familiar, run affairs, govern, domineer."

Gave me a letter from Bucke. "Keep it—there's nothing particular in it—but I know you like to keep the run of these things." I asked W. a question or two about Conway's old letter. First he had me read the letter aloud.

14 MILLBORNE GROVE, BROMPTON,
LONDON, ENGLAND, Feb. 1, '68.

My dear friend, I have but a moment in which to write to you, if I save the mail. My object is to ask you, in behalf of Hotten, whether it is consistent with your will that the selection from your works made by Rossetti shall be sold in the American market. Hotten has written to me that if so he will give you one shilling on each copy sold in America. He hopes the prefatory essay may attract purchasers there. I have read it and it is excellent. The volume will be out next week; it is very neatly done, and quite as large as your last edition (American). Hotten writes that when expenses are paid, you will have a percentage on each copy sold here. I have assumed to be your financial agent here. I hope you will answer about the sale in America by return mail. Rossetti is much pleased with your letter to him. If you see O'Connor please thank him for sending me The Ghost and The Carpenter—which we (wife and I) think extremely interesting and dramatic. You will see in the February Fortnightly I have (in reviewing Swinburne's Blake) had something more to say of your work—which is to me the more I read it (as I do daily) the Genesis of an American Bible.

Faithfully yours
M. D. CONWAY.

P. S. I will watch for reviews when your book appears, and send you any that are valuable.

The letter was addressed to W. in care of the Attorney General's office. W. said: "Conway closed with a striking thought." I asked: "Has he stuck to it?" "Sometimes I suspect not: I don't mean that he has gone back on me (he has not): I mean that he don't look upon me with quite the fullest favor of his earlier enthusiasm. Conway has done me good turns which I would be an ingrate not to acknowledge. Conway, you will notice, does not call the Leaves a new Bible but the Genesis of a new Bible. That's more like sense than to make monopolistic claims." "No matter what has come more is yet to come." "That's what I would have said, Horace, if you'd given me time. I don't intend it for cant when I say in my book that my best lesson is the lesson by which I am myself destroyed." The letter from Hotten connects with the Conway letter here and there.

> LONDON, 5 February, 1868.

Dear Sir, I have taken the liberty to send you by this post a copy of Mr. Swinburne's new book upon William Blake, poet and artist—a great but neglected genius who was counted as a madman by his contemporaries here sixty years ago. As Mr. Swinburne makes mention of yourself in this, his most recent published composition, it is but right that you should see what is said. But irrespective of that I feel assured—from what Mr. M. D. Conway tells me—that the book will interest you.

Mr. Conway will have told you of our intention to publish an English edition of your "poems"—or rather a "selection" from them—edited by Mr. W. M. Rossetti, one of our most able critics and himself a poet. In about a week I shall send you a copy by post. It makes a handy volume of about 440 pages, and will I think be a favorite here. Mr. Rossetti's introduction is most admirable and gives great satisfaction to your admirers and his friends.

Now, we want the privilege of selling copies of the "selection" in the United States—if you will allow us: and I have told Mr. Conway that I would give you, or your agent, a royalty of one shilling (or twenty-five cents gold) upon every copy sold in your country.

I imagine the sale of this "selection" in your country would serve as whet, or stimulant, to readers to secure copies of the complete works. I really don't think it would materially interfere with the sale of the latter.

On this English edition I will ask your acceptance of a share of our profits—after the original outlay in paper, printing, and binding, has been returned to the publisher.

I was greatly gratified this afternoon in having almost the first copy of Mr. Robert Buchanan's new volume of essays placed in my hands. I was gratified because in the middle of the book his admirable paper upon your poems—the article which recently appeared in the Broadway—is given.

I think in conclusion that I ought to apologize for sending this familiarly written letter to you, as I am but a trader—a bookseller—and have only an acquaintance with your books of some years' standing to offer as an excuse. True, the first copies imported into this country were at the order of the undersigned; but that, it is feared, will not in any way palliate the liberty now taken.

Yours very obediently:
John Camden Hotten.

W. said: "Hotten didn't know that I in the main like traders, workers, anyone, better than authors. The author class is a priest class with esoteric doctrines: I do not easily mix with it—I refuse to condone it. This is a part of the so much that went towards producing my English editions: the story is not to be all told offhand—the cat has a very, very long tail." W. said: "I am still holding Wilde back—you shall have it to-morrow." W. also said this evening: "Some day I will tell you the real story of my life: then you will open your eyes." I looked at him, supposing he was smiling. He was dead serious. "What do you mean?" I asked. "I can't commence now—some day I will explain."

Sunday, September, 9th, 1888.

Not one of W.'s best days. Very close, rainy, debilitating. I went down at seven. He lay on the bed, but knew me, dark as it was. "I know your step no matter how lightly you tread." Stayed on the bed for full half an hour. Talked very readily and easily. He wanted to get up at once but I objected. He did finally do so and go to his chair. He closed the blinds of the shutter. Adjusted the arm of the gaspipe and turned the key. Could not find a match. Fumbled about, upset the clothes-basket in which he throws his waste papers. He never said a word. Black enough to blind an owl. I then broke in and got the gas lighted. W. said: "I can generally pilot myself about here, but the devil gets into things (or me) now and then."

W. rarely reads his poems to anybody. To-night read An Evening Lull to me. His voice was strong and sweet. He never recites a poem (his own). I never had him do it for me. Occasionally he will cite a line or two. "I don't know my poems that way: any one of you fellows probably could repeat more lines from the Leaves than I could." Again: "I never commit poems to memory—they would be in my way." He further remarked: "I don't revise my revisions too much—polish: I don't hold it to be principally important to develope special technical flavors. Studying for recitation is mainly technical—tends to reaction: encourages formalism. I keep as far away from the mere machinery of composition as I can."

W. gave me the Wilde letter. I thought he might say more about it. He said little: only this: "It seems all straight and honest to me. I have been told a thousand times what Wilde is but I do not see why Wilde is not what he is and I am not what I am with both of us friends according each other a mutual respect. There is no parade in this note: it wears the simplest clothes—has no sunflower in its button hole—has in fact a cast of virgin simplicity, sincerity. Read it for yourself: see if the letter does not bear me out." He said nothing while I read. He had endorsed the envelope in blue pencil: "from Oscar

Wilde early in '82." The postmark was Chicago, March 1. The letter was written in New York.

1267 BROADWAY, NEW YORK.

My Dear Dear Walt—Swinburne has just written to me to say as follows.

"I am sincerely interested and gratified by your account of Walt Whitman and the assurance of his kindly and friendly feeling towards me: and I thank you, no less sincerely, for your kindness in sending me word of it. As sincerely can I say, what I shall be freshly obliged to you if you will assure him of in my name, that I have by no manner of means relaxed my admiration of his noblest works—such parts, above all, of his writings, as treat of the noblest subjects, material and spiritual, with which poetry can deal—I have always thought it, and I believe it will be hereafter generally thought his highest and surely most enviable distinction that he never speaks so well as when he speaks of great matters—Liberty, for instance, and Death.

"This of course does not imply that I do, or rather it implies that I do not agree with all his theories, or admire all his work in anything like equal measure—a form of admiration which I should by no means desire for myself and am as little prepared to bestow on another—considering it a form of scarcely indirect insult."

There! You see how you remain in our hearts—and how simply and grandly Swinburne speaks of you, knowing you to be simple and grand yourself.

Will you in return send me for Swinburne a copy of your Essay on Poetry—the pamphlet—with your name and his on it—it would please him so much. Before I leave America I must see you again—there is no one in this wide great world of America whom I love and honor so much. With warm affection, and honorable admiration,

OSCAR WILDE.

When I looked up after reading the letter W. asked: "Am I not right? Does he strike a false note? It all rings sound and true

...ssay on Poetry — the
pamphlet — with
your name on his
on it — it would
please him so much.

Before I leave
America I must see
him again — there is no
one in this wide great
world of America
whom I love and
honour so much..
                with warm
        affection, and honourable
            admiration,
                Oscar Wilde

A PAGE FROM AN OSCAR WILDE LETTER TO WALT WHITMAN

to me there. Everybody's been so in the habit of looking at Wilde cross-eyed, sort of, that they have charged the defect of their vision up against Wilde as a weakness in his character." I told W. Harned liked Old Age's Lambent Peaks "a whole lot." He replied: "So do I, if I may be allowed to say it: to me it is an essential poem—it needed to be made." Said he "had a letter from Rhys." "He is off in Wales somewhere or was—having a good time, flitting about, seeing his own people, new things, fresh incidents. But he says nothing about our fellows—about the fellows we are interested in over there." Again: "I have another letter, too—from Rolleston: you know him?—he is the Epictetus man. He says he has in hand now a batch of the German proofs for the German edition of Leaves of Grass. You remember, the edition is not to be complete, to include all: is simply to be made up of translations of a few of the poems—Knortz, Karl Knortz, rendering a number and Rolleston doing the rest. What will the book come to, do you think? It excites my curiosity. I want your father to see the proofs if they are sent me—want his opinion." Rolleston asked for Knortz's present address. W. says of Rolleston: "We have never met but he has made me from time to time notable tenders of affection." Said of Rhys: "He has many solid, estimable qualities: lacks brilliancy but possesses substance: should come to something (I can't say what) in the finish." Then suddenly he laughed. "All the foreign mail comes the same day. I did not tell you I got a copy of the Star—London Star: it contains a notice of me drawn out by Herbert's picture in the Grosvenor Gallery." Here he paused and laughed again most merrily. "And it is very funny: the fellow who writes the notice (a very good notice it is, too: among the best)—Clarke—William I take it—says the picture is much like and all that except that Walt Whitman has no Italian curls in his beard: 'Italian curls' he calls them. How cute! How direct!"

Harned tells me Gilchrist on his call last week criticised the Eakins portrait "generally if not sharply." W. asked me:

"Do you know exactly what he said of it?" adding without waiting for my answer: "But it's of no importance: of no importance at all what he thinks of it"—then saying rather apologetically: "I should not say that—should not say of no importance: it has an importance—an importance its own: has the sort of value which goes with the usual, the commonplace—as telling what technique purely, the schools, traditions, would say of such a piece of work." My father had said he was not entirely satisfied with the flesh of the portrait—it lacked in purity. W. replied: "It is good to hear that and it is in effect true I have no doubt. My own impression summed up is, that the painting is a genuine piece of work—a quite extraordinary piece of work: may one day be considered (as somebody has said here to me) even a great production. I can very easily see why the average run of critics should make faces at it—some of 'em hideous faces—why it is inevitable, necessary, for them to do so, considering their philosophies of style: but Eakins is not the man to be choked off by a few unripe or over-ripe dissenters." He said after another pause: "I am much mystified anyhow by Herbert's visit at this time. No doubt he has a big egg to crack and will crack it—but what it is, what it will all amount to—there I'm stuck."

Has sent the Hicks piece off to the Herald. Asked for my Holmes life of Emerson. "I have never read it but I should." "Morse says it's a better life of Holmes than of Emerson." "Good! That's more than likely—far more: and that's a thing that might just as pertinently be said of Herbert's picture: if it don't give me it gives Herbert. Often enough an artist floats out into his picture to the utter destruction of his subject." The Star quotes a post card recently received in England from W., who guessed it belonged to Rhys. W. read some proofs of Annex pages today. I went back a day or two to remind W. of the Rossetti letter. He said: "Read it to me: let me hear it again: I get a heap from letters, things, as I sit here, you reading, I just listening. It's getting to be a delicious lazy habit with me: you are spoiling me." I read.

LONDON, 5 Jan., 1886.

Dear Whitman, I received your note of 30 November, and have been intending to write for some little while past.

You and I have both suffered a loss in the death of that admirable woman Mrs. Gilchrist—a strong, warm nature, full of sympathetic sense and frank cordiality. I look round the circle of my acquaintance for her equal. Much might be said on such a topic: but often a little is as good as much.

The subscription has continued going on, in much the same course as previously, as you will see from the enclosed list. In the Athanaeum (and I believe Academy) of 2 January a paragraph was put in, to serve as a reminder to any well-wishers: perhaps it may be expected that a few will respond, and that we may then regard our little movement as wound up. I shall always esteem it a privilege to have borne my small share in testifying the respect and gratitude to you which are due to you (I might say) from all open-minded men and women in the world—and from the shut-minded too, for the matter of that.

My wife and children are away at Ventnor (Isle of Wight), as the London winter threatened to be too much for my wife's delicate chest. I expect to join them within the next few days, staying away some three weeks or so. As I may be a little hurried these last remaining days, it is possible that I may not just now pay in the £23. 16. 6 shown in the enclosed list—assuming as I do that this point would not be regarded as material. However, the utmost likely delay would not be long.

I have seen three or four times Mr. Charles Aldrich of Webster City, Iowa: he told us of his interview with you shortly before he crossed the Atlantic. We liked him, and would gladly have seen more of him: but this apparently will not be, for he must now be just about to sail back from Liverpool to New York.

Yours always truly,
W. M. ROSSETTI.

W. said: "Rossetti is the kind of friend who never forgets the market basket: he does not bombard the needy with affectionate regrets—he feeds 'em. This is to say nothing, either, of the spiritual quality of his succor." He said: "Charles Aldrich is my good friend: he has ideas, faiths, which lead him affectionately my way. Rossetti mentions Mrs. Gilchrist. Well, he had a right to—almost as much right as I had: a sort of brother's right: she was his friend, she was more than my friend. I feel like Hamlet when he said forty thousand brothers could not feel what he felt for Ophelia. After all, Horace, we were a family—a happy family: the few of us who got together, going with love the same way—we were a happy family. The crowd was on the other side but we were on our side—we: a few of us, just a few: and despite our paucity of numbers we made ourselves tell for the good cause. These letters get me talking, don't you see?" I thought this a good time to read the Trowbridge letter to him. He did not object—in fact settled himself comfortably in the chair to hear it.

SOMERVILLE, MASS.
Jan. 6th, 1865.

My dear Friend. I have been thinking much of you lately and wondering where you were (for I heard some time since that you had left Washington), when the New York Times came, with your long and interesting communication. I do not yet, from reading that, understand very well where you are, and I send this at a venture. If this reaches you, please let me know your address, and I will try to send you something to help along your good work. I sent you, some time last summer, by private hands, a copy of Great Expectations and two dollars in money, but could never learn that they reached you: did they? How are you now?

A great change has taken place in my life since I saw you. My dearest friend has left me leaving in her place a little boy, now eleven months old. A superb little fellow (although I say it); and in him I have great comfort.

I went three times to find Dr. Le Baron Russell, with your note in my hand, but failing each time, I gave him up.

I am now trying to withdraw from the arena of popular literature: only the necessity of coining a livelihood has kept me in it so long. I feel that, if I live frugally and sincerely, and do not use up my mental energies in rapid writing, I may be able to do something excellent. I am about getting out a volume of poems—or, as you would say, prettinesses.

Sincerely your friend
J. T. TROWBRIDGE.

W. asked as I concluded: "Is that all? It's good enough to be more. Trowbridge has had his knock-downs—bad ones—but he has always managed to get back on his feet again—to recover his mettle. He'll never set the world afire with his stories and poems—especially the poems (he puts the word 'prettiness' in my mouth, talking about them, you noticed) but he has a quite inimitable talent which I am led to believe within its own range and as subserving its own purpose amounts to a mastership. Trowbridge has a human side of which I am very fond. He took a real interest in my hospital work—contributed to it with more than words—with more than literary compliments. In these later years I have sometimes suspected Trowbridge is not quite so well satisfied with me. He says nothing to make me feel that way—except perhaps his saying nothing at all."

Monday, September 10th, 1888.

8 p. m. W. talked brightly this evening though he said he was not feeling bright. "I was in terrible shape when I first woke up this morning but I afterwards gathered myself together." Harned was in during part of our talk. W. said: "Come often, Tom: come whenever you can: I miss you." Discussed binding for November Boughs. I opened the package I had brought containing one of the two folded sets of the book I had got from Ferguson today. W.'s eyes were large with desire. "What's that? What have you there?" he asked, reaching both hands out as if to take the sheets. When I

exhibited my prize he exclaimed: "Handsome! it completely satisfies me: that is the book—the real, living, undoubted book!" at the same time turning it over and over fondly and in a spirit of undisguised exhilaration. "Horace—the deed is done! My blood, your blood, went to the making of this book! Some men go the North Pole to do things—some go to wars—some trade and swindle: we just stayed where we were and made a book!"

Afterwards, when Harned entered, and asked W., "What's the thing in your hand, Walt?" W. passed it over, saying: "It's the book, Tom: November Boughs: the whole book: our newest baby. Look at it: look at that—that title-page: haven't we made a ten-strike?" adding after a pause: "I believe it at least: as I say, I never count upon material success until I have it right in my hands—am paid in cash for it (the money paid down is usually a pretty convincing argument.) So now the ship is in at last and the cargo delivered and my last doubt is gone. Horace will tell you, Tom, how many times—hundreds of times—we thought the whole caboodle was going to wreck: how often and often it looked as if we could never get the wheel of the ship manageable again." I said: "That's your best printing so far." He replied: "So I should say myself, except, perhaps, for the '55 edition. Oh! if the big book only comes to as much. I am doubtful: the paper is not first-class for the purpose."

He alluded to the sale of the horse and buggy. "Well—I've sold the nag. Did you know it?—both know it? Corning bought it. I first offered it to Bucke who refused it." Bucke had asked me whether W. was vexed at his refusal. W. laughed: "Oh, no! tell him no. He wrote me frankly—I saw the weight of his argument. He was indeed very affectionate—offered to take the animal, the mare, and keep her till she died, if I had any sentiment about it. I have for long now seen how useless it is to attempt to keep it. Here I had a chance to make a sale— made it. Corning was in earnest to buy, I was in earnest to sell—so we struck a bargain."

W. still harping on Gilchrist. "Why did he come over? He has not told me: some big art scheme, perhaps: perhaps no

scheme at all—simply an Irish ambassador business over again
—the secret is that there is no secret: the scheme is that there is
no scheme. There's something mysterious about it, I admit.
He came in yesterday, made some inquiries down stairs, and
went off again without seeing me. There's something back of
it all: it's hardly like him to hurry in and out in that way. When
he was in America last year he would come over here and
stay and stay, sometimes three or four hours, and would want
to talk all the time. I joked with Mary about it: perhaps he's
over to get married—or perhaps for worse reasons even than
that!" He laughed. Turned to Harned. "Tom, what did
Herbert say about Eakins' picture?" Harned replied: "He
didn't say much: he did say, however, that the picture falsified
you—was a dangerous picture to make current." W. rejoined:
"I can hear Herbert say that: I do not wonder: it seems the
most natural thing in the world for him to say. If he had had
another opinion of Eakins' picture he would have painted a
different Walt Whitman picture himself. The two pictures
sort of bark at each other, they are so unlike." Harned asked:
"How do you account for it? Has jealousy anything to do with
it?" "Jealousy? Something, maybe, but not much. Not
jealousy—not wholly or even chiefly jealousy. The fact is,
Herbert is in the London swim—likes the swell crowd—endorsing its codes, sharing its worships, sailing by its beacons. He
belongs with the Royal Academy nabobs: the Sir Frederick
Leighton kind of reigning monarchs (that's him, ain't it?)—
adept (ah! a miraculously skilled man) in technique, style, tradition: a great man according to existing rules—really of some
importance, as all of them are. Herbert is in with that class—
is imbued with its interests, crotchets, idiocrities—not one of them,
of the whole London crowd, caring for origins, sources, inspirations, direct. It seems to me that explains Herbert's case.
How could they appreciate Eakins, who breaks utterly away
from the old, the outworn, the merely traditionary? Then we
must remember that Eakins' picture is severe—keeps close to
nature—slurs nothing—faces the worst as well as the best.

In short they don't know, don't understand: they haven't the taste for it. Give a man who is fond of poor whiskey, rum: give him the fine brandies, Johannisberger, Pommery Sac, and he'll spit 'em out, won't like 'em—won't stand by them on any account."

W. said: "The doctor comes in and says, this is poor stuff for you to be reading—referring to the Carlyle book you brought me and the Emerson correspondence: but it does not depress me—not in the least—though I am very sensitive to smiling faces, cheery looks. Some people come in, sit on the sofa across there—treat me to a list of their woes or tell me some doleful story. The books do not have such a black influence over me—are on the contrary inspiring—put some rich blood into my poor veins. The Carlyle—Froude's Carlyle—is its own excuse for being: I do not sympathize with the howl against it. What justifies it to me is the fact that that is Carlyle—that and nothing else: just Carlyle: not a picture of what he should have been but of what he was: my simple criticism of Froude's life would be, that it gives the man as he was, growl and all." I read this to W. as a note I had recently written about Carlyle: "To me the explanation, the justification, of Carlyle himself, as of the Lives of Carlyle, gloomy as they might sometimes seem to be, lies in the fact of his supreme honesty: every page of every book is honest, square with his native sense of right and truth. I read clean through his growl, his complaint, his dyspepsia, to an underlying pathos of treatment that seems to vivify and glorify his work and entitle it to universal respect and adhesion." W. said: "That is first-class: read it again." When I was through he added: "That is good—splendid—the whole truth in a nutshell: better than all else that has been said. John Burroughs ought to hear that: it seems to me to throw a light on Carlyle. Let me tell you, Horace: write the gist of that to John sometime: take some afternoon—fifteen minutes of some afternoon—or an evening, now the evenings grow long and winter is coming—and write that out—a copy of it—just as you read it to me—and send it to him. It will touch him as it has touched me: it seems to say something he has himself long had in him to say and has not said."

Told W. I had read Drum Taps over again today. "And what was your main thought as you read?" "My main thought? It was this: that Bucke is wrong when he says that Drum Taps already shows a falling off in the power of the Leaves." W. took this up at once: "Horace, you are right—Doctor is wrong. Bucke has certain whims and he always keeps them well to the front—certain ideas of poetry, for instance, which he clings to at all hazards but does not seem able to justify. I have several times tried to get a statement from Bucke—something I could understand—(convincing, if so it might be)—but all I could get from Bucke was—it is so because it is so." W. added: "Doctor sometimes assumes it all—that he knows the whole story—tries to put me down five by six in a doctrine—but somehow I do not yield to such treatment. My last, my final, my conclusive, message (conclusive for me) is in A Backward Glance: the steel of its strength is there—the screw-point—the heart-spot of it, too—is there, in that, where I say, 'But it is not in Leaves of Grass distinctly as *literature* or a specimen'—and so on (you remember the passage): that's me—the last of me if not the first—doctrine or no doctrine, Bucke or no Bucke. Taking it in that spirit—freely, bravely, according to its design—with that paragraph and others closely connected—you will see that all my parts cohere—that there are no loose joints: one reason explains all: Leaves of Grass—(intact, unbroken, not a comma removed) from first to last—from the very earliest poems to the very latest—from Starting from Paumanok to Sands at Seventy. Doctor is too much for dogmas, too much for seeing it all and more too—drives the steed mighty near to death sometimes. I am for caution—for never claiming too much—for always allowing for a beyond." I waited for him to go on. Still thinking of Bucke he said: "When you visit Doctor, as you will some day, don't miss the drive over his farm. You must go for several weeks when you go at all—don't go for too short a stay. Doctor goes once a week all over the farm—inspecting, inquiring, instructing, learning: learning not the least result of his trips. The farm covers a thousand acres, and good land, too. Doctor has his theories about keeping the patients at work—theories which time, experiment, have served to confirm."

W. gave me two letters received from Bucke. "He seems determined not to let a day pass without writing, which is grist to our mill, to be sure." He called my attention to one passage in the notes: "I suppose you have not read Robert Elsmere by Mrs. Ward. It is quite a book and I believe has made quite a stir in England. I am just reading it. It is calculated to make the modern Britisher think." Had he read the book? "No—no: I do not seem to connect with it. I have looked at it a bit here and there—only peeped, so to speak." Harned said something which seemed to W. to express a distrust of the people. W. blazed out: "You're a hell of a democrat, Tom." T. explained. W. was mollified. "I got the idea started wrong," he said. He endorsed my set of November Boughs sheets: "Horace Traubel Sept. 10, '88." W. spoke of Ellen Emerson as "the old hag." I demurred. He repeated it: "She is a nasty old hag—a Puritan gone to seed." I said: "She has been regarded as Emerson's right hand helper." He shook his head. "Not so: interferer." But he liked Edward. "Edward is a noble fellow all through, so far as I can see—a man much after the father's own style."

W. gave me a Baxter letter. It was in a Boston Herald envelope endorsed: "List of Contributors to the Boston Cottage Fund." He said: "I particularly want you to have it. It is a letter of *fact:* not sentiment—not talk: *fact.* I want you to know how the thing was done—how, when, by whom. It is an *American* fact—would please Gilder to know about: this wouldn't 'gall' Gilder—God bless 'im! Gilder always contended 'that it's nonsense to tell Englishmen Walt Whitman is in danger of starving to death': that he has plenty of friends right here in America to see him through. Anyway, this cottage business is an argument on Gilder's side. I don't seem to have things to say about it to you: it arouses in me unspeakable recognition."

THE HERALD, BOSTON, Oct. 8, 1887.

My dear friend: I have yours of yesterday and enclose a list of the subscribers. I cannot send the amount since it was understood that the individual sums should not be made known and some of the largest givers expressly made that stipulation, on the ground that it might be unjust to those who could give but little and yet in proportion gave even more largely than themselves. You will see that some are from outside Boston. Mrs. van Renssalaer is, I believe, the only representative of New York, but if there had been anybody there to take hold we could have got many, I am confident. Mrs van Renssalaer is a genuine friend and hearing of the project specially sent me word she wished to subscribe. She was visiting here then.

Saw Kennedy yesterday: has been working hard reading proof. Saw Dr. Bartol the other day and he spoke warmly of you.

What glorious October weather!

Faithfully yours,

SYLVESTER BAXTER.

Baxter added a list of the subscribers:

J. T. Trowbridge, C. A. Bartol, William P. Wesselhoeft, Mrs. Ole Bull, L. N. Fairchild, Albert B. Otis, A friend, W. D. Howells, John Boyle O'Reilly, A friend, T. B. Aldrich, Mellin Chamberlain, Mrs. Annie Fields, Lawrence Barrett, Edwin Booth, Laurence Hutton, James R. Osgood, Susan C. Warren, Frank Sanborn, Linn Boyd Porter, Albert A. Pope, Mrs. S. A. Bigelow, Daniel S. Ford, Roberts Brothers, Samuel L. Clemens, Charles S. Gleed (Topeka), A friend, Francis Tiffany, H. R. Dorr, Arlo Bates, E. B. Haskell, Charles S. Sargent, M. G. van Renssalaer (New York), Charles Eliot Norton, George Fred Williams, J. R. Chadwick, (Mr.) Bromley,

Hugh Cochrane, Charles Levi Woodbury, T. R. Sullivan, J. J. Roche, A. P. Brown, Arthur Macy, Benjamin Kimball, W. S. Kennedy, Sylvester Baxter.

I said to W.: "That's an honor list you ought to be proud of." "I am proud—or humble. It's a chapter in my personal history that must not be lost sight of. I do not say much about it myself but you are at liberty to exploit it all you choose. If there's anything I like less than gratitude it's ingratitude. You will not misunderstand me."

Tuesday, September 11th, 1888.

7.45 p. m. W. not well today. "I am holding my head up but that's all." Said also: "It is my admonition constantly repeated to myself: 'Boast not of to-morrow!'" When I entered he was reading his Carlyle—laying it down and monologuing more or less about Carlyle: "Froude's Life don't change my opinion: I still keep pegging away at the book. It fascinates me. A wonderful story, if no more—but *more*, too." He asked me: "Did you send Burroughs that Carlyle bit?" "Yes —the substance of it—not the exact words." He added: "The exact words were good enough. As you say, John has put out invaluable things about Carlyle—but the best points yet remain to be stated: the indicative, final, conclusive, points. Your own item on Carlyle last night quite settles some things for me—as I think, forever: it surprised me with a new, a true, decision. I am not sure myself about Carlyle's final place— what it must finally come to—whether to be acknowledged beyond his present fame or to fall short. I am disposed to think of him as more significant than any modern man—as in himself a full answer to the cry of the modern spirit for expression. This chirpy, self-satisfied age, full of vaunt, boast—so certain of all facts or no facts—stood in need of just such a man —a man full of scorn, complaint, contempt—lashing it into good manners by his fury." I read him a note I received from Stedman today—this:

NEW LONDON, SUNDAY,

Sept. 8th, 1888.

Dear Mr. Traubel, I am on a kind of "Sentimental Journey," needing a week's rest, among the haunts of my youth—and thus happen to be passing Sunday at this old port. My son has sent me the final proofsheets of the passages which I selected from Walt's poetry for the Library of American Literature. Will you kindly show these to him, and then return them to me —% C. L. Webster & Co. 3 East 14th str., New York City?

The problem was to give a really characteristic and sympathetic representation within the utmost space that could be allotted. (You see there are 149 other authors in the same vol. —the space for each averaging only 3½ pages. I have given Walt *twelve*.)

So I begin with the *American* note—the New World; then the cosmic and radical, following with human heroism, evolution, &c. &c. Then, for pure lyric splendor and sustained flight, the long passage from Out of the Cradle. Next, my favorites, for imagination—vitality—feeling, among his *complete* short poems: The Frigate-bird, Ethiopian, O Captain, Old Ireland, Platte Canon, &c.; then through the Vast Rondure, to broader life and immortality. Thus I suggest, at least, an epitome of Whitman's course in thought and song, from port to destination.

My love and constant honor to the grand old bard of whom the last tidings that reached me were satisfying. Next week Cassell & Co. are to give me a decision about the Calendar. As I said before, I am not hopeful for this year.

Sincerely yours,

EDMUND C. STEDMAN.

When W. heard: "I have given Walt twelve," he smiled happily: "That does me proud." When I read, "the grand old bard," he exclaimed: "Ah, did he say that: I am in luck indeed!" And in conclusion: "So you think Stedman means well—is affectionate? Yes, *does* well. I guess you are right: Stedman has been fair to a degree—has sized us up generously. I take all this as a feather in our cap"—handling and lifting up the proofs—"another point gained—won, I may say. Ah! we are getting along. I take all this as significant for our cause." W. said as to Stedman's reference to the calendar: "Well, I don't care for that: that's the least concern of all." Much moved by Stedman's good-will. "Aside entirely from the question of going into the book or not—the bandying of literary standards and reputations—aside from all that is the love Stedman excites in me by the consistent affection and consideration that he demonstrates. I would not be worth while if I failed to respond to that in kind."

Gilchrist was over again today but again went off without seeing W. W. said: "He seemed only to want to ask questions —said he would come again. I wonder what it means? I have some of his mail here." He handed me a letter from Bucke. "A bold hand," I said, half aside. He exclaimed laughingly: "A damnable hand, I think: that address on the envelope is the best of it. The Doctor has the worst vice of penmanship—running two, three or four words together with one stroke of the pen." Bucke, who expects to get rich off the water meter, says in his letter: "This may be the last annual report I shall write." "God forbid!" cried W.—"we want Maurice poor or not at all!"

W referred to Johnston, New York. "He is loyal beyond loyalty—he is faithful in the worst and the best. I have always felt that Johnston belonged to our circus—could be relied upon whatever happened to show up at the right time and do the right thing. Johnston has some of the failings of the business man"—I broke in: "Yes, and all the virtues of the lover." W. shook his finger at me: "There you are again! Why didn't you let me say that? Some of the failings of the business man and all the virtues of the lover. Well, that's the truth, even if you do say it." He asked my advice about portraits for the complete Whitman. He turned to the Linton portrait. "You like that, don't you?" "Oh yes" "So do I—I always have liked it." "That is one," he said, following up the subject: "and this must go in, too"—pointing to the 1855 portrait: "Then," he added, as if still somewhat in doubt, "I will use the Specimen Days picture—the one holding the butterfly, and the little cut belonging to November Boughs—perhaps even one or two more, though of that I am uncertain." Discussing title page he asked: "Isn't it title page enough if the book is signed and delivered?"—but: "I suppose I should really design a title page: there are many formal reasons for a title page." Wondered if it would not be well after all to keep the marketing and imprint of the big book himself? "I might sell Dave some but not use his name as publisher." I suggested: "'Author's Edition' sounds well—it cuts off the last suspicion of business." "Why—yes: so it does: I like the thought of it." W. will write to Linton about the use of the Linton cut. Decides upon a wine-colored cover for November Boughs. "That color is a fad with me just now. Nothing will satisfy me but to get it on something that belongs to me."

The time approaches for W. to come to terms with McKay. He says: "I'm going to leave that largely to you. I must spare myself as much of that worry as possible." W. will make offers to McKay for copies of November Boughs in bulk. He is afraid he will charge Dave too much. "Let Dave alone for taking care of himself," said Harned: "Dave or any other business man, for that matter." "I quite understand that it is my business to watch my own dunghill." After a pause: "I do not expect to come out cash whole on the book: I am satisfied to get the book out on whatever conditions. November Boughs is my final word—my closing up thought. The complete book celebrates my final technical blow-out." W. will probably give McKay a contract on November Boughs but is disinclined to renew the general contract for five years. He says: "My spark'll go out any day now: I don't want to tie you fellows up: you may find reasons for going to another publisher. I wouldn't advise you to go but I wouldn't put my corpse in your way if you were disposed to make a change." Asked me to see that the corrections in L. of G. and S. D. are properly made before the big book goes to press. "I am willing to rely upon you to sustain the integrity of my book."

W. gave me three letters tied in a string: his draft of a letter to Thomas Dixon, and letters to W. from Burroughs and Lathrop. "Take them with you—read them: they contain 'material.' John's account of his visit to Concord is quite memorable. Lathrop's letter is unique—good in general, silly in one particular. His suggestion that I should disguise my literary self in order to secure entrance to a volume of anonymous poetry is too good to be forgotten. But you will ask me questions about the letters before you finally put 'em away, no doubt—so I will not try to anticipate you."

W. was both jolly and serious about a squib he saw in a newspaper saying: "If Walt Whitman had written a volume of My Captains instead of filling a scrapbasket with waste and calling it a book the world would be better off today and Walt Whitman would have some excuse for living." W. commented in this way: "I'm honest when I say, damn My Captain and all the My Captains in my book! This is not the first time I have been irritated into saying I'm almost sorry I ever wrote the poem. It has reasons for being—it is a ballad—it sings, sings, in a certain strain with a certain motive—but as for being the best, the very best—God help me! what can the worst be like? A whole volume of My Captains instead of a scrap-basket! Well, that's funny, very funny: it don't leave me much room for escape. *I* say that if I'd written a whole volume of My Captains I'd deserve to be spanked and sent to bed with the world's compliments—which would be generous treatment, considering what a lame duck book such a book would have been! Horace, that fellow deserves a medal: he's given me a mad dig between the ribs." W. was very vehement as well as very good natured about the matter. W. handed me a letter—an old letter—from Baxter with these words: "This should go with the letters I gave you yesterday: it relates to the same incident: it will help you to get your history ship-shape. File it away."

The Boston Herald,
Boston, Mass., June 21, 1887.

My dear friend: Yours of the 18th received, and in response I enclose a check for $373. I hope to be able to send you more in a few days by calling in the amounts already subscribed as speedily as the pressure of my journalistic work will permit. Had I more time it might progress somewhat faster, but I regard it a privilege to be able to do what I can, and I only wish more energetic hands and a more eloquent tongue might be in charge.

We all want you to suit yourself thoroughly in the matter and we hope you will soon find yourself domiciled amid surroundings after your own heart.

I have had a call from a bright young German-Japanese, your friend Hartmann, who is on his way back to Philadelphia from Europe. It is satisfying to see your friends numbered among such diverse races.

Faithfully yours,
Sylvester Baxter.

Wednesday, September 12th, 1888.

7.45. p. m. W. still reading Carlyle in London. Now in the final chapters. Examined the Stedman proofsheets today, making some, though very few, alterations. "My impression is a good one though I have a holy horror of elegant extracts. Still, I accept it—I see its meaning—am satisfied to have the affair just what it is. And Stedman is such a good fellow, too— so affectionate." What message had he for Stedman? "Give him my love: tell him I enter into the spirit of his work"—then he stopped: "No, don't say it that way: give him my love— then tell him: Walt Whitman is still in his prison here, not mentally broken down or dispirited, but physically all done for."

Corning came in with Harned. The former went off in a few minutes. Corning asked: "How's your health, Mr. Whitman?" "Indifferent good, indifferent bad," he replied: "The doctor recommends cheerful people, cheerful books, cheerful everything—all things to be light, happy, reassured—and I do not see that I can disagree with him." Then alluded to the Carlyle book. He regarded Carlyle as being "gloomy pabulum, full of growl, darkness, venom." "Carlyle," he added, "was satisfied with nobody—not with poets, reformers, writers—not with uncommon people or common people: was a damnable, dyspeptic, Presbyterian, temperament—all the more nasty, horrible, to me because I insist upon a more affable attitude towards society." Corning made some allusion to Carlyle's domestic relations. W. turned that down vigorously. "I make nothing of that. My complaint (what right have I to complain?) is of a more personal nature. Carlyle's very existence was an insult to the Almighty—a slap in the face of the universe. But there's more than that to Carlyle: I do not hide the fact from myself: gleams of suns—almost paradisaical haloings. And then, as Horace has been putting it to me here, and profoundly too, I think—we must not forget the immense overwhelming pathos of it all. I could not disregard it: indeed, I fully comprehend, gladly allow, it. Then I'm so much an optimist myself—born so—constitutionally an optimist—that it may be just as well to have some quotations from the other side —to have some one indicate that things are not all they might be: as the old lady says in the story, 'not all sugar:' that they need mending, need labor, need a devil of a thinking, before they can be set to order." Corning said: "How can you account for the friendship of Emerson and Carlyle? They are such opposites. It is a surprise to me." "No—no," said W., "it does not surprise me: I can easily see why it should be so: Carlyle is not all told in what I have just been saying. Besides, I am myself fascinated with this book—fascinated, hate to put it down—am absorbed, forget myself, in the book. The great fact which I never forget as I go along is that the Carlyle of this book is just the man Carlyle: bad as this may seem it is honest: from top to toe, with every hair of his head, Carlyle—Carlyle the man—no trimming, no trimming—no dressing: compensating for all his sins in a grand integrity. The worst of this book is its monotony: its utter want of relief: it is a blank, blank horror and no release. In the hospitals at Washington I had multiform experiences—horrors, phantoms: the agonies unspeakable of the sick men: these things, other things, all of a nature to overdraw a man's store of sympathy: but there you could buckle to" —here he slapped the arm of his chair—"lend a hand, take part in the daily work of the world: there are even outlets in work for emotional tempests: in this book there's none of it— none of it at all: this book is the book of sitters and talkers."

W. quoted the letters of acceptance of the Presidential candidates. He had read both—Cleveland's first, then Harrison's. "I am not impressed by either letter of itself. Harrison's is a shrewd bid for votes: I shouldn't say there was anything at all in Cleveland's. I would not be at all surprised if Harrison pulled through—things at first doubtful have now shown signs of going his way. Besides, the time has not yet come for the next real thing to be done: the wheel must turn many times before the great day is here. And yet, if after all the noise, doubt, expectation, Cleveland should be elected I for my part would be gratified: for, you know, I am for Cleveland: he goes in my direction." Harned queried: "I thought you were for Harrison?" "No Tom—I am not: I got over all that if I ever had it. If I found the masses in this country making a decision for Cleveland, I would be happy—it would compensate for many defeats—it would make my optimism feel proud of itself. Harrison stands for broadcloth, three millions, finger bowls, Presbyterianism, and all that: and from one point of view it may be said that all the poisons, venoms, bigotries, of that old system—all its ugly parade of castes and elect persons—may still be needed. I may concede that something is to be said for broadcloth, finger bowls, service—even Presbyterianism: I hate them like the devil myself, but they are genteel (the dude-life, collar, tie, make-up)—and one half: oh! three quarters, of the sociology of America consists in keeping genteel. The crowd sleeps—it will yet wake up—yet come to know where its real interests lie and put in an irrefusable demand for them. I think some of our American voters are an unlikely lot. In the West and South and South West there is a great mass of voting put through with which don't seem to me to morally count for much. I like these fellows, too, in most of their ways: know them, have gone round with them: illiterate, rough, tall—drinking bad whiskey, belly way in"—pressing his own: I laughing: "You can't do it—it ain't in you!" and he: "It's so, I'm sure." Harned spoke up: "Regular Be-Jesus boys?" W. laughingly: "No, not just that sort—though I know them, the Be-Jesus boys, too: in New York—stevedores on the wharves: I am soft for them, too—the real genuine fellows: but there's a rough gang, set, in New York—wicked, poisonous, snaky, filthy—oh! a dangerous gang. Perhaps to elect Harrison means to put them down. But I am at sea on all that. We want to go on and on until we hit the real trail—then go on again. Protectionism, one nation against another nation, property all of it in a few hands, none of it in the many hands—such things, conditions, ask questions which America must answer—yes, answer in the right voice, with the right decision (answer for democracy's sake) or leave our republic to go to hell for its pains. Tom, I enjoyed Dudley at your house: Dudley holds to protection with some reasons for it: but the protection of profit —the protection of the swell proprietors—I guess I don't care a shucks for that: I guess I'd just whip it out of the temple with cords any day if I could."

Harned said something which disparaged my politics. W. said: "Horace is a good deal of an anarchist." "And you, Walt—what are you?" He laughed but answered at once: "I must be a good deal of an anarchist, too—though anarchist only tells a part of the story." Harned asked W. some questions about Tennyson. W. said: "It is queer how cautious, almost cowardly, he is of his words—how he feels his way. When Herbert came over I insisted upon it: Tell me what Tennyson said—tell me the very words—the exact words, verbatim—and the very manner of the words if you can. And Herbert repeated this one sentence: 'Tell Walt Whitman I send him my cordial esteem and remembrances.' There was nothing more—not a word more: and Herbert swore to 'em—said he knew he had made no mistake. It seemed to me spare if not formal. We on this side go farther—talk out more freely—are more spontaneous: we say always, I send you my love, or, Give him my love. Even Emerson, circumspect as he was, always did it that way: when sending remembrances to me or through me it was always, the 'love' of it—'take my love'—'heart-felt love.'" Harned asked: "Does Gilchrist see a great deal of the big bugs over there?" W. replied: "Herbert knows them all over there: is in with snobs, lords, writers (good and bad: mostly bad), artists—meets them, meets Tennyson: says Tennyson in these later days is more get-at-able—get-about-able—especially among the art classes."

I had verified Ferguson's bills for composition and printing N. B. W. examined them—then looked over his spectacles at me. "They are all right? I will make you out a check for 'em to-morrow." A minute later he added: "There's no time like the present time—I might just as well do it now." Thereupon took his check book from his inside vest pocket and filled out a check for $246.98. Handed it to me: "That settles it—let it get dry." W. sold his buggy and horse to Corning for $130. Corning spoke of the "honor" he enjoyed. W. smiled that off without a word. W. said of Herbert: "He seems to avoid me—seems to be afraid I might ask him what he came over for." Not yet ready to have me go to McKay to treat about N. B. "I am more than ever persuaded to leave a publisher's name off the big book. I would like you to go to Dave with a book already bound and containing only my personal imprint." Harned spoke of somebody who "has money." W. looked up: "Has he money? Good! He must be happy. Ain't a man happy with a million?" Gave me note from Bucke dated 10th. "Bucke is making a big fight against alcohol in his annual report. He says: 'I expect to give the alcohol men a black eye.' Here's luck to Maurice's fist!" W. gave me a little note reminiscent of Lord Houghton's visit in 1875.

York Farm, Branchtown P. O.,
Philadelphia, Pa., Nov. 3d, 1875.

Lord Houghton proposes to visit Mr. Whitman next Saturday
Nov 6th and would be obliged to him to inform him what hour
would be the most convenient.

I remarked the poor hand. "Yes," said W., "he belongs to
the tribe of illegibles: it is a big tribe!" Then he said: "I have
a longer Houghton letter somewhere: it was written to Miller
and sent to me by Miller. It will turn up somehow someday.
Lots of my fish fight shy of my rod for a long time but I eventually
game them all." I kicked to W. over something he says in the
Dixon letter about the preface to the first edition: "I do not consider it of permanent value." "In what way do you wish us
to take that?" He replied: "Any way you choose." "But you
have taken a big lot from the preface and put it into your poems
where it seems to me to have immense value." "Yes—that,
too, is so. I had no notion when I wrote to Dixon that the preface would come to be regarded by my friends as permanently
anything in itself. I was mistaken—some of them have even
said it is the best thing I have done. But read the letter to me:
let me see how my negative comes in there." The letter was
addressed to Thomas Dixon and was sent from Washington.

June 30, '70.

I must render you thanks for the box of books, as they have
at last reached me in good condition. The delay in their arrival
is unaccountable. But they are welcome, and will all be read
in due time, with sincere gratitude to the donor.

Both your letters also reached me, and were cordially welcomed. I should have acknowledged them at date, only that for
many weeks I have been disabled from writing and from my clerical work by reason of a wound in the right hand, which is now
better.

There is nothing new or noteworthy in my own affairs. I

still remain in the Attorney General's office here—still enjoying good health. I keep freshening and shaping my books at my leisure, and hope to put them in type the coming year.

You speak of my prose preface to first Leaves of Grass. I am unable to send it you having not a copy left. It was written hastily while the first edition was being printed in 1855—I do not consider it of permanent value. I shall send you (probably in the mail that follows this—certainly very soon,) a piece written some while since by me on Democracy—in which Mr. Carlyle's "shooting Niagara" is alluded to. I shall also send an article by an English lady, put in print here, that may interest you.

I am writing this at my desk in the Treasury building here, an immense pile, in which our office occupies rooms. From my large open window I have an extensive view of sky, Potomac river, hills and fields of Virginia many many miles. We are having a spell of that oppressive heat which so much falls upon us here.

W. said again: "I may have underrated the preface: it appears to have some very likely friends. At the moment it seemed vital and necessary: it seemed to give the book some feet to stand on. After the first call I saw no permanent place for it in the Leaves. I keep it in my prose volume. As you say, a heap of it —all the best of it—has got into my later verse, one place or another. O'Connor would say to me: 'Walt, you never can get any perspective on yourself: you always like yourself when you're silly.' The impulse, the demon, the something I can't deny, draws me to do something—so I do it with a cheerful spirit. I withdraw in the same spirit when the time comes." When I left with Harned, Baker, Mrs. Davis and Musgrove were sitting in the kitchen talking together. I went to Harned's for half an hour—then went home, where I found Baker had already arrived. Baker said: "Mr. Whitman came down stairs after you left. He surprised us all—was half way down before we knew he was coming."

Thursday, September 13th, 1888.

7.50 p. m.   W. reading Carlyle still—takes it up every evening.   "I stick to it as much in spite of myself as because of myself."   He sat with his right side towards the light, his book held quite near his face: always reads with his eyebrows lifted, glasses high up.   I entered very quietly and stood in the middle of the room.   Finally he saw me.   "Is it a spirit?" he asked.   Smiled.   Put the book down on its face.   "Is it a spirit? Why, my boy, I didn't hear you at all!" He looked at my burden.   "And what have you there? Something good, I'm sure."   "It's from   John,   Walt."   "John   who?"   "Burroughs."   "Ah! John Burroughs again? Still thinks of us here in our prison. John is good to us—good—good."   The basket had been sent to me in Philadelphia: was filled with grapes, "the mere sight of which," W. said, "makes my mouth water."   He stuck his nose down over the basket: "And the odor, too—it is deliciously fragrant!"   Finally he said: "You'll write to John?   Give him my love and all that: tell him they came and that I knew why they came."

I asked him how he had been.   "I last—I last: that is about all I can say.   It has been a long day: I have sat here, read the papers, dozed: this morning read some things about Proctor— his work, his death.   It seemed to me sad—his death—if that can ever be said of death.   [He died in a hospital in New York of yellow fever.]   He was prone to write—to get into the papers: his name was everywhere."   I protested: "Yes—but decently so: he was not a notoriety seeker."   W. said at once: "No indeed—he was not: I did not mean that he was.   I always thoroughly esteemed Proctor—put him up very high: he had such a fair, judicial mind—was imbued with the scientific spirit: always calm, rational, genial.   I read all his pieces—all of them. When they came in the papers and I had no immediate time to read them I always carefully put them aside to be taken up as occasion offered.   Proctor was of a beautiful type: the modern man of science type: they mean the best things to the world: they never parley with the conventions—they never pledge themselves to schools." I said at this point: "And Weld is dead, too—Hastings Weld: you remember, you have told me about him." "Oh! yes! Weld is dead—and he's a horse of another color, too. I knew him: he came here: a queer, dandified-looking little fellow: like Haweis, the English preacher. Weld persisted to the last in his adherence to old English customs of toilet and dress—wore a wig—shaved (I should think every day)—seemed prim and waxy." How was Weld as a journalist? "I knew he was in some way connected with The Ledger—was *au fait* there—but there was nothing in him—no power: not first rate, not second rate; no original quality whatever."

We talked of the tariff and the Maine election. W. said: "I'm not greatly interested in ballots anyhow. Oregon, Vermont, Maine, tell nothing: we have yet to hear from the larger, the significant States: New York, Illinois, Michigan, Ohio—even Tennessee: things there are not so one-sided. That tariff taffy and tall talk gives me the belly-ache. Dudley's about the only man believing in the tariff I could ever hear with patience. He's the best of the lot: has a show of reason on his side. Dudley says for today, this hour, this minute, these present exigencies, these facts right under our feet, the tariff is the best policy, the only policy—here we must stop. For certain classes this is the thing needed. Dudley states it this way: the tariff means profits, profits make a prosperous nation, therefore the tariff is just and right. This is the protection ideal and the protection reason: what do you make of it? I am done for: such logic staggers me. The whole thing is hoggish—put on hoggish foundations. My pocket, your pocket, houses, rents, grounds. We are often asked: Why should we do anything to help the English, the German, the Hungarian workman? Why should we? Why *shouldn't* we? It looks as good one way to me as another. I am not ashamed to confess that I am willing to have the foreign workman live. Home industry! Whose home? What home? I am not slow to say—am not afraid to say—I consider men en masse—

for benefits as well as for other things. Some one has said 'mugwump' is the Indian name for captain. For my part I am willing to accept the name with all the orthodox odium attached, if it is necessary, though I do not label myself. It is easy to call names—I rejoice in being free. Let these tariff gymnasts have their laugh—their sneer and scorn—today, for they won't have any reason to laugh or face to scorn tomorrow. Today things are their way, but God help 'em after the wheel has gone round a few times more. Back of all else in me is *feeling*—emotional substance: I *feel* this to be true—feel this must in the nature of things be so—feel that in its good time freedom, light, will come on this question. More than all else I enjoy the sight of rebellion—of men who stand aside from parties (yes—I may say, from churches, too—sects)—refuse to be labelled, rejecting any name that may be offered them: the vast floating vote, ready to nip things in season, to cast their weight where most needed, at critical moments, with no formal pledge or party alliance. I remember one of my last talks with Emerson. That subject came up: we stuck to it—stuck to it—like paste. I found Emerson as happy as myself in discovering the inherent health of the masses of the people—in reading the signs of the coming of a new political dispensation: some new readings of democracy in the common life of the world."

Picked up a Bible at his feet. "Look at that: what noble type—how good to look at! The English still do the best printing. I do not think it's from a superior mechanical equipment so much as from a superior conscience." I asked: "Do you find the Bible worth while for a steady companion?" "Yes—it lasts—comes back to me. I have had this particular book about me now for twenty years—always have it by me to read—even lately have had constant inclinations towards it." He had this to say about type-writing: "It seems to me ridiculous—robs us of something: for my part I would as lief, or rather, have the worst from a man's hand than the best from a machine." I asked him why he went down stairs last evening. "Oh! I took a sudden notion: it was like a brief flash: so I up and went: only

staying a minute, however. Things are the same down there."
He gave me a letter from Bucke. "It contains no news but it
is a bit of good health—nice to breathe in, to taste of. He pays
you a nice compliment, which is not a compliment but the truth
—I want you to notice it." Bucke's compliment was this:
"Yes, I do not know what we should all do without Horace.
He is a grand fellow and sticks to his guns like an old soldier."
The Lathrop letter given to me by W. day before yesterday was
as follows:

> 41 Bowdoin st.,
> Cambridge, Mass.,
> April 20, 1878.

My Dear Sir, I saw Mr. Burroughs in New York, lately, and
he encouraged me to believe that I might get from you some
news of your new book. I am anxious to see some proofs or
early sheets, in order to write an account of it to the London
Academy. If it is possible, will you oblige me in this matter?

I have confessed to Burroughs my admiration of the spirit
you have breathed into the air, to enlarge and stimulate the
after-comers, the young writers of America. At times I have had
an intense longing to express my gratitude to you yourself; and
it was a sharp disappointment to me that I could not come down
to Mrs. Gilchrist's last summer, with the young Englishman,
Carpenter, to meet you.

But I am not gifted with the faculty of praising. When I
greatly admire I am most likely to be silent; and I never felt it
quite the time to speak to you. Well, this time has not come now;
it hardly comes at all. The secret of our reluctance to make
acknowledgment to those whom we owe much in the spiritual
way is, probably, that we know it is impossible ever to give ade-
quate utterance to such matters; and to speak at all is almost
to obscure the sentiment instead of revealing it. If I myself
could choose, or had done anything, I would by preference take
silent recognition, though personal expression of appreciation
is certainly a great balm, at times.

In writing now, I have another project to advance, besides that of seeing your new book. I am getting up a volume of poems to be published anonymously by Messrs Roberts Brothers, of Boston. Of course they are of the older and prevalent fashion. They are by a number of poets, some of whom are very well known. I don't know whether you will feel like participating in this scheme; but there are some advantages about it which may strike you. If they do I would greatly like to have you send me two or three short pieces with a view to insertion in this book. Owing to the general character of the collection, however, your contribution would have to conform to the more usual rhythms at least as far as Captain, my Captain! Have you anything lying by you—especially of a patriotic tone? There is time enough yet; the copy will not be prepared for the printers until September. But, if you look favorably on the plan, please let me know before long.

I think you have corresponded with Albert Otis, a lawyer of Boston, whom I know. You have more appreciators here than you suspect.

Meanwhile, the new book.

Very sincerely yours,

G. P. LATHROP.

W. laughed over Lathrop's proposition. "He wants me to appear in a disguise. I do not believe even disguises would disguise me. You might as well suggest that an elephant should masquerade as a fox." W. said to me mysteriously tonight: "Some day when you are ready and I am ready I will tell you about one period in my life of which my friends know nothing: not now—not to-morrow—but some day before long. I want to tell you the whole story with figures and all the data so that you may make no mistake about it." I have no idea what he refers to. He saw my blank face. "Of course you do not understand an allusion so vague—but you ought to know: I have made up my mind to confide in you to the fullest extent." I looked for more but he added nothing. Gave me a couple of sheets of manuscript containing original draft of My Captain. "I ought to have destroyed it, but your face always hovers around to rebuke me when I think of destruction so I laid it aside for you. After our talk about the poem the other day I feel nasty enough to do anything with it. But if you will promise not to bring the manuscript back I will promise to let you take it away."

Friday, September 14th, 1888.

W. spent a bad day. Reading Emerson-Carlyle correspondence when I went in. Done with the Carlyle life. "You may as well take it home with you to-night." he said, as he looked about the floor for it. "Yes, take it. Have you the letters of Jane Carlyle—'the final memorials' as they call them?" I could get the book for him. "Do that, then, if it can be done without trouble. While I am in for it I want to go right through with these books—the whole of them. Nothing that I read seems to change my opinion of Carlyle. The Carlyle books are rather black reading: but, for all in all, I get along reasonably well with their gloom. Carlyle was not first of all a cheery presence —he inspires, when he does inspire (and he often does that) by the vehemence and sweep of his faith." Did he wish to read Conway's Emerson and Carlyle? "Hardly—at present: sometime, maybe. I shrink from Conway."

W. spoke of "the overplus of politics in the papers." Picked up a copy of the Book Maker and pointed out heads of Harrison and Cleveland. "As for me I shall be satisfied if Harrison is elected and satisfied if Cleveland is elected: my own faith (if I have any faith at all, which I doubt) is in Cleveland: but whatever the result the greater end I am after will come some day just as well." "What end?" "Some real democracy—a world-democracy: brotherhood (universal comradery): things these damned huckster parties at the best (and they have their virtues) never even dream of." W. read a W. W. parody in the Presbyterian Journal. Laughed over it. "It's not at all bad." He has finally decided to make price of complete Walt Whitman six dollars. He will call it an "author's edition," and put no publisher's imprint on the title page, though in the page of ads he wrote today it is announced as for sale by McKay. He will autograph the whole six hundred. "Perhaps I shall get a hundred up my own extra best way: I can do that without hurt to the rest and make a penny or two by it." W. is going on in this work without consultation with McKay, whom he tries to treat fairly and with courtesy. "I want to make this an author's book. Sometimes I think all books should be author's books. We have got the whole author business twisted into all sorts of devilish business tangles. The author needs to be rescued from the publisher." "Who will rescue him?" "He will rescue himself". "How?" "I don't know—but he will do it. He will some day make his own books, cover and all." Paid Ferguson today. W. said to me: "Keep a sharp lookout on all our affairs. I depend upon you absolutely—your cuteness, which—let me tell you the truth—is more than considerable." W. asked: "What about the Burroughs letter I gave you the other day? You have not mentioned it since." I still had it in my pocket. Produced it. "Is there anything you wished to ask me about?" "Do you remember its contents quite clearly?" "I think I do—but to make sure, read it to me." This I did.

ESOPUS, N. Y.,
Aug. 10, 1877.

Dear Walt, I am back only a few days from a three weeks' trip to Canada. The morning after my return some wretch poisoned my dog and the loss has quite upset me. I have not been myself since. Then I am out of sorts in body and wife is away under the doctor's care, so that I am not having a very good time. We travelled—Mr. Johns and me—about twenty-three hundred miles, and excepting a week spent in the woods north of Quebec, the trip was a good deal of a bore. We went by the way of Boston and I ran about there some. I called on Guernsey of the Boston Herald and found him a very likable young man—in fact a thoroughly good fellow. He said he had written to you but had received no reply yet. I told him you were probably away in the country. I liked the looks of Boston much. We poked about Cambridge some and then went over to Concord and spent a night there. I found Mr. Sanborn and was cordially received. I had seen him the day before in Boston. I like Sanborn all except his lofty coldness and reserve. It seems to be the style out there to affect ignorance of everything you are interested in. He showed me the home and some of the haunts of Thoreau, and then his grave and that of Hawthorne. He took me to see Alcott, whom I liked. Alcott praised my Emerson piece, but Sanborn appeared not to know anything about my writings. We were at Alcott's only a few minutes. He spoke in a friendly way about you &c. We passed by Emerson's house and I admired his woodpile. I did not feel like calling on him of my own motive. Alcott said he was well. I liked Concord, but I don't see how any great thing can come out of that place.

I got the Library Table with Blood's sanguinary review of my book. It is very petty criticism and I think I can stand it better than Blood can. He evidently wanted to pitch into my Eagle, but was afraid of the claws. I hope I shall see you soon, as I must go to W. this month unless the heat is too oppressive. Write me how and where you are.

Ever yours,

JOHN BURROUGHS.

W. said: "That's a suggestive picture of Concord. I wonder if he would stand by the letter if he saw it today. That touch on Sanborn is explicable but only deals with his surface. Sanborn is God's own! We often catch 'em in moods—bad moods and we hate 'em, good moods and we love 'em. The love may be as unreasonable as the hate. Though John is simple and true he is not a sample of the comrade par excellence: if he lacks at all (I suppose he does—we all do) it is on that side. He would not for such a reason make himself a companion to whom a stranger would surrender on sight. I had something the same feeling he had when I was in Concord. 'I don't see how any great thing can come out of that place.' I didn't see it, either—but it came: and so the case must rest." William Ingram—"the dear old Quaker man," W. calls him—wrote this note to W.:

TELFORD, BUCKS CO., PA.,
Sept. 12, 1888.

Dear Friend, I send today by express a basket of fruit. It ought to be emptied right away. The golden rod on the top will make a bouquet for you. Let me know if the two bottles of wine got broke. I hope you are feeling better. Mrs. Ingram still keeps weak but is able to be around. I am kept very busy looking after the fruit. We all send much love.

From your friend,
WILLIAM INGRAM.

The bouquet was on the table before W., who remarked: "Ingram is the best salt of the earth: he is the finest sample of the democrat—of the plain self-sufficient comrade: a real man among real men: thank God, not professional—only human. He don't write about books and philosophy, though he is a philosopher. He just sends much love. I have thousands of ornamental letters that send me no love at all. 'We all send much love.'" W. gave me a letter from Bucke dated 12th. It contained a reference to the marriage of a young nephew of his wife's. "I know the young man," said W.: "he is a rather fine sample of the Englishman, Scotchman. Kittermaster is in the business line. The English business men seem superior: they are not so quick, nervous, as our fellows, but more solid—though we will come to all that, too, in time: our commercial hysteria is only a temporary shadow: it will pass off." I consulted W. about some errors in Specimen Days not indicated by him on the sheets sent to the printers. "Make the changes if you think they need to be made. You see to all such matters: I am absolutely in your hands."

The big book is already on press and will all be printed by the middle of next week. W. has not "yet settled with" himself "as to the character of the general title-page: yet it will come: everything to me finally must please the eye—must commend itself to my sight." Mr. Coates writes me—says he wants more books. W. exclaimed: "Books? God speed you!" Kennedy writes me another of his little notes. Read it to W. Kennedy enclosed some newspaper slip about Hartmann. W. said: "I have more hopes of him, more faith in him, than any of the boys. They all seem to regard him as a humbug—or, if not that, a sensationalist anyhow or an adventurer. I can't see it that way. I expect good things of him—extra good things: not great but good. The Boston fellows seem to be particularly strong against him: some of them seem to think that if he is not a bad egg he is at least the raw stuff of a bad egg. That sounds very familiar: lots of the most amiable people have from time to time anonymously written me the same facts about myself."

Read him a long letter from Morse, now in Chicago. Morse complains of Frank Harned's poor photos of the busts. "Sidney is right," said W.: "The pictures are poor—I see they won't do." I said: "I am sorry the Morse head is not to go in the books." "So am I: but the books are now about done with— we can't alter the plans. Morse's time will come—he is secure: I have no fear that this work will be lost. A time for both—for the Hicks and for the Whitman—is bound to come. As to what you have said, Horace—I quite agree with you. I too see the great features in that portrait—that it is seamed over and over with tracings of power and truth: in fact, I may say I am willing to go down to the future, to be judged of in days to come— the long, long hereafter—by Sidney's head—by that more than any other—more than all others." Kennedy spoke in his note of Baxter's departure with Prof. Edward Morse to attend a Congress of Archæologists abroad. W. said: "I am surprised at the absence of Dr. Brinton's name from the list of delegates. Brinton is the best one of them all: the first person I always think of in connection with that science." I took him back this even-

ing Parodies and the little Australian volume of labor poems.
W. was hit hard by one passage in Morse's letter—this:

"Love to Walt. I'm real glad, with your help, he has been
able to get out his book. I should like to gather up all that
remains of his material in a final waft of the spirit. There has
been enough biography—enough analysis; now there needs a
spirit touch or soul interest—not explanation or vindication, but
ideal summary under ideal light. I know what that means but
can't tell anybody who doesn't also know."

W. made me read this a second and a third time—his head
bent forward to listen. "That is good enough to go with the
best," he said: "it is Sidney as he is in elect moments. We want
to preserve it: it is for next year and any year as well as for this."
As I left W. asked: "Did you write John about the grapes?
They were oh! so fine! Send my love for them: tell him we sit
here and enjoy them and the thought of them—of him."

Saturday, September 15th, 1888.

W. in forenoon quite indisposed. Then got better again.
In the evening when I came I found him talking with Harned in
a cheerful mood. They were on politics. W. radical—said:
"The parties are getting behind the age." Again: "The
masses are all going wrong just now but they will have a waking-
up some day soon. The people have got a lot to wake up to:
they are fleeced right and left and everywhere: they are long-
suffering: sometime they will get up in their wrath and slay the
monsters." Henry George speaks at the Academy of Music
to-night. W. said: "I would like to be there—I think a heap of
George." The Record speaks of Talcott Williams as a free
trader in disguise. W. demurred: "I do not believe it—he is
ultra the other way I have no doubt." Harned pointed to the
stove on which were a couple of bottles. "Who sent you the
wine, Walt?" "Ingram, Tom—William Ingram: they came
down from the country. Let's open one—shall we? Will you

take a glass?" Took up a bottle. "You won't do like a fellow I had here a little while ago: he sat across from me, as you do—saw me open the bottle for him—then said he was a temperance man, or something—never drank at all." W. took a corkscrew out of his pocket and handed it with the bottle to me. "Open it, Horace." I laughed. "Do you carry the corkscrew about with you, Walt?" "Yes." Harned said: "That's bad, Walt—they'll throw you out of the temperance society." "They can't—I never was in." I asked: "But didn't you write a temperance novel once?" "Yes, so I did—for seventy five dollars cash down. And, by the way, that seventy-five dollars was not the end of it, for the book sold so well they sent me fifty dollars more in two or three weeks." I mentioned the fact that Appleton's Journal had called attention to the moral inconsistency of this episode. W. was a hypocrite: consorted with roughs: what sort of a fraud was he anyway? W. said: "Yes—that's so! What is Walt Whitman anyway? A pretty tough customer." Tom drank. W. did not touch the wine. Tom remarked: "It's sour, Walt." "Yes, Ingram knows what I like."

I quoted something said of Proctor by the Press the day he died. W. had seen it. "Yes, it was good—favorable—but today they take another tack." Harned asked: "In what way?" I explained: "They question his standing among scientists." W. thus continued: "Yes, that's the grunt, but it amounts to little. For my part I thoroughly trusted Proctor: he was modest, made no claims for himself, went quietly about his work, wrote well, was possessed of extraordinary knowledge. Of course, if a fellow starts out to discern specks on the sun he'll find them—oh! he'll find all he wants of them: he can take any of the big names and throw them if specks will throw them: Shakespeare, Bacon, Milton, Emerson: there's lots to be said if that's all they're after. Why, I anticipate the day—you will live to see it, Horace, I haven't a doubt—I anticipate the day when some wise man will start out to argue that two and two are not four but five or something else: history proving that two and two couldn't be four: and probability, too: yes, more than that, the wise man will prove it out of his own consciousness —prove it for somebody—for a few: they will believe in him— a body of disciples will believe: then, presto! you have a new religion! What a horrible mess the critics of the world would make of things if the making of things was (as God knows and thank God they are not) in their hands. When I think of the critics I never fail to be reminded of Heine's canon of criticism. Oh! it is superb—splendid. Heine would ask: What did this certain man stand for, set out to do? And then would ask further: Did he do that—do it honestly, his own way, with success? The code of the newspaper critic has nothing of Heine in it. Every whipper-snapper of a reviewer, instead of trying to get at the motive of a book or an incident, sets out sharply to abuse a fellow because he don't accomplish what he never aimed for and sometimes would not have if he could."

I called his attention to several errors in Specimen Days which he had missed. But he thought it was too late to correct them now and he would let them go. "But there is one thing, above all, I wish you would see done. On page thirty-one of the Leaves the line containing 'show to me a cent' should read, 'show me to a cent.' It has I believe gone through every edition from the first wrong. It quite loses its pith in the change." I said: "I found it, Walt, and it is already corrected." W. looked at me: "You did? Damn you—you're quite a detective!" Took up a copy of the Leaves and showed the error to Tom. "It is a saying with the proofreaders, that there never has been a book without a mistake—never—never—from the earliest records of printing: never a book absolutely correct—technically, mechanically. Prizes have from time to time even been offered for correct editions, in Bible printing especially: but the prizes are all unclaimed to this day."

I repeated to W. a remark made to me today: "Ain't it strange that all these God damned literary fellows are free traders?" W. was hilarious: "No—not strange—only natural: more significant than strange: a badge of honor. Congratulate mister whoever-he-is: he has hit a nail well on its head. I am not always the apologist of the literary class but I think this would be one of the best feathers in its cap." Picked up the Pall Mall Annual containing Gilchrist's Whitman and called my attention to Richmond's portrait of Bismarck. "Don't you think that's good? fine? I like it tremendously: that is, for a portrait: done in a style I accept."

W. said: "One day early in the week I sent off four letters all of them upon matters I had hoped to know about at once. One was for copyright: but then there's a good lot to do about the new library building down there and I suppose poor Spofford is at his wit's end to make things meet nowadays. I wrote to Knortz, too. Did I tell you about the German edition? Oh, yes! it comes along splendidly: Rolleston expects much of it. I wrote also to Linton for a cut: at New Haven. I have had no answers." Spoke of the Glasgow edition of Specimen Days: Wilson and McCormick's: all printed here but the title page. W. said: "They are poorly bound over there. Dave sold them sheets cheap—unusually cheap: but he was fair about it—let me know what he was doing and I didn't object." We discussed title pages for the complete W. W. W. said: "We must proceed very deliberately. I shall have to try my hand at a design or two." All of November Boughs and a part of L. of G. for the complete W. W. now printed. Read this to W.:

"Chevreul, the French savant, has just celebrated his one-hundred-and-first birthday. When asked the secret of his longevity, he replied: 'There is no secret; there can be no rule of life; what is good for one may not be good for another. We must study what is best for us individually. For example, my parents lived to be more than ninety years old, and they drank wine; from my childhood wine has been disagreeable to me. Like Locke and Newton, I have never cared for any beverage but water, and yet I am president of the Wine Society of Anjou.'"

He made me read it a second time showing renewed interest. Then he said: "Them's my sentiments—every one of them:

there can be no rule: every man must be a rule to himself."
Asked me: "Did you bring Jane Carlyle?" And when I said:
"My friend who borrowed it has not brought it back" he assented: "Oh well—but bring it as soon as you can. I am of
the Carlyle humor just now. It may not come back to me soon
again." I reminded him of a supplementary volume of the
Emerson-Carlyle correspondence. He said at once: "Ah!
good! bring it down to-morrow." W. handed me some drafts
of letters pinned together: "You may put them away or throw
them away just as you think best. They will give you a little
biographical data, maybe—and that would be some excuse for
keeping them. Before you came around I used to burn most of
such stuff up: you are responsible for the idea that there is a
reason for preserving it." The letters were to Freiligrath,
Buchanan (two), Carlyle and John Morley. I will put them
here in the order in which they were pinned together. On the
back of the second Buchanan letter W. wrote: "Sent B the N Y
letter of July 4 '78 (to Olean, Scotland)." On the back of the
Carlyle letter he had written: "To Carlyle with Dem Vistas &
Am Inst. poem." On the reverse of the Morley letter was this:
"letter to Mr. Morley reach'd London probably New Year's
day."

ATTORNEY GENERAL'S OFFICE,
WASHINGTON Jan 26, 1869.

[FREILIGRATH]

I have sent you today by ocean mail a copy of my Leaves
of Grass—not knowing whether you have received a package
sent you by a friend of mine some ten weeks since. I should
be well-pleased to hear from you. My address is——

Sept. 4 '76.

R. BUCHANAN.

I forward you by Express today same address as this letter
the package of Books (see list on other side)—I wish Tennyson to have a set and have enclosed one, and would ask you
to do me the favor of seeing that it is safely transmitted to

him. Notwithstanding the disclaimer in yours of April 23 I also send a set for Richard Bentley in response to his kindness and generosity: (if anything I know not of prevents its reaching him, I wish *you* to keep it for yourself.)

Please see that the photograph is given to the School of Art, with my affectionate respects.

Trusting to your kindness to see that they are carefully sent to the subscribers.

431 STEVENS ST COR WEST
CAMDEN N JERSEY U S AMERICA
April 4 '76

ROBERT BUCHANAN—

My dear friend—I merely want to say that I have read your letter in the London *Daily News*—all your three letters—and that I deeply appreciate them, and do not hesitate to accept and respond to them in the same spirit in which they were surely impelled and written.

May God bless you and yours,
WALT WHITMAN.

Sept 3 '72

[CARLYLE]

Dear Sir: Following an impulse of the moment, I have just mailed to you two little books of mine—writing this to introduce them—and taking permission to personally offer, as it were, from America true respects and love.

Dec. 17, '68.

JOHN MORLEY.

Dear Sir: I send you an original piece of mine, in hopes it will be found available for say the March Number of your Magazine. The price is four pounds—twenty dollars—in gold—and four copies of the number in which it is printed, sent me by mail.

Please send me an answer, with decision, by next or succeeding mail.

My address is to Attorney General's Office, this city.

327

I found this phrase cut out of the Freiligrath letter: "I have seen your piece about me, and—" I asked: "Do you make a prior draft of all letters?" "Of all? No: Of some? Of particular letters? Yes. I have never been a copious letter writer. I rarely write to anyone to say just: 'How do you do?' I seem to need more reason than that to write." I objected: "But sometimes a letter in which you say only 'how do you do?' may be the most necessary and valuable letter to the fellow who receives it." W. did not answer offhand but finally said: "I have no doubt you are right: I do not cite myself as an example." I asked him: "Did Carlyle ever make any bows in your direction?" He laughed: "Not one: I was outside to Carlyle: he could not divine what I was up to: I think I was no more to Carlyle than any other disturber of the peace—no more than the cock that crowed in the next door back yard and bothered the life out of him." I mentioned Anne Montgomerie. W. said: "Yes, she comes sometimes—brings flowers—kisses me: but she don't come enough. You're always harping on her: I think you folks have serious intentions towards each other. What's Anne Montgomerie to you, or what are you to Anne Montgomerie, that you should love each other as you do?" He laughed a lot over his paraphrase. He added: "A boy can do a lot sight worse than have a girl: he may *not* have a girl—that's a lot sight worse." I exclaimed: "And that from a bachelor!" He snapped back half in fun and much in earnest: "Not too much of a bachelor, either, if you knew it all!" This fling was so dead set with its teeth shut that I thought he might go on some on the subject. But he was silent and I went home.

Sunday, September 16, 1888.

W. woke up this morning feeling bum, but rallied a little towards noon. Very close, oppressive, today. Sat in a chair eating some grapes when I entered (1.15 p. m.). "I have been frugal today." Then he added: "Sit down—get that chair and bring it here." He resumed eating his grapes. "Tom just left: he went to church this morning: Corning spoke on formalism, tradition, and what is the opposite of that: a fruitful subject: and Tom says the sermon was good. But—the best sermon is a bit (more than a bit) doubtful to me." Took him the supplementary volume Emerson-Carlyle correspondence. "I am mighty glad to get the book: it fits in with my present mood." Had been reading Hugo (translation: Canterbury Poets): "He always appeals to what is deepest in me." He is gradually gathering his books about him again—getting them from down stairs, the other room, &c. Reads miscellaneously, "to kill time," he says. Told him I had written Kennedy this morning speaking of W.'s ups and downs. He said: "I don't know what will come of it: but this much at least, is settled—we will get the books out: we have won that much." He proposed sending As a Strong Bird to Myrick. The books were piled in the next room on the shelf. I offered to get a copy. W. expostulated: "No—I will do it: I can put my hand right on it: and it always does me good to move about a little." Took up his cane, rose painfully, and crossed to the other room alone. Upon getting back to his chair he wrote in the book: "Mr. Myrick, from Walt Whitman, Sept: '88." "Give him that: he should have it, something, from us: I want him to know I respect and love him."

W. questioned me searchingly about the George meeting I went to last night. "What did George say? Was he outspoken? —no hedging?" And after my replies: "Good for George! It's a fine thing to have a man talk straight instead of crooked: you must have enjoyed it. I think George must be right: I, too, for example, feel that with free trade—absolute free trade —war would be less frequent—would perhaps stop: and what a universal step ahead that would be!" W. asked what books I had home "connecting in any way with Emerson, Thoreau and so forth." I spoke of several. "A mine! a regular mine! I shall have to make drafts upon it!" Asked particularly for Sanborn's Thoreau. "I may have read it but I think not. You see I am daily going out on new voyages of discovery." He said after a bit during which we sat quietly without a word: "I have decided to have the title pages as you suggested: the three, each dropped to the center—then a main page, enclosing all. As you say, that would unify the volume. As to what the general page should be, I must have a set of the sheets in my hands before I can fully make up my mind what to do."

W. said to me: "I like your interest in sports—ball, chiefest of all—base-ball particularly: base-ball is our game: the American game: I connect it with our national character. Sports take people out of doors, get them filled with oxygen—generate some of the brutal customs (so-called brutal customs) which, after all, tend to habituate people to a necessary physical stoicism. We are some ways a dyspeptic, nervous set: anything which will repair such losses may be regarded as a blessing to the race. We want to go out and howl, swear, run, jump, wrestle, even fight, if only by so doing we may improve the guts of the people: the guts, vile as guts are, divine as guts are!" I said to W.: "Neither do you refuse praise." "No—why should I? I am willing to have praise that belongs to me but I would not go out of my way to get it." "Isn't there something higher even than honest praise?" "You mean appreciation? Yes—that is higher —that is the highest of all." We talked a little about an old letter from Rossetti:

5 Endsleigh Gardens, N. W.

13 November, '85.

Dear Whitman, I read with great concern the statement in your note of 20 October that you are "in poorer health even than of late seasons": it would give me and others the sincerest pleasure to receive pretty soon a statement to the reverse effect.

Since I wrote last to you little sums have been accumulating in my hands: I enclose an account of them, amounting to £31: 19. Within the next few days I shall take the usual steps for postal remittance of this amount, and will send you the papers.

In the letter of Miss L. Agnes Jones to me (more especially) there are some expressions which I think you will be pleased to read. I don't know this lady: she writes from 16 Nevern Road, Earl's Court, London.

"The necessities of persons one knows, and may be bound to

do all he can for, are so near and pressing that to give money to help on the efforts of those who try to realize one's ideals is seldom possible; and, even in sign of one's gratitude to one who has partly reformed our ideals, is less so. . . . Yet Walt Whitman should have those to whom it is at once instinct and natural inevitable duty not to count any cost, or weigh this claim with that; but to break the alabaster, and pour the ointment, with no thought but of *him*. Has he not? This is a long apology for sending five shillings: it seemed so poor and ungenerous to send, unless I had said what gratitude it may yet stand for. Walt Whitman knows better than most that the sense of spiritual gain can seldom find the expression it longs for; and that it may forever remain unexpressed in material terms, and yet be present and abiding. I have so often wished to thank him."

I grieve to say that Mrs. Gilchrist has been much out of health of late, and I fear still continues so. No doubt you have details from headquarters.

Yours in reverence and affection,

W. M. ROSSETTI.

"That is in a sense a woman's letter," said W. "Though the women are by no means always on my side, when they are they are. I like Rossetti's signature: 'yours in reverence and affection'—especially the 'affection.' Leaves of Grass is essentially a woman's book: the women do not know it, but every now and then a woman shows that she knows it: it speaks out the necessities, its cry is the cry of the right and wrong of the woman sex —of the woman first of all, of the facts of creation first of all— of the feminine: speaks out loud: warns, encourages, persuades, points the way." I broke in: "And marriage? What of marriage?" "I don't know what about marriage (the state, the church, marriage) but about love—well, love will always take care of itself: it does not need censors, monitors, guardians." "And free love?" "Why—you are catechizing me! Free love? Is there any other kind of love?" "Would less law mean less responsibility?" "No—more: more responsibility."

W. is very familiar with the formal classics in a general way. In our talk today he referred at different times to Aristophanes, Plato, Socrates, Marcus Aurelius, the Bagavad Ghita, Euripides, Seneca. Once he quoted the Bible. He also advised me to read all I could "in Buddhist and Confucian books," saying: "Tackle them anyhow, anyhow: they will reward you." I had a pink in my button hole. He called me over to him. Took the flower. "You let me have this," he said: "you don't need it: you are going out into the open air: leave it to me here in my prison: it is a ray of light." He stuck it into the lapel of his own coat and slanted his eyes down affectionately towards it. Day hot. "It is close—sultry: I make the best of it. I seem to have a journey to make: I push on—push on. There is a journey's end: it does not appal me." He said again: "Don't forget the Jane Carlyle. And the printers—well, use your judgment with them: they are rather in your hands than mine." I kissed W. as I left. He seemed very grave. "Some kiss some day (maybe some day when we both least expect it) will be a last kiss. Good bye! Good bye! God bless you!" I find the My Captain manuscript W. gave me Thursday to contain some variations. I will copy it here literally without argument.

MY CAPTAIN

The mortal voyage over, the gales and tempests done,
The ship that bears me nears her home the prize I sought is
     won,
The port is close, the bells I hear, the people all exulting,
While (As) steady sails and enters straight my wondrous vet-
     eran vessel;
But O heart! heart! heart! leave you not the little spot,
Where on the deck my Captain lies—sleeping pale and dead.

O Captain! dearest Captain! get up and hear the bells;
Get up and see the flying flags, and see the splendid sun,
For you it is the cities shout—for you the shores are crowded;
For you the red-rose garlands, and electric eyes of women;
O Captain! O my father! My arm I push beneath you;
It is some dream that on the deck you slumber pale and dead.

O Captain! dearest Captain! wake up
    & hear the bells;
Wake up & see the ~~shining sun~~, & see the
    flags a-flying; splendid sun
For you it is the Cities ~~want~~ — for you the
    shores are crowded;
For you the red-rose ~~rosy~~ garlands, and ~~the many~~ electric eyes
    of women;
O Captain! O my father! my arm I ~~place~~ push
    around you;
It is some Dream that on the deck
    you ~~sleep~~, slumber pale ~~cold~~ & dead.

FIRST DRAFT MANUSCRIPT OF ONE VERSE OF WHITMAN'S "MY CAPTAIN"

My captain does not answer, his lips are closed and still,
My father does not feel my arm—he has no pulse nor will;
But his ship, his ship, is anchor'd safe, the fearful trip is done,
The wondrous ship, the ship divine, its mighty object won,
And our cities walk in triumph—but O heart, heart, you stay,
Where on the deck my captain lies sleeping cold   dead.

And cities shout and thunder—but my heart.

And all career in triumph wide—but I with gentle tread,
Walk the deck my captain lies, sleeping cold and dead.

My captain does not answer, his lips are closed and still,
My father does not feel my arm, he has no pulse nor will,
But his ship, his ship is anchor'd safe—the fearful trip is done,
The wondrous ship, the well-tried ship, its proudest object
            won;
And my lands career in triumph—but I with gentle tread
Walk the spot my captain lies sleeping pale and dead.

When I spoke to W. about this manuscript he said: "You
don't like the poem anyway." I explained: "I don't say that. I
think it clumsy: you tried too hard to make it what you shouldn't
have tried to make it at all—and what yon didn't succeed in
making it in the end." W. laughed and responded: "You're
more than half right." "Technically it conforms neither to the
old nor the new: it is hybrid." W. laughed and said: "If you
keep on talking you'll convince me you're the other half right
also! The thing that tantalizes me most is not its rhythmic imperfection or its imperfection as a ballad or rhymed poem (it is
damned bad in all that, I do believe) but the fact that my enemies
and some of my friends who half doubt me, look upon it as a
concession made to the philistines—that makes me mad. I
come back to the conviction that it had certain emotional immediate reasons for being: that's the best I can say for it myself."
On the reverse side of the two sheets of paper containing the
My Captain draft was this stanza:

And by one great pitchy torch, stationary, with a wild flame,
    and much smoke,
Crowds, groups of forms, I see, on the floor, and some in the
    pews laid down ;
At my very feet a soldier, a mere lad, in danger of bleeding to
    death—(he is shot in the abdomen,)
I staunch the blood temporarily, (the youngster's face is
    white as a lily ;)
Then before I depart I sweep my eyes o'er the scene around,
    —I am fain to absorb it all,
Faces, varieties, postures beyond description, some in ob-
    scurity, some of the dead.

W. quizzed me: "I guess you like this better than My Captain."
I asked him: "Shall I lie to you or shall I tell you the truth?"
"You needn't do either: I know anyhow: you do like it better."
He stopped as if for me to say something. I didn't. Then he
smiled and added: "I like it better, too—but you mustn't tell
on me."

Monday, September 17th, 1888.

8 p. m. W. described this as one of his very worst days—
"tarry, sticky, depressing." Rallied towards night. Cheerful.
Went down stairs yesterday after I left—alone. Stayed half an
hour in the kitchen talking to Warren Fritzinger about his voyages. Warren is a sailor. Musgrove says the trip greatly exhausted W. W. handed me a couple of letters from Bucke. "I
kept them here for you: they will interest you. Doctor is worked
up about Carlyle: he says: Don't read him: he's not the food
for you now: Carlyle is a bad egg—both Carlyles are bad eggs—
fretful, dissatisfied, disquieting." I questioned: "But you didn't
agree to all that?" "Yes, I would be willing to say all that and
then to say: There's something more: let's not be too quick and
end matters just there. Carlyle was satisfied with nobody,
nothing: no god existed for him: reform was a sham, democracy
a humbug, civilization a lie: everything was turned helter-
skelter: everything was wrong ended—everything meant despair—dead death. But the question returns and returns

again: was not Carlyle more than that? was he not true, the
honest reflex of some incontrovertible fact? And there I
stick." I asked: "Don't society sometimes need the whip of
the master?" "Yes indeed—that was what I was about to say.
I am not so sure Carlyle will last: many people—not the meanest
—put a negation on Carlyle. There's Bucke—a sagacious,
catholic spirit: he shakes his head: he does not acquiesce in
Carlyle. I make no rule for myself about reading: I read what
comes to my hand—what pleases my mood. I can't say that
the Carlyle books oppress me: they are black enough, but they
are also more than black." Reading Emerson-Carlyle correspondence this evening. I took him the Jane Carlyle volume.
"I persevere—am fascinated—whether for good or evil."

W. has been looking into Carrington's translations of Hugo.
"Take the book for a few days—look it over—see what you can
make of it. Carrington is skim milk. I am not surprised, however, to find his work poor. Carrington is just such a man as
could not translate Hugo—do it justly: a man of no marked type
—proper, dressing two or three times a day: a clergyman: that
style of a creature with all that it implies. The best renderings
of Hugo were Mrs. Gilchrist's. She put the Legende des Siecles
into English: copied it for me—showed it to me—while she was
here. It was nobly done. Do you know it?—the Pan and Deity
business? Oh! how superb it was—how it opened up the great
mines!—rich with ore: finer even than the French to English
renderings of my French friend in Washington years ago." I
named Ben Tucker as enjoying a big reputation for French
translation. "Yes, I have heard of that, too—Morse spoke of
it." I told him I had read some translations made from Hugo
by Bayard Taylor. He never gets interested in Taylor. W.
added: "They charge Hugo with a lack of decorum—God
knows! He was of masculine genius. There are some signs of
flare, peculiar Frenchiness, in Legende des Siecles, but after that
a real sublimity of power. As to the charge of nakedness made
against Hugo: the charge is made and made again: it is always
a weak charge: O'Connor always had a drastic way of dispos-

335

ing of it. I remember an evening company in Washington: great heat of debate, babble of voices, dissenting discordant opinions—mostly antagonizing Hugo—and William's final breaking in (just at the right moment and place in the talk) with the exclamation of Heine: 'But, madam, we are all naked under our clothes!'"

W. received a copy of the concluding symposium piece in The American: The Poetry of Walt Whitman: a Rejoinder, written by Frank Williams. "It is the most parsible of the lot—better than all the rest put together—better than Frank's own first paper. My objection to them all would be that they take up verses centuries old, debate them by rule and measure: they mean this or that or the other: and then formulate the result in a doctrine or standard to which you must ever after conform or be damned. As long as they persist in such a method of criticism they had better let the Leaves alone. There are standards by which we may be judged, but they are not such standards: they must be contemporary, not antique, standards." Bucke is still asking what brought Gilchrist over? B. suggests that there's a woman in it. W. once said the same thing in a joke. Now, however, he shakes his head. "No—not that: I should say, just the desire to take up stakes and move. Such times come in every life—yours, mine, anyone's. Carlyle in the mood of rebellion just got up and away—went off on a dismal moor—anywhere, anywhere, the place not imperative: the hour had struck for him to go and he obeyed." Perhaps G. had come on a Whitman mission of some sort? "I hardly think so. What could it be? Perhaps to be around in case of my serious sickness—to watch, to care for, me: but that is provided for."

Coates gave me ten dollars more for another set of the Centennial edition. W. spread the note flat on his knee and said: "The portrait of somebody or other on a ten dollar bill always has a lucky look!" Coates had made some hint to me that he and some one else had wondered if they might not buy up the residue of the Centennial edition and so help W. in his need. I had replied that W. was not in such pressing need—that he would like well enough to sell the books but not by any false pretense. I explained all this to W. who said: "You did right—perfectly right: I am not in any need whatever—neither am I greatly flush. Coates has done so much more than well as it is that I would hesitate to have him do better from any fallacious fear that I might be in dire straits. This does not mean that I would not like to or am not willing to sell the books: selling books is what I am here for: but when I sell 'em I want to sell 'em honest." Said again: "I have been a little worried: a man out in St. Louis somehow got a spurious edition of the Leaves and wrote telling me about it: so I took and sent him a copy of the Osgood issue— one of the few I thought I had—the 'author's edition' I got bound up here. Now, when I come to look more into the matter, I find it possible I sent him the last copy I had. Another may turn up but if it don't I'm in a stew." Baker was over to-night. Felt W.'s pulse and reported it "good." "Do you say so?" asked W. Baker nodded assent. W. then: "No matter how bad I feel that ought to satisfy me. I always like you fellows to tell me I am well." After B was gone W. said: "He's a gentle fellow—was a sweet nurse: it was like good health to have him touch me." W. called my attention to this in Bucke's note of the 14th.

"I hope you will settle down to the notion of issuing the big book *yourself* without the intermeddling of any publisher—print four or five hundred copies—get them up in all ways in first class style—number each—sell for ten dollars—advertise in the N. B. and perhaps in the Critic and Pall Mall Gazette—let Horace do all the work except the autographing—make it a solid remembrancer of yourself to your friends—make it as *personal* as possible."

W. said: "We have anticipated Maurice on almost every point: he comes a day after the fair. But his Carlyle letter is very vigorous and worth while: it presents a point of view—a valuable point of view: is partial, fragmentary, a piece instead of the whole—but significant—an impression that we can't skip or pass by as being useless." This is the Bucke letter:

LONDON, ONTARIO, Sept. 14, '88.

All quiet here and another perfect autumn day. Your card of the 13th came this morning. I think it is wonderful how perfect your handwriting keeps through all your illness and feebleness. No, I would not recommend Froude's Carlyle to a man who needed cheering up. I read it a few years ago and it nearly gave me a fit of melancholia. I look upon that same Carlyle as being (or having been?) one of the worst "cranks" that ever lived. And he certainly had about as bad a time of it for eighty-six years as any man ever had in this world. Nothing gave him pleasure, nearly everything gave him pain. As long as his wife lived her presence only seemed to add to his worry and gloom; as soon as she was dead he was more gloomy and worried more than ever because he had lost her. He was a bad sample and she was little (if any?) better. He couldn't even live with his favorite brother John. I think his ignorant old mother with her pipe was the best of the lot; think I could have liked her. I should like to know C. by and bye to see what he is like in the next world but I never expect to care much about him. Love to you.

R. M. BUCKE.

I said to W.: "Somebody here the other day said you swore by Doctor Bucke—that you always said yes when he did and all that." W. replied: "Did they? They were very shrewd: they found us out in a great secret. You know how I say yes to the Doctor—and to you, too, for that matter. I have always been taken for a great quarreler—almost a brawler—rather than a bower and scraper: I was never accused before of being too willing to train in with other people. My dear mother used to say to me: 'Walt—does thee not sometimes—just sometimes, Walt—look for differences where there are none?' Dear mother!"

Tuesday, September 18th, 1888.

7.45 p. m. W. not improved today. "I was cheerier when you came last night—you braced me up (Horace, you always do)—was brighter: thought the depression had worn out its welcome: but this morning I was back at the old stand again feeling as choky and sticky and heavy as hell. It went on so all day until about an hour ago: then I commenced to grow better. The evenings are my best times." The Jane Carlyle lay open face down on the floor. Pointing to it I said: "You won't read all the letters: I have kept on saying to myself that you wouldn't." "Neither shall I—you are right: but I want to run through them." I found a copy of the '82 edition of the Leaves in the parlor. Took it to W. He was jubilant. "Hurrah! the country's saved!" Gave me a short letter sent him by Swinton in 1865—September 25th of that year. "It's John in his most amiable mood: it is very warm—very ardent. John is often mistaken for a cynic by people who only half-know him."

Friday 6 p. m.

My dear and great Walt. As you did not come up yesterday afternoon I did not expect you today.

I hope to be present when you come up for this package. I would be did I know when you would come.

I want to see you that I may get another copy of the Leaves and subscribe an X for the expense of their publication.

I am profoundly impressed with the great humanity, or genius, that expresses itself through you. I read this afternoon in the book. I read its first division which I never read before. I could convey no idea to you how it affects my soul. It is more to me than all other books and poetry.

The poem in the Broadway has supreme passages and thoughts but it does not seem to me perfectly artistic.

Art, as applied to poetry, simply means the best, highest, most natural, most effective form of expression.

I salute you as the poet of my heart, my intellect, my ideality, my life.

Yours,

J. Swinton.

W. said: "I want you and John to know each other: you are fellow radicals. John is as much interested in the labor question as you are: he is a veteran—has long been loved and hated by the combatants one side and the other: is rather revolutionary, as you yourself are." Harry Fritzinger talked some with W. while I was there. W. was asking him questions about the Chinese in California. Harry is a sailor—lived for some time in San Francisco. W. felt that he was here getting "some intelligent impressions at first hand." "They are not dreams— they are not politics—they are actual experience." Kennedy sent W. a couple of copies of the Christian Register marking papers of foreign travel by Augusta Larned. W. said: "He no doubt sent them in kindness of heart but I never read such papers. Who is Augusta Larned? Perhaps a friend, a correspondent, of Kennedy's." I tried to explain who she was. He then went on: "Well—I don't know her: it may be that the pieces are good: Kennedy must have thought there was something in them."

Musgrove entered with a letter, which proved to be from Logan Smith—so W. thought without reading it. Written from an unpronounceable place in Wales. W. laughing said: "One thing is sure, Logan: when I write back to you I will address to London. Such a name deserves to be ignored." Letter was long. "And anyhow, I won't rassle with it now: it's a job in itself for to-morrow." Told him I had sent The American to Doctor Bucke. "I must confess that I don't think the best things about Frank's paper. It really contains nothing to startle anyone who looks at things as we do." "Do you require to be startled?" "No—not that: but I like the individual touch. I thought Frank's piece the best of the cluster though not the best of any cluster: the best of that set:

containing the suspicion of something or other, I don't know what. Agnes Repplier is bright, smart, quick, knowing—and that is the trouble: especially the smartness, from which I always shrink. Smart people, merely intellectual people, professionals, writers as such, cannot comprehend Leaves of Grass— none of them: might as well let it alone." "You think Miss Repplier extra clever?" "Did I say extra? no, I didn't say extra: I only said clever, or something to that effect. She strains for brilliancy—tries hard and harder and hardest until she gets her wit just where she wants it." "You wouldn't say that of Ingersoll's cleverness and wit?" "Oh, Lord no: the Colonel is chuck full and only bubbles it out: he just moves and spills over." I stopped for a minute. So did he. Then he said: "A man or a woman who strains to be brilliant generally ends by being simply impertinent: I'm afraid Agnes is impertinent. That crowd and our crowd start out from quite opposite premises: our roots, our aims, our ways, our results, are never like theirs—are never really understood by them. That is why the friendliness of the Coateses surprises me: their extreme friendliness. It may be that they are Quakers and the Quaker in them finds itself attracted to the same thing in me. Frank is himself way above that American paper in style and size— way above it. I think I have told you how splendidly the Williamses have always received me in their home? Their home was a sort of asylum (like the old churches, temples) when so many homes were closed against me. They were like the Gilders—they were not afraid even in the days of greatest outcry to ask me round, to have me cackle and rub feathers with them in their own coop."

Had today fixed up the books for Coates "with mine own hand." Autographed them. Then put this label in his hand on the package: "$10 Centennial Edn. Two Vols: *Leaves of Grass* and *Two Rivulets* bound in half leather & Italian boards containing Autograph, Portraits (three from life) Personal Memoranda in Secession War and Democratic Vistas." Then said: "I have about a dozen sets of the Centennial edition ready:

am willing to sell them if a purchaser should appear. I don't see why Coates should want them. You had better persuade him against it. Don't let the poor man load up with Leaves of Grass: let him take warning of us: see how we have suffered all these years from our great overstock!"

After a brief silence W. said he'd "bet" I couldn't tell who his chief visitor was today. I didn't bet. I only looked inquiringly at him. Then he said: "Gilchrist was over—Herbert: this time for a genuine visit—real—long. He did not, however, explain the mystery of his appearance in America: talked very well, with great optimism. I have it from some one else that he is a correspondent or something of that sort. You know, Europe is on the qui vive as to affairs in this country: they don't know America, she is a specter, a nightmare, to some of them—a puzzle to all. What does it all mean? Why hasn't America long ago gone to the devil?—and if she hasn't she ought to. She has the fastest locomotives, the biggest prairies, almost illimitable space—elbow room: has fought down the most stupendous rebellion: has had riots, Ku Klux, and hell's own pother again and again: develops an independent, almost cocky, citizenship and vast unprecedented processes in machinery: and still hangs on. What does it mean? And then, this year, there is the political hub-bub—the general excitement: the people just as much in it as the leaders. Now, it may be that Herbert came over to tell them about such things."

I wrote to Burroughs last week to this effect: "W. will never be better than he is now: if, therefore, you are so disposed, come down: you want to see him: Dr. Bucke is afraid any day may bring a serious turn: take your chances now—even if you see but little of W. come now." Burroughs was coming in the summer. W. advised against it. Said then: "Don't tell him till I advise." He does not "advise." Today I received a postal from Burroughs saying he would be down this week, probably Wednesday. I said to W. this evening: "It's pretty near time for Burroughs to come." "So it is. Well—he will come: do not hurry him." After a silence: "Yes, he'll come.

I love John. We have not of late seen as much of each other as I would have liked. John has lived a little too close to the New York crowd—has been a trifle touched by it: is a little bit here and there under its sway. They don't let you alone—they press themselves upon you: there is no escape: you've got to yield or say no with your clenched fist: they don't recognize any mild negative. But John's faithfulness, affection, are beyond question. Our relations with each other have always been comradely—largely and directly personal." Then dwelt upon his life in Washington and intimacy with Burroughs there. "The mornings: shall I ever forget them? And John's wife—and the unmatchable griddle cakes—the best in the world—no one's could equal hers (and at that time I set more store by such facts than I do now). Burroughs would come in for me and take me home with him—for breakfast: Mrs. Burroughs managed things then—kept some of the department clerks—and there was always a rub with the precious coffee—that, too, the best on earth: and then the hour's talk after the meal—the sweet talk. They were precious days! I can never forget them: precious, sacred days." He then described Burroughs to me: "He is plain, large, not heavy—a farmer in appearance, a little hesitating in speech—a little more and it would be a stammer: cordial, endowed with a good voice—timbre to it: of habits all simple: just such a man as you like, I like: contented with what comes: fare frugal as a Jersey ploughman's, or a country innkeeper's. John wins on you by just such qualities. They say of him—I know it of him: when there's a particularly hard job of work to be done on the farm, he does it himself—reserves it: he has hands there to help him, yet he chooses his own place, and that generally the most difficult one." I asked him if he had seen B. since the New York reception: "No—he was there then—all the time I was—a couple of days—short, but enough for both, I guess. And that's another thing about the New York boys. They look upon it as the great need—the supreme fact—to meet with, to gaze upon, celebres: to gossip about them, to take them to dinners, to swell their peacock tails and strut about with them." I said: "Your book acquits you of that weakness." "Weakness? Madness, you mean. So it does. And if it does not, I am sure I stand personally acquitted—acquit myself. I have no interest in mere distinction—in what the world calls greatness—in the professional elects—the superior author of this, the superior author of that, the superior author of the other: they do not fool me—their feathers are at the best only good for easy weather."

I said to W.: "What I like about you, Walt, is that though you often talk strong you never talk sore." He looked at me fixedly. "I hope you are right—I hope you are right: but are you right?" I replied: "I haven't thought that today alone—I have thought it always: it is not a judgment for one day alone—it is for all time." He was very fervent when he exclaimed: "Thank God for that! thank God for that! I would rather talk weak then talk sore. Thank God for that!"

Wednesday, September 19*th,* 1888.

7.45 p. m. Harned already there when I called. W's "Howdy—howdy?" cordial. Shook hands. Had had a hard early morning but afterwards the trouble dissipated. Now bright though somewhat fagged. Said Burroughs had arrived today. "He looked thinner than when I last saw him but was bright, cheery." Then he added: "You fellows had better remain: John went over to hunt up Herbert—said he wanted to see Horace and he would come back in time to do so—but it is now late and you had better wait here until John turns up again." Expressed great interest in Burroughs' visit, taking it more calmly than I had expected. Engaged us in talk, a good deal of it politics—free trade, his own conviction that things are "bound all right and therefore must come right in the end."

Handed me Buxton Forman's production of Shelley's Masque of Anarchy, fac simile of the original manuscript. It wore B. F.'s autographic dedication to W. W. said: "Herbert left that with me yesterday. It came from Forman himself. It seems the fellows over there have a Shelley society, and they want to know what Walt Whitman thinks of Shelley." Then after a brief wait: "That's what Walt Whitman would like to know himself." He said further as Harned quizzed him: "No indeed Tom: I am not a reader of Shelley—I don't come so near him, or he to me, as some others." Harned alluded to a handsome Shelley once possessed by W. "Yes, I had that: you mean the one in red canvas? I sold it—a friend of mine came here one day and wanted it badly, offering to buy it: so I let him take it away." Tom spoke of its value: "It must have been worth four dollars, American money, at least." But W. demurred: "No— or if so, I didn't get that for it—didn't charge much." After- wards he exclaimed as Tom read a verse from Shelley: "Oh, how fine! But I know nothing about Shelley—at least not enough to go on record with formally about him. I think O'Connor speaks for me in that—makes what I regard as a perfect statement of critical truth. He brings together spirit and matter: on one side Rabelais, representing all that is carnal, beastly, of the earth earthy: on the other Shelley—a wind, a perfume: pure, ethereal. That is a rare piece of abstract description: no one but O'Connor could have so touched it with vital fire." And O'Connor, he believed, was "the most catholic, comprehensive, of all critics. He has a place for every one—will not banish a soul: not any one of them —Shelley or any other." I asked: "Even Longfellow?" "Yes, even Longfellow. I know how quick he always was to resent my exceptions. There was Poe: I had often to say so and so not entirely commendatory and O'Connor would at once cry out— no, no, that is not the thing to say: that must not be!" W. stopped a bit—then cried: "Poe—poor, wonderful Poe!" and quoted: "And the fever called living is conquered at last"— saying pathetically and looking at me: "How full that seems! how true, far-reaching!" He added then: "Shelley is interesting to me as Burns is, chiefly as a person: I read with most avidity not their poems but their lives: the Burns letters, for instance."

We talked of Henry George and his advocacy of free trade. W. interested, asking a lot of questions—what does he say? how does he propose to do it? and so forth. Then would say "good" and again "good"—and once: "It makes a man feel better to know somebody is saying that thing for him." Then suddenly, while we still "harped on" George, he reached towards the table saying as he did so: "My Australian anarchist friend has a poem about George: did you see it?" With his hand on the book he said: "And do you know, Horace, there's poetry in that book—poetry after all?—fire—strong places, passages: without any tricky art, but natural, sustained." He reflected further (we had in the meantime discussed the oddities of his style— broken lines, Whitmanesque and yet not): "After all, if a fellow is to write poetry the secret is—get in touch with humanity— know what the people are thinking about: retire to the very deepest sources of life—back, back, till there is no farther point to retire to." He said that Adams' inscription in the volume sent him was "genuine, hearty, and interesting." "I had another Australian socialist here to see me—Bright: it was full two years ago. I think it was John Swinton who sent him. After he had gone back he delivered an address on Walt Whitman. I had a copy—he sent it to me: and it made me blush: I threw it back of the bed—it was so full, so full, of praise. Then I guess I lost sight of it—put it into the waste basket or burnt it up or sent it to Bucke." We laughed at the way he connected Bucke with its disappearance. "Well, I send all sorts of things to Bucke: I know he likes to have everything, pro or con. Bright was a keen, cute fellow—I liked him—liked him to come: but he did me up too large." I suggested: "That's the way you get square for the malignancy on the other side." He first smiled, then was serious: "The extreme that, the extreme this? I guess it is so—guess that explains it." Harned read aloud Adams' poem on Swinburne which dwells upon his apostasy, &c. I said: "It is natural for the socialist fellows, the democrats, to feel so: Swinburne has in recent years taken a sudden turn against his old loves and ideals—some say with an object." W. at this point: "Yes, I have heard it so said—the laureateship in view, it is hinted: but I don't think that is the case." There was a mystery in it but he was not prepared to side against Swinburne's motives. "Herbert might tell us something about that: Swinburne is intimate with the editor of The Athenaeum—derives many of his inspirations from that source, I am told. Herbert is in with all that sort of life in London: all the polish of it, the glitter: he might know."

W. informed me that the Herald would not use his piece. "Habberton wrote me that I did not quite understand what they wanted. He intimated that their design was to help me along —give the book a lift. On Monday the Herald gave me a notice about so long"—indicating three or four inches on his hand— "for November Boughs." Said he was "not disappointed" —"expected as much." Told me he had written to Morse— "a short note." (Afterwards when Burroughs and Gilchrist and Harned were with us he suddenly picked his notebook up from the floor, took off the rubber—putting it about the arm of the chair—opened at a certain page, and said to me: "Laflin street: that's right?") Said he had "something peculiar" to tell me about H. G.'s picture. "He puts it at three hundred pounds. And did you know—I guess none of us did—that the head there (and in the book, too) is not the head he painted here?" Explained: "The crown of the head in the Camden picture was too near the edge of the canvas: therefore Herbert made new measurements and a full new copy." I suggested: "It can't have been changed much or we would have detected it." "It wasn't," returned W.: "in fact it is in one sense the same picture." Harned told a story of a fellow suing a client of his for a hundred and thirty-five thousand dollars. Harned had asked—why didn't he sue for that many millions—he would be just as likely to get it. "So with Herbert's picture—why didn't he ask three thousand for it?" W. exceedingly amused— laughed for some time before he could say what he wanted to— then: "Don't be too hard on 'em, Tom: let the London crowd have its swing, though I guess it'll have it whether we say so or no. The picture is not all bad—has good (indeed, very superior) qualities: and then, you know, they want Walt Whitman a certain way—will have him that way whatever is said—however wide of the truth it may be." He spoke of "the sublime confidence of Englishmen—the mountainous egotism: and it is sublime—grandly so—so grand I can't help but admire it." Tom said he had asked H. G. about European art—where it was most highly developed, G. replying: "Undoubtedly in England." W. shook with gayety: "That's a sample of it—just what I've been saying."

W. entirely satisfied with my arrangement of bastard titles. Also with Oldach's promise to get us four show copies of November Boughs in covers by Saturday. Delivered the books to Coates, repeating to him what W. had said about the copies left. Coates thought he knew several people who would like to have sets. W. facetious: "God speed 'em in their like!" A package of photos of Bucke's children on the table—tied together. Harned picked them up—looked them through—finding a picture of W. among them—a Sarony picture. W. saw it and at first said: "Why, where did that come from? I don't remember myself how it happened"—but after a little thought: "Yes I do, too." Looked long and long at the Bucke portraits—remarked the family resemblances.

Got a short note from Donaldson asking for some written opinion from W. on the Catlin volume of Indian remains, &c., either accompanying or sent some time since. W. said he had known Catlin: "That picture on the wall over there was his: he gave it to me over forty years ago. He was an interesting old codger—a lithographer—gave the second half of his life all up to these studies—became proficient, accumulated a vast deal of information." Of the two portraits in the volume W. commended the younger. "Catlin was already old when I knew him." I asked: "Well—will you gratify Donaldson? will you write?" And he said: "Yes, I guess so: I am willing to bear my testimony to the old man—say a good word for the old man." Was it to be long? "No—five or six or a dozen lines at the outmost." Did not "think however" that he "would read Donaldson's immense book." Picked it up and looked at it with mock horror. Said about the Catlin picture: "I had that stowed away ten years, and when it came out it was in that shape. And there is the other, too: I took the better part of two days putting it together. I should have our man up on Market street frame them both—Neumeyer—and superintend the job myself."

After the foregoing, in the midst of one of W.'s sentences, we heard a step down stairs and the vestibule door opened. W. looked at me and said: "There's John now"—which proved to be true: John and Gilchrist, who came in together. After greetings I swung the lounge around. B. sat at one end, I at the other. Harned took his chair again. Gilchrist sat on the bed. Walt serene, questioning. Had Burroughs had his oysters, &c? Offered him "home hospitality" down stairs. Talked of viands: of oysters chiefly—where to get them in Philadelphia and how. Afterwards prompted by the noise of bands, &c. on the street (Democratic Cleveland and Thurman demonstration in Camden to-night) talked of the tariff. W. very lively—went over the ground much traversed by him of late. No discussion because all were free traders, except, perhaps, Harned, whose faith in the tariff is not pugnacious. W. told his "good story" of the Benton-Calhoun duel. "John Forney used to repeat it to me with great gusto." After a shot apiece, "each admitting to the other that he knew nothing about the question at issue—the tariff question—each in fact doubting if anybody knew," &c &c. W. hugely moved with the humor of it. "And if not then, how or why more now?"

At one point, when Burroughs had spoken of "solidarity" among the nations, W. said almost solemnly: "Yes, solidarity— that's the word: that's a noble view to take of it: the federation of the world." Curiously, however, after W. had tired a little of the persistent talk on the one subject he suddenly turned to Burroughs with an utterly foreign question. This got us out of the rut. He handed B. November Boughs (in sheets) and spoke somewhat of that. Finally he seemed to suffer from too much talk. I suggested we should leave. W. looked at me gratefully. It was proposed that all hands should go up the street to the meeting. B. asked W. if the long talk did not weary him and he said he thought it did. Then away—Burroughs to come in the morning again. W. said: "Not before ten—you know I stay in bed late"—or words to that effect. B. asked what time he went to bed usually. Thought to-night he would "go right away." But evidently thought better of it—for an hour after and more when we returned for B.'s valise left in the parlor the light was still up in his bedroom. Cannot stand much consecutive strain—listening, reading, talking. Burroughs reports an impression of great change in W. but thinks he looks better than might have been expected. B. will stay over till Friday morning, putting up at Harned's. Went after leaving W.'s to Harned's—saw big torchlight parade from that point. Talked much of Walt. Burroughs advises more energetic, even drastic, nursing—rubbing, massage, and so on.

Thursday, September 20th, 1888.

7.45 p. m. After we had left him last night W. had a bad time of it—what with the extra visiting and the noise of the paraders: had not got to sleep until way in the morning. He said: "It seemed as if all the fiends out of hell were loose: some bright particular devils sent here for my especial benefit. I suppose we may expect the disturbance to be kept up now for a while: this seems to be one way people have of eliminating from themselves some of their superfluities." He laughed the whole matter off—his usual way of clearing the atmosphere. Yet the bad night had told on him, so that when he got awake this morning he was in miserable shape. Burroughs came along with Harned by and bye but was not admitted to W.'s room. In fact W. closed people out all day. For when Burroughs came back with Gilchrist in the afternoon W. still said "no"—he would see nobody. Once, in the forenoon, he spoke very gravely to Mrs. Davis about his condition. She describes him as looking extra dreadful. She had asked him how he was. He said to her: "Mary—I am near my end: the end of the rope is plainly near at hand." His manner affected her deeply. She broke down and cried in his presence. When I arrived he sat reading the Bible—calm, serene, smiling: reached out a cordial hand—gave me his "Ah, Horace! Howdy? Howdy?" once more and closed his book and laid it aside. When Burroughs came with Gilchrist Mary went up stairs and announced them. He instantly said he could not see them. She demurred. He then cried vehemently: "No Mary —that would be the last straw: it is impossible." Now he said to me: "The instant you came into the room and hung your hat on the bed post I felt better. How do you account for that?"

W. looked about for a Bucke letter which he wished me to have. "Bucke gives me a heap big advice—more and worse of it—about the big book. He has rubbed up against London publishers—has notions of London fineries in bindings, editions de luxe, and all that, which I do not share at all. He wants my book to be personal. It is personal enough already—the most personal of all books ever published: the very heart of a man— of me: the expression of the most intimate facts of a life and its subtlest, profoundest emotional backgrounds. I have no sympathy whatever with handsome books (handsome whether or no), showy appearances, unique styles, costly dressings, merely for themselves. I never had any desire to set myself apart—to claim special privileges, exceptional attentions. And this would be a late day indeed, and the worst day, to make a turnabout. My wish has been to merge myself with the masses, be a drop in the ocean, mingle with the bulk: I have not sought, do not seek, any distinction—any rare exaltation." He stopped for a few minutes. I did not feel like breaking in. Then he added: "Tell all of them this for me—tell even Bucke: tell them this book, this big book, this signatured book compassing all, is my final utterance—my last attested episode of self-expression: full, correct (we hope it will be that), conclusive. I see no reason for having it more than that, let bark what dog may: the personality of the book, if it has any (and if it hasn't that what has it?) must be construed in the light of what has gone before, of what originally resided in my motive, of what has guided my hand in its long apprenticeship to an ideal, rather than by anything I can put into the book now."

Then he suddenly said to me: "Horace, I do believe you're the only one of all the fellows—of all, of all—who is willing to let me do as I please." I said: "That's not because I always agree with you." He laughed and replied: "I know—I know: but you never interfere, you never push in, you never take me by the neck and shake the life out of me for disagreeing with you about the use of commas or the sizes of margins or the colors of muslins on the backs of books." I said again: "Sometimes I think you do fool things." He assented: "Yes, I do: and sometimes the fool is right and the wise man is wrong, too, as you know"—I nodding—"though as for that, Horace, I don't suppose I make more than my quota of mistakes or possess more than my own modest quota of the virtues. What I mainly, chiefly, mean is this: that somehow you do not insist upon yourself in such a way as seems to exclude me. I like to have a hand finally in decisions connected with my own course of life, don't you? Doctor is magnificent—I love him (do I love anybody better saving maybe only William?)—but he sometimes charges an awful fee for his advice."

Burroughs has said to me here about W.'s version of their last meeting day before yesterday: "That was an error—I rode with him to Glendale in the summer of last year to see Gilchrist." W. concerned some for imagining Morse may think himself slighted by W.'s recent silence. "Sidney thinks I have gone back on him: God bless me! how ridiculous! I'd as likely go back on my mother. I hope he will accept my letter: he will some day see my position." I remarked: "I have explained everything to him." "Well—that is good to hear. I have a thorough-going belief in Morse and his work." "Walt, I would not worry about that. When the books are done you can send him copies with his name and your name together in them and then he'll understand all." W. said: "That we will—that we will: I wish I had the books ready to send now."

I told W. that Burroughs seemed to be but little impressed with the Eakins picture down stairs and no better impressed with the Morse bust at Tom's. Gilchrist dismissed Morse with a "no—no" and a deprecating wave of the hand. W. replied quickly: "I can say for myself—I care little what either of them says about the portraits: I am too well persuaded myself, have been too long thinking it over, to be shaken out of my conviction by the shrug of anybody's shoulders. And you think Herbert dismisses it with a sneer? Well—that is not unexpected. It is like the case of a fellow who has long been fed on one dish—who resists every proposition for a change: swears there is no other. I confess I am surprised that John takes a stand against Eakins and Morse: but that just emphasizes another of the differences in John—that he is not quite so stern about his principles as was the case long ago: in that respect he has lost ground. Morse has put great work into the head—the head of me: I would be willing to stake anything on it and on the Hicks, too, for that matter: and there is the big Emerson, also—don't let us forget that, either: the best of the two Emersons without a doubt— at least I like it best." What objection had he to the little Emerson? "Objection? None. Only I feel like saying this about it: it is canny—perhaps laying too much stress on that point: canny to that degree, I might say, that if it were more so it would be too much: just on the borderland."

Morse has been telling us of a portrait of W., a sketch, that he made west there in an hour from memory. W. said: "Tell him to send it on." "Morse says he don't think it would please any one else but thinks it would please you and me." W. laughing replied: "Just the thing: that's a concluding point in its favor. Well—if I may say it without irreverence—that's like pleasing God Almighty himself." He spoke rather doubtingly of his health. I sparred him: "But you must brace up, Walt: you know there are six hundred books to sign." Laughed. "You are a good needle in my side: you prick the life back into me: yes, I will live: I hereby resolve to live! But I can't live without an effort: I have now to force myself whatever I do: this horrible inertia is robbing me of all instinctive, voluntary, power." Urged me to take the Catlin book home and look it over. "You should have it at least a week. You won't want to read it but will find it full of interest at certain points. Catlin was a wise, informed, vital character—devoted, oh so devoted. I don't remember where we were when he gave me that picture"— pointing to the wall—"whether it was in New York or Washington, but it was before the War, maybe as many as forty years ago. The subject of this book always attracted me—indeed, fascinated me: does so still." Turned over the pages and commented on the portraits, pausing as he came to the Indian pictures: "As for them, you will not find them interesting from the art side, but from the human side: the side of experience, emotion, life. What is it that appeals to me in Egyptian art? Nothing technical, purely technical: at least, not to me: no, no, no: something human, everyday—a bit of strange distant history— a touch of human struggle reflected in the work of an ancient people."

W. showed me a wee draft of a note written by him to Schmidt in 1874. He said of it: "I found it here in the mess and read it. It was written fourteen years ago and more—speaks of my sickness then—the worst, darkest, doubtfullest, period of my life, all told—in some ways possessing features not unlike my present experience. I was having hell's own time then as I am now with the outlook bad if not quite desperate." I broke in: "Remember the six hundred and shut up." He laughed heartily. "Damn you, why don't you let me finish? Read the letter for yourself: you will see that I am not making too much of my troubles: the letter is cheerful—and I am cheerful today. The fact that I am consciously staring death in the face don't make me less cheerful: even death has its advantages—and death has its to-morrow. What do you suppose keeps me alive? My interest in the books and my consideration for you! If anything happened either to the books or to you I'd give in without further protestation—rather welcome the release. But read the letter." I found he had kept a record of his correspondence with Schmidt on the back of the letter. I will quote it: "letter to Rudolph Schmidt Jan 25, '74—wrote also March 4, '74 and sent Redwood Tree and Columbus—wrote also March 19, '74—also April 25 sending note and C. Petersen's piece. Also June 11 enclosing Song of the Universal—American Humor—Southern letter &c. Also about Aug. 29, '74." The letter follows:

Jan 25 '74.

My dear Rudolph Schmidt, Your letter of Jan. 2, has just reached me here. I am always glad to hear from you. Write oftener. I have been very ill, just a year, from paralysis and cerebral anæmia—I have been at death's door. I sent you a paper with acct four or five months since but as you do not allude to it I suppose you did not rec. it. I send another by this mail. I have sent you several papers and magazines. I am not in bed but go out a little every day, and shall probably get well again yet, but remain paralyzed yet—have bad spells in my head, and walk with great difficulty—ameliorate very, very slowly. Still I write and publish a little.

What about Björnson? Is he coming to America? If so give him my address and tell him to come and see me. It is almost a part of Philadelphia where I live on the opposite side of the Delaware river. When you write or send Democratic Vistas, direct here. Write me from Germany.

What did I hear a while since of some great German university putting up for discussion? I have no thought of visiting England. In a letter two years since Tennyson kindly invited me to come and accept his hospitality—which aroused some thought of it in my mind—but it has passed over.

W.'s eyes brightened when I told him of the progress made by the printers with our books. "So I may expect copies of November Boughs to-morrow or Saturday? Good for you! Good for me! Good for everyone! But I will not believe it until the books are in my possession. Keep your hand on the throttle-valve, Horace: don't let your vigilance sleep for an instant! I am entirely dependent upon you to carry our adventure off with credit."

Friday, September 21st, 1888.

8 p. m. W. not bright this evening though he has been better today than yesterday—"but only a very little—a shade better: though, as you understand, a little is a great deal in my case." Harned in this evening. Burroughs started off for Sea Bright this morning. "It was to visit Johnson," said W.: "Johnson of the Century staff—an old-fashioned first-class fellow doing the work of a general utility man there." Burroughs still complains of insomnia. I had a long talk with him last night. W. said: "I thought he was all over that insomnia deviltry long ago. Dear John! I do not question his loyalty: he is true as a die! The damnable insomnia—what causes it? There was Lindell's wife, too—she was bad, very bad." "Lindell's wife is much better." "Do you hear that? That's good news—better news —best news! Tell Lindell for me that I am glad to hear of her luck. Herbert Spencer, too, seems to be a victim of the same complaint. I have belly aches and head aches and leg aches and all other kinds of damned aches but I hain't got no acheless insomnia: thank God for that!" I said: "You are chipper this evening. You show the effects of not having to endure tariff symposiums and torchlight parades last night!" He was merry over this. "Very good—and true enough to be good, too, Horace: I seem to have got past the age, and the health, when I can stand debating societies and political jubilations without hurt. Life simply drags along with me: there's drag, drag, drag— but nothing more substantial." I said Burroughs had asked me if W. thought well of Kennedy. "What did you say?" "That you did—very well." "That was right: that will do very well for an answer. Yes indeed we do—all of us."

W. had his hat on and wore a red tie. "You have a sort of out-doors and youthful look to-night, Walt." "Do I? That's worth believing. I'll get into the hat and tie habit: maybe that'll help to keep me alive." Burroughs had brought him an apple phenomenal both for size and beauty. It still lay on the table. "Why don't you eat it." "It's too grand: I hate the idea of not having it just where it is so I can look at it." W. spoke of Donaldson as "a rare raconteur: among the very best: perhaps the very best. Burroughs tells some Greek story of two armies, one of them nearly conquered yet not despairing. A moonlight night comes on: the weaker combatants are under arms, not knowing what to do. All at once, on a new angle of the moon, the position of the enemy was revealed by the glint on their spears. Then an assault—a victory—the tide turned! When it comes to a story Donaldson can give you that glint: or if not a story then just a bit of current philosophy: he can give you that glint: he has the genius of that glint." He talked again of his physical decadence. "Bucke says your letters are better today than any time since you were taken sick." "Ah! But Bucke don't know all—or half of all! There's many a dangerous spot beneath the fair surface of the stream." Could not get his mind off Burroughs. "What a singular thing that insomnia is— the most horrible affliction I can think of."

Found a pile of well on to a thousand copies of the Linton portrait in the back room but sheet too small to fit into the big book. W. said: "That's infernal tantalizing. I should not have left the cut so long in New Haven, where Linton has it. I have a bad habit of dropping things about in that way and often of forgetting where they are: leaving them here and there on deposit, so to speak. Linton once used this portrait in a book he prepared for Bohn—asked my permission, which I granted. I like it—always have liked it. The printing bill at the time was a startling one: that is why I regret to have to waste these sheets now." Alluded to Gutekunst pictures of his father and of himself: "They are first-rate: they satisfy my sense of photographic righteousness: I have given many of them away—the pictures of myself—because, on the whole, to a person who gets only one picture, this picture is in more ways than any other spiritually satisfactory and physically representative."

Has spent part of the day making up packages of the Centennial Edition. Is happy over the intelligence, brought by Burroughs from Gilder, that W.'s prose piece will undoubtedly appear in October. Copyright not yet received. "Where did our dollar go? If any fellow needs that dollar more than I do, let him have it. I don't object to losing the dollar but I do object to the delay. The minutes to a man in my straits are golden. How can I do much, shut off here from the world, from the light and air of the common life, so precious (yes, so necessary), day in and out, and night—and the vim of me all gone!" I said: "If you keep on practising putting on such a poor mouth you'll get yourself penniless again." "Ain't I penniless—in health?" "No—you've got a fortune left and you know it." He looked at me. "Horace—you're more right than I am in that: yes, there's a fortune left and I will draw on it." I said to W.: "Were you sorry to see John go?" "Yes and no: yes—because it would be nice to have him live nearer: no—because we were about talked out for the present. I am no kind of a social being just now. I seem to have only one thing in mind—only one: the book, the book, only the book—and you, who are my other self pledged to the same single undertaking: you and the book— you are in my mind day and night. Besides, though John is wholesome in general he carries about with him just now a slightly depressed air, to which I seem to be extremely sensitive." W. started me looking over the table for some letters which I didn't find, but in the course of my search I turned up a draft of a letter written by him in 1867 to Rossetti which he said I might "take along and put away" if I thought it "likely to be of any biographical use in the future." I sat right down where I was and read it.

Nov. 22, '67.

I suppose Mr. Conway has received and you have read, the letter I sent over about three weeks since, assenting to the substitution of other words, &c. as prepared by you, in your reprint of my book, or selections therefrom.

I suppose the reprint intends to avoid any expressed or implied character of being an expurgated edition—and hope it will simply assume the form and name of a selection from the various editions of my pieces, printed here. I suggest, in the interest of that view, whether the following might not be a good form of Title-page: "Walt Whitman's Poems Selected from the American Editions By William M. Rossetti."

When I have my next edition brought out here, I shall change the title of the piece, "When lilacs in the Dooryard bloom'd," to "President Lincoln's Funeral Hymn." You are at liberty to take the latter name, or the old one, at your option, (if you include the piece in your reprint.)

I wish particularly not [only] that the little figures numbering the stanzas, but also that the larger figures dividing the pieces into separate passages or sections, be carefully preserved as in copy.

It is quite certain that I shall add to my next edition (according to my plan from the start) a brief cluster of pieces, born of thoughts on the deep themes—Death and Immortality.

You will allow me to send you an article I have printed on "Democracy"—a hasty charcoal-sketch of a piece, but indicative, to any one interested in Leaves of Grass, as of the audience the book supposes and in whose interest it is made.

Allow me also to send you (as the ocean postage law is now so easy,) a copy of Mr. Burroughs' Notes and some papers.

And now, my dear sir, and with uninterested candor, you must just make what use, or no use at all, of anything I suggest or send as your own occasions call for. Very likely some of my suggestions may have been anticipated.

I asked W.: "Didn't you after all come to the conviction that the Rossetti book was in effect an expurgated edition?" "Yes I did: I never gave my assent to any abbreviated editions which I didn't live to regret. After all, the Rossetti book was a piece-meal affair—an apology: it said to the British public: here you are good respectable readers, here is this American Walt Whitman pruned so as to make a decent member of your household: your sons and daughters are safe with this book: we have shaved off the mane of the lion, we have drawn his claws and teeth: now, behold, you have one of yourselves, whom you may welcome with an unfearing heart. I do not say Rossetti intended it for that but that's what it came to. I never have had any reason to be other than proud of Rossetti: his attitude towards me has been consistently noble, considerate, even sacrificial—no man could have been more truly another man's friend and brother." I said to W.: "I've been waiting to hear the big story you were going to tell me." "You'll hear that in due time—not to-night. That cat has too long a tail to start to unravel at the end of an evening: we'll need a whole night for it."

Saturday, September 22nd, 1888.

2.30 P. M. W. sitting in chair reading Lippincott's Magazine. Had been examining literary notices in closing pages. Was not bright. Woke up this morning with headache—something unusual for him. How was he? "Oh! nothing to brag of." Day cool, beautiful: thought that assisted him a little. I had with me a package of books—November Boughs—five copies, secured from binder this noon, still damp when I unfolded them to Walt. His whole face lightened into a smile. "So that's the book?"—and again: "Here it is at last—and after such a siege!" Turned it over and over, radiant with satisfaction. "Yes, it is better even than I expected it would be—satisfies me —gives me peace." Things still to be looked to here and there. Advertisement not yet in. "It belongs in—I consider it a part of the history of the book—integral. I had thought we might have a book like this"—picking up the Epictetus—"but our book is so much bigger I don't know whether such a cover would do." Turned the book over and over. "Well—it will do: I approve of it: it is our dear child come safely at last through the great storm." He took a copy he meant for me and wrote on the fly-leaf: "Sept. 22 '88 Horace Traubel with the best memories and thanks of Walt Whitman"—saying as he handed it back to me: "It's not very strong, very emphatic: but then I'm not very strong, very emphatic." I quoted

Emerson: "The superlative is the fat of expression." W. said: "Thank you for that—and thank Emerson. It's just like Emerson, too: that's the Emerson I knew: sinew without fat: if anything (though I guess not) too much sinew: reserved, reticent, always sweet, almost a disciple of silence. You know me and know I never quite go off about things—am not explosive, extravagant. Gesticulation, physical emphasis, facial grimacing, more prevalently distinguishes southern peoples than peoples north. Yet Americans are sometimes very actively exclamatory—perhaps not the most so and yet just as surely not the least so." I spoke of Salvini's remarkable physical mobility. "Well—that's the actor's part—that's his power. My friend who used to translate Hugo for me—he would sit at the other side of the table and talk across—was very lively, very animated —almost danced some of his verses out."

Gave me two letters from Bucke. "You will want to see them—take them along: they are simple, affectionate, vigorous —and, thank God, not literary." If there is any business afoot which W. must imperatively watch he pins some memorandum concerning it to the hanging end of the table cover. Looked over several bills and reminders there this evening. "I had a paper from Boyle O'Reilly: I have sent it off to Bucke: it came yesterday or day before. Boyle is a brave man among brave men: Horace, you would cleave to him if you could get together." Burroughs suggested that W. should eat clams. Was he favorable to clams? "Ah! you forget I am a Long Islander or you would not ask the question. But then, as to liking clams— that's another thing: I don't like things by premeditation: but if a good thing turns up on the table I am not averse to liking it. A girl off in the country sent me a jar of jelly: I didn't first of all ask myself whether I liked it: I just ate it up. After it was all gone I asked myself: 'I wonder if I like jelly?'" Then he added: "Let's try the clams: get a small jar first: it can do no harm: if it won't cure neither may it kill. 'What might cure Henry may be fatal to Camille': that is a line in a novel or a play somewhere." W. has received his copyright from Washington. "Now we proceed under the seal of authority." I read him this letter received by me from Stedman today:

44 EAST 26TH STREET,
NEW YORK, Sept. 21st, '88.

My dear Sir, At length I have received the enclosed report (accidentally disfigured) from Cassell & Co.—the third firm which I have labored with on the subject of the Calendar. It plainly reached my hands too late for this year. Yesterday I received Ticknor's Calendar, edited by Miss Sanborn, for 1889. But the objections made by both Scribner and Cassell are not so much against the lateness of the season, as against "Calendars" in general. They say these are no longer a novelty, and for the moment do not sell well. Mr. Scribner told me he would rather publish the Whitman Calendar than any other he had seen—but he will not publish any. Doubtless we can place this one somewhere for 1890! Am glad to hear better news of Walt's health. Tell him I have made the amendments which he indicated on those proofs. With cordial regards,

Sincerely yours,
E. C. STEDMAN.

The Cassell report enclosed was merely formal. W. said: "Stedman is generous—is always doing things for people: I am not grateful for I know he would resent gratitude—I am only happy for knowing his good-will to be so near and constant." I said: "I told Stedman you personally cared little about the Calendar." "You did, eh? Well—you told what was true: I wouldn't turn on my heel for it. That's the reason it seems like an outrage to worry Stedman with it." Passed an old Dowden letter over to me. "Maybe you would like that. It's Dowden all over: always under rein—never slap-dash and let go: but loyal, hospitable, insinuating. I don't know what kind of a man I like most—one kind of a man or another kind of a man. I guess I like all kinds most." I started to read the letter to myself. W. said: "Read it aloud—it's just as easy for you and better for me." I said to W.: "You're still your mother's boy Walt!" He laughed and answered fervently: "Thank God for that, Horace!"

> Dublin, November 21, 1882.

Dear Mr. Whitman. Your card and Progress have just arrived. I rejoice that with the ill tidings of your recent prostration comes good news of your recovery. May this better condition continue! You annex your friends so closely that your health and strength becomes part of theirs.

I send you the Academy with my notice of Specimen Days. I closed my review with a wish that you might try a voyage across the Atlantic. It would be a happy thing if we could have you here for a while, where you would find a bedroom, books, and, in summer, flowers and birds, besides a friend or two. Think of this. In London, I am sure, your welcome would be hearty.

Please notice a few lines by the editor of The Academy (I suppose) on p. 362. Who his informant was I do not know.

> Most truly yours, dear friend,
> Edward Dowden.

I said: "I know one thing in that letter that hit you hard." "So do I. What was it?" "The sentence, 'you annex your friends so closely': that's my guess." "You fire right home— that's the thing. Isn't that better than writing books?" "But don't it come to you because you have written a book?" He hesitated an instant before replying. "It might be put that way but I prefer to say, *because I have lived a life.* Don't you think *living a life* the most important thing after all?" I accepted his amendment. "I suppose you would say, Walt, that the trouble with most books is that they have not lived a life?" "Precisely: that comes first: all else follows or don't follow: living a life—a life of service, love—that is the first article in every noble faith."

Evening. Went down with Harned. Up into the bedroom. W. not there. Found him in adjoining room, in the darkness, fumbling about for something. As he came through the door on his way back he saw us. "Oh! it's Tom and Horace! Welcome both—welcome both!" Had his hat on and wore his red tie. Walked laboriously to his chair. Prefers not to be helped. "It's a job for me to take the shortest journey." W. handed Harned a copy of November Boughs. "It's all good but that lettering on the cover: that's weak pea-soup, dish-wash. Oldach tried for his worst on that and succeeded." Talked with Harned about Burroughs' insomnia: "That's an agent of the devil. I am mystified: why should John suffer from insomnia? John always seemed to me rugged, hearty, strong, with good digestion and a clear head." Harned said: "Why, it's so bad, Walt, that Burroughs has an idea he may have to undergo an operation to get rid of it." W. dissented: "An operation? Oh no—not that: tell John not that: anything but that: that's worse than all. I say, damn the drugs—damn operations!" He stopped. "I guess that's too strong but that's what I meant to say in effect. There's one habit of John's with which I never could sympathize: his disposition to rush off and have something done for him by a doctor the minute anything is the matter with him: to consult medicine men, take things—potions of some sort. Nature abhors all that—abhors it especially in a fellow like John, whose good body, good brain, seem to demand saner correctives. I have often met instances of that insomnia horror but find that it is usually of short duration. Indigestion accounts for fully nine-tenths of all our ailments and yet it cannot be that with John. We all love John and all hate his troubles. I thought after John had been here awhile the other day that there was a great absence in him of that buoyancy, spring, spirit, which had always been to me a source of delight. John is sweet—equable: breathes out the life of pears, cherries, grapes— odors of wildwoods, too. And by the way, when he was here he asked if I would have more pears, and I said no—or, if not more pears, grapes, and I still said no—and then if neither pears nor grapes, how about cider? And there he stumped me. Cider? I asked him: 'Have you cider?' and he answered: 'I

haven't but everybody up there has: I can get all I want.' So
I shouldn't be surprised to have it come to you over there in
Philadelphia some day—a barrel of it: and you will come along
here some evening with it on your shoulders, like the little
mountain men in Rip Van Winkle."

I picked up the Jane Carlyle book. W.'s marker was stuck
into it about half way through. "So you're going to read it
after all?" I asked. W. took the book out of my hands and
said: "Yes and no: though go through with them—take a
glance at each letter—that I must do. It is like a case with a
fellow who has bad bowels: I must keep at him to get at the
bottom facts." Was he interested, after all? "No—I think it
about the stupidest stuff that ever was put into print." Harned
asked: "Why was it printed, then?" W. replied: "Lord only
knows: because the world wanted it, I suppose—wanted and
would pay for it." But Mrs. Carlyle was for him "one of those
smart people, capable of saying sharp and bitter and bright
things—the sort no one could ever expect me to feel any thorough
interest in." He regarded it as "a horrible dose, taken all in all:
the whole Carlyle matter, in fact, very hard indeed to bear.
Sour, discontented, vinegary, grunting—what a horror it is!
As you heard me say the other night, the Carlyle rumpus is a
reproach to the Almighty: think of it, that any man could stand
in the presence of the great globes and say, all this is humbug—
stand and rail at everything, all men—the whole constitution of
the existing universe: nothing left in the wreckage to satisfy the
soul—nothing to offer reassurances—nothing that would compensate for defects or to make up for evil. There's no use talking,
they were both bad eggs—Jane, Thomas: bad eggs indeed.
And yet I see underlying all that, pervading all, pathos: pathos,
as you said the other day so finely, Horace: here everything is
pathetic: no matter how deep you dig, how wide you cut, how
high you go, there's the pathos of it, the awful pathos of it,
staring you in the face. Yet I keep always asking myself
another question. Why the hell didn't she marry some strong,
healthy, manly Scotchman—some fellow who loved her and

could be lived with?—then all this vinegar might have been turned into sweet channels—might have been spared or converted to beneficent uses. Carlyle seemed to forget that other men had mothers, too: he didn't have sympathy for other men's mothers: he was dull—did not see the big things in others—in Mill, for instance: and he never saw radicalism clearly: all the radicals, democrats—no matter how disinterested, pure—were to him damned shams, arrant knaves, spectres of night: and civilization itself, modern life and hopes, more than all the fresher spiritual lights, aroused in him sorry forebodings of reaction. Life is not so bright that anybody should wanton with it—should keep its shadows too much to the front. Carlyle spit out everything—perhaps to his peace, though to the world's pain."

Harned said: "Walt, you've gone at a great pace: you've rubbed all the fur off Carlyle's back." W. laughed. "Well, Tom, look what Carlyle has done to me: he has left me with hardly a hope left, for all my great faith, what with the green envy and devilish venom of his growl. Yet I know more's to be said—much more. I always tell myself after speaking freely of Carlyle—there is more yet to be said: he was needed, he was great, he was important to this age perhaps beyond any other." I cited a story repeated by Emerson to Whittier. Emerson told Carlyle about a lecture manager who tried to get him to deduct something from his fee for the lecture after it was delivered. Carlyle took his pipe from his mouth and exclaimed: "And why did you not put a bullet through his doorty brains?" W. enjoyed the story. "Well—I could forgive Carlyle much for that—that's a classic!" Harned asked W.: "Walt, do you find that John Burroughs is as fond of your friends as you are?" W. answered very slowly: "That's funny, Tom: I've been asking myself such a question. I feel that John is loyal to me even if he is not loyal to my friends—is not afraid of me, though he may be a little afraid of some of my friends. Don't you see, you're a dangerous lot—William, down in Washington, and Bucke, and Horace here, with enough revolution in him to make a good Mexican!'"

Sunday, September 23rd, 1888.

7.15 p. m. W. reading Pardoe's Court of Louis Fourteenth. "I feel a bit better today but you notice I wear no extra feathers in my cap." The morning papers published extracts from the Diary of the Emperor Frederick William—cabled from abroad. "Ah! the good Emperor! His time had not come yet—Europe was not ready for him. The moral greatness of Frederick always impresses me profoundly." I told him Burroughs had left word that the substance of the Carlyle papers which W. advised him to put into a book had already been so used. "Then I don't think I ever got the book," said W. "Two or three weeks ago I made up my mind to go into the Carlyle matter—go to the bottom of it—if it had a bottom—sift all its wheat from its chaff. If John had sent me such a book I know I should have taken to it first. I endorse all he said in those papers: his torch lit up the whole scene: it was like the best light in the worst darkness. Carlyle is still a Carlyle mystery to me. I have long had these doubts and they remain unshaken by all I have recently read." I advised W. to read the letters. "They show the best Carlyle—Carlyle real, loyal: they are the letters to his mother, father and brothers." W. said quickly: "That's surely stuff for me to read: nothing is more likely to exploit the interior best of a man." I remarked: "I admit all you said last night, and yet Carlyle has done me good." "I am glad to hear you say that, Horace: he has done me good, too—immense, incalculable good: that is what I always allow whatever has been denied: the substance of his message underlying all its often misguiding words: the precious something unwritten, unsaid: the fact below the fact. I have often taken up cudgels for Carlyle. I remember two or three occasions at Pearsall Smith's —stormy occasions—when I had to rally the stampede and declare for Carlyle in vehement terms."

I was in Germantown today. Many inquiries everywhere concerning W. "It does me good to sit here and think there are people, even groups of people, unknown, never met, even unsuspected—who ask for, remember, me. Kennedy used to go about a good deal in Boston, years ago: you know the time—it was when he wrote the famous letter: 'there is a solid phalanx of enemies wherever I turn.' Kennedy is easily riled: he goes into the most orthodox circles: some word is said— maybe a very innocent word: he takes it up, defends, assaults, fences, and then a battle is on. There was a little clipping of Kennedy's piece on Sanborn's Thoreau in the Press today." Clifford gave me a scrap on W. from the N. Y. Press. W. read it. First he said: "No, no, that's not me." Then: "There seem glints of things here and there"—then, after reading on: "Oh what bosh! I never said that—it don't sound like me—I don't talk so peacocky." Finally, he said: "This fellow is friendly but he hasn't got the correct line on my history." It was given out mostly as an interview, mainly purporting to be in W.'s own words. "The ideas seem like your ideas Walt." "So they do—mostly: but I never talk in that way."

"Long white hair, long white beard and moustache, a florid face, with blue eyes alive with fire, a gigantic frame withered, a shirt thrown open below his corded neck, gray coat and trousers, shoes tied with leather strings, is the picture that Walt Whitman presents to a visitor. An inkstand and pen are on the table before him, and a lead pencil is on the window near him. His old white hat lies on a chair. His tone and manner are cheerful, and he responds to the expression of sympathetic interest in him.

"It is now thirty years since Walt Whitman began to write. He is nearer, but scarcely nearer, popular appreciation than when he began. There is something pathetic in his uncomplaining attitude towards the persistent misapprehension which attends all he does.

"He said recently, in speaking of this: 'I set out with a design as thoroughly considered as an architect's plan of a cathedral. None of the poets have touched exactly what I wanted to do. It seemed to me that all had fallen short of getting down deep into the appreciation and sympathies of the mass of mankind. Of course, in a brief conversation I can only suggest what I mean. Shakespeare's poems of war and passion, Milton's allegories and the poetry of men like Tennyson and Longfellow—in fact, all the poetry I had ever read, seemed to fall far short of touching the people of the world in their very cores of understanding and desire.

"'I set out to illustrate, without any flinching, humanity. I proposed to myself a series of compositions which should depict the physical, emotional, moral, intellectual and spiritual nature of man.' This man was to be himself. 'I had to deal with the physical, corporeal and amative—that part which is developed between the ages of twenty-two and thirty-five. It is that part of my endeavor which has caused the harshest criticism and prevented candid examination of the ensuing stages of the design. Still I have gone on adding, building up, preserving, so far as I am able to do in my original intention. I suppose I fail, as many others have failed, in fully expressing myself. The difficulty is not in not knowing what a man wants to say, but in formulating it. I am not embittered by my want of success. It is so different from the accepted forms of poetry that it could not be expected to make its way. I have been most kindly received in England both by periodicals and critics. My last volume is in response to the interest of my friends abroad.'"

W. gave me a set of the Centennial Edition. "It makes me feel rich," I said. He replied: "If you feel richer taking than I do to give you must feel like a millionaire." Pointed out a pile of the books over on the floor. "I am trying to get them in shape for selling," he said. W. is a slow answerer but he always answers to the point. That is, if he wants to answer at all. Sometimes he don't. Then he will say he don't want to in so many words or will tell you what a long tail that cat has and so get off your chase. I asked him: "What comes before comradeship?" He answered: "Nothing." I asked: "And after?" "Nothing again." This apropos of a letter he gave me. It was one of the rough drafts a few of which he seems to have kept. I will put it right in here.

April 15, 1870.

DEAR BENTON WILSON.

Dear loving comrade, As I have just been again reading your last letter to me of December 19, last. I think I wrote to you on receiving it, but cannot now remember for certain. Sometimes, after an interval, the thought of one I much love comes upon me strong and full all of a sudden—and now as I sit here by a big open window, this beautiful afternoon, every thing quiet and sunny—I have been and am now, thinking so of you, dear young man, and of your love, or more rightly speaking, our love for each other—so curious, so sweet, I say so *religious*— We met there in the Hospital—how little we have been together —seems to me we ought to be some together every day of our lives—I don't care about talking, or amusement—but just to be together, and work together, or go off in the open air together— Now it is a long while since we have been together—and it seems a long while since I have had a letter. Don't blame me for not writing oftener. I know you would feel satisfied if you could only realize how and how much I am thinking of you, and with what great love, this afternoon. I can hardly express it in a letter—but I thought I would just write a letter this time off-hand to you, dearest soldier, only for love to you—I thought it might please you.

Nothing very new or different in my affairs. I am still working here in Atty Gens office—same posish—have good health— expect to bring out new editions of my books before long—how is the little boy—I send my love to him and to your wife and parents.

I looked at W. There were tears in my eyes. I said: "You did not ask me to read that aloud and I'm glad you didn't." "You mean you couldn't have read it?" "Yes—and that you couldn't have heard it read." His face was very grave. "Horace—it is true—it is true: I can't live some of my old letters over again." I said: "These letters of yours to the soldiers are the best gospel of comradeship in the language—better than the Leaves itself." "Comradeship—yes, that's the thing: getting one and one together to make two—getting the twos together everywhere to make all: that's the only bond we should accept and that's the only freedom we should desire: comradeship, comradeship." He had made up a little bunch of old letters for me tonight—"brands plucked from the burning," he called them. They were from Nelly O'Connor, William O'Connor, Cyril Flower, Henry Clapp, Sylvester Baxter, and W.'s own draft of a letter to Elijah Fox. I stuck them in my pocket. As I kissed W. on leaving he said: "All our good nights are precious to me—and our good mornings."

Monday, September 24th, 1888.

8 p. m. W. reading Ibsen's Pillars of Society. "Some one in the Walter Scott Company sent it over to me." Laid it down. Shook hands with me. "Perhaps it was Rhys. I am not greatly impressed. It seems to me to have been too prettily done though it is no doubt much more powerful in the Norwegian— hardly seems apposite when rendered in English. I doubt whether I would ever care for the play." Better today. "I'm not feeling like a whole mob but I do feel a bit sassy." Also said: "I have great faith in my power of endurance. I have no doubt now but I shall hold out my time—that is, I shall not hasten my death by anything I do." Gave me a couple of letters from Bucke. "They are so bright, cheerful, elastic: and he is so faithful—writes again and again and again. Bucke is my only constant correspondent left: William writes very rarely— is not able to write." I took him a proof of advertisement to go in November Boughs. He at once proceeded to revise it.

Referred to Boyle O'Reilly. "He is staunch with the staunchest: he is a man of whom we can be sure: his whole life has been a life of loyalty—to persons, to causes, nobly most of all to his own principles. There seems to be quite a cluster of Boston folks who mean me well—are eligible to accept, acknowledge, my cause—make my cause theirs: quite a cluster. There was a man who borrowed from my Old Ireland poem, or happened nearby when it was around and got unconsciously infected —anyhow, was tainted with it. O'Reilly brought the question up in The Pilot. I was not inclined to make anything of it—but there is a right and a right and it may be well to have it understood. You remember the charge that Longfellow stole Hiawatha from the Finnish. What does that come to? Little. I can scarcely say I have read Hiawatha with attention and knowledge—read it from start to end. I knew Selma Borg: she used to say Hiawatha was a most brazen theft—absolutely stolen—shamelessly. I confess the idea never excited me, one way or the other. I always felt that Longfellow had his reasons and reasons and that they were sufficient whatever they were."

We talked of November Boughs. Who should get the first copies? "I will let you attend to that mostly, Horace. I must send copies to my sisters, niece, O'Connor, Mary Costelloe, John Burroughs"—here he stopped an instant: "also the Doctor, Kennedy, Morse"—pausing again: "I suppose there will be others, too, but I wish to send these first and particularly. I shall let Dave send to the rest—the papers—except that, perhaps, I shall personally send a copy to Julius Chambers, of the Herald, to whom I have taken a special shine." How close did the Critic Gilders stand to him? He said: "Not very: I never considered them warm: theirs is rather a hectic flush of admiration. You know, Horace, there are some who in the natural order couldn't accept Walt Whitman—couldn't appreciate the inmost purpose of his art: it is the absence of affinities. Lowell, with his almost steel-like beauty, and Higginson, with his strict, straight, notions of literary propriety—I could call them enemies, creatures natively antipathetic." How was it with Richard Watson Gilder? "Burroughs, when he was here, spoke of Stedman and Gilder as 'coming over'—says Gilder has grown into a very warm appreciation—confesses that nowadays some of my lines haunt him. I don't think John quite takes it all in. I should say Stedman—yes: Stedman is affectionate, warm-blooded: but Gilder—well, Watson is a bit too much impressed with the importance of parlors, literatures, singing. I have no doubt about Gilder—about his genuineness. He is rich on the emotional side—approaches me that way. Gilder is essentially a troubadour singer, realizing grace, music, prettiness: he lays his emphasis upon that. As for me, that is just the thing in which I seem to take no particular interest. If there is anything whatever in Leaves of Grass—anything that sets it apart as a fact of any importance—that thing must be its totality—its massings. I respond to no other explanation: no other explanation comes up to my purpose—tallies the long steady pull of my many years of adhesion to a first purpose. I chose the fundamentals for Leaves of Grass—heart, spirit: the initiating passions of character: chose that it should stand for, be, a human being, with all the impulses, desires, aspirations, gropings, triumphs, that go with human life: comprehended at no time by its parts, at all times by its unity." He was very earnest. Then he went on: "Leaves of Grass is not intellectual alone (I do not despise the intellectual—far from it: it is not to be despised—has its uses) nor sympathetic alone (though sympathetic enough, too) nor yet vaguely emotional—least of all this. I have always stood in Leaves of Grass for something higher than qualities, particulars. It is atmosphere, unity: it is never to be set down in traits but as a symphony: is no more to be stated by superficial criticism than life itself is to be so stated: is not to be caught by a smart definition or all given up to any one extreme statement." The Cyril Flower letter was addressed to W. at Washington:

FURZE DOWN,
SURREY, S. W., July 16, '71.

Dear Mr. Whitman. Tennyson writes to you by this mail. He lays upon me the blame of not having written to you sooner and I am willing to bear it. The fact is the books went to his London address and were not forwarded.

Yours affectionately,
CYRIL FLOWER.

"I think it was then that Tennyson invited me to visit him in England. It was a tempting offer—it pulled at my heart-strings: my friends over there all said, come, you will have an ovation—the time has arrived for you to come: I was almost on the point of taking passage—then something inside me said very plainly, *stay where you are Walt Whitman:* said it in ways, in words, in warnings, I had no right to, could not, misunderstand. Even some of my friends here said, go: and some were angry when I decided not to: but my own heart never was in doubt about it—never said anything else than stay, stay, stay. The incident has no other history than that." I said to W.: "That O'Connor letter you gave me yesterday was of a most extraordinary character both for beauty and power." He answered: "It's wonderful, don't you think, Horace? The very handwriting is a stroke of genius, to speak of nothing else. Can you name any man in the literature of England or America capable of writing such a letter—any man? When William gets on his real high horse—his high horse of high horses—he completely fills the stage: there is no use for any other performer. This amazing effect is not secured by arrogance but by sheer force and vehemence of self-expression. I confess that it staggers me —leaves me without a word." I said to W.: "I want to study that letter some more before I put it away." "It will bear study: William never loses caste at close quarters: he always more than holds his own."

Bucke writes this: "I do not doubt you often feel bad enough and I know you are very sick—worse luck. Still, it is grand to see you keep up as you do—never giving up to the last—I think it is immense—something for us all to be proud of and to take to heart—and the world will take all this to heart one day and will be the better for it." I said to W.: "It's worth dying for, Walt—to live that way." He said: "If you'll remember that I'm only living to sign the six hundred books, you won't feel so proud of my courage." Gently laughed. I asked W.: "Walt, do I come too much?" He reached out his hand and

took mine. "Does the fresh air come too much? Thank God
for the fresh air!"

When I mentioned the Clapp letter W. said: "Henry was my
friend: he had abilities way out of the common: he seems to be
forgotten except for the few men and women who were his
associates. I can see how Henry in another environment might
have loomed up as a central influence. He was always in trouble—always behind in his finances: had to put up the most heroic fight right along to keep the Press alive. Somebody some
day will tell that story to our literary historians, who will thenceforth see that Henry cannot be skipped, for the Press cut a significant figure in the periodical literature of its time. I have
often said to you that my own history could not be written with
Henry left out: I mean it—that is not an extravagant statement."
W. had written on the envelope: "Henry Clapp to me in Boston."

N. Y. Monday May 14, '60.

My dear Walt: I spent much time yesterday reading your
poems, and am more charmed with them than ever. I think
you would have done well to follow Mr. Emerson's advice, but
you may have done better as it is. At any rate, the book is
bound to sell, if money enough is spent circulating the Reprints
and advertising it generally. It is a fundamental principle in
political economy that everything succeeds if money enough is
spent on it. If I could spend five hundred dollars in one week
on the Saturday Press I would make five thousand dollars by the
operation. Ditto you with the L. of G.

You should send copies at once to Vanity Fair, Momus, The
Albion, The Day Book, The Journal of Commerce, Crayon—
also to Mrs. Juliette H. Beach, Albion, N. Y., who will do you
great justice in the S. P. (for we shall have a *series* of articles)—
to Charles D. Gardette Esq, No 910 Walnut Street, Philadelphia, to Evening Journal, Philadelphia, and also some dozen
copies to me to be distributed at discretion. Do not hereafter
ask the editors to notice at any particular time or *at all:* for the
effect is bad.

I want to do great things for you with the book, and as soon as I get over my immediate troubles will do so. But just now I am in a state of despair even in respect to getting out another issue of the S. P. and all for the want of a paltry two or three hundred dollars which would take the thing to a paying point, and make it worth ten thousand dollars as a transferable piece of property.

Yours in haste,

HENRY CLAPP, JR.

W. wants a stove—a wood stove.   Asked me to look about for it.   "That little stove is burned out: it was put here once, years ago, by my sister, when I was sick: brought in a hurry.   I am likely to be tied right here in this room the whole winter if I live at all.   Some days I get doubtful about myself but I have a notion now that I may drag on several years on my present low level of life.   It is a conservative level—conservative to the last degree—but suffices for some purposes, of which we will make the most we can."   Asked me what sort of a service Clifford conducted in his church.   Smiled, pleased, when told of Clifford's informalities.   "He makes pretty free and easy with religion, then—don't he?   Why shouldn't we?   Religion ceases to be religion if we have to do anything else with it.   My wonder is, that Clifford can do so much as he pleases and still please the people: I would be surprised if I heard he could go on with this policy successfully for any length of time.   Clifford has an Emerson way about him—or maybe it's the other way about: Emerson had a Clifford way about him: anyhow, Clifford, in his immense catholicity, in his pith—in his big sympathies, (even in his occasional overdone phrases), suggests the Emersonian flavor—though I admit that Clifford takes liberties—decided liberties—where Emerson would not."

Tuesday, September 25th, 1888.

7.45 p. m.   Bad day today.   The folks were in a state of quiet anxiety about him.   Trouble with his stomach.   Must have felt rotten, for he expressed a wish to have Dr. Osler come over. This is the first time that he has asked for a doctor himself. Said to me: "I have been wishing all day Osler would come over." It's odd why Osler does not come over. I wrote him Saturday suggesting that he do so. He has not seen W. since early summer—since the day he said: "Well, Mrs. Davis, your old man is better: I am sure he will live over the summer." Baker met Osler and advised him to see W. Musgrove went over and left a note at Osler's this evening. Osler was absent. Harned was in.

When I entered W.'s room Mrs. Davis sat on the sofa and they were talking together. W. sat in his chair, his hat on. He was as always cordial. Shook hands with me—motioned me to a seat. "Is it raining?" he asked. Mrs. Davis left. Had been reading Pardoe's book again. "I tried to do some work today but gave it up. I have been much upset." I said: "This is one of your bad days?" "I only have two kinds of days—bad days and days not so bad." "And good days?" "No good days in the real sense." Asked me what I had done today. I told him I came empty-handed—everything went wrong today with both binders and printers: and I had no mail. He laughed. "That sounds shady enough to be my report: no mail, nothing at all. Yet let me see." Picked up a couple of letters—one from Kennedy and one from Rhys (nearly a year old): "Oh, here is something but not much." Read me part of Kennedy's letter. Talked rather weariedly—somewhat confusedly here and there, as on that Saturday night in June. "It is the cool weather—I am sensitive to it—it came all of a sudden." What had I done about the stove? I found one. "It will cost seven dollars." He asked: "Is it worth the money?" Then he added: "We will not need the stove at once: it will be warm weather again, perhaps for a month yet." He drew his coat tightly about him. "That is a good little stove over there," he said. "But didn't you tell me last night that it was burnt out?" "Yes, that's so—burnt out: but if I sit here and watch it it will do very well: I would not like to leave it alone—it would be risky." I tried to get him to say, "buy the new stove." He wouldn't do so—put it off. I warned him about colds. "I will be careful, Horace—I will, I will: I, too, know how important it is for me to fight shy of colds."

Told him I had written to Stedman expressing his thanks. Satisfied. Was worried some about the books. "On a day like this the six hundred signatures look like a mountainous job." Expressed interest in a paragraph from one of Bucke's letters: "I am reading Carlyle again—Chartism, Past and Present, &c &c. Looking into French Revolution. He is a grand old fellow but not one of the immortals. There are just two great modern books—Faust and Leaves of Grass." W. laughed mildly. "Is it a joke?" "No—I was thinking that was a modification of Doctor's partisanship! I am wondering why he included Faust!" W. adding: "Maurice always goes far enough and on days when he feels particularly good he goes too far." Musgrove came in for an instant. W. asked: "Where have you been?" He had really just got back from Osler's but did not say so. Later W. said about Osler's non-arrival: "It's all right any way—it's all the same, whether I get help or not—all the same: if I get it well and good—better perhaps: if not, just as well if not quite as good." Admitted he felt much relieved this evening. "I'm worse than an old woman with my complaints. I am very dependent on you, Horace, for all the work of the books: if you fail me all will fail—I might as well give up the ghost." The Baxter letter given to me by W. Sunday was about the cottage fund. W. said: "You should take it and put it with the other letters on the same subject: they belong together. That man Law mentioned in the letter excites my affection but I do not seem to connect him with Pfaff's."

THE HERALD, BOSTON,
Aug. 2, 1887.

My dear friend: I enclose for the cottage $285 in two checks of $50 and $235 respectively. On the former you will see the signature of one of the best of your Boston friends—Dr. Wesselhoeft. This will make $788, so far, I believe and I think the remaining $12 will be forthcoming soon.

I wish it might have been done so as to enable you to escape this hot weather altogether, but I hope you can contrive to get away before the summer ends. Shall you get some house that is already built, or do you propose building?

Would you not like in the house a nice fireplace where you could sit and toast your toes before a nice open fire and dream with open eyes as you look at the blaze? I think you would like that better than an ugly black stove that scorches all the vitality out of the air. If the idea pleases you, my friend, Jack Law, the Chelsea tile-maker, would like to send you a handsome set of tiles for it. Law knew you in the old Pfaff days, when he was a landscape painter, but says you probably would not recognize him by name. Very likely you might remember his vigorous expletives and great enthusiasm!

I think I may go on to New York next week and run over to Philadelphia when I shall drop in on you.

Oh! about Hartmann. He was altogether "too previous" and hardly appreciated what he had undertaken. He did not know how to go to work and appointed officers of a society which had not been organized! We all had to sit down on him and the matter is in abeyance. I hope it may come to something later. You may remember I wrote to you last winter about the idea of a W. W. Society

Faithfully yours,
Sylvester Baxter.

"I pray God it may be very much later," said W. of the W. W. Society: "What do they want of a Walt Whitman Society, anyway? Are they to dig a hole for me and close me in?" I said: "They are bound to come—Walt Whitman Societies." "Then God help me—I am lost!" "That won't be because you are lost—it will be because you are found." He looked at me. "How do you make that out? Do you justify a Leaves of Grass creed?—boards of explicators?—this line means this, and that line means that, and God damn you for a fool if you don't say so too? Do you go in for that, Horace?" "No—for nothing of the kind—nor will the Societies. They will go in for fraternity without a creed—love without a creed. Do you object to that?" "No—I don't: but can you hold societies together with no more than fraternity as the article of faith?" "Why not? If we can't then I don't want Walt Whitman Societies any more than you do. If we can I want to see Walt Whitman Societies all over the world." W. was very still after this for several minutes. I wondered what he would finally say. I wanted him to say more. At last he spoke. "I say, God bless fraternity, Horace: what else could I say? I stand for that if I stand for anything—fraternity, comradeship: and I suppose that if you can make societies that stand for the same thing (if you can, do you hear? if, if) then I am bound to wish them luck, whether they bear your name or mine or whatever name they bear."

I said to W.: "That letter to Elijah Fox you gave me the other day is better than the gospel according to John for love." "You have read it? You think it says something?" "Don't you? Didn't you mean it to say something?" "Yes I did—what to me is the most important something in the world—something I tried to make clear in another way in Calamus—yes, something, something." His manner was very fervent. I said: "The letter does not seem like words—it seems like life: it is the collateral for Calamus—the thing that made Calamus possible or went to verify it." W. then said; "I want you to think that way about it if you think about it at all: if the matter has a meaning that is its meaning." This is the letter we talked about:

BROOKLYN Saturday night Nov 21, '63.

Dear son and comrade. I wrote a few lines about five days ago and sent on to Armory Square, but as I have not heard from it I suppose you have gone on to Michigan. I got your letter of Nov. 10th and it gave me much comfort. Douglass I shall return to Washington about the 24th so when you write direct to care of Major Hapgood, paymaster U S A, Washington D C— Dearest comrade I only write this lest the one I wrote five days ago may not reach you from the hospital. I am still here at my mother's and feel as if I have had enough of going around New York—enough of amusements, suppers, drinking, and what is called *pleasure*.—Dearest son: it would be more pleasure if we could be together just in quiet, in some plain way of living, with some good employment and reasonable income, where I could have you often with me, than all the dissipations and amusements of this great city—O I hope things may work so that we can yet have each other's society—for I cannot bear the thought of being separated from you—I know I am a great fool about such things but I tell you the truth dear son. I do not think one night has passed in New York or Brooklyn when I have been at the theatre or opera or afterward to some supper party or carousal made by the young fellows for me, but what amid the play or the singing I would perhaps suddenly think of you,— and the same at the gayest supper party of men where all was fun and noise and laughing and drinking, of a dozen young men and I among them I would see your face before me in my thought as I have seen it so often there in Ward G, and my amusement or drink would be all turned to nothing, and I would realize how happy it would be if I could leave all the fun and noise and the crowd and be with you—I don't wish to disparage my dear friends and acquaintances here, there are so many of them and all so good, many so educated, traveled, &c. some so handsome and witty, some rich &c. some among the literary class—many young men—all good—many of them educated and polished and brilliant in conversation, &c—and I thought I valued their society and friendship—and I do, for it is worth valuing—But Douglass I will tell you the truth. You are so much closer to me than any of them that there is no comparison—there has never passed so much between them and me as we have—besides there is something that takes down all artificial accomplishments, and that is a manly and loving soul—My dearest comrade, I am sitting here writing to you very late at night—I have been reading—it is indeed after 12, and my mother and all the rest have gone to bed two hours ago, and I am here above writing to you, and I enjoy it too. Although it is not much yet I know it will please you dear boy. If you get this you must write and tell me where and how you are. I hope you are quite well and with your dear wife, for I know you have long wished to be with her, and I wish you to give her my best respects and love too.

Douglass I haven't written any news for there is nothing particular I have to write. Well, it is now past midnight, pretty well on to one o'clock, and my sheet is mostly written out—so my dear darling boy, I must bid you good night, or rather good morning, and I hope it may be God's will we shall yet be with each other—but I must indeed bid you good night my dear loving comrade, and the blessing of God on you by night and day my darling boy.

W's last words to me to-night were: "Good bye—bye—bye! And you'll watch all things for two, eh? And see a little more about the stove? I am taking you for granted in all ways, Horace, don't you see? Good night!"

Wednesday, September 26th, 1888.

7.50 p. m. W. improved today. Osler over but not alarmed. W. reading Gilchrist's life of Blake. Asked me: "Do you know much about Blake? You know, this is Mrs. Gilchrist's book—the book she completed. They had made up their minds to do the work—her husband had it well under way: he caught a fever and was carried off. Mrs. Gilchrist was left with four young children, alone: her perplexities were great. Have you noticed that the time to look for the best things in best people is the moment of their greatest need? Look at Lincoln: he is our proudest example: he proved to be big as, bigger than, any emergency—his grasp was a giant's grasp— made dark things light, made hard things easy. Herbert's mother belonged to the same noble breed: seized the reins, was competent: her head was clear, her hand was firm. Her husband had designed an introductory note or two: she carried out his idea—neglected nothing—was afraid of nothing. The

Blake book"—he tapped it with his hand—"is charming for the same reason that we find Froude's Carlyle fascinating—it is minute, it presents the man as he was, it gathers together little things ordinarily forgotten: portrays the man as he walked, talked, worked, in his simple capacity as a human being. It is just in such touches—such significant details—that the profounder, conclusive, art of biographical narrative lies. Such elements rightly unified seem to make a vivid picture of anybody we know or are interested in."

He spoke of Dickens. "I never met him but saw him. The first time in a theatre—then again in some other public place. I did not hear any of his readings." After this bit of talk he suddenly went off on another strain. "Osler was over today—did you know? They have clapped a plaster—a mustard plaster —on me. Something has helped me today—I don't know what. Osler made light of my condition. I don't like his pooh-poohs: the professional air of the doctor grates on me. It is like the case of a rich man who loses half a dollar and says grandly to the man who finds it: never mind—never mind: keep it: I've lots more than I want. The doctor says: Never mind about that health business—I'm seeing to all that. When a man gets old he has confirmed habits—has ways of his own which the winds blowing however hard or righteously could not displace: they are his to last out his life. They all give me good advice which I can't follow. I am as the boys say 'an old rat' and must be left to die in my own way."

W. spoke of a visit today from "Professor Hamlin Garland of Boston." "He came in—the doctor said for two minutes (only two minutes) but he stayed half an hour at least—seemed to be so interested he would have stayed longer." W. laughed. "Mr. Musgrove was on nettles—the man so overstayed his leave." "What is he professor of?" Smiled and replied: "That would be hard to tell—literature or something kin to it —I don't know. I think Kennedy knows him—I don't know but has written about him to me. I have heard from him— know him in a way, too—but on the personal side we have naturally not seen each other. Garland has lectured on Walt Whitman. I asked him if the people didn't protest against it: he said, no, no, they cried for more! And now it occurs to me I had intended to ask him to send me a good report of his talks, lectures—if one is given anywhere. I have always been curious to see what he says—once started to write him but did not know where to address my letter. I am more than favorably impressed with Garland. He has a good voice—is almost Emersonee—has belly—some would say, guts. The English say of a man, 'he has guts, guts'—and that means something very good, not very bad. Garland has guts—the good kind: has voice, power, manliness—has chest-tones in his talk which attract me: I am very sensitive to certain things like those in a man. Garland seemed to be enthusiastic about Leaves of Grass."

At this juncture W. added: "This has been reception day: we've had lots of 'em here." "Lots of what?" "People, people." "Who—besides Osler and Garland?" "Why—a real live member of parliament—Summers is his name: he said he was Liberal—junior whip under Gladstone and those fellows." "Is he a reader of Leaves of Grass?" "I think he is—yes, he said something about it while he was here. He brought a letter from Mrs. Costelloe—and by the way, I sent that off to Doctor Bucke in my letter today—(he always likes enclosures). Summers hit me hard. He made a grand show-up—had fine ways—was young, strong, optimistic. I have always seriously asked myself whether Gladstone knows anything about Ireland after all—is really bent upon any policy of benefit for Ireland: knows himself what he wants or Ireland needs. I thought to myself today: this is my opportunity—this is your opportunity, Walt Whitman—so I turned to Summers and put it directly to him—the straight question: told him my own suspicions—asked him as one of them, as coming in contact with the men right at their work—Do you, Summers, think better of this—know better?—and so on. His answer was, that Gladstone realized the condition of Ireland, saw something had to be done, was doing what he could, what the moment suggested—or words to that effect." I shook my head over the reply. W. then continued: "It was, indeed, not an answer to my question, but it was about the best, perhaps the only, answer he could have made to it except he pleaded guilty and made a confession, which I didn't expect him to do. Summers was going from here to Washington—then not farther west than Chicago: said he might stop in again on his way back to New York. I was writing to Bucke at the moment Summers arrived. I added this as a sort of postscript: 'How curiously the traveling Englishman is like the best of our educated Americans'—something like that."

He gets a lot of fun out of the Herald's column of last Sunday on W. W. "The Herald piece about us," he calls it. Added: "They set us down there in good style. I wonder who wrote it? It purports to come from Philadelphia—it is not signed—has a strong smell of the pot-boiler—an air of fraternization. It is friendly—as we used to say at Washington, we are there on our own terms. He has caught some points and made the most of them." No word from Bucke today. Gave me a letter from Morse: "It's mighty fine but too little about himself—what he is doing there. That's what I want most—personal chat—the concrete Morse who goes about seeing people, doing things. From what I'm able to catch on the fly I find he is better pleased with Chicago than with the Eastern cities—finds vent there for things cribbed here: will probably stay, get contented, it may be, and settle at last. Morse is another wandering Jew. What he says there about the Lincoln I read over to myself two or three times it was so good." I had for him this evening a set of sheets of the big book, now all printed except the general title. Very greatly interested. Handled them affectionately. "Is it all here?" he asked—and turned one signature after another over on his lap. "We are fortunate—we've done a pretty clean job, considering." He pointed to the bastard page of Specimen Days and Collect. "We had a devil of a time over that curious inscription: we couldn't get suited: at last one day I sat down and with a big, coarse, ragged pen, scrawled this." "Where did you do that?" "Whether at the printer's or McKay's or here I don't remember—in town somewhere, I'm certain." Was much in favor of having his advertisement in the book. "It's as much a part of the book as the reading pages."

Bucke is still, W. says, "harping on the idea that I caught cold that night on the drive to Pea Shore. I don't agree with him but I let every fellow have his say, then have my own opinion anyhow. I always trust my own feelings: they don't delude me." Has decided to have me order a stove to-morrow. I cautioned him again about taking cold. He drew his coat about him, put on a mock shiver, and said: "All right—I'll obey." Liked the size of the big book. "It's about right in bulk: we made a good guess on the paper after all." He had received a tariff circular. Showed it to me. "They warn us: if Cleveland is elected the country will go to hell. To hell it may go then, for all I care. If the country can't stand the truth it should go to hell, the sooner the better. These liars tell their lie so often they think it's the truth. Let them go on believing there's no day of judgment. Woe be! Woe be!" He asked me: "What do you make out of the word 'hogged'? It's not pretty to the ear but it sounds as if it might have sense. The word 'mugwump' don't seem so plausible to me—not so obvious. I think Amelie Rives was the first in my observation to use the word 'hogged': still, it sounds like a street word: she probably borrowed it from the street: the street words are often the best. Mugwump is stupid—means nothing itself: as used, it points its finger at a man who leaves a party—tries to make a shame of the thing—a shame of that which should be, is, a glory. I would like to write something powerful strong about the hugger-muggers who fling the word about in opprobrium." "You might make the old-line editors mad if you did that." "I'd rather make them mad than try to please them: think of trying to please the politics of Charles Emery Smith! I'd have to give up Leaves of Grass first."

W. again referred to Morse's letter. "It came along like a whiff of the prairies: it did more for me than plasters—more than doctors. You will want to take good care of the letter: Morse is so invariably cheerful, so inevitably placid, it wouldn't be bad to have him for a steady diet. He was a refreshing presence to me the months he spent here."

CHICAGO, Sept. 2, '88.

Dear W— I was pleased to get your brief word about yourself, even though you report your imprisonment. I am glad you have been able to bring your books so near completion. No one could have done it but yourself with the same satisfaction to your friends. There seems to be a sort of providence in one's life who has the courage to peg away, and to wait when he can't peg. Somehow the pegging gets done at what finally seems to have been the right and opportune moment; and the result abides.

I went yesterday to hear Prof. Swing preach. If you don't know about him Horace will tell you. He said some bright things. One: "Many a promising lad goes through Cambridge and Oxford and on through time into oblivion quoting his Greek and Latin. And many a poor unfriended boy rises up out of the gutter where he was born and climbs into the heights of knowledge and wisdom. Verily, the spirit cares for its own" (or words to that effect). Chicago has better preachers than Boston. There is greater inspiration in their utterances. They seem to be spiritually more awake—alert. Foregleaming, foreseeing! The great vast bulk of a city weighs on the senses like a nightmare, but if one don't care a button for his five senses, he can escape into a great liberation of mind and spirit. "What is your city with its temples and walls? I can tear it all down and build it again in three days," said Jesus. How the old sense-ridden Jew must have glowered and foamed! "Why, it would take a hundred years to build the walls alone." Chicago has been a-building for fifty years only, and what a wonderful spread it has made! I like it, I enjoy it. The boulevards stretching miles and miles, white and clean—yes, as far as the eye can reach—make me stop and look up and down them for a long time. I don't care much for the great buildings—from the tops of some of them you can almost touch the moon.

The Lincoln statue is good. The face has a vast deal in it. The figure is Lincolnish. I have seen it now three times and I find a little fault with its eternally standing there before that chair. The chair part is, as the critics would say, "a bold conception," but whether 'tis not an infraction of the old Greek admonition as being "too bold?" I believe on the whole I would not have put it there or anywhere. The modelling is strong but a little too much done. The hair, however, is better than represented in the engraving. On the whole, I know of no other public statue as good. But in the streets here I find some half dozen ·statues (Scott, Burns and others) done by some unfamed fellow for one hundred dollars each in gray sandstone, that far surpass it. I find myself always stopped by them with a half-defined expectancy that they are going to say something to me. By the way, this stone would be just the thing for your bust.

Well, I should like to see you, that I might at least lay aside this scratchy pen, and say and hear you say. But——. I have no studio yet but am on the look for one, with some encouragement of work. Rent here is way up. Kind remembrances to your faithful housekeeper. With wishes and wishes, truly,

MORSE.

W. said: "If Morse had got a better start in sculpture he'd have been the high jinks in the business: now he only kind of hangs around the edge. He has the capacity—all capacities but one, I might say: he is not quite steady enough at one thing ever to get the best out of it. He writes well—very well— but don't write best: he speaks well—very well—but don't speak best: and so with sculpture—his trade: he models very well—very well—but just misses modeling *best*. He gets around about too much as my dear mother used to say—don't root anywhere long enough to grow."

Thursday, September 27th, 1888.

7.45 p. m. W. not greatly better. Still complaining of his stomach. Still "plastered up," as he says. Cheerful—almost gay. Laughed freely. Fire in the stove—the first of the fall. Took the chill off the air. He looked a lot more comfortable in consequence. The new stove, ordered today, not yet come. W. signed my sheets of the book. I gave him two dollars from Fred May for a copy of Speciman Days. "Professor Garland, who was here yesterday, said he always started with Specimen Days if he wished to win some one over to Walt Whitman." May is a Jew and has had trouble with orthodox Jews because of his radical ideas. W. said: "If that's the kind of fellow he is he must be one of us," and then added: "He'll understand —he'll see." Spoke again of the Herald piece. He was not "drawn" to it but liked its "friendliness." Laughed over the Bryant "slip." "In the headline it said: 'He thinks Bryant America's greatest poet,' but in the piece itself there is no reference to Bryant. Evidently it was crowded out—set up but not used."

I asked W. how he first came upon Dr. Bucke. "I would have to think awhile before I could say. Quite by a growth, a struggle, on his part, I guess: he tells how slowly he came over." Remarked how most of the strong friends he had found had "approached by degrees, first with questions, afterwards with lessening qualms." Expressed his unsatisfied curiosity over the German renderings of poems from L. of G. "I have always wished to know what a real live German—a German born and bred—would make of me." Said he had Freiligrath's translations there somewhere. If he could find them wished my father "to go over them and report." Had not heard from Knortz in Rolleston matter. "Knortz is a German and a scholar—I should prefer to have his opinion even to Bucke's." Spoke of opponents of L. of G. who "had never read the book." He remarked the frequency of that vice—"people everywhere condemning writers before they have taken the trouble to read them." Instanced the case of one who without reading it dismissed Donnelly's book with a negation. He reflected: "That is quite common: Leaves of Grass has had that experience from the start."

Showed W. a parody in Danbury News. "It is amusing," he said, "not more." Talked of portraits for the complete W. W. No final arrangement yet agreed upon. "I will look the book all over to-morrow." I asked him: "What was the sheet you pinned in the corrected copy of Specimen Days?" "What do you mean? I remember none." I looked for and picked up the book. "This, I mean," opening at one of the index pages, where he had pinned a little sheet of suggestions as to where to put portraits, &c. He laughed: "Caught, sure. But I don't see when I did it: I am always getting up schemes—they come and go: there are many, many of them: fugitive schemes, for good or bad, for foolishness or wisdom." My father is reading Bucke's W. W. W. poked his cane about the floor until he turned up a copy in paper covers. Referred to page 74. "Fix this if it is so in your copy"—pointing to an "it" dropped out at the foot of the page. "I put no bad construction on errors of that kind—care nothing about them: but they make O'Connor mad as a hare—he's in a fury about them: and I can even imagine John Burroughs taking issue on such a nicety. O'Connor is always sensitive on that point." Alluded again to the Englishman Summers, "his answer that was no answer"— "that strange evasion, when I asked my question, that Gladstone realized Ireland's condition, saw that something had to be done —ending nowhere, leading to nothing." He enlarged some upon Summers. "Mrs. Costelloe wrote that he would give me an inside view of English politics. Had I been well I might have availed myself of the chance, listened, enjoyed hearing what he had to tell, though 'inside' views rarely tempt me. Summers seemed like a lively fellow—a good believer, a sparkling lieutenant—evidently having a value in just that place they have given him. But then, no view of any one man could be satisfactory—no view, outside or inside—no one version standing alone. It is as if America was to be revealed, stamped, in any one person, one statement—as if she was not a result of countless contributions, gifts from all quarters of the earth, coming like the weather."

I gave W. some notion of Burroughs' estimate of Arnold as developed in my talks with B. during his visit. B. asked me whether W. had ever read Literature and Dogma? "I had the book once—I don't know but it's here yet: some one sent it to me—I guess Doctor—Doctor Bucke. I attempted to read it— read along some considerable pages, chapters perhaps—then gave it up. I have no interest in such books—none at all. That matter there which he writes about is old, old—not only a thrice told but a three hundred times told tale. If I do at times concede a point and read arguments of that kind it is only for a vacation: I never go back to them: once done it is forever done. But Scott I can take up every year—The Antiquary and The Heart of Mid-Lothian in particular. They are a rest to my mind—are always fresh, new—give me the quiet, the peace, I crave." But he did "not doubt John Burroughs had very important reasons for his espousal of Arnold." B. had said to me: "Arnold was the man for England—for present English life—the flower of its native soil: that W., on the other hand, was for America—America's absolute self—the first product of its soil, the most significant promise of its future." But W. was not impressed with this exposition. "I can never realize Arnold—like him: we are constitutionally antipathetic: Arnold is porcelain, chinaware, hangings."

W. thinks Burroughs "does not nowadays do full justice to his own genius." "I feel, in spite of what he says (and he would resent it, if it was told to him, I know) that John has been bitten by the New York poison. I am sure of it—sure what I have frequently told you is true—will hold good. No doubt John is unconscious of it—absolutely so: yet for all that the mark of it is there. They have their orthodoxies—their measures, lines—those fellows: John has never done anything to countervail them—is therefore admitted to the sanctuary. I am not likely to be deceived on that score—I know the breed too well." Again he said: "Take John's estimate of O'Connor—it falls very short of the truth—short of the short of it: shows a failure to penetrate to the deeper roots of the man: especially misses his size—especially misses his steadfastness: his utter alienation from the conventional usages and shams of our age. This is where John misses it—though it is only fair to say that he hits it quite often in other places—yes, oftener hits than misses. Now, John has too many radical qualities—too many radically noble points, traits—traits established, irrefragible as facts in nature, the universe itself—to be destroyed by his imperfections: I know that there is in these enough to offset all that could be said adverse to him: in such a man the little weaknesses—and in John they are little—can do no harm. For years past he has seemed to be unable to get adjusted to the immensities of William's perspective. Why is it? I have tried to say—yet I suppose my explanation—like explanations in general—does not explain." He asked me: "Do you notice that sickness has such different effects on William and John? John exaggerates his trouble: William, who is much worse off, makes light of it—seems not in the least spiritually affected by it: his courage remains undaunted—indeed, if anything, fierier."

We talked of Ingersoll. W. said: "They are telling me to beware of Ingersoll. Rot! Rot! Why shouldn't Ingersoll beware of me? That's as good said one way as the other. Dr. Bucke has told me of an aunt he has—lives in England: conventional, prejudiced, straight-laced. Doctor was over there once, years ago—was staying with her—and asked one Sunday about the Methodist church in the place—where was it? who preached there? She asked him sharply: 'Are you going there?' He said: 'Yes!' 'Well,' was her reply, 'if you go to that place you need not come back here.' She wanted no dissent. My friends may say that to me when I say hello to the Colonel, but I say, damn my friends if their friendship means that!" Advised me to keep in touch with Bucke: "Write to him—write often—write to-morrow: he is hungry for things from this quarter—

things, small and large, whatever signifying." W. gave me an interesting old letter of Swinton's—all smeared and crushed—which he took from under a tumbler on the table. "Read it," he said: "read it aloud."

KAATERSKILL, N. Y., Aug. 12, 1882.

My dear Walt— Nine years ago I delivered before a German Society of New York city a lecture on American literature, in which a great deal was said about you. Last winter, after the manuscript had lain all these years in a trunk, I spoke it twice again—before the Philosophical Society of Brooklyn and that of Williamsburgh. But now comes the fun for you. Some months ago, I sent the lecture, by invitation, as an essay to the great literary magazine of Russia, the Sagranitschuy Viestuik of St. Petersburgh. There it was put into the Russian language and into the Olympian Magazine. Now I have the magazine, and you have a very heavy puff in the organ which is studied by all the powerful and intellectual classes of Russia—about a quarter or a fifth of the whole article. I guess this is your first introduction to Rooshia, to the Czar and his subjects—and I am sure it would be satisfactory to you. You will never read it in the beautiful Russian—for it is indeed a dreadful language; but it is enough for you to know it partly.

I have been staying here for a week and shall leave in two or three days; but back in the city by the end of the month.

Yours truly,
JOHN SWINTON.

When I was done W. said: "That has a real sound: it seems to take me way off into a strange country and set me down there. But William says I'm as much for all countries as for one and I suppose I am so that I should not feel like an alien even over in that great Tartar empire." W. asked: "What have you done with the O'Connor letter I gave you some days ago?" "I still have it—am still carrying it about in my pocket· it is too fine to put away right off: I've been showing it to people." He said:

393

"I carry it about in my heart—carry it—yes: and William, too. William is fresh every day: never seems to get stale with time."

Friday, September 28th, 1888.

7.45 P. M.   W. sat reading Lewes' Goethe.   Spoke of it with applause.   "I like it—like the preface, particularly: he says there at the start, know you all, I am a friend of this man and yet I will hide nothing to confuse the verdict on his life.   That's good.   Of course the book's written approvingly—in that temper."   He once had an abridged edition.   "I liked it well— so well I was not satisfied until I had got the full book.   Lewes confesses himself a worshiper—I like his candor."   He has "read the book more than once."   Has been reading Miss Pardoe's book again.   "I tell Dr. Bucke I do it as an antidote to Carlyle—to Mr. and Mrs. Carlyle.   Here is another world— a world of glitter, it is true, but also of optimism—everyway opposite to the gloominess, irascibility, of Carlyle and his extreme dissatisfaction with the condition of the world."

Stove came today.   The room was very comfortable.   W. had shifted his quarters from the table east to the table by the windows near the bed.   Harned dropped in.   W. still complains of the pain in his stomach.   "It is in the right side, significantly—I think," he said.   Asked W.: "Before your paralysis of 1873 your digestion was always good?"   "Yes, perfect: too good, too good."   Spoke of the Herald piece again.   The writer said W. revised what he gave there as expressed opinions of W.   W. said to me: "That is not true: and yet, to any one who knows reporters as you do that claim explains itself."   Had he revised Morse's notes on W. W.?   "No—but it might be well if I did.   I am confident Morse would do me no injustice. Sidney is honest.   But there was Hartmann—he, too, did some business of the reporting sort.   He gave some of his notes to Kennedy, who sent them to me.   They were absurdly warped: everything that should have been straight was crooked.   He put Carlylean fire into my mouth—made me saturnine: said things for me I didn't say for myself.   I am doubtful of the manner of these talks, too: I am not literary—not soft-edged—not polished. I doubt if talk is ever quite so clear, direct, as the reporters make it. If there is vitality in talk—not too much study—there must be ease—therefore offences against the rules of speech. Yet Emerson was a clear instance of the careful talker. His characteristic feature was being toned down: his invariable manner, wariness—consummate, perfect, prudence—yet not deceit (no—that word don't even come in sight)—an abiding caution as to what he was saying, as if in warning: be in no haste to commit yourself—to say things not justified by your deeper consciousness. I know I am different: there is no smell of preparation about my conversation: I would disdain that. Emerson was not Socratic. Socrates was perhaps the most wonderful individual who ever lived in the great masterful quality which distinguished four or five—I guess there are not more—of the foremost English judges." What was that? "Ah, this!" working his forefinger with a spiral movement downwards to the floor: "The clear eye which winds safely about and through all snarls and sophisms to the honest roots of the case—no distraction whatever being allowed to confuse the vision or obscure the issue. More than that, these fellows had the advantage at the start of knowing what they were after. Now, Socrates was so: would confuse all Athens by his innocent questions. Socrates would convict a man out of his own mouth." Here followed an inimitable description of the reported methods of Socrates—his "do you think this or that so?" and "if so, why so?" and "if this, then of course something more?" and "if something more" then "not something less"—"till at last," W. exclaimed with a most vehement and amusing gesture, "the poor devil had got himself into a snarl from which escape would be hopeless."

W. said: "I am not surprised at the personal facts the Herald fellow got hold of: I have become public property." Told W. I knew McKay had told people how much he had paid W. in copyrights. "And exaggerated it, I'll be bound!" he exclaimed. The Herald writer said he first visited W. in 1885 and had been to see him repeatedly since. W. says: "No matter how many hints he throws out I am not able to identify the writer." The Home Journal, N. Y., reviewing Olive Schreiner's book, says: "The Story of an African Farm contains more poetry than most poems. Page 259, for instance, where Lyndall describes the various forms of life unknown to her which seem to percolate through her consciousness, is in itself an exquisite poem, which Walt Whitman might be proud to own among the best of his rhymeless rhythms, teeming, as it does, with picturesque contrasts such as Swinburne might not disdain to fashion into enchanting arabesques of melody." W. remarked: "That fellow offers us a little feather which we may stick in our cap. It is like an unexpected friendly hand."

I picked up a copy of the Long Islander and called Harned's attention to it as W. W.'s child. W. said: "Yes: and I consider it the best country paper I ever came across—concerns itself only with country news from all the towns around—and crowds that in thick." He thought it good for a country editor to "have wit enough to not try to compete with the big dailies," adding: "The Camden papers haven't discovered that yet—the Post, Courier." Mrs. Coates has sent him a poem, type-written: The Promised Land. "The letter that came with it was very hospitable, forth-giving: I liked it: indeed, the letter was a better poem than the poem: a real poem, in fact." Harned expressed a wish for loose sheets of the big W. W. W. said: "You shall have them, Thomas"—putting affectionate emphasis on 'Thomas' (H. being usually Tom)—"and I don't know but there will be others like-minded to be taken care of." W. said Gilchrist had been over but not upstairs. "He don't come here, in this room—don't seem to want to exploit himself." A letter from Dick Hinton on the table caused some talk. W. said: "Dick's an anarchist—something like that—wants to upset society—send it to the devil or some other—knock things all helter-skelter: but he's a good fellow—and they were always very kind to me—Dick and his wife, both."

W. going through complete W. W.—the whole book—with a

vigilant eye. "So far as I have gone I haven't come upon a single mistake. We'll get conceited if we are too correct. A few errors are salt for the spirit." Harned said he would specially bind his sheets of the book for his center table. W. looked heartily disgusted. "Don't do it, Tom: it might happen to you, too." "It? What?" "Didn't I tell you? About Chase? He went in to the parlor of a friend—a woman—and found a copy of Leaves of Grass on the table. She was a reader of the Leaves (God bless 'er!). Chase picked up the book and asked: What is this here for? She was up in arms at once: What are *you* here for? she asked: and they had a hot quarrel. Tom, don't play with fire." Harned told W. that at the Hoffman House in New York on Wednesday he was put into the bridal chamber—the only room left. "What luxury!" W. said. "I, too once had a taste of such grandeur. I refer to the reception of 1887. I had it bad then—and was glad enough to get away from it, too!" He threw his arms out wide. "A whole suite of rooms: crowds of people: rush: and such an utter weariness at the last! It was near midnight—I was clean gone: then John Fiske happened in and wanted to discuss the subject of the immortality of the soul. I saw that if I stayed a minute longer it would be all up with me. I called Billy and said: 'I'm nearly tired to death: take me somewhere—anywhere: take me to my room.' I diverted Fiske to Pearsall Smith, saying: 'Here's a fellow who knows all about such things'—and went off, leaving them there to their talk: and for all I know they're still on the spot whacking away at each other." W. then added on the general question: "I'm satisfied with Epictetus—'what is good for thee O Nature is good for me': indeed, I am sure that whatever death is it is all right. We should all accept the Benton-Calhoun solution—that there is no solution: no man ever knows here, no man ever came back to tell us." Burroughs asked when he was here: "Is Walt still of the same firm faith in personal immortality?" W. said: "Am I? I have no doubt: I guess I am." Harned said something disparaging of spiritualism. W. put in: "Don't do it, Tom: we can't wipe the spiritualists out."

Signed May's copy of S. Days. At one moment he said: "I shall be glad when this cursed book is out. Carlyle always cried and fussed like the devil when he started a new book and went on so about it like a half maudlin old woman until it was finished: I threaten to follow suit." Harned protested: "But Walt, this book has helped to keep you up—given you something to live for." W. then said fervently: "Yes, indeed, Tom—you are right: it has: I have realized it time and again." Harned told W. he was reading George's book on the tariff. But W. shook his head. "Not figures, Tom: figures are a great lie—a great trial: and besides, I don't try anything by figures, statistics: free trade proves itself to me by other arguments. I should say the best free trade argument is the tariff literature itself." I quoted Robert Porter's logic—if American steel rails cost thirty two fifty per ton and English twenty two fifty why not buy the American output and keep both money and rails on this side the Atlantic and be so much the richer for our wisdom? W. was uproarious: "Ha! ha! ha!—and yet, Horace, that would be a very taking point at a meeting—the boys would think it awful sweet: they would applaud the roof off the house. It is a good thing there are fellows like me—an extreme among extremes—on the one side, and Dudley across there on the other: Dudley, with his undoubted statistics, perfect in themselves."

W. is very patient when things go bad or wrong. Being sick he says: "Well, it's a comfort to think I'm not as ill as I might be." If there is something wrong in the book: "Well, thank the Lord it's na worse." Some one overcharged him: "No matter: stomach it and be grateful to your stars he hasn't made it bigger." He never admits that any real luck is against him. "Nothing is so bad it might not be worse." Gave me an envelope containing note and verses from Dalton: called the verses "queer"—asking me: "What, if anything, can you make out of them?" The O'Connor letter I have carried about with me was written December, 1864. W. was then looking for an official job in Washington. He got numerous letters of introduction at the time. He gave me another of them to-night. It was written in W.'s own hand and signed by another. When I spoke to W. of this he laughed and said: "Yes, I had to tell Hall what to say about me: he was satisfied: when he looked at it after it was written he said: 'You might have said more—made it stronger—and I would still have signed it.'" This is the note:

The bearer, Walt Whitman, of Brooklyn, desires an appointment. No man in the United States is more competent or more deserving than Mr. Whitman. He was born and raised in my town, and is well known as a literary man, and to me and to the citizens of Brooklyn, for fifteen years past, for his benevolence, righteousness and ardent patriotism—is a steadfast Republican, voted for Mr. Lincoln, has two brothers in the army, and the family is poor.

Geo. Hall.
Late Mayor of Brooklyn.

I said: "I'm afraid you're no longer 'an ardent Republican.'" He laughed: "I'm afraid so, too: if politics keep on going from bad to worse, from worse to worse again and more of it, I'm in danger of becoming an ardent anti-Republican." "That is, an ardent Democrat?" "No—the alternative is enough to make me shudder: I'll have to go unsworn until something worthy of my ardor turns up: Japhet in search of a father."

Saturday, September 29th, 1888.

7.15 P. M. Received from Ferguson today bastard titles S. Days and Nov. Boughs. Oldach promises some bound copies latter on Tuesday. All sheets of complete W. have been shipped to Oldach. Got bill for stove from Spear today: nine twenty five. W. reading Gilchrist's Blake. "I find it always has new charm: it is so simple, so direct, so true: so rich in what are considered the minor but what I consider the significant features of experience." Laid book down. The fire burned cheerily, the room was comfortable (out of doors it was very chilly, a damp wind blowing). His hand was warm, his color a good flush. "Howdy—howdy?" He said he had been going on with the sheets today. "So far again, no error!" "There are one or two sheets of the book not as well printed as I should like, but all in all it is fine." He had been "cogitating" what portraits to use and where to put them. Had struck upon one for the frontispiece—profile. "What do you think of that? Like it? I thought so!" If finally chosen it will have to be reproduced —"yes," he said, "and by the photo-engraver—like the others." "There should be something," he added, "to differentiate the book—something its own: perhaps this would secure it." We discussed the general title. "I have something new, entirely new: let me show you." Has been asking himself also whether he should insert an advertising page. "If we do it must be peculiarly ours—like that in November Boughs—a part of our history. But we must take each step with exceeding care. This will be my last utterance, my final message: in it, then, I must aim for the utmost excellence compatible with my financial means and physical condition." Was vigorous and clear in all his talk. Gave me a letter from Bucke and called my attention to the last paragraph:

"I am reading Past and Present. Funny, isn't it, to see a man of the nineteenth century who thinks better of the monastico-feudal life of the twelfth century than of the industrial life of today? And by his own showing they must have been a bad lot, those monks and knights. And see Froude's Henry VIII— especially as to the monks!"

W. said: "Bucke hits square between the eyes. Carlyle often lays himself open to destruction. I seem to have all sorts of feelings about Carlyle, from freezes to thaws and back again." W. sat me down and asked me to read him the O'Connor letter again—the old letter. I still had it in my pocket.

WASHINGTON, D. C.,
December 30, 1864.

Dear Walt: I have been constantly hoping to have you here again and now begin to see something more than a glimmer of fruition. Ashton has spoken (at my instigation) to Mr. Otto the Assistant Secretary of the Department of the Interior in your behalf, and Mr. Otto says that if you will write a letter of application to the Secretary of the Interior, he will endeavor to put you in.

Now, dear Walt, do this without delay. The object of your writing the letter is to get a specimen of your hand. Pick out, then, a good pen and write as fairly as you can a letter formally applying for a clerkship. Then enclose a copy of this letter to Ashton, so that he can follow it on to the Secretary. The first letter you will, of course, mail to the Secretary direct. Do this as soon as you can. We shall fetch it this time. I have every confidence that you will get a good and an easy berth, a regular income, &c., leaving you time to attend to the soldiers, to your poems, &c—in a word, what Archimedes wanted, a place on which to rest the lever.

I shall wait anxiously to hear that you have sent on the letters. Have been thinking of you constantly for months and have been doing everything I could to secure you a foothold here. For a long time deceived (I must think) by Swinton's pretensions to influence and by his profuse promises, I hoped to get you either one of the New York State Agency Assistantships or the place of an Assistant Librarian in the Congressional Library (the latter would be really a sinecure if the right one was got). But who follows Swinton follows a will-o-the-wisp, and though I followed him remorselessly every blessed day for several weeks, and gave him neither rest nor peace, as the saying is, I got nothing except promises. Since I gave him up I have been badgering Ashton, who is a man of another sort, as what he has done shows. The difficulty was to get the right thing. He secured me some little time ago a place in the Post Office for you, but I declined it, because I thought it was not the proper place for you. I think a desk in the Interior would be first-rate.

I told Ashton there was nothing I would not do for him if he would carry this affair to a safe conclusion. He has been very good and anxious in your behalf. He would have given you a desk in his own office if a vacancy had occurred as expected.

Don't forget to do as I tell you immediately.

I never answered your letter of September 11th, but, dear Walt, I always think of you, though I write so seldom and so badly. You are never forgotten. I read your poems often, I get their meaning more and more, I stand up for them and you, I expound, define, defend, vindicate, justify them and you with all the heart and head I have whenever occasion demands.

I got the Times with your long letter about the Hospital experiences, which I read with a swelling heart and wet eyes. It was very great and touching to me. I think I could mount the tribune for you on that and speak speech which jets fire and drops tears. Only it filled me with infinite regrets that there is not a book from you, embodying these rich and sad experiences. It would be sure of immortality. No history of our times would ever be written without it, if written with that wealth of living details you could crowd into it. Indeed, it would itself be history.

I saw your letter about the prisoners. It was as just as powerful. I have been hearing for a fortnight past that it is the Secretary of War's "policy" which prevents exchange, and if this is true, I pray from my heart of hearts that it never may be forgotten against him. Reddest murder is white to an act like this and its folly is equal to its crime. It would be demonism of another kind indeed than the Southerner's, yet as bad, perhaps worse, because sprung from calculation rather than hatred.

Such things make one sicken of the world.

I write this letter at intervals between the press of office work, which has driven upon me in spasms today, but pretty severely when it did come. Any incoherencies in it, you may refer to the obfusticated state which such hurryings have induced in me.

Farewell, dear Walt. I hope to hear from you very soon. We are all tolerably well at home. Eldridge comes every evening. We often talk of you. On Christmas you were wanted to make the dinner at home perfect. We all spoke of you. On

Thanksgiving it was the same. At dinner that day I said
"I wish"—and stopped. "What?" said Nelly. "I know,"
chirped little Jeannie, "he wishes Walt was here." Which was
true—that *was* the unuttered wish.

Let me hear soon.

Your loving
W. D. O'CONNOR.

I looked up as I finished. W.'s face was very grave and there
were tears in his eyes. I wondered if he would talk more about
the letter but he did not seem inclined to and I did not press it.
The letter was addressed to W. at Brooklyn. O'Connor used
Ashton's frank. Williamson writes a letter proposing to buy
manuscripts. W. says: "There's nobody I'd rather sell manuscripts to but I'd rather sell them to nobody." Williamson
sent money for a book which he never got. W. says: "It is my
habit, nearly always, when I send away a book, to write a postal
saying I have done so and asking for an acknowledgment. In
most cases I get replies—in this case I did not. Williamson
has been a good friend—he has shown his love in the most practical ways: just a while ago he sent me five dollars. Tell him
for me that he's a buster: tell him he shall have a set of the sheets
untrimmed and welcome—twice welcome, three times welcome.
Horace, I've had God's own luck with my friends no matter
what my enemies say about me."

Morse wrote me a long letter, date 27th, describing his present ways and means in the West. W. intensely interested.
The instant I told him I had such a letter he put aside everything,
looked at me, settled himself in his chair: "Read it—read it all,
if you can—all you feel like reading: come over to the light."
—and as I shifted my chair to his side: "Yes, so: now let us hear
what Sidney has to say." As I read W. made his comments.
It took half an hour for me to get through. W. extra bright.
At one moment he said: "That's not worthy of Sidney"—at
another: "How interesting! how pathetic!"—and again: "Good!
good! that has the true ring." Morse spoke of his poverty.

403

W. said: "A few dollars between him and the world! Why didn't he say so? Why did he go away? There was enough here to do all he needed done: I would have done it, a part of it: gladly, proudly. Morse should be sustained in good work he is busy with. It is the duty of his friends to see him through. Tom did a lot in that direction when Sidney was here. He has in my presence urged Sidney to take up quarters in his house. But Sidney is proud: artists, poets, men of the finer temperament whatever they do, are all proud—proud after a true fashion, not ignobly proud. But then I admit that an artist should be in his own quarters—where he does not interfere and is not interfered with. My plan was to put up a shanty for Sidney where he could have it all his own way—work, study, write, peg away at whatever and however he pleased. Indeed, I have not abandoned the idea even yet: if he comes East I will set him up." Morse at one point spoke of the "she-devil" loose in the churches —in Blake's, for instance. W. laughed: "I have heard of that creature—what is she?" M. wrote: "Of all W's friends, I know of only Bucke, you and Harned that really believe in the bust." W. exclaimed—"Oh! Sidney! Sidney—my poor fellow!—there you are wrong—wrong! They all like it: all the bright particular fellows: all the folks who squarely realize me. What of Kennedy, who thinks it a 'revelation'? And there's Baxter: and across the ocean, Mrs. Costelloe, who writes of it as a great work—thinks it elemental, I should say from her words." When I came to the concluding passage of the note—"Give my love to Walt: For all his friendship I have sacred room, and for yours" —W. said: "Horace—read it again"—and I did so—and he still said: "I want to hear it once more"—and so I read it a third time. Then there was a little note in the corner: "I'd like to make a bust of W. here all by myself that no eye should see till it was in plaster, and then send it to W. with permission that if he thought it not equal to or better than the others, to have it smashed into smithereens." As before, W. asked me to read this over again. "Ah! Sidney! you should not mistrust me! Yet," turning to me, "I doubt if he will ever do better than with the heads he did while here." I said: "That's what I wrote today." W. said: "Bucke says he fluctuates between the two heads—now he likes one, now he likes the other." I said: "I don't—I prefer number two, first and always." "So do I, Horace—I vote all my proxies for number two, first and always, as you say. What do you think is the main difference between the two busts?" "The second is the better portrait." "That's my say, too—the better portrait: I never waver from that conclusion." I suggested: "I consider it phenomenal. You can't tell how a great poet writes a great poem—neither can you tell how Morse struck upon that head." W. exclaimed: "That's splendid: true: deep."

W. asked me: "Do you know Bartlett up there in Boston? Well—it was through Bartlett I came to know Millet—got to him: through him I went out to Shaw's. Bartlett is a man of strong likes and dislikes: very prominent among the dislikes was an awful dislike for poor Sidney. Yet Bartlett never really knew Sidney. Sidney's work in Boston there years ago was very open to criticism, and it's that Bartlett judged him from. Now, however, Morse's whole life, manner, has broadened out. He has demonstrated distinctive powers—a rugged power—crude, too, to be sure—rarely to be found among the artists—and a magnificent abandon—utter abandon!" W. exclaimed, throwing his coat open and opening his arms wide: "and the certain, secure swing that he has caught at last"—gesturing: illustrating: "It all tells of the growth in concentration and finesse of a genius that should be cherished."

So W. talked the main part of the hour of my stay: evidently deeply moved by Morse's straits—evidently desiring to go on record as his sponsor. Before I left W. asked me about St. Gaudens, of whom Morse had spoken as getting the contract for the fifty thousand dollar Logan statue. Was St. G. American &c? Also expressed great pleasure in M.'s opinion that St. G.'s Lincoln was a commendable piece of work. Donahue, who is to make the Shakespeare, is new to us both. I left with W. a Nineteenth Century sketch of Millet. Said he had read much about Millet "in scraps"—little "connectedly." W. said: "I've got a little present for you." What was that? "Just this." Handed me a yellow envelope containing some little Washington portraits of Grant, Sherman, Sheridan, and Stanton. "They are old, worn, faded, but interesting. They are still in their own original envelope." He also handed me a stereoscopic card arranged with two portraits of himself—J. Gurney and Son, New York. "That picture seems to have been liked—I don't know but I like it myself. William thought it 'a trifle weak', but I don't think it so. I can't always be a roaring lion!"

Sunday, September 30th, 1888.

Morning, 11.15. W. just done breakfast. Had slept later than usual—to 11 from 9.30 last night, nurse said. W. said: "It was only half-sleep, however, all night." Sat in the chair. Hair rather in disorder. Pale. Eyes languid and weary. Talked clearly but as if with strain. Said instantly to me: "Sit down: sit down on the sofa over there"—then asked: "It is a good deal colder this morning?"—feeding a few bits of wood to the fire at the same moment. Ate some toast. Musgrove came in and handed W. the Press. He said: "I have eaten little: there was little to stimulate me to eat." I said: "I'm afraid the Press won't do much towards stimulating you: it's full of tariff this morning." W. returned: "I supposed so: I saw Blaine was to speak"—adding: "The Press is of all the papers I know the meanest, most malignant, most lying—a searcher after hidden blackness, a suspicioner of motives, a pecker at the foibles of humanity: a sort of journalistic imp of Beelzebub." I laughed. "My—your sleep must have been a soothing one!" He laughed with me. "Well, Horace—that was maybe going it pretty strong even on the very nasty Press, but it does make me mad as a hornet every time I look at it." Then I asked: "Hasn't it stimulated you after all? It has brought the red back into your face!" He nodded: "That's certainly a cheerful way to look at it, Horace: I may after all have something to thank even the Press for."

From a Portrait by J. Gurney & Son

WALT WHITMAN
(About 1865)

He handed me the Millet piece I left last evening. "I have read it all through—read it last night. It was the first chance I had to get a connected consecutive recital of the facts of Millet's personal history. I know his pictures—a dozen of them, the originals: maybe more, maybe less: but owed all the rest of my knowledge of Millet to fugitive items in the newspapers and magazines—here and there—over ten or a score of years. Millet seems to have lived a sad sort of life—sad, but never meanly sad: on the contrary, a heroic, beautiful, life. The thing that first and always interested me in Millet's pictures was the untold something behind all that was depicted—an essence, a suggestion, an indirection, leading off into the immortal mysteries." I said: "I have often explained my adhesion to you in almost the same words." "Is it so? Well for me if you are right and if it is so. I take it as the glory, not the shame, of the best work—its essential crown, confirmation." "Do you not feel as if you had somehow dipped in the same spiritual stream?" "Yes I do: I have no doubt of the resemblance." I added: "As I read that sketch it seemed as though a thread of your own life ran clean through it from end to end." "That," said W., "would no doubt be more easily obvious to you than to me—to anyone looking at it from the other side of my ribs." Quoted something from Schiller about the backgrounds of art—I did not catch it. Then added as to Millet: "He had an abiding remembrance of his origin—parents: father, mother, grandmother."

He said of Morse's Hicks: "I consider it a powerful piece of work: no one is better qualified than I am to say so." Monologued at some length about Bucke. He thought B.'s Whitman "rather too eulogistic," adding: "Even I shrink from that. So when I hear that somebody takes exception to it I rather sympathize with the exception. Yet it is not to be forgotten that there were circumstances attending the production of the book which explained its extreme laudation. It was written to stem the tide—to stop the inflow: a sort of damn-you-take-that retort and impetus: effective, too, unquestionably, for its purpose and time." He explained Bucke's growth towards him as being

"made by perfectly easy and almost measured graduation."
"He was much given to Oriental studies—mysticality: dived into
them deep, oh so deep!—and coming along fresh from that,
falling upon me, upon Walt Whitman—the things he had been
dreaming about embodied right here in his modern world and in
an American—it was a revelation of convincing significance.
Then there is a curious likeness between us—between all of us,
for the matter of that—all our crowd, who, most all of us, came
to our religion, our peculiar faith in America, by a common way.
Doctor's is before all a religious nature, yet is enough concrete,
too, to be safe against monasticism. I have been reading Miss
Pardoe's book. The Louis XIV men and women, when they
got tired of things, when life palled on them, went, the women
into the nunneries the men into monasteries. Bucke, any man
like him, I, you, would find another avenue of escape. Concrete?
That he is, too: serious, deep, fervent, steadfast: he enjoys
dinners, travels, sights—but that is not all (indeed is only the
surface of all): after that there's an undertone—more than an
undertone—oh! so sacred—the explicating note." He thinks
Bucke "has a healthy way of looking at the universe." "He is
impatient of disbelief—the disbelief in ends: in that, too, we
find that he comes close to us—again explains why he has joined
our clan. He looks at life not from the standpoint of an hour, a
day, a month, even a year, but as the creative power itself—
over ages, cycles of ages—perceives then that everything is self-
explained, self-justified."

W. went on in this way for some time. There came up the
question of Bucke's affection for Ingersoll: "I am aware of it,"
said W.: "I know he looks on Ingersoll as religious—religious
in some larger sense than common, It may be that he puts more
stress upon Ingersoll than I would—perhaps he does: though I,
too, like Ingersoll, value him, see he is a right word put in.
But allowing for all that can rightly be said commendatory of
Ingersoll I still persist in saying that there's more to be said than
Ingersoll says—more, far more." I asked: "But wouldn't you
say that of any man: can any one person state the whole case for

the universe?" W. returned: "You are right—you call me to
order: it's well not to forget a point so good—an item so conclusive in my philosophy." He spoke of the picture struck upon
yesterday for frontispiece and alluded to last night. "It was
made seven or eight years ago—made by Spieler. I think I am
the only one who likes it—all of them object. Even Sidney was
not warm over it at all. But my own eye selected this from a
number taken—I grew to like it and in the end to order copies
struck off for my own use. Here they have lain ever since."
This talk over the picture led to Spieler himself. W. never forgets the artist in his art. "Spieler has the fine German make-up:
I like it much: large body—not heavy—black hair, good eyes,
frank. And Spieler's son was very kind to me—considerate—
I liked the boy, too." Spieler made the photo used in the Centennial Edition. "Very few liked it, but it has virtues."
Thought S. a good workman—"I favored the man, approved
his methods." Spoke of flesh-tones, in photos and paintings. "I can forgive the bad tones of a photo—in a painting
they are inexcusable. If Eakins' picture, as somebody has said,
has such defects of tone then it is my business to reconsider my
notion in its favor." I received this letter from O'Connor
yesterday:

WASHINGTON, D. C.,
Sept. 28, '88.

Dear friend: I got yours of the 26th, yesterday, but was so
ill I had to go home, and could not answer. Today I am a
little better, but can only dimly see with one eye, the other being
closed with nervous exhaustion, so must be brief.

Before I can fully reply anyhow, I want you to tell me (of
course in confidence) whether John Burroughs said anything in
objection to my speaking at Walt's funeral. I do not ask you
in any unkindness to John, not out of curiosity, but only because
the answer will enable me to understand the matter more clearly
than I can now tell you.

Also tell me as fully as you can what he said about Stedman and

Gilder in connection, as you say, with people, "coming over or about to come over," to Walt's cause. This, also, may have a significance only discernible to me at present.

Excuse brevity. I feel today in my generally purblind and bunged-up condition very much like a combination of Cyclops and the man who fought in the Kickapoo campaign.

Yours faithfully,
W. D. O'CONNOR.

8 P. M. W. not improved—looked ill—said headache continued. I had taken a run out to Boozer, at Primos: a walk with the children in the woods. W. asked me about it—was pleased: "Nothing could be finer than vigorous walks—even on a cold day in winter." Has finally decided instead of frontispiece to use head for the title-page itself, putting lettering above and below. Questioned me also: would it be advisable to include heads of his father and mother in big book? He thought it was about time, anyhow, for him "to gather his equipment together." He had "cuts here and there and everywhere"— and when he wanted them they were never available. "Now we are waiting for Linton, who is away off in England somewhere, our letter having to be forwarded." "I consider with regard to all these portraits that the end to be gained is to have my own view gratified, not that of the purist or artist." He "had no idea where the 1854 and butterfly plates were deposited." Asked that I look them up through McKay. I saw the parade (Republican) in Philadelphia last night. He was very inquisitive. What was my impression of it? "You like to see all that's going on? So did I, once: so do I still: if I could get about now I would probably join you in many such excursions." Was reading the Bible to-night. W. talked but slightly except as concerning the book. When W. strikes the well days, he sometimes says: "There's plenty of time—let us go along leisurely." But when he strikes the sick days he says: "Hasten things: push them through—we have no time to lose." Took with me when I left Spieler portrait for reproduction.

Monday, October 1st, 1888.

7.45 p. m. W. relieved today. Headache gone. Digestion improved. The difference was at once apparent in his talk. He cheerfully told me to bring up a chair and sit down. Then asked what I had done today. Brown asked for a darker original for reproduction. We afterwards searched for it. Was in to see McKay who had a letter from Dillingham asking for a copy of November Boughs and terms. McKay asked: "When will the book be ready?" I answered: "Next week." W. assented. Harned came in. W. said: "As I have been feeling the past week I would have sold myself and the whole edition pretty cheap. And yet—what a precious thing is a good day!—a free day!—no money can measure its value." He commended McKay for his Americanism. "Except in cases like Pepys and Shakespeare he confines himself to American books." I asked him if he had read Pepys. "Yes: Dave sent me a set: it is pretty small ware and yet curiously fascinating." The Century turned up today. "I am relieved: the piece appeared: I am glad I felt nervous about it all along: I was in honor bound to keep back November Boughs until the magazine was out." Asked me: "Have you seen Roosevelt's paper—ranche paper? It is interesting: I like it: he gets pretty near the truth. He don't write it exactly as I would, of course: that's because he don't enter into it—puts on his glasses before he looks at it— writes it with a little the touch of a dude. Still, there is something-alluring in the subject and the way it is handled: Roosevelt seems to have realized its character—its shape and size—to have honestly imbibed some of the spirit of that wild Western life."

Said he had had visitors. I looked inquisitive. "My niece and sister were here today: nothing would do but I should let them have a copy of the book. And do you know, Horace—no one likes the frontispiece—nobody but one or two of the women. All the boys turn up their noses—smell something wrong—think it won't do." Harned put in: "I must confess myself I don't think it high art." W. at once rejoined: "We don't put it there for high art. Does any one call the book itself, call me, high art? It serves our purpose—is appropriate: in keeping with what it goes along with." Said he wished one hundred copies of N. B. for his own personal use. To sell? "No—not to sell—to give: I have lots of nieces and sisters and others. Then there are friends who send me extra amounts—ten dollars instead of five, five instead of two: I like to throw a book or two in occasionally: it is right, necessary, to do so."

He took up the bundle of Spieler portraits to look for a dark one. There were several odd portraits in the same package. Handed a Sarony picture to me. "How does that strike you? Take it along. It is one of the strongest of my good-humored pictures. Some of my pictures are strong but too severe— don't you think so? This is strong enough to be right and gentle enough to be right, too: I like to be both: I wouldn't like people to say 'he is a giant' and then forget I know how to love. It would be no consolation to me to be a giant with the love left out." Then took up another picture. "And that? That's what I call the Quaker picture: see? the sombrero— the nice adjustment of light and shade." Shoved it back into the package. "Here is the street—the 1855—figure: the one we are to use again." Then he passed one after the other of the Spieler pictures along until we had struck upon a copy that seemed sufficiently well preserved for our purpose. I had proposed that instead of using type we might have my father free-hand the necessary lettering about the portrait. W. favorably disposed. I was looking fixedly at the portrait in my hand. He noticed it. "What's the matter?" "I was thinking that if we put above this portrait 'Walt Whitman complete' they'll laugh at us." W. himself laughed: "Do you know I have felt that same thing myself?" I then said: "But you don't mind clamor: you won't care?" "Yes, I will care, too: I don't believe in lending myself to the scamps—in making their occupation easy for them." He did in fact consider the matter quite serious. Said he "would put the title by for another day to study the chances out." I said: "I guess I should keep one of these pictures?" He nodded assent. "Yes, keep the one on the card" (he had mounted it yesterday): I had another in my hand. "Shall I give this to Tom?" He looked doubtful. "On the whole, I'd rather not: if I do I won't have enough for my own purpose." This was an intimation of some new publishing project. "Have you still other plans in view?" "Yes—I had been thinking of something: you know, I am always scheming, surveying—putting in my stakes for new claims: I suppose I'll go on being like that until they nail down my coffin lid."

Speaking of McKay, W. predicted a bright future for him as a publisher. "I should not like to say he will be a millionaire, but he'll be a hundred-thousander, without a doubt." Dave had certain "canny" ways which were "bound to put him on top." McKay had given me today for Walt a set of his Emerson just out—two vols—first and second series: half calf. W. much gratified. Handled the box fondly—took books out several times while we stayed—and as I was leaving he asked me to hand them to him again. Started to read. "I shall like them—read them: they are precious to me." Spoke approvingly of good big type and open page. Then of an edition shown him once at Washington by Burroughs. "John said, 'keep them—use them: I have more books than I know what to do with.' And I did. But bye and bye I got sick—the doctor warned me: 'You'd better pack up and get out, or, it'll be a coffin.' So I put my stuff together and came to Camden. That was in the first period of my paralysis. I left my goods behind me until two or three years ago, when I came into this house. After all those years—fifteen or sixteen years—you can imagine how much reminiscence was awakened in me (some ugly, some beautiful) when I turned the mess all over again. Among the very first things to show up were these books—these Emerson books, John's. Five volumes, I think: smaller type, larger page, than in this book: you may be sure I packed them back to John at once." He desired me to tell McKay that he had decided to have Dave take charge of all his books. "I will give you some definite ideas to-morrow—then you can go over and fight it out with him." McKay had asked, how many copies N. B. were to be sent to papers? Garland, calling last week, had said to McKay: "Tell W., tell him I said it, that a hundred copies at least should be sent to the papers." But Walt is disposed to let D. attend to that for himself, making him the offer of one thousand copies at forty-three cents.

Tom remarked that Senator Frye was in town, talking tariff. W. said: "They need him: I begin to tremble for them—the prospects are dimming—don't you think so, Tom? They're holding up their hands—and isn't it fear, fear, with them? The noise, fury, clatter, at the start confused, puzzled, us a little: now the air appears to be clearing." Yesterday's Press contained a paragraph on Gilchrist called out by his probable appointment to a professorship at the Academy of the Fine Arts. W. said: "That's Talcott's piece—he wrote it: Talcott Williams. I do not think Herbert came to America expecting this thing. Herbert has been over several times. He is always bright, handsome, but don't talk with me much more than at first about his purposes." McKay tells me Gutekunst has the plate for the butterfly picture and Adams the steel plate (1855). Tom had been speaking of a fifteen dollar binding put on a Byron. W. asked: "All on one book?" "Yes." "That's extravagant!" Asked what tooling was—had read of it in connection with rare bindings. Said he would bind his "complete" W. in half calf—save for cost. "It would break me up." "Dave has a way of trimming everything down—prices—costs." Here was the Emerson. "Printing, paper, both inferior to ours: yet looks well, though not rich." Tom happened to say something about his law library. W. asked: "I never saw that, did I, Tom?" He had not—it was remote in the house. Said quietly: "And never shall, I guess: never am to get out again." W. gave me another of his war-time recommends—this one from Preston King. He laughed over it. "I was pulling eminent wires those days," he said. This is King's little note:

WASHINGTON, Feb. 13, 1863.

The Bearer Mr. Whitman of Brooklyn N. Y. is recommended to me by Hon Charles Sumner who knows him personally; he also has letters from well known Gentlemen which he has shown to me. He desires employment of a clerical character or in some way in which he can be serviceable to the Government. He has testimonials of character which he will show. I commend him to the favorable consideration of any of the heads of Departments who may want his services.

Very Respectfully

PRESTON KING.

The King letter was addressed to General M. C. Meigs, Quartermaster General. I said to W.: "You had to rassle for that job." "So I did—quite considerable: even Emerson intervened." "Emerson?" "Yes, even Emerson—in a letter to Seward: and come to think of it I have the letter about here somewhere today—I don't know where." "The original?" "Yes—it was never delivered: and I tell you, Horace, when it turns up, it'll be a pretty gem for your crown!" "Do you mean that it is to come to me?" "Who else could it come to? Aint everything coming to you?" He laughed. I put in: "Everything but that big story you were going to tell me: that's not coming very fast." He was grave at once. Took my hand in his: looked me straight in the eye: "That couldn't come fast, Horace—that's too serious, yes—sacred: that must come in its own way, in its own time: but it will come." W's good night more than usually tender. He kissed me. Said again: "That must come in its own way, in its own time."

I had a talk with Osler today—the first since his return. He said: "I can see no reason why Mr. Whitman should not live for months, even years." Yet seemed confident of mental changes as time wore on. On the other hand while there might be no reason for instant fear everything was uncertain. "*Carpe diem* should be his motto—make hay while the sun shines." Said he would be over to-morrow. Considered the past week's experience in no way alarming. Yet advised me, if W. had work that should be done, it would be well to have it done as quickly as possible.

Tuesday, October 2nd, 1888.

8 p. m. W. has had a tough day of it again. Looked down-spirited—referred to his "dulness." "A bad day again," he said: "but sit you down and let us hear what you have to say." He said he did not know how to account for these varied ups and downs. "It's not 'this cursed book' with me, as with Carlyle, but, I guess, the being cribbed, confined, and for so long." He said further, on my questioning: "Indeed, the books, rather than hindering, help me—are important aids." But he had "felt it dawning" upon him "even more positively" that he was "not good for much any more." I tried to rally him with the encouraging side of Osler's talk yesterday—that O. was surprised to find him so well—that he had more resilience than O. "had suspected"—that W. was "undoubtedly more vital and tenacious than even his friends had supposed." W. said: "That certainly is encouraging: if it shall all eventuate in that— all the experience of these four months—we shall be repaid— well pleased." I added: "And you know, he had no motive to hide anything from me, over there in his office, alone"—W. saying further: "That's true—that is to be considered." Still, his face was not bright, his voice not strong. His pulse "was way down" as he said himself.

Had been reading Emerson today, "but not greatly," "had little mind for it." Nurse says W.'s bowels are open but much of the food passes through undigested. Mrs Davis reports less emphasis in his calls for food, though sometimes of some things he partakes heartily. My sister sent him in a jar of the clams recommended by Burroughs when here. He has sipped a little bit of wine—mostly the sour wine sent by Ingram (who, by the way, was over today and had a talk with W.). I told W. Osler advised: "Never let his bowels be closed more than two days." W. laughed heartily: "I will 'let': it's not a question of 'letting': if that was all there was about it, the matter could easily be settled." Illustrated his thought with an anecdote of a friend in Washington—an incident "more apt," he said, "than agreeable or polite." He gave me two letters from Bucke— 28th and 30th. Then rooted among his papers until he found a slip from Kennedy containing this from Edmund Gosse in the October Forum:

"Never simple, never easy, never in one single lyric natural and spontaneous for more than one stanza, always forcing the note, always concealing his bareness and lameness by grotesque violence of image and preposterous storm of sand, Lanier appears to me to be as little a poet of genius as any ambitious man who ever lived, labored and failed."

I read that aloud to W., who then said: "I got a paper from Kennedy: he sent this with it—this dropped out. I don't see that it needs to be taken very seriously: Gosse don't seem to take himself seriously: why should he take any one else so? My feeling about Lanier is not that he is empty but that he is full—but rather full of sound than of sense: and as to his artificiality— how can any fellow, Gosse included or excluded, save himself from artificiality if he writes according to the canons?—the canons themselves being artificiality piled on artificiality ages come and gone?" I said to W.: "I wrote Kennedy today: told him our big book would not be out for a month yet." W. looked at me then at himself, so to speak, seeming to count the days. "A month? Yes: I suppose that's as good a guess as anyone could make at this stage of the game." W. had me read a bit out of Bucke's letter of the 28th:

"I note all you say about my W. W. Your wishes will be religiously respected. I did think of considerable changes (for I am certain the book will sell by and bye) but was never set on them and less so lately. Yes, I shall leave it stand as it is and add under a later date what else I may have to say."

I asked W.: "What were you advising him to do?" "Oh! to let his present Walt Whitman alone—not to attempt to recast it. I do not object to supplementary pages but I like this book for just what it is, incomplete though it may be." Talked of portraits. "The butterfly picture could not have cost much or Dave would not have used it." Had changed title page. "I wrestled with the puzzle we turned up yesterday. Think of choosing a title page with the legend 'Walt Whitman complete' or 'complete Walt Whitman' sprawled across its face! All the funny men in the land would be down on us in a minute! Yet we almost did it." He had made his design on a thick piece of paste-board. Head in the centre. Above the head: "Complete Poems and Prose of Walt Whitman." Under the head: "Author's Edition with autograph, portraits from life, last revisions, &c. 1855—1888." I was to take this to my father who was to make a design for it. W. much disappointed because Oldach had no books for us today. O. complained that some of the material had not come. None, then, till Thursday. W. put on a face of mock dismay: "Thursday is years off to a man who is as impatient as I am." Got Ferguson's bill: one hundred seven dollars for press work on the big book. W. said: "That's easy compared with what I expected: I have been anticipating impossible charges." Tried to catch phototype man at Gutekunst's today but missed him. Osler not over according to promise. W. spoke of his "fiber" as a thing he owed to his parents. "I started well—was lucky: had a father, a mother, as they had fathers and mothers, strong, wise, temperate, pure." Read that Ingersoll is to speak at a memorial meeting for Proctor: "Good for Ingersoll—good for Proctor! I still actively feel the tragedy of Proctor's death." W. gave me drafts of old letters to Conway and Hotten, 1867–8. "Both are about English publication: I was trying all I could then trying hard against formidable obstacles, to bring out independent English editions." On the outside of the Conway letter W. had asked himself this question: "Did the letter or copy ever go?" I asked him: "Did it?" He answered: "I still ask my old question: did it ever go?" The letter was written in pencil.

July 24, 1867.

Dear friend. I avail myself of an opportunity to send you, by the hands of Mr. Philp, just starting for London, a copy of my Poems prepared with care for the printers, with reference to republication in England. The Introduction is written by William O'Connor. All is sent you, so that in case there comes any opening you may have a proper copy of latest date, prepared by me, to publish from. Of course I do not expect you, and would not permit you, to make yourself the job of running around and seeking after a publisher; only, please take charge of the copy—I hereby clothe you with power over it, and should any good chance befall, it is what I should wish a London edition set up from.

Mr. O'Connor has shown me your note of April 30th last to him. I wish to send you, as also to those other friends and well-wishers whom it seems I have in England, my true thanks and love.

Many serious and wonderful things have occurred in our dear country since you and I last met, my friend. But of these I will not now talk. I too have had many deep experiences since.

Mr. Philp starts from Washington this evening so I must cut short my letter. I will add that I remain well and hearty. For occupation I hold a pleasant clerkship in the Attorney General's office—of pay sufficient and duties agreeable and consistent with my tastes. I may write you, by mail, further about the book, and other matters. Write me on receipt of the copy. Farewell.

W. said: "With all the fussing and fretting I never got a complete edition of Leaves of Grass done in England: with all my friends there—all their heart, all their loyalty—I only appeared there in pieces, extracts, bits, expurgations—except, of course, where they bought the American books. I was always fishing for a full invite but was never more than conditionally received. I suppose the publishers saw no market. In later years I have not cared because now the sheets are sent over and the full book appears on that side with an English imprint: but time was when I did hope that I might be done straight out and unabridged in an English book. The fact is, I am probably not any more popular there than here: it may even be that counting the sales of the Leaves complete many more books have been sold in America than in England. Anyway you look at it, I'm not a bloomin' success from the market point of view. I find that with regard to the abridged books I hate 'em more and more. I hate the idea of being put somewhere with the harm taken out of me, as good house-wives alter Tomcats to make them respectable in the neighborhood." The Hotten letter was written from Washington, enclosed in an envelope of the Attorney General's Office.

Feb. 18, 1868.

Dear Sir: In response to your letter of the 5th instant, which has just reached me, I have to say that I accept the proposal in it respecting your English publication of my poems—and hereby agree that you have the privilege of selling that publication in the United States, on payment to me, or my agent, of a royalty of one shilling, (or 25 cents gold) upon every copy sold in the U. S. Of course it is distinctly understood that this grant from me does not affect my copyright here but that said copyright in each of its particulars and in the whole, is absolutely and fully and exclusively retained by me.

It is not improbable that a very handsome and steady sale of the English volume may be effected here, by the right business manipulation, a moderate, judicious advertising &c.

My book has never been really published here at all and the market is in a sort vacant of supply. I will suggest something to you on these points in a future letter.

I received yesterday a letter from Mr. Conway conveying

your proposition, to which I mailed an immediate answer, to the same effect as herewith.

Accept my thanks for the William Blake. It has not yet come from the post office, but I know it will prove to me a profoundly interesting study and a handsome gift. It is, in fact, a book I was wanting.

After the reception of the copy you speak of—my own volume —(now probably on its way)—I shall doubtless have occasion to express genuine pleasure—with gratitude both to its editor and publisher.

And now, my dear sir, please accept with my trust in the success of the enterprise my kindest respects to yourself personally.

Asked W.: "Did you never feel you were 'really published' until Osgood took the book?" "I would say that—yes: Osgood was the first to really push the Leaves in the regular and general way: he threatened to sell a lot of the books: but the state stuck in its nose—smelt our bad smell—found we wouldn't do—and we ran for our lives: ran, but took our plates with us: and then, what radical Massachusetts was too good to do conservative Pennsylvania was bad enough to do, and we were safe."

Wednesday, October 3rd, 1888.

8 p.m. W. had a dictionary on his lap. "What's timbre?" he asked, before he had even said "how do you do?" I laid my hat down. We shook hands. He was still looking at the book: "I have sort of an idea but can't state it." Then he smiled: "Oh, yes! now I see: timbre, timbre." He put the book down. "And how is everything with you today, Horace?" I said: "The Doctor has been over and improved you." "Been over? yes—and given a very encouraging twist to things." Still shook his head. "But, improved? I don't know. The Doctor talks— I accept his talk—but that don't conclude the matter. The shoemaker tells his customer that the shoe just fits but the customer feels the pinch: the fellow who wears the shoe always knows

most about the pinch." Still, he is brighter. Musgrove says he has seemed to be more at ease ever since the Doctor was here.

I showed him the title page my father had drawn. He looked at it quietly—was greatly interested. "It's beautiful!" he exclaimed: "Beautiful!" Then as he thought further: "Yes, splendidly made—too splendid for me: too ornate"—and in conclusion: "If I was to see it somewhere, done, in its place, I should acknowledge, accept it: yet it's too fine for me—for me to premeditate: I must not use it." He laid the drawing down: "Horace, I guess we'll have the head made plain, alone, and then do the lettering in type." Letter today to me from Morse. Full of personal gossip. W. said: "That's the kind of letter we look for—personal notes, news." Morse suggested Blake should review N. B. for Unity. W. took Morse's new address and said he would send a book to Blake. Photo on the lounge. I picked it up. It was Gilchrist's W. W. inscribed to W. by G. W. said: "That's the picture—the London picture—Italian curls and all. How do you like Walt Whitman as fixed up for proper London society? But what a photo it is! that, at least, is up to standard. Herbert was here today for some time—talked, sat about, was cheerful. The professorship is an assured thing now—he told me so: seventy-five dollars a month—that will pay his way."

I asked W. if the bit from Gosse did not remind him of things he had himself said of Lanier? "I can hardly see how that can be: I know so little about him—have read but detached pieces, here and there, in papers, magazines." I explained: "I mean things you have said about the art side of Lanier—the obviousness of preparation in all he wrote." W. then: "Oh yes! that is likely: but then I say that of all of 'em: it's not the thing that's to be said but the way in which to say it they most care for and emphasize. Lanier, Matthew Arnold—men of that stripe—are after style, expression, phrase: to them the fact I most and first welcome comes last." I asked him: "Is Gosse friendly?" "Yes—rather so—kindly. He has been here—sat right across there opposite me—had a long pow-wow with me one afternoon two or three years ago." Did Gosse seem especially absorbed in L. of G.? "No—I guess not: am sure not: he is in great part Philistine, you know." As friendly as Dowden? "Oh no! no! Dowden, in fact, believes in me—at least in some significant measure: opens the door, asks me in. Gosse is on the other side of the house: he don't train in our code or want of code: he belongs to the present and past orders not to to-morrow and the day after."

Bucke writes: "Johnston has written me for a likeness of myself to be used in an article on Walt and his Friends." W. said in answer to my inquiry: "I know nothing about it beyond what we find in the Doctor's letter. I expect to learn more about it as it develops. Johnston is bright, quick, demonstrative, enthusiastic, unswerving: loyal to the last degree; a money-maker but a generous sample of the breed. I count him as in our inner circle, among the chosen few. Johnston has a transcendental side strongly marked and that's where he spiritually connects with our crowd: he is free, progressive, alert. Johnston has had several wives—they liked me, I liked them: I deem that important. Often you hear it said: 'He likes so and so but the wife is opposed.' In this case the wives were on my side. Alma, the present Mrs. Johnston, is a wonderful woman; she is a convincing woman: when I look at her I think: now I know what womanhood means when it comes to its own. Johnston has a daughter, May: a most quiet, unassuming girl: she appeals to the fatherhood in me. And talking of daughters, girls—I have no little curiosity to see Ingersoll's two daughters, of whom I have heard so much—though I suppose I never shall."

Has read of the Archæological Congress abroad: partly from having known of Baxter's participation, partly from interest in Brinton's movements. "It must be an absorbing, fascinating study when a fellow is once initiated." Speaking of conscience, he said: "It must have developed as had other organs or faculties. Still—the development theory does not account for it all. Remember," he added: "be bold, be bold, be not too bold." He always shies at purely physical theories accounting for life. J. Foster Kirk in today. "He came with what appeared to be his daughter." Kirk, he said. "was evidently badly broken up by that accident" (knocked down by a team on the street). I questioned him. "Did you ever put anything into the old Lippincott's? did Kirk approve of you?" He replied: "Never a thing there—and Kirk never endorsed me: never caught even a glimmer of me: the old Lippincott never knew Walt Whitman." Yet he confessed: "I cannot count Kirk among downright enemies. Kirk may have been melting a little: I don't know. I have always felt Kirk was one upon whom I could not count —that is all. He has evidently of late years been impressed by what he has heard from my friends—good friends they are, too —many of them in Germantown. These friends won't have active opposition—not even the sign of it. It makes me think of some species of buck of which I have read somewhere: he stands on tip-toe of expectation: the faintest whinny at some vastly distant point—the very sniff of a foe: (sounds no other animal—even the cute, sharp, ones—would hear, suspect:) and he's off to battle—eager, dauntless. That's the way of some of my friends." Kirk had written of Charles the Bold? W. broke out vigorously: "Yes, he has—and I consider that a poisonous, insidious book: all such books, in fact: Carlyle's Frederick, Cromwell." I asked in surprise: "How's that?"—and he added: "Well, I suppose I had better not say more—could not perhaps make out my case." Yet he did say more. "I may instance things meteorological, physiological, theological: could any one of them alone reveal life, the universe? To judge of history as if all could be brought, expressed, in one fact—one little branch of knowledge—in one person! I am very impatient of stories which imply the concentration of all historical meanings in single eminent persons. I have read but little from Green —know practically nothing of him at first hand—yet I am convinced that he was on the right track—was not a great-man historian—was not a disciple of the masters this and the masters that and the devil take the people at large."

Talked again of the reference in Bucke's recent letter to "wishes religiously respected" in regard to his biography of W.

"It was not greatly important, I suppose. I advised, counselled, him: keep the book as it stands intact: if there's more to be said, say it supplementally: if you are full of this thing, are moved to pursue it, do not, at the worst, touch what is already done. I have felt this deeply. It is important to show what the book grew from—all that contributed to its formation—the adverse statements. Indeed, the book—this book—is among the few that frankly accept the facts of opposition—gives them a hearing direct. I like the book: I want this put on record, want it borne testimony to, positively, for me, as my concluding admonition."

I told him Bucke wrote me as if he had been greatly pleased with the Herald column. "Especially the last part, Walt— the part the fellow says you revised and you say you didn't." He flashed out instantly: "Nor did I: never touched it—knew nothing about it." Then, picking up a card from the table: "This is from Garland: he says he has considerable difficulty in getting me a copy of that Herald." And as he reflected further he turned to me quickly as I was leaving and with great earnest- ness said: "There's that last paragraph—the bad taste of it: I 'never had a love affair', he says. 'Taint true—'Taint true! Why, just these last two weeks I've been in a great worry: a young fellow wants to come on here—I don't want him to come. There's a little fortune hanging on it—thirty or forty thousand dollars—I don't want him to sacrifice it for a sentiment." Then after a pause he resumed on the same tack: "But some other time—to-morrow—some night when we are free—I'll tell you— give you a glint: a glint—more perhaps: it is a story, a long story —important!" I hung an instant in the doorway, waiting to see if he would say more but he did not. So, with my, "Well— good bye": and his own—"good bye—good bye, boy: I'll see you to-morrow again?"—we parted. There was some- thing deeply stirring in his manner. This must be the "big story" he has intended to confide to me.

W. gave me earlier in our talk this evening with only a brief allusion to their significance ("put these in with your biographia:

they are side lights or front lights or lights somehow on much that has gone before and will yet come in our talks") two letters, one of these Swinton to W. and the other Swinton to Grant (this a copy in W.'s hand, the original having been delivered) relative to the exchange of George Whitman (1865).

NEW YORK, Feb. 5, [1865].

My dear Walt—I most cheerfully write the note you request to Gen. Grant, though I do not know that it will be of any service. I enclose it to you, for the reason that in the new aspect of the Exchange question you may not think it worth mailing. Since your letter was written, the statement has been published (and you have doubtless seen it) that Grant has made the arrangements for a general exchange which is to be begun immediately, and carried on with all possible promptitude. It may be, and I trust will be, that under these circumstances your brother will be at once exchanged in the general mode. However, I leave this for you to decide by what you may have heard when you get this. Hoping you are now in health and that your lost brother may be soon restored to you and his mother

I remain yours

J. SWINTON.

THE TIMES OFFICE,
NEW YORK, Feb 6, 1865.

TO THE LIEUTENANT GENERAL
COMMANDING ARMIES UNITED STATES:

I respectfully and earnestly ask the Lieutenant General, in behalf of a deeply distressed mother and family, that he will give directions that one of the special exchanges be made in favor of Capt. G. W. Whitman 51st New York Vol.—and another in favor of Lieut. S. Pooley 51st N. Y. Vols. The former has been in active service for four years, has borne himself bravely in battles east and west, including Vicksburg and Jackson, and has an aged widowed mother in deepest distress. Both of the above officers have been promoted from the ranks for brave conduct on the field, and both are now, or were lately, in C. S. Military Prison, Danville, Va.

In giving the order of release the Lieutenant General will be gratefully remembered by the prisoners, by their parents and friends, and by his

Devoted admirer
JOHN SWINTON.

Thursday, October 4th, 1888.

7.45 p. m. W. reading. Carried on my shoulder twenty copies of November Boughs, which I put down on the sofa. "Books, eh?" queried W., as he shook my hand. At once began to question me about the day. What was his own condition? "I begin to realize that I must resign myself to the inevitable—the sooner the better." I opened the package and piled the books at his feet. "Tribute paid to Caesar," he laughingly remarked. Then added: "Horace, you are loyal, loyal: I would not accept all this from you but that I love you and I know you love me. That sort of relation seems to square all things up." Endorsed a book for Bucke: "Dr. R. M. Bucke from Walt Whitman the author with memories and affection Oct. 4, 1888"—saying of it: "That'll do for Doctor, won't it?" Also said he would send a copy to Morse at once. Wished me to go to McKay and make him a proposition on N. Boughs: "Offer him the edition for forty-three cents per copy: tell him we have a thousand to deliver any time he says so. The future will have to be governed by some other arrangement. I do not expect any big sale of the book: it may strike a popular fancy, but that is doubtful: the Hicks piece might interest a few Quakers—at any rate, somebody had to do the job and I volunteered as the victim. If I can come out any where near whole I shall be more than satisfied and a lot surprised. Tell Dave I aim to be generous—to do more than is right by him."

Gilchrist's Whitman stood on the mantlepiece. W. asked that I set it on the table—it had started to warp. As I conformed, I said: "You think it has no great sum of virtues to risk."

427

W. laughed: "Well, it's not bad: the body of it, belly, the hands there, the light as it falls: if it was not for the hair—the curls— even the face might pass. No—no! Herbert didn't do the picture bad because he wasn't able to do it better but because the people over there demanded a certain kind of Walt Whitman and he gave them what they wanted. I look less to technical points than others. A man's got to know how to do a thing of course, but he's also got to know what he wants to do, and wants to go about doing the job without excursions into technical ornament. The trouble with Herbert's portrait of me is mainly with its ornament." He laughed gently and added: "Of course I can be told that I'm a fool, but that's nothing new. I think I am more ready to be pleased with the work of the photo-engraving company than the most of you are. Then there's that etching made by the New York man: most people would think it good, rich: I think less of it than of almost any picture I know. Tom spoke the other night of high art: the little picture here in November Boughs was not high art. I know it is not high art: I was not looking for high art: though I am not stone blind, either: I make some admissions even for high art. But if high art is low everything else I don't see that I care to make any use of it. Then sometimes a picture which is elementally very simple, crude, has something to say, says something, in fact, which no amount of added finesse would strengthen or improve."

Called at Gutekunst's today. Found they did not have the butterfly negative. Afterwards traced it to Broadbent and Taylor's, who will look it up. W. said: "What a siege of it!" Also saw steel-plate printers, who will charge us fifty cents a hundred. Brown will do the title portrait for us in ten days. To be oval. "I prophesy its success," said W., "though, as you know, prophesy is not my long suit." No word yet from Linton. "You know Linton—or know of him?" I had read some things of his in The Radical. W. added: "Yes—that's Linton—that's the man: and that work in the magazines was fine, fine—amazing, delicate. Linton is a good fellow—a good friend: I hold him in real esteem. You know he is a divorced man? His wife is the celebrated woman who writes novels: I guess you know all about them. When Linton made the cut he wrote me that if he had been rich he would have made it for nothing but as he was not he would charge me fifty dollars for it. I sent him the fifty dollars. Afterwards he asked permission to use it in the Bohn book. It looked well there: I had no objection. Linton is radical—a liberty-lover. He was poor, as he said, like the rest of us—not in want but always in straitened circumstances: he was one of the folks to whom every five dollars received or given out is somewhat of a serious matter. Although my philosophy includes conservatives, everything else being equal I prefer the radicals as men and companions."

Suggested that I should look up a mounter of photographs. "I've got a heap big lot of pictures here which I think of having some one put on cards." My foot struck a book. I reached down, pushed aside the newspaper that hid it, and picked it up. It proved to be one volume of the McKay Emerson. "Ah!" I said: "it has joined its fellow-treasures on the floor." W. said: "Yes—it is being initiated." Then he added more seriously: "You may doubt it but I have been reading it a little—looking through it, at the least." Then, turning his eyes upon me as if desiring an answer: "As I read, an old feeling came back to me—a feeling returned after the lapse of many years—a feeling that the book is a little, just a little, antique." Then, after a very brief pause and some evident thought: "And here and there signs of preaching—just a little of it: don't you perceive it?" I answered: "Yes—preaching like the last paragraph of your Hicks." W. shook his head: "I should be sorry to think I preached too much." "It's not 'too much,'" I rejoined— "sometimes the preacher is needed—somebody needs to be shaken up—covenanter style." W. here remarked: "Well, a man insensibly falls into it—I, too: no one is entirely free from danger. It was unmistakable in Father Taylor and Elias Hicks. Perhaps the most remarkable trait in both was their dead earnestness—an awful sense of the gravity of their message.

Hicks would unconsciously fall into the canting sing-song tone—then come to realize his danger—recover himself: turn about quick as that"—flinging arm and body—"shake the thing off." W. added to this graphically: "And his audiences always accepted it—comprehended what he meant." This brought up the question of Emerson's optimism. "It is sometimes complained of as too general." W. said dissentingly: "No—no—it could not be—it can do nothing but good—be nothing but right. I have no patience with people who start out to blacken the face of the earth. Whether it is constitutional or what not with me, I stand for the sunny point of view—stand for the joyful conclusions. This is not because I merely guess: it's because my faith seems to belong to the nature of things—is imposed, cannot be escaped: can better account for life and what goes with life than the opposite theory."

Said to me about the book: "And precious little in it for you so far—nothing but work, work." I carried his sentence along: "Nothing but love, love." He looked happy. Reached out his hand. "Horace, I understand that—I understand:—it removes all my doubts." Gave me a letter from Bucke dated First and pointed out the opening sentences: "Horace Traubel has sent me (just to hand) Herald of 23rd ult. Have been reading the piece on you and like it well. Who is the author?" W. said: "That's just it: who is the author? The author, whoever he is, says I am the author—that I said all the things he says I said and in the way he says them: but I don't see it that way. But if all you fellows agree in liking the thing I suppose I don't count." W. produced an old letter from Johnston, saying of it: "I talked with you about Johnston yesterday: well, this will show you the practical nature of his camaraderie. Johnston is always turning up the pennies but spends the pounds with a certain sort of abandon. He is the kind of a man who might play with riches and die poor—though he's mighty comfortable fixed, I should imagine, as things are going now. This letter gives you a little look in on Johnston for one thing—then adds a point or two of history for keeps."

150 Bowery, New York, Mar 24, 1887.

Dear Uncle Walt: Over two weeks ago I determined to let Major Pond manage your lecture. He is "up" in that kind of business and knows just how to do it. He said I might calculate three hundred and fifty dollars as the cost—the output, and he would guarantee to fill a hall. I at once assumed the responsibility and became security for the three hundred and fifty dollars. He then tried to get Chickering Hall but it was engaged for April 14th and also for every afternoon and evening about that date. We have at last settled upon the Madison Square Theatre for the afternoon (four o'clock) of April 14th. I must pay the seventy five dollars for the Theatre the moment it is engaged, and I will do so the moment I receive a telegram from you to-morrow saying, "all right, go ahead." Please wire me at once on receipt of this.

Alma is here with me and is well and says: "Lots of love and thanks for the nice letter received at Equinunk."

Ever yours sincerely

J. H. Johnston.

W. asked me: "Do you remember that I gave you some time ago a draft of a letter I wrote Freiligrath when I sent him the Leaves? Yes? Well—here is a letter of William's connected with the same affair: you had better take it and put the two together." I started to read the letter to myself. W. said: "Let me hear it, too—read it aloud."

Washington, D. C.,
September 16, 1868.

Dear Walt: I was very sorry not to have seen you yesterday before you left, because the enclosed answer came from Westerman, and I wanted to consult with you as to the steps to be taken. I think a package ought to be made up at once for Ferdinand Freiligrath, and we can send it through Westerman, reimbursing him for the expense of transportation. I suppose it would be best to have it done by my agency, and I suggest that I write

F. F. a letter, (to go with the package) explaining things generally, and making him as far as possible master of the situation. What do you think? I am sorry I did not know you were going yesterday, because we could have arranged all better than now.

Preserve the enclosed. I think the sooner we do what is to be done (if anything) regarding F. F., the better.

I write hurriedly, just on the edge of mail-time. No letter from you today at the Attorney General's. I hope you'll have a good time. Give my love to your mother. John came in yesterday and bid me tell you to come up to his house before you left. I did not then know you had gone. He will be disappointed.

Affectionately yours,
W. D. O'Connor.

Friday, October 5th, 1888.

8 p. m. W. reading Symonds' Greek Poets. Laid book face down, open, on a basket of old paper. Seemed a trifle depressed. He had a letter from Bucke this evening. Bucke has heard from Osler, direct. "He says he finds you 'decidedly better,' 'brighter mentally and physically holding your own,' 'the pain, he says, points to nothing serious.'" W. said: "I confess I do not wholly like or credit what he says—I do not fancy the jaunty way in which he seems inclined to dismiss the troubles. Still, that may all be a part of his settled policy—I do not object to cheer. I don't know whether it's from getting down to hard pan or is a theory, but, whatever, Osler pursues it, and it is right—it is inspiring. Still, I know my own condition—don't need him to tell me about that—can't be fooled." I protested: "But, after all, allowing for exaggerations, hasn't he said enough to encourage us?" "Yes." "Then why ain't you encouraged? During your worst days last June you always kept on saying, 'We won't fight the battle with the worst end in view.' Why don't you say that now?" W's face broke out into a smile. "I must have said something like that—it sounds like me; it is well for a fellow to be reminded

of himself now and then." He still insisted: "I know my condition better than any doctor."

I stooped to the floor and picked up a copy of November Boughs. He noticed what I was doing. "Do you find water on it?" he asked. I said "Yes." "Ah! I fell to-night—had a cup of water in my hand." He must have seen some alarm expressed in my face for he went on instantly: "It did no damage—it was not serious. It happened this way: I was at the stove there, turned, caught my foot in this shawl on the floor: as I am not steady anyhow I just bowled over. I wasn't hurt: the worst was I spilled water over one volume of the Emerson— the handsome Emerson. I had considerable difficulty getting up on my feet, and to the chair, again, but called no one—preferred managing alone." (Musgrove down stairs heard the fall but it did not sound heavy enough to be W. W. had not said a word to him about the accident). W. gave me a letter from Buxton Forman. "Take it—forward it to Doctor Bucke. There are things in the letter you will like to see, hear. Forman is on our side: is friendly, appreciative: is a man obviously of talent and power."

46 MARLBOROUGH HILL, ST. JOHN'S WOOD,
LONDON N. W., 26 Sept. 1888.

Dear Walt Whitman: I have had it in my mind, concerning Leaves of Grass, to tell you a tale which will perhaps afford you a quiet moment's amusement now while you are preparing Autumn Boughs for us.

Many years ago, probably about 1871, when the first enthusiasm for your wonderful book was on me,—the first and last enthusiasm, I should say, for it has endured uninterruptedly,— I was at the house of George Hy. Lewes and "George Eliot," and was enjoying one of those short earnest tête-a-têtes that she found means to accord somehow to each of her room full of visitors.

I asked her what she thought of L. of G.; and Lewes, coming up at the moment, remarked in his flippant way, "Let me see, the author wrote Heel-taps, didn't he?" Letting this poor jest pass, I pursued the serious talk with G. E.—found she knew hardly anything of L. of G., and urged her to read it. She said she had glanced at it but was impressed that it had "no message for her soul." I ventured a respectful demurrer and made way for the next tête-a-tête-ist. A few weeks afterwards, she sent me by young Lewes, who was then an official colleague of mine, a handsome and characteristic message. She had been *reading* Leaves of Grass: had found that the book *had* a "message for her soul" and thanked me for the part I had taken in pressing on her attention its scope, meaning, and original force. I do not pretend to quote her words except those in inverted commas. The rest were only reported to me by a tolerably inaccurate young man; but the drift was certainly as given above.

Now I have often thought she must have made some such acknowledgment to you direct—seldom as she wrote to any one in those "Priory" days. Did she or did she not?

Always, dear Walt Whitman,

most sincerely yours,

H. Buxton Forman.

Forman put on the margin above head of letter: "Excuse the unreadableness of a scrawl written in the only available quarter hour of the day, on the underground railway, with that most hateful of modern inventions—a stylographic pen."

"Well," I asked, "did you ever hear from her direct?" "No —that was the last of it." Then he added, after a moment's thought: "I had similar intimations given me by other people who knew her in London. But while I might have some message for her soul, as she said, I do not think that as a whole I would ingratiate myself in her affections. We stood for the same things up to a certain point but there parted company, she to look back and around, I to look ahead." I said: "Her idea seemed to be that we should do all we can to make this sad world less sad, yours that we should do all we can to make this joyful world more joyful." He repeated the sentence after me and seemed to be turning it over in his mind: "That's probably the whole story in a nutshell, except"—I put in: "What is the 'except'?" He answered: "I don't want people to think my joy does not contain sorrow—does not allow for it and realize its rejuvenating force. With that admission made I stand by your statement. They speak of George Eliot as a 'meliorist'. That would be no sort of a word to express my attitude towards the universe: that word contains an apology—an apology: and an apology is an impertinence. George Eliot was a great, gentle soul, lacking sunlight."

I inquired: "Have you had many visitors today—or any?" He put on a rueful face at once: "Yes, hosts of 'em"—adding, the next minute: "None, however, who concern our fortunes." Yet Hunter was one of them and when he got talking of Hunter he warmed right up. "He came in, was chatty: I enjoyed him. He told me of some New York edition of the Encyclopedia Brittanica for which he had been chosen to write various articles. I thought the American edition was made in Philadelphia? However, Hunter is to do it—just what I say: is to write War articles—three or four of them anyway." Here he stopped and fingered his penknife a little: then removed his glasses and laughed quietly: "It struck me while he was here —I smiled to myself about it: can't help smiling now to recall it— struck me as odd, to say the least, that he was selected for that service—to do that precise job of work. He is to write up Sherman, Thomas—McClellan, too, I think. I guess you know, Hunter was a Rebel—hot, hot: what they call dyed-in-the-wool: sees everything through that one glass, colored by it, nothing at all coming to him from any other source. That question of the War is the only one over which we threatened to come to words. I know I have roused up once or twice when we got on that subject: I have tried to keep shy of it: but Hunter himself is a challenge—he won't let you avoid it."

I told W. that Hunter resented his reference to Lincoln's death as a "murder." H. had heard W. read the lecture at Unity Church. W. now exclaimed: "Well—I'm glad I did not hear him do that—I hope it will never come up while he is here: I am afraid it would irritate, provoke, me. That is a delicate, almost a forbidden field: I am easily stirred there—my nerve for that is very near the surface: you don't need to step on my corns—it's enough to be near them—to arouse me. Yes, it is a trifle absurd to give Hunter such commissions. Yet I do like him so much I can forget the things in him I don't like. Hunter is cheery, canny, buoyant—helps a fellow up steep places: possesses the best traits of the Scottish character—which are the best of the best anywhere, all nations, to say the least of them. What interests me in him is his point of view, which he entertains no matter who howls or who praises. The Scotch point of view differs from all others—has its own way of arriving at results: it is subtle, cool, discriminating. The Scotch are wholly unlike the Germans: Hunter, for instance, shows none of the German traits—is neither ideal nor sentimental. The German will probably never comprehend the Scotch—could never take to Robert Burns." I said: "Schiller did." "Oh!" he replied: "He was a poet: of course, all poets would. But take the German intellect—German scholarship, learning: the average student among the Germans: I do not imagine that Burns or any other characteristic Scotchman could make himself any too welcome to German culture. For that matter, I am not sure that Burns can anyway ever be internationally recognized. Of course, I acknowledge him: I doubt if anybody includes more than I do: I have room for them all: I am a great accepter." "But will the democratic masses speaking other tongues ever put him among their classics?" "I should say no. But how I love him myself! He is as dear to me as my old clothes!"

Getting back to Hunter again W. said: "I did not finish: the Brittanica folks want him to write me up, too—Walt Whitman. Now, what do you think of that?" W. waited for my reply. I said some things. Then he went on: "He asked for help— wanted to know authorities: I referred him to Bucke's book— told him I would be glad to give him a lift over rough places: advised him to consult with you on doubtful points from time to time." I asked W.: "Has he what you call a spinal appreciation of Leaves of Grass?" W. replying: "I don't know about that—could not say: but I know for myself that I catch his criticisms, opinions, as they fly, and have cause to value them—they often seem to go deeper than the opinions of some avowed Whitmanites,"

I detailed to him the results of my talk today with McKay. McKay liked the book—not the binding. Said of the latter: "That's a hell of a mess!" Had, however, consented to take over one thousand—nine hundred and fifty at forty-three cents, fifty free—amount to be paid January 10th. W. said: "I don't insist upon keeping the cover that way forever. We meant to do something different and have done so. My own taste in books is for very narrow margins and as small a page as possible —making all books books for the pocket so people would get into the habit of carrying books about with them and reading books when they read at all in the open air." How did he wish to settle with McKay. "I don't know: by our old contracts there were settlements to be made every six months—May first, November first—but they have not been made so, probably because I have not insisted upon it." He then asked: "Did you say January 10th? I would rather have the money now than then." I suggested that we might ask for McKay's note. W. could get that cashed. He said: "I leave that to you—do as you think best—I want the money and am confident that you know just how to go about getting it." W. advised me to insure the sheets of the books. McKay thinks our plates would be safer in the Sherman vaults. Broadbent today said he wanted forty dollars for six hundred butterfly prints. W. cried: "Broadbent may crack his knuckles for his forty dollars: I could not think of it: the book is already costing more than I calculated for." That set us off again discussing pictures. I have convinced W. that he should autograph the six hundred first signatures of the books before they are bound.

Osler said to me when I spoke of this: "I am not an alarmist—on the contrary, I expect your old man to last for years—

but I would advise you to provide for contingencies by having this matter pushed through at once." W. signed my name in the two volumes 1876 edition which he gave me Sunday week back. I sent off Bucke's N. B. today. W. thought Spear had done him up on the stove. "I've half a mind to send him eight dollars and let him whistle awhile for the rest." Laughed. "But what's the use? I guess I'm getting mean—that's all!" He then said: "If you have the sheets sent to Camden address them plainly to Walt Whitman as well as to the street number. That catamount next door—down—has made his number 328 —built some little house on six or seven feet of his lot and given it a full number, so throwing me out!" He said "things sent to" him "simply by number had gone wrong—many of them." "I wrote to the City Surveyor about it a year ago, and he said he would have it set right—but has not done so. '328' belongs to me, by every right of precedent recent and remote."

Saturday, October 6th, 1888.

W. read some but wrote more today. Bucke is exuberant over Osler's report. W. shakes his head: "Go slow, Doctor Bucke—go slow! As I said before, the fellow who wears the shoe knows best whether it pinches or not. Osler's cheer, instituted of malice prepense, has a place, is not to be sneezed away: but I, too, know when the wind blows north. For some time I have succeeded in maintaining myself on a low level of comfort: now the enemy is at work again: I feel myself going down hill." Mrs Davis wants to get the room cleaned. Would he retire to the parlor some day while this was being done? "Yes—down stairs—but not to the parlor: to the kitchen."

Forman's note came up again. "So you did not get that letter from George Eliot?" "No, not a word—not a word. I am sure George Eliot had an affinity for me—some impulse in her own nature towards me. Mrs. Gilchrist more than once spoke to me about it: she knew Mathilde Blind and knew from her many things about George Eliot. Then I am sure George Eliot was tampered with: her instincts, her large vision, her rich nature all through, rebelled against, appealed from, restriction. But she lived in the midst of crowding conventions, in relations with those who at the end tried to explain away any preference she may have shown for me. She once adopted a motto from the Leaves and more than one of her friends have made some show as if to apologize for it. I do not think Forman's quotation of Lewes' flippant jest ended the matter for Lewes. There was more to Lewes than that: that was only one of his many sides." I asked: "Do you consider the Forman incident conclusive?" He answered: "I do: it serves to confirm numerous things that have gone before." I asked again: "You stand by your statement made to me yesterday about George Eliot?" "Yes—every word of it: I have said nothing today to contradict it." Then added: "I started to say to Bucke (I wrote to him today) that I would enclose that letter and then happened to think you had it. Will you send it on to him?" Characterized Forman again as "a man of considerable power without any considerable individuality."

I mentioned O'Connor in some connection. W. said: "I had a letter from him yesterday: didn't I tell you? I meant to. I sent it on to John Burroughs today and advised him to pass it on to Bucke." How is O'Connor? "In a pretty bad way just now, I should judge: down with almost total blindness." What was the cause of O'Connor's trouble? "I know of none—in particular. When we were together in Washington he was one of the lithest men you ever saw—like Dave McKay, a little, in build, in physical grit. You don't know probably—I have never told you, I may tell you now—we regard it as a sort of secret: do not speak of it—never at least on the outside: Bucke says O'Connor has locomotor ataxia—that is his opinion, his theory, after much thinking over it. You would not guess such a thing from William's appearance. You have seen the picture down stairs: he is magnificent, he is strong: Horace, he is even beautiful: that is correct—beautiful is not the wrong word. Well, he is all that in life and more too. There seems to be no cure for his trouble, though its victims enjoy long immunities from any active experience of its symptoms: its fatal results may be delayed." Had Bucke ever spoken freely to O'C. on the subject? "No—not a word of it: if he had been asked he would have done so. O'Connor has stopped with Bucke up there in London but said nothing on this line—asked no questions: so there was silence on both sides. Bucke probes things to the bottom: always wants to face the last possibility—is an austere investigator who is not to be fooled and does not want to fool himself. I am not sure that Bucke has got to the end of matters—not sure that there's not more to be known: I don't absolutely adopt his theory —in fact, any man's theories, even my own. I always leave a loop-hole of escape—a way open for retreat or advance. Now, all this is only for us to know with each other: it must not go beyond us." Then talked generally of O'Connor: "He is one of the rarest, richest combinations of intellect and feeling: I doubt if there ever lived a man more superbly endowed: intellect and feeling—with feeling, perhaps, and rightly, somewhat predominant. O'Connor is hot with the world-fire and is full of magnificent possibilities, potential achievement. I know of no one—have never met any man or woman, not a single person— in whom there was such a vigor, such a depth and fervent innate power, and at the same time such an exquisite sense of literary and art form. Yet O'Connor, too, hot, impassioned, is in addition to that, like some of the famous jurists—Matthew Hale was one of them—gifted with the power to spread aside the obstructions to truth and go straight to his point. O'Connor is a man to tie to, to set store by, to reckon upon. Nothing can escape him—nothing evade him: he has an eye that sees clean through things." "Yes," he added, "an almighty, always prescient, eye."

McKay said to me today, again: "This is a hell of a book for shape," &c. Complains of flexible cover that although it might please the Whitmanites, probably would please them, it would have no public or popular attraction. McK. had seen Oldach about this. O. had stopped binding after the first hundred copies. McKay ordered a copy done up his way—stamping

changed, gilt top added, edges clipped, stiff cover—to be submitted to W. for approval. Said Lippincott, Porter and Coates
and others had "laughed the book out of face." All of which
—in fuller detail—I gave to W.—who listened intently. While
McK. had been laying all this out to me I had asked: "Then if
W. W. insists on the present form you won't take the edition at
forty-three cents?" But he wouldn't say that. I knew he looked
for a sale—wanted to handle it—in fact, he finally said so. He
might insist, however, upon removing his name from the title
page. W. remarked: "I see: Dave was determined to see it
wrong: started out for that. Still, we're not dead set for that
cover: if he can give us another that is better, why, we may take
it. I know that's not a cover for the conventional eye, but I
think the time has come for authors and publishers to break
through the rules that have been laid down for them." I had
suggested to McKay what I had previously suggested to W.—
stamp the peculiar "November Boughs" of the title page on the
cover, and McKay adopted the idea. McKay is to pay himself
for all extra expenses over our first arrangements if W. accepts
his changes. McKay proposed coming over Tuesday with book
and to make settlement with W. on old matters. W. agreeable.
"Tell him I will expect him Monday or next day." I had advised
McK.: come in forenoon towards twelve or afternoon from half
past one to four. W. said: "That is exactly right—that is my
time." Prepared today to insure our sheets. Ferguson protests that his vaults are as good as Sherman's, contradicting
McKay: says the best evidence of his faith is in the fact that he
carries no insurance on them. W. sometimes is testy in trying
to make small economies. We quarreled a bit about the cost of
the stove. Read him a letter I had from Williamson:

NEW YORK, Oct. 6, 1888.
Yours of Oct. 4th. I am sorry that I asked for the manuscript,
or at least part, as I was not aware that Mr. Whitman kept it
intact, and on no account would I have him break it, much as
I desire it, but if at any future time he should care to part with

any manuscripts that he has, and you should know it, let me know the value he would put on them and I may become the happy owner of them. I always feel a little delicate in meeting anyone in a matter of this kind as not knowing what is the owner's desire about keeping them. Give Mr. Whitman my kind regards and hopes for his returning strength.

I remain, yours,

G. M. WILLIAMSON.

W. said: "I would like to humor Williamson but don't see how I can do it. He will have to content his 'happy owner' soul with patience: I can give him no hope. That whole mania for collecting things strikes me as an evidence of disease—sometimes of disease in an acute form: though I know Williamson for an exceptional man in a bad crowd. And indeed, that is what makes a remarkable matter more remarkable—that a man such as we know Williamson to be should care a damn whether he was the happy owner of a manuscript—any manuscript—or not. Well, give him my love: that is real: and if he is satisfied to be the happy owner of my love he owns it—tell him so—and welcome, welcome." I gave McKay an order on Ferguson for the plates of Sands at Seventy, which are to be added to future issues of the Leaves, the plates to be returned by March 1st. No word from Linton yet about the cut. "I wonder why?" he asks. In the meantime he turned another old Linton letter over to me. "You will read it and know what to do with it: whether to keep it for history or throw it away for nonsense. By the way, you'll have to put up some more shelves in your house—won't you?—if we keep on with this thing."

NEW HAVEN, CONN.,
July 1, 1885.

My dear Whitman: I see by the papers that you may be going to England. If you do go, you must see William Bell Scott, the painter and poet, the first (unless Dante Rossetti were earlier) of your English admirers. He will be glad to welcome you.

442

And I glad to give you a note of "introduction" when I know you are going. We are old friends and regular correspondents, and I had much delightful time with him in England and Scotland during 1883 and '84, being then across the waters.

You will tell me too if I can be of any other use to you. I may be visiting the dear old land again next year, probably having to look after the bringing out of a book on Wood Engraving.

As I am writing I think of something to send you, which ought to have come to you before. It is a bit of home-production, setting up, printing, binding and all. You'll not value it less for that.

Need I say that I am glad to see a good report of your health and that, however drifted off, as seems too generally our human fate, I am always pleased to think of you. Let me hear from you and believe me always heartily yours

W. J. LINTON.

W. said of the trip to Europe: "I didn't go—thank God! It might have been fatal. I seem to need to end, as I began, on this side of the Atlantic: that being toted around, feted, treated, would have done me no good: it is the sort of thing that of all things I am most averse to. Then there is the book! it has had to be guarded against all counter-inspirations."

Sunday, October 7th, 1888.

7.45 p. m. W. not mending at all—stays just as he has been. The nurse's daily report, as I enter and nod to him in the parlor, is, "tolerable, tolerable"—and Mrs. Davis only too frequently shakes her head. W. himself appears to have abandoned hope of gaining strength. The question comes back, day to day— how long can he maintain himself at this level? He sat by the light reading the New York Tribune which Harned had brought him. He complained of the dearth of matter of interest. Did he read Harrison's speeches? No—he had "no interest that way." Yet had to have the papers: "They are as necessary as my food." For an instant W. seemed to forget today is Sunday.

He asked me: "What have you learned today?" I reminded him and he remarked: "That's so: but one day is like another here." Then he said: "If you ask me how I am, I can say, 'I am here—the day is passed:' that is about all I can say." He added: "Corning and Tom came in some time ago—have been gone a couple of hours I guess: Tom brought the magazines in"—pointing to copies of N. A. Review on floor.

W. is to read Ingersoll's reply to Manning. The Ibsen book did not interest him. He cut a few pages of it—"tried to make it go"—but since that day weeks back it has been laid aside. Tonight, when I referred to the subject, he expressed no interest in the book. Gilchrist was over and up stairs today, but stayed merely a short time. I mentioned my trip to Germantown today and quoted affectionate inquiries made after W. He asked: "Who were they?" and then: "They were curious, were they?—curious to know how I am?" I demurred a little: "It was not curiosity, Walt, but affection!" He repeated my sentence and then said earnestly: "I know—I know: there's Clifford: I'm certain he means it—means every word. All I have seen of him—heard of him—of what he thinks, does— convinces me that he is a man of force—generic, a first-hander." But he laughed when I said I found it difficult to describe his condition. "I do not wonder: it would be hard for me to tell the story myself." Then he said: "Horace, when you hear me growl take me by the neck and shake the black devils out of me. I know these people are my friends—respect the work I have tried to do. If I failed to respond to that feeling I would be a damned lie to myself. Some days, with this long tie-up, the long imprisonment (the beautiful sweet days outside that I so hunger for and can't go to) the irritations overcome me and I say things. Lucky is the man who never says things!"

"I wrote Kennedy today," W. remarked—"a long letter— for me,"—and then—"and I have sent him a book, too—sent one also to O'Connor." Said he had used ten-cent stamps. "It is more convenient—and besides, I like the stamp—it seems to me the finest of the whole Uncle Sam series." I told him I had sent off Forman's note. W. then talked a bit more about George Eliot. "There is no doubt if she had had a perfectly free pen she would have made some acknowledgment to me in the key of Forman's allusion to her. But she was nullified— by Lewes, first—then by her second husband, Cross. I never seem to have any but the best feeling for Lewes—he is a man I respect: a man of a thousand parts."

W. has frequently advised me to read Fanny Wright's book, A few Days in Athens. Today I borrowed the book. He said at once warmly: "I am glad—glad. They used to say— they would say still—that it is a green book. It is crude: it might in a certain sense be said—crude as the Bible and Homer are crude. There are some people who are shocked at the bare mention of her name: there has always been a sort of goody-goody taboo of her morals." "Did she ever do anything or stand for anything that shocked you?" "Oh dear no! No indeed! Fanny Wright (we always called her Fanny for affection's sake)—Fanny Wright had a nimbus"—encircling her pictorially with a sweep of the hand—"a halo: is almost sacerdotal." "Yes, they may object to her—object as the priestly class would object to Jesus, Socrates. She was one of the few characters to excite in me a wholesale respect and love: she was beautiful in bodily shape and gifts of soul. Her book about Epicurus was daily food to me: I kept it about me for years. It is young, flowery, yet has attributes all its own. I always associated that book with Volney's Ruins, which was another of the books on which I may be said to have been raised."

Referred to Hunter again: "I have seen a good deal of the Southern people—know them well, love them well, would not misjudge them. Yet I believe in nationality, too—internationality, for that matter: not the breaking away of peoples but the coming together of peoples—ever more and more the coming together. The War stirs me up—the causes of the War—its consequences: fills me with emotion: possibly because I have been very close to the most painful phases of its tragedy—in the hospitals, in the midst of the most extreme manifestations of its suffering. There is another point to this story which interested me greatly: the publishers have informed Hunter that the word 'Rebel' is not to occur in the vocabulary of the book—he is to make 'Rebel' 'Confederate' every time."

W. spoke of photographers. "They have photographed me all ages, sizes, shapes: they have used me for a show-horse again and again and again: they make the pictures and sell them: but as for paying me—well, they don't worry about that: all except Cox, the premier exception, who, I shouldn't wonder, has paid me as much as a hundred dollars and more in royalties." Sent me hunting over his table for a letter from Bucke. Bucke says he will be down shortly on meter business. W. advised me to show the letter to Harned. "Doctor thinks he's going to get rich: God help us not to get rich! Doctor thinks riches would make him a free man: it would do exactly the opposite— put him into the bonds of the worst slavery. God help us not to get rich!" I said: "We don't need to advise God on that subject—he keeps most of us poor enough without special dispensations." "For reasons," said W.—"yes, for the best reasons. I will amend my prayer: God help us not to want to get rich!"

W. said autobiographically: "Most of my friends have been thinkers—people of the highest, though not of the professional, poetic nature. The great literary leaders—most of them—had no idea that I could be taken seriously and refused to condone my existence. If God Almighty was willing to be responsible for me, well and good: but as for them—they would have no Walt Whitman: their skirts were clean." Said Bucke was "a German scholar": "He will not admit of translations—not even the best: not even Taylor's." Gave Harned a copy of N. B., writing in it: "T. B. Harned from Walt Whitman with thanks, affection and best memories." Also sent a copy by Harned to Corning. Wants to see McKay. "Tell him what I have said about the book—that we are willing to hear all his objections and even to change our plans if it may seem wise to do so." W. asked: "Do you remember that we talked the other night about

English editions and that I remarked that after all their talk in England they had never been willing to make a complete Leaves over there? I have put you aside some correspondence I had with Ellis back in the seventies on that subject. You will construe it as a confirmation of your argument and I don't question your right to do so." There were three letters—one a draft from W. to Ellis and two from Ellis in return. W. wrote from Washington.

Sent by Steamer, Aug. 12 '71.

F. S. Ellis, publisher, 33 King st, Covent Garden, London: I take the liberty of writing at a venture to propose to you the publication, in a moderate-priced volume, of a full edition of my poems, Leaves of Grass, in England under my sanction. I send by same mail as this, a revised copy of L. of G. I should like a fair remuneration or percentage.

I make this proposition not only to get my poems before the British public, but more because I am annoyed at the horrible dismemberment of my book there already and possibility of something worse.

Should my proposal suit you, go right on with the book. Style of setting it up, price, rate of remuneration to me, &c, I leave entirely to you. Only the text must be sacredly preserved, verbatim.

Please direct to me here as soon as convenient.

London, W. C. Aug 23, 1871.

Dear Sir: I thank you very much for your letter received this morning. Its frank and pleasant tone makes me regret even more than I should otherwise have done, to feel myself obliged to say at once that I do not see my way to bringing out a complete edition of your poems in England. I admire them so very much myself that I should much like to do it but there are certain pieces (among those which I admire the most) which would not go down in England, and it certainly would not be worth while to publish it again in a mutilated form, nor of course would you wish it. W. M. Rossetti is a great admirer of your poems and a man by no means squeamish yet you see he did not venture to publish them without alteration in England. I think he was wrong: they should have been published complete and with your sanction or let alone. May I keep the volume you send me? If so I will remit you the price for I have tried in vain to get a complete edition through Trübner's.

I am Dear Sir

Yours faithfully

F. S. ELLIS.

LONDON, Aug. 24, 1871.

Dear Sir: When I wrote to you yesterday I quite forgot to mention that Mr. Swinburne had for a long time been very much concerned that not knowing your address he had been unable to send you a copy of his Songs before Sunrise. As I think it possible that by this time you may have got the books I send you one of the special copies printed on fine paper, of which only twenty-five were struck off, and shall feel much gratified by your acceptance of it.

Dear Sir, Yours faithfully,

F. S. ELLIS.

"Yes," I said to W., "that's rather on my side. It looks a little this way: as if you had more literary support in England and more popular support over here." W. said: "It's an open question but your statement sounds very plausible."

Monday, October 8th, 1888.

8 p. m. W. reading Boston Transcript. "A monotonous paper," he said, "but on rather a high level: monotonously good, we might say." I had with me the six hundred and more first folds of the big book. As he saw my big bundle he asked: "What have you got there—what is all that?" I replying: "Some work for you to do." "Ah! the sheets! Hurrah!"

Then he stopped himself: "I'd better wait until I get them all signed before I yell hurrah!" Fixed the sheets carefully on the floor within reach. Contemplated them with pleasure. "This looks like getting something done: I'll be getting quite proud of myself by and bye—or of you, rather, for you are the one who is oiling the machine and keeping the fires up these days." Talcott Williams over today. Saw W. W. has been reading his collection of reviews of Bucke's Whitman. Has them in a scrap book. "I feel a trifle snappier today—as if I might even be sassy if there was any call for it." Harned came in. Gave McKay W's message today. McKay will be over in the morning. Insured our sheets for four hundred dollars. W. acquiesced in my disposition of the various business matters. He leaves all such things mostly to me. He will say: "I trust you to do that"—or: "I must leave that in your hands"—or: "If I fool with that something will go wrong"—and so on. Once he laughingly said: "Do it, do it your own way: if you don't do it right I can say damn you, and that won't hurt."

Said of Bucke: "He is very enthusiastic over the complete book—expects great things from it: I hope he won't be disappointed: I'm not so sure of all that myself." When I said: "McKay thinks November Boughs will sell," W. replied: "Let him go on believing there's no hell!" Still adhered to his faith in the cover as it is. "I, for my part, am satisfied—fully satisfied: would let it go at that. Dave got two or three people to pooh pooh the book (maybe hypnotized them into doing it) and that ended matters. While I am willing to meet Dave half way I'm not willing to take off my hat to his sneers. I'd venture to say that nine out of every ten people who happened into a book store would take a fling at anything they saw there that was novel or new. The casual observer is always a critic first—and but rarely a good one, either."

Tom said: "There's nothing in this book, Walt, to shock people." W. replied: "Perhaps—but, Tom, that's the very point which will be criticised by my friends—that it don't shock them: contains nothing to shock them." Gilchrist's picture displayed on the table elicited from Harned some praise for its technical merits. W. nodded: "Yes, yes—that is mainly so, Tom. How admirable it seems in that light, at a little distance, sufficiently removed to give it atmosphere." Then he said vehemently: "But I never, never had those curls on my head—never! The head is not so bad if you can rescue it from the curls. The picture needs to be sent to a barber. I have a notion I like the photograph better than I would the original: it is a masterpiece. Herbert has drawn the body superbly: its light and shade is striking—across the clothing, the hand: all that is done with power, without fault." Said of politics: "I have the wish if not the hope of Cleveland's election. The Democrats in New York have got to fighting among themselves: it is too bad—they must unite." Harned gave W. Dudley's love. W. said: "Dudley is probably the chief tariff culture man of the country—the marked man above all the rest in a big crowd. His lucidity: his arguments, his absolute belief that they are, all in all, conclusive: his unshaken nerve, unshakable: it is all admirable—admirable to me. I don't go a cent on the views themselves—I only like to see how Dudley sticks to his guns: I'd do anything I could anytime to chuck the whole high tariff caboodle into the Atlantic." W. today received a letter from Queensland: "It is a hello from way off in a far country: it is a sweet letter to me in a sweet class: they come from time to time—many of them: a sort of profession of faith—interesting, notable. I would rather hear such news of my book than have the celebres celebrate it. Read the letter: it'll do you good. Read it to me—I want to hear it again." So I read:

GIRL'S GRAMMAR SCHOOL,
MARYBOROUGH, QUEENSLAND, AUSTRALIA.
Aug. 7, 1888.

Sir. You have had, I do not doubt, many a letter of warm appreciation from people of eminent talent, but I am only what I think in America you call a "school marm" and of no "eminence," but I expect it's the average intellect you most want to touch as they form the bulk of the living beings. I have only had the pleasure so far of reading two of your books, Leaves of Grass and Specimen Days. They are both moral tonics in their joyous healthiness and seem to me just the antidote that is needed to all the morbid self-analysis and sickly sentimentality of the present age. I never read them without feeling more strongly than ever what a beautiful sane thing human life is. I wish, as I am a woman, you had told us more of your views about us. I wonder what your ideal of woman is. I should not have ventured to write to you only I see you are "alone" and that is a word which always touches me, specially now, when as an English teacher in a new land I am without one friend near me. A thousand thanks my dear Walt Whitman for all you have written. I shall always be your debtor.

JESSIE TAYLOR.

The Press yesterday contained some further extracts from Frederick William's diary. W. read them with great interest. "It seems sorrowful to think that he did not live to do his full work. But that was not to be—not yet: he was too good for the aristocratic crowd—too superior: was probably fifty, at least fifty, perhaps a hundred years, ahead of his time. The diary seems to me to change the face of things—of things, I, for one, have deemed settled. Some of the Germans cry 'fraud' at the diary: to me it seems thoroughly genuine: it bears the soul-marks of the Emperor. Bismarck at the start endeavored to throw discredit upon its authenticity—but he is silent now: he knows that any further opposition would be a boomerang. Bismarck is angry because it is for him a letting down. It seems that the one fact which to me always justified them—the Emperor, the old Emperor and Bismarck—the only virtue which justified, excused, explained them—is really to be credited to another." Then he did not suspect the diary? "Not at all—it is straight—it is full of light—it confirms what has always been my opinion of conditions in Germany and of Frederick." He here went into a monologue on German affairs—"the

451

cavorting about of the young Emperor." "There must be a strange seething mass back of court externalities: all official Germany is aroused now, expectant of great events. There is a vast area of unrest back of settled things we see: a vast, unseen, unsuspected force—a host of strong men and women, determined to see that things do not perpetually go wrong. This is the simple crowd of the people—the latent finally self-sufficient democracy from whom all rulers by force in all countries are soon to hear the inevitable outcry for justice. The patricians, the rulers, the kings, think they save the state, the nation: no, no—they are but the parasites—the people, the crowd, save all or all is lost. It was much the same way with Abe Lincoln here: a vast area, soaked with an atmosphere of vigilance, determination, to see the right thing through. I was in Washington at the time—heard all the dark threats, saw the head-shakings—heard the half-toned stories, whispers, disturbing suspicions. It all meant, if you betray us,—if you prove unfaithful—there'll be hell to pay—and in fact we had hell to pay, but that in unexpected places." "Now," he continued, swinging his arm indicatively, "over in Germany there is just such a vast mass of the populace back of all, responsible at last for all—at least, feeling itself so—and not Bismarck himself would dare defy it. I seem to catch glints there of perturbation near the throne: it is a power not all revealed, yet certainly not all hidden, which will one day break out in some opposing form constituting itself a menace to the continuance of the empire. All hail the people! all hail that day!"

He had read Cardinal Manning's N. A. Review paper on the Ingersoll-Gladstone controversy. He said: "What most struck me in reading it was that it was one of the most curious pieces in all the annals of literature: it irresistibly recalled Abe Lincoln's exclamation when some one—some self-important official—[Harned suggested "Sumner," and W. said "Yes—that might be"] had been in and had his say and gone: 'God Almighty has been here!' Anyone who has read history knows what it is hard to think the Cardinal don't know—knows that the popes, take them all in all, were a pretty poor mess—hard cases, indeed —what Tennyson's Northern Farmer would call a 'bad lot.' I read this deliverance with unusual care—quite categorically in fact: it was such a remarkable case of a man turning in on himself: moral, spiritual, inversion." "The Cardinal has no shred of a case left after he gets through with himself," I put in. "Do you say so, Horace? So do I: that was what I was trying to say all the time but I was so long getting it out you had to come to my rescue."

I asked W.: "Were you a trifle hard on Sumner just now?" "I did not mean to be: Sumner was wide open to criticism— invited, courted, it—but after all was big, strong, faithful, true-blue." The Century this month contains a Nicolay-Hay instalment of Lincoln history which goes over the controversy with McClellan. "It would take a good deal." said W., "to persuade me from my conviction—my old conviction, born at the time and never by any later developments shaken—my old conviction that McClellan straddled. I was on the spot at the time—in the midst of all the controversy, the suspicion, the tension and the patriotism: and from it all, fairly and sternly, I drew my estimate of McClellan. He thought, the time will come when these sections will be united again—(he saw it: we all saw it—knew it was sure to be)—then the lucky man, he thought—the man with most power—will be the man who dealt most gently with the malcontents." I said: "I do not think The Century piece means to imply that—they are not so severe: their intimation is that McClellan was incompetent." W. was unmoved. "I see no reason for forgetting or denying indubitable facts. Lincoln was not hasty in action—far from it: had almost infinite patience: always waited a long time (an extra long time) before proceeding to extreme measures. He was mighty when aroused. I have seen him both ways—angry as well as calm: more than once seen him when his whole being was shaken up—when his passion was at white heat. I do not believe that he would have taken the position he did towards McClellan except for some reason the logic of which could not be denied—some last reason of all reasons which the most conservative man would find he must obey."

W. asked me if I had heard about Sanborn's summary dismissal from the State Board of Charities of Massachusetts? He said: "He has always been very kind to me—and his wife, too. He is in the front of educational and charitable matters the world over." Why was he removed? W. guessed: "He is too tolerant, too catholic, accepts too much. There's my friend William Swinton, John's brother: I used to be very intimate with him: he has suffered from an experience somewhat like Sanborn's. Twenty-five years ago (he had been a good deal of a traveler, wanderer—was in California at the time, I think)—twenty-five years ago William made up his mind that he was going to make some money—so set about to see what to put his hooks in. After considerable uncertainty he became a maker of school-books—books of a superior cast: they really were ahead of everything that had so far been made. Recently he made a compend known as Outlines of History. I have seen it—think I have it here: and therein, in a definition of 'indulgences,' lurks all the trouble. His definition was harmless enough: to you fellows, to me, to anyone not hopelessly bigoted, it would be axiomatic—no one would dream of questioning it—but there was fierce sectarian antagonism aroused and now it has been decided that Swinton's book must go." I expressed some curiosity over a little picture of W. that I found on the table. He was quite willing to have me take it away. "It's stiff, a little too much up and down, but a really good likeness I suppose. You can put it into your collection and mark it Exhibit number something or other: if you can't call it a picture you may call it a curio. Who took it? I don't just recall the name of the photographer. Horace, I have been photographed to confusion."

Tuesday, October 9th, 1888.

8 p. m. W. reading the Mrs. Carlyle letters. Held the book sort of in the air as he read. Eyes wide open. Hat on. Entire attitude one of great interest. Light burned brightly. Saw

From a Photograph

WALT WHITMAN
(During the war)

me—laid the book down: "Howdy? Howdy?" extending his right hand. They had cleared the room up a bit today. Complains some of his eyes. Fire burns in his room. Very hot but calls the room "just about comfortable." Likes to keep the stove door open—to feed the fire from time to time. Still hates to be helped. "I'd rather die helping myself then live being helped." Brings back the long nights of last winter: the little stove, the one now displaced, never able to heat the room: he sitting here, a pad on his knee, writing, sometimes—sometimes a book: and then our talks—the sweet cherished talks on all subjects under the sun. Now he sits on the same spot a different figure: less virile, subdued: waiting in his own way for "an inevitable release." This creature of out-doors, this open-air god as I once called him to his own great amusement, now sits in a closed room, sensitive to drafts, feeling warm on cold days and cold on hot days. The contrast hit me hard to-night when he said: "Ah! Horace—is it hot here? and is it not cool out of doors?" and then further: "Clear, did you say? and do the stars shine? And the moon? is it a half moon? Oh! it must be one of God's perfect nights!" ending the matter with a deep sigh.

W. is passing through another period of depression—expresses no hope of getting round again. Yet he talks freely and with power. He laughs about that. "I am getting to be a sort of monologuer: it is a disease that grows on a man who has no legs to walk on." Seeing him reading the Carlyle to-night I asked: "Is it possible?" He answered: "Yes indeed: as Burns says somewhere of the birds, 'they flit from place to place,' &c: which is just my case for reading—getting anywhere, everywhere, something to feed the mood of the moment. Mrs. Carlyle? Don't be too hard on her, Tom. And then you know, Emerson cutely says somewhere: if there's something, some hard thing, which you absolutely don't want to do, absolutely hate to do, go do that thing, do it thoroughly, do it at once. I don't suppose it would work well to apply such a principle to reading, and yet I do so on occasions—often read books that do not particularly interest me because of an end beyond the book that I have in view: on that principle I am reading Mrs. Carlyle's letters."

McKay over today. Paid W. one hundred dollars on royalties. Had with him a copy of N. B. in stiff covers. W. assented to the change. "Dave was only here a little while: everything was satisfactorily arranged." I asked: "You didn't sign any of the sheets today?" W. said at once: "Didn't I? I did indeed —full a hundred—yes, and did them up in twenty-fives." Clifford proposes to review N. B. for some paper. W. said: "Let them fire away. But I'm more anxious to get the book to the people." "Sure—but the one helps the other." He admitted that: "Sometimes I'm as blind as two bats." Gave him a postal I had from Kennedy today. Read it aloud, slowly, clearly. "That all sounds genuine—very Kennedy-like: chatty, newsy" —and when I said: "Of course—he is always genuine," W. fervently added his assent. I pointed out the frontispiece portrait of Emma Lazuras in the Century. "A beautiful face," he said: "and a beautiful engraving, too. Who is this T. Johnson who does the engraving? He's a hummer! we ought to know who he is. A man who does work like that is our man—belongs to our church, is an initiate in our school. T. Johnson! We must ask Gilder why we don't know T. Johnson." Had not met Emma Lazurus. "I know little about her or her work: but her face is an argument. I must ask Alma Johnston about her: she knows most every woman in New York who does public things. By the way, the Johnstons were here the other day— did I tell you? No? Well—I shouldn't have missed that: I was glad to see them. Johnston is very bright—very American."

Osler has been appointed to a professorship at Johns Hopkins. W. said: "That seems like his size: Doctor Bucke says he has A one credit everywhere in the profession." Had he noticed Lounger paragraph in last Critic correcting Herald misstatements? "Yes, yes—I read it: but I did not know—or forgot if I did know—that the Herald man spoke of Stedman in that way." The Lounger put it thus: "Again it is suggested that some day Mr. Stedman may atone for the injustice he has done

the old poet.   It is needless to say that he has long been a warm
personal friend of Whitman's and a great admirer of his work."
W. said on this point: "It is of course not true—there were other
things in that article not true: Stedman has always been affectionate, honest, loyal.   Stedman wrote that piece for The Century: it was not satisfactory to my friends, but was in fair
spirit, and was the truth as Stedman saw the truth, which is all
anybody could ask.   Stedman has especially of recent years been
eager to do me any service in his power.   That Herald man seems
to be capable of doing a lot of damage when he gets started.   I
am glad The Critic saw fit to make a counter statement."

When he found to-night that Oldach will charge us twelve
instead of ten cents for the covers he said: "That looks like a
gouge.   I am done with him."   I laughed.   He asked: "What
the devil's the matter now?"   I only laughed again.   "Oh! you
think I'll get over my kink about Oldach.   Well—maybe!"   He
wonders if the engraving people are "going to fool us, too, with
extra charges."   Has an economical streak today.   I do not
take it seriously.   Told him: "You will recover: you're never
mean for long at a time."   Even the insurance man came in for
a kick.   He thought the premiums should go for more time.   I
was irritated and cried: "Keep your darned money until you
can give it out without a growl."   Then he straightened up, was
himself again, and said: "Well—have it your own way: you
usually do: I'll be a pauper yet."   "Better be a pauper than a
miser."   He was all right by this time.   "Amen! Amen!"
Every now and then I have to fight him in the same way in one
of his moods of unreasonable economy.   W. called me "an
impertinent hussy" in one of our encounters to-night.   Advised
me: "Don't let the process people dicker with the portrait:
they're liable to try to fix it up if you don't cry hands off.   Such
people never can be made to do an informal thing without a fight.
They are not willing to let nature alone—they want to assist her:
they want to give a man curls when his hair is straight or make
it straight when his hair curls—always working by contraries.
Look what Herbert did with my face when he got it over in

London: look how he dressed me up—put the barber at work on my hair—put it up in curl-papers and flung me abroad in the exhibitions as a social luminary. I should think they would like a man to come in his own dress and with his own manners not as remade by tailors and turned into a grimacing monkey repeating the platitudes of the parlors." Then he added: "Herbert knows how to paint but he has not learned that other important thing, how not to paint." As I left W. gave me an old letter from Cyril Flower and his own draft of a delayed reply.

Wednesday, October 10th, 1888.

8 p. m. W. reading a letter from Kennedy. Musgrove goes daily to post-office after tea to get what mail comes in after the last delivery. W. sat me down at once and catechised me. I picked a pamphlet off a crowded chair. It was Lathrop's Gettysburg Ode. Had W. read it? "No—only glanced through it a few pages. I guess it's not remarkable, especially in that shape, but he took it there, it was the thing for the moment—the soldiers liked it, would have it preserved: so here it is." L. had written inside the pamphlet: "To Walt Whitman, from his friend and admirer, George Parsons Lathrop, Oct. 9, 1888." I asked W.: "Do you rank him with your friends and admirers?" "He has always been cordial to me—seemed to have my personal interests at heart: beyond that I do not know. I have understood, however, that Lathrop's wife is a reader of Leaves of Grass—Rose Lathrop. I have never met her but have met and known him. Lathrop is not morbid, as Hawthorne was—is more ready to meet the world half way—dine with it—that sort of thing: is evidently a likable character. I have an idea Lathrop was at the New York reception. He was the man deputed by the St. Botolph Club years ago to arrange for my lecture in Boston—my lecture on the murder of Lincoln. I delivered that lecture first in New York—made fifty or a few more dollars from it: then repeated it in half a dozen places—twice in Philadelphia—again in New York in 1887. The St. Botolph high jinks came off in the Hawthorne Rooms—a hall a good deal like

our Morgan's Hall, yet handsomer—more fitted for culture, refinement, well-dressed ladies, and all that. It was crowded, crowded—people standing—as if all the town who frequented places of that kind came out. It was the best woman audience I ever addressed. These particular women were of the large sort—came because they were sympathetically, emotionally, moved to it, not because it was the thing to do. I always associate my Contemporary Club evening with that: the New Century rooms (don't you call them that?): the little raised platform —the people all about, men and women in all postures (a rim of women about the platform itself). That night brought into my head an old line—'And they gathered at the feet of Gamaliel.' I don't know where I got that from—no doubt years, years ago, at some camp meeting: 'and they gathered at the feet of Gamaliel': they came, young and old, rich and poor, men, women, children—he glad to gather them and they glad to come. There will be no more occasions like that: my time is gone—my time for gadding about on speechifying expeditions."

W. had been reading some about Emma Lazarus today. "She must have had a great, sweet, unusual nature. I have meant to look more into her work: all I know of her has been casual—the things that come to you here and there in the magazines and newspapers. I never met her—several times came near doing so. It may be gratuitous to say so—no doubt is— but I have randomly, wholly at random, believed she did not wish to meet me—rather avoided me. It may be gratuitous to say this, but I have had reasons for feeling its truth—good reasons, though reasons rather emotional than concrete. If she did deliberately set about not to see me she was put up to it." I said: "You are not singular in the opposition you have met." "No indeed, I am not: I am but one creature in a process that involves many." Added as to Emma Lazarus: "She was as you say, quite different from the great body of professional women —from Miss Repplier, for instance, who is vitrolic—who thinks it her purpose on earth (that she was so made—God made her) to be vitrolic, say bright things, provoke a laugh."

Asked me when the title portrait would be done. "I am aware that many do not like that picture but I consider it a hit. It is appropriate: the looking *out:* the face *away* from the book. Had it looked *in* how different would have been its significance —what a different tale it would tell! I am not looking for art: I am after spiritual expression. Consider it in that way: I am not literary, my books are not literature, in the professional sense: I am after nature first of all: the out look of the face in the book is no chance. I know my argument may be taken to pieces by the logicians but I know what I am about and can put it together again." I gave him Register containing Cooke's little paper— A Lover of Nature—treating of Burroughs and calling W. "that remarkable poet" and one of B.'s "spiritual forefathers." W. expressed the desire to read it. He had never seen Cooke's Emerson nor remembered Cooke's visit to Camden, a year or so ago, and staying at Harned's—meeting with W. there and in W.'s own home.

Talked business. He approved of what I had done and proposed doing with McKay. "The publishers have us in their hands," he said, "and I trust Dave"—then after a pause: "But I don't know—I don't know. Think of it—Dave tells me he has printed twenty-two hundred copies of Leaves of Grass—new copies. What did he do it for?" No contract exists now with McKay. "He prints editions each time upon my special grant," explained W. W. said: "I shouldn't wonder but that had something to do with it: the more he prints the more valuable each grant becomes! Shrewd Dave! I feel drawn to Dave McKay because he took me up at a time when I was very poor and everybody else passed me by. Not Dave in name though in fact: Rees, Welsh and Company, to whom Dave was really right-hand man at that time. That was immediately after the Massachusetts affair: the books sold a-hellin'. Dave's early payments put me in this house: a good lump from royalties and a lift from George Childs. I do not mean that Dave was my publisher from affection: I could not have expected that anyway: he made money out of the Leaves, no doubt. But money or no money no other publisher at that time would touch me. I shall never forget Dave's good will—nor his good sense, either, for it was good sense for a young business man to take up the Leaves while it was getting such a heap of gratuitous advertising. I had been living with brother George in Stevens street then: the house was to be given up: I was to be adrift. I had to look out for something: there were reasons why boarding was not to be desired: I saw this house: it seemed to answer my purpose— was within my means: so here I came, have been ever since." "Did your books before that period net you anything in particular?" "Nothing at all—the opposite: I got them out generally at my own expense. Then publishers went back on me— and dealers, jobbers. There's one guilty man in New York— a Liberal publisher: he knows how guilty he is: and another one over there, just as bad or worse—and then Holy Dick, to crown the pirate gang. Experience has shown me how little an author has his fate in his own hands." W. had endorsed the Flower letter he gave me yesterday: "from Cyril Flower Paris, after the German siege '71." I will include this letter and his answer in today's memoranda:

Furzedown, Streatham,
Oct. 20, 1871.

My dear Mr. Whitman: I have just returned from a long tour in Germany and France to find a pamphlet of yours awaiting me sent I hope and presume by you. I say I hope for there is no line accompanying it and yet I think it is your writing on the cover. If you have sent it then am I not forgotten.

I have often wished, I may say even longed, to have from you a few, a very few, lines to tell me of your well being, a little of your doings and of your recollection (if it is not too much to ask) of one who is always your sincere friend and lover and who travelled many a mile to see and speak with you. I even hoped against hope that you would brighten us in England this summer, but it passed and neither you nor word of you came. Many

and many a time and oft as steamer after steamer arrived I
wondered, does he come or write? Enough.

Mark you: if to you I am indebted for the pamphlet I like
it much: it strikes me as so simple, pure and powerful and
reminds me as so much of your work does of all that is sweet and
good and noble in the world. Somehow when I read you or
think of you I feel once more the cool never to be forgotten breeze
of a boundless prairie; my lungs seem to open and I respire
more freely. I feel perhaps freer for the time and less material
and then again I feel that I hold in my hand clasped strong and
tight and for eternity the great hand of a friend—a simple good
fellow, a man who loves me and who is beautiful because he loves
—and with the consciousness of that I feel never alone, never
sad—and much more I feel: but to what purpose do I write
thus?

I will tell you a little of what I have seen but it must be very
little as I only returned late last night after a long journey and
find much to occupy me. Paris, the gay, the beautiful, is no
longer either. It is terribly sad and horribly ugly. Great wounds
as it were over the face of it—ruins at every corner—streets black-
ened with petroleum. Shop window after shop window in the
most busy and flourishing quarters still smashed and unmended
—patched up with paper. Houses torn by shells. And the
people on the streets and in the boulevards no longer the Parisians of old but a sadder—may we hope a wiser—people.
So many thousands are in deep mourning that this gives as it
were a funeral touch to it all. Then the palace of St. Cloud
is a skeleton—not a window, not a bit of roof, is left of it. The
old Tuileries, too, look fearful with their picturesque walls, and
in the distance the grand, almost sublime, ruins of the Hotel
de Ville look reproachfully upon you. To me Paris was sadden-
ing—still more Metz and Strasbourg, which are alike what the
French call abimé—literally razed even unto the ground. The
soldiers, all that remain of them, look small, ill-fed, ill-clothed,
and are I heard over-drilled. In Strasbourg a Prussian band
plays magnificently every day at a certain hour but as yet no

one has been seen to stand and listen to it. Hatred is no word for the feeling between them.

The Prussian soldiers are really splendid fellows. I think you would very much like them. They are so manly and simple—perhaps too warlike, but that is of course the fault of their education, for their temperament is it seems to me very domestic and affectionate. Blind as Frenchmen always are to their own faults Parisians seem to be dimly conscious that it was Paris much more than France that forced the Emperor by its mad clamor to undertake the war which has ruined both the Emperor and the Capital.

I will write again when I hear from you. In the meantime I remain dear Mr. Whitman

Forever affectionately

CYRIL FLOWER.

Feb. 2, '72.

Dear Cyril Flower: You may think yourself neglected—perhaps forgotten—by your American friend. Not at all the latter, believe me. Twenty times during the last year I have promised myself to write you. I am still here at Washington—everything much the same as when you made your brief visit here. I continue well and hearty, in good spirits: spend much more of my leisure in the open air than reading or studying, or in-doors at all. I am very soon going on to New York to bring out a new edition of my poems (same as the copy you have, only in one volume)—shall remain there until about 7th of April—then to return here again where my address will be—— Your two letters duly reached me at the time and were very welcome. Tennyson has twice written to me—and friendly hearty letters. He invites me to visit him. I shall mail you my latest piece in a magazine to be out presently. Dear Cyril Flower I send you my love and hope you will not think hard of me for not writing before.

Thursday, October 11th, 1888.

8 p. m. W. exceedingly cheerful. As usual reading when I came. Quick to salute me and cordial in his "take a seat and

tell me what you know new." Less lethargic than for days, eye clearer, voice full. He sat by the light. Conversed for over an hour. Harned has not been in for several days. Still working on the sheets. "I have finished and done up fully two hundred of them. They're a big job but I'm trying to prove I'm bigger than the job." Gave me back the Register. Has read Cooke. "I read it—it is good—simple, discriminating." Asked what I thought of Early English Metrical Romances. "It is a text-book for me—a sort of work-tool: I have made use of it time and again." Saturday's Critic contained four references to W. I asked: "Did you see them all?" He shook his head: "I guess not—a couple of them." I indicated to him Harding's dissertation on Arnold and the one place in it in which he indicated a resemblance between A. and Whitman. W. was laughing before I had finished. The idea of the Arnoldian likeness excited him. He said: "I have not read the piece, but that is a good reason for doing so now." As to the Critic's commendation of his Century Memoranda, he remarked: "I saw that: it was well-put: the War piece will hold its own." Further, as to the allusion to W. as one of Mrs. Gilchrist's friends: "Yes —I am frequently alluded to in Mrs. Gilchrist's book. Just today I came across an old Herald—Boston Herald—in which Kennedy referred to that book. I sent it off to the Doctor: you know he collects all sorts of scraps, memoranda, anything, appertaining to our affairs: I send him many many odds and ends with that in mind. Kennedy tells me he is to review November Boughs for the Transcript." Said: "I feel guilty: I have not yet sent books to Burroughs and Morse: I will not delay much longer: John can wait and Sidney will have to. God bless Sidney!" I asked: "And John? God bless John?" "Yes— why not? God bless John, too!" No acknowledgment of the book from Bucke. W. interprets B.'s silence: "Doctor is very busy—has a hand in a dozen pies at once: gets up his reports, has the inspector there, lectures students, fools with the water meter, sees everybody and goes everywhere: and now another thing: the devil of whiskey is upon him: he is persuaded, don't drink whiskey, none of you, young or old, sick or well—don't touch it, don't have it about, don't even look at it." Had he read Bucke's pamphlet on the subject? "Probably, but I don't remember: I guess I was not convinced: I go on as I have gone on. You can't make rules of diet or rules of anything else to suit everybody. I am more likely to have feelings than theories about things: I was never a man to drive doctrines to death— to take up with fads, special providences, whims of diet or manners." Handed me this letter to look over:

SHEFFIELD SCIENTIFIC SCHOOL OF YALE COLLEGE,
NEW HAVEN, CONN., Oct 9, '88.

WALT WHITMAN:

Dear Sir: Shortly after posting your first letter to Mr. Linton I received word from him to forward the block to Mr. Arthur Stedman of Webster and Co. In acknowledging its receipt Mr. Stedman said that as soon as an electro could be taken it would be returned to me and I have seen nothing of it yet. I have heard nothing further from Mr. Linton with regard to the block —there has been hardly time—but will take the reponsibility of sending it on to you as soon as I get it.

Very truly yours

T. W. MATHER.

W. had written an answer advising that the cut be hurried a little and sent either to him or to me. Had kept letter open in order to include my Philadelphia address. Read it aloud, carefully, with fine enunciation, and in a strong voice. Then gave it to me. I mailed it over the river later on. W. said: "I have heard from Kennedy, for one: he has the book, Look at this letter: why, it says all and says more too. Sloane often writes such scratchy letters that wobble all over but this is fine and keeps to the road. Read it." I did not know that he intended me to read it aloud. W. cried: "Don't be selfish—let me hear it, too." "Why—I'll bet you read it a dozen times today before I came."

He only smiled as he said: "I shouldn't wonder but I can hear it again without hurt."

UNIVERSITY PRESS,
CAMBRIDGE, Sept [Oct?] 9, '88.

Dear W. W. The precious volume November Boughs arrived last night and drew forth an exclamation of delight from me as I untied the package at the supper table. The portrait was a real surprise, and I value very highly the portrait of E. Hicks—a remarkable face. A god-sent man of the old heroic stamp.

The mélange of the volume exhibits a range and strength that I had not thought to be so marked when I read the pieces separately as they came out. The very mass is wonderful, considering that they emanate from a semi-invalid.

I thank you deeply for the beautiful volume and for its inscription, and the good nice Sunday-afternoon letter. I devoured the new poems and prose pieces bit by bit, stealthily, today, having the book, disguised by cover, in my drawer, whence I took it out to read from time to time.

I notice a deepening shade of the sombre and of pathos throughout the latest bits of poetry. But it is better so: it completes your picture of a typical man—a man complete, clear through the opiate shades to the gates of death.

The plaster bust I still hold in trust. Mr. Sanborn accepted it for the Concord School. But as the School is closed for the following year, I suppose he neglects to call for it. I shall take occasion to speak of it (indirectly) some day, and follow his directions. The bust shall surely go into some gallery or I'll be busted myself.

I hope to write a notice of the Boughs for The Transcript.

Sorry indeed to hear of O'Connor's bad state. We all need out-o'door life continually. I am also so sorry to hear so much of your bad digestion and lethargy. Don't you think you ought to take a railway sleeper for Florida this winter?

Affectionately and admiringly your friend
W. S. KENNEDY.

W. had me read the passage about "your picture of a typical man" a second time, and said of it: "That's the truth, the whole truth and nothing but the truth: if some of the enemies of the Leaves could get that into their noddles—and some of its friends, too—we'd all be in a more amiable frame of mind and my ship would sail out its journey with less jars." Now he handed me a third letter. "From O'Connor at last! Not a long letter—but his: and that seems like saying enough. This has been a busy day for me, Horace." William's letter was indeed brief.

LIFE SAVING SERVICE,
WASHINGTON, D. C.,
Oct. 9, 1888.

Dear Walt: I was delighted to get yours of the 7th, with the welcome November Boughs. My eye is now under battery treatment (assault and battery treatment, you would think to look at it!) and just as soon as I can recover my sight a little better, I will plunge into the volume, which now invites me through a thick blur. I hope David McKay will do better with it than he has done with your other books. I long for you to have a good publisher.

More anon. The weather here has turned very cold, though bright, and I am barking with influenza. November bow-wows! (Isn't this insulting!)

I hope you keep comfortable. Nelly sends her love.

Always affectionately,
W. D. O'CONNOR.

"He is apt to go off about things in general, not to submit peacefully to them," said W. "Do you mean he is not as even in temper as you are?" "No—I didn't mean that: I guess I didn't say it right. I should say he was quite as easy-going as I am: it is not that." He stopped as if to gather the threads of something together. Then went on: "Now I've got it! Oh! you have turned my memory back to an old story. Did I ever tell you? Years ago, one day, I met Dana, Charles A. Dana, the Sun man, on the street: it was in New York: it was at a period when Dana's public utterances were particularly irascible: he was finding fault with all things, all people, nobody satisfying him, nobody hitting his mark: Grant, particularly, a great national figure, subjected to constant castigation from Dana— word-lashing: the latest, though not the last, of Dana's hates. You know, I aways liked Grant, he was so reticent, modest— so philosophical: so imperturbably accepted events, people. Well, that day, with Dana: the instant I saw him, I made for him, talked my loudest, saying: 'What in hell is the matter with you, Dana, that nothing satisfies you—that you keep up an everlasting growl about everybody, everything?' something in that strain. Dana waited till I was through and then took me by the lapel of the coat: 'See here, Walt,' he said—I think he said it almost in that way—'see here, Walt: have you spent all these years in the world and not known, not learned, (as I have) what a sorry, mean lot mankind is anyhow?'"

W. laughed long and heartily: "It is a Carlylean humor: things all wrong, a bad smell in the car, bed bugs at home, the cocks noisy next door, a huckster crying his wares in the street, a little bit put out at the stomach, a cold in the head, somebody's unruly children—such things, any things, liable to throw the balance of humor to the bad. Carlyle was chronically victimized by this defect of temper. William was in a trifling measure afflicted in the same way. It is often said: better to have this ire out than in. I am not so sure about that: I question whether a fellow has any excuse for hitting out right and left fore and aft on the slightest provocation. While it might do him good to hit what about the man he hits? Yet I believe O'Connor's abounding spirits will hold on to the last—his inclination to see a bright side to the darkest event: his ability to make the very best always of the very worst bargains. Look at that letter we have just read: he is in a devil of a pickle and yet he has the time and the courage to joke about it. You can't kill such character—dead or alive it has immortal resources." I said to W.: "I used to regret that I missed going to college." "You regret it no longer?" "I see now that I was in luck." "Good for you: you were in luck: you made a providential escape: for a fellow with your rebel independence, with your ability to take care of yourself, with your almost nasty resolution to go your own road, a college is not necessary—would in fact be a monster mountain of obstruction. As between a university course anyhow and a struggle of the right sort in the quick of everyday life the life course would beat the university course every time." Still harps a little on Oldach's "gouge." Oldach has dropped his quotations a quarter of a cent a copy—but says he won't go a bit lower. W. says: "It's still a gouge—but it's not a matter of life or death either way." I said: "That's ugly in you, Walt." He looked at me questioningly. "You mean that you think Oldach right and me wrong?" "Yes." Resumed his good humor: "Outvoted again! The decision of the meeting is that the gouge is not a gouge!" I kissed him for good night and left.

Friday, October 12th, 1888.

7.45 p. m. Reading the Mrs. Carlyle letters. Laid the book down. Said: "The day has been a slow one: I have been sleepy, tired: have not done anything—have not (don't get mad now!) signed a single copy of the elect six hundred: I have, however, read some more in the sheets of the complete book, finding no errors, however." The Standard this week quotes W.'s anti-protection piece from Specimen Days. W. looked at me quizzically: "Henry George's paper?" I said: "Yes: and I suppose you still stand by that doctrine?" "Do I? still stand by it? I should hope so: you might just as well ask me: do you stand by yourself? My ground is a peculiar one: I know nothing on the other side of the question—the side of statistics, money, politics. I am a free trader by a sort of instinct. I do not concern myself technically about the problem. I build up my conviction mainly on the idea of solidarity, democracy—on the dream of an America standing for the whole world: an America without slaveries, without exceptions, without castes: an

America standing for all rather than for one here and there. I doubt the justice, I always have doubted the justice, of selecting a few men from the whole mass of the people, a few favored men, and presenting them with all the benefits. Protectionists call my position millennial: you heard even Dudley up there at Tom's speak of it as quixotic. So it goes." I received a note from Stedman this morning:

New York, Oct. 11th, 1888.

Dear Mr. Traubel, In our "Acknowledgment" page we give credit to the publishers now publishing and selling the books of authors—the books from which we quote extracts. To what publisher, or publishers, shall we give acknowledgment, as the present publisher or publishers of Walt's poem? Kindly answer at earliest convenience.

I am delighted to hear of Whitman's comfortable spirits, and that his strength has been equal to the completion of the task of getting the November Boughs through the press.

Who writes such stuff about him and me to the N. Y. Herald? See the N. Y. Critic of Oct. 6th among the literary and personal notes.

Sincerely yours,

Edmund C. Stedman.

"Sure enough, such stuff!" exclaimed W.: "I wonder why Bucke so easily swallowed The Herald report: he seemed to like it. The worst of it is, it is so damned familiar I haven't even the suspicion of an idea who wrote the stuff. I suppose if I inquired of Julius Chambers or Habberton I could find out but I would not do that. One thing we do have to concede the scamp—his good nature: he writes in a friendly fashion: it's that geniality which saves the stuff from immediate death. I am always non-plussed in trying to decide what to do when the liar breaks loose. Shall I up and call him a liar? shall I make a noise or keep quiet? I turn the thing over and over in my head each time and always end by admonishing myself: keep quiet—and I have kept quiet through practically my whole career—almost utter silence—and have never had occasion to regret it. I admit I am not above being annoyed—things sometimes are too infernally barefaced to be passed over without some interior resentment. After a little while I will kick the bucket: then all sorts of reports, stories, will spring up." He hesitated a moment—then went on (I thought with an almost consecrating earnestness): "Doctor Bucke will tear his hair out —what little hair he has left—at some things said: and you'll get mad: but I'll be beyond it all—beyond it all." In conclusion he said: "You will write to Stedman?" and then upon my saying "yes": "Well—give him my love: tell him I know as little about that Herald author as he does: tell him I am thick-skinned (I think you can say, we are thick-skinned) and can stand all that is put upon us—the worst."

I asked W. a question about the steel plate used in the first edition and since. That made him reminiscent again: he gave me an almost absurd account of the sale—or disappearance— of that edition. "I don't think one copy was sold—not a copy. It was printed in Brooklyn—I had some friends in the printing business there—the Romes—three or four young fellows, brothers. They had consented to produce the book. I set up some of it myself: some call it my hand-work: it was not strictly that—there were about one hundred pages: out of them I set up ten or so—that was all. The books were put into the stores. But nobody bought them. They had to be given away. But the ones we sent them to—a good many of them—sent them back—did not want them even on such terms." "Yet," he said, "I was popular among some of the dealers then—they liked me. Beecher wanted to buy a copy. The dealer didn't know how much it was—asked me: I said: 'Give Beecher one.'" Had Beecher ever acknowledged it? "No—but he stole most terrifically from it." Added: "I once heard Beecher under curious circumstances: from across the street while Plymouth church was undergoing repairs of some kind: he hit me so hard, fascinated me to such a degree, that I was afterwards willing to go far out of my way to hear him talk. I said something about Beecher—that he stole from Leaves of Grass. Do you ever think, Horace, what infernal plagiarists the big fellows are—big lawyers, big preachers, big writers—even Shakespeare, Longfellow: how much they borrow and never pay back?" I asked again: "So you do not know what became of the first edition?" "It is a mystery: the books scattered, somehow, somewhere, God knows, to the four corners of the earth: I only know that they never have been in my possession."

W. said to-night that he thought he had best read Conway's volumes on Emerson and Carlyle. I have them both. "I may as well push it on to a finish now that I have started the Emerson-Carlyle business. I have no doubt Conway has much to say which it is worth while to hear. He knew both men—was close to them both. Then it can be said of Conway, he has improved much in late years—his style, his authority." He gave me some points which he wished me to argue out with McKay. "I wish to do everything that is reasonable for Dave, throwing in his way what I can: I want Dave to feel I am sticking by him." "You do not entirely endorse O'Connor's feeling about McKay?" "No—I do not: and yet William is right, too. The point is that I have had no choice of publishers: the big fellows whom O'Connor wants do not want me." Bucke acknowledges his copy of N. B. "The Doctor was pleased—you will see what he says about it: he is almost too willing to accept: I like to win after a tussle—I don't like people to bow down to me without question." I quoted Bucke's kick: "I note the two corrections (p. 37—An Evening Lull) and think the poem should have been left as it was." W. said: "I see his idea but don't assent to it. I was in miserable shape the day I wrote that little thing—was in no shape at all. Bucke argues that the verse of that day with its mistakes reflecting my unsteady intelligence was more honest than the poem as today corrected in a more lucid mood. That looks like speeding a good theory to its own worst ruin." W. gave me rough drafts in his hand of short notes (all old) to Routledge, Conway and Dowden: "They look useless but if you find them useful they are yours."

Saturday, October 13th, 1888.

7.45 p. m.   W. "in a cloud," as he said, today: at least, in forenoon and part of the afternoon: but "gathered together again" later on: "made up my mind to think no more about it." Had not been idle, either.   "I signed a good many of the sheets today: will have them all finished in two or three days."   Still reading Mrs. Carlyle.   I took him Conway's Emerson.   I wrote Stedman today.   W. has at last heard from Linton.   This is what Linton writes:

> 4 TRAFALGAR SQUARE,
> LONDON W. C.
> Oct. 3, 1888.

Dear friend: Your card to New Haven followed me on here, where I have been for some months, looking after the production of a work on wood engraving.

The enclosed letter seems to have anticipated your request. My answer to it has crossed the letter enclosing yours. In reading that I wrote also home, telling them to look for and forward the block to Stedman.   I presume it before now has gone to him.   Will you write him for what use you yourself need of it?

I am glad to see your hand again and anyway to hear of you. I hope you keep in fair health and in as much prosperity as may be necessary for the poet.

For myself, after some five years' work on a book concerning my own especial art, I am now waiting for the return, which may give me a sufficiency, or may not.   At seventy-six, or close upon it, one need not be very anxious.   I keep in good health.

Give me a few words of yourself.   The above address will find me for some months to come.

> Always heartily yours,
> W. J. LINTON.

Linton enclosed Arthur Stedman's letter in which I was quoted as saying: "The Linton cut still belongs to Walt Whitman, who gives freest consent to its use for any of the purposes of the book." W. gave me Bucke's letter of the 11th: "Bucke is no fool, as they say: is busy—head and ears in things. See what he says there of William—towards the end." Bucke wrote: "Burroughs forwarded me O'Connor's letter to you of 5th. He is a grand fellow, that—the grandest of all your friends: a hero." I said to W.: "You endorse it of course." He answered: "He is grand, sure enough—a hero, sure enough: I am not afraid to cite William in capital letters." I also read W. Bucke's reference to the complete W. W.: "Guess it will be the sacred text by and bye. The first folio of S. is valuable but I guess after a little that autograph C. W. of W. W. will lead it in the market." W. laughed in his quiet way. "Maurice is a monster boomer: he could make you feel a lot too big about yourself if you didn't look out. Dear Maurice!" W. went back to O'Connor. "I am much concerned about him—it worries me: I don't like that eye business." Heine had had a like experience. "Yes," said W., "it's that: I fear for him—fear there is something back of it." Gave Mrs. Davis a copy of November Boughs and sent one to Clifford. "It's not for me to be anxious whether the book sells or don't sell, but whether it holds an answer within itself—whether it consists with the whole—fits with the ensemble—enters the Leaves total without a jar." I said: "I liked November Boughs better in the proofs than in the copy: I like it better now in the book then in the proofs." He looked at me earnestly: "You honestly think that?" "Yes, honestly—without qualification." He then said: "Well, it is sweet—it is helpful to my soul —to hear that from you: it is the best thing you could tell me— the dearest hint of confirmation. For my own part, I cannot explain my faith in the book: my satisfaction, if I may say so, is intuitive—not to be reasoned about yet to be insisted upon. I can never accept a book for any surface importance it may have: I trust November Boughs for its long reach. If we eat a meal, the point to be considered is not whether it is good while we eat it, but whether it is good an hour after, good a day after, good a month after, good a year after: yes, good for life—the whole of life. By that test all things must be tried—will float, will go under, by that test."

Saw McKay today. Dave is still making complaints which excite W.'s resentment. McKay said W. admitted the frontispiece was badly margined. W. replied: "Dave is mistaken— I did not. When he spoke to me I may have nodded my head: when people advise me I have a way of saying 'yes, yes', as sort of signifying that I hear: that, often, is taken for assent. It is a trick I have—you know it well—of avoiding discussion when I don't want to go to the trouble of formally throwing them down." Then as if annoyed: "Well, let Dave do as he chooses: I am willing to keep every one of the books myself—keep them here." Found our title page head done at Brown's today. Brought two proofs. W. signed one for me. Looked at it again and again. "It is superbly done!" he exclaimed—"it resembles the beautiful medallions we sometimes see. Every tone comes up, yet not sharply: it is both mellow and firm (is velvet and iron)—has a quality that gives it both appeal and hauteur. Yet, just as indubitably, those Italian curls on the top of the head are not mine." "Indeed," he thought, "here is the Grosvenor gallery, Herbert Gilchrist, London parlor fellow at work." It recalled Hollyer's etching just at that one point: "It impresses me that the same hand has been at work on both. Yet the virtue of the picture—the effect of it—is so great, so unquestionably true and excellent, that this one point may be overlooked if necessary—if it cannot be remedied. In fact, Horace, when you see him Monday, say to him just as I have said to you—just these words: 'Walt Whitman never has had, has not now, Italian curls—or the semblance of 'em.' So that if there is a way by which the prominence of that aberration may be lessened advise him to have it done." He was dead in earnest about this: "Why didn't the fellow let the thing alone as we sent it? It's the old story of the artist trying to improve on nature again. The artist argues: if he hasn't Italian curls he ought to have—just as the London fellows do.

As a portrait, on the whole, barring this nonsense, it is a magnificent copy, equal to the best things they do by that process."

I had today paid Spear's bill for stove and charged to the fund. I said to W.: "If you find the bill, tear it up." He started to say: "I intended having you pay it," but I interrupted: "It is paid already—it is settled for you by your friends." He looked at me quizzically: "How's that? Who does it?" I explained: "The same people who put the nurse here." He was touched deeply. "And who are they?" he asked, earnestly: "tell me?" "No, I can't," I replied: "A group of us, a group of your friends, who are pledged to keep you comfortable the rest of your days." "It is so good! Boy, boy—who are they?" I got up from my seat and made a move towards the table, afraid that unless I did something physical I would give way to the feelings excited by his unusual display of emotion. "Never mind, Walt—I can't tell you any more about it: tear up the bill." And then for some minutes there was absolute quiet: he looked about the room and out of the window and towards me. He fooled some with his pen, which he took up and laid down. He played a bit with his big penknife. Finally he broke out: "God bless you all, whoever you are! God bless you all—all!" And then he stopped. No more was said on the subject. But his manner all the rest of the evening was more than ever affectionate—full of suppressed feeling. He did add later on just before I left: "Horace, you have done many things for me but this last lays over them all. God bless you!"

I spoke of Calamus as "supreme among love-poems in the English language." He said : "There seem to be various ideas on that subject. The South has produced love poems, songs, sweet, delicate, true: Paul H. Hayne was one of its poets— Cooke (was it Pendleton?): men of that stamp. It is a fact, of course, that they were piano tunes: still, they were good in their range. But there is a more rugged—a universal—sentiment which has most largely and primarily to be recognized in the basic big chants of the affections." Alluded to Boker: "He is pretty genuine, after all: the fellows say he holds off—will have nothing of them: but I don't know. Boker is genuine, has quality." I spoke of Francesca da Rimini, commending it: "Yes," said W.: "it is excellent: I have seen it, enjoyed it." The Critic this week discusses Gosse's Forum paper: Has America Produced a Poet? without an allusion to W.—though naming some undoubtedly inferior celebrities. Near the close it says: "The number of those who, whether erroneously or not, are of opinion that America's greatest singer is still alive and 'in voice' is perhaps not inconsiderable." W. said: "That must be Lowell—you are right." I asked him questions which led him to add: "There are some of them—the editors, writers—whose policy it is studiously to ignore me—to settle me passively by abstaining from any mention of my name. But I look upon the discussion of such questions as mostly profitless though we all take a curious interest in them."

Referring to something he was to send to Bucke: "I make one note serve for three or four before I am done with it: I get them to pass it along." After leaving W. I stopped awhile with Mrs. Davis in the kitchen. I was there ten or fifteen minutes. We heard a noise on the stairway—rushed into the hall—found W. at the first landing above on his way down. He had started out all alone. Hates assistance. He came along feebly, Mrs. D. on one side and I flanking him. Arrived in the kitchen W. took a chair. He was in decided good humor though looking tired. To me (I stood there hat in hand) he said: "Stay, stay, Horace —sit down." Remained about twenty minutes. Gave Mary some "sound advice" as to how to preserve pictures. Talked of the German Emperor's visit to the Pope. "Emperors, presidents, are humbugs—nothing in themselves, possibly much in what they stand for. The Emperor's wanderings may help along to keep peace in Europe. That, surely, would be worth a crown's weight any time. They should make their madness useful. The Emperor should go to Paris," he further said— "show himself there: see what would come of it: nothing but good, I'm sure. It is true I care nothing for him—have been thinking of him as a bad egg." How about the anti-German feeling in France? "Ah!" he said, "they would not disturb him: no man, no nation, placed on its honor, would violate the courtesy implied: the amenities due such an incident."

Speaking of the labor disturbances in Chicago: "It seems to to be a big welter—confusion: we will go from bad to worse until one day we are landed in a revolution." Suddenly he picked up his cane and made a move as if to rise from his chair. As he did so, we spoke of his coming down some day to take dinner, he smiling and saying: "That's a good idea: some day I shall adopt it." Then: "Well, I guess I'll go up to the den again: I've been here long enough—am satisfied." He walked into the hallway, saying to me as I followed: "I can get along very well but you should stay by me: Doctor is very earnest about that—'don't go up or down stairs alone' he says and says" —then went toilsomely up, I along. When at the top he said: "Well—that will do," but seemed to think further—"but as long as you are this far you may as well go farther"—and at the doorway of his room: "Come in—you are nearly there—you might fix the window for me"—showing exhaustion. Finally he got over to and sank heavily into his chair. "Harbored again, at last!" he said slowly. I closed the window. Shook hands with him again. Left him there—the light half up—he resting his head on his hands. This was his fifth trip down stairs.

Sunday, October 14, 1888.

7.40 p. m. W. sat in his chair, the light turned half down, his head resting on his hands. I had not shaken him out of his abstraction. Stood at the foot of the bed a minute. He looked up, saw me: "Ah! Horace! is that you? Sit down— sit down!" I asked: "What's the matter, Walt? are you not well?" Smiled. "Yes and no. I have not had a breezy day of it: the long confinement here in the one room—four or five months of it—is telling on me badly." Lindell gave me money for a copy of N. B. Would W. autograph it? "Yes, certainly: don't I autograph everything? And Lindell can have what he asks for from me. I shouldn't accept money from him for this book anyway." Signed the book. At Germantown to-day. Clifford gave me his portrait. W. looked at it searchingly and with pleasure. "It is a splendid face—strong, courageous. Clifford deserves to be looked at, he presents so inspiring a front." Also showed him a portrait of Charles C. Burleigh given me by Edward, his son. "Yes, that's the man: what a beautiful face. I know his work, heard him speak. I can see him now: the Tabernacle there in New York, the abolition meetings. It's the man—the same man." The subject of the title portrait came up. "See here," he said, handing me a sheet of paper: "I've made a note on the subject which I want you to take over and read to Brown." This was his pencilled memorandum:

"The head is generally satisfactory and even fine—the main *mar* is '*the top-knot and Romeo Italian curls*' (as a cynical person here calls it all) at the crest of the head and towards the forehead —Can this be *combed out* (so to speak) more in consonance with the copy?—*Some hair should be left there brushed back*—but *not* in a top knot or Italian curls—which are not now and never were worn there in that way—If remedied, corrected, *it should be done with great delicacy*—not to spoil it as existing. W. W. leaves it to you muchly—and thanks you all for the taste and care and success already achieved."

W. then added, addressing me: "Why do they all set to and curl my hair? Look at that picture of Herbert's over there now. Look at those twinges of hair about the forehead: they make me up as if I was to figure as a snake-charmer." Said again of Mc-Kay: "Repeat to him what I said yesterday—give it to him straight—do not apologize for it. You have to knock some people down before they understand that you are saying no." Was it just the thing for authors to market their own books? "I used to have trouble with myself about the dignity of authors —whether it comported well with the rest of him that an author should peddle his own books. I got bravely over all doubts on that point. My theory is that the author might be the maker even of the body of his book—set the type, print the book on a press, put a cover on it, all with his own hands: learning his trade from A to Z—all there is of it. The literary craftsman should not be so helpless with his hands."

Expressed curiosity to see the Critic piece on Gosse. His copy not yet here. "I guess the Critic people haven't much money. I always have had a soft spot for the paper—for the Gilders, in fact: of course chiefly for Watson—dear man!—and the Mrs. Gilder, his wife, who has shown me distinguished good will at all times." How had they paid him? "Oh! often my own price sent them with the piece. There were times when I named no amount myself, when they did not pay so well. Still, in the main, they paid well. I don't know who for, but they sent to me several times for written copies of poems. I did not send them, of course—it is not my practice. I did years ago do that thing for John Hay: copied My Captain for him: he paid me handsomely for it. Hay is a good friend—I have known him a long while." Who did Gilder wish his copies for? "I don't know—some lady this or that, who is collecting autographs. If I was inclined to do that thing, of course I would be willing to do it for Joe Gilder—for his sister." In this connection he had more to say of Hay: "John has helped me more than once in princely fashion. Ah!" said W.—"I think John sent me thirty dollars for one book in 1876—that was the amount?"—pausing thoughtfully: "And it was a friend in need: I was sorely down just then: a friend in need—Hay and one or two others: sales abroad of the ten dollar book—lifted me out of all the trouble, deep trouble, of that period."

What had he been reading to-day? "Not much: not as much as usual: Tom was in, brought the Tribune: that and the Press have been about all. And by the way," W. continued, "I have sent the Tribune off to Bucke—sent it this evening: and now I am sorry I have done so. The Tribune contained a piece which you should have seen: I intended to have you take it first." He described "a fellow" who went during the War "from the Southern Confederacy to London—there edited the Index, the organ of the Confederacy abroad. This man came back to New York afterwards—became intimate with the Stoddards (Dick Stoddard, you know)—and it is, as I understand, Mrs. Stoddard who publishes these notes, which are interesting and vivid because they seem so thoroughly spontaneous, even awkward. They are jotted down like my notes: at the time—or the next minute —on the field—the memory not being much trusted. It reads like this: I went here, I went there, met so and so: met Carlyle, met Tennyson, met Browning: they looked well, ill—said one thing, said another: and so on." At this point W. paused. On resuming he said: "It was for the Carlyle portion of this stuff that I had meant to save the paper unluckily sent away. But no doubt we'll hear more about it—the other papers will take it up." He considered the Carlyle evidence "conclusive." I questioned: "Has it finally convinced you?" "No—confirmed: it goes along with all the rest."

By a natural stop and transition he then spoke of Hunter. "Hunter told a story when he was here last which is to the same effect. You know how cheery Hunter is—how well he can tell a story, laugh: what a good voice he has. Hunter knows all the Scotch country well. It was in one of the Carlyle neighborhoods. Mrs. Welsh was dead: her effects were to be removed, Carlyle superintending—irascible, nasty: had an immediate altercation with the hired mover: the boss mover arrived and neatly turned the tables on Carlyle: asked him, 'Do you want these things moved?' 'Yes.' 'Very well then, leave the room—we can't do it while you are here.' Carlyle got off the scene: afterwards invited the movers, boss and hired, to dinner, but all hands refused." In the midst of this story W. had suddenly turned my way: "It's a long tale: shall I go on?—do you want to hear it?" He saw the hat in my hand—thought I was impatient to go. I said: "You bet!" Then he went on: "I consider it so markedly significant I want you to hear it—want to tell it to you. I know Hunter tells it better—much better: he so enriches it with his Scottish twists of expression. You see what it all points to: sourness, chronic sourness, over all things: nothing, nobody, under the whole heavens, worth his consideration: all a devil of a bad lot." "And yet," he continued, "I know this don't upset you: you seem bound to excuse Carlyle whatever is produced." I explained: "Not exactly that: I am only loyal to a principle which you yourself endorse." W. laughed: "I see that you stick to your point: it is a good one. John would always say (you know I endorse him in that): consider Carlyle scientifically: we have talked about it: consider him scientifically, judicially—not as if he was a man with one side only but as if he was composite." I added here: "Yes—the balance after he is summed up." W. then concluding: "True: true: Carlyle was three thousand miles away: Carlyle lived under peculiar local conditions: Carlyle is dead: such things: let us remember all that."

The three drafts of old letters W. gave me the day before yesterday were brief. The one to Conway was endorsed: "Draft of note to Conway about personalism—went March 18, '68. Looked over July 29, 1885."

WASHINGTON, March 18, '68.

My dear Conway. I send the accompanying article in hopes you can do me the favor to dispose of it to an English magazine. The one I first think of is the Fortnightly Review. If not that some other. I place the whole business, price, &c. in your absolute control. Only understand that the piece is to be published here in the Galaxy for May. Some English magazine for May is what would suit best. In haste.

WASHINGTON, Aug. 22, '71.

Dear Mr. Dowden. I have received your kind letter and your review in the Westminster, and thank you heartily. I wish to write to you at more length, and may do so before long. I take real comfort in the thought that I have such friends in Ireland including yourself. I wish to hear more of Mr. Tyrrell, whom you speak of.

WITH WALT WHITMAN IN CAMDEN

WASHINGTON, Jan. 17, '68.

EDMUND ROUTLEDGE:

Dear Sir: In compliance with request in your name in letter from George Routledge and Sons, New York, of December 28th and my own reply thereto of December 30th, I send you herewith a poem for the Magazine, if found acceptable. For my own convenience and to insure correctness I have had the manuscript put in type and transmit it to you in the shape of a printed proof. The price is one hundred and twenty dollars in gold, payable here, and I should like thirty copies of the magazine sent me here. It is to be distinctly understood that I reserve the right to print it in any future editions of my book. Hoping success to the Magazine, and that my piece may be found acceptable for it, I remain

Respectfully &c yours

WALT WHITMAN.

Advised me to take Ibsen's The Pillars of Society and read it: "Take it—take it for a long while, take it for a long while"— then, laughingly: "Take it for good if you can make good out of it." "You don't seem to take any great shine to Ibsen." "No —it seems that way: and yet I realize him to be an immense power: he is dynamic, vital: I do not seem to find the exact place for him." "But you think he has a place?" "Do you?" "Sure—don't you?" He said quickly: "Sure—sure—but where is it?" I remarked: "You don't often give puzzles up: you generally find some way to solve them." He shook his head: "Did I say I gave Ibsen up? I'm a little slower than common making him out—that's all."

Monday, October 15, 1888.

7.45 p. m. W. reading. I had a dozen more copies N. B. Oldach had bound up sixty-five copies in the flexible covers. W. had a letter from Mary Costelloe today. "I have sent it on a long journey," he said: "first to Burroughs, by whom it is to be sent to O'Connor, who is to send it to Bucke: I am sorry I

did not keep it—you should have had it to start with." Kennedy
sent him Christian Register again. He does not read it: "It
has no blood—it's like something dead." Long Islander came
to-day with a tariff supplement. "To what base uses we have
come at last! Think of it—I started that paper!" Added: "The
tariffites are commencing to raise the devil—trying to scare the
crowd, which, unfortunately, will be scared." W. said:
"Before you go open the bundle: I want to send copies of the
book to Blake and Sidney." I proceeded at once to do so.
Asked him: "And John, too—shouldn't he have one?"—he
saying in reply: "Certainly, certainly—one for John, too: John
should have had it long ago." He took the copies I passed over.
"Should I write in these?" I nodded: "Something—yes," and
he saying: "Well—here goes?" taking his pen and dipping it in
the ink. In Blake's book he first wrote "fiend" for "friend":
laughed over it: "That strikes a tragic note!" He waited for
himself some time before he decided just what he wished in
Burroughs' book. I asked: "How about Stedman, Walt:
don't you forget Stedman?" He answered at once: "Sure
enough, sure enough: one for Stedman, too." He graded
the inscriptions. To Blake he was "his friend the author."
To Morse he was the same friend "with affectionate memories."
To Burroughs it was "with love and memories." To Stedman
it was "from his friend the author" again. "With Morse's and
Burroughs' gone, Walt, the inner circle are all supplied." He
was leaning forward, putting the last book open down on the
floor, as I said this: stopped right where he was, looked up at
me thoughtfully, said: "Yes, I think so—are now supplied"—
then lifted his head. Said again: "I might have said more to
Stedman: I always feel very loving towards him: but I don't
like to pile it on to a man who may not like it. Stedman
seems to be warming towards me year by year."

Brown wants to make another trial for the title plate. Acknowledges the justice of W.'s objections. W. says: "Well let
'em try again: if it comes up better we'll be in big luck—if it
don't then I'll be mad at myself. But here—see here—look at

this: can you beat this?" Held out towards me a large photographed head of Bucke. "Ain't it the best thing that could be?—Bucke in and out, up and down: and this is taken by some little man with no reputation at all. It seems to me these little fellows beat our city men: some of the strokes of these out-of-the-way fellows are masterly: look at this—and there was Clifford's picture the other day. The city photographers like things toned down, polished, in the mode." Harned asked: "Is Burroughs quite friendly to Bucke?" W. replied: "He ought to be—I'm quite sure he wants to be. John gets a little cynical as he grows older: he seems to incline a little bit more towards conventional things, conventional people—likes the radical fellows rather less: this seems to me like giving up valuable prestige. John gets to New York—gets nowhere else: goes down to the city—sees the men there—the literary class: hears only one thing. A man who tries New York on has got to be careful: he may very easily find himself in a false suit of clothes." Then of Bucke: "Bucke's great point—greatest point of all—is his wonderful frankness, candor, openness. Gilder always strikes me as a man of the same sort: not so virile as Doctor, but frank, open—a man to be everyway counted upon. Gilder seems to be coming on: is a bigger man than he was—by far bigger than when I first knew him. He likes fine things a little too well—that's where he misses the mark: is a little too much concerned about lightness (deftness) of touch, delicatesse. Yet he is an ideal editor—he knows how to put two and two together any time without a mistake. I do not mean by that that The Century is my ideal of a magazine: it is ideal of a kind: that's what I mean: granting its purpose it's perfectly done, almost."

Brown himself to-day referred to the "Romeo curls" as "an unwarranted liberty." W. said: "I didn't use those words—yet I don't know but they're justified." Received Liberty to-day. Read the Appleton-Tucker-Morse correspondence. "I sent the paper off to Charles Eldridge—you know him?—off in New Mexico: he is always interested. I see that Sidney—I did not know it before—that Morse is pretty well committed to

Anarchy—that he is in fact possessed by it, fully endorsing it. I knew his inclinations that way but I thought he had only been touched by it incidentally—that it was not a chief thing with him. Yet I might have known better—might have seen the truth. Morse is such a mild mannered revolutionist you never quite realize that he is also very forceful—that he can when necessary strike a blow that hurts. When Morse was here last year, at the time of the Anarchist trials, he was at white-heat—I could see it: full of suppressed feeling. As the day for execution approached it was easy to be seen that he was deeply troubled. I think he was even angry with me because I did not take more interest—show more concern. I had my own way of looking upon the transactions of that exciting period: I did not want to see them executed—I wanted to see them reprieved." Why? "Well—much for reasons I would have urged for Jefferson Davis and those associated with him: for our own sakes, all our sakes—America's, humanity's. But the men were hung. It passed away: it was a tempest, a storm, furious, making waste—and afterwards a clear day. I never wished the severe penalty enforced: to me, too, it was grievous." I asked what had been his emotional experience at the time of the execution of John Brown. "About the same as this—much the same: a little stronger, it may be, but the same: not enough to take away my appetite—to spoil my supper." "Did your friends understand this at the time?" "Some of them—yes: some of them thought I was hard-hearted. My brother George was much more excited at that time than I was: George, now up there at Burlington: he thought it a martyrdom." "So did you—didn't you?" "Yes—but not the only one: I am never convinced by the formal martyrdoms alone: I see martyrdoms wherever I go: it is an average factor in life: why should I go off emotionally half-cocked only about the ostentatious cases?"

I read him a letter I had received from Morse to-day. This passage occurred, descriptive of a modeling talk in Chicago: "I modelled Cleveland, and in response to a question as to how he would look after the election, I said, 'Thus—perhaps,' and changed him into Harrison in the space of about three minutes, strange to say, getting H. better than C. Then I fixed H. into John Brown, and Brown into Mephisto. Blake and Dr. Thomas thought it 'masterly' but 'twas a simple twist of the wrist." W. did not wish to leave this till he "had it down fine:" laughed most unreservedly—described it as "witty—genuinely witty." Morse has an idea that he could make a good Whitman from a gray stone common out there. Urges: "Raise a hundred and fifty dollars and let me go on with it: then put it in Phila-delphia somewhere." W. asked: "Where? Where would they have me? They have no room for me." Yet he wished to "chew upon Morse's suggestion"—to see: "if I have anything at all, and what, to suggest." Then he asked if Morse knew what had become of the Concord bust? This led to some talk of the Concord School. W. described a drive past one day: "Sanborn came out to the carriage—urged me in—to see—yes, go on the platform, if I elected: to talk, too, I suppose: but I would not have it—not hear of it: it was a thing everyway impossible. The Concord School was always a sort of ghost-land to me." McKay thinks he will sell a thousand copies of the book, "at least." W. says: "Let him try it on—let 'em all try it on: let 'em believe there's no bad place!" W. handed me an old Swinton letter. "Read that—it refers to some old-time people: Greeley, Ripley."

NEW YORK, Oct. 19, 1870.

Dear Walt— I delivered the book to Mr. Reid for the Tribune —and had some considerable talk with him about a review article. I was afraid of Ripley but Reid confirmed my impression that Greeley is or has been favorable, and he agreed to speak to Greeley, and see what could be done in the premises. The conversation was exhaustive—that is to say, I exhausted the powers I for the time being possessed—and the upshot was the rather limited result above mentioned. In any event, if the matter goes to Ripley it will have gone to him by a friendly line.

I read the Vistas—not in the morning but at night. There are very good and striking ideas, with plenty of opportunity for difference of opinion and criticism.

Yours,

J. SWINTON.

Tuesday, October 16, 1888.

7:45 p. m. W. lying down, the first time since early summer at this hour. The light burned faintly on the table. There was an uncertain fire in the stove. Room very warm. W. not asleep. At once saluted me. Gave me his hand. "Move up a chair." I sat this way at the side of the bed during our whole talk. I asked: "Why are you on the bed? Are you sick?" "No—it has no such significance at all: it only means that it was my humor to lie down: that is the whole mystery." No sign of the Linton cut yet. Is just a little impatient for it. He suggested: "It may be you had best write to Arthur Stedman stirring him up a bit." McKay to-day showed me M. P.'s Press review of N. B. W. asked: "Who is M. P?" adding after my answer: "Well, I never met him myself. What is the value of the piece?" M. P. prints the concluding paragraph of the Hicks in full. W. said: "That seems to bear you out—they all seem to confirm you—to pounce upon that." I said further: "He seemed to know that the Hicks was at one time proposed for a magazine article. How did he know that?" "From Walsh: at least, I suppose that is the case. I hope Walsh won't feel sore to see it in the book: I intended it for him: if I hadn't got into trouble he would have had it: as it was I was glad to get it out in any shape." M. P. referred to it as "made up from notes." W. acquiesced. "Yes—that is about right: that's what I would say myself: happy me to have had that much to go by! I would hate to have Walsh feel that I had been guilty of a breach of faith: he will understand, I'm sure."

I told Walt that William Lloyd Garrison was to speak in Philadelphia on the 31st. "What is he to talk about?" "The tariff." "Against the tariff of course?" "Of course!" "Good!

good! just like his father. I never met the father—never spoke
to him—yet saw him often in meetings: heard him. He was,
yes, a good speaker: interesting: I might use that word 'effective'—an effective speaker: and earnest, too, naturally—dead
in earnest: earnestness is the quality necessary first and last if
you want to attract and move the people. Garrison always
spoke like a man who had a story to tell and was determined to
tell it: he never seemed to have any doubts about the splendor
and efficacy of his doctrine. He was of the noblest race of revo-
lutionaries—a man who could accept without desiring martyrdom: he always seemed to me to belong where he was—never
seemed gratuitous: the splendid band of his companions never
found their confidence in him misplaced. Like all men of the
real sort he was modest, simple—never had to look beyond his
natural self and employ the artificial weapons of rebellion. I
rank Garrison way up: I don't know how high, but very high."
I said: "You never associated with that radical crowd." "No:
but that wasn't because they were too radical: it was because
they were not radical enough."

Publishers' Weekly has borrowed our frontispiece cut of N. B.
Dave says: "I'll bet you my cover won't cost more than a cent
more than yours." In connection with Morse's Cleveland-
Harrison quid W. says: "Sidney has a rich strain of genuine
humor: it tells for much in an affair like that." W. complains
of his eyes: "They don't seem to be satisfied with the light I
provide for them." Thinks of having me get him a lamp to
use instead of gas. W. pointed to a copy of the Boston Transcript on the floor: "There's something in it about Frank Sanborn. Frank says they can't discharge him! yet he is dis-
charged. There is a legal point involved—a conflict of authority." Havelock Ellis in the Preface to the Ibsen book says:

"It is only by the creation of great men and women, by the
enlargement to the utmost of the reasonable freedom of the
individual, that the realization of Democracy is possible. And
herein, as in other fundamental matters, Ibsen is at one with the

American, with whom he would appear at first sight to have little in common. 'Where the men and women think lightly of the laws; . . . . . where the populace rise at once against the never-ending audacity of elected persons; . . . . . where outside authority enters always after the precedence of inside authority; where the citizen is always the head and ideal; where children are taught to be laws to themselves; . . . . . there the great city stands!' exclaims Walt Whitman."

I asked W. if he had seen that. "No—was it there? If I had known I surely should have hunted it up. I did not read the book. I looked into half a dozen pages of the preface and the beginning of each of the three plays, in no case finding myself interested, and so stopped. My impression of the work was that it was light: that may have come from the loss by translation, but I doubt it." Harrison Morris had telephoned me—could he see W. W. sometime, and report to him how the Century piece was received? I had been doubtful but promised to refer it to W., doing that this evening, W. thereupon saying: "You will have to excuse me to him; tell him I am sick—very sick. Somewhere there's a phrase—'dog with a sore head.' It is very apt: I am that dog: tell him so. He will understand: you will tell it to him kindly—for me, kindly"—then, after a pause: "If he has anything to say, why can't he say it to you? Tell him that, too." Still talks of the Bucke and Clifford pictures: "I am a little doubtful of my own pictures: after that picture of Clifford and now Bucke a fellow has got to be very careful what he accepts: he must not allow himself to be too easily satisfied." Told him I was going to have a Whitman gallery in one corner of my room. "Shall I help you out?" he asked. Then said: "You know the Cox portraits? Have you one of them? No? Well—they are not all of them satisfactory to me: I had eight or ten and kept only two. My own choice right through has been the one I call 'the laughing philosopher.' It was that I sent to Tennyson—and he liked it well, I have understood." After a bit he added: "If Tennyson happened in here some day—came unannounced—what a talk we would have! I suppose he would want to light his pipe: and though I have never smoked I would almost want to smoke with him to celebrate our meeting in fit style."

W. referred to Bucke's objections to the changes in An Evening Lull: "I do not share his regret—I am confident the piece is right as it stands. Bucke and O'Connor—I don't know if Bucke as much as O'Connor—are most severe on that point: O'Connor especially. They have eyes as sharp as hawks: resent any change of text—even the slightest: contend that every change is harmful—has been and must be for the worse. They snap and snarl like mad dogs the instant I make the slightest revision." "My rule has been," W. continued, "so far as I could have any rule (I could have no cast-iron rule)— my rule has been, to write what I have to say the best way I can—then lay it aside—taking it up again after some time and reading it afresh—the mind new to it. If there's no jar in the new reading, well and good—that's sufficient for me." Then personally of Bucke and O'Connor: "Bucke accepts mainly through his sympathy—his emotion. O'Connor does all that and does more. For brilliant mental equipment O'Connor is the pride of the flock. He has an essentially honest mind: is possessed of the most severe literary integrity: his learning is vast: probably no man alive enters more thoroughly into the Elizabethan spirit—the literature, thought, life, of the age of Bacon, Shakespeare. William can see truth at a glance—can instantly probe to the heart of experience, fact. His sense of literary propriety is exquisite—yet remains conjoined with the most thorough-going individuality." He stopped and looked up at me with a smile. Took my hand. "That may seem extreme about William, but it's not so extreme as not to be all true. If you don't believe it say so and I will tell you the whole thing over to-morrow again, and next day—and next." Laughed quietly to himself. Suddenly lifted his head off the pillow: "That reminds me, Horace—I laid an old letter of William's out on the table for you over there." I started to get it: "Yes

—on the other side—off towards the window: Is that it? Good! How does it start off?" I took the letter from the envelope and read the first sentence. "That's the letter: take it along: it's a lively letter, Horace: full of sting and sweetness." Leaned over W. and kissed him goodnight. He said: "Kiss me again." Then said, not sorrowfully, only seriously: "Some night it will be a last kiss, Horace."

Wednesday, October 17, 1888.

7:45, evening. W. reading Memoirs of Bewick. "It is autobiographical," said W: "simple, plain, interesting." "Are you particularly interested in artists? You read a lot about Blake, Millet——". He replied: "I suppose I am, but not necessarily. The book just accidentally turned up—I have had it for years: so I tackle it again. Why do I read? Here I sit, all day long, days in and out: what else have I to do?" He handed me a copy of Alden's Literature: "Kennedy sent it on in a bundle: I took it up—saw that piece on Thackeray by Guernsey—started it— read the whole thing." "Did it seem to be of any special value?" "No—not that: I got started: kept on because I got started. I must fill up the time in some way: it's greatly a matter of chance what I read: a book may turn up, like the Bewick—a long, long time mislaid: then I am at it again. My reading is wholly without plan: the first thing at hand, that is the thing I take up." Had he finished the Mrs. Carlyle letters? "Yes—and for good: done with them: there isn't the slightest possibility of a revival of interest: take them away for forever." Picked up the Bewick again: "I like the make of the book—the open page: it is all leaded out—has a liberal look. Every book ought to be leaded, double-leaded, triple-leaded: we ought to have respect for each others' eyes: though sometimes a fellow has so much to put into a book he has to forego his esthetics very largely." Again he said: "I read by fits and starts—fragments: read in moods: no sequence, no order, no nothing." Had he seen the Critic piece talked of the other day? "Yes, at last: I read it, not carefully, but clearly enough to give me its main notions. I think people generally attach more importance to that sort of writing than I do." Asked me: "Have you met Gosse?" No. "Well—if Gosse did not mention me it must have been by order." "Whose order?" "Metcalf's: You know about Metcalf? He was at one time on the North American Review—left there, I don't know whether voluntarily or by Rice's command, going I don't know for what: started his rival affair." "But why do you suppose Metcalf objects to you?" "I can say I am certain of it: Metcalf has no time for me: has always been of that feeling—was so when on the Review." "You never had anything in the Forum?" "No—never: would not send them anything."

We are expecting Bucke's visit. W. expressed interest in Bucke's report. "He always sends it on. Of course that drink argument this year won't hit me—I care nothing for it. I am more interested in the patients—their number, their work, all that. You remember, I have been up there—I know the lay of the ground." Speaks of "the gloomy news all around"— explaining: "There's poor O'Connor—I get to thinking of him days at a time: his condition is miserable—dangerous: I look ahead with fear: and there's my sister up in Vermont—she's having hell's own time, between her viper husband and a thumb she lost years ago which is now troubling her again." Asked him about the autographs: "I haven't signed any for two or three days but I'll get at it to-morrow or next day and finish the job." Then said: "I've about decided to have one hundred of the books made up at once." Asked him if he had any visitors to-day. "Yes—one of the right sort: Frank Williams: he was over. He stayed with me but a few minutes but they have lasted for hours. Horace—you fellows mustn't make any mistake about Frank; he's one of the saints of the calendar." No sign of the Linton cut. I wrote to Arthur Stedman to-day. I had a postal from Burroughs this morning:

WEST PARK, Oct. 16, 1888.

I hope you will continue writing me such notes as these, "My food nourishes me better." I shall certainly see our great friend again. I am pretty well—work now with better heart. I had a few days by the sea with Mr. Johnson after I left Camden. My love to W. W.

J. B.

W. asked: "Is the postmark West Park? I don't know why, but West Park and West Farms always mix themselves together in my mind. I know nobody at West Farms: the name simply got into my noddle in some inexplicable way. How queer it is with the mind: it gets a false impression—then there's an end: can never wholly eject the interloper." Turning again to Burroughs: "If you write to him give him my love: that will be all for this time. I do not remember writing the line John quotes, though I have no doubt I did write it. I have written him I think twice since my sickness set in: if I did write that I don't know what called it forth." W. called my attention to a copy of the Yonkers Gazette containing two sonnets (marked with blue pencil) by W. L. Shoemaker: September Sonnets: The Valley Pathway Blue. W. spoke of S.: "He was here a week ago: came up: I liked him: an old man—rather past the age of vigor —but discreet, quiet, not obtrusive." Then added: "Take the paper: give the sonnets more careful reading: they are not bad—good, rather: I was attracted. He sent me the paper after he had gone home."

Brown thinks they are making a new plate for the title. W. says: "Maybe I've put my foot in it: maybe I'd better kept my mouth shut." Osler said to me: "Carpe diem should be his motto." I had not repeated this to W., who to-day said to me: "Carpe diem is my motto." I told him I had sold another book. Laid the money on the table. "Don't let it get lost," I said. He laughed: "Never fear. I lose other things but I never lose money." He went searching among his papers on a chair near by, finally producing a letter and handing it to me: "It's from Jerome Buck, lawyer and so forth: warm, warm: he got the book. Now he writes to say how-do-you-do and here's luck! Read the letter: it's quite after your own heart. Tom

494

tells me Buck is a clever lawyer." W. then asked: "What did you make out of William's letter—the one I gave you yesterday? It was written in one of his most vehement moods. William's enemies always felt that an earthquake had occurred after he had blown one of his lambasting blasts. Have you got the letter in your pocket there?" He had seen me make a motion as though to get it. "Good! Good! read it to me: I want to hear it again." He fixed himself in the chair as if to enjoy himself and I read. He repeatedly broke in with, "Good!" "That's every word true!" "That's right, give 'em hell!" "Now, William, don't be too hard on 'em!" "Chadwick! heaven help 'im!" and several other exclamations which I do not recall.

WASHINGTON, D. C. Aug. 19, 1882.

Dear Walt: I got your card of the 6th, and duly the new edition of the book arrived, for which I am much obliged. I have now all the editions, except the second, which I hope to possess some day. The weather has been until yesterday so fearfully oppressive that I have unwittingly delayed acknowledging the book, having been almost sick with the heat. I sent a blast against Comstock to the Tribune on Friday, apropos of his threats in that paper of the 6th, which I suppose you saw. They may not print it or they may to-morrow. Whitelaw Reid being away is against me. We shall see. The article is brief, but a scorcher. I debated before sending it, holding your interests in consideration, but concluded that Comstock means mischief, and thought prudent to make him feel the talon as a warning. If he meddles with your book in New York, I will do my utmost in all directions to have him removed from his Post Office agency, and I think I can raise a tempest that will darken him forever, if I try.

It is splendid, the way the Rees Welsh edition sells. I am delighted.

Much obliged for your interest about the Florio Montaigne. I only asked because I saw Welsh dealt in old books. There has been a boom in Montaigne in late years, and it is not so easy to get hold of the earlier editions now. I have been re-reading him lately. It is immense. I can hardly doubt that Bacon is the true author—the book so fits into his scheme. That chapter, On Some Verses in Virgil, is tremendous, and backs you greatly.

I thought Gilder of the Critic was a friend of yours. His taking up for that miserable Chadwick against me, misrepresenting and falsifying my argumentation, was anything but friendly. The Index did a rascally thing lately in reprinting Chadwick's letter verbatim, without my reply. Dr. Channing went up to Boston and saw Underwood, the editor, and gave him a piece of his mind (the Doctor thinks it "a crushing reply.") Underwood excused himself for not printing my answer on the ground that it was too personal! When you remember how Chadwick assailed me as a liar, you will appreciate this delicious reason. Upon hearing of it, I wrote Underwood a note in which I gave him cantharides, or, as the Long Island boys say, "hell under the shirt." To which he rejoined in a whining letter saying he meant to do me no injustice, and would print a reply from me to Chadwick if I would write him one and make it short! In conclusion he begged me to remember that his paper was "small." To which I had a mind to answer, "Very." But I have not again written him, being quite satisfied with letting him know what I thought of his fair play.

Dr. Bucke has written me about his book. Can anything be done to make Rees Welsh publish it? I wish it could be done. Now is the time, when public interest has been awakened, and persecution is yet possible.

That is a sick article of Gordon's you sent me. But will have something to say on that point yet.

I have a card from John Burroughs on his return.

I was sorry to see the item in the Tribune of the 15th, saying that your book had been proscribed by Trinity College, Dublin, through the efforts of one Galbraith, described as a Fellow of the College, and a damned low fellow too, I should say. The news made me fear the possible effect here. Strange that I

From a Photograph by W. Kurtz

WALT WHITMAN
(1860)

cannot find the alleged letter to Marston in any of the Boston papers. It was in Dublin, either at this College or the University, that Tyrrell lectured on you, glorifying the book they now proscribe. "So runs the world away."

Good-bye. I hope to hear that the third edition is already called for!

Faithfully,
W. D. O'CONNOR.

W. said: "Looked back upon from these days of peace that sounds like the report of a commander in chief off the field of battle. William was always in the thick of danger: was always the first in and the last out of a fight."

Thursday, October 18, 1888.

4.35 p. m. Down with Clifford: first saw W. in his room— sitting at table, started into his afternoon meal. Clifford had come over: would he see him? He looked at me: "Who?" "Clifford." "Oh! if Clifford is here he must come up, if only for a minute or two." Talk meager—only about ten minutes. W. looking bad—eye dull, manner listless. He told me at once: "I am not very well to-day." As usual on ill days he asked anxiously concerning book matters. Had the Linton cut come? Asked that twice. When Clifford came in and had greeted W. there ensued a little talk, mainly about foreign visitors to America. It came about naturally. W. had asked me to tell him about Arthur Stedman. I described A. S. as he had been described to me—eye-glasses, deafness, &c. W. exclaimed: "Why—he's almost up to Gosse! Gosse wears glasses," &c. Then looking at Clifford and throwing his head back as a laugh escaped him: "Yes, Gosse—and what a hell of a fellow he is, too, to come across here to tell us about America! What a damned set of roosters come over here anyhow to tell us what we are! We don't know that ourselves! Gosse, Matthew Arnold—such fellows!" Here he referred to Lord Houghton as "a man of another ilk."

Clifford asked—had H. been here and to Camden? W. answering: "Yes: and a true man he was, too: Lord Houghton, Moncton Milnes." W. continued: "I could get about better then than I can now: he was in to see me: was plain, ate a baked apple —enjoyed it: afterwards we strolled out on the streets together. I could closely observe him as we went along: his manners— frank, open—to workmen, laborers, anybody we met." W. afterwards said: "He was a traveller—a born traveller." "It is by such things," W. further said, "that I estimate a man."

I quoted an incident of the last birthday night—Harrison Morris' trip to Philadelphia with Kennedy: M. telling me afterwards how simply Kennedy had invited him up to a street stand to take a glass of lemonade. W. asked; "That was Kennedy?" "Yes." "It's like him—it's like our fellows: our gospel means simplicity of life: Houghton was characterized by simple impulse and let it go—was not always drawing himself in—belonged naturally with the gang who can resign themselves to a ten cent meal —sit down to it as though there was nothing else in the world but to just do that: entering into, surrendering to, that." Spoke of "the indefinable attractiveness of some men: we cannot describe it any more than why we are attracted by a tree, a field, a boat, a road—only we know that it is and that is all."

W. clear, bright. Asked us about the weather, asked Clifford about his trip, very briefly—spoke quietly of Bucke's photo, which I had picked up and handed to C. He had stopped eating when we entered—did not eat while we remained. C. said he came over if for no more than to shake hands and thank him for the book. W. said: "If there came no more of it than that that would be enough: I can chew on that—respond in kind to that, at the least," &c. Perfectly frank and loving talk on both sides: a little joking, too: we all the time hat in hand— finally, good-bye: and then the brief call was past.

8 p. m. I took W. Conway's Carlyle. Found him reading— stood full two or three minutes beside the bed before he raised his eyes and saw me across the room. Then we shook hands, he cordial as ever—brighter than in the afternoon. Took the

Carlyle book from my hands—looked at picture of Mrs. C. "How good it is—favorable—how Scotch. Don't you see that—the Scotch? It gives quite another impression of her. How much better this is than the picture in the book of letters!" I remarked a resemblance to T. Carlyle, W. putting in: "I see it too: it is undoubtedly there. It is a remarkable face: a face that speaks beautiful things for itself." I exhibited to him the book I had secured from Weston: Fanny Wright's A Few Days in Athens. W. regarded the portrait in the book affectionately. I spoke of her as "evidently beautiful." W. shook his head: "No—no: she was more than beautiful: she was grand! It was not feature simply but soul—soul. There was a majesty about her. Yet this is rather a youthful picture: I did not know her so young. There were people who objected to Fanny Wright as radical and all that. She was sweeter, nobler, grander—multiplied by twenty—than all who traduced her." Then he handled the book fondly (Mendum, Boston)—looking it all over, cover and inside. "How familiar it looks, feels: the edition seems to be the same I knew: the same plates. I guess they have printed them again and again from the same plates adding this portrait." He asked finally: "Are you going to leave this with me?" I answered him: "Yes, if you want it." I knew he did want it but he said he would wait when he found that I had not read it myself.

W. still persists with his careful reading of the sheets of the big book. Is now far in Specimen Days: says he has not yet found one error—that it makes him happy to think he "has been in such good hands." He explained to me his trouble of the afternoon: was glad Clifford came—sorry he "could do no better for a talk." "I don't know what from, but my head was struck by a strange qua'mishness. That was just the moment Clifford came: the climax—the stomach sick, too—head and stomach together." He had been "a little mystified by the trouble" it came upon him "so entirely without warning." "When you came in I was just about to tackle the meal—see if it would help me any." Then he continued: "I had been signing the sheets when suddenly I gave out: whether from leaning over, turning round (as I had to do in fixing the sheets) I do not know." "The sensations for awhile were anything but comfortable—I had ceased eating when you came in. But the meal finally did the business: eased me: I find myself much improved this evening."

Harned was in during a part of our talk. I gave him Bucke's picture to look at, as I had Clifford, W. saying, meanwhile: "It is a study in shadows—beautiful, compensating: the deep shadow, and every feature shining through, clearly, vividly." I said to W.: "I have never known you to speak of any woman as glowingly as you do of Fanny Wright." He answered quickly: "I never felt so glowingly towards any other woman." "Are you sure?" He was very serious as he said: "Quite sure: she possessed herself of my body and soul: I have said much to you about her—much, much: but I have not said a word that I would not stick to—not a word that is not rather under than over the truth." There was some banter between W. and Harned over the prospective reviews of the book. H. said: "There'll be lots of criticisms and they'll be interesting reading." W. responded: "Yes, for the first two or three: then they'll be a bore—then we'll send the bore to Dr. Bucke!"

Read W. a short note I had from Williamson in which I find this referring to N. B.: "You may imagine me this evening with paper knife and slippers enjoying its pages." W. laughed: "Slippers and paper knife sound rather big for November Boughs. Why not jewel case, also?" Called my attention to a little silver knife he had in his hand: "Somebody gave it to me as a fruit knife: I have put it into general use: look at the swell handle: I use it for everything but an axe." Harned not in since Sunday. W. said: "You must look out: the next thing you know we will court-martial you for desertion." H. said that he had seen Jerome Buck in New York yesterday. W. said: "He wrote me a brotherly letter in which I take a brotherly pride. Did you see it? No? Horace, have you still got the letter about you? Read it to Tom—read it to me: I want to hear it again."

NEW YORK, Oct. 16, 1888.

My dear sir: Please accept my lasting acknowledgments for the copy of November Boughs so kindly sent me through the persuasion of our friend Mr. Harned. This expression of your goodness I did not expect nor deserve. I sought only through Tom Harned a line from your hand to place in my copy of Leaves of Grass. 'Tis many a year ago that I learned to love your noble, honest, robust nature, and the immortal lines that flowed from your virile and vigorous pen. Your poetry above all others is stamped with intense sincerity and rugged beauty and I love it for its entire absence of pretense, cant, affectation and hypocrisy. If you ever come my way I know a place hard by where a bottle of the reddest Burgundy may be found that will dispell the November chill of age and make our hearts as joyous and generous as its own ruddy hue.

JEROME BUCK.

W. asked H.: "How's that for high? Don't you think we might enjoy that Burgundy if we had it here some night?" Harned laughed: "You told me the other day that you had given up all tipple of all sorts, Walt." W. in mock severity: "So I did, Tom, but that's no reason for you to rub it in." W. said he had no idea where Ellis had got his Whitman quotation for the Ibsen preface. "I know nothing about my books: Bucke would know —he knows everything of that sort: he can quote the text like a priest." Clifford had spoken of the title page portrait to-day— that the "curls" were, to him, not an insuperable objection, &c. W. remarked: "He is right there—nor are they. I consider that portrait a perfect piece of work. But while the curls may not be absolutely damning they are an inexcusable tampering with the individual." W. gave me a Bucke letter of the 16th. "Doctor says: 'I, too, am uneasy about O'Connor!' It would be strange, so strange, if William should beat me out after all.'"

Friday, October 19, 1888.

7.50, evening. W. reading The Century. Laid it aside. Brighter even than yesterday. Asked at once for "news".

I had secured some copies of the steel print to-day—the 1855 picture. Was very much pleased. "It's the best work yet from that plate." He signed a copy for me: "Walt Whitman in 1855." I asked W. if Sam Longfellow had been over at any time during the years of his connection with the Germantown Unitarian Church. "I think not—never once. Yet I have met Longfellow—several times: that was long ago. He had a little church in Brooklyn: I lived there at the time—met him, heard him preach. His brother, you remember, came over to see me in this house. About the same time that Longfellow was preaching in Brooklyn I fell in with Brown, the sculptor—was often in his studio, where he was always modelling something— always at work. There many bright fellows came—Ward among them: there we all met on the freest terms. I have been in contact with the Longfellow circles, but they were literary, polite: I was not their kind—was not au fait—so preferred not to push myself in, or, if in, to stay in. The Brown habitues were more to my taste. There I would meet all sorts—young fellows from abroad stopped here in their swoopings: they would tell us of students, studios, the teachers, they had just left in Paris, Rome, Florence: one sparkling fellow in particular I fancied: he spoke of Beranger—I was greatly interested; he either knew Beranger or knew a heap about him. In this crowd I was myself called Beranger: my hair had already commenced to turn gray. My mother and sister would say to me: You're an odd one, Walt: whereas everybody else seems to try all they can to keep young you seem to glory in the fact that you are already beginning to look venerable." I asked him if he shaved at that time. "Very little: in fact, I may say, practically never." Getting back again to Longfellow: "No—Sam was never here—at any rate, I can't remember him here: yet away back he was a student of Leaves of Grass, I was told—liked it, called it Greek—said I was the most Greek of moderns, or something like that. Others have made similar comparisons—still others have observed what they thought was a resemblance to the Hebrew. Sam, however, was not, as I understood him, making allusion so much to the form as to the spirit of the book—the underlying recognition of facts which were the peculiar property of the Grecian. That was all long, long ago. I have heard nothing of Sam for many years—seen nothing of him: whether he still entertains those old views I do not know. That standing portrait of me was much hatchelled by the fellows at the time—war was waged on it: it passed through a great fire of criticism. There was Launt Thompson: you know him? he came to Brown's studio though not in my time. They were big, strong days—our young days—days of preparation: the gathering of the forces." I promised to bring him Sam's Life of Henry which he said he would like to read.

Clifford yesterday spoke to me of "the sublime quiet and confidence—faith—" of A Backward Glance. Harned quoted Jerome Buck as calling that "the piece of a disappointed man." Clifford retorted: "Buck may call Whitman senile and all that, but if he said such a thing he don't understand the situation. A man who can say at the end of a career like his that he can afford to wait a hundred years for confirmation is in no way or measure a disappointed man—could not be—but is on the contrary filled full and run over with reassurance and faith." I repeated all this to W., who manifested great interest. W. turned to me and asked: "And what do you say about that, Horace?" I said this: "I do not find one note of disappointment or despair in the whole book." He then said fervently: "I hope not—indeed, I can say, I believe not. But I am willing to entertain Buck's opinion—it is one of the factors going to make up the great sum. Indeed, there are passages in A Backward Glance which might be so interpreted if they could be taken as the index of the whole, but they could not be so taken: one of Milton's angels, swooping down on some desert spot—some arid plain (everything being in gloom, horror)—might take that as typical of the whole earth: but there is more to be considered than that: that is a mere speck on the great expanse." Clifford made some comparison of W. with Carlyle, which led W. to say: "I have no time for despair—not even for the fidgets. If my friends would understand me—

if the group of my friends wished to recognize the salient meanings—if they thought it worth while—I should say they must consider how much I carry in me that is peculiar, indigenous, to America—and America cannot afford to despair, to get gloomy, whatever comes to the top."

I quoted Emerson as being very much of W.'s own optimistic spirit. "Yes—he was very beautiful, very serene: there were always new revelations of it in our intercourse. Did I ever tell you the story of a visit he paid me once on the way to lecture at Newark? Emerson called—I was in Brooklyn at the time: it was early afternoon: he was free from then on to the lecture hour: he said to me at once: 'I have a lecture to deliver at Newark this evening: I therefore have three hours to spend with you.' I invited him to take a bite or two, but he answered: 'No—it is but a little after dinner: I am stopping at the Astor House: you don't want anything now? Nor do I.' I was entirely satisfied. He asked me how we should go: we lived three miles from the ferry: I answered him that I would rather walk. He was agreeable to that: so we went along in that way talking: the long stroll being very happy, memorable. We went to New York—to the Astor House. Emerson left me here: took me into the office: spoke of his engagement in the evening—of his anxiety to be on time: said that he would go out for a few minutes—see about the trains, make sure of everything: meanwhile I should go to his room. He left—I looked up one of the hotel men. I asked him if he knew Mr. Emerson's room. He said, yes. I then asked: Have you the pass-key? He said again, yes. I then told him what I wanted. He was reluctant. I asked: Will you open the room for me so I can wait there till Mr. Emerson comes? He still hesitated. I asked: You won't do it? and he answered: I'd rather not." W. stopped here—laughed heartily—took some liberal gulps of water from the pitcher on the floor. "After about ten minutes Emerson came back—took in the situation at a glance: seemed anxious, annoyed, flustrated—even inclined to be angry. I was not a bit mad myself—I was thoroughly composed, satisfied: on the contrary,

I commended the waiter: he had done the one thing the right kind of a man in his position was bound to do. We went up to Emerson's room together—Emerson still seemed exercised—made no attempt to disguise his annoyance. We sat down. Emerson said: 'We have had quite a long walk: you must be thirsty: wouldn't you like to have something to drink?' I answered 'yes.' So we had some drink together, I can't now remember what. Emerson still continued in a sort of fretful mood: I saw there was danger he would break loose on, be sharp to, the waiter. I think I said to him—I am sure I said to him—about it: 'Let it pass—don't say anything about it: he did his duty—that was all.'" Did Emerson see it? "I should say so—like a flash." Then added: "Why, Emerson had the cutest, justest, brain of all our world: saw everything, literally everything, in right perspective—things personal, things general. We got into some discussion at dinner: were perfectly free together: sometimes things would get hot, stormy (for us): we differed sharply in some things—never hesitated to express our differences—doing so this day rather loudly—more positively than usual. The question up was of national character: Emerson had just published English Traits—naturally was full of the English—English power, characteristics, and so forth. We talked and talked: Emerson inclined to favor the English—to accept them in a more favorable light than the Scotch-Irish. My own choice would have been hard to tell—I embrace, include, all. I am especially fond of the Scotch, though I can never be partial in the last analysis to one nation as above another: fond of the Scotch, who, after we admit their gloomy, despotic, reverse side, are still to be credited with some of the most marvellous qualities of which any race can boast. At one moment, the discussion running along this line, Emerson was saying: 'I like the English—I do not like the Scotch so well: and as for the Irish—': here he suddenly stopped (suddenly, as Hicks used to haul himself to in the moment of his canting spells): I didn't know what had happened. A young waiter who had been standing back of us left the room. Emerson looked at me quietly and said: 'I was going to say more—more about the Irish: but it suddenly struck me that the young man there was himself Irish and might not find what I was going to say pleasant.' It was thoroughly characteristic—just like him: like his consideration, courtesy, unfailing tact. His temperament was almost ideal." Then he said: "Whatever may be the truth of what Clifford says about me I hope there may never stray out of my work anywhere a note of dissatisfaction, disappointment, despair: indeed, I may say I am sure there does not—sure of it."

W. dissented from the idea that Tennyson's brother "was a greater poet than Alfred." "It could not be proved—therefore it is easy to say. The same thing was said about Emerson's brother. I like to hear people say things but I don't always say yes." I quoted Disraeli's retort upon those who criticised the sins of Byron: "Gentleman, remember his youth." W. exclaimed: "How good! how noble! Disraeli was a man of brilliant qualities who cannot be dismissed with a sneer." Talked about portraits of himself. He mentioned a painting. "The other picture," he said, "is in oil—belongs to my sister in St. Louis." Who was the artist? "Libbey," he answered, even going so far as to spell the name out for me: "Libbey: he was quite young—a friend of mine: Walter Libbey: bright, versatile, full of promise, it was everywhere recognized: but died young with nothing practically accomplished—not even a name won." He spoke pathetically of this episode: "The painting is even of earlier date than the steel, I think. The steel came from a photo—the photo from what would be called a chance." How was that? "I was sauntering along the street: the day was hot: I was dressed just as you see me there. A friend of mine—Gabriel Harrison (you know him? ah! yes!—he has always been a good friend!)—stood at the door of his place looking at the passers-by. He cried out to me at once: 'Old man! —old man!—come here: come right up stairs with me this minute'—and when he noticed that I hesitated cried still more emphatically: 'Do come: come: I'm dying for something to do.' This picture was the result. Many people think the dominant

quality in Harrison's picture is its sadness: even Bucke has said
something of the kind—and others, too." W. gave me a postal
from Kennedy. It read this way:

BELMONT, Oct. 18, '88.

I send you the Transcript with my notice of November Boughs,
hastily pencil-scrawled between jobs on my proof-desk. I have
really no time to myself now—except a sleepy hour o' evening.
The same Transcript contains a good big piece by young Sadakichi Hartmann. Your card just received. Thank you. Be
sure to tell me about O'Connor when you hear. I asked
Traubel to tell you that Wilson (Glaswegian) had written me
about my book.

Cordially yours,
W. S. KENNEDY.

I have received a letter from Arthur Stedman. He says he
has sent the Linton cut to Mather. Stedman intimates that
Linton's folks are in some doubt as to who owns the cut. W.
says hotly: "I have no doubt on the subject myself: just you
tell them that the cut belongs to Walt Whitman—that it was
paid for, every cent, just by Walt Whitman."

Saturday, October 20, 1888.

7.45 p. m. W. very much more active to-day—brighter, more
cheerful, than for many days. Received Transcript containing
Kennedy's notice of November Boughs. I asked W. what he
thought of it. He said: "Very much: it is short but there are
touches in it which I would not like to miss—points well to have
generally known, well to get said." He handed me the slip of
paper. "Read it—read it now: it's worth your while." And
he added: "You should put that among your papers: it is an
item helping along the elaboration of your records." This is
what Kennedy wrote:

"Walt Whitman's new volume of poetry and prose, November
Boughs, is out in handsome shape—flexible dark-red covers,

new and unique portrait of the poet at seventy years, from life, and a rare portrait of Elias Hicks, to whom Mr. Whitman devotes some pages of reminiscence. The poems are entitled, 'Sands at Seventy.' Many of them bear the stamp of full power —such as With Husky Haughty Lips, Fancies at Navesink, etc.: others show marks of the advancing lethargy of age. The whole melange is a remarkable work to have been forged in a sick room. Walt Whitman is exhibiting an astonishing tenacity of grip on life. His brain is as clear in its thinking as ever, and his handwriting bold and strong as of old. He ought to winter in some pleasant Southern city where he could sit by open windows. But as he has not come down stairs out of his chamber more than twice in several months, it is probable— nearly certain, in fact—that he would not be equal to a journey of any kind, even if inclined to take it. He is in the care of affectionate friends, one of whom, Mr. Horace Traubel, formerly an editorial writer on the Boston Commonwealth, is in constant and affectionate daily attendance on him, and has helped him put through the press the volume November Boughs and a forthcoming six-dollar edition of his complete works."

I told W. that McKay ridiculed the reference to "a rare portrait of Elias Hicks:" "That damned thing!" W. replied: "That is the business point of view: I think the head a good one, don't you? Dave is a business man, and though business men are infernal cute some ways most ways they are like tom-cats lost in the woods." To-day's Press announces a review of N. B. for to-morrow. W. said: "I am not very curious." The Times review by Seilheimer also expected for to-morrow will be put aside. "Seilheimer? That's a new name to me. Lambdin used to be managing editor of The Times. He was strenuously opposed to Leaves of Grass—bitterly, malignantly, opposed." I asked: "Was it so bad as that?" "Yes—so bad: even worse. Have you ever experienced the rankest enmity of one who opposed you with all weapons honest and dishonest without seeming to know why: with no square reason opposed you: you, you, just you—foully, bitterly, you: men who find a stab in the back none too good to use in furthering their malicious designs? I have always regarded Lambdin as that kind of an enemy." I remarked: "I understand that Seilheimer himself is none too friendly." "Then," said W., "he can give us a column of cussing: cussing is often of more value than the other thing." "You don't seem to think so in the case of Lambdin." "That is not cussing—that is downright personal vituperation and assault. Did you ever hear me kick about honest opposition? That is as good to me, as good for me, as anything else honest: but Lambdin's objections to me, like Stoddard's and some others', is rather of the offensive personal order." W. then again: "Julius Chambers used to be on The Times, but he is always exceedingly friendly." W. gave me a letter he received to-day from Hamlin Garland. "Garland also seems to have intended sending something to The Transcript about the book but Kennedy has cut him out. Garland writes a very interesting note."

JAMAICA PLAIN, Oct. 18, 1888.

Dear Mr. Whitman: I began a course of twelve class lectures in Waltham yesterday in which I take up Walt Whitman's Message. I never have any difficulty in obtaining respectful listeners upon that theme. I hope to speak many times upon it. I had a very friendly letter from Mr. Burroughs. I am sorry I did not see him as I came through. I want to say also that I did not write that little notice of your book in Transcript. I am waiting till you send that autograph copy—then I will write a goodly review for Transcript or elsewhere. I have not seen Kennedy since returning—nor Baxter. Hope to do so soon. At the earliest possible moment I intend to get that article into shape concerning your work as a landscapist. I do hope you'll keep gaining in strength, as Burroughs wrote me you were.

With grateful esteem,

HAMLIN GARLAND.

W. said: "Garland seems to be getting actively on our side: he seems to swallow the lump without gagging over it. That's the only safe sort of a rebel: the rebel who has to try to be one or wonder why he is one or asks himself if he hasn't made a mistake —that sort of a rebel had better go back home and lock his door —he's not quite the ilk for our stern brotherhood." I asked: "The Walt Whitman brotherhood?" "That, maybe—yes: but not more that than the Horace Traubel brotherhood or any other man's brotherhood. The chief thing is the brotherhood— not any particular member of it." Dave speaks of H. G.'s picture of W. as "a caricature." W. protests: "That is too severe: take away the curls, the Italian curls, which I haven't, and it's not so bad: even of the curls they'd say: 'Damn 'im, if he aint got 'em he'd ought to have 'em'." I saw Brown to-day. The title is not yet done. W. said: "I'll punch myself if the first plate is destroyed and the second is no good!" Linton cut arrived from New Haven to-day, addressed to me. I asked W.: "You don't keep an account book?" "Mercy, no! it's unheard of! I've got nothing to keep account of!" W. will send McKay a bill for one thousand copies of N. B. at thirty-one and a quarter cents. Gave me a copy of the soft N. B. for Talcott Williams— endorsed it. I looked over his shoulder as he wrote "You write his name a good deal more clearly than he would." He laughed. "As a printer I am bound to: there is no excuse for illegible writing in a printer—not the slightest."

Letter from Blake to-day acknowledging the book. Blake says: "I am enjoying Morse exceedingly. We go along brotherly. It will turn out well for him here I think." W. remarked: "That good news about Sidney rejoices my soul." I asked W.: "Walt, are you in earnest in saying you have a big story to tell me some day?" He grew very grave at once: "Yes, Horace— dead in earnest: you have no idea, no suspicion, of it, but you ought to know it all. I find it hard to steady my nerves for it— it means so much to me, will mean so much to you, means so much to others. The cat has a long tail—a very, very long tail." It did not seem to me there was anything for me to do but be silent. He looked at me intently. Then he reached his hand out and took my own, holding it: "We won't go on with it to-night—not to-night: I am not enough myself to undertake it to-night: it involves so much—feeling, reminiscence, almost tragedy: it's a long, long story: and I don't want you to know only a part of it—I want you to know it all: when I start I want to finish: so we must let it go over to some day, some night, when I am just in the exact mood to speak and you are just in the exact mood to listen. I want you to get it right when I tell it—not wrong: which implies, as I have just said, that you must be in the mood to hear right what I want to tell in the right spirit." I reached over and kissed him good night. He called "good night" to me several times as I went to and out the door into the hallway: "Good-night!" "Good-night!" His voice was full of emotion.

Sunday, October 21, 1888.

7.20 evening. W. lying on the bed, dressed, I entered very quietly: stood there without a word. He had been dozing. Started up. "Come in! Come in!" After we had shaken hands he described his day: "I have kept busy—have been down stairs for a bit, read, written some, kept wide awake." Then he asked: "And you—what have you done with the day?" I had been far in the country on a long walk. I said something about "the joy of going on and on and not getting tired." This aroused him. "I can fully realize that joy—that untranslatable joy: I have known its meaning to the full. In the old days, long ago, I was fond of taking interminable walks—going on and on, as you say, without a stop or the thought of a stop. It was at that time, in Washington, that I got to know Peter Doyle—a Rebel, a car-driver, a soldier: have you met him here? seen him? talked with him? Ah yes! we would walk together for miles and miles, never sated. Often we would go on for some time without a word, then talk—Pete a rod ahead or I a rod ahead. Washington was then the grandest of all the cities for such strolls. In order to maintain the centrality, identity, authority, of the city, a whole chain of forts, barracks, was put about it and roads leading out to them. It was therefore owing to these facts that our walks were made easy. Oh! the long, long walks, way into the nights!—in the after hours—sometimes lasting till two or three in the morning! The air, the stars, the moon, the water—what a fulness of inspiration they imparted!—what exhilaration! And there were the detours, too—wanderings off into the country out of the beaten path: I remember one place in Maryland in particular to which we would go. How splendid, above all, was the moon—the full moon, the half moon: and then the wonder, the delight, of the silences." He half sat up in bed as he spoke. "It was a great, a precious, a memorable, experience. To get the ensemble of Leaves of Grass you have got to include such things as these—the walks, Pete's friendship: yes, such things: they are absolutely necessary to the completion of the story."

I made some reference to a silent, inarticulate walk related as having been taken by Emerson and Hawthorne. W. said: "The reference to Hawthorne brings back to my mind a story once told me by a friend in Brooklyn, a lawyer, a reader of Hawthorne, who arranged to pay him a visit in company with another person—a celebre, I think, though who I can no longer remember. They gave Hawthorne notice of their coming— were there punctually on the minute: they knocked at the door (knocked, I believe, a second time): finally the door was opened by a child or a servant who asked them in. Hawthorne was not on hand at the instant but came in right afterwards with a bottle of wine in each hand—so—which he had been hunting in the cellar. He said to them that they had had a long journey and must certainly be ready for some entertainment—something of that kind. Now, while Hawthorne brought in the wine he said little or nothing during the stay of his visitors. Hawthorne was an extremely reticent character: I have read somewhere the story of his slipping off at nightfall and going silently among the sailors at Salem—to the inns frequented by them. The story has the air of being authentic—I believe is authentic."

I picked up a card lying on a pile of papers: "Charles Leonard Moore." W. noticed it. "That's one of the callers: I don't know the name—don't know him: they come in groups, often: come to the door, inquire, go off again. No doubt I often turn away angels—turn away people I would like to see—ought to see: but then, I am feeling too bad nowadays to make too many exceptions to my rule." No word from O'Connor. W. says he is afraid "William is on the down road—is not long for this world." The Press article on November Boughs written by Melville Phillips was on W.'s table. He spoke of it. To the remark that the Hicks "notes" are "disjointed indeed" W. said: "I would take no exception to that: indeed, do I not say the same thing myself?" M. P. calls the concluding paragraphs of the Hicks "the most brilliant bit of prose Whitman has ever written." W. turned to me: "You were the first discoverer of that world! And did you not say that Clifford commended it, too? I recognize only too well the scrappiness of the piece taken as a whole. Bucke writes accepting it all—allowing for no deductions whatever: but I am not so easily satisfied as that: I need more convincing proofs of myself than I find in the Hicks." W. said again: "For myself I consider A Backward Glance my right bower." Asked me whether I thought Kennedy had "sent Doctor that Transcript piece." I sent copies of to-day's Press to both of them. W. nodded: "That is well. Doctor is hungry for every scrap—Kennedy not so much so, though expectant, curious. O'Connor never seemed to care particularly for curios of that description. Doctor must have a perfect museum of curiosities—a curious mess: everything, all sorts, good and bad."

Talked of the title page portrait again. "Sometimes it impresses me that I made a mistake in condemning the head." Then he added: "In any event, if the second trial should turn out bad, we can go back to the first: I should say, take the first, curls and all!" When I originally suggested no publisher's imprint on the big book he was favorable. Then from time to time he seemed to waver a little: saw his precarious state and doubted his ability to market the edition at first hand. To-night, however, his answer to my renewed questions on that point rejoiced me: "No—no—no name at all—mine alone: this will be my book." "I sat down to-day." he said, "and codgered my brains trying to get words for the title page that would thoroughly express my idea." Finally he hit upon what is now the third version, with "complete" above the head—then this below: "Poems and Prose of Walt Whitman —1855–1888: Authenticated and Personal Book (handled by W. W.)—Portraits from Life—Autograph." "This is to be final." My previous notes show his earlier experiments. "I like it because it succeeds better than either of the others in stating the wonderful personal nature of the book. As for the rest, I trust all in your hands—you come into personal, direct contact with the printers—their shops—know what is there, what can be done." W. assented to my proposition to write to Arthur Stedman telling him the Linton cut belonged absolutely to W. W. and would not be returned to New Haven: that the Stedmans were welcome to it for use any time. Just before I left he said: "Horace, I got through with all the sheets to-day: they are all signed—and some over. I feel as if I had at last got home from a long voyage." His several designs for the title page made for the printer are very clear-sighted. They provide for everything. Showed one of them to me but I was not to take it until the portrait was ready. He handed me an old war-time Trowbridge letter: "That, too, was written while I was hunting a job in Washington: still harping on my daughter: you have the other letters—take this, too."

Monday, October 22, 1888.

8 p. m. W. not at first lively but melted out. Harned there. Asked me: "What do you know in our affairs?" The cut for the title not yet over from New York. Saw McKay and told him W. had sent Williams a book. Ordered an electro of the Linton to be done to-morrow or next day. Acknowledged receipt of cut to Mather and wrote Arthur Stedman as arranged for

yesterday. W. said: "That sounds fine—as if everything was rounding up in great style: you have a knack of doing just right, Horace." I laughed. "You don't always say so—sometimes you damn me." He was quite serious: "But if you count up the God-bless-yous on the other side the damns would make a poor showing." No word from Stedman, Morse or Burroughs, acknowledging the books. But W. says: "We've got to give a fellow time to make up his mind about our virtues." I am to get Myrick to experiment with a title page. W. gave me his original pencil design and a second design made on a copy of the rejected portrait.

Opened and read to us notes from Rhys and Kennedy. Laughed quietly: "Their letters came in the same mail—they didn't fight: you remember, Horace, that the two fellows quarreled like the devil when Rhys was here? Rhys is still with the Walter Scott Company: there's a lot of gold back of it—a great heap—and David Gordon, I think David, is mate of the ship. Kennedy's letter is long, unusually long, and gushing—gushing: a sort of confession. Why shouldn't you take it along with you and bring it back to-morrow so I can answer his questions?" He had been reading a letter as I entered. I said: "Go on with it." He replied: "No—I don't need to: I have been worried for several days: one of my near relations is in trouble: so I opened that note with trembling. The first line settles it: I am relieved—there is improvement." I did not question him. He did not say who was sick. Called my attention to four memorandums he had made up for McKay. Harned looked them over: "They are a trifle irregular, Walt." "You mean legally?" "Yes." "To hell with that: they're morally straight—moreover, Tom, morally unmistakable." H. laughingly replied: "I guess they are Walt—and yet I've known many a case where a slight technical error made where the intent was obvious overthrew a good claim." Then W. said: "The more true that be the worse for the laws! The best part of the laws anyhow, Tom, don't help, are in the way of, justice." These were W.'s mems:

I

328 Mickle St Camden New Jersey Oct: 22, 1888. David McKay Dr to Walt Whitman. Copies of November Boughs (1000 copies are furnished) 950 at 33 cts $313.50 Received payment

II

Mr Oldach, give as he requests the "November Boughs" to Mr David McKay—and he will pay you the binding—except for 100 copies wh. I will pay you

WALT WHITMAN

III

CAMDEN Monday Evn'g Oct. 22 '88

Dave I don't see how I can make the books bill any less than 33 cts (and you to pay the binder)—they cost me more than that —and *that* was what—10 cts binding—I calculated from what Oldach sent specifically (though he now makes it more now)— I have to request you will sign the memorandum and send back to me by Horace—I send the order on Oldach.

WALT WHITMAN

IV

PHILADELPHIA, Oct: 23 1888.

Memorandum

I have agreed with Walt Whitman to buy from him Nine Hundred and Fifty copies of "November Boughs" printed book, for Three Hundred and Thirteen dollars, fifty cents, ($313.50)—which I agree to pay said W W on January 10, 1889. I am to have the privilege of printing further copies of said "November Boughs" from W W's plates during the years 1888, 1889 and 1890, on giving him twelve (12) cents royalty a copy. Of the present batch I am to have fifty (50) copies free for editors' copies.

W. said to me: "You'll have difficulties but I leave the matter all with you: fight it out in the best way you know how." I alluded to Fanny Wright's book, which I am now reading. W. asked: "Don't you find something of damn certainness in it? She got along beyond that after a time: she was young when she wrote that book—eighteen, I think. She went beyond Epicurus himself and he would have commended her for it. Epicurus, all the big fellows, the sages, then, now, always keep themselves free for new impressions—new lights. Look at Emerson saying: 'This is so and so—seems so and so to me to-day: What will happen to-morrow I cannot tell.' There was Darwin, too—I always put the two together: Emerson, Darwin: Darwin was sweetly, grandly non-opinionative." Spoke of F. W.'s style, W. saying: "She had got pretty well soaked with the teachings of Epicurus before she wrote the book else she could not so well have caught the trick of his style. And at the worst, at the best, I like the style—the style of all the greatest sages—Epicurus, Epictetus, Emerson, Darwin: the modesty—the readiness to yield, to see what they might have excuses for not seeing. All modern science is saturated with the same spirit, and in this exists its excuse for being."

Suddenly W. asked: "Did I tell you fellows that I had a letter from The Critic the other day?" Then: "No—I guess not. They wanted to ask a question. Their question was to this effect: Has America produced a poet now living worthy to be added to the galaxy of the great English writers—the writers whose position is unquestioned—universally, everywhere, admitted?" I said: "That is Gosse's question." W. repeating: "Yes, it is." We asked what his verdict was—if he had given any? "Yes— a sort of one: I don't know if they will think it one." He then added: "I regret that I sent the letter to Bucke: you should have seen it." We still insisted: "What did you tell them?" He laughed quietly: "I won't tell you: I might say, it will be in print next Saturday—see it there." Who were the "assured" writers? W. replied: "Thirteen: let me see if I can name them. There were Chaucer, Spenser, Shakespeare, Milton, Dryden,

Pope, Gray, Shelley, Byron, Wordsworth, Keats: does that make thirteen? At any rate, they were named." After this he broke through his mock reserve: "I answered them—I kept no copy of my answer. What I said amounts to this: I believe we have: believe that Emerson (Emerson without a doubt) with Bryant, Whittier, Longfellow—perhaps also some of the Southern writers—writers of single poems—deserved to be ranked high—deserved to go along with the list of great English stars: except, it may be, as affecting the case of Shakespeare: Shakespeare, exceptional beyond all others—unprecedented: himself an age, an epoch: the Shakespeare-Bacon creations."

This led to some discussion of Gosse, W. saying: "Yes—Gosse: ready to pronounce on all subjects, yet himself—what is he? He is not even second or third or even fourth rate." I asked: "As critic?" W. replied: "As anything"—adding: "What has he to give him authority in any direction?" Harned asked: "Has Gosse been here?" W. saying: "Yes—once: and strange to say, we made almost an afternoon of it, and it was a good afternoon, too. I inquired of him about London matters—of the dudes, dandies, there—the literary guild, books, places. I rather liked him: he was agreeable, gentle, lymphatic: so lymphatic the lymph stuck out of every inch of his body, top to toe: a creature of finesse, the very aroma of drawing-rooms, hangings, conventionalisms, good-breeding." Gosse had remarked Poe's great influence upon English writers. W. said: "He means in technique—of all things, metrical niceties! Gosse's applause of Poe is like admiration for a shop window crowded with delicacies: is like a polite Episcopal preacher's estimate, analysis, of a Catholic priest. Gosse is like the typical English clergyman—polite, oily, sweet—oh! so sweet, so very sweet and inoffensive: like an English clergyman, a clergyman of the state church, a man who trembles before a vulgar word—for whom to go into the market, hear an oath, come into contact with the roughs of the street, is hell itself—hell enough!" Had Gosse any personal interest in L. of G.? W. said: "I don't know—not much, I guess: yet his allusions to me have been kind—I can say kind: he goes to see the Costelloes in London—likes them, they him, I believe: indeed, I like him myself. He assumes the same position towards me that Stedman does here in America." W. modified this immediately: "I mean—as Stedman did occupy: for Stedman is showing more and more consideration—has shifted his affection my way greatly in recent years." W. described a London Quarterly reviewer who had a couple of years ago "handled Gosse without gloves." "I thought it rich—of its kind the finest thing I know in the English language." Who had written it? He did not know. "I did once know—someone from over there told me: but I have lost the name: the thing was printed anonymously, I believe. It was much like Ingersoll—full of resource, life, fire: I say like Ingersoll—but only partly: this was bitter—Ingersoll is always suave, suave—good-tempered, open-armed: this man acid-like." It had struck W. as "a wonderful exposure," and he concluded: "Gosse can never fully recover from that attack."

Spoke of lack of excitement over the election: "I read things about it here and there but it is all of the hell-take-the-other-side order and I make nothing worth while out of it." Harned asked: "Do you read Blaine's speeches?" W. replied quickly: "No indeed—I've got too much respect for the clock." Then he added gravely: "It's coming about that we need a new politics—something of the human to supplant the political order: and it will come, too—maybe not soon, maybe not for some time: but it will come—it must come: without it our democracy will go to the devil—nothing can save it." He announced: "We have a new inhabitant in this room." We looked at him inquiringly. "It's a mouse—the first of his race." Asked me about the Trowbridge letter—said: "I'll have quite a dribble more documents of that period to turn over to you from time to time: so get ready." Then added mischievously: "But I forgot—you're always ready!"

Tuesday, October 23, 1888.

8 P. M. W. reading Illustrations—an English periodical.

"I have been trying to find out what it is: have got this far"—indicating: "It seems to be an advertising sheet." Talked for over an hour—one of the best, most vigorous, talks for a month. "I count this one of my very best days, taking it altogether." Gave me a copy of Open Court which Kennedy had sent on. Returned W. Kennedy's letter. He asked me again: "Gushing, isn't it? Too much so, don't you think? How does it strike you? As a confession of faith? Some one here the other day said Kennedy was no kind of punkins anyhow: I said, Kennedy was not to be sneered away. Then they said: 'He has done nothing of note'—to which I answered: 'Well, what does that matter? It's in him—he's young—as Disraeli said of Byron: remember his youth.'" Kennedy writes pointing out some spelling errors in N. B. W. says: "I attach little importance to them: I do not know that I would go a great way to correct them."

Saw McKay today. He acquiesced in W's. new price for N. B. No "fighting it out" necessary. Asks W. on the other hand to sign a paper giving McKay a right to sell N. B. until the end of 1890. W. says he will keep the signed sheets in the house and only send them to the binder's when necessary in small lots. W. is still reading the sheets of the big book. After having gone over seven hundred pages he found one error. "That's pretty good for my book," he said. I had a proof of the title portrait with me at last. After having seen that it was a success, I wrote at once to Bucke to say so and to say that I expected W. to be pleased and to spend a happy evening with him in consequence. I had ordered a reproduction of the original without any accentuation of light and shade whatever, much less changes. When I handed the sheet out to W. he looked at it for a moment with a very anxious face: then broke into a serene smile. "I am satisfied," he said. Then he went on: "What does it express? Does it say anything to you? To me it has a charm in what it don't say—because it says nothing in particular—suggests, what? Not inattention, not intentness, not devil-may-care, not intellectuality: then what is it?" He studied it that way between his own questions and answers.

"It is truth—that is enough to say: it is strong—it preserves the features: yet it is also indefinite with an indefiniteness that has a fascination of its own. I know this head is not favored, but I approve it—have liked it from the first." He added: "I think we must get seven hundred of these printed: six hundred or so for the book—a hundred for me." Then he looked at it gladly once more. "It is fine indeed: I am almost tempted to put it in the book as it is, without the lettering." But then: "There has been a place set for it and there it should go." Decided to get electro of title-page engraving. W. gave me fifteen dollars for several matters now about done—saying: "You should have that, anyhow—there's little enough, nothing, for you, but work, work, work." Then: "You've heard the story of the valet who was packing up for his master? The master asked him: 'Are you sure, now, that you have everything belonging to me—every scrap of my property?' and the man looked at him and answered: 'Yes, my lord—at least!'—and I think you should take a lesson out of that yourself."

W. discussed an argument he had read for a universal language. "Language cannot be made by Gosses—cannot be manufactured: must grow as the trees grow. I can say I doubt the compatibility of a universal language—yet, I honor, respect, the ambition of those who idealize about it. I am inclined to feel that it goes with evolution, is incident to progress, that there should be different languages." He had "no closed theory on the question." "Many whom I know—the wisest, often, of people I know—consider that if a universal language ever comes it will be the English. There are multiplying doctrines of human solidarity to which a common language would be of great benefit, but no tendency to any general convergence of tongues seems to be at present observable. I often put the case of the orthodox church in a similar way: the fact that it exists—that there are Methodist, Episcopal, Baptist churches—is proof that here are people who need something thus provided for. So I say—let it be, let it go, let it grow! Language is a thing which takes its own path of growth—may some day merge all tongues into one tongue but will not do so by an edict of scholars or a pronunciamento from the universities. A universal language has a lot to provide for—must provide for the Asiatic and the African as well as for us—must not cast out any nation, any people, however remote. I do not say a universal language may not grow but I am sure it cannot be deliberately made piecemeal by scholastic machinery."

Kennedy writes that he gets "despair" from reading Hugo—that Hugo "depresses" him. W. replies talking with me about it: "That is extraordinary: I never supposed anybody regarded Hugo as a pessimistic force. I have not felt it so. I always have looked upon Hugo as a man among the first forces in literature—in the literature of aspiration. Yet Les Miserables has a good deal to do with horror, convicts—hopeless convicts—with that phase of life. It may be that Hugo exalts, toplofticates, the ragamuffins too much. But that is only one side of the question. Hugo cannot be judged simply from one phase of his work. While I allow that Kennedy is right as a critic—sees enough as a critic to warrant that he should state his experience—I don't regard the thing in any serious light: even if it exists, it does no hurt: I accept it." W. went on expositing at considerable length, defending Hugo against wholesale charges, yet permitting slight deductions. "I can imagine O'Connor taking issue—taking the matter into his hands—defending Hugo: what a flash!—how he would flame up! O'Connor would say, Hugo's real heroes were the cavaliers, the ladies, the gentlemen, lords: in America, it was the wise, the imposed, task, to exalt the common people—to make much of the multitude: Hugo, in Europe, in France, whether to do this thing or another, was the man needed by Europe, by France, to meet a certain crisis of his time." W. said again: "Hugo's immortal works were the dramas, the plays, the poems: least accessible, yet greatest of all—greater than the novels, stories, orations. I have described to you how I used to get at them." He had no fear at bottom that Hugo unduly exalted the common people. "No—he knew what they needed: what was there to respond. He filled his place: like Napoleon with his guns, served with the set purpose of genius; all the equipment at hand: armament: weapons of all sorts: it was but for him to set to—to go on—to effect his ends. I am ready to recognize a complaint that I also may be said to have unduly patronized the masses. I have often been accused of undervaluing the leaders —of exaggerating the importance of the *miserable*—of unreasonably exalting the rank and file. Military men have often taken me up on that score—have said: 'If you will look, you cannot but see that officers are as important as men'. I might say 'yes' to that: yet I see more than that, too."

I read W. Dr. B's. letter of 20th. There occurred this passage: "No, Gilchrist has never written me; I did not praise his picture last year, and I have a feeling since that he thinks of me somewhat as the Bishop thought of Gil Blas under similar circumstances." W. laughed most heartily: then, as if to satisfy himself, went over the story half in soliloquy, with great unction, himself. "And the Bishops are not all dead yet: they still crop up to remind us of the faithfulness of the old story." Bucke had written also of the probable demise of Pardee within a few weeks, and of O'Connor's remarkable failure of the past few years. W. shook his head gloomily: "It is bad—bad: bad all around—bad news: and Pardee is a very worthy man (Bucke thinks a good deal of him, I think)." At this point he hunted among the papers and found Dr. Bucke's letter to him (20th)— saying: "Here—take this along with you: there are things in it for you to see—things about the books: Doctor often writes with great pith straight to the end." Bucke says: "The complete works take time, a lot of time, but that is all right—take time, enough of it, and have it right. It is worth taking pains about. It will be a standard book for many a day. To many and many it will be a sacred, and altogether priceless, volume—a bible of the bibles—a resumé of them all." W. said: "Go to the plate men: thank them. We will pay their bill later on but they must be thanked at once." This is the Trowbridge letter given me day before yesterday: W. says of it again today: "It throws a little side-light on the stage—helps to show you what a few of us were about those days."

SOMERVILLE, Feb. 12, 1864.

My dear Walt Whitman. I have not seen your friend Babbitt since he left the Mason Hospital (about the time I wrote you before); but I have been there to inquire about him. Three days ago I called, and a soldier who had recently seen him reported him as gradually regaining his strength, though not his voice. He is able to go out a little. He is with, or near, some good friends of his, who are no doubt a comfort to him.

What you write me of yourself and of your experiences, interests me, and makes me almost envy you the privilege of being with our noble unfortunate soldiers. You ought to write the epic of this war. By the way, has anything been done with Drum Taps? O'Connor said he would communicate with Carleton on the subject. I have spoken to one publisher here about them; but he did not bite.

An item of great domestic importance to us will perhaps interest you. A boy was born to me yesterday—a lusty little chap, fat, well-formed, weight ten pounds. Mother doing well thus far. I have seen the new moon over my right shoulder to some purpose lately.

A few days ago I wrote a letter about you to Secretary Chase. I hope you will yet hear from him. He acknowledged at the time the receipt of the book you handed him; so I knew the package must have reached you. I am heartily glad if the books have been put to any use. How is your friend Brown who was to lose his foot?

Give my love to the O'Connors.

Good bye. Your friend,
J. T. TROWBRIDGE.

Wednesday, October 24, 1888.

8 P. M. When I called, found the vestibule door unfastened and apparently no one about—neither nurse nor Mrs. Davis nor

any other. W. reading when I entered. Shook hands and asked me at once: "How did you get in ?—was the door open ?" and then: "Mr. Musgrove went away several hours ago—has not appeared since—so I sent Mary to the postoffice." I had never heard him in all the months before express any desire for the presence of a nurse—even care where the nurse might be—but this evening he said: "I do not like his staying so long and saying nothing: when he goes off for any length of time he should leave word,"—not disagreeably said, or irritatedly. He insists on that evening mail: it is always a matter of greatest interest to him. Mrs. Davis entered a few minutes after to say there was nothing. He was satisfied. Said there had been no mail to-day anyhow—not a letter, not a paper—"no letter even from Bucke." Still professes great satisfaction with the little picture.

McKay has sent copies of N. B. to some papers. W. said: "I don't attach much importance to sending the book broadcast: a half dozen papers in New York, wisely chosen—they seem to be required—and one or two in Boston and Philadelphia and Chicago: why should we go farther than that? There will be enough reviews and to spare by and bye—at the best they offer no attraction to me. I do not agree with Dave that the book will sell: it may have a purchaser here or there but will get no vogue. I never have sold to any extent except on the two or three occasions when the law got after me and stirred up a sort of indecent curiosity concerning my work. In the case of the big book my design is to get everything safely into authentic shape before speculating upon the money returns. Bucke calls this my 'bible.' Call it that—call it anything: it is important for me just now to get it out, leaving its fate to the world. My anxiety is all centered at one spot—to get the job well done before I receive another blow between the eyes making any further literary work altogether impossible." "You have said you didn't believe you would ever receive such a blow." "Yes—so I have—and I still say so: but I want to provide for the other contingency." Showed him another proof of title page text. He liked its general appearance. He regarded it dubiously at one spot. Pointing with his finger to the lines below the portrait, "authenticated," &c., he asked: "Didn't I have the word 'revisions' there in the copy? Was it not there?" then answering himself: "Yet I guess not." I said: "Well—put it in now." He hesitated a minute, looked at me, then shook his head: "No: if it was there I might say it should stay there, but as it is not there I am not moved to insert it." Then asked about the line "Walt Whitman": "Is it too big?" Finally satisfied with it.

Mentioned Lippincott's. "The whole of that Rebel editor's diary appears in the November issue. I sent it to Dr. Bucke—tore out the leaves: rolled the rest of the magazine up with some other papers and mailed it to the Asylum. You know, I send a bundle of stuff—papers, odds and ends—every week." He pointed across the room to the trunk: "You might throw those leaves out in the hall-way: they commence to smell rather strong: Musgrove objects to them strongly—I suppose I should yield: but I like anything that savors of the open air—flowers, anything. Some one kindly brought that bunch of green in the other day: I have derived great pleasure from it." W. is worried some over O'Connor. "I'm afraid something pretty serious is the matter with him: Bucke is down in the mouth about it all: Bucke is very shrewd—knows. I look into my mail hoping to get some intelligence to cheer me but the chances of that are very slight." He turned to the table picked up a letter written so faintly with thin ink it was almost impossible to decipher. "What do you think of that?" Then leaned over and pushed books and papers about on the floor until he found an envelope addressed in his own hand and postmarked "Burlington, Vermont." "Is there any excuse for that going wrong?" he asked, and indeed there was not. "Yet it went to Englewood and came here a day or two belated marked 'Missent.' It is about my dear sister at Burlington. Doctor handed me the letter while you were here: I opened it just after you had gone—hurried as best I could to the door to call you back, thought you could read it for me: but you had got away. So Mary came up: she has cute eyes: she read it for me—studied it out. It is written by a woman who helps my sister: my sister has jaundice —is in bed—can do little for herself: I have been in a great worry about her." Here he picked up the letter again: "And then this letter is very indefinite, too: I sent some money and other things I wished her to have—but there is no word of acknowledgment here."

He returned me this evening the Mrs. Carlyle letters and two volumes of the Emerson-Carlyle correspondence—third volume missing; could not with his "best efforts hit upon it in the mess on the floor." Tom Harned had said something about reading them. W. said: "Let him go at it: it's a great mixture—there are a great many things in that pot." He is "glad" he has "taken it all in now that it is done." I asked if he had yet examined the Conway books. "Yes, I have read them—as much of them as I care to: they're too much in the essay line to suit me. Conway always excites both my interest and my suspicion." We spoke of the "Hobby Horse Guild" periodical which I casually picked up from the floor. "It's whole virtue is in the printing and paper," he believed: "See the printing! and this paper"—feeling it: "As for the matter, it's poor enough, I guess: I do not read it." He pointed to a picture—Rene's Honeymoon: "See this—see the pictures: what are they? Not for us, at any rate. But as for paper and printing—where can we find another periodical like it: where such splendid paper, such press work? Surely not in America. The book is produced by a circle of young fellows over there—artists, writers: seems to me to show some color of affectation—style." He asked me further whether I didn't think anyhow that "the English artists are bitten with the ambition of richness, luxury?" "Yet these fellows," he reflected again, "are most of them poor enough, I guess; work for a living, some or all of them—get pay for all their work." "Was William Morris one of them?" he questioned himself. I doubted, and he said: "He appears at times —you'll find his name in some of the numbers: if not one of them, they hang on to the tail of his coat, anyhow." He referred to Rhys. "I don't think he mingles with that crowd: his circle is quite another: he gets into generally wholesome connections." A little later in my stay W. handed me an English letter with the remark: "You will like to see this." He had drawn his blue pencil across both pages. Laughed. "It seemed such a nice sheet of paper I thought I would use the back of it for something or other: afterwards it occurred to me that the letter really belonged to you: now you have it. It came from that Hobby Horse crowd we have just been talking about." This is the letter.

LONDON, Oct. 1, 1888.

Dear Mr. Whitman—I have asked our new agents for America to send you a copy of the October number of the Hobby Horse, hoping you may find something in it to interest you.

I am glad to hear from Mrs. Costelloe that you have recovered from your late illness. Ernest Rhys, who is now away in Wales, brought back golden accounts of the delightful time he had in America and during his stay with you.

I do not know if you write much fresh work now. But if you would see your way to send us some little contribution of your own for our Magazine, nothing would give us greater pleasure. Unlike in so many ways as our own efforts may seem to your poetry, we have a *very* genuine and great admiration for your work, and to see your name on our pages, although the contribution be only a few lines, we should regard as a distinct privilege. I believe you are aware that the Hobby Horse is entirely a labor of love.

Now that Herbert Gilchrist is in Philadelphia I suppose you see him often. Pray give my love to him and say I am expecting a letter saying where I may write to him.

Sincerely yours,

HERBERT P. HORNE.

I said to W.: "That don't sound degenerate." "Did I say degenerate? Hardly: that certainly would not be the word: I

would say, rather—disciples of finesse—advocates of taste, laces,
bindings, ornamentation—protagonists of filigree: tailor-men—
an estheticism that far from meaning beauty means to me only a
sickly sweetness: that's more what I meant." No word to
either of us about N. B. from Burroughs, Morse, Stedman or T.
Williams. W. said last: "How can I ever pay my debt to you?"
I asked in return: "How can I ever pay my debt to you?" He
took my hand, pressed it—then said: "How can we?" I finally
suggested: "Let's pair off and say no more about it either side."
He nodded a smiling assent: "You have a way sometimes of
settling my difficulties for me. Yes, let's pair off." "It's easy
for love to pair off," I said. He added: "It's easy for love to
do miracles!"

Thursday, October 25, 1888.

7.50 p. m. W. reading. Laid his book down. Looked
mighty well. "Yes—I'm a trifle chipper—better than on some
of those summer days, anyhow." Brought along the remaining
copies of flexible N. B. Piled them with the others on the floor.
W. at once said: "I have a letter from Hamlin Garland: he
got the book (you know I sent him a book): is grateful for it—
all that: has been spending an afternoon with Howells—thought
Howells should have a copy." I asked: "Did you send him
one?" "Yes—addressed it to a little place—Nahant." "Have
you ever been in affectionate relations with Howells?" "No—
not affectionate: not that: but friendly—always friendly. You
remember the St. Botolph Lincoln affair in Boston? I was in
Boston that time for a week—put up at the Revere House:
Howells came to see me there—was happy, cordial: came a
number of times." "Was he a good talker?" "That I could
not say: we had no real chance to get thoroughly acquainted
then: I think I would get along better with him now. That
was before I came into this house—probably '79 or '80. I have
it in my memorandum book here—the date: can get it if we
need to. It was quite an occasion: everybody came: all the
lights—the literary luminaries. Aldrich? Yes, he came, too.

I had a sort of reception time set—an hour or two when I had it made known these visits would be agreeable—say, between eleven and one or two: and they came—had the entree: came with a vengeance. It had to be gone through with but it seemed like a lot of fol-de-rol. I guess I made it evident I wouldn't turn a damned inch on my heel for any of them." I asked if he had autographed the book he sent to Howells. "No—I did not: did not write a word in it: made up the package, addressed it simply: the Doctor has just taken it to the post-office. Howells will know who it is from: no doubt Garland will take care of that—has doubtless written to him and led him to expect it." Handed me Garland's letter:

JAMAICA PLAIN,
Oct. 24, '88.

Dear Mr. Whitman: I am overjoyed to receive your volume and autograph. Be sure it will be read and heralded to the world. I saw Mr. Howells yesterday—spent the afternoon with him discussing reforms, literary progress, etc. He spoke of you again with a good deal of feeling. I think it of very great importance that you send him an autograph copy of November Boughs. If it has not been done don't fail to do it at once. If you send it immediately upon receipt of this letter address W. D. Howells, Little Nahant, Mass. If you do not send until next week address W. D. Howells, 330 East 17th st., New York City. And I will write him again about it. He is more than friendly to you and all progressive movements.

With deepest regard—

HAMLIN GARLAND.

W. said of the letter: "Take it—keep it: if there's anything in it I have forgotten about tell me. See—it's written only on one side: how good that is! that's my method: I rarely write on the reverse side of the sheet. I find no difficulty with Garland's handwriting—I like the swing of it." We had spoken of Aldrich. W. took up the subject again: "Aldrich always brings back to me with great force Nat Willis: I knew Willis—met and talked with him often. Everything with Nat was polish, grace, beauty. He was a handsome man—stately, impressive: when young, beautiful—though of a beauty I did not, you would not, like. Nat was really a dandy—yet not simply or only a dandy: neither was he a man of power: he was a man we could not leave out altogether—could not entirely skip: that's about the most, best, I could say of him. He was agreeable—we got on well together: but God help me what a contrast we must have presented!"

W. handed me a copy of the Springfield Republican containing a notice of November Boughs, "They are all friendly up there. I want to tell you what to do with that: take it with you, show it to Dave, then"—I finished the sentence for him: "Mail it to Bucke." He laughed. "I see you know without my telling you. Well, do it that way. Tell Dave, too, that I have myself sent out half a dozen editors' copies." In reply to my expressed suspicion that there was someone on the Christian Union interested in ignoring him W. said: "I don't know who it can be: it can't be Lyman Abbott: Lyman Abbott was always friendly to me—to Leaves of Grass. I know that is the policy of some of the editors but there's no use objecting to it—that's just as legitimate as endorsing us: we must excuse it—it's their way: they think they are in honor bound to pursue that policy. Society would go to pieces if its guardians didn't protect it against the inroads of rebellion."

We discussed Bucke's reference to his re-reading of Cooper. W. expressed great interest, especially after I told him Cooper was just as fresh as ever to me. Questioned me closely. How was I impressed with Cooper's "outdoorness"—and so forth? Then: "I do not wonder that he lasts—that you still find yourself drawn to him. He is justified by what you say: Cooper was a master-man in many very significant ways. Cooper had a growl—the cynicism of Carlyle, without the top-lofticalness with which Carlyle carried it off: and there was a healthy vigor in everything Cooper did—even to the libel suits he had so many of, up in New York. I always liked the make-up of the man.

Cooper could take his own part magnificently: let a scribbler go for him and Cooper would hit back, with great effect—sued, went to court. Cooper knew law even if he was not a lawyer, and was pretty keen in his perception of legal propositions. Have you got the Cooper stories: the Leatherstocking tales? The Last of the Mohicans, chiefly?—and The Wept of Wish-ton-Wish? Can you bring me that? It is beautiful indeed: and The Bravo, too—I remember that: the wonderful, splendid Jacopo—who can forget him? It is years and years since I read Cooper: now the mood comes back to me, I should like to take him up again." He asked me: "Do you ever find Cooper long-winded—tiresome? I have always regarded Cooper as essentially fresh, robust, noble: one of the original characters—the tonic natures. Over in England, among the fellows, there's a word they use—'guts': if a man is a man of power they say he has 'guts'. I think Herbert brought the word to me: that was the first I heard of it. Well—Cooper has guts. I never met Cooper—I never met him to talk with: at least I think I did not; but I heard him. He was a good, sturdy, man in appearance: had the appearance of a farmer—a brainy farmer: not very tall, not very stout: good belly—carried himself well. Unlike Irving, Cooper had a remarkable personality, and, as I have said, he had Carlyle's cynicism to some extent, though he was never gloomy—was always as strong and sweet as sunlight. Irving, on the other hand, suggested weakness, if he was not weak: was pleasant, as you say, but without background. I never enthused over him: Irving was suckled on the Addisonian-Oxford-Cambridge milk."

I quoted something Bryant said about Cooper—that he was "our first man," &c. W. said: "Ah! Bryant! did he say that? Bryant is himself the man! Of all Americans so far, I am inclined to rank Bryant highest. Bryant has all that was knotty, gnarled, in Dante, Carlyle: besides that, has great other qualities. It has always seemed to me Bryant, more than any other American, had the power to suck in the air of spring, to put it into his song, to breathe it forth again—the palpable influence of spring: the new entrance to life. A feature in Bryant which is never to be under-weighed is the marvelous purity of his work in verse. It was severe—oh! so severe!—never a waste word— the last superfluity struck off: a clear nameless beauty pervading and overarching all the work of his pen. Bryant the man I met often—often. He was not much of a talker, would not impress or attract as such. His voice was a good one—not deep —not fascinating—not moving, eloquent. Bryant tried lectur- ing. He was a great homeopathist—a great Unitarian: at the time of the homeopathic excitement he delivered two or three lectures on the subject. But I don't think he liked lecturing himself, and he did not prove a success with others. He was an American: that is one of the palpable facts: thoroughly Amer- ican, patriotic: moreover, he had a tint of the Scotch left—a trifle hypochondriac—a bit irascible. I have often observed marked traces running through the Scotch character of general hypochrondriacism: Burns? yes: and Carlyle. Bryant bore the marks of it. I know it is not invariable: there are exceptions: but in the main its existence cannot be questioned."

W. led the way at this point to his Critic note weighing the relative merits of our great poets. "Of late days I have put Bryant first of the four: Bryant, Emerson, Whittier, Longfellow: in that order. The Critic piece will show. You put Emerson first? So did I, years ago—for many years—but I have been led to make a change. But my revisions of old opinions are con- stant, so that perhaps I shall revise the list again before I am done for. At any rate, I feel the uncertainties attending this method of reasoning—its unprofitableness—and how can an end even be reached?—then it is true, what you say, Horace: among the giants, what matters a little more or less—who can draw a line?" I had said: "No more than between two fine mornings: we suck them in giving no reasons." He said earnestly: "That is fine— true: nothing can be added to that."

W. gave me Bucke's letter of the 23d and called my attention to the paragraph referring to O'Connor: "I have written a long letter to O'Connor to try to cheer him up a bit. I fear he is in a bad way. That paralysis of the eyelid (ptosis) I fear will not let up. It is an extension of the disease (schlerosis) that has troubled him so long and a disease of this kind is a good deal more in the habit of going forwards than backwards." W. said: "Yes, Doctor—I believe you are right! Horace, there is a cloud hanging over William—over us all: a fatal black cloud. I am not in the habit of anticipating disaster, but I can't help seeing that William's persistent trouble is gradually sapping him of his last hold on life. I look forward into the next few months with fear—great fear."

Friday, October 26, 1888.

8 p. m. W. always reading. Laid his book down. "Howdy? Howdy?" As for himself: "It has been a miserable day: the day has looked down instead of up." Again: "I woke up doubtfully—did not get my good night's sleep: then I missed this morning's nap—the nap between eight and nine: I could not take it: it seems to be getting indispensable. Lately I have had a persistent pain in the belly—a gnawing away at the stomach: a pain in the head also—perhaps the one hanging on the other." Said he had sent Mrs. Costelloe a copy of the book today. This suggested my remark: "Garland asked that you send an autograph copy to Howells." "Did he say that? I did not read it that way. However, I would not have done it even had I known."

Brought him over half a dozen books in stiff covers. W. examined a copy intently. "I see that the cover is an improvement—from their standpoint decidedly an improvement"—then turning it over—"yes, rather stylish: gilt top—this"—putting his finger on McKay's monogram—"this especially so. It's not me, exactly—not me: is out of kelter with my other books: still, I see Dave's point—yes, see it. And anyhow, Oldach did all he could to make our cover look bad." Talked about the title page still. Liked the appearance of it as electrotyped. I asked: "Do you notice that your title page specifies no place of issue? Did you intend that?" He answered quickly: "Ah! is that so? that's the case, is it? I had not noticed it—was not aware of it. No—I did not intend to omit it—neither did I intend to insert it. I wrote down what came into my head at the time—what then seemed required." I said: "Call it America: America is the place." He laughed in an approving way: "Yes, but that would sound egotistic—make too much of a spread: one has to be careful of that."

I asked him now as he asked me a day or two ago: "Do you think the 'Walt Whitman' on the title page—the name—is too big?" He shook his head. "No—I had my doubts the other night but they were only momentary doubts. I see clearly that it is about right as we have it now. The book is anyhow greatly personal: there never was a more personal book, in fact: in that book Walt Whitman is everywhere and perpetually being brought to the fore. Besides, the book is large—makes a fair bulk—will stand the racket. My usual course has been to subordinate the title page to the contents of the book itself. My purpose has been, to put into the book a living personality—to give it verve, pulse, human fibre—whole, entire. My name there —at the worst it can do no harm: Walt Whitman is so positive a force in the book that this arrangement of the title seems well in accord with his general methods and principles. I am accused of egotism—of preaching egotism. Call it that if you choose— if that pleases you: I call it personal force: it is personal force that I respect—that I look for. It may be conceit, vanity, egotism—but it is also personal force: you can't get me to quarrel over the name. It is of the first necessity in my life that this personal prowess should be brought prominently forward—should be thrown unreservedly into our work. If I said 'I, Walt Whitman' in my poems and the text meant only what it literally said, then the situation would be sad indeed—would be very serious: but the Walt Whitman who belongs in the Leaves is not a circumscribed Walt Whitman but just as well a Horace Traubel as any one else—personalized moral, spiritual, force of whatever kind, for whatever day; it is force, force, personal force, we are after." He added very emphatically: " I am one with Kennedy's opinion, that a writer, to reflect life, nature—be true to himself, to his art (if we may say that)—must throw identity, overmastering identity, personality, verve, into his pages. Kennedy says it well: you have seen it there in the note—there in Bucke's book? I don't know if it has been elsewhere so well said. To throw a live man into the book: you, your friend, me, anybody else: that is the background, the heart-pulse, of Leaves of Grass."

W. said he had tried to explain to himself how it was the Transcript (Boston) would receive Kennedy, when Kennedy came as the spokesman of Walt Whitman. "The Transcript is the properest, nicest sheet going: I read it: it has some interesting points: is well respected in Boston. My surprise is, how they can receive me? I have friends there, I guess: Chamberlain, for one, perhaps—perhaps others." Had finally decided that the cuts to go into the big book should be limited to four—title-page, steel of 1855, Linton engraving, November Boughs frontispiece. Till the title-page success was assured W. had not completely settled this point. Said: "Even the Linton cut has its place: has some relation to the text. You know it? All the pictures now have a significance which gives them their own justification. This is so, whether the fortunate (or unfortunate) reader sees it or fails to see it." W. in handing me letter from Bucke which came today, said: "He speaks there of a change of the nurse. Does he say anything more definite to you? He says he has written you. What does he say?" This was Bucke's letter to W.:

LONDON, Oct. 24, '88.

There is no doubt Dr. Osler thinks you are doing well or he would be over oftener. If he thought you failing or very ill he would not neglect you I am sure. He is an exceptionally able man, and we must admit (whatever we may think or feel) that he knows as much about your condition as any one does (including yourself). I do not hear good accounts of your present nurse (Musgrove) and I have just written to Horace about a young man whom I can fully recommend who is willing to go from here and take the place. His name is Edward Wilkins. I know you would like him. He is a real good, nice looking, young fellow. I have known him some years. He is as good as he looks. I expect to hear from Horace at once on this business. I hope you will approve of the change. I am sure you will be pleased with it when made.

Affectionately,

R. M. BUCKE.

W. then remarked: "Well, I assume that you fellows know. I wrote the Doctor that I left it with you and with him to decide." I questioned him a little about Musgrove, but he would only say: "I am not indisposed to a change: I judge from what Doctor says that Edward Wilkins is my man. I like the air that Doctor gives him." This was decided enough. I knew his habitual reserve and consideration: how unwilling he is to say a harsh word in such a situation. It settled with me at once what I had been in some little doubt about at the time of the arrival of Doctor B.'s first letter on the subject. W. was not willing to make a special complaint against M. "If he is somewhat rough, it is out of the kindness of his heart I have no doubt." Here W. handed me a letter from Stedman. "Take it," he said: "you will like to hear what he has to say." Then, following that thought of S. up: "He writes a warm note: the book came—it was his birthday—conquered him—he likes it—likes it all: shape, contents, air. Stedman grows more and more affectionate: is coming up: steadily forward, the last few years notably. And you should see him, Horace: he is a man you would like: his regard is a thing to put value upon."

44 EAST 26TH ST.
NEW YORK, Oct. 25, '88.

Dear Walt, Your seasons outlast mine. Your book, always to be handed down and transferred by my clan, reached me on my fifty-fifth birthday, and made me wonder that your Novem-

537

ber Boughs still hang so rich with color while my October Leaves are already pale and wilted. I am very grateful for your remembrance, and touched by it withal. In many respects this collection (so strikingly and fittingly put up) is one of the most significant—as it is the most various—of your enduring works. Rest tranquil, as you ever are, in the ripeness of your harvest and fame—well assured that, whether your pilgrimage is still to be long or brief, you "shall not wholly die." I am always more and more your reader, and

Your attached friend,

EDMUND C. STEDMAN.

Speaking of "the reasons for Hugo's being what he was," W. remarked: "I might say of him what I have often said of Millet: he did what he found right at hand. Millet had the peasants at his doors—Hugo the varied, often loathsome, criminal life of the cities." W. referred to "O'Connor's short note" sent on to Bucke with the Costelloe letter and forwarded by B. to Camden. "Bucke is exceedingly despondent: has the darkest fears—no confidence whatever. But then Bucke does not take sufficiently into account O'Connor's remarkable physiological qualifications. O'Connor is better calculated than I am to stand shock—this, another: is built a little taller than your father, but much like him otherwise: has resistance—power to get up and up and go on! Bucke don't allow for O'Connor's overflowing measure of vitality. O'Connor is deeply, broadly based in the soil: has roots like the roots of a great tree, casting out immense arms underground around rocks, into crevices. It is this positive physiological property, rootedness, for which Doctor fails to account."

Reference being again made to the Springfield Republican review W. said: "There's too much of the battered old veteran business—who could have expected this or that?—and such stuff. If I should give my friends who write any counsel on this point (and I shall not: you know that) I would say, say nothing about it! Of course it would do no good to protest—the scribblers will have their way. Kennedy's screed in the Transcript seemed right enough because Kennedy spoke as one who was near and personal. The general comment on the book is of the pity-the-old man order. It is good discipline for a man in the face of such an abuse of criticism to sit down and keep cool. I would rather be damned than be saved by pity." W. expressed a wish to see Sheridan's Sedan piece in Scribner's. "I am sure it will appeal to me—parts of it, at least." Some one writing of Sheridan's later portraits remarked that "his face has become more intellectual." W. shook his head: "No—never intellect: that's hardly the word. Sheridan never expressed intellect. Physical heroism was common during the war: indeed, was notable on both sides, in all classes—men and officers, poor and rich, all. This was so rich a quantity that the time came when they needed to be held in, reined—not only the men but the officers, too—officers worse than men, if anything. In all this, brains did not rule—none of it, in fact. As I have often said of the land in America, it is indefinite, infinite—you can call for as much as you want. In true greatness as an accepter of things, Grant, of all men in the War, all leaders, I am inclined to credit most: his composure, adaptedness. For war simply in the concrete— except as it expressed some spiritual fact—my aversion always amounted, amounts to, abhorence."

Clifford had written me—date 25th: "Walt might be amused to know how when I showed Hilda his picture, she kept crying: 'Dear old gentleman—want to kiss him!' And she did again and again." W. said: "Yes—I remember—it was her beautiful pictures you brought me back in the summer! We commence life all over again and again with the darling children." Clifford had also written: "The more I read and think of Walt the more I revere and love him." W. replied also to this: "Tell Clifford his words are sweet to me more because they come from him than because they seem to make much of my work: I would rather have such a man send me his love than put a crown on my head."

Saturday, October 27, 1888.

7.45 evening. W. sitting up talking with Harned. W. said: "My day was bad but I came up smiling this evening." Discussed the Sackville West excitement. "The use they are making of his letter is natural but despicable. These fellows argue—these Republicans: this is a Roland for your Oliver— we give you West for Burchard: but it is an utterly base agitation. Take West's letter of itself: it's harmless enough—in fact, if it was worse I should still say: let it be, let it go! And whatever the case proves it in no way compromises Cleveland: Cleveland is no more responsible for West's writing than he would have been for his not writing—no more than Blaine for Burchard. Besides, why should it be out of place for him, for any man, to speak his mind? Should not freedom commend it, or, if not commend, excuse it? My only thought has been, how could a man in West's position write so insipid, so stupid, a letter? How could he have been so green—been taken in so easily? Had he no eyes, no ears? So far as the sentiments of the letter are concerned, they are harmless. They are weak, peurile, tepid. It was the most cowardly and sneakiest thing to get hold of the letter—use it—in that way. Look at that headline in The Press: 'The British Minister tells an American citizen how to vote in the coming election.' As if West was telling anybody anything he didn't know already." Harned said: "Blaine claims that the woes of Ireland are owed to British free trade." "Tom—that's damn fool rot—that's not only not true: that's not anything like the truth. What do you suppose Blaine cares about the big question anyhow? Blaine wants votes—votes— votes—no matter how they're got. The prime question is: What can I say—what word, what thought—which will gain most votes in Maine, Texas, Pennsylvania? It is in the nature of the politician, the schemer, the plotter, to degrade his warfare to the level of the lowest weapons of controversy and gain. I have spoken of Blaine: I don't know but Cleveland acts from the same motives—though I should perhaps not say that: I

have not the same evidence of it.   Blaine is a typical politician—
sees everything for its end in prestige, power, property: Blaine
of all Americans most eminently today enforces that observation.
Take the West letter—the use he makes of it: a palpably dishonest bid for Irish votes.   And it will have some effect, too.
An Irishman hates England—at least, the English government.
There is a vast aliment of wind, foam, gas, an immense fund of
it, running through the Irish character, along with truly admirable, lovable, brilliant traits: a great deal of what an Irishman
thinks, feels, does, rises out of that.   It is such a consideration
which explains to me the noise over the West letter.   Blaine
everywhere seeks to say that which will most touch, draw upon,
this emotionalism—this one-sided quality."   Here W. turned
to Harned: "What was it Tom: that trouble in the court house
here with the English visitors that time, not many months ago?
Wasn't Tom Curley in it?   It has escaped me a little—the
details of it.   What were they here for?"   T. explaining: "They
came, as favoring arbitration"—W. nodding: "Yes, I remember
now"—and Tom describing the interruptions of Irishmen
present, concluding: "The fun of it was the visitors were all
Home Rulers—every one of them."   W. exclaimed: "Bad!
bad!—wasn't it?   I remember: I had Bonsall tell me about it
and was very strong in my denunciation of it at the time."

Harned asked W. if he had read Ingersoll's reply to Manning
yet?   W. answered: "Yes—all of it."   Then T. inquired:
"Don't you think Ingersoll uses him up?"   W. repeating H's
words: "Yes, he uses him up—completely.   He uses them all
up.   Who is there to cope with him in that line?"   W. "excused"
himself however, "from any kind of sympathy" with Manning.
"He harps on one string—one monotonous string.   He goes
too deep into the Popes for me: takes them up A to Z, lauds
them—never qualifies"—adding after a pause, and with a
gesture and look towards Tom: "And yet everybody knows
they're the damnedest set of scoundrels out of hell—the earth-
hell: and that's hell enough!"   Then: "You know, Elias Hicks
would say, there's no worse devil than man, and he was right,

undoubtedly right: neither is there any worse hell than we make for ourselves right here." He quoted a more optimistic line from Hegel and added: "I repeat that verdict—maybe come back to it in the end: but in the meantime I believe Hicks was right. You know there's a streak of bad in us along with the good—a streak of very bad: we can't ignore it: it forces its presence upon our attention: though man finally is much more than the sum of all his villainy—much more: I always wind up with this consoling observation."

Harned had been over in New York—seen Jerome Buck again—talked with him about two unpublishable letters of Franklin and Washington. W. was amused, but skeptical. "I allow all you will on that, but must still put the main part of such gossip down to the inventive faculty: yes, fully nine-tenths—I may say, forty-nine fiftieths." He continued: "I have had plenty of experience going to show I do right. You both know many of the Lincoln stories: the thousands of them given currency, laughed over, brought down, accepted. I think few of them are entitled to respect. It is true, James Parton once told me—told me in conversation—that the true life of Washington could not be printed—no respectable North-ern publishing house or public would be responsible for its appearance. Yet I know too much at first hand not to see origins, explanations, that take you below the superficial ugli-ness of these stories. As I was saying, take Lincoln. I can speak from knowledge of those department fellows. When I was in Washington, there were about two thousand of them, full half of whom had nothing to do. All day long these boys would loaf about, talk together, invent stories—invent filthy stories: their minds ran upon such themes. A fellow would sit at his desk—the fellow with something to do: along would come somebody: 'Have you heard the latest?' The busy man would look up with surprise: 'No, what's that?'—then his visitor would likely come closer—whisper: 'Have you a minute to spare?'—and generally it would be 'yes'. Then he would take a seat, draw up his chair—'listen'—and tell you some story."

W. laughed: "I have often seen it done: been a party to it—a victim!" And added: "Then in a day or two the story would turn up in the papers foisted on Lincoln—fastened to him—thenceforth to take a place among the 'facts' of his life. This sort of thing does throw a doubt upon all history—eats away at its foundations. What does somebody say? 'I know it's false'—'Why?'—'I found it in a history!' That is great logic. My experience with life makes me afraid of the historian: the historian, if not a liar himself, is largely at the mercy of liars."

Some one had sent him a tariff pamphlet "giving both sides." He said: "I won't read it: would have to change a very old habit to read it." North American today contained a study of W. W. by George Rogers. Harned read it while he was with us. Passed it over to W. with the remark: "It's darn green, Walt" —W. thereat saying: "I don't doubt it: studies mostly are:"—asking then: "And who is George Rogers? Do either of you fellows know who George Rogers is?" Not being enlightened he laughed: "Well—I will see for myself when I read this fling in the morning: I will know his size and shape. The best way to get to know a man sometimes is not to get acquainted with him." Gave me a letter from Bucke. "Nothing special in it." Note to me from Arthur Stedman today asking for the Linton cut, which I sent to him.

W. referred to his "big secret" this evening again: "I am daily more anxious to have you know the story—all of it: it belongs to you by right of our sacred association—and when the proper moment comes you shall be made acquainted with all its facts. There are best reasons why I have not heretofore told you—there are also best reasons why I should tell you now. It's not so much that I desire to confide a secret to you as that I wish you on general principles to be made familiar with the one big factor, entanglement (I may almost say tragedy) of my life about which I have not so far talked freely with you." I waited for more but that was all he said—except that, seeing inquiry on my face, he concluded: "Not to-night, Horace, dear boy—not tonight." Finally I said: "Walt, you seem to be getting a little steadier every day—a little more reliable for work." He smiled. "Sometimes it looks that way: but on the whole I am only passably well—am in fact downcast, physically speaking. I have seen the iron collars on the slaves in the South—bits on the wrist here, a chain—back of the collar a spike: the effect of all not pain, not anguish, but a dull weight —making its wearer incapable of effort—bearing him down. It is such a collar I wear day by day: a burden impossible to shake off—vitiating all my attempts to get on my feet again."

Sunday, October 28, 1888.

7.45, evening. W. reading Tribune. Had "passed an average day." Ate well. Harned had brought in The Tribune. I had the November Scribner's along with me. Instantly looked over the Sheridan paper—From Gravelotte to Sedan. Exclaimed over the frontispiece: "What a strong, a beautiful, picture!" Tried to interpret the decorations: "This is an army corps, this is probably foreign," and so on until he finally said: "I guess I know very little about it anyhow." He spoke of the portrait of Arnold that went with the Birrell essay. Would he read the essay? "Perhaps—it may occur to me to do so: it may occur to me: I would have no original impulse to do it: would not deliberately start out to read anything more about Arnold." Looked at the portrait again—shook his head: "No, no—he was not for me: yet he must have been because he was: there is no better reason, and no worse: indeed, that is sufficient."

W. told me that he had "sent a McKay book to Doctor Bucke," adding: "I sent it off to-day: Musgrove just a short while ago took it up to the post-office." Then spoke of my copy. "Won't you take it now? Yes, take it now." I picked up a book and took it over for him to sign. "What shall I put into it? You don't want your own name? You will want to give it to somebody?" I replied, laughing: "Well, put my girl's name in it then: she comes next, anyhow"—W. interrupting and shaking his pen at me—"or first!" proceeding then to write in the freest hand: "Anne Montgomerie from the author W. W. Oct: 28, '88"—and concluding: "She's as sweet and dear as an unsoiled flower: I'm sure she comes first." Then he said: "That was not all I sent Bucke: I wrote him a postal—also forwarded some papers: the North American you brought me— then the Times: you saw the Times yesterday? It contained a notice—so much of it, perhaps"—indicating a few inches on his coat sleeve—"half a column, maybe. All the critics say about the same thing just as if they consulted together and agreed to: one fellow starts so and so—they all follow. The North American man has evidently written without reading the book: he is markedly sophomoristic: I am sorry for anybody who thinks he ought to read it." Then with a twinkle in his eye: "But they are all good from the publisher's point of view: they say that Dave McKay is the publisher—that he lives and publishes in Philadelphia—that the book is so much per copy— and all that: so you see the newspapers are not without a market importance. I object to the harping all around on my sanity, sickness—such things: it is remarkable, Walt Whitman has lived all these years and is still sane: it is a miracle, Walt Whitman has been sick and sick and sick and has managed not to die: he is a wonder, this old old man, who has saved his soul from the raging decay of the body: such things, again and again copied, repeated. Why should they come in at all? What have they to do with the real question, which is whether the book is a book and deserves respect as such?" I read this to W. from the New York Home Journal:

"Walt Whitman's new volume of poems, November Boughs, is another proof of the fact that advancing age does not necessarily imply decay of intellect. Mental activity is indeed the surest buckler against senility. Some of these poems might have been written in the full vigor of manhood. The aged poet seldom leaves his room, but he receives kindly care and attention from many friends, one of whom, Mr. Horace Traubel, is in daily attendance."

He said: "There it is again: wonderful old man: hi there Walt—think of it: you're entitled to be an idiot but you're some punkins! Yet I like the paragraph on the whole: it sounds well: is very friendly, circumspect: and see that one sentence there: 'Some of these poems might have been written in the full vigor of manhood!' That sounds better than an excuse—better than 'it's pretty good considering'—and so forth." Again: "Some of the many who used to fling their darts at me have of late been silent—holding in: whether for good or not I hardly know." "Have they changed their opinions?" "No—not at all: their silence is from policy." I asked him about The Critic. "I do not count upon it as any too neighborly or affectionate though it is by no means unfriendly. I think Joe Gilder takes the business view of me entirely: if I succeed, if I sell my books, good for me, approved!—if I do not, bad, bad! Yet I trust Joe: I imagine his paper has a hard tussle to get on: indeed, I am surprised it lasts at all: it is kept up on a pretty high plane where everything like popular support is out of the question: they might vulgarize it and make it pay but they won't do that. It is Jennie Gilder, the girl on the staff, who is more friendly to me—more likely to decide doubts in my favor." "Your note did not appear in their issue of last week." "Ah! perhaps it will not show up at all: Joe may decide not to use it—that it is not exactly what he wants. I wonder, I wonder?"

W. has prepared lettering for title page, wiping out the last ornament—two stars, one on each side of "complete." Wrote these instructions to the printer in the corner: "Abt like this. I leave however mainly to your taste and judgment—I want to see proof—pull two impressions—I want your pressman to keep up as good a *strong* color as can be maintained *without clotting or muddy*." More favorable letter from O'Connor to-day. "He is cheerful: has not yet regained control of his eye-lid: how that recalls Heine—Heine the wonderful! William speaks of 'a week'—expects a change in a week—is still having battery treatment. He is cute—knows what may come—may defy the prediction of the doctors—Bucke with the rest." Then, after

From a Photograph by W. Kurtz

WALT WHITMAN
(1860)

a pause, as if to qualify his speech: "At least, we hope so." Remarked O'C.s "imperturbable spirit:" "He keeps it up—his letter is full of life: why, he is still joking, making fun: probably will make light of his danger to the very last."

Showed W. Olive Dana's article on Stedman, with portrait. "It appears to be intelligently written," said W., "and this portrait resembles him fairly. Stedman is of good size—not large nor heavy—not small. I have every reason to regard Stedman with warmth, acceptance, even affection: he is truly good to me: effusive, almost: seeks to be of service, to prove his faith: is open, transparent, genuine." "Indeed," he asked, turning his eyes up to mine (I was over his shoulder): "Don't you think this picture bears me out?" W. added, again: "Ed is the best talker of the lot—readiest. It's not that he says bright things: not that particularly: but readiest—readiest to say what forces its way up. He is popular—popular as a man —everybody likes him: you would: you would want to be with him: in a sense he has the fine spirit of the camerado." I alluded to John Burroughs' statement while here that Gilder and Stedman were "coming over," W. responding: "Did John say that? He did not say it to me, or at least if he did I did not pay the right attention to it at the time. I do indeed see the drift that way in Stedman though not so positively in Gilder, whose human feeling towards me, noble brotherly feeling, I cannot question. John seems a little afraid of me, if I may say it: seems afraid I have done something or may do something to offend them. I remember at the time Stedman had that long piece in the Century he appeared to have caught the idea—I was told so, told by several—that I was mad: had trodden him under foot, so to speak. I was always troubled over this rumor. Nothing could have more misrepresented me. I regarded the piece as thoroughly friendly, thoroughly courteous, thoroughly fair—if not more. It is clear to me still: I had it in my mind at the time (did not say it, probably, to anyone: I don't think to John: I know not—certainly not—to Stedman): I don't care this"—snapping his fingers—"what any of them think, this way or that. Yet all my feeling was in good temper. It had been free criticism and I never resent free criticism—in fact, no man has had more of it, no one has held himself so open to it —and I may add that I have got some of my best points from it. I am only too glad to be read and examined as Stedman has read and examined me. After a long experience with men who neither hoped for truth nor would see it, it was like daylight to meet with such treatment as Stedman accorded me. I have an appreciation of Stedman that does not require me to put him into the seventh heaven of flattery."

Speaking of Bucke's book, Man's Moral Nature, W. said: "It is a grapple: I find it tough up-hill work. I can see how valuable the book should be to anyone who is interested in such studies, as I confess I am not." W. handed me a couple of old Burroughs letters with the remark: "You may find a way to make these fit in with your collection: if you can't there's another thing you can do with them: do that." I said: "You wouldn't give them to me if you had the slightest notion that I would do that other thing." Laughed roundly. "That's so: I wouldn't." I looked at the letters: said: "There's a lot of difference in the handwriting of the two letters." One was dated 1864, the other 1886. "Yes: John originally wrote a hand like a boarding school miss: his hand has grown strong as it has matured." I sat back on the bed and read the letters— this one first:

TREASURY DEPARTMENT, WASHINGTON, Aug. 2, 1864.

Dear Walt, I am disconsolate at your long stay. What has become of you? On returning the 7th of July I found you had gone home sick. You have no business to be sick, so I expect you are well. I was so unlucky as to be sick all the time I was home—and most of the time since I came back. I am quite well now, however, and feel like myself. Benton and I looked for you at Leedsville, as I wrote to you to come. If you have leisure now you would enjoy hugely a visit up there. I hope you are printing Drum Taps, and that this universal drought does not reach your "grass." But make haste and come back. The heat is delicious. I have a constant bath in my own perspiration. I was out at the front during the siege of Washington and lay in the rifle pits with the soldiers. I got quite a taste of war and learned the song of those modern minstrels—the minnie bullets—by heart. A line from you would be prized.

Truly yours,

JOHN BURROUGHS.

"How excellent that is," said W.: "'The heat is delicious: I have a constant bath in my own perspiration.' I know what that means. Times have changed: now I dread what then I rejoiced in: I am afraid of the severe heat—it subjects me to an awful strain. 1864! A quarter of a century almost come and gone since that was written! Do you notice John's ladified hand of those days? Now his writing has a grip on itself: it stands for something creative—for the grown John—for the master, not the pupil, of experience." Burroughs' other letter was this:

WEST PARK, N. Y., April 3, '86.

Dear Walt. I received the books all right, also your letters and card. I am just back from Roxbury where I went a week ago to make sugar in the old woods of my boyhood; had a pretty good time, though too much storm. Only my brother is now upon the old farm. I have to go back there at least twice a year to ease my pain. Oh, the pathos of the old place where my youth was passed, where father and mother lived and died, and where my heart has always been.

I have been pretty well since I saw you, except that I have been off my sleep a good deal. Just now I am having a streak of sleeplessness. I do not quite know what to make of it. Today is my birthday, too; I am forty-nine today. I hope spring finds you better. I lately heard from you through J. W. Alexander, the artist. I think he will make a good picture of you. He is a fine fellow. I am glad to hear of the projected new book. I hope it is to be a reality. Your title is good. My book, Signs and Seasons, will be out this month. I do not think much of it—the poorest of my books, I think. No news with me. I hope to see you in May, as I go to Kentucky. I hope you will not try to face the summer again in Camden. It is very imprudent. A bright afternoon here with remains of last night's snow still lingering. With much love

J. BURROUGHS.

"There is a little of the let-us-cry character about John's letters," said W.: "you would never catch William standing in any such attitude of apology towards life: his acceptance of life is always vehement and conclusive: I always feel in William's presence (in the presence of one of his letters, too) that I have the best right to live. It is always wonderful to me—the inexhaustible fund of his energy. Sick or well, sad or glad, William is the same man—cheerful, tonic, like a strong wind off the sea. John is rather more of the contemplative type—is quietistic (too much so, I should say): is a trifle too conscious of his ills. It takes more than a few kinds of people to perfect a world, don't it? That's how we get in—eh, Horace?" "Good night" after that and I slid out.

Monday, October 29, 1888.

8 p. m. "Not one of the darkest, not one of the brightest, days." Reading Cooper. Read him two letters I had from Bucke to-day. W. welcomes the thought of Ed. Wilkins. Bucke gloomy about O'C. W. says: "Maurice is too conclusive by far: let's take another guess, a good guess, for William: I don't want to say the worst until there's nothing else left to be said." Had been reading the Scribner's but not the Birrell paper on Arnold: "It did not strike me: I was not impelled to it: but I read the railroad piece"—B. B. Adams, Jr., on The Everyday Life of Railroad Men—" it was exceedingly interesting: I took it in from beginning to end." How about the Sheridan? He nodded affirmatively. "That—yes, of course: and

it was everyway worth the time consumed." A newspaper suggests that S. had not written the paper. W. said: "I don't believe that myself: I think Sheridan wrote it: I seem to see his hand: it is the touch of a man who was there, on the spot—strong, active, vivid." Pointed to the frontispiece portrait of Sheridan. "They who contend that Sheridan is a numbskull make a mistake: it will not do to dismiss him in that style: he can't be puffed away: he was not the very greatest but he was quite a size." Admired the pictures in the magazine—especially one picture in the Adams article representing a railroad yard at night. "I looked a long time at that—a long time: it was compensating. It more and more strikes me, year and year, that art is advancing towards its democratization with unprecedented strides: take such a magazine in evidence—every picture good, suggestive."

Again discussed the critics of November Boughs. "The pathos they discover in the book—the whole crowd—is purely imagined: they have all dipped their pens in the same ink: they have been feeding on newspaper talk for so long they've got the newspaper perspective, which is cross-eyed to say the least. They know that I am physically in a precarious condition: they imagine that condition as prevailing in the book—read it into, force it into, the book—when, as a matter of fact, as you know well enough, all that stuff was written before I was sick— nearly all of it: very little has been added since." Clifford writes W. again: "The predominating quality of November Boughs is of confidence, of victory." W. says: "A bugle note, eh? that is better—that is Clifford." Some reference was made to Byron. Had he outgrown Byron? "No indeed: I stand where I have always stood: it has been a settled conviction with me for forty years." "But you have 'revised' on Bryant." "I know—but I have never had any two moods about Byron: I have for so long acknowledged his extraordinary genius it's not likely I'd take a turnabout at this late day: my faith has stood every possible assault, suspicion, treachery: is utterly without compromise."

After some general talk about "extreme, wholesale criticism," W. explained: "It is easy to get askew with writers—to reason, we don't like 'em, they're not for us, therefore they're of no use to anybody at all. But that is as bad as the priestly anathema. It is illustrated in my friend Mr. Smith—Pearsall Smith: he has the greatest horror of Carlyle: Carlyle was no good: Pearsall wouldn't hear to him on any condition. It is especially easy to get askew with a man like Carlyle: we should guard against it—for with a nature strongly perverse in some things there often goes the highest manifestations of nobility." W. here made some personal reference to Smith as "a good fellow: hospitable, kind: level-headed, too—truly my well-wisher, I do believe."

Arthur Stedman sends me sheets of notices of his father's Library. I showed them to W. who read some bits and looked through the whole stuff casually. On the last page were opinions from Howells, Whittier, Higginson, Tyler and others. I said to W.: "Here are words from your friends." First he said "Oh! Ah!"—then, putting his finger down on Higginson's name: "Yes, here's one of them—over the left!" Then he spoke of Whittier's note. He said: "Whittier cannot be considered my enemy: he is friendly: not an early comer—among those who come in at the round-up!" He spoke of Whittier's "severe moral tone:" "puritanic, even," but: "It is genuine—wholly, beautifully genuine." I alluded to Whittier's "moral eye" and W. smiled: "That moral eye did not prevent him from slopping over Burns: he did that at the first: he does it still—has done it this year." W. spoke of novelists, novels, novel-reading. He had "never seen Thackeray"—had not "heard him lecture." "I have read Vanity Fair and liked it: it seemed to me a considerable story of its kind—to have its own peculiar value. But Thackeray as a whole did not cast his sinker very deep though he's none the worse for that." He had read Dickens more generally: "But Dickens had something the same make up as Conway: if a story is not interesting make it so." I suggested that there was some difference between the obligations of a story writer and a historian. This W. acknowledged: "I concede that: but a man may be as false to human nature in a novel as false to dates and so forth in a history." "But your general feeling towards Dickens—what is that?" "Of great admiration—very great: I acknowledge him without question: he will live."

Had he read Robert Elsmere? "No—nor have I much curiosity concerning it: though I am of course perfectly familiar with the discussion it has aroused: we have to be—the noise is so loud we can't help but hear it: but I don't seem to be tempted to dig into deep ground after its mysteries. Now—George Eliot was another matter: she was fundamentally vital, vitalizing: I have read her with great assiduity—she is convincing. Have you read Scenes from Clerical Life? They make up probably a couple—maybe more—good-sized volumes: as stories they are the most fascinating of all. I want to ask you, Horace— what was the character of her essay on Heine? I have no doubt I should read it—it would appeal to me: I always stand up for Heine—am hotly inclined his way: resent all the puritan criticism of his character as a man and his significance as a writer: am eager (more than willing) to recognize his high estate: to excuse (if excuses are needed, as they are not) his improprieties, his erraticism, his strayings off from conventional standpoints, as with Byron, Burns, Goethe. I find Heine everyway interesting—the simplest facts about him as well as the gravest." I asked W.: "Have you read many novels?" He answered with emphasis: "Cartloads of 'em—cartloads—when I was younger: indeed, that was a most important formative element in my education, nurture."

W. did not meet Tyndall, Huxley or Spencer on their visits to America. "So far as I know none of the English scientists except Clifford have ever taken any shine to me." Then said: "I am glad enough, indeed, to see that Spencer's health is getting better." I wrote Bucke to-day to have Wilkins here so he could take Musgrove's place Monday morning next. Also told him to send Kennedy his extra copy of the North American. W. said to me to-night: "You'll be speaking for me many a time after I am dead: do not be afraid to tell the truth—any sort of truth good or bad, for or against: only be afraid *not* to tell the truth." I said. "I promise not to help send you down into history wearing another man's clothes." He nodded and said fervently: "That's all I could ask, Horace."

Tuesday, October 30, 1888.

7.45, evening. W. reading quietly—poems of Walter Scott. Appeared bright. Had the day gone well? "Yes—mostly so: I can only say—I have got through it and here I am." Reported to him that I had word from Arthur Stedman of the safe arrival of the cut: that I had conferred with Bilstein but got no proofs from him as yet. W. questioning me concerning details of these and other matters. Then settled into general talk. I took him down the George Eliot volume containing the Heine piece. Was interested at once: looked over the pages casually—laid the book on his lap open: "I must read it—I am sure it will please me." I think W. is incapable of irritation on such a point, but the absence of acknowledgment from Burroughs and Morse as to books sent them excites his remark. "They'll come up," he says, however—"come up in their own time." He had spoken last night of Spencer. Here are two paragraphs of the note touching his health written by him to J. A. Skilton of the Ethical Association of Chadwick's church:

"I am glad to say, and you will be glad to hear, that I am considerably better than when I gave to Dr. W. J. Youmans the impression you quote. Leaving London in a very low state about a month ago, I have since improved greatly, and am now in hopes of getting back to something like the low level of health which I before had, though I scarcely expect to reach that amount of working power which has been usual with me.

"The information contained in your letter was, I need hardly say, gratifying to me both on public and on personal grounds. The spread of the doctrine of evolution, first of all in its limited acceptation, and now in its wider acceptation, is alike surprising

554

and encouraging; and doubtless the movement now to be initiated by the lectures and essays set forth in your program will
greatly accelerate its progress."

After reading the first paragraph W. said looking up at me:
"Well, I hope it will stay so: but he is doubtful of it himself."
Then, as he read paragraph two he put his finger index-like upon
it: "How fine the spirit of this!—let it be said, let it be heard:
it seems to me this and that or so and so: how does it strike you?
—so goes the letter. This spirit of science: what a glory it has
added to the world!" I described a highly-wrought, over-ardent
Republican I had met in the forenoon who said: "If Cleveland
is elected, if the American people elect that damned sneak, then
I say let them have their fill: I hope they'll see riots, strikes,
bloodshed, starvation!" W. highly amused. "That's a refreshing
idiot, sure enough: I didn't know anybody cared that much
about the election either way: I thought we were just in a cold
scramble for office and didn't mind the morals one side or the
other a bit. Well—let them who are of the blood to do so keep
hot: America, the world, life, will go on unconcerned to inevitable conclusions. I don't think the fate of America hangs
on the issue of a Presidential election—of all Presidential elec-
tions: the fate of Europe on the speeches of kings: indeed,
these are the least, not the most, significant integers of historic
progress: I say always that it is not a bit significant what the
aristocrats, the swells, the kings and presidents, do—that it is
everyway significant what the people do. When the people
some day get stirred up as they must and will—it is inevitable—
the rulers themselves will realize that nothing they can say
contravening popular equality and right can count for much."
W. gave me Bucke's letter of the 28th: "There's nothing in the
letter—nothing new: but it's pleasant to have, to read, to hear,
one may say: one virtue it has (it is the Doctor's virtue)—it
keeps moving: movement, activity, life, is in every fiber of the
Doctor's body. Doctor's trip east here is still among the ifs:
he will come, will not come, to-morrow, next day, if, if, if."

Harned made some reference to the saying that Von Moltke "is silent in six languages." W. said: "I don't take that without a question: I don't know whether I believe in reticence—the common idea of it—as a principle: that it necessarily indicates extra fine points and all that. A man in public life, living in the public eye, may need to be careful what he says, how he says what he says: Bismarck, for instance, Von Moltke, Lincoln, Grant. There may be public reasons for reserve, for silence: but after that is said a good deal more may be said and better said. Indeed, it is my principal objection to the infernal noise created by the Sackville West letter that it takes reticence for granted—absolute silence: that men in positions of prominence must not have opinions or, having 'em, must not tell what they are. I for my part can see no reason why West should not have his say—why any man should not have his say: any man, diplomat or other. What is the notion of sense or justice which dares to stand in the way of the freest utterance of faith? I believe in the freest expression of opinion all around, all times, here, in Europe, yes in Asia, wherever men choose or happen to think or choose or happen to want to talk. It seems to me a grand heap more dignified for West to write that letter than for Cleveland to give ten thousand dollars to the campaign fund. Dignity may become a bugbear. Arnold complained of Lincoln that he lacked distinction. Is this the co-eval word—this, with dignity? What did Arnold mean? That must be an English quality: what is it? how do you tell it when you see it? I for my part am distrustful of any personal rules or public customs which interpose barriers between the leaders and the people. I like all fraternization between leaders, people, the masses: no travesty of reserve. It was charged against Hayes, too—want of dignity, going about the country speech-making, talking to crowds—President Rutherford Hayes. But this never troubled me. I read all the speeches—they were genial, good-natured, sensible, helping things along—South, North—especially South—Oh! I think they did much good there, simple as they appeared. I was in St. Louis at the time—sick: I liked the speeches—liked them much though

they were much criticised: I thought them just the right thing."
Cleveland's speeches of last year he had not "so closely watched,"
and now "remembered little about them." "But in all instances
—Houston (they pronounce it Hueston down South), Hayes,
others—I am sure frank intercourse is the best intercourse,
whether here, you with me, I with you, or among public men or
between public men and the people. I have not the beginning
of a feeling of resentment over the West letter."

I referred to some one's criticism of W.—that he "must
have led a wild early life" instancing one case the quotation of
which had set Bucke off. W. took the thing smilingly: "That
is a familiar story: I am not a saint—have never been guilty of
setting up for a saint. I find some of my friends—some of the
ardent eulogists—making very many claims for me which I
would not make for myself. Neither do I feel that I am such
an awful sinner: I have made mistakes—many of them: led
an average human life: not too good, not too bad—just a so-so
sort of life. I don't spend much time wondering whether I
should not have been better or might not have been worse."
W. said as I was going: "I've been looking over a heap of old
things the last few days which I'll probably eventually turn over
to you for safe keeping or for destruction—whichever you may
decide to be for the best." Then he added: "I know what you'll
do: you'll save every scrap of paper and lock it all up in a safe."

Wednesday, October 31, 1888.

7.30, evening. Reading a paper. When he looked up he saw
I had a bundle in my hand. "Here again! How the days pass!
How are you?" Talk very long and free. Told him I had writ-
ten to Burroughs saying he was better than in the summer.
He shook his finger at me: "Be careful what you say—don't be
too sure about me: some day when you come you will find that
I have slipped cable and am gone." Opened my bundle and
showed him what I had. Three printed impressions of the
Linton and one hundred of the title page portraits—also proof of
complete title page. He put on his glasses and got right down to

business. "They are all satisfactory. You find me a great skeptic—don't you? I am very conservative: I don't say I have won until there is no doubt of the victory. Many disappointments have taught me not to be boastful: I have no peacock feathers to exploit. The Linton cut comes up here as it never has before: the paper seems just right, the ink seems just right: the picture is a revelation—is a new birth." His comments on the title page were equally earnest. "This ought to please my friends, but I am not sure it will: there's Bucke, as whimsical and kinky as hell: and Burroughs is about as bad. Doctor will be coming along in a few days so we can keep this to surprise him with. I want you to thank the printers for this work: they did it—we owe our chief debt to them." Then he started to quiz himself and me about the lettering at the foot of the page. "Is it too large? Can it be too large?" I shook my head. Then he asked: "Does it betray eccentricity?" Finally taking his glasses off and looking at me: "For this book I guess the name is not too large: I have looked at it again and again with considerable anxiety—asked myself: does it seem like affectation, display?" Then he added: "I have suffered all my life from the misjudgments of people who looked with suspicion upon all I do. I am not concerned to please them, but I am anxious to come to conclusions satisfactory to my own soul. My ways are very methodical: I have been much criticised for that: but my ways are mine and are necessary to me. I need to isolate myself— to work along very undemonstrative lines: I can never rush: I must proceed in a leisurely manner as if I have all the time there is."

W. said again: "We received Tom's letter to-day"—he said "we" with a twinkle in his eye—"the letter to Mr. Musgrove, telling him of the change that has been decided upon. I saw the letter—the Doctor brought it up to me: he don't like it much— he calls it getting the bounce." W. is eager for the change. Yet he hates to have Musgrove's feelings hurt. "He has been most kind to me—tried to serve me, tried to anticipate my wishes: I feel personally grateful to him." W. received a long letter from Bucke to-day talking about the change in nurses. Gave it to me to read. "I will answer it to-morrow: I must look carefully into it." He said later: "Doctor is what the boys call boss for details: he goes in for care in the minutest particulars: I suppose that belongs to his scientific training." Musgrove came in with a letter. It was from Burlington, Vermont—news about W.'s sister. He read it at once, saying: "Excuse me," and then smiling with the remark: "The news is good news—thank God for that! It is from my sister—I have been worried about her. She has never been here: she is frail, delicate—gets about but little." Talked of what he called "family physiology." "The race has mainly been a powerful one: sickness at minimum: fortunate, blessed. Look at my own great strength. Jeff is quite as large as I am I suppose: stronger—twelve years younger: is in perfect health. We went on the New Orleans trip together: I shall never lose the immediate memory of that. Jeff was with me: he did not thoroughly enjoy it—enter into it: was much sick—on the Mississippi was subject to dysentery: what is worse than dysentery to a traveller? But I myself kept in perfect health—enjoyed perfect physical nonchalance, in fact: was moved by nothing: was absolutely season and climate proof: up to my fifty-third year: proof against all material, digestive disturbances. After that came the Washington earthquake: they called it inflammation of the veins induced by handling a more than ordinarily gangrenous wound: a sort of malarial trouble followed. Then I achieved a recovery again, or what I thought recovery: by and bye the '73 almost total collapse. Up to this fifty-third year I had lived immune. I feel even now that the long-arriving effects of my last June trouble are not clearly defined. I have no confidence in a rally. The time is past for that. The only question is, when will come the final effect?"

He alluded to friends "who come pleased and go angry" for his not seeing them. "I think this has particularly happened to the South Jersey folks: they return home hurt—only half-believing." Some get mad when I advise them not to come. He said:

"I know of no better thing to say than this—that the doctor vehemently, positively, prohibits—won't hear to my having—visitors: and as far as we can we must observe this advice." I said I thought Morris was a little hurt at not being received on a recent call. W. said: "I am sorry. He had something to tell me—somebody's opinions or what not—opinions of my pieces? hadn't he? You know—probably he will know—that I care nothing about such stuff—would not even under other circumstances encourage anybody to come as the bearer of such news. Yet if I was well I would invite Morris to come—to come often: he is clever, bright, active, quick, interested in all things—and most kindly, besides. When you see him again give him my love—tell him this for me."

W. was very earnest as he said: "By the way Horace, I have been reading the book you left last night—the George Eliot book. It is wonderfully interesting—I have read two or three of the pieces—read them almost verbatim: the Heine, the piece on Young. There were things revealed to me which I never realized in George Eliot before—for one thing a subtlety of surpassing greatness. It was with a good deal of pleasure that I read the piece on Young. Young deserved it all. I never knew George Eliot could let herself out so: it was something to learn that if there was nothing else to be gained by it: yet there was more—oh so much more. She is profound, masterful: her analysis is perfect: she chases her game without tremor to the very limit of its endurance. It is all a wonderful specimen of dialectics—excites my most thoroughgoing admiration. Her paper on Heine has likewise thrown out hints of things or things not known to me before."

W. remarked that he "often cudgelled with" himself to know "if the final summing up—the last conclusive message—has yet been delivered with respect to Heine." He found his own admiration of Heine "a constantly growing one": "I look on him as a genuinely great soul—not yet justly measured: hot, turbulent, but gifted highly—perhaps as highly as any modern man." He respected Heine as "combining in himself the distinguishing elements both of Burns and Byron—and then powers clearly super-added. Both those influences seem to stream into Heine: yet he was great in learning, culture: knowing in all things—literature, science: was Hellenist—full of fact, circumstance: as packed with it as Goethe, Carlyle. Yet Heine was always warm, pulsing—his style pure, lofty, sweeping, in its wild strength. Heine knew more than Burns. It becomes a familiar reproach to speak of Heine's 'mockery.' It does not disturb me: I never find myself shocked, repelled, by it. They call it 'mockery': I think there should be another word for it—that there is, though I can't recall it now: for Heine deserves a better word. They may call it a trick with Heine: a trick: but whatever it be called it is very effective. It seems to belong honestly to Heine —is quite in its place in him: is not an importation. I remember one of his stories—it is in point (maybe I am not any too clear about its details any more): its purport, spirit, is sharp, strong, as a knife-cut—a master-stroke of incisive symbolism. It is all in a picture: it is a quiet night: I am alone: overhead are the stars: afar off I can see the moon-lit horizon—a fort, strange dark shrubberies between: along the parapet of the fort the dim figure of a sentry on duty: oh that the sentry would shoot me!"

It was wonderful, the simple sweet feeling W. put into the recital—his voice deep, his finger pointing into space, his eye animated. He asked me: "Do you remember it" Then: "At any rate it illustrates Heine—the 'mockery' as they call it." He went on to explain: "I knew in my early days in New York a couple of young fellows, writers, who practiced the same art. No doubt it was upon a suggestion from Heine: two or three verses pathetic, serious—then the break-off: 'oh that the sentry would shoot me!' I did not know at the time that the idea was borrowed. When I did come to know it took from their work the value I might have—had in fact—attached to it. I then realized in them the weakness that always inheres to what is not first, initial, original. What you said yesterday about Heine's culture was very cute, Horace: if it don't hit the nail on the head it at least shows where the head can be found. I find in Heine a superb fusion of culture and native elemental genius. I consider it the bane of the universities, colleges, that they withhold, withdraw, men from direct, drastic contact with life. The best gift to our age so far is what we have come to know as the scientific spirit: it is just in this thing that the universities must fill out if they are to be centers of rising influence. Whether it all came from Bacon—from the work attributed to Bacon—as some are disposed to claim, or whether it is the result of painful slow evolution, of long accumulation, I don't know—I am not knowing enough to settle: but that it is here, that we have got a hold on it, that I know full well. It is the crowning glory of our time that this new evangel has appeared. There is no salvation if not in that: it is an appeal to nature, an appeal to final meanings—to facts, to the sun itself: it is an absolute surrender to the truth: it never asks us: Do you want this thing to be true? or, Is it ugly, hateful? but, Is it true, and if it is true that settles it. That's all there is to it—that's all there needs to be to it: that's enough. Here science and literature are one, as they everywhere and always should be one in fact, and it is here, in such a noble equipment, that Heine lustrously shines. Brilliants, gems, crystallizations, in the requisites of a writer—bright epigrams, splendid learning, eloquent roundings-off of phrase—all these, I can see, have an importance, too, though second-rate, third-rate, at the best. But in all imaginative work, all pure poetic work, there must especially come in a primal quality, not to be mentioned, named, described, but always felt when present: the direct off-throwing of nature, parting the ways between formal, conventional, borrowed expression and the fervor of genuine spirit. Heine had it—so do all the big fellows have it. More than any other agent, science has been furthering it." Was it not also in Leaves of Grass? W. exclaimed fervidly: "Oh! I hope so, I believe so: it has been in the air: I have sucked it in as the breath of life: unconsciously, not by determination, but with full recognition now of its great value, of its wonderful significance. Yes, Leaves of Grass would lose much if it lost that.

that is the ground underlying all: the fact, the fact: that alone: the fact devotedly espoused, sacred, uplifting! The whole mass of people are being leavened by this spirit of scientific worship— this noblest of religions coming after all the religions that came before. After culture has said its last say we find that the best things yet remain to be said: that the heart is still listening to have heart things said to it—the brain still listening to have brain things said to it—the faith, the spirit, the soul of man, waiting to have such things of faith, spirit, the soul, said to it. Books won't say what we must have said: try all that books may they can't say it. The utmost pride goes with the utmost resignation: science says to us—be ready to say yes whatever happens, whatever don't happen: yes, yes, yes. That's where science becomes religion—where the new spirit utters the highest truth—makes the last demonstration of faith: looks the universe full in the face —its bad in the face, its good—and says yes to it."

I gazed at W. His face shone—he regarded me with great love. I kissed him good night and withdrew. "Good-night!" he called after me: "Good-night! Good-night!"

INDEX

INDEX

(1)

THE GREATEST LIVING ACTRESS.

Memories of My Life.

By Sarah Bernhardt.   Profusely illustrated. 8vo.   Ornamental cloth, $4.00 net ; postage 30 cents additional.

The most famous of living actresses, Sarah Bernhardt has lived life to the full as a builder and manager of theatres, author, painter and sculptor.   She turned her theatre into a hospital during the Siege of Paris.   She played French classics in a tent in Texas.   She wrote "Memories of My Life" with her own hand, and with her own inimitable verve.

"Great is Bernhardt, and great is any true description of her life, for nothing more fascinatingly brilliant could have come from the mind of the most daring of fictionists.   The autobiography is as interesting to those who care nothing for the theatre as to those devoted to it."
—*Baltimore Sun.*

"It is the work of a genius which feels and sees with instinctive insight and understanding, and puts into words such a bright and varied panorama of life as it has been given to few authors to portray."
—*Cleveland Plain Dealer.*

"Out of an overflowing reservoir of reminiscence the author pours out a flood of anecdote and of dramatic story, and she always gives the idea that she is only skimming the surface and that other treasures lie always below."—*San Francisco Argonaut.*

"The book is interesting and entertaining from cover to cover, and is related with a vivacity that is engaging."—*Toledo Blade.*

"The eventful life lived by Madame Bernhardt both on and off the stage is told with great charm.   Not only has the greatest actress of her generation more to tell than the majority of persons who write memoirs, but she has the gift of recounting the things that have befallen her with a real literary skill."—*Publishers' Weekly.*

REMINISCENCES OF A SCIENTIST.

The Autobiography of Joseph Le Conte.

With Portrait. 12mo. Cloth, $1.25 net.

Professor Le Conte was widely known as a man of science, and notably as a geologist. His later years were spent at the University of California. But his early life was passed in the South; there he was born and spent his youth; there he was living when the civil war brought ruin to his home and his inherited estate. His reminiscences deal with phases of life in the South that have unfailing interest to all students of American history. His account of the war as he saw it has permanent value. He was in Georgia when Sherman marched across it. Professor Le Conte knew Agassiz, and writes charmingly of his associations with him.

D. APPLETON AND COMPANY,

NEW YORK. BOSTON. CHICAGO. LONDON.